DRAMA
PRINCIPLES & PLAYS

DRAMA

PRINCIPLES & PLAYS

EDITED AND WITH AN INTRODUCTION BY
THEODORE W. HATLEN
UNIVERSITY OF CALIFORNIA, SANTA BARBARA

ACC
APPLETON-CENTURY-CROFTS
NEW YORK / DIVISION OF MEREDITH PUBLISHING COMPANY

667-2

Library of Congress Card Number: 67-14571

ACKNOWLEDGEMENTS. The line drawings on pp. 63, 88, 158, 294 and 372 are from Kenneth Macgowan and David Melnitz, *The Living Stage: A History of the World Theater,* Copyright © 1955 by Prentice-Hall, Inc.: Englewood Cliffs, N.Y., and are used by permission of the publisher.

PRINTED IN THE UNITED STATES OF AMERICA
E42290

PREFACE

Reading a play well is often more difficult than seeing it well performed. In order to experience the full impact of a playwright's work, a reader must himself visualize and create all its dimensions. In a theatrical production the burden of interpretation is largely carried, with greater or lesser skill, by the director, actors and designers. Through speech, movement, gesture, rhythm, scenery, costume and lighting, the meaning and emotion of the play are communicated to the audience. The solitary reader misses the emotional contagion of a responsive audience, the atmosphere created by light, sound and speech, the cumulative effect of climactic action, and the personal qualities of the living actor. As an individual, you must exercise your imagination with cues from the printed page alone. To help you envision your own production, this anthology goes beyond the texts of the plays.

The opening section surveys the starting points and purposes of drama, its genres and techniques. This account may be read straight through, or piecemeal, and either before or after your own recreation of a play.

Each play is introduced by pictures of theaters and productions as well as an historical headnote. To enhance your understanding and appreciation, study the illustrations carefully and try to visualize the action of the play in relation to the theater architecture and stage setting. Note carefully also the stage directions, and attempt to imagine the characters' movements and stage business. Rereading some of the most arresting scenes aloud may help you to sense the emotional content of the play.

A group of review questions follows each play. These queries are not intended to form a rigid pattern for classroom discussions or examinations so much as to serve as examples of the kinds of questions pertinent to analysis. Individually they should provide points of departure, more or less useful, for investigating the varied facets of dramatic technique.

Finally, a glossary offers compact definitions of critical and technical terms and gives cross-references to appropriate passages in the discussion of principles at the beginning of the book.

As a reader you have the opportunity for thoughtful analysis of the meaning, structure and symbolic aspects of the drama at your own pace. To appreciate a play fully is to realize that it is more than an evening's diversion in the theater, more than so many words on a page; it is at once a personal statement of the dramatist and a clue to the culture that produced it. The twelve plays that follow are an invitation to a wide range of feeling and thought.

I am grateful to the various persons and institutions for their assistance: to Professor William Melnitz of the University of California, Los Angeles; to Professor Wendell Cole of Stanford University; to Jules Irving and Susan Bloch of The Repertory Theater of Lincoln Center; to Eva Maria Duday of the Deutsche Sektion des Internationalen Theater—Instituts; to David Thomson of the Stratford Shakespearean Festival of Canada; to Anne Richards of the Minnesota Theatre Company; to the Victoria and Albert Museum; to my associates in the Department of Dramatic Art at the University of California, Santa Barbara; to William Reardon, Marty Swing, Richard Baschky, Angus McBean, Mrs. T. J. Grosser, Sandi Lane, and Edna Hatlen.

TWH

CONTENTS

part one PRINCIPLES

THEATER AND DRAMA / TRAGEDY / COMEDY

chapter one THEATER AND DRAMA

Origins

Man has always sought ways to enlarge his world. He reinforces his own strength with a weapon—a stone, a club, a spear, a gun, a rocket, a bomb. He acts as far as he is able to insure good crops—he tills the land, plants the seed, irrigates the soil, and then, realizing that he is subject to forces beyond his control, invokes divine intervention to provide him with a good harvest. He links himself to the present with his mate and children and tribe. He projects himself beyond the grave with rites of passage which will insure him of an afterlife. These attempts of man to widen his experience and strengthen his power result from a complex cluster of motives—his needs to communicate, to survive, to understand, to secure recognition and status—which represent the basic longings to which he gives expression by means of his religious ceremonies.

It is in such rituals that we find the basic elements of drama—music, song, dance, costuming, impersonation, mimetic action and communal performance. Drama could not begin without the disciplined construction of an orderly sequence of words and actions representing a real or imaginary experience. But not all ritual becomes drama, because often the rites continue on as functional activities, never attaining the detachment necessary to transform them into works of art which can exist for their own sake. It was in ancient Greece that the remarkable transformation from ritual to drama took place.

It would be convenient if the steps in the origin and evolution of Greek drama were clearly marked and recorded, but unfortunately much of its background is obscure. However, certain inferences can be made from the evidence at hand.

Aristotle in his *Poetics*[1] informs us that "Tragedy . . . was at first improvisation . . . originating with the leaders of the dithyramb. It advanced by slow degrees; each new element that showed itself was in turn developed." It seems clear from this statement that the rites were at first spontaneous expressions of the participants when they summoned the gods or rhapsodized on the coming of spring. The dithyramb seems to have been at first an improvised choral ode, a song of spring, which later became enriched as a part of a ceremonial rite in honor of the god Dionysus with the addition of dance and written verses by such poets as Pindar and

[1] All quotations from Aristotle are from S. H. Butcher, *Aristotle's Theory of Poetry and Fine Art* (London, Macmillan and Co., Ltd., 1907).

Arion. Dionysus was the god of vegetation, wine and fertility—an appropriate divinity for representing man's oldest needs, food and family. Primitive societies invented rituals around seasonal celebrations in their efforts to induce fertility, good hunting and bountiful crops. In Greece, these objectives were centered in a single god whose relationship to fertility was not confined to vegetation, but included human fecundity as well, as is clearly evident from the phallic rites associated with Dionysus. The legend of this god tells of his death and subsequent rebirth as a young man—a symbolic representation of the calendrical cycle of the death of the seed as it is buried in the ground in winter and its rebirth with the coming of spring. Some scholars, in tracing the origin of drama, emphasize the seasonal celebrations of seed and harvest. Others suggest that the roots of drama are to be found in the commemorative rites honoring dead heroes. In any case, the rituals from which drama emerged carried the emotional fervor of man's deepest urges and gave symbolic representation to his longest thoughts as he sought to orient himself to the universe.

In Aristotle's statement concerning the origin of Greek tragedy, he notes that "it advanced by slow degrees; each element that showed itself was in turn developed." We know that tragedy as a specific form was first mentioned in the seventh century B.C., that a century later its improvisatory nature gave way as tragedy became serious and more formalized, with poets writing verses in its form, and that by 534 B.C. it had developed sufficiently in form and substance so that Peisistratus inaugurated competition in tragedies as a part of the spring festivals in Athens.

The improvised dithyrambs probably were performed on threshing floors, just as today the Greeks make use of threshing floors as places for dancing. The altar of Dionysus was in the center and the dancers moved about it in a circular formation, setting the pattern for the orchestra circle of the later, fully developed theater architecture. At first the dithyrambs were a communal activity: everyone got into the act. When some of the worshippers broke away from the circle and became onlookers, it was possible to make the performance more specialized, with only the more proficient taking part and utilizing prepared verses and passages instead of the previous improvisations. As the spectators became more numerous, the locale of the celebration was moved to the base of an adjacent hillside so that the audience could more easily see the action. The separation of the participants from the viewers enhanced the possibility of developing an attitude of detachment in the audience, so that their enjoyment then included not only what was done, but also the *way* in which it was performed. As writers added their imaginative contributions, the original utilitarian basis for the ritual—the invocation of the supernatural to secure growth and fertility—lost some of its emphasis and the ceremony began to exist for its own sake, thus giving new freedom and sanction to the performers and poets.

An astonishing innovation then took place. Thespis appeared as the first actor. He broke away from the chorus and added the dramatic potential of impersonation. Instead of describing Dionysus, he became Dionysus, and in antiphonal response with the chorus and leaders he enlarged and enriched the ritual as a dramatic medium. When Aeschylus added the second actor another new thrust forward was given to drama, because the additional actor enabled the dramatist to *show in action* a dramatic conflict rather than merely talk about it. This primacy of action became a central tenet of Aristotelian criticism. The second actor enormously increased the potentialities of theatrical tension, which the playwrights were quick to exploit. Sophocles' addition of the third actor further enlarged the scope of the dramatist, providing him with the means of complicating his plot and devising more complex structural arrangements of his tragedies. As actors were added to the performance, the emphasis of the production shifted. While at first the chorus was the essential theatrical element, as the dramatic form evolved the playwright focused his attention on the speech and actions of individuals, so that by the time Greek tragedy had reached its "golden age" the chorus had assumed a mere supporting role to the protagonists, in whom the dramatic conflict was now centered. In part this shift in emphasis was due to the change in dramatists' selection of materials; as they drew more and more heavily upon Greek myth and legend for their characters and situations, the individual roles became so powerful that they dominated the chorus.

The evolution of the physical theater was from the dancing circle, which all of the participants occupied, to three separate areas —the orchestra circle for the chorus, the huge theatron for the audience, which eventually became quite remote from the performers, and the *skene,* where the actors carried on the essential action of the play.

Play-giving, which was a religious obligation and celebration, centered in an annual spring festival called the City of Dionysia. On the opening day of the festival, which lasted for five or six days, a processional carried the image of Dionysus from his temple to the theater. The actual performances took place on the last three or four days, when each playwright presented three tragedies and a satyr-play. The productions were under state control and financed in part by wealthy patrons. The Athenian audience comprised practically the entire free population of the city, excepting the women. The people came early in morning and brought their day's food with them. As they watched the plays they knew that each was presented for one time only—a magnificent outpouring of talent and effort in honor of Dionysus.

Like tragedy, Greek comedy had its origin in rituals honoring Dionysus, but its development was separate. Playwrights and actors limited themselves to one type. Aristotle says that "comedy also sprang from improvisations, originating with the leaders of the phallic ceremonies which still survive in many of our cities." Old Comedy, which became the important feature of the Lenaen festival, was officially recognized in 486 B.C. and reached its height of development in the comic genius of Aristophanes, as seen in such extant plays as *The Frogs, The Birds* and *Lysistrata.*

Just as Greek drama grew out of the rites performed in honor of Dionysus, so drama in the Middle Ages developed from the ritual performed in honor of the death and resurrection of Christ. Antiphonal singing was a part of the liturgy of the church as early as the fourth century, but genuine dialogue arose from the practice of inserting lines, known as tropes, into certain parts of the mass. An extant manuscript shows the introduction of a trope into the Easter service in the early part of the tenth century. From these tropes, which included mimetic action and the use of costumes and properties, serious plays developed through the addition of scenes, until long and complicated dramas were written and performed to dramatize the entire life of Christ.

As drama and its production became more complex it was moved out of the church and the various locales required in the expanding stories were represented by a series of "stations" or "mansions" placed in a churchyard or market place. Entire cycles of stories from the Bible and the lives of the saints placed so heavy a burden on the church for production that drama eventually passed into secular hands. In England, for example, the trade guilds, which often made use of "pageant wagons" to represent the various places for the action, took on the responsibility for producing plays. For a time drama existed precariously in the efforts of traveling companies of amateur players performing nondescript plays in improvised quarters. Ultimately the quality of drama improved markedly; the players, under noble patronage, became professionals working in the established theaters of Shakespeare's time.

Appeals

Why do people go to the theater?

The sources of the theater's appeal are manifold, and no doubt the dramatic experience is very often a blend of several satisfactions. Let us suggest four of them.

First, much of drama appeals to an audience because it tells an entertaining story. Plays and performances exist on the game level. There is nothing serious intended by the playwright. The audience finds no secondary or residual meaning—no food for thought, no universalizing experience. If the play holds the spectator's attention, arouses laughter or excitement, the play has fulfilled its purpose for him. There are many theatergoers who insist on this level of appeal. Hence most drama is journalistic rather than literary, concerned with the surface aspects of make-believe rather than with a penetration of reality. Those who support the popular theater often reject drama that deals seriously with life. Their attitude is indicated in their complaint that "there are enough troubles in this life without having to suffer in the theater; when I go to a show, I want to forget my problems." While this point of view is not conducive to the elevation of drama as a significant form of art and communication, it represents the prevalent attitude that dominates motion picture and television fare. Although great works of drama make far more demands on an audience, no successful dramatist has been able to ignore the need to engage the theatergoer's attention. The theater must contain an element of the theatrical; drama must be dramatic, and usually this involves story appeal.

Man has always found delight in sharing tales of adventure and excitement, struggle and conflict. From his very primitive days around the fire he has enjoyed hearing what happened next. He listens with rapt attention to eye-witness accounts or to those who have a gift for recreating an experience. But even more compelling is his desire to see the events for himself. Thus the word has been joined to action; narration has become dramatization. The spectator shares the story vicariously when he sees it reenacted. Drama may take many forms, but the story element persists as a basic appeal. In many instances modern fiction writers have rejected the importance of the narrative. They have shifted their attention from plot to character penetration and delineation, or to the creation of atmosphere and environment. Likewise, the naturalists in drama and our contemporary "absurdists" have attempted to write plays that neglect or subordinate the story element. But their efforts have not met with general acceptance and it seems likely that man's interest in a sequence of events with a beginning, a middle, and an end will continue to be a primary means of attracting and holding an audience.

Second, the audience finds pleasure, in witnessing an achievement, in considering the manner in which a thing is done. The theatergoer may take naive pleasure in the illusions created by the designer and the technical crew through their skillful use of canvas, lumber, paint, and light. As a connoisseur of performances, the spectator will find pleasure in comparing Sir Laurence Olivier's Hamlet with that of Sir Maurice Evans or Sir John Gielgud. As a knowledgeable theater enthusiast, he notes the effectiveness of the ensemble acting, the director's adroit use of pace and rhythm, the actor's ability to react as well as to speak, the appropriateness of the scenery in reinforcing the mood of the play, the expressive use of movement and business, the psychological and emotional content implied by the groupings of characters. The enjoyment that an informed spectator feels at a fine performance of a great play stems in part from his recognition of the achievements of the interpreters in translating the essential values of the play into theatrical terms.

A third satisfaction provided by the theater has already been suggested earlier—its function as a means of extending ourselves beyond the narrow circle of everyday existence. Most plays elicit an empathic response from the spectator. He "feels into" the action. His sympathies are aroused as he identifies himself with the characters and action before him. He becomes emotionally involved in the outcome. He often sees in the play universal patterns of behavior that parallel his own. In short, drama becomes a way of enlarging our experience, with all of the concomitant emotional overtones enhanced and augmented by theatrical production, so that in the end we act out the play for ourselves.

Fourth, the dramatic experience can also be a spiritual one. As Aristotle suggested, tragedy is serious, of a certain magnitude; it is elevated in scale and it evokes a catharsis —a purging away, a cleansing of the ignoble, the mean, the base. The great works of drama depict great characters exploring the great issues of life. Greek tragedy was a declaration of faith; it exalted mankind. "Wonders are many, and none is more wonderful than man," sang Sophocles. The sufferings of Antigone, Oedipus, and Prometheus were positive statements about the Greek view of life. The medieval dramatist in composing *Everyman* had the high purpose of presenting the process of salvation to mankind. In the masterpieces of drama, good and evil are ruthlessly examined, choices are made and judgments rendered which indicate the distilled wisdom of the race. Man's loftiest ideas and aspirations have been the significant content of drama. Thus, the theater in times past has been an institution of edification and spiritual stimulation, and in our drama today we can sometimes find affirmation of the dignity of man and the greatness of his spirit.

The Conventions of the Theater

Drama, like all other forms of art, is conventionalized. That is to say, there are certain common agreements between spectator and theater-worker as to the manner of creation and production—certain ground rules that determine how the game is to be played. In painting, there is the convention that pigment is applied to a flat surface within a regular framework. Music is a conventionalized combination of sounds and rhythms that make almost no pretence of imitating nature. The spectator, as he enters the theater, becomes a partner to conventions in order that the drama can take place. He enters into the situation imaginatively by what Coleridge termed a "willing suspension of disbelief." In our contemporary theater, the spectator of a legitimate modern play generally expects to see onstage characters and settings that resemble those of life: the speech suggests normal conversation and the characters' behavior follows familiar patterns. Actually, much of what the playgoer sees and hears is arbitrarily conventionalized even if the dramatist has written in a realistic style. Performer and audience tacitly agree that they will be separated from one another: the audience occupies the auditorium; the actor remains on stage. The separation of these two entities is facilitated by the darkened auditorium and the lighted stage, the architectural features of the elevated stage, a curtain that opens and closes, and the proscenium arch itself. There is also a psychological barrier at work, known as the "fourth wall," a contemporary convention that developed with realism, in which the actors pretend that the audience does not exist and avoid direct communication across the footlights. Actually, the performer employs specific techniques to assure communication with everyone in the theater—by speaking louder and more clearly than in normal conversation, by turning his face at least partially toward the audience, by exaggerating his gestures and facial expressions. The drama itself is conventionalized. Its compressed structure, the arrangement into scenes or acts interrupted by intermissions and set changes, the climactic order of the action usually involving only a few characters—these are arbitrary practices of the playwright. Even the scenery that gives the illusion of actuality, with all the clutter and detail of real life, is patently artificial in the arrangement of exits and entrances, the grouping of furniture so that it "opens out" toward the audience, the arbitrary use of lighting, the enlarged scale of set pieces, the very use of scenic materials itself.

Conventions are not rigid, however. They change from time to time and even from one style of drama to another. In musical comedy, for example, everyone expects scenery that is frankly theatrical, performers who break into song and dance at the slightest provocation and to the accompaniment of a large orchestra, and a chorus of interlopers who hover in the immediate background ready to join instantly into the action of the production. In contemporary "arena," or center-staged productions, the audience is asked to accept such conventions as the absence of scenery, the intimacy of the surroundings, and the different kinds of movements and groupings which result from the playing area surrounded by spectators. As modern playwrights become increasingly dissatisfied with realism, more and more attempts are made to free the theater from restricting conventions. For example, scenery is becoming frankly theatrical instead of representational. Now, for instance, a fragment of a wall may be picked out of the darkness by light to serve as a setting that a generation ago would have required a complete interior with three walls, a ceiling and practical doors. Dramatists are using freer forms for their plays. Dialogue may be poetic; asides, soliloquies and direct address may be reintroduced. Acting is oftentimes quite stylized, or the separation between spectator and performer deliberately broken down. The point is that theater conventions are subject to change as those who work in theater seek ways of expressing themselves more interestingly and completely, and as the established practices give way to new ones the spectator is obliged to make a corresponding adjustment.

Fashions in theatrical conventions have differed from time to time, and in order to understand the drama of any period it is essential to know the conventions underlying its productions. In the Greek theater, for example, performances were given outdoors and in the daytime as public ceremonies. Only three speaking characters appeared on stage at one time, and men played all of the female roles. Actors wore masks, special headpieces and footgear, and the plays dramatizing ancient legends and myths were written in verse. Greek dramas, presented usually in a single permanent setting with a simple story that occurred in a short space of time, also displayed little or no violence onstage. In the Elizabethan theater, like the

Greek, all roles were played by male actors in an outdoor theater in the daytime with little or no use of illusionistic scenery. The plays, written in verse, were quite different from the Greek drama in form and content. The play usually was a complicated one involving several plot lines, comic matter was mixed with serious, high-born characters with low, and the playwright had openly ransacked history and literature for material that would tell an exciting story. Because plays were performed by professional actors in theaters whose dimensions and arrangement placed the actor in close proximity to the spectator, the subtleties of the language could be exploited. In addition, the convention of the large, unlocalized platform gave the dramatist a great deal of freedom in staging an animated and complicated narrative.

In each age, theater conventions have varied according to the influences of the playwrights, actors, audiences and physical theaters, and in turn, the conventions have affected all elements of the drama. In evaluating any drama, therefore, it is essential to recognize these conventions because of their influence in shaping the play and its production.

Elements of Drama

In the previous sections we have suggested the appeals of drama and the variety of ways for studying its nature, among them analysis of dramatic structure. Let us examine the specific elements that constitute such a structure. In this discussion we will follow a pattern set down by Aristotle in his *Poetics,* perhaps the most significant and influential work on dramatic criticism ever written. Aristotle categorized drama into the following six elements, which are listed here in their order of importance as he viewed them:

Plot
Character
Thought
Diction
Music
Spectacle

We will not argue the relative importance of each of these items, but the student can use these six elements as a convenient frame of reference, not only in this chapter but in all considerations of dramatic literature. Hence, familiarity with Aristotle's dramatic categories and their component parts is necessary for subsequent discussions.

Plot

Plot is, in Aristotle's words, "the life and soul of tragedy." As the formal aspect of a play, it is for the playwright what composition is for the painter and composer, namely, the arrangement of parts into a consistent and logical pattern. A play is not a series of separate events ordered chronologically like a timetable or the minutes of a meeting. Just as a motion picture editor arranges a meaningful sequence of film clips by relating each frame to every other, so, in a similar way, the playwright composes his events and builds the structure of his play. Dramatic structure is a concatenation, or linking of actions into an indivisible chain. Plots have varied from the tightly knit, simple structure of Greek tragedy to the loose episodes of medieval drama, bound together by a theme, to the complicated action of the Elizabethans, who employed several sets of characters involved in a welter of overlapping situations, to the naturalist's attempt to avoid all semblance of structure in "slice-of-life" plays, and finally to contemporary experiments in expressionistic, "absurd" and "epic" drama that have little regard for disciplined construction. But despite differences in composition, the underlying pattern of Western drama reflects Aristotle's concept of organic unity—a series of actions that an audience can accept as "necessary and probable." Most of our plays involve human beings caught in decisive moments of struggle and conflict. Tension is increased as the drama moves toward a climax and an ultimate decision. In a Greek drama the central character finds himself in a situation that requires him to choose among courses of action and to endure the often dire consequences of his choice. Antigone must decide whether she will disrespect the funeral rites due her dead brother or bury him in defiance of the king's edict. Oedipus decides, whatever the cost, to rid his kingdom of the cause of the plague. Once the tragic hero makes a decision, pressure is brought to bear upon him, he refuses to be diverted from his course, and catastrophe ensues.

A play is composed of a series of units. Major divisions are the acts, which in turn may be divided into scenes, and these may be separated still further by a director into a series of "beats." "Scenes" in the French sense refer to any new grouping of characters. "Beats" are a director's device for separating small units of action for rehearsal purposes, such as the appearances of the ghost in the first scene of *Hamlet,* the "dumb show" and "pantomime" in *Miss Julie,* or the picture auction in *School for Scandal.*

Greek tragedies have simple plots with a series of episodes involving two or three speaking characters, as for example in *Antigone*—Haimon and Creon, Antigone and Ismene, Antigone and Creon, Ismene and Antigone, and the guard and Creon. Between each of these episodes, which are of only a few minutes duration, the Chorus chants lyrical passages. In a compressed modern play such as *Miss Julie* the entire action is centered in three characters with only the interruption of the peasants' "ballet" to break the tension. These simple plots are in marked contrast to Shakespeare's structure of *Hamlet,* in which more than a score of characters are directly involved in a variety of locales over a considerable span of time. But in each of these plays, the dramatist puts each scene or episode in its appropriate place in the sequence of action so that it is causally related to what happens before and after. It is this process of devising and arranging incidents that controls the progression of the action and which makes the art of playwriting a difficult one.

The plot is arranged to produce a cumulative effect by giving the play tension and emotional momentum. In addition, the plot provides explanation and meaning for the sum total of the parts. What incidents lead to Miss Julie's swift destruction? What events occur between the first view of Hamlet with the King and Queen at court and their deaths at the end? What changes our initial impressions of Charles and Joseph Surface in *School for Scandal?* The plot raises and answers these questions by providing the critical incidents that account for changes in the characters' fortunes.

In the nineteenth century the French critic Brunetière offered his celebrated "law of the drama," in which the basic tenet is that a play presents "the spectacle of the will striving toward a goal." While this concept is difficult to apply to all kinds of drama, there is a hard core of truth in it. Most plays do, in fact, deal with a group of characters striving toward goals—goals such as status, power, wealth, security, recognition, or affection. Usually the character is prevented from realizing his goal; obstacles are in his way and opposition often breaks into sharp and open conflict. Note the clashes in each episode of Antigone, beginning with the contention between the two sisters, then the clash of Creon and the guard, and finally of Creon and Antigone; the conflicts progressively build the emotional impact of the play as Sophocles dramatizes Antigone and the King, each striving toward a goal and running headlong into each other in the process. Similarly, Hamlet strives toward the goal of avenging his father's murder and, in the process, clashes with the King. In comedy, the traditional plot is centered around a pair of lovers who are separated by social and economic barriers, parental disapproval, misunderstandings, a third person, or a cloud on his or her reputation. The pattern of action is concerned with eliminating such obstacles, as for example in *The Miser* where the lovers are initially thwarted by the greed of the father, Harpagon.

John Howard Lawson, in his *Theory and Technique of Playwriting,* advanced a theory of drama built on conflicts: "The essential nature of drama is a social conflict in which the conscious will is exerted . . ." Like Brunetière's theory, Lawson's contains much validity, although it seems inapplicable to works by Chekhov, Maeterlinck, and the current "absurdists," whose drama appears to be organized in a circular fashion rather than a linear one. Often these plays create a mood or show characters incapable of striving toward a goal, or who perhaps deny that a goal even exists. In Beckett's *Waiting for Godot,* the characters take no positive action. They do not know where they are headed. In Ionesco's *The Leader* the playwright dramatizes the act of waiting, but with the expectation that "the Leader" will come. The plot of Tennessee Williams' *The Glass Menagerie* is notably free of dynamic action, being, as the playwright says, "a play of memory."

A common characteristic of all drama is the prevalence of *tension*. Without it, drama has little chance of holding attention. Usually, as Brunetière suggests, tension grows out of "striving toward a goal," and even in those plays of mood or those that lack striving, a sense of intensified feeling still arises from the expectancy of an arrival. In *The Leader,* the arrival does in fact take place, but the pattern is one of a joke—tension is aroused and given a sudden release in an unexpected direction. The same holds true of the plot of Beckett's *Play Without Words.* In Chekhov's plays, where most of the characters are frustrated and incapable of taking action, a sense of tension grows out of their dissatisfaction with their lives and conditions. They have memories and aspirations that are at odds with the hard facts of their present existence.

Generally speaking, each person will tend to form his own "theory" of plot, to derive his own emphases according to his separate analysis. For the purpose of such analysis plot may be said to consist of eleven basic aspects:

Exposition
Discovery and Reversal
Point of Attack
Foreshadowing
Complication
Climax
Crisis
Denouement
The Unities,
- of time
- of place
- of action

It is well to remember that although these aspects of plot may be separable in discussion, they may often coincide in any given play. The climax and crisis, for example, may occur at the same time, or exposition may be used for foreshadowing.

EXPOSITION

When the curtain rises on a play, the dramatist faces the problem of capturing his audience's attention and providing necessary background so that it can understand subsequent action. He must show who the characters are, what their relationship is to one another, what motivates them, and usually some aspect of their environment. This is *exposition*. Notice in *The Miser* how quickly Molière sketches in the character relationships and the conflict. In *Miss Julie* Strindberg's first line is nearly a plot summary: "*Jean:* Miss Julie's mad again tonight: absolutely mad!" Likewise, Sophocles in the opening speeches of *Antigonæ* gives the audience important background information. The first scene of *Hamlet* is a classic example of exposition, crammed full of antecedent information skillfully blended with dramatic action.

In most contemporary plays in which the dramatist is endeavoring to create the illusion of actuality, he ordinarily introduces his exposition into the play as an organic part of the action rather than as obvious information. Because exposition usually bulks rather large in the first act of a play, the writer must find ways to capture and hold the audience's interest while unobtrusively providing this necessary material. Many playwrights find it difficult to get their action underway, with the result that the opening scenes tend to drag. The television producer, conscious of this tendency in the opening moments of a play, often has resorted to the technique of beginning a production with an excerpt of violent action from the climax of the play in order to "hook" the spectator into the story.

Playwrights have used a variety of expository devices, such as "feather-duster scenes" of two minor characters bouncing information off one another toward the audience, or dumb-shows, confidants, narrators, choruses, asides, soliloquies, prologues, and all sorts of visual aids including slides, charts, maps, and motion pictures. The stage setting also serves as a means of providing background material for the audience. The modern dramatist takes considerable care to describe the locale of the play. Note, for example, Strindberg's explicit stage directions for the *Miss Julie* setting.

DISCOVERY AND REVERSAL

The playwright, in revealing his characters' motivations and objectives, their relationships, and their feelings, must possess the ability to invent and organize a series of interesting and compelling *discoveries* about his characters. Exposition is a part of a general discovery process, but it deals primarily with antecedent or background material whereas discovery *per se* includes events that may happen during the course of the action onstage, as for example Antigone's death, Ophelia's drowning, or Claudius' guilt. Notice the number and variety of effective discoveries in *Hamlet*—the ghost's revelation of the murder, the guilt of Claudius, the madness and death of Ophelia, the pirates' attempt to slay Hamlet, the death of Polonius, the poisoned sword and drink. Discovery scenes may be those of recognition, such as in *The Miser,* Act v, scene 5, when Anselm is reunited with his children. Sheridan created two particularly effective scenes of discovery in *School for Scandal;* in the picture auction Sir Oliver realizes the goodheartedness of his nephew, Charles, and the screen scene serves both to unmask the duplicity of Joseph Surface and to convince Lady Teazle of the genuine affection of Sir Peter.

A *reversal* is a turning about, a sudden change in direction. Aristotle thought that discovery was most successful when it coincided with a reversal, as in *Oedipus the King* when Oedipus discovers the truth which brings on his catastrophe.

POINT OF ATTACK

Once the playwright provides sufficient background to hold the audience's attention, he starts a chain of events that constitute the main action of the play. The *point of attack* refers to that moment in the play when the precipitating force sets the mechanism into motion. The equilibrium that ordinarily exists at the rise of the first curtain is disturbed, turbulence results and a period of adjustment begins. Horatio meets the ghost of Hamlet's father; Creon forbids the burial of Polyneices; Miss Julie orders a servant to dance with her —these are characteristic points of attack, in which an inciting force triggers the course of action.

The location of the point of attack in the story is related directly to the physical theater and its conventions. The more flexible the stage, the freer the dramatic form and the greater the opportunity for an early attack and the presentation of a great deal of action. Medieval and Elizabethan playwrights, for example, exploited the freedom provided by their stages to tell complicated stories with many scenes and characters, while, in contrast, the Greek dramatists felt obliged to begin their stories as near as possible to the major crisis. In the most modern plays, because of the expense and limitations of staging a play, the tendency is to use a compact plot. As a consequence, the contemporary dramatist is likely to employ a relatively late point of attack.

FORESHADOWING

In the exposition we have observed how the playwright must furnish the audience with background material. He also has the task of preparing the spectator for future developments. He does this by *foreshadowing,* that is, he makes the subsequent action credible by supplying carefully inserted clues in early parts of the play. Everyone is familiar with the techniques of foreshadowing, or "planting," employed by a mystery-story writer when he takes pains to drop hints—the butler is left-handed; the revolver is hidden in the desk drawer; the chauffeur has an assumed name. The dramatist is likewise obliged to prepare the audience for acceptance of the developments of the action.

Foreshadowing has several purposes: to make events appear believable, to build suspense, to create tension, to reveal character or aid in the development of climaxes, crises, and complications. It may also announce an entrance or establish atmosphere. Within the first thirty lines of *Hamlet,* for example, several references are made to the "dreaded sight," which has appeared twice before, as a means of preparing for the ghost's entrance and of rendering appropriate atmosphere. Strindberg skillfully prepares for Miss Julie's suicide by the slaughter of the bird and the presence of the razor. Warnings by Teiresias and the Chorus anticipate the catastrophes in *Antigone.* The absurdists, in order to make their point that much of modern life is meaningless, build up expectations through foreshadowing only to let them collapse into nothingness. But in general, the dramatist's use of foreshadowing indicates that he is aware of the need for an organic structure to his plot so that no turn of events will seem extraneous or incredible. The playwright values suspense more than surprise, and, while dramas may use the unexpected, good craftsmanship requires that the chain of events be foreshadowed.

COMPLICATION

A *complication* is any new force introduced into play which affects the direction of the course of action. Once the playwright has selected his characters, determined his theme, and planned the beginning and ending of his play, he constructs the plot through a series of complications. The point of attack, for example, is the first complication. Macgowan considers the complications so important that he says they are "the lifeblood of ninety-nine and ninety-nine hundredths percent of a play."

Let us consider for a moment the analogy of a three-stage rocket. Its destination is determined, its course charted and launching prepared. The mechanism is fired and the rocket is projected into space, but the initial impetus is insufficient to keep it moving; additional thrusts are needed from second- and third-stage firings to send the rocket soaring into its trajectory. In a similar way, the dramatist decides on his objective and sets his course of action. He precipitates the initial motion by means of a complication (the point of attack), but the plot, like the rocket, needs additional force to keep the mass moving forward and upward. Additional complications, like the rocket's secondary and tertiary firings, accelerate and increase the action until the play reaches its highest point. The thrust of a play follows a cumulative and climactic pattern from the introduction of the first complication to the major crisis, when the protagonist's fate is settled. Complications are utilized by the playwright in order to create a "straining forward of interest," to use George Pierce Baker's apt phrase. Their purpose is to intensify the emotions, arouse suspense, to illustrate and determine what happens to the characters—generally, to provide the building blocks of the play's plot structure.

Romeo falls in love with Juliet, but the situation is complicated by the enmity between the two families. This hostility is aggravated when Romeo slays Tybalt, causing a new complication, the banishment of Romeo. A further complication is raised when Juliet's father insists that she marry Paris immediately. In order to avoid this development, a plan is devised for Juliet to feign death through the use of a magic potion. But the letter disclosing the plan is not delivered to Romeo and the action is again further complicated. Romeo learns of Juliet's apparent death, goes to her and takes poison. Juliet awakens to find her lover dead—the final complication. She joins him in death, and this is the final action of the play. Shakespeare, like most playwrights, begins his play with a character trying to reach an objective, but complications intervene and require, as the play gathers momentum and intensity, a continuous readjustment of forces. This readjustment process is the heart of plot, and it is out of complications that the conflict of forces becomes apparent.

CLIMAX

The *climax* is the culmination of a course of action, "the maximum disturbance of the equilibrium," "the moment of the most intense strain," "the crisis of maximum emotion and tension."

Actually, a play is a series of climaxes with moments of stability and adjustment in between. The action surges forward and upward, the tension mounting through minor climaxes, until the major climax is reached and the emotional impact of the play reaches its strongest point. The structure, in this respect, may resemble a boxing match between two opponents of similar strength and skill. In each round, there may be moments of climactic action with first one fighter gaining the advantage and then the other. In between the peaks of action are relatively quiet moments, rest periods between the rounds. In the frantic last round, the major climax is reached when one boxer succeeds in knocking out the other.

Notice the climatic pattern of action Strindberg employs in the seduction in *Miss Julie*. First we hear about her exploits with the servants at the dance; then she appears in person at the servants' quarters; she drinks beer (a servants' drink); she orders Jean to remove his livery and to sit with her; she removes something from his eye; she openly flirts with him and admires his French, his dancing, his physical strength. One by one, in scenes of gradual intensification, the barriers are removed between them. Similarly, her suicide is a carefully ordered structure of climatic action. This is basically the usual pattern of dramatic writing—an ordered sequence of mounting tension culminating in a major climax.

CRISIS

Although the terms *crisis* and climax are sometimes used interchangeably because they may occur at the same time, we shall consider a crisis to mean a time of decision, a turning point, or a crossroads. After an accident, a patient hovers between life and death; he is at a moment of crisis and possibly of climax. A batter steps to the plate with the score tied and the bases loaded. The count reaches three balls and two strikes. The game is at a point of crisis and possibly at its climax too.

A crisis involves a clash of interests. The protagonist is faced with alternatives that will determine his fate. Hamlet, sword in hand, must decide whether or not to slay the praying Claudius; Antigone must choose to bury her brother's body or obey the King; Laura learns that the "gentleman caller" is already involved with another girl. Sometimes a character makes his own decisions; sometimes they are thrust upon him. A crisis may lead to good fortune or to disaster depending upon the nature of the play and the author's intent.

A play, which is usually made up of a series of crises growing out of a series of complications, reaches its major crisis toward the play's end. Resolution of this crisis determines the ultimate outcome of the entire sequence of actions. A dramatist creates loaded situations which dramatize his characters caught in critical moments of their lives. For a time the outcome is in doubt; the protagonist teeters on the brink of success or failure. The hero's moment of suspension, before a decisive action occurs and settles his fate, is the final crisis.

DENOUEMENT

The *denouement* is the ending of the play, the final resolution. Julie takes her own life; Hamlet avenges his father's death at the cost of his own life; Oedipus goes into exile; Abby and Eben are united; Tom runs away from Amanda and Laura; Romeo and Juliet are joined in death. It is the unravelling of the knot that the complications have formed, the committing of the protagonist to his ultimate fate. As a segment of the play, it occurs from the major crisis to the final curtain.

The denouement's function is to restore order, to unify and complete the course of action, and to provide an ending that seems necessary and probable as the result of the antecedent development. Indeed, the play's denouement is a fairly good index of the skill and integrity of the dramatist. The inept playwright may find his characters in an inextricable situation and resort to an implausible suicide, or to some other violent action, with the mistaken notion that these acts in themselves are "dramatic." In legitimate usage, violent action is the credible result of the characters themselves and their previous actions. Another kind of faulty ending occurs when the playwright uses an outside force to intervene and unsnarl the entanglements. The hero is incapable of working out his own salvation, so he must be rescued by the Cavalry, the Coast Guard, the Marines, the King or a miracle from on high. Still another weak denouement occurs when the playwright suddenly changes, for the sake of shock or surprise, to a direction which is contrary to his characters or violates the preceding action. As we have already suggested, however, the "absurdists" oftentimes deliberately twist the ending because the strange effect produced coincides with their view of life. Note, for example, the endings of *The Leader* and *Act Without Words.* Another questionable, though sometimes amusing denouement is the indeterminate ending in which the characters and the audience are left in doubt as to the outcome. Pirandello, in *Right You Are If You Think You Are,* makes an acceptable use of this device, but ordinarily the spectator likes to have the major questions answered before he goes home.

While the denouement of comedy usually shows the protagonist successful in overcoming obstacles to reach the land of his heart's desire, the denouement of tragedy often shows disaster. The denouements of both comedy and tragedy, however, frequently involve a complete reversal of the hero's status.

THE UNITIES

Most dramatists have sought some means of creating *unity* in their plays—some way of providing a central focus. Aristotle suggested unity in an interlocking arrangement of the incidents with a "beginning, middle, and end." During the Renaissance, scholars insisted on imposing on the dramatist the alleged "classical" unities of time, place, and action. Actually, Aristotle mentions only time and action. He does not, as we have mentioned earlier, set down rules for dramatic composition; rather, his observations record the practices of the Greek playwrights of the preceding century. Aeschylus, Sophocles, and Euripides did not write according to law-like rules, but constructed their plays to meet the conventions of the theater and their own imaginations. They did not regard drama as a fixed and unchangeable form, but created their plays and methods of presentation to suit themselves. The notion that playwrights must observe rules or conform to the unities has had very little acceptance in the theater except in the neoclassic drama of France and England in the seventeenth century. In general, playwrights have written for popular approval rather than for academic acceptance.

Unity of Time. Aristotle wrote that "Tragedy endeavors, as far as possible to confine itself to a single revolution of the sun, or but slightly to exceed this limit." The Italian scholars of the Renaissance misapplied this *unity of time,* warping it to mean the portrayal of a maximum of twelve hours, and preferably of only the length of time which the play itself took. The Greek playwrights usually were close to Aristotle's observation, although there are several instances of plays requiring a longer span of time. Greek dramatists were not concerned with strict adherence to chronology. Their interest was centered on portrayal of characters and ideas rather than confining the action within a specific amount of elapsed time. Dramatists in other periods of theater history have felt free to use all of the time they needed. In practice, and as a natural concomitant of the compact nature of drama, the playwright has tended to restrict his action to a relatively short space of time. It will be noted that the majority of the plays in the text follow the unity of time.

Unity of Place. Aristotle said nothing about *unity of place,* although it was customary for Greek tragic writers to use a single, or at the most two locales. Perhaps the continual presence of the chorus influenced this practice. Perhaps the fact of drama performed in a single locale set a precedent; or again, perhaps outdoor performances during daylight hours without the means of making rapid shifts of scenery conditioned playwriting. But more likely, a play which was centered on a few characters shown in the climatic and critical stages of their careers required no change of scenic background.

In medieval drama, the playwrights attempted to tell a complicated story and to put all of the action onstage. Shakespeare, and his fellow Elizabethans, followed this tradition. Furthermore, the architecture of the theater and the tastes of the audience encouraged the playwright to move about freely in time and space. Thus, *Hamlet* has a variety of action in several locales over a considerable space of time. Similarly, Brecht in his "epic" drama *The Caucasian Chalk Circle* uses a wide latitude of time and place. While there are numerous plays that require freedom to move from place to place, the general tendency of the dramatist is to concentrate his action in order to keep his focus clear.

Unity of Action. Aristotle said that the plot should be simple enough so that it might be held easily in the mind of the spectator. *Unity of action* means that the drama deals with a single course of events, involving little or no extraneous material, no mixture of comic and serious matter. The most important ingredient in the concept of unity is that all parts of the play be organically related. Again quoting from Aristotle: "The structural unity of the parts is such that, if any one of them is displaced or removed, the whole will be disjointed and disturbed. For a thing whose presence or absence makes no visible difference is not an organic part of the whole." It was, in fact, the practice of the Greek writers of tragedy to create simple, well-articulated plots. But the history of drama reveals that playwrights have often ignored the unity of action as Aristotle defined it, particularly in Elizabethan England where the physical theater, with its unlocalized platform, permitted the use of complicated stories and actions, and where the medieval tradition of mixing comedy with serious drama was an accepted practice.

You will find examples in this text of complicated action in *Hamlet* and *The Caucasian Chalk Circle* and simplicity of plot in *The Glass Menagerie, Miss Julie, Antigone, The Miser,* and *Desire Under the Elms.*

In Elizabethan drama, playwrights often achieved a kind of unity of character by focusing the action on one dominant figure. Others have sought a unity of idea by selecting only those characters and incidents that were germane to the development and projection of their theme. Still others, ignoring structural unity, have achieved a unity of atmosphere. In any case, most dramatists have been cognizant of the need for finding some means to suggest a singleness of purpose or effect in order to clarify and organize their creative efforts.

Character

In placing character as his second element, Aristotle started an endless argument. Many critics and playwrights insist that character is the most important element of drama. The controversy will undoubtedly continue, since there are valid arguments on both sides, but more importantly, the point needs to be made that plot and character are not mutually exclusive. Good drama requires both good plot and good characterization, for in the last analysis plot is character in action and plot, in turn, is the result of what people are. The sequence of events is rooted in the characters' wills, desires, and objectives that are revealed in effective drama by skillful selection and organization.

The nature of the dramatic method and the conditions and conventions of the physical theater have exerted important influences on characterization. Unlike the novelist, who can demonstrate character by a wide range of incidents over a span of many years and under many conditions, who has, in addition, the opportunity to describe the character at length and to indicate the secret thoughts coursing through his head, the playwright must select a few key incidents that occur in a short space of time and in a few locales and must reveal character only by speech and behavior. The dramatist has no means of commenting directly on character. As a result, the characters in plays must be simplified, their qualities made clear in a few telling scenes. Because of the compression of the medium, characterization in drama often becomes one-dimensional, especially in farce and melodrama, and in the minor roles of most all plays.

As in all other aspects of drama, characterization has been exposed to a variety of fashions. In Greek, Elizabethan, and Japanese drama, the roles of women were played by men. Medieval drama often made use of allegorical figures representing single attributes of character, such as Wisdom, Greed, and Gluttony. Contemporary dramatists of realistic and naturalistic persuasion have endeavored to create the illusion of complicated character by piling up a wealth of physical details, by capitalizing on the significant trifle, and by searching for the psychological meaning beneath the act.

High tragedy deals primarily with "men as better than they are" but who, through some flaw of character, are led to great misfortune. Low comedy, on the other hand, deals with "men as worse than they are" but not with men who are altogether vicious or depraved. Medieval characters ranged from God to the Devil, from purest saint to most abject sinner. Some characters have been drawn on a heroic scale, masters of their fate, working out their destinies by dint of their own resources; other characters have been treated as hapless victims of an unfortunate heredity and environment, incapable of taking action, defeated, frustrated, and resigned. The expressionists have experimented with split personalities and characters effaced of all aspects of individuality, reducing them to X or Mr. Zero. During the last quarter of the nineteenth century, under the impact of the scientific method and the new developments in psychology, the playwright has generally become concerned with delineating characters with rich inner lives and complex motivations. Ibsen, Strindberg, and Chekhov were particularly successful in creating figures with the "stamp of life" upon them. Observe, for example, how complete a sense of character Strindberg creates with Julie and Jean in a very short space of time. Dramatists in the twentieth century have continued to strive for the creation of solid characters whose motivations conform to the findings of contemporary psychology, with the result that many of our plays give the effect of case studies. Our modern writer is also interested in the interaction of characters, and his plays exploit the tensions and turbulence that result from the impact of one upon the other.

While he is restricted in scope, the playwright's very use of selection and heightening give clarity and directness to his figures. The fact that he is confined to a very few events places great weight upon them. The characters are brought into sharp focus because onstage all of their behavior is significant. The playwright cannot afford the diffuse haphazardness of real life or the leisurely indirectness of many novels.

Character may be delineated in four ways. First, by appearance, since the actor's physical qualities give an immediate stimulus to the audience. Many modern playwrights have a very specific image in mind and thus describe the character's appearance in considerable detail, as for example in the plays of Shaw.

Second, by speech, for the kind of language employed by the person, his manner of speaking, his voice quality, his inflection pattern, pitch, rate, and general vitality, all say something about him. The dramatist takes great care to write dialogue that makes an immediate impression about the characters. At the beginning of *Miss Julie,* Jean and Kristin have just been commenting on their mistress' behavior and are then able to establish her vacillating nature in just three lines. Similarly, in *The Glass Menagerie,* Amanda immediately indicates her character in her own opening speeches. Although dialogue in most modern plays gives the impression of the give and take of normal conversation, some playwrights have found long speeches of reminiscence useful as a means both of conveying antecedent information and of revealing character to the listener. *Miss Julie* is a first rate example of this technique, as is the lengthy dialogue of Amanda and Tom in *The Glass Menagerie.* Before the advent of realism in the nineteenth century, it was common practice for the playwright to use soliloquies and asides to let the audience know what the characters were thinking, as in the celebrated speeches of Hamlet. Molière makes an amusing use of the aside in Act I, scenes 4 and 5, of *The Miser* when Harpagon, thinking himself alone, talks to the audience about his treasure, only to discover that there are other characters onstage who might have overheard him.

Third, through a character's external actions we have clues to his inner motivations. Sometimes the playwright may choose to create an initial impression that is misleading or ambiguous and then gradually reveal the truth as the play progresses. Charles and Joseph Surface are not at all the same characters at the end of *The School for Scandal* as they appeared to be at the beginning. The more usual practice, however, is for the playwright to set the key to a character from the outset. Molière's Harpagon in his first appearance in Act I, scene 3, is shown as a testy skinflint, and the rest of the play goes on to detail action-by-action the completeness of his avarice. Miss Julie also indicates her character from her first entrance: she goes to the looking-glass, then strikes Jean in the face with her handkerchief, and a moment later plays the coquette by praising Jean's dancing.

Fourth, by what others say about a character and the way in which they react to him, we may begin to form an opinion before he even appears. We have already noted Jean's opening line about Miss Julie's madness; the gossip that follows between the two servants provides a further damaging portrait of their mistress.

The sharpness of a character's image is in part dependent upon the structure of the drama. Plays written for a theater that permitted most of the essential action to appear onstage gave the playwright a greater opportunity to create a vivid and complex character than do those plays confined to a minimum of action. For example, one reason that Hamlet is such a rich and interesting character is because we see him in combination with so many other characters—Hamlet and the Ghost, Hamlet and Horatio, Hamlet and Ophelia, Hamlet and Gertrude, Hamlet and Polonius, and so forth. When we contrast this variety of character exposure to that of Antigone, we realize how limited the Greeks were in delineating complex characterization. Some playwrights, notably Shakespeare, possessed the ability to sketch memorable characters in a very few lines, but most dramatists have felt the need of developing their roles at length in order to achieve personages that are convincing.

The credibility of a character is enhanced by the performance of the actor. The personal attributes of the performer add a dimension to the play which is difficult to describe and often impossible to predict in advance. In the hands of some actors villains have become heroic, heroines insipid, comic characters dull, and minor roles have run away with the play. It is a commonplace of the theater that flat, pedestrian material has, on occasion, been made by the actor to seem rich and captivating stuff, that talented performers have taken superficially contrived parts and infused them with the warmth and glow of scintillating life. In a sense, the playwright's conception of character is at the mercy of the actor. To the latter's credit, he very often extends and enlarges the original sketch into a fully rounded portrait.

Thought

The third Aristotelian element, *thought,* refers to the reasoning aspect of drama. Thought is more than the intellectual content, since a character's reasons for his behavior are bound up with his emotions. Plays are not objective debates, mere presentations of factual data and logical arguments leading to a clear decision. Characters in drama make subjective decisions under pressure, while enmeshed in webs of conflicting emotional entanglements. In this respect, dramas are like the experiences of life with all of their complicating networks of feeling and meaning beyond the immediate moment.

In his opposition to Antigone, Creon presents arguments to support his edict. The episodes between him and Antigone, Haimon, the Chorus, and Teiresias nearly become organized debates. Hamlet attempts to think his way through his perplexing problems, and Tom, in *The Glass Menagerie,* explains his reason for running away from home. This rational background constitutes the thought element of individual characters.

In addition to the rationale of individual characters, thought also concerns a play's theme—a kind of "golden text" that summarizes the moral and indicates the symbolic meaning of the play as a whole, such as "love conquers all," "murder will out," or "niceness pays." Drama does not, however, always lend itself to such neat copybook maxims. A given play may convey a variety of interpretations to an audience. Most of Ibsen's contemporaries were profoundly shocked at Nora's decision to leave her husband and children, although her action is entirely credible to most of us today. Some people regard Antigone as headstrong and foolish in openly defying Creon and thus deliberately choosing to die. The ideas of great dramas have, of course, been sources of endless critical contention. What is the true interpretation of *Hamlet?* Is Shylock a comic or tragic figure? Is the tragedy of *Antigone* really that of Creon? Where varied interpretations of a play's meaning exist, the dramatist obviously did not openly make a statement of his theme. Unless a drama is freighted with an explicit message, it is open fairly to personal interpretations, and the individual reader and spectator is challenged to search his own mind in evaluating it.

On the other hand, the express purpose of some dramatists is to illustrate a theme. Medieval drama, for example, which was a sort of visual aid designed to frighten people into salvation, patently stated the point of the story. In the best known of all medieval plays, *The Moral of Everyman,* a Messenger prepares the audience to receive the moral in a prologue; at the end of the play a Doctor appears to reemphasize it in these words:

> This moral men may have in mind;
> Ye hearers, take it of worth, old and young,
> And forsake Pride, for he deceiveth you in the end,
> And remember Beauty, Five-Wits, Strength and Discretion
> They all at the last do Everyman forsake,
> Save his Good-Deeds, there doth he take.
> But beware, and they be small
> Before God, he hath no help at all.

The outstanding German playwright Bertolt Brecht viewed the theater as a social force and thus deliberately avoided attempts to evoke emotional responses in order that his audience might be more aware of his political ideas. You will notice the interruption of continuity from time to time in *The Caucasian Chalk Circle.*

One of the most important contributions of Ibsen was his concern with dramatic themes that would provoke thought and discussion. His approach to the element of thought is clearly evident from the preliminary notes he made when in Rome while contemplating *A Doll's House.* In "Notes for a Modern Tragedy" he wrote:

> There are two kinds of spiritual law, two kinds of conscience, one in man and another, altogether different, in woman. They do not understand each other; but in practical life the woman is judged by man's law, as though she were not a woman but a man.
>
> The wife in the play ends by having no idea of what is right or wrong; natural feeling on the one hand and belief in authority on the other have bewildered her.
>
> A woman cannot be herself in the society of the present day, which is an exclusively masculine society, with laws framed by men

and with a judicial system that judges feminine conduct from a masculine point of view.

She has committed forgery, and she is proud of it; for she did it out of love for her husband, to save his life. But this husband with his commonplace principles of honor is on the side of the law and regards the question with masculine eyes.

Spiritual conflicts. Oppressed and bewildered by the belief in authority, she loses faith in her moral right and ability to bring up her children. Bitterness. A mother in modern society, like certain insects who go away and die when she has done her duty in the propagation of the race. Here and there a womanly shaking-off of her thoughts. Sudden return of anxiety and terror. She must bear it all alone. The catastrophe approaches, inexorably, inevitably. Despair, conflict and destruction.

Although Ibsen, in describing his method of working on a play, acknowledges that he began with a clearly stated theme, he took considerable pains to present his thought by implication, indirection and innuendo rather than by direct statement. As a consequence, the spectator is not overly conscious of Ibsen's themes. Unlike the medieval writers, Ibsen did not point to a clear-cut solution to the problems he raised. His purpose was to provoke thought rather than to persuade the audience to adopt a specific plan of action. An interesting example of Ibsen's intention occurred in *An Enemy of the People.* In one scene in the original version, Dr. Stockmann alludes to biology to prove that there are certain individuals "bred" to superior comprehension of truths, and who, therefore, are natural leaders. This view has been taken by some to suggest that the playwright was a fascist. When Ibsen was attacked with this argument, he replied, "I do not mean the aristocracy of birth, or of the purse, or even the aristocracy of the intellect, I mean the aristocracy of character, of will, of mind—that alone can free us." Following Ibsen's example, many modern playwrights have found their source material in contemporary problems. The content of the plays of our day is often a direct reflection of contemporary thought as the playwright weighs values and motives by which men live, seek for individual fulfillment, or search for reality.

All playwrights, in representing men in action, dramatize their significant behavior and decisions, thus providing insight into the ways by which men live and move and have their being. In tragedy, the dramatist is concerned with the profoundest problems and the most elevated concepts of mankind, with the relation of his characters to their gods, the meaning of justice, the probing into good and evil. In comedy, the playwright may exploit the ridiculous aspects of human conduct. In some forms of drama, notably farce and melodrama, the dramatist may have little or no interest in the secondary meaning of the actions of his characters. The personages of his plays are concerned only with the actions themselves, not with the meaning of the actions. In creating this kind of drama the playwright has little reference to actuality except to require the external appearance of real life. He freely manipulates his characters according to the exigencies of his plot and excuses his essential dishonesty of thought and motivation on the grounds that he is concerned only with theatrical values.

Whatever the purpose of the playwright, the action of significant drama is as meaningful as an experience of life itself. The choices that the characters make, their behavior and motivation, and the sequence of the events of the play are all rewarding subjects for investigation. The playwright's attitude is inferable from his treatment of plot and character. He may be humane and sensible like Shakespeare and Molière; he may write with the scathing satire of Ben Jonson, the compassion of Chekhov and Hauptmann, the zeal of the early Odets, the incisive and perplexing probing of Pirandello, the bleak pessimism of Sartre and Beckett, or the comic audacity of Shaw. A play, then, is more than a passing diversion unrelated to life. It is, rather, a significant revelation of the human condition.

Diction

Aristotle's fourth element is *diction,* by which is meant the language of the play, the words the actors speak. The function of diction is to provide a means for communicating the characters' thoughts, and ultimately to convey the playwright's total meaning to the audience. As John Howard Lawson says, "Speech puts the actual impact of events into words: it dramatizes forces which are not seen." In modern drama, the dramatist has a utilitarian basis for his dialogue. His lines must, as someone has suggested, "Advance the plot, delineate character, or get a laugh." Good dialogue is a means to an end, not an end in itself, for the real merit of the drama does not reside so much in wording as in its solid structure, in the sequence of the plot, in the integrity and vividness of the characterization, and in the meaning of the action behind the facade of language.

Discourse in drama must be clear, because the language must be immediately apprehended by the listener; in the theater, one cannot turn back the page or pause to weigh and consider a line before hearing the next. The dialogue must be interesting despite the need for simplicity and economy. It should capture the spirit of life and character. As the Irish playwright, Synge, put it, "In a good play, every speech should be as fully flavored as a nut or an apple." Diction must be appropriate to the character and the situation, for lines do not exist in the theater as separate entities. They are always in context. They grow out of the emotionally charged incidents of the plot. The language of drama must be dynamic, its presentation a form of action. The dialogue thus shows the character's relationship to others, reflects the progression of the action, indicates what is happening inside the characters, reveals their suffering, growth or decline. It is a means of articulating the clash of wills and the conflicting motivations. It is also a means of establishing locale, as for example O'Neill's use of the New England dialect in *Desire Under the Elms.* In high comedy, agile dialogue, with characters shooting barbed verbal shafts at one another, may be a substitute for physical movement. The dramatist needs the poet's feeling for language—a rich imagination, a felicity for provocative imagery, an awareness of the weight, texture and arrangement of words. Dramatic dialogue is not contemplative or static; it is harnessed to action and change. Finally, good dialogue must be suited for oral expression. The lines must give the actor a basic pattern for performance. They must reveal fully the character's emotions and motivations as the actor interprets them before the audience.

Much of the serious drama preceding the nineteenth century was linked to poetry. The Greek and Elizabethan masters of drama were poets as well as playwrights. Their works, therefore, have an added literary and linguistic dimension, and their use of verse seems particularly appropriate to the elevated tragedies of high-born characters. In modern times, however, poetry gives way to prose when the naturalist and realist bring onstage contemporary, commonplace figures in the everyday pursuits of life. Many have lamented the absence of poetry in the contemporary theater; sporadic attempts have been made to recapture some of the enrichment of poetic speech, notably in the works of Maxwell Anderson, Christopher Fry, Bertolt Brecht, T. S. Eliot, and Federico Garcia Lorca. Although modern drama lacks elevated language, it is not true that all plays written in poetic form were successful. Indeed, the use of verse in the past was often puerile and ostentatious. Many poets had no sense of dramatic form or theatrical awareness. Oftentimes, their preoccupation with the language retarded the action, filled their plays with linguistic clutter, thus making the drama unstageworthy. The general use of prose in the contemporary theater has resulted in stage speech that tends to be flat and pedestrian, filled with the clichés of commonplace conversation. On the other hand, current emphasis on functional speech has produced texts of directness and clarity. In the hands of some modern playwrights, the dialogue is often vivid and evocative, as for example, in the plays of Tennessee Williams and Samuel Beckett. As Bernard Shaw points out, the modern drama has gained in what he calls the "discussion" element of drama. Shaw, of course, was especially fond of ventilating controversial issues, and his plays are full of shafts and barbs about all manner of problems, as is evident in *Major Barbara.*

Most modern playwrights tend to center their attention on dramatic experiences in which characters analyze and describe forces at work upon them. They do not simply pass through a series of adventures without cerebration. They talk over the issues and expose points of view, thus adding substance to contemporary dialogue. Consider, for example, the discussion elements that do so much to expose character in *Miss Julie.*

Over the years dramatists have utilized a variety of dialogue devices. One of the most interesting, devised by the Greeks, is *stichomythia,* that is, short lines of alternating dialogue. The Greek dramatist employed stichomythia as a method of building tension much as a motion picture editor uses rapid intercutting of film clips to increase intensity in exciting moments of a picture. Molière, in the seventeenth century French theater, achieved comic stichomythia by breaking lines of dialogue into short bursts of speech by means of interruptions. You will find an example of this in *The Miser,* Act I, scene 3, and Act IV, scene 5.

Another linguistic device, one much favored by Shakespeare, is the soliloquy, a solo speech, generally an introspective analysis or a pondering of a future course of action. Playwrights, aware of rich psychological life beneath the surface, also used the convention of the soliloquy to reveal workings of the mind. The neoclassicists in France often replaced this device by the use of confidants for each of the leading characters, so that private thoughts, aimed at the ears of servants, friends, and duennas, reached the audience.

The use of extended narration for recounting offstage or antecedent action has been used from the Greeks to the present day. Effective examples are the messenger's description of the deaths of Antigone, Haimon, and Eurydice. Miss Julie's extended description of her family background is another case in point. In *The Caucasian Chalk Circle* you will note the use of a story-teller to bridge the action. An ingenious adaptation of the soliloquy is used by Beckett in *Krapp's Last Tape,* in which a single character contrasts his old age with his earlier life by listening to and commenting upon an old tape-recording of his voice.

A number of new playwrights have appeared recently who refuse to conform to established techniques and conventions of the theater. These so-called "absurdists" are of special interest in their rejection of dramatic structure and in their use of dialogue. Beckett, Ionesco, and Pinter, in particular, have written stage speech which, while intentionally pedestrian and hackneyed, is nevertheless remarkably evocative, as for example the dialogue in Ionesco's *The Leader.* Their use of clichés in short segments of sound, combined with frequent pauses, is strangely expressive in performance. At times this kind of dialogue has been used to satirize the vacuity of commonplace conversation. At other times the very flatness of the language has served as a kind of desperate cover to conceal the fear of silence.

Other dialogue devices have been used from time to time in the theater such as choral speeches, antiphonal passages between a leader and a group, staccato, telegraphic fragments of speech in expressionistic plays, extensive monologues, prologues and epilogues for exposition, foreshadowing or commenting on the action, bits of poetry, and involved conceits and epigrams. But the primary form of diction in most drama is compressed dialogue, which despite its conventions, gives to the listener the impression of natural speech.

Music

Aristotle's fifth element is *music,* which refers to all of the auditory material of a play, including sound effects and the tonal patterns of the spoken words. Music encompasses all aspects of sound—pitch, rate, quality, duration, volume, and rhythm. We remember that Greek drama had its origin in choric dithyrambs, in which music, chanting, and dancing were integral parts of the performance. The speech of the Athenian playwrights was created in rich patterns of verse in which the sound, texture, and cadence of language were significant aspects. In the Oriental theater, music continues to play an essential part in the total effect. The language of the Elizabethans often was rich in lyricism that broke out into song. Melodrama was originally linked to music, and even though the spoken word came to dominate the genre, musical backgrounds were used to accompany exits and entrances of major characters and to reinforce the tensely emotional mood of the scenes.

In our contemporary drama, naturalism and realism have rejected music per se as an artificial intrusion, but even in realistic drama playwrights have occasionally made telling use of sound to enhance the mood of their plays. Chekhov, for example, was very conscious of the use of sounds in *Uncle Vanya.* In the final act of the play, a melancholy atmosphere is reinforced by the click of the counting beads, the scratch of the pen, the churring of a cricket, the tapping of the night watchman's cane, the soft strumming of a guitar, and the bells of the carriage as Dr. Astrov makes his departure. Strindberg too was aware of the evocative effect of music. In *Miss Julie* the dance and chorus music offstage reinforce our awareness of the Midsummer Eve celebrations, and the sound of the bell heightens emotional feeling at the play's end. Other modern dramatists with a keen ear for the expressiveness of sound are Eugene O'Neill, Tennessee Williams, Maurice Maeterlinck, Federico Garcia Lorca, and Sean O'Casey. The nonrealistic playwrights, particularly the expressionists, have freely introduced music into their plays, as Brecht does in the songs in *The Caucasian Chalk Circle.*

The spoken word of all kinds of drama is allied to music in its appeal to the ear, and all successful playwrights have been mindful of the importance of rhythm and sound.

Spectacle

The sixth Aristotelian element of drama, *spectacle*, refers to all of the visual aspects of production—scenery, lighting, costume, makeup, and the business and movement of the actors. A glance at the descriptions of the stage settings and properties of the modern plays in this text will indicate how essential spectacle is for recent playwrights.

The kind and amount of spectacle have varied throughout theatrical history. In the Greek, Elizabethan, and Japanese Noh plays, virtually no representation of locale is required except that supplied by the architecture itself. Nonetheless, these plays are rich in spectacle, particularly in the use of striking costumes and in the action of the performers. The Greek chorus, the use of dance in Noh and Kabuki drama, and the vivid use of the entire ensemble in panoramic movement in Elizabethan plays, enhanced the visual appeal of the performances. With the development of the prosenium-arch theater during the Renaissance, a taste for pictorialism, for elaborate use of enormous and complicated settings, was cultivated because the arch provided a picture frame behind which changeable scenery could be devised. The realistic and naturalistic movements in the late nineteenth century gave spectacle a new importance in production because environment was widely accepted as a conditioning force in determining behavior. Hence spectacle came to assume an organic, psychological role in the theater, reinforcing the meaning of the play and serving as an expository device to relate character to its social milieu. This view of the function of spectacle is the current one, although there has been a tendency to temper the fashion for complete and factual representation of actuality by increasing simplicity and theatricalism, as for example in *The Caucasian Chalk Circle.*

While at times spectacle has dominated the stage, dwarfing or competing with the actor for the audience's attention, our present attitude is that visual aspects of theatrical production must provide appropriate psychological and physical environment for the drama, create atmosphere, and serve the actor's needs as he performs the play. Inasmuch as a play is intended to be acted, the display and the environment of that action contribute heavily to the impact of the play as theater.

chapter two TRAGEDY

Works of art are not subject to precise scientific classification because the artist, in this case the dramatist, works with a personal bent. He may also vary his style from time to time to suit a variety of purposes. We can, however, distinguish between drama that is serious (or at least makes a pretense of being serious) and drama that is intended to evoke laughter. Serious drama is usually termed tragedy and lighter drama comedy. In this chapter we will first discuss the nature of tragedy and then that of melodrama, and finally that species of play occupying a middle ground between tragedy and melodrama, which we will call *drame.*

Tragedy is a strange and mysterious country despite considerable efforts made to fix its boundaries and establish its configurations. Each adventurer must find his own way through an entangling jungle of conjecture and a luxuriant undergrowth of verbiage surrounding this territory. There is no short cut, no easy known way, because tragedy is a quality of experience each man must come to know for himself.

The first to chart his course and mark the way was Aristotle, who in his fourth century B.C. work, the *Poetics,* sought to guide those who followed him. Although he found his original directions by the genius of dead-reckoning from relatively limited observation, we may still trace his progress with profit, so clearly did he designate his landmarks. As a consequence, we will continue to refer to him frequently, as we have in the preceding section. Aristotle's work is, however, open to varied interpretations and misinterpretations, partly because of his language, which is at points hastily constructed and even contradictory, and partly because of his examples, a number of which are from plays lost to us. Aristotelian doctrine, therefore, should be regarded as a lamp in the darkness, not the source of all light.

Aristotle places considerable emphasis on the structure of tragedy. Excellence of form in all kinds of art was a source of aesthetic pleasure to the Greeks. They saw things as parts of a whole. They delighted in the organization of a unified structure. Thus, while the *Poetics* is an analysis of tragedy, Aristotle's discussion frequently concerns all forms of dramatic writing and can serve as a commentary on play-making in general.

Aristotle & Tragedy

Let us turn our attention to Aristotle's very significant definition of tragedy and then examine his terms.

> Tragedy, then, is an imitation of an action that is serious, complete, and of a certain magnitude; in language embellished with each kind of artistic ornament, the several kinds being found in separate parts of the play; in the form of action, not of narrative; through pity and fear effecting the proper purgation of these emotions.

The origin of the word *tragedy* is a matter of conjecture. "Tragos" in Greek means goat; "oide" means song. Tragedy was associated with goat-song or goat-singer in its early stages. The terms "tragic" and "tragedy" as we use them in everyday speech have little to do with "tragedy" as a form of drama. A person may speak of the "tragic" death of a small girl in an automobile accident. While tragedy usually involves catastrophe, it is not the calamity itself upon which attention is focused in drama. Death may even seem incidental, as in *Hamlet* when it occurs to such secondary characters as Polonius or Laertes. The validity of genuine tragedy is not concerned with the act of violence, but with what that act says about life—the struggle of the protagonist, the issues at stake, the effect of his suffering.

An *imitation* is not a mere copy, but is a created work of art fashioned by man. Its relation to reality is that the course of events of the drama are "necessary and probable."

An action refers to a sequence of incidents joined together into a unified whole. An action is the thing done.

Tragedy has been called the drama of *high seriousness*. It deals with the most profound and universal problems of man—his purpose and destiny, the nature of good and evil, a man's relationship to forces greater than himself, the consequences of individual responsibility. Tragedy is never frivolous, trivial, or mean. It goes far beyond diversion or amusement to investigate spiritual values and struggles.

Tragedy attains *magnitude* in the heroic stature of its characters, through the use of poetry, by the universality of its meaning and the loftiness of its ideas. Tragedies are elevated; they possess scale and scope far beyond the petty vicissitudes of daily existence. Magnitude of character is realized in tragedy through the use of high-born characters, persons of nobility and prominence who occupy "exposed positions;" people who, as Aristotle said, "are better than we are," such as the daughters of the king in *Oedipus the King* or the son of the dead king in *Hamlet.*

A tragedy is *complete;* it has a beginning, a middle, and an end. Each of these parts is causally related, thus creating a unified effect and a plot that is a well-articulated structure having no extraneous material. The course of action is a "necessary and probable" linking of antecedents and consequents. Such unity and wholeness were fundamental to the Greek aesthetic view of life.

"By *language embellished with each kind of artistic ornament,"* Aristotle explains, "I mean that with rhythm and harmony or song super-added; and by the kinds separately, I mean that some portions are worked out with verse only, and others in turn with song."

The chief difference between the *dramatic* and *narrative form* is a result of the manner of presentation. A narrative may be written or told; drama must be presented with impersonation and action—it is "a thing done." The dramatic form puts the creative work of the playwright before an audience in the theater by means of the actors' performance.

Pity, fear, and *proper purgation* (*catharsis*) are terms that have perplexed and intrigued scholars and critics for generations. Although we will discuss these special effects of tragedy at length later, let us here state that *pity* goes beyond mere pathos to include the compassion that accompanies shared grief, and that *fear* transcends sheer fright to convey a sense of anxious concern and profound reverence. *Catharsis,* or *purgation,* suggests purification—a release of emotional tension that results in tranquillity.

With Aristotle's definition in mind, and acknowledging its shortcomings because of his limited basis for observation, let us consider some important principles that characterize tragedy.

Plot

Aristotle lays great stress on plot—the "soul of tragedy." He discusses at length the essentials of dramatic structure, such as the necessity for a unified and complete sequence of interlocking action, the just proportions of the plot, and the proper use of such devices as reversal, discovery, and recognition. So broad is his consideration of plot that it may be applied to all forms of drama as well as specifically to tragedy.

What aspects of plot apply exclusively to tragedy? Certainly, Aristotle's concept of unity of action—a plot simple enough to be held easily in the mind of the spectator—does not apply to *Hamlet* or to most Elizabethan drama. Shakespeare and his contemporaries disregarded unity, moreover, by blending comic and serious material, combining high- and low-born characters, mixing verse and prose, freely interweaving plots and sub-plots on the flexible Elizabethan stage. The general answer, then, is no, the structure of tragedy does not have its own special form. The plays of the Greeks, the Elizabethans, and the neoclassicists are too divergent in structure to fit a single pattern.

Certain generalizations, however, do apply to the treatment of dramatic materials. Tragedy usually deals with a positive and active protagonist caught in sharp conflict with opposing forces. In the ensuing struggle, he suffers greatly and moves from good fortune to misfortune, never in the opposite direction. Tragic conflicts are of a particular kind. The struggle does not involve such mundane considerations as economic or sociological problems. The struggle is ethical, spiritual. Oftentimes, the tragic hero is placed in a situation in which the courses of action open to him are at war with the moral order he has accepted. Tragic actions thus arise from inner conflicts that test the protagonist's integrity.

In the organization of the incidents, the playwright must solve the customary problems of plot construction; he must create climaxes, crises, reversals, discoveries and so forth, but always with a view toward what the events reveal about the hero. The interest is not only in the incidents themselves, but in what is going on inside, the effect on the protagonist's soul. When the dramatist adopts the opposite stance and makes the external action his primary concern, he writes melodrama. The writer of genuine tragedy constructs a plot that emphasizes "inwardness."

Because tragedy is relentlessly honest, the dramatist does not contrive to save the protagonist from catastrophe or spare him from suffering. Once Antigone has defied Creon's edict she is sent relentlessly to her doom. Shakespeare does not spare Hamlet from suffering or death. The playwright shows life as it is, not as one wishes it might be. Evil is shown along with the good. In the treatment of character, the protagonist is neither the white-washed, idealized hero of romanticism nor the black-hearted villain of melodrama. Man is shown as a mixture of clay and stardust. The tragic hero is usually an admirable character, but he possesses a flaw and his imperfection links him to us. In short, tragedy rests on a solid basis of integrity, making no concessions to desires for wish-fulfillment on the part of the audience.

Tragic Catharsis

The most significant element that distinguishes tragedy from other forms of drama is the tragic effect. Just what it is in tragedy that gives pleasure through pain is difficult to determine. Friedrich Schlegel felt that the tragic tone was one of "irrepressible melancholy," as the audience is consoled and elevated through witnessing human weakness exposed to the vagaries of fate and natural forces. Arthur Schopenhauer saw the meaning of tragedy as resignation and renunciation in the face of a miserable and desolate existence. On the other hand, H. A. Myers asserts that tragedy appeals to us because it satisfies our craving to discover, even in moments of utmost suffering and evil, patterns in life which are truly representative of life and therefore just.[1] What constitutes the tragic effect is thus capable of many interpretations.

Our individual sense of the tragic is complex and highly personalized; it is arrived at through our experience and awareness. In such plays as *Hamlet* and *Antigone,* as we seek to interpret the play with our experience and with our attitudes about life, we perceive values beyond what is explicit in the story and stage action. The play's events are raised to a universal level and move us, as Professor Alan Thompson says, ". . . to the impassioned contemplation of ultimates."

To understand the tragic effect, it is necessary to keep Aristotle's words "fear and pity" before us. What did he mean by them? Pity is not simply pathos, a soft sentiment of sorrow for one who is weak or unworthy. Pity is not contemptuous or patronizing. Implied in tragic pity is an equality, a sharing of grief. We enter into the experience of another through our sympathy and our fellow-feeling. We feel pity for the tragic hero as an act of compassion. Similarly, the meaning of the word fear must be extended beyond that of sheer fright or terror to include anxious concern, solicitude, awe, reverence, and apprehension. In tragedy, fear is not merely a hair-raising, spine-tingling reaction of the nervous system; it is an emotion that warms the heart and illuminates the mind. Fear carries a sense of wonder. The terms fear and pity, therefore, must be thought of in their most human and universal context, as involving a general concern for others rather than a private and personal identification with disaster.

Aristotle obviously intended that catharsis should be therapeutic. The tragic effect on the spectator is to purge away his fear and pity, to give him a sense of release and tranquillity. He is cleansed and exhilarated when he is liberated from his own emotional entanglements and disturbing passions. Fear gives way to certainty, even though that certainty is death. Pity goes beyond feeling and becomes understanding. The spectator leaves the theater "in calm of mind, all passion spent." The end result is, as Northrop Frye suggests, that the audience experiences a "kind of buoyancy." Or again, in Edith Hamilton's words, "the great soul in pain and death transforms and exalts pain and death." Myers universalizes the meaning more explicitly:

> These are the main features of the tragic spirit. It lifts us above self-pity and reconciles us to suffering by showing that evil is a necessary part of the intelligible and just order of our experience. It lifts us above the divisive spirit of melodrama by showing that men are neither naturally good nor inherently evil. It saves us all from the pitfalls of utopianism and fatalism. It teaches moderation by showing that the way of the extremist is short, but at the same time it shows the man of principle that an uncompromising stand is not without its just compensations. And most important, it teaches us that all men are united in the kin-

[1] Henry Alonzo Myers, *Tragedy: A View of Life* (Ithaca, Cornell University Press, 1956).

ship of a common fate, that all are destined to suffer and enjoy, each according to his capacity.[2]

The Tragic Hero

Another Aristotelian concept of fundamental importance to the understanding of tragedy is the nature of the tragic hero. The tragic hero is a good man, but not free from blemish—"an intermediate kind of personage" who, while not preeminently virtuous, is not depraved. His flaw is an error in judgment. This flaw, *hamartia,* has been the source of considerable controversy in that it appears to be neither uniformly applicable to all tragedies nor consistent with the variety of characters involved in catastrophes. How does one equate the suffering of Prometheus with that of Oedipus? Antigone with that of Medea? Hamlet with that of Macbeth? The degree of guilt seems to have little or nothing to do with justice. All tragic figures suffer greatly. Frequently, their fall seems to proceed not so much from crime and punishment as it does from cause and effect. They suffer because they occupy positions of responsibility. The tragic hero is a man of good intentions whose catastrophe may be the result of a flaw, not of guilt. He may fall because he errs as well as because he sins. He often elicits our pity because of his "undeserved misfortune." In this connection, we think of the protagonists who suffer beyond all desert—Julius Caesar, Antigone, Electra, Oedipus, Othello, and Lear. Tragedy does not exist to demonstrate justice. On the contrary, it may serve to remind us of the hard fact that much of life is filled with injustice. It is a mistake, therefore, to look to tragedy for a neat apportionment of reward and punishment. Some Greek tragedies deal with protagonists whose judgment is flawed by emotional pressure that causes them to lose their sense of balance and proportion. The Greek view of the good life was based on a sense of completeness and moderation in which the passions were controlled and tempered by reason. The tragic flaw is in the loss of the hero's sense of perspective. Caught in a web of circumstances, he becomes an extremist: he loses sight of the golden mean, fails to keep his balance on a high place, and at last slips to his downfall.

Aristotle's view of the tragic hero, and of his flaw, must not be regarded as an inflexible and all-inclusive definition. To make his concepts fit the few extant Greek tragedies, not to mention the plays of Shakespeare and his contemporaries, takes considerable stretching and straining. Aristotle is thus a frame of reference for discussing tragic heroes and their qualities rather than a rigid measure by which a play may or may not be justly labeled a tragedy.

The tragic hero is a man of significance, who in representing universal human qualities, represents us. He is an active agent rather than a passive, submissive victim of accident or fate. He struggles and suffers mightily, and in his travail affirms the greatness of the human spirit.

[2] *Ibid.*

The Creation of Tragedy

Tragedy, because of its defining characteristics, requires rather special circumstances for its creation. While numerous attempts have been made to write tragedy at many different times, playwrights in general have failed to ascend the heights because of deficiency of talent, shortness of vision, or prevailing circumstances that stunted their spiritual growth. Tragedy is thus *rare.*

What seem to be the social conditions

conducive to the writing of tragedy? Both the Golden Age of Greece and the England of Elizabeth I were periods and places of great intellectual stimulation. The human spirit was exalted, mankind ennobled. The world was no vale of shadows, but an exciting place full of enormous possibilities. Life was not bland or filled with despair. Man was dignified, hopeful, secure in his faith in the future and himself. He could extend himself in many directions. The spirit of such ages was congenial to tragedy because these cultures affirmed the world and dignity of human life. The atmosphere of these times seems to conform to three basic assumptions that Oates and O'Neill give us as necessary for the creation of tragedy: "First, the dignity of man; second, the freedom of his will and his responsibility for the use which he makes of that will; and third, the existence in the universe of a super-human factor."[3] Such assumptions are positive expressions about life and its meaning. When the philosophical climate of an age rejects one or more of these points of view, tragedy of an elevated and affirmative nature is difficult to create.

Our modern temper with its doubts and skepticism about man and supernatural forces is considered by some to be inhospitable ground for the nurture of the tragic spirit. The political practice of raising the proletariat to a dominant position has changed our fashion in heroes from high-born and romantic characters to common, contemporary men. The materialism resulting from the Industrial Revolution has not only worked against individualism, but also has shifted our sense of values to a high regard for products and possessions. But most importantly, the impact of science has forced modern man to reorient his thinking, to question traditional Christian morality, to look with skepticism upon the dignity of man and see him rather as a part of the animal kingdom, "red in tooth and claw." The psychologist has caused us to look upon human behavior as a conditioned reflex. He studies the mechanism of conduct and explains man's choices and decisions on the basis of his emotions and drives.

The appropriate forms of expression which resulted from these changing attitudes were, as we shall see, realism and naturalism. The effect on drama was to drive out poetry, to emphasize the conditioning of behavior from a standpoint of heredity and environment, to depict contemporary characters involved in social problems in which interrelationships were extremely important, and to create a new significance for accurate representation of specific locale because of its influence on the action. It is obvious that these conditions were inhospitable to the creation of high tragedy. Among our contemporary playwrights, Arthur Miller, although dealing with the common man, has been most ambitious to recapture the tragic spirit. Miller's concept of tragedy is expressed in these terms:

> "I think the tragic feeling is evoked in us when we are in the presence of a character who is ready to lay down his life, if need be, to secure one thing—his sense of personal dignity. From Orestes to Hamlet, Medea to Macbeth, the underlying struggle is that of the individual attempting to gain his 'rightful' position in society."[4]

While Miller's plays faithfully demonstrate his philosophy of tragedy, his emphasis on environmental conditioning and the force of social pressures narrows his vision so that his protagonists remain earthbound despite their great suffering. The existentialists have written seriously about the human condition, but they have been restricted because their protagonists are cut off from outside forces, even from their contemporaries. The lack of faith and the restricted range of spiritual exploration negate the elevation of tragedy. Now

[3] Whitney J. Oates and Eugene O'Neill, Jr., eds., *The Complete Greek Drama* (New York, Random House, Inc., 1938), p. xxviii.

[4] Arthur Miller, "Tragedy and the Common Man," *New York Times,* February 27, 1949, Section II, p. 1.

the "absurdists" have taken a yet more extreme position by denying even themselves and dramatizing life as being futile, meaningless, and grotesque.

John Mason Brown describes the difficulties of writing modern tragedy, although he does see some hope:

> A period of realism and an age of prose are not the only hindrances. The lost or dwindling religious faith of many people; the encroachments of such a materialistic and earthbound theology as Marxism; an increasing uncertainty as to accepted or acceptable standards; our living with the threat of mass annihilation; adjusting to the great changes in the stresses and basic concepts of our economic and social life; the emergence of the "little man" as the new hero for hero worship; the shrinkage of the individual's importance under the pressures of super-states or ever-growing bureaucracies; indeed, not only the notion but the realization that the century belongs to the common rather than the exceptional man—all these factors, widening or limiting, which have altered tragedy along with everything else. Because of them, one wonders if the tragic blueprint, cherished for so long as an ideal, has not, at least in part, become a glorious anachronism.
>
> Not that tragedy is dead or will ever die. Or that Man has lost his touch with the heroic. No one who has watched men, women, and children rise to the terrible trials of these past years can maintain that Man has become mean. The bigness of the so-called "little man" in the face of such trials and of daily living is one of the most hopeful facts of recent history. It is simply that the heroic has become different in scale and kind, and for this very reason tragedy needs to be rediscovered for our own times and in our own terms.[5]

Whether or not great tragedy can be written today is a matter of controversy. Certainly, the temper of our times seems alien to the great traditions, although in the plays of Arthur Miller, Ugo Betti, and Paul Claudel we catch glimpses of an ancient grandeur, and in modern biography considerable evidence of man's spiritual capacity raises him again toward the tragic heights.

[5] John Mason Brown, "American Tragedy," *Saturday Review*, August 6, 1949. Reprinted by permission of the publishers.

Significance of Content

Tragedy achieves significance because it is concerned with the deep and abiding questions and problems that have perplexed man throughout the ages. As Nicoll says, tragedy puts us in ". . . contact with infinity. If we are religious, we shall say it is in contact with the vast illimitable forces of the universe. Everywhere in tragedy there is this sense of being raised to loftier heights."[6] Tragedy is thus concerned with man's spiritual nature. It confronts suffering and evil with relentless honesty in such a way as to reveal both the weakness and nobility of man, his strength of will, and his capacity for suffering without breaking in the face of inevitable doom.

Although tragedy involves suffering, evil and death, it is a positive statement about life. As Nicoll says, "Death never really matters in a tragedy. . . . Tragedy assumes that death is inevitable and that its time of coming is of no importance compared with what a man does before his death."[7] Death may

[6] Allardyce Nicoll, *The Theory of Drama* (New York, Thomas Y. Crowell Co., 1931).

[7] *Ibid.*

overtake the protagonist, but he is spiritually victorious. He is not an abject, craven victim of fate who goes cowering to his doom. The principles for which he lived and died survive his passing. The hero dies; heroism lives on. We admire the audacity of a man who, disregarding human frailty, reveals an astonishing capacity for suffering in matters of the spirit. His action, an affirmation of life, sustains our faith in mankind.

Professor H. A. Myers asserts that "tragedy best expresses its conceptions of the orderly and absolute nature of values;" and Professor Francis Fergusson observes that tragedy "celebrates the mystery of human nature and destiny with the health of the soul in view."

Tragedy is not the drama of small souls. It does not concentrate on man's physical environment or his welfare, nor with his getting and spending, his thing-collecting. On the contrary, tragedy lifts our vision beyond petty cares and mundane anxieties by forcing our attention to the great issues of life which bear a relationship to our spiritual welfare. Antigone is caught between her sacred obligation to the dead and obedience to the King. Entangled in a set of strong moral sensibilities, Hamlet bears the awful burden of avenging the death of his father. The conflicting characters in *Antigone* and *Hamlet* occupy places of great responsibility in contrast to the rather narrow lives of Tom and Amanda in *The Glass Menagerie,* of Eben and Abbie in *Desire Under the Elms,* and of Jean and Miss Julie in *Miss Julie.* In contemporary serious drama the characters seem to be playing for small stakes and the effect of their suffering is personal rather than of great consequence.

The significant content of tragedy gives this form of drama a sense of universality. The effect of the play goes beyond the particular characters and the immediate circumstances to achieve an atmosphere of broad application. If even kings may suffer, how vulnerable are we? To the Greeks and Elizabethans the fate of the ruler was connected directly with that of his subjects. To witness genuine tragedy gives us not only a sense of elevation to our own separate lives, but also an acute awareness of our common frailty and humanity. The tragic hero's struggles and suffering thus ennoble and humble those who share the play.

In order to attain magnitude and elevation, however, let us remember that tragic events must be removed a step from our own lives. To perceive their great scope and grandeur, a certain amount of distance and perspective is required. High tragedy conveys a sense of aloofness and detachment, which in its most severe expression threatens to throw a chill of austerity over the drama and its characters. On the other hand, the problems dealt with by tragedy are so universal and the protagonist's suffering so intense that we are drawn quite naturally into the action.

Melodrama

The writer of melodrama is not interested in the literary aspects of drama; essentially he is an adept storyteller and craftsman with a shrewd sense of pace, rhythm, a feeling for climactic action, and an understanding of the audience for which he writes. Logic does not interest him so long as his script gives the impression of credibility. He achieves this credibility by involving his characters in exciting action and by creating the illusion of actuality through the use of realistic backgrounds, appropriate costuming, and dialogue that suggests the speech of everyday life.

Melodramatic plots rely on strong story lines because the writer knows that his audience is not primarily interested in probing character, listening to bright parlor talk, or considering perplexing social problems. His clientele wants to see familiar characters involved in stories told in scenes of clear and vigorous action. Hence, melodrama exaggerates climaxes and crises so that its structure becomes a series of peaks of action rather than a well-knit steady progression of logically related events. Characters are shown facing overwhelming odds—trapped, dangling, or marooned—holding out until help comes—the last bullet, the last drop of water, the last morsel of food, the last cent. Stock melodramatic situations include escapes, ambushes, shipwrecks, murders, duels, drownings, explosions, battles, rescues, fires, executions, rendezvous and all manner of natural phenomena—storms, avalanches, floods, eruptions: any situation, in short, that places the characters in physical jeopardy.

In *Hamlet* Shakespeare approaches the techniques of melodrama in his use of the duel with the poisoned sword and drink, and in the gothic atmosphere surrounding the appearances of the ghost. Strindberg carefully manipulates the arrival of the Count and Julie's violent death after the fashion of melodrama, but neither Shakespeare nor Strindberg exploit violence for its own sake. The techniques employed are organic to the plays and are not injected as sheer spectacle.

Melodrama no longer occupies the central position that it did in the legitimate theater of the nineteenth century, but it continues today to have a very wide popular appeal in motion pictures and on television. Much of our current melodrama is much more sophisticated than that of a century ago. The visual aspects are far more credible, and the action may be psychological as well as physical. But the essentials of melodrama are almost always present in our "westerns," "whodunits," and our stories of war and adventure.

Professor H. A. Myers in his *Tragedy: A View of Life,* makes an interesting statement about character when he says, "In the black-and-white world of melodrama men are divided in two sharply opposed classes, represented by the unblemished hero and the unspeakable villain. . . . The first premise of melodrama is that there are two distinct kinds of men: the first premise of tragedy is that all men are essentially the same." [8] Nineteenth-century melodrama and our contemporary motion picture and television plays of action testify to the validity of Myers' observation. Characters are generally good or bad one-dimensional figures who pursue their objectives in a straight line, without thought, development, or psychological complexity. They do not think; they act. And as a result of their thoughtlessness, they become involved in all sorts of absurd entanglements, such as being caught on a train trestle at midnight without a lantern or match, lost in the snow barefoot, or ensnared by the villain because they misjudged the character of their adversary. The writer of melodrama has little or no concern with delineating characters as substantial individuals who respond to the events in which they participate and who are conditioned by their environment and past experiences. Melodramatic characters are simple in heart and mind; they are objects of desire with whom the audience can readily identify itself. Hence, the heroes and heroines of melodrama are not the elevated figures of great tragedy; they are humble people drawn from everyday life. The villains, however, are often outsiders—foreigners, members of the upper crust, unscrupulous men of wealth.

[8] Meyers, *Op. cit.*

The impact of melodrama relies heavily on music and spectacle. Melodrama, originally linked with music, has continued that association as a principal means of eliciting emotional response. In the nineteenth century, special theme music was used to announce entrances and exits of leading characters and to create the atmosphere for emotionally loaded scenes. With the coming of realism to the theater during the last quarter of the nineteenth century, music nearly disappeared. The makers of silent motion pictures soon learned to provide appropriate scores for piano or organ, and with the advent of sound films and television music has continued to be an important aspect of the production.

In the first half of the nineteenth century, theaters made use of two-dimensional stock pieces consisting of backdrops and wings, on which were painted a variety of backgrounds such as a kitchen, a palace, a prison, a grotto, a woodland glade. This system possessed two virtues—it was economic, and it made shifting rapid and easy. To change to a new setting, the backdrop was raised and the wings were slid back along their grooves to uncover the scenes directly behind them. Throughout the country theaters were equipped with stock sets, so that a touring company needed to bring only its special effects and costumes along. But as the taste for sensational novelties grew, productions became increasingly elaborate and expensive. Metropolitan stages became more complicated with bridges, traps, elevators, moving platforms, and various kinds of paraphernalia for producing fires, floods, explosions, and all manner of astounding displays. Two-dimensional scenery was replaced by built-up solid pieces, making the sets substantial and difficult to move. The producer David Belasco actually bought pieces of buildings and moved them intact onto the stage. Playwrights were obliged to create scenes calculated to exploit visual sensations. While sensational scenery called attention to itself, it was also used for more than pictorial representation. The setting was functional in that it served the actor's needs in particular scenes. A waterfall was not simply shown as an enlarged calendar picture for its visual appeal; it became a factor in the action when the hero struggled to save the heroine from plunging to her death. A railroad trestle was set on stage not merely for the novelty of showing a train, but also as a weapon of the villain who tied the heroine to the tracks while the approaching light and whistle of the train were seen and heard. The setting was an essential part of the action. Hence, a considerable amount of ingenuity was required by the stage mechanic to devise effects that were not only visually credible, but also utilitarian enough to be used in chases, fights, and escapes. The motion picture, the ideal medium for exploiting action, has shifted the elaboration of scenic requirements from stage to screen.

Drame

Most serious modern playwrights have not aspired to scale the heights of tragedy, nor have they been content to confine themselves to sheer melodrama. They have tended to write middle-class plays for a middle-class audience, dealing with contemporary man in commonplace circumstances. This vast body of dramatic literature defies definition because of its great diversity, its technical experimentation and its mixture of several forms of writing at once. Some critics simply use the general term, drama, but we prefer, as a lesser evil, the French term *drame,* by which is meant a play of serious intent which deals for the most part with contemporary life. Just as realism has been the dominant mode of modern drama, likewise, the *drame* has been the preponderant form used by such writers as Henrik Ibsen, Anton Chekhov, Maxim Gorki, Sean O'Casey, Eugene O'Neill, Luigi Pirandello, Jean Anouilh, Clifford Odets, Arthur Miller, and Tennessee Williams.

Drame is allied to melodrama in that the playwright often attempts to involve the spectator in the action through identification with the characters and through suspense and tension. *Drame* differs from melodrama in that it may be interested in the realm of ideas—the issues at stake may be sociological and philosophical in implication, as in *An Enemy of the People.* Characters may be involved in genuinely significant action. The effect of a *drame* may be to provoke thought and discussion after the curtain has gone down.

Drame is allied to tragedy in its seriousness of purpose, in its relentless honesty of treatment, in its concern with the meaning of human conduct. *Drame* differs from tragedy in its narrowness of vision, often with its emphasis on material, with temporary or local conditions that deny it universality, with its mechanistic or deterministic sense of values, and with its general lack of elevation. Frequently, the writer of *drames* is fascinated by the psychological complexities of character. His *dramatis personae* are not the stock characters of melodrama; they are individuals with subtle and complicated motivations. They are also not the tragic heroes of great stature who fall from high places, but are ordinary people painfully searching for meaning and security in a baffling world of shifting values.

Modern drama has been notable for its experimentation, but the bulk of serious theatrical fare falls in the general area of realism. It may be profitable to give some attention to this mode and departures from it.

Although playwrights throughout theater history have often intended to give their plots and characters the feeling of actuality, it was not until the nineteenth century that *realism* as a specific literary theory emerged. The intellectual revolution that was brought about by the advance of science and industrialism placed emphasis on the physical and material aspects of life and created the climate for realism. The works of Darwin, Freud, and Marx challenged the traditional views of man. He became an object of scientific study. His life and behavior were viewed as susceptible to explanation according to naturalistic laws and principles. Heredity and environment were conditioning factors behind his actions. The realist relied on meticulous observation, analysis, and recording of specific details. It was his mission to see, hear, and report everything.

This intellectual revolution had a profound effect on drama and the theater. The writer of popular nineteenth-century melodrama dramatized simple people in a complicated plot based on physical action. The realist reversed this method by showing complex characters in a simple plot involving psychological action. He caught the semblance of reality by making all aspects of his work seem logical and free from theatrical contrivances. The painted, two-dimensional stock sets gave way to the "box set," a setting of three continuous walls with practical doors and windows and the furniture properties of real life. Relying on observed facts of everyday existence, he brought the drama closer to actual experience. But the effect often achieved was to make the plot plausible at the expense of narrowing the scope of action and slowing down the pace. Critics of realism complain that in order to condense the action within a solid framework cluttered with detail, the realist sacrificed the free play of his imagination and trapped himself in the stuffy atmosphere of middle-class interiors.

The realist's interest in character caused

him to probe into the complexities of motivation. He discarded the stock figures of the popular nineteenth-century theater because they did not jibe with his concept of behavior as rooted in the pressures of environment, the dynamics of childhood, and the interaction of biological drives and social inhibitions. A new gallery of characters, the ordinary and the downtrodden, took a central position on stage. They were shown at the critical moments of their lives, not necessarily those of violent physical action as in melodrama, but of the inner crises that penetrated the social façade and gave insight into their desires, aspirations, and frustrations. The effect on playwriting was to deal with people of small stature, who were sometimes victims of circumstances, incapable of taking action against the forces that impinged on them. But the writers of realistic *drames* did contribute to the theater integrity of character and a concern with sound psychological motivation.

While realism has been the dominating mode of the contemporary theater, the *drame* has also moved in other directions. Two offshoots of realism were naturalism and expressionism.

The "naturalists" shared with the realists a similar background, but the former were much more emphatic in their mechanistic and deterministic view of life. Man is regarded as animalistic, a product of callous nature. The naturalist stresses the sordid and somber aspects of life; his characters are twisted rejects, the social outcast, the moral outlaw. The naturalist breaks sharply from the realist in his preoccupation with the ugly and squalid side of life. Émile Zola, the champion of naturalism, clamored for drama based on the scientific method, free from theatrical trickery. Attempts were made to write "slice-of-life plays," in which the usual dramatic structure was rejected in order to give the impression that what happened on stage was unorganized actuality.

In 1888 August Strindberg wrote *Miss Julie,* terming it "the Swedish drama's first naturalistic play." This *drame* is an excellent example of naturalism in its conflict of wills growing out of complicated motivations, the powerful use of biological drives, and the general atmosphere of amoral depravity. But technically the play does not follow strictly the tenets of naturalism. It is carefully structured toward a powerful climax, embodies careful foreshadowing and exposition and exhibits a clearcut beginning, middle, and end. In a very powerful way it displays nonetheless the naturalist's approach to character.

A second derivative of realism is expressionism, in which the dramatist argues that reality lies within. The observed facts of conventional behavior do not really show the vast jungle of primitive feelings and drives hidden beneath the surface. Hence, the expressionist strives to project the essential qualities of objects, experiences, and people from the inside out. The expressionist's method is to suppress the details of actuality and to experiment freely with ways of conveying his feelings, often in fantastic, distorted fragments. He flings open the windows of the mind and allows the spectator to look in upon the private, disordered, associative processes of his characters. In Rice's *The Adding Machine,* Mr. Zero's crime and punishment are shown; Kaiser's *From Morn to Midnight* tells the story of a bank clerk's theft, orgy of spending, and death; O'Neill's *Emperor Jones* is a kaleidoscopic depiction of the disintegration of a fugitive through fear. The events often are shown from the subjective and disoriented point of view of the protagonist caught in a nightmare world of grotesquerie. Expressionism never dominated the theater because of its lack of story appeal and its sometimes baffling use of symbols, but its bold theatricalism and effective use of light, form, and color make it a fascinating treatment of the *drame.*

Current playwrights seem to be increasingly impatient with the literal narrowness of realism and have struck off in many new directions, including the "absurdists," who are represented in this volume by Beckett and Ionesco. Another modern innovator writing in a serious vein was Brecht, who rejected the realistic mode to write "epic drama"—plays that are not concerned with the personal conflicts of an individual but with the dynamics of social forces at work, as in *The Caucasian Chalk Circle*. Since Brecht was a man with a message, he utilized all the resources of the stage as visual support for his ideas.

chapter three COMEDY

Comedy wears many masks, appears in many guises, from the ill-fitting tattered rags of the drunken hobo to the elegant evening clothes of the most sophisticated aristocrat to the overdressed finery of the fop. Comedy makes many appeals, from the belly-laugh to the well-concealed smile. Its armor includes such a variety of weapons as the rapier, the slapstick, the barbed shaft, and the custard pie. It may invoke warm and sympathetic general laughter, or it may castigate a victim with a hard and ruthless derision. Comedy speaks many languages—epigrams, conceits, puns, obscenities, *bons mots,* double-meanings, and the gesture vocabulary of the silent mime. The field of comedy is broad enough to encompass many variations—the romantic comedy of Shakespeare, such as *As You Like It,* and his dark comedies like *A Winter's Tale;* the high comedy of Sheridan's *The School for Scandal;* a musical comedy such as *My Fair Lady;* a farce like Molière's *A Doctor in Spite of Himself* or his character comedy, *The Miser;* a Shavian satire, *Major Barbara;* an intimate revue, *Beyond the Fringe;* an Aristophanic thrust, *Lysistrata;* or a Jacques Tati pasquinade, *Mr. Hulot's Holiday.* And comedy includes the prefabricated television fare of Lucille Ball, Jack Benny, Danny Kaye, and situations built around the bewildering behavior of adolescents, the antics of their parents, and "fun in uniform."

The Nature of Comedy

To define comedy is first to acknowledge the difficulties and hazards of definition. What may make one person laugh may make another grieve. The lively oak of comedy cannot be crammed into a flower pot of simple definition when one considers all of its roots and branches, its variegated fruits and foliage. We usually label a play that ends happily as a comedy and one that ends unhappily as a tragedy. But even this broad generalization breaks down in some instances. Euripides chose to end *Alcestis* happily; Dante calls his great work, with its elevated theme and treatment, *The Divine Comedy.* While classicists and neoclassicists keep tragedy and comedy separate, many playwrights, notably the English, blended comic and serious matter together, as in *Hamlet, Dr. Faustus,* and *Macbeth.* Aristotle, in his *Poetics.* makes an important distinction in saying that in tragedy men are shown as "better than they are" and in comedy as "worse than they are." As Northrop Frye has pointed out, the qualifying words Aristotle uses for good and bad are *spoudaios* and *phaulos,* which have a figurative connotation of "weighty" and "light." Lightness of touch is certainly one of the hallmarks of comedy.

Perhaps it is sufficient to say that comedy has as its purpose to delight, entertain, or regale an audience through the presentation of characters, situations, and ideas in the spirit of fun. As tragedy achieves its catharsis through fear and pity, so comedy aims at its special catharsis through amusement and laughter that keep man close to sanity and balance, that remind us of our human frailties and keep us humbly aware of what we are rather than what we might wish ourselves to be.

Kinds of Comedy

The problem of classification is also especially acute in comedy. Playwrights have a way of ignoring arbitrary pigeonholes and of mixing various kinds of comic matter to suit their dramatic purposes without regard to academic convenience. For example, Aristophanes frequently uses all manner of obscenities and physical humor characteristic of farce, but he blends this material with satirical thrusts at the ideas of his contemporaries, thus filling his comedies with political and philosophical ramifications. The perplexed scholar, in an attempt to catalogue this variety, has been forced to use the label of "Aristophanic" comedy. Shakespeare is similarly difficult to categorize because he writes in such a variety of ways—farcical, romantic, and "dark" comedies, sometimes mixing different styles in the same play.

The easiest generalization to make is that at the low end of the scale is the physical comedy of farce and at the other end the high comedy of manners or ideas. But the problem with the gradations in-between, as well as with the two extremes, is, as we have already noted, that they are not mutually exclusive. Moreover, playwrights have compounded plays of all of the elements, blending them in various fashions so that they defy neat schematic compartmentalization. The juices of comedy have a way of bubbling over, penetrating all kinds of chinks and crannies. They are difficult to cork up in logic-tight containers. The safest conclusion seems to be that comedy ranges between high and low, between the physical and intellectual, and that it differs in kind from play to play according to the playwright's purposes. Perhaps the most essential ingredient for all kinds of comedy is the point of view we shall discuss subsequently as "the comic attitude."

Purposes of Comedy

Many thinkers consider comedy to have a useful and moral aim. Goldoni regarded comedy as a means to correct "faults and foibles;" Hazlitt, "to unmask ignorance and deceit;" Meredith, "to vindicate reason, common sense, rightness and justice, for no vain purpose ever;" Shaw, "for the correcting of pretentiousness, of inflation, of dullness." The French philosopher Henri Bergson, in his entertaining book *Laughter,* summarizes this function of comedy as the drama of criticism in these words: "Laughter is, above all, a corrective. Being intended to humiliate, it must make a painful impression on the person against whom it is directed. By laughter, society avenges itself for liberties taken with it." [1] When comedy serves such a purpose, the object of laughter is usually unsociable.

[1] Henri Bergson, *Laughter,* trans. by Cloudesley Brereton and Fred Rothwell (New York, The Macmillan Co., 1917).

This has little to do with morality, since we are inclined to laugh at a character's eccentricities rather than his vices or virtues, except insofar as they make him ludicrous. A comic character's deviation from the norm in speech, manners, or appearance causes us to laugh because we want to keep him in line. This corrective use of laughter is, of course, not confined to the theater inasmuch as the fear of ridicle is one of the primary forces in causing the members of society to conform. Hence, in comedy, the butt of the joke, by implication, suggests the sin of antisocial behavior.

But the purpose of comedy is not always critical. Laughter is shared in those situations when we laugh *with* a character rather than *at* him—a character who may be fully aware of his weakness, yet is appealing because we are reminded of our common human inconsistency. As instances of this kind of comic appeal, we think of characters caught in circumstances where they are embarrassed, fearful, and confused. Our laughter often becomes a bond of sympathy, not of ridicule. We do not isolate such characters from our approval; we share with them our universal experience as human beings. While some comedy is critical, it also exists on the level of sheer entertainment and delight and serves only secondarily as a means for releasing tensions and inhibitions, a purpose Freud saw, however, as the primary reason for the phenomenon of laughter.

The Comic Attitude

Max Eastman has devoted considerable attention to analyzing the conditions essential for the "enjoyment of laughter" in his book by the same title.[2] He observes that humor depends upon the existence of a favorable circumstance, and concludes that "the condition in which joyful laughter most continually occurs is that of play." Laughter is not aroused by those situations where feelings are violent or deep. As a part of his evidence, Eastman cites the native response of a child who may welcome shock and disappointment as a pleasurable experience provided that an atmosphere of play has been established. If the child is teased, however, when he is tired or hungry, the fun is over; the atmosphere of play has been destroyed. Eastman's point of view is pertinent to our understanding of the comic attitude. How much emotional involvement should the audience be made to feel during a comedy? What is the basis for the comic attitude?

In Shakespeare's romantic comedies, the sentimental plays of Sheridan and Goldsmith in the eighteenth century, and in many of our contemporary works, the spectator is invited to enter into the emotions of the characters. We become concerned about the fortunes of the protagonist, and our sympathies and hostilities are aroused by the playwright's treatment of his characters; we take pleasure in seeing the hero achieve his objective, which is often accompanied by the jingle of money or wedding bells. The characters may be laughable, may at times appear foolish and weak, but the playwright does not criticize them. He treats them with tolerance and indulgence—the comic strip humor of "Peanuts." We laugh with the characters rather than at them, and our laughter is without malice.

[2] Max Eastman, *Enjoyment of Laughter* (New York, Simon & Shuster, Inc., 1942).

On the other hand, Bergson argues that "laughter has no greater foe than emotion . . . Its appeal is to the intelligence, pure and simple." Myers supports Bergson in this view by saying, "without detachment, we cannot realize the effect of comedy, which transforms the frustrations of reason into laughter." This point of view is well taken, especially at the extremes of the comic scale—low comedy and high. In most farce, our enjoyment stems from the action itself, the momentary laugh, the sudden release. We recognize that farce is a form of play; we do not take its actions seriously. These are prefabricated characters racing through the convolutions of plot; they are not real people. No one experiences any genuine pain; the feelings do not penetrate the grease paint. Thus a detachment is achieved because we consciously watch the actions of an artificial world.

High comedy has a different basis for objectivity. Its appeal is intellectual. The reaction to it arises out of perception and insight rather than emotion. Sentiment is fatal to the aesthetic attitude required for intellectual wit and satire. Occasionally, the playwright lashes out too vigorously at his characters, stirring up an undertone of bitterness which destroys the comic effect. When Ben Jonson laid bare the human follies of avarice in *Volpone,* his unmerciful treatment of the brutality and viciousness of his characters threatened to dissipate the spirit of laughter. When Molière attacked greed in *The Miser,* he was careful to exaggerate the niggardliness of his protagonist so that little emotional attachment was possible. The character of Shylock in Shakespeare's *The Merchant of Venice* presents a perplexing challenge to the actor because of the wide range of emotions; he is at once an object of ridicule and at the same time a human being whose deep suffering intrudes upon the comic atmosphere.

The comic attitude requires a just sense of proportion so that the essential lightness of spirit is achieved, just as Eastman suggested in play with the child. The audience of comedy cannot be pushed too hard in any direction. Excessive sentimentality, bitterness, depravity, exaggeration—any conspicuous straining for effect, any flat dullness or heavy-footed plodding—upsets the niceness of balance which is so necessary for comedy and which makes comedy the most difficult of all the forms of drama to perform. In the words of Hegel:

> Inseparable from the comic is an infinite geniality and confidence, capable of rising superior to its own contradiction, and experiencing therein no taint of bitterness nor sense of misfortune whatever. It is the happy frame of mind, a hale condition of the soul, which, fully aware of itself, can suffer the dissolution of its aims.[3]

[3] G. W. F. Hegel, *The Philosophy of History,* trans. by J. Sisbree (New York, Colonial Press, 1899).

Sources of Laughter

The sources of comic effect have given scholar, critic, philosopher, and psychologist endless ground for speculation, and although their efforts have resulted in no uncontroversial conclusions, we may find something of value in their ideas. Among the various comic theories, let us briefly examine the three which Allardyce Nicoll cites in his *The Theory of Drama* as the most prominent, and understand at the outset that a good deal of their validity depends upon personal interpretation and careful selection of examples. The three theories may be summarized as derision, incongruity, and automatism. You will recognize immediately the tendency of the theories to overlap because of the mercurial nature of comedy.

Derision

Aristotle's observation that comedy deals with men as "worse than they are," implies a comic theory of derision or degradation. It is ordinarily used as a form of criticism to combat pretentiousness or ignorance. Its objective is to keep men balanced, humble, and human. The legitimate targets of derision are pomposity, hypocrisy, and sanctimoniousness. As in life, laughter is used to keep people in line, to insure conformity to a socially acceptable code of behavior. The satirist has always regarded comedy as a salutary scourge to castigate awkward behavior. Notice the use of comedy as criticism in the plays of Molière, Sheridan, and Shaw in this text.

Greek comedy ridiculed physical deformities as well as those of conduct. Comic characters were intentionally distorted and misshapen in appearance through the use of masks, phallic symbols, and padded costumes. A man's attempts to rise above himself were often counteracted by the reminder of his biological needs. Aristophanes delighted in mocking men and gods by exhibiting them in all kinds of embarrassing physical situations. He was ruthless in aiming his shafts of wit at all levels of life. The pattern of derision, including all manner of physical humor, coarse gags, barbed insults, and eccentric behavior, has continued throughout dramatic literature to the present time, especially in farce. The satirist exploits situations in which characters are debased and reduced to objects of scorn by such stock devices as physical beatings, bodily functions—situations in which man is caught off-balance, red-handed, under the bed, in the closet, in his underwear—in any of the circumstances of life in which he is exposed, his dignity punctured, his flaw revealed, reminding everyone of his kinship with the animal world. Even the most serious moments of life are not free from the threat of derision. For example, the sacred liturgy of the church was burlesqued by medieval performers in their *Feast of the Asses*. In a contemporary film, Jacques Tati in *Mr. Hulot's Holiday,* reduces the solemnity of a funeral to shambles when his leaking inner tube is mistaken for a wreath, hissing and writhing during the somber ceremony.

Degradation of character often involves a reversal of status. The deviant from normal social behavior wins the prize; the inflated person is brought down from his pedestal. Such common offenders against common sense and decent humanity as fools, fops, hypocrites, bumpkins, louts, misers, philanderers, braggarts, bores, and battle-axes are ridiculed into limbo because of their deformed behavior, their lack of wit or excess of ambition, greed, lust, or stupidity. And authority of any kind, when it becomes unbending and heavyhanded, is fair game for the barbs of satirists because the common man finds release and enjoyment in the discomfiture of those above him.

Incongruity

Perhaps because it is the most elastic and extensive theory of comedy, the idea of incongruity has the widest application. Incongruity is the result of the tension or dissonance created by setting side by side two objects or people that are markedly or unexpectedly different, such as a large, fat woman matched with a small, skinny man, or a person out of place with his surroundings, say, someone wearing a bathing suit at the opera or formal clothes on the beach. The laugh-producing quality of the contrast usually depends on establishment of some kind of norm so that the degree of difference is emphasized. A distinct gap between the expected and the unexpected, between normal and abnormal, between intention and realization, results in comic discord and inconsistency.

Incongruity may take various forms—of situation, of character, or of dialogue. The comic situation based on incongruity presents a contrast between the usual or accepted behavior and the unusual or unacceptable. A typical pattern is to place a character in unfamiliar surroundings that reveal his social incongruity, such as a country bumpkin in polite society, the socially elite in bucolic surroundings, an intellectual among barbarians, a clown or an inebriate in a dignified gathering, a sailor in a harem, a coed in a men's dormitory, a tramp in the mayor's bed. Some examples of incongruous comic situations are the father's failure to know his own children in *Major Barbara,* the extremely usurious demands made by Harpagon in loaning money in *The Miser,* and, in *The School for Scandal,* the wife hiding herself behind a screen in another man's house to keep her husband from discovering her presence.

Incongruity of character also involves a contrast between the ideal and the real, or between appearance and actuality: the miser's ridiculous attempts to serve as genial host while saving money on food and drink, or his ludicrous efforts to woo Marianna. An aspect of incongruity of character which also fits Bergson's automatism, described below, is the inflexible character whose one-track mind separates him from the norm. An excellent illustration is again Harpagon and the miserliness which colors every facet of his life.

Incongruity of language occurs when the dialogue is in sharp contrast to the social context, such as the sudden interjection of vulgarity into a polite conversation, or when the language has the opposite effect to that intended by the speaker. Still another use of incongruous language is speech that is unexpected or inappropriate to the characters, such as refined epigrams spoken by rustics or wise sayings from the mouths of children.

Incongruity in its various forms suggests imbalance and disproportion; there is the implication of an upset equilibrium, "the disconnecting of one idea from another, or the jostling of one feeling against another."

Automatism

One of the most imaginative and provocative theories of comedy is that advanced by Bergson in his book, *Laughter,* in which he claims that the essence of the laughable is automatism—"something mechanical is encrusted on the living." Man becomes an object of laughter whenever he becomes rigid and machinelike, whenever he loses control of himself or breaks contact with humanity.

Automatism of character occurs when an individual loses his human flexibility and his behavior becomes mechanical in its repetition, or when a man becomes a puppet, no longer in control of his actions. The gist of Bergson's thinking is indicated by these representative statements about comedy and character:

> We laugh every time a person gives us the impression of being a thing.
>
> Any individual is comic who automatically goes his own way without troubling himself about getting in touch with the rest of his fellow beings.
>
> Rigidity, automatism, absentmindedness, and unsociability are all inextricably entwined, and all serve as ingredients to the making up of the comic in character.[4]

Bergson's point of view on one-sided characters is similar to that of Ben Jonson's comedy of "humours," in which he ridiculed those characters who were guilty of some imbalance, some excess.

> As when some one peculiar quality
> Doth so possess a man, that it doth draw
> All his effects, his spirits, and his powers

[4] Bergson, *Op. cit.*

In their conflluctions, all to run one way
This may be truly said to be a humour.

In such plays as *Epicene, Volpone,* and *The Alchemist,* Jonson makes comic figures of those who have lost control and succumbed to some individual trait of character that causes eccentric and antisocial behavior. Molière, in bringing low those guilty of excess, derided those who were too ambitious in *The Would-Be Gentleman,* those who were too clever in *The Affected Young Ladies,* too exacting in *Le Misanthrope,* too gullible in *Tartuffe,* and of course, too parsimonious in *The Miser.*

Bergson's theory is an interesting extension of the idea of incongruity, the jostling together of the human and the mechanical. By his ingenuity and persuasiveness, Bergson makes quite a plausible case for automatism, especially in regard to the comedies of Molière, but like other comic theories, automatism does not explain all of the sources of laughter, nor is it appropriate to all kinds of comic effect. Automatism must be recognized, nevertheless, as one of the explanations for the phenomenon of laughter, and we are indebted to Bergson for his stimulating analysis.

From the preceding discussion of representative theories of comedy, a case can be made for derision, incongruity, and automatism as significant factors in the comic effect. It is impossible, however, to fix comedy in a single rigid mold, even though recurrent patterns and mechanisms show through its diverse forms. The many faces of comedy will be increasingly evident as we consider its structure and content.

Plot

Good comedy requires skillful plotting. A comedy is not simply a loosely knit accumulation of situations and gags. Laughs must be carefully timed and built, situations contrived and an appropriate atmosphere established. A comedy playscript is a score for playing, and, just as the composer must be fully cognizant of the possibilities of his music in the hands of musicians, the writer of comedy must, in a similar way, be fully aware of the techniques and resources of the actor which will animate his material. The comic writer is acutely concerned with man in his social environment. Basic patterns of comedy depict a character who deviates from the norm or who is out of place with his surroundings. The implicit contrasts and conflicts require adroit delineation of the social milieu in order to expose the laughable elements of conduct. Tragic writers may concentrate on heroic figures isolated from other characters and unaffected by their behavior, but comedy exploits the interaction of characters, the human scene, the group situation, the juxtaposition of characters. Comedy is more involved with the particular than with the universal. Its emphasis is on the here and now, not the long view. The playwright frequently develops timely allusions, local references, and contemporaneous characters. His material must have a sense of crispness and spontaneity. Comedy must not smell of the museum or the dead past. Hence, it is difficult for a comedy to survive its time and place of origin because many of its most telling targets are soon gone.

A typical Aristophanic plot shows how the leading character becomes inspired with a ridiculous idea that is vigorously opposed by others. The idea is tried out and the results are demonstrated. The play ends in revelry. In the subsequent development of comedy, the original pattern persists. A character strives for an objective but is thwarted because his goal is an impossible one, or because he misjudges his objectives and his opposition, or because he fights with the wrong weapons. His problem is solved when misunderstandings are cleared up and his true character emerges. The play ends happily, often with the lovers united in an embrace, a vestigial reminder of the orgiastic celebrations of Greek "old comedy." In any case, the comic plot usually involves an imbalance caused by the presence of some ridiculous element of error, ignorance, or ambition. The resultant conflicts and contrasts create comic tension that is released in laughter.

The plots of most comedies are made up of sharp complications that require careful craftsmanship in the use of exposition, climaxes, crises, discoveries, and the denouement. The tangled threads of action must be kept clear to the audience. This is tricky business in plays of rapid action, mixups, and misunderstandings. In previous centuries, the playwright's task was made much easier by the conventions of the aside and the soliloquy, which allowed the playwright to communicate directly with the audience in informing them of the schemes and tricks of the plot and of the disparity between the truth and the pretense. The climaxes and crises of comedy demand technical mastery because the high points of the action often involve a social situation in which a number of people are caught in the same net, obliging the playwright to deal with very complex materials. Frequently, the emotional peaks are those of action and discovery, which require the playwright to have a strong sense of visual humor. Climaxes must be built and sustained without prolonging them beyond the limits of the material. The denouement must seem the logical result of the preceding action. The playwright's touch must be deft and sure to keep the pace rapid and to create the special climate of comedy which will insure laughter.

The materials from which comedies are made are venerable ones, as old as the theater itself. The sources of comic effect which the classic playwrights Aristophanes, Plautus, and Terence used to delight the audiences of Athens and Rome are still the stock in trade that you can see on your television or motion-picture screen tonight. Similarly, the devices of comedy which the playwright uses are well established. Let us consider three very common devices for evoking laughter, realizing that these are representative examples and by no means an exhaustive list.

Comic Devices

One of the most reliable comic devices is that of teasing or "gulling," which may take a variety of forms, such as the delay of news employed by Shakespeare when the nurse withholds Romeo's message from Juliet, or Molière's use of gulling in *The Miser* (Act V, scene 2) when Mr. James teases Harpagon with the slow revelation of truth about the loss of his casket. Another form of teasing occurs whenever characters are intentionally placed in embarrassing or awkward situations. A famous example is *The Taming of the Shrew,* at the point where Petruchio exposes Katharine to a series of teasings before "taming" her. After he has rudely taken her away following the wedding ceremony and has kept her from food and sleep, Petruchio tests Kate's subservience in this scene as he takes his starved, fatigued, and unkempt bride toward home:

PETRUCHIO: Come on, i' God's name; once more toward our father's
Good Lord, how bright and goodly shines the moon!

KATHERINE: The moon! the sun: it is not moonlight now.
PETRUCHIO: I say it is the moon that shines so bright.
KATHERINE: I know it is the sun that shines so bright.
PETRUCHIO: Now, by my mother's son, and that's myself,
It shall be moon, or star, or what I list,
Or ere I journey to your father's house.
Go on, and fetch our horses back again.
Evermore cross'd and cross'd; nothing but cross'd!
HORTENSIO: Say as he says, or we shall never go.
KATHERINE: Forward, I pray since we have come so far,
And be it moon, or sun, or what you please;
And if you please to call it a rush-candle,
Henceforth, I vow it shall be so for me.
PETRUCHIO: I say it is the moon.
KATHERINE: I know it is the moon.
PETRUCHIO: Nay, then you lie: it is the blessed sun.
KATHERINE: Then, God be blessed, it is the blessed sun:
But sun it is not, when you say it is not;
And the moon changes even as your mind.
What you will have it named, even that it is;
And so it shall be so for Katherine.

Another familiar plot mechanism of comedy is inversion. The entire play may be based on the turn-about of a downtrodden character who ultimately achieves status, as in such plays as *Born Yesterday* and *The Solid Gold Cadillac.* Note how the lovers take the dominant position at the end of *The Miser,* and in *The School for Scandal* how the statuses of Charles and Joseph Surface are reversed as a result of the action.

Another well-worn comic device is the use of the unfamiliar. A character or group of characters is placed in new surroundings or are engaged in unaccustomed activities. One form of this device is the process of teaching an inexperienced and oftentimes inexpert person; see, for example, the English lesson in Shakespeare's *Henry IV* and the dancing lesson in Molière's *Le Bourgeoise Gentilhomme.* The humor may be heightened by the additional twist of having the instructor as ignorant as his pupil. The awkward, embarrassed, or shy person making an adjustment to a new experience is used again and again for comic effect, such as that of the girls' first night in their basement apartment in *My Sister Eileen,* or Christopher Sly's adjustment to royal treatment in *The Taming of the Shrew.*

Perhaps these examples of comic devices are sufficient to indicate some of the mechanisms of comedy. In the discussion of farce, additional comic patterns will be cited. The point is that the plots of comedy make use of fairly standardized devices that over the years have consistently produced laughter in the theater.

Character

Because comedy wears many guises its characters differ from each other considerably, not only in kind but also in treatment. A comic character may be the unconscious butt of ridicule, as is Harpagon in *The Miser* or Dogberry in *Much do About Nothing.* Sometimes, a character may be conscious of his plight and share his discomfiture with the audience, as does Falstaff in *Henry IV.* Again, a comic character may, through his wit and insight, direct the laughter toward an idea or situation, as does Undershaft at the "poor but honest" concept in *Major Barbara.* Sometimes a character may be comical because of his reversal in fortune, as for example Charles and Sir Peter in *The School for Scandal.* A character may be comical because of his eccentric behavior, his lack of wit or judgment, his peculiar cast of mind, his delightful facility with language, his engaging animal spirits, his charming manner, or his buoyant attitude toward life. Character varies with the playwright's purpose.

Comic characters tend to be psychologically uncomplicated. The playwright is frequently more concerned about developing the intricacies of plot than he is about revealing depth of character. Hence he sketches his figures lightly or else resorts to easily recognizable types. The dramatist may deliberately create one-sided roles as a means of showing his characters' inhumanity in their fixations and inflexibility. Again, he may purposely keep his characters in the simple mold of stock figures in order to prevent excessive emotional attachment that might destroy the light atmosphere of comedy. As character becomes more genuine and complex, drama moves away from comedy.

The writer of comedy is closer to surface reality than the writer of tragedy. The comic dramatist is more concerned with the immediate, the temporal, the commonplace. Hence, despite the fact that characters in comedy may be types in that they are psychologically simple, they may give a superficial effect of actuality to an audience, especially when acted by consummate comedians whose personal attributes enlarge and deepen the original image of the playwright. Furthermore, the very nature of comic material is rooted in the kind of action that gives to the actor license and latitude to transform a spare outline into a full figure.

Bergson describes the comic character as one who is "generally comic in proportion to his ignorance of himself. The comic person is unconscious." Such character has a blind side that causes him to react in a ludicrous fashion. Harpagon, for example, is quite unaware that he is a comic figure. But, as we mentioned before, Bergson's point of view is too narrow for universal application. All comic characters are not unconscious or ignorant of their shortcomings. As we suggested earlier, laughter is shared with the character when we borrow some of his humiliation as the inept lover, the raw recruit, the bashful swain, or the shy maiden. Falstaff's follies infect us all. We do not laugh at him to punish him or to change him; we laugh because of the Falstaff in us. Laughter stems from sympathy as well as ridicule. Numerous comic characters, especially those from classic and neoclassic comedy, do fit neatly into Bergson's theory, but scores of comic roles, particularly in English and American plays, arouse our sympathy and affection only; a few of the examples are Rosalind in *As You Like It,* Viola in *Twelfth Night,* Billie in *Born Yesterday,* Marlow in *She Stoops to Conquer,* Professor Turner in *The Male Animal,* Charles Surface in *The School for Scandal,* and Tony in *They Knew What They Wanted*. The kind of response, whether critical or sympathetic, which a character elicits from an audience varies with the playwright's purpose.

Thought

Most comedy does not bear a heavy burden of thought. The playwright is much more concerned with satisfying the needs of those spectators who come to the theater for diversion, who wish to avoid facing someone else's serious problems—spectators who, in short, have no immediate interest in receiving intellectual stimulation from the theater. They want to have a good time, to laugh and forget themselves. Because this attitude represents the dominating taste of those who come to see a comedy, the comic writer's efforts are concentrated on interesting the audience in a series of light-hearted actions and sympathetic characters whose involvements are not to be taken seriously. While laughter at such comedy may imply our acceptance of a code of behavior and a system of values, our attention is not centered on weighing the merits of conventional morality except insofar as it serves as a frame of reference for displaying the incongruous. In most comedy, the playwright is not questioning values; he is exposing ridiculous behavior. For his purposes, the comic action itself is more important than any deeper meaning the action may have.

A particular kind of comedy, however, reverses the point of view and makes of it a drama of criticism in which the appeal of the play is intellectual. This is known as high comedy. High comedy, social comedy, or the comedy of manners—each is a special form of drama with its own particular emphasis and techniques—are all the very antithesis of farce or low comedy in that they appeal to a limited, cultivated audience rather than a general, undiscriminating public, and in that they stress dialogue rather than action. High and low comedy do, however, possess one important similarity: both require an attitude of detachment, a freedom from emotional involvement.

High comedy is written for an audience that is urbane and sophisticated and possesses a commonly accepted code of behavior, which is a matter of manners, not morals. Indeed, the Restoration audience was notorious for its immorality and licentiousness, and yet the period produced the most brilliant high comedy in England literature. It was the purpose of the high comedies of Congreve, Wycherley, and Vanbrugh to mock those who violated its manners. The objects of laughter were the gauche, the outsiders, the pretenders, whose absurd or awkward behavior caused them to lose their sense of balance. Ridicule was not a moral indictment but a reproof for antisocial conduct. In other periods of theater history, writers of high comedy have directed their criticism at more universal targets, like the foibles and follies of their age. Aristophanes scorned the militarists; Sheridan and Molière attacked hypocrisy and pretense; Shaw delighted in exposing the sham behind the sentimental and rigid precepts of Victorian behavior. High comedy is therefore a social weapon. Its implications extend beyond the immediate chuckle; its aim is to evoke thoughtful laughter. It is intended to have a residue of meaning. Writing in the *New York Times,* S. N. Behrman, a most successful American writer of high comedy, sums up the playwright's point of view in this statement:

> What makes the essence of high comedy is not the furniture of the room where the action takes place, but the articulateness of the characters, the plane on which they talk, the intellectual and moral climate in which they live . . . One of the endless sources of high comedy is seriousness of temperament and intensity of purpose in contrast with the triviality of the occasion.[5]

The techniques of high comedy rely heavily on language. Since it is addressed to an intellectual and cultivated audience, this kind of comedy employs bright repartee, conceits, epigrams, double-meanings, and all of the refinements and subtleties the writer can command. Note the scintillating repartee throughout *The School for Scandal* and *Major Barbara.*

High comedy is an esoteric form of drama created for a particular kind of audience and demanding a special style of playing that is facile, suave, and artificial in keeping with the hothouse atmosphere of the play itself.

[5] S.N. Behrman, *New York Times,* O.12, 59, II, 7.

Comedy in Performance

More than other forms of drama, comedy depends upon performance for its full effect. The timing of the actor, his ability to play a piece of business, to project a laugh line, to bring out the risible qualities of situation and character without destroying the light atmosphere—these are all needed for the complete realization of comedy.

To achieve its effects comedy employs a wide variety of language devices, from cleverly turned conceits and *bons mots* to crude puns, insults, vulgarisms, and deformed words. We have already observed some of its comic uses of diction in derision, automatism, and incongruity. Most successful comic writers have excellent ears for dialogue, and they take apparent delight in their verbal skill. Shakespeare as well as other Elizabethans was especially fond of exploiting language for comic effect. The rich texture of the rustics' speech in *A Midsummer Night's Dream,* the word-play of the doorkeeper in *Macbeth,* the banter of the grave diggers in *Hamlet* are all memorable in this aspect. Even in translation Molière's comic dialogue is notable for its tempo and cadence, and Shaw's repartee is incisive with its surprising twists and turns as he elaborates an idea. Sheridan, an acknowledged master of bright conversation, gives thrust and parry to the dialogue throughout *The School for Scandal.*

The famous interrogation scene in Oscar Wilde's *The Importance of Being Earnest* depends for its full effectiveness on an actress who can convincingly reproduce Lady Bracknell's aristocratic speech as it modulates among tones of impersonal cross-examination, disapproval, dismay and utter disgust, as well as on an actor who can convey the mingled tones of eagerness, bewilderment and persistence on the part of the young suitor, Jack Worthing.

LADY BRACKNELL: . . . Are your parents living?

JACK: I have lost both my parents.

LADY BRACKNELL: Both? . . . That seems like carelessness. Who was your father? He was evidently a man of some wealth. Was he born in what the Radical papers call the purple of commerce, or did he rise from the ranks of the aristocracy?

JACK: I am afraid I really don't know. The fact is, Lady Bracknell, I said I had lost my parents. It would be nearer the truth to say that my parents seem to have lost me . . . I don't actually know who I am by birth. I was . . . well, I was found.

LADY BRACKNELL: Found!

JACK: The late Mr. Thomas Cardew, an old gentleman of a very charitable and kindly disposition, found me, and gave me the name of Worthing, because he happened to have a first-class ticket for Worthing in his pocket at the time. Worthing is a place in Sussex. It is a seaside resort.

LADY BRACKNELL: Where did the charitable gentleman who had a first-class ticket for this seaside resort find you?

JACK: (*gravely*) In a hand-bag.

LADY BRACKNELL: A hand-bag?

JACK: (*very seriously*) Yes, Lady Bracknell. I was in a hand-bag—a somewhat large, black leather hand-bag, with handles to it—an ordinary hand-bag in fact.

LADY BRACKNELL: In what locality did this Mr. James, or Thomas, Cardew come across this ordinary hand-bag?

JACK: In the cloak-room at Victoria Station. It was given to him in mistake for his own.

LADY BRACKNELL: The cloak-room at Victoria Station?

JACK: [*with deliberately oppressive honesty*] Yes. The Brighton line.

LADY BRACKNELL: The line is immaterial. [*moved to perorative sonorousness*] Mr. Worthing, I confess I feel somewhat bewildered by what you have just told me. To be born, or at any rate bred, in a hand-bag, whether it had handles or not, seems to me to display a contempt for the ordinary decencies of family life that remind one of the worst excesses of the French Revolution. And I presume you know what that unfortunate movement led to? As for the particular locality in which the hand-bag was found, a cloak-room at a railway station might serve to conceal a social indiscretion—has probably, indeed, been used for that purpose before now—but it could hardly be regarded as an assured basis for a recognized position in good society.

JACK: May I ask you then what you would advise me to do? I need hardly say I would do anything in the world to ensure Gwendolen's happiness.

LADY BRACKNELL: [*modulating into withering forthrightness*] I would strongly advise you, Mr. Worthing, to try and acquire some relations as soon as possible, and to make a definite effort to produce at any rate one parent, of either sex, before the season is quite over.

JACK: [*with a primitive unconcern for Lady Bracknell's social demands*] Well, I don't see how I could possibly manage to do that. I can produce the hand-bag at any moment. It is in my dressing-room at home. I really think that should satisfy you, Lady Bracknell.

LADY BRACKNELL: [*as though contemplating an obscene horror*] Me, sir! What has it to do with me? You can hardly imagine that I and Lord Bracknell would dream of allowing our only daughter—a girl brought up with the utmost care—to marry into a cloak-room, and form an alliance with a parcel? Good morning, Mr. Worthing! (*Lady Bracknell sweeps out in majestic indignation.*)

One of the most puzzling aspects in the performance of comedy is the variety of response from audience to audience. A comic line or piece of business may arouse boisterious laughter at one performance and at the next be greeted by cold and stony silence. Friday and Saturday night audiences invariably outlaugh a Monday or Tuesday night one. Young spectators are more demonstrative than older ones, and a scattered audience is less susceptible to laughter than a closely packed one. Within a given audience some individuals may often be convulsed with laughter while others remain aloof and unamused throughout the play.

In general, any easy social gathering helps create the climate for comedy. Laughter is a gesture that is social and contagious, but the audience must be in a light mood, easily susceptible to the courtship of comedy. Spectators must be wooed and won, not coerced. The comedian can lose the comic sympathy of his hearers by making them conscious of his efforts to be funny. Begin by saying to someone, "I'm going to tell you a very funny story," and you double your difficulty in getting a laugh because you have engaged the listener's critical faculties and he has focused on the means of your telling rather than the end. Let one performer in a comedy strain for effect by being "consciously cute," and he is likely to alienate the audience for the production as a whole.

Comedy is a framework for action. The inanimate script is brought to life by the performer, but his skill is dependent upon the craftsmanship of the playright. As the critic A H. Thorndike says:

> Comedy finds its purpose aided by skillful use of words as well as by gesture and mimicry. It avails itself of the arts of the theatre and of literature. It delights in song as well as dance, in epigram as well as grimace, in paradox as well as slap-jack, and it can stoop to punning as readily as to buffoonery. Whatever can be used in verse or fiction to amuse and delight can be employed in the drama with the additional advantage of impersonation. It combines the humor of words and voice, of the audible and visible. Its form and movement, construction and texture, person and speeches, are all dependent on literary art. Its greatest creative triumphs are won by the pen.[6]

[6] Ashley H. Thorndike, *English Comedy* (New York, The Macmillan Co., 1929).

Farce

Just as the counterpart of tragedy is melodrama, the counterpart of high comedy is farce. As a form of drama, farce is very old, and as for its universal appeal, it has been and continues to be, along with melodrama, the most popular kind of entertainment presented in motion pictures and on television.

The purpose of farce is to entertain; the appropriate response to it is continuous and unrestrained laughter. Farce has little intellectual content or symbolic significance, is not concerned with presenting a message, has slight residue of meaning, and makes no pretense of demanding serious consideration. In the journalistic fare of the theater, farce is the comic strip of the *Zam-Bang-Powie* school. Its appeal is simple, external and spontaneous.

Farce may involve a complete play such as *The Comedy of Errors* and *Charley's Aunt,* or its techniques may be injected piecemeal into other forms of drama, as in *The Miser*. Critics may disparage farce as a degraded form of drama that "though it makes the unskillful laugh, cannot but make the judicious grieve." Farcical devices and characters have been employed, nevertheless, not only by dramatic hacks but also by some of the most preeminent playwrights, including Shakespeare, Molière, and Aristophanes.

The script of a farce must be regarded as a scenario for action. The distinctive essence of farce can be realized only in performance by accomplished comedians before a live audience. The gags, tricks, and devices that seem so absurd and flat in print may, in the hands of talented performers, move an audience to gales of laughter from which even the most sophisticated theatergoer cannot remain aloof, even though, on later reflection, he may wonder at his lack of judgment in responding to such stuff.

Because the enjoyment of laughter is one of man's favorite diversions, farce is the most popular of all forms of comedy. It demands no intellectual insight, no awareness of a social norm, no linguistic sensitivity in finding nuances of meaning—all of which are necessary for understanding other forms of comedy. The response to the farce is immediate and direct, offering no strain to the mind. Hence, this kind of laughing matter has a very wide appeal. The language barriers are slight because the performer in farce often expresses himself in the universal vocabulary of gesture and action. The enacted story is itself a kind of language which finds a ready audience.

Plot

Farce is the comedy of situation. A good farcical plot is one that provides maximum opportunity for a series of complications, even though it has obviously been contrived and manipulated by the playwright. The structure of farce is a framework for vigorous, rapid, and exaggerated action in which the characters move rather than think and where getting a laugh justifies nearly any means. Once the engine is cranked up and set in motion, the speed is accelerated, and by unexpected blowouts, backfirings and explosions, the mechanism careens crazily through space, gathering momentum until it finally lurches to an awkward but happy ending in a cloud of steam with all of its parts still spinning; and while we have witnessed a whirlwind of activity, the machine has not really moved an inch in any direction.

The skill of plotting farce is determined by the dramatist's ingenuity in inventing a variety of entanglements to give the comedian a chance to play for laughs. The playwright usually exploits a basic situation that is highly improbable and atypical: a woodcutter reluctantly consents to become a court physician in order to cure the king's daughter of a feigned illness; two long-lost twin brothers, whose servants are another pair of twins, strive for reunion; two young Communists sharing a one-room apartment fall in love with each other's newly-wed wives; a shy writer of greeting-card verses becomes involved with a gang of race track touts because of his skill in predicting the winners; a young man wages that he can tell the complete truth for twenty-four hours; a genial husband undertakes the precarious responsibility of simultaneously maintaining two separate wives and families, one each in Wilmington, Delaware, and Philadelphia, Pennsylvania. These are characteristic plot situations employed by writers of farce. Inventing a farcical plot requires ingenuity in manipulating situations, plus a shrewd sense of the theater. The playwright must know precisely how, when and where to tickle the audience. An example of a plot which illustrates the materials and organization that characterize this kind of comedy is the medieval farce, *Master Pierre Pathelin*.

An impoverished lawyer, Pierre Pathelin, assures his wife, Guillemette, that he has a plan for procuring some cloth. He visits the draper's shop, where he flatters the shopkeeper into giving him a piece of cloth. The draper is wary about parting with the cloth on credit, but Pathelin allays his fears by inviting him to visit his house, where the draper will get his money and share a roast goose dinner. The scene ends when Pathelin walks off with the cloth, leaving the draper to gloat over the price. Pathelin brings the cloth home to his delighted wife. When his dinner guest arrives, Pathelin climbs into bed, and his wife informs the hapless draper that her husband could not possibly have purchased any cloth —he has been seriously ill for some weeks. The draper goes away but returns immediately to find Pathelin feigning a ranting fit of madness. The draper becomes convinced that the devil has hoodwinked him. Another facet of the story then develops; the draper brings a shepherd into court, accused of having eaten several sheep belonging to the draper. The shepherd engages Pathelin to defend him, who feigning a toothache, masks his face until the draper makes his accusation. When Pathelin suddenly reveals his identity, the draper loses his wits and attacks the lawyer for stealing his cloth. The case becomes hopelessly lost in the confusing tangle of the two arguments. The bewildered judge tries to restore order by questioning the shepherd, who, following Pathelin's counsel, answers all questions by bleating like a sheep. The judge abandons the trial; Pathelin has succeeded. The distraught draper dashes off saying to Pathelin: "I am going to your house to see if you are here or there." When Pathelin demands his fee from his client, the shepherd's only reply is continued bleating. The trickster is himself victim of his own trick.

Earlier in the chapter, three representative theories of comedy were cited—derision, incongruity, and automatism—and three characteristic devices were discussed—teasing, inversion, and the unfamiliar. These theories and devices are also applicable to farce, although their use is generally on an elementary level. Low comedy exploits the physical aspects of man. His body, its desires and functions, are a primary source for comic material. Farcical situations usually depend upon visual humor—man is shown as the victim of his biological nature, not only sex but any drive, appetite or situation that makes him appear ridiculous, causes him to lose his balance, his control of himself or of his circumstances. Farcical characters move in an active physical world; they are out of place in the rarefied atmosphere of intellectual pursuits.

Familiar farcical devices are found in such standard patterns as mistaken identity, the funny costume, "caught in the act," or physical beatings or violence, but the action should not evoke genuine suffering in either the performer or the spectator. To elicit the audience's sympathy, or to give the effect of real pain, is to destroy the atmosphere for laughter. "A situation in which the actor really suffers," as W. H. Auden has pointed out, "can only be found comic by children, who see only the situation and are unaware of the suffering, as when a child laughs at a hunchback, or by human swine."[6] The comic possibilities of a situation are, moreover, enhanced when the recipient of the violence deserves chastisement for his antisocial behavior, such as Harpagon in *The Miser*. Farcical literature is filled with all kinds of fights, duels, beatings, spankings, combats, accidents and tumbles. Standard gags are the "prat-fall," the black-eye, the sore foot, and the use of a cream pie.

Character

Farce usually deals with simple stock characters, often from ordinary walks of life. The romantic aspects of the story are frequently carried by pasteboard figures who have a talent for bumbling into awkward situations. The main burden of the comedy is in the hands of two kinds of characters—crafty manipulators, who keep the action going, and awkward, unlearned or unsuspecting characters, who are the targets of laughter. The manipulators are often tricky servants or parasites living by their wits; those preyed upon are rustics, foreigners, foolish old men, hypocrites and poseurs of all kinds. Low comedians may be a part of a farce, or they may be introduced into other kinds of plays, such as melodrama, for comic relief. In English comedy of the late eighteenth and early nineteenth centuries, low, farcical characters were injected into the plays in such roles as farmers, sailors, and Irishmen. Their ludicrous antics met with such popular favor that they frequently ran away with the show.

The speech and behavior of farcical characters is simplified as they race through the contrived mechanism of the plot. They do not think—they scheme, manipulate and act, often in devious ways, but always toward clearly defined objectives. Because farce involves so much acting based on situations, the actor is given exceptional opportunities to develop a full pattern of behavior. The playwright's original sketchy design may be filled out and enhanced by the lively performance and personality of an imaginative comedian so that, in the theater, the character becomes a memorable one.

Thought

The writer of farce does not have a message. His aim is to divert the audience's attention by providing a pattern of comic behavior; his manipulation of character and situation aims only to serve his comic purpose. At the play's end, questions are answered, misunderstandings cleared up, the tangled threads of the story unravelled.

Because of its gay disrespect for conventional behavior, farce is sometimes criticized for its immorality; but actually farce is amoral, unconcerned with ethical implications, because the actions of its characters are removed from life and exist only in the theater through an unspoken agreement with the audience. Although farces may often include implicit criticisms of society and its mores, as for example attacks on pretentiousness and hypocrisy in works by Molière, Labiche, and Feydeau, they do not depend for their exis-

[6] W. H. Auden, "Notes on the Comic," in *The Dyer's Hand* (Random House, 1952), p. 371.

tence on such moralizing elements. They exist primarily as means of entertainment.

Diction

Diction in farce is undistinguished by any literary pretensions. The linguistic devices of low comedy are puns, repetitions, "tag lines," wisecracks, insults, vulgarisms, and deformed language. Although the language of farce is non-literary, it requires a special talent. The dialogue of farce must sharply distinguish each character and accompany or thrust forward the action rather than impede it. Laugh lines demand a feeling for the flavor and cadence of language, for its angularities and crispness. The playwright must have an excellent sense of theater in order to pace his dialogue, build for laughs, make effective use of repetition, and realize the comic possibilities in arranging the incongruities of human speech. Writing effective farcical dialogue may seem an easy task to the reader but actually it is an exacting and rather rare skill.

Spectacle

Farce makes little demands of stage scenery except in occasional plays when the locale is an important aspect of the comic situation. In general, the main interest is in the actions of the character. The set designs should not hamper the actor but should give him ample space and opportunity for vigorous and rapid movement. The visual aspects of costume may be important in some instances and in nearly all cases the playing of farce will appeal to the eye in the use of pantomime and stage business. In farce, the fun is in the doing. Note the farcical comedy business called for by the stage directions of *The Miser*.

part two PLAYS

ANTIGONE / HAMLET / THE MISER / THE SCHOOL FOR SCANDAL / AN ENEMY OF THE PEOPLE / MISS JULIE / MAJOR BARBARA / DESIRE UNDER THE ELMS / THE CAUCASIAN CHALK CIRCLE / THE GLASS MENAGERIE / THE LEADER / ACT WITHOUT WORDS, I

ANTIGONE

Sophocles (c.495-406 B.C.)

TRANSLATED AND EDITED BY
PETER D. ARNOTT

Sophocles was born at Colonus, near Athens. He stood high in the esteem of his contemporaries both as a playwright and as a man, being elected as one of the ten Athenian generals during the Samian War.

Sophocles followed the dramatic practices of Aeschylus and added the third actor. Although he wrote more than 120 plays, only seven are extant. In the yearly competition he won twenty-four victories and never finished lower than second. Sophocles is not regarded as being as original a thinker as Euripides or Aeschylus, but his mastery of dramatic techniques made him the greatest of the Greek playwrights.

Antigone (c.441 B.C.) is the earliest of Sophocles' surviving plays. His masterpieces, *Oedipus the King* and *Oedipus at Colonus,* deal with Antigone's ill-fated father. Other surviving plays of Sophocles are *Electra, Philoctetes, The Trachnioe,* and *Ajax.*

Aristotle praised Sophocles as a dramatist who "saw life steadily and saw it whole." At the first dramatic festival following the death of Sophocles, the playwright Phrynichus paid this tribute: "Blessed is Sophocles, a happy and fortunate man who died after a long life; author of many beautiful tragedies, he came to a beautiful end and lived to see no evil day."

The Greek theater was made up of three main elements: the orchestra circle where the chorus danced and sang, the *skene* or stage-house where the actors usually performed, and the *theatron* occupied by the audience. It was a huge theater; the orchestra measuring more than 75 feet in diameter, and the 80 tiers of seats in the Theater of Dionysus on the Acropolis accommodated at least fifteen thousand spectators.

The dimensions of the theater compelled the actor to solve the problems of projection. His style of performance was necessarily enlarged by broad gesture, clear speech, and the use of masks, headdresses and footgear to increase his size and expressiveness. Such exaggeration ruled out the illusion of realistic acting. This does not mean that the audience thought of the style as artificial; the actor's integrity and sense of conviction, and his ability to convey emotion and interpret the feeling and meaning of great poetry, gave his performance validity despite the conventions of the theater.

All roles were played by male actors, and no more than three speaking characters appeared onstage at once. The performance of the chorus, retaining the circular movement of the original improvised dithyramb once performed on the threshing floor, was stylized in the use of dance and song. The length and positions of the entrances and exits and the huge orchestra placed great emphasis on choric movement and affected its direction and quality, whereas the rhetorical nature of the drama, and the convention of not portraying violent action onstage, committed the actor to an emphasis on oral interpretation of the lines.

D. Harissiadis

BELOW. "But will you kill your son's appointed bride?" Ismene pleads for mercy for her sister. Here the players are situated in the *skene*.

D. Harissiadis

LEFT. Antigone, played by Anna Synodinou in the 1956 Epidaurus Festival of Ancient Greek Drama.

D. Harissiadis

D. Harissiadis

ABOVE. The Chorus and the orchestra circle came to be extremely flexible dramatic elements. Here, in a recent production of *Hecuba* played in the ruins of the Theater of Epidaurus, the Chorus portrays the Erinys, or Furies, whose mythological function is to hound down those who flee from justice.

LEFT. A view through the entrance arch of the Theater of Epidaurus. Antigone and the Chorus can be seen confronting each other in the orchestra circle, from the 1956 Festival production.

BELOW. This artist's reconstruction of the Theater of Epidaurus indicates the general layout that was typical of classical Greek theaters. The orchestra circle, at center, is of hardened earth. Surrounding is the theatron, which seated approximately 15,000. The *skene* and entrance arches can be seen on the right. Even today this theater is said to have excellent acoustics.

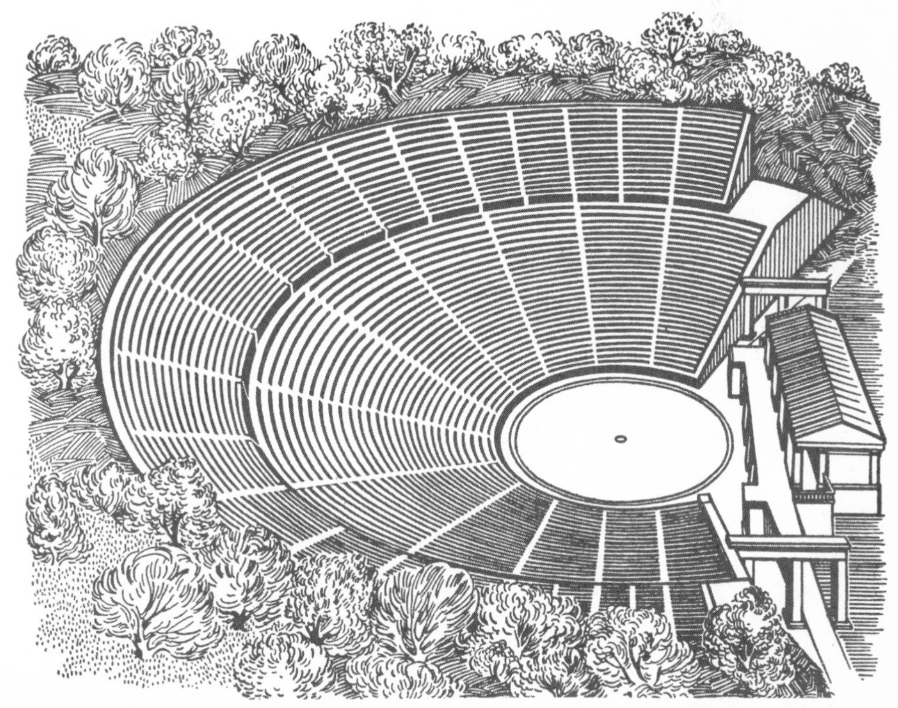

Drawing by Gerda Becker

(From Macgowan & Melnitz, The Living Stage, *©1955 by Prentice-Hall, Inc.)*

Characters

ANTIGONE, *daughter of dead King Oedipus*
ISMENE, *her sister*
CHORUS *of Theban elders*
CREON, *uncle of* ANTIGONE *and* ISMENE, *King of Thebes*
GUARD
HAEMON, *son of* CREON, *betrothed to* ANTIGONE
TEIRESIAS, *a blind prophet*
FIRST MESSENGER
EURYDICE, *wife of Creon*
SECOND MESSENGER
GUARDS *and* ATTENDANTS

SCENE: *Before the palace of* CREON *in Thebes*

ANTIGONE

[*Enter* ANTIGONE *and* ISMENE]

ANTIGONE. Ismene, my dear, my mother's child, my sister,
What part of Oedipus' sad legacy
Has Zeus not laid in full on us who live?
There is nothing bitter, nothing of disaster,
No shame, no humiliation I have not seen
In the number of your sufferings and mine.
And now what is this order which they say
Our leader has announced throughout the city?
Do you know? Have you heard? Or do I have to tell you
That what has happened to our enemies
Is threatening to fall upon our friends? 10

ISMENE. I have heard no word of friends, Antigone,
To bring me comfort or to bring me pain
Since the time we two were robbed of our two brothers,
Dead in one day, and by each other's hand.
And now the Argive army overnight
Has disappeared, I am no nearer knowing
Whether my luck has changed for good or bad.

ANT. I know, too well. That is why I wanted to bring you
Outside the courtyard, to talk to you alone.

ISM. What is it? Trouble, you do not need to tell me.

ANT. What else, when Creon singles out one brother
For a hero's grave, and lets the other rot?
They are saying he has laid Eteocles in the ground
With every rite and custom that is fitting
To give him honor with the dead below.
But Polyneices' body, that was killed
So pitifully, they say he has commanded
Should not be mourned or given burial
But lie unburied and unwept, a feast 30
For passing birds to gorge on at their pleasure.
And so, the rumor runs, has our good Creon
Decreed for you and me—for me, I say!
And is on his way here now, to spell it out
To those who have not heard. He does not take
This matter lightly. Anyone who disobeys
In any way will die by public stoning.
So there you have it. Now we shall soon find out
If you are a true-born daughter of your line,
Or if you will disgrace your noble blood! 40

ISM. But, my poor sister, if things are as you say,
What ways and means have I to set them straight?

ANT. Ask yourself, will you work with me, help me do it?

ISM. What adventure is this? What do you have in mind?

ANT. Will you help this hand of mine to lift the dead?

ISM. You mean to bury him? Against the law?

ANT. Bury my brother? Yes—and bury yours,
If you will not. No-one shall call me faithless.

ISM. You would not dare, when Creon has forbidden it!

ANT. He has no right to keep me from my own. 50

10 **That what . . . friends?** the bodies of the warriors of Argos, who had aided Polyneices in his attempt on Thebes, had been left unburied; this punishment is now to be extended to Polyneices himself, although a Theban born

ISM. Oh sister, think of how our father died,
Hated, despised, and driven by the sins
He had himself laid bare, to turn his hand
Against himself, and strike out both his eyes.
And then his mother, wife—which shall I call her?
Knotted a noose, and took away her life.
Then the final blow, two brothers in one day,
Unhappy pair, each shedding kinsman's blood,
Lay hands on each other, and made one in death.
60 Now we two are alone. Think how much worse
Our deaths will be, if in despite of law
We brave the king's commandment and his power.
Let us not forget two things—that we were born
Women, and so not meant to fight with men;
And then, that we must do what our masters tell us—
Obey in this, and other things far worse.
I, then, will ask the kingdom of the dead
To pardon me; since I am no free agent,
I will yield to the powers that be. There is no sense
70 In meddling in things outside our sphere.
ANT. I shall not persuade you. You would not be welcome
To help me now, even if you wanted to.
Be what you want to be; but I intend
To bury him. It is a noble way to die.
I shall lie with him for love, as he loved me,
A criminal, but guiltless; for the dead
Have longer claims upon me than the living.
There is my lasting home. If you think fit
To dishonor the gods' commandments, then you may.
ISM. I mean them no dishonor; but when it
80 means
Defying the state—I am not strong enough.
ANT. Let that be your excuse. Now I shall go
To heap the earth on my beloved brother.
ISM. Antigone, no! I am so afraid for you!
ANT. You need not fear for me. Look after yourself.
ISM. At least tell no-one what you mean to do.
Keep it a secret, I shall do the same.
ANT. Oh no, denounce me! You will be in far worse trouble
For keeping silence, if you do not tell the world.
ISM. You have a hot heart where you should
90 be shivering.
ANT. I know I am giving pleasure where I should.
ISM. Yes, if you can. But you ask too much of yourself.
ANT. When I have no more strength, then I shall stop.
ISM. No point in starting, when the cause is hopeless.
ANT. Go on like this and you will make me hate you,
And the dead will hate you too; you give him cause.
Leave me alone with my stupidity
To face this dread unknown; whatever it is,
Anything is better than to die a coward!
ISM. Then if your mind is made up, go. You
are a fool, 100
And yet your own will love you for it.

[*Exit* ANTIGONE; ISMENE *retires within the palace. Enter* CHORUS *of Theban elders.*]

CHORUS. Light of the morning sun, brightest that ever yet
Dawned upon the seven gates of Thebes;
Eye of the golden day, at last we see you
Rising over Dirke's streams,
Turning to rout the white-shielded warrior
That came from Argos in his array,
Winging his feet, and sending him flying home.

Polyneices' contentious quarrel
Was the cause of his coming here, 110
Winging over our country
Like an eagle clamoring,
Sheathed in snow-white feathers
With mail-clad men and waving plumes.

Over the housetops hovering, howling before
Our seven gates for blood to slake his spears;
But before he could suck his fill of Theban
Blood, before the Fire-god's flame
Leapt from the logs to embrace our ramparts,
He left, so loud the roaring of the war-cry 120
Behind him, as he fought the Theban dragon.

Zeus hates nothing more than a boastful tongue.
When he saw them coming, a mighty stream
Arrogant in their clanging gold

105 **Dirke** river on the west of Thebes

He brandished his thunderbolt and felled the man
Who had scaled our ramparts, and stood at his goal
With the cry of victory on his lips.
And over he tumbled, torch in hand,
He who a moment before
130 Had come at us like a man possessed,
Running berserk, with the hot breath of hatred.
Earth rang with his fall, and his threats went wide.
Then the God of War, our good yoke-fellow,
Lashed out, and assigned
To each of the rest their several deaths.

Seven captains stood before seven gates,
Matched against seven, and left their armor
In homage to Zeus, the arbiter of battles,
All but the ill-starred pair, who, born
140 Of one father and mother, leveled their spears
At each other; both won, and both fell dead.

But now the glorious name of Victory
Enters our chariot-proud
City, to laugh with us in our joy,
Let us put all memory of past war behind us
And visit the temples of the gods with song
And with nightlong dances; Bacchus, whose steps
Set the meadows dancing,
Come down to lead the procession!

[*Enter* CREON]

150 But here comes our country's ruler,
Creon, Menoeceus' son, our new lord
By the gods' new dispensations.
What counsel can he be pondering
To summon the elders by general decree
To meet in special conference together?

CREON. Gentlemen, the state has been in troubled waters,
But now the gods have set us back on course.
My summons came to you, of all the people,
To meet here privately, because I knew
Your constant reverence for Laius' throne, 160
And then, when Oedipus became our king,
After his death, I saw their children
Secure in your unswerving loyalty.
And now this double blow has taken both
His sons in one day, each struck down by the other,
Each with his brother's blood upon his hands,
The throne and all its powers come to me
As next of kin in order of succession.
But you can never know what a man is made of,
His character or powers of intellect, 170
Until you have seen him tried in rule and office.
A man who holds the reins of government
And does not follow the wisest policies
But lets something scare him from saying what he thinks,
I hold despicable, and always have done.
Nor have I time for anyone who puts
His popularity before his country.
As Zeus the omnipotent will be my witness,
If I saw our welfare threatened; if I saw
One danger-signal, I would speak my mind, 180
And never count an enemy of my country
To be a friend of mine. This I believe:
The state keeps us afloat. While she holds an even keel,
Then, and then only, can we make real friends.
By this creed I shall make Thebes prosperous;
And in accordance with it, I have published
My edict on the sons of Oedipus,
That Eteocles, who died a hero's death
While fighting to defend his fatherland
Should be entombed with every solemn rite 190
With which the glorious dead are sent to rest.
But his brother Polyneices, who returned
From exile, with intent to devastate
The country of his fathers, and to burn
The temples of his fathers' gods, to taste
His brother's blood, and make the rest his slaves,
Concerning him, it is proclaimed as follows:
That nobody shall mourn or bury him,
But let his body lie for dogs and birds
To make their meal, so men may look and shudder. 200
Such is my policy; foul play shall never
Triumph over honest merit, if I can help it,
But the man who loves his city shall receive
Honor from me, in his life and in his death.

CHORUS. Such is your pleasure, Creon, son of Menoeceus,

125 **the man . . . ramparts** a famous incident in the Theban story. Capaneus, one of the seven heroes who marched against the city, dared to defy Zeus and for his presumption was struck down at the moment of his triumph

Concerning our city's friend and enemy,
And you have the power to order as you wish,
Not only the dead, but the living too.

CREON. Then see to it my orders are obeyed.

CHORUS. Lay this responsibility on someone younger!

210

CREON. No, not to guard the corpse; that has been seen to.

CHORUS. Then what else are you asking me to do?

CREON. Not to side with anyone who disobeys me.

CHORUS. No man is fool enough to ask for death.

CREON. That is what you would get. But hope of gain
Has often led men on to their destruction.

[*Enter* GUARD]

GUARD. My lord, I won't say that I'm out of breath
From hurrying, or that I've run here all the way,
For several times my thoughts pulled me up short
And made me turn round to go back again. 220
There was a voice inside me kept on saying
"Why go, you fool? You're certain to be punished."
"Idiot, why hang about? If Creon hears
The news from someone else, you'll smart for it."
Arguing like this I went at snail's pace,
And so a short road turned into a long one.
But in the end, go forward won the day.
There's nothing to say, but all the same I'll say it.
I'm certain of one thing, at any rate,
That I can only get what's coming to me. 230

CREON. What is it that has put such fear in you?

GUARD. First let me say a word on my own account.
I didn't do it, nor did I see who did,
And it isn't right that I should take the blame for it.

CREON. A well-placed shot. You have covered yourself
Well against attack. I see you mean to surprise me.

GUARD. A man thinks twice before he tells bad news.

CREON. Then tell me will you, and be on your way.

GUARD. Well, here it is: the corpse—someone has buried it.
The flesh, and did whatever else was fitting. 240
And gone away; he sprinkled dry dust over

CREON. What are you saying? What man has dared to do this?

GUARD. I don't know. There was no mark of a pickaxe,
No spade had been at work; the ground was hard,
Dry and unbroken; we could find no tracks
Of wheels; he left no trace, whoever did it.
And when the man who took the morning watch
Showed us, nobody knew what to make of it.
The corpse was out of sight—not in a tomb
But sprinkled with dust, as though someone had thrown it 250
To avoid bad luck. There was no sign of wild beasts
Or dogs around; the corpse was in one piece.
Then we all started cursing each other at once,
One sentry blaming the next; it would have come
To blows in the end, there was no-one there to stop us.
First one had done it, then the next man, then the next,
But we couldn't pin it down, all pleaded ignorance.
We were ready to take red-hot irons in our hands,
To walk through fire, to swear an oath to heaven
That we were innocent, had no idea 260
Of who had planned it all, or done the work.
In the end, when there was no more point in searching,
One man said something which made every one of us
Shiver, and hang our heads; we didn't see
How we could argue with him, or if we listened
How we could save our necks. He said we couldn't
Keep the thing dark, but we must come and tell you.
So we did; and I was the unlucky one.
The lot picked me to receive the prize.
So here I am—about as pleased to be here 270

As I know you are to see me. Nobody
Has any love for the one who brings bad news.

CHORUS. My lord, since he began, I have been wondering
Could this perhaps have been the work of heaven?

CREON. Be quiet, before you make me lose my temper.
Do you want to look like fools in your old age?
What you suggest is intolerable,
That the gods would give this corpse a second thought.
Why should they try to hide his nakedness?
280 In reward for services rendered? When he came
To burn their marble halls and treasuries,
To burn their land, make havoc of its laws?
Or can you see the gods rewarding sinners?
Never. No, there were people in this town
Who took it hard from the first, and grumbled at me,
Furtively tossing their heads, not submitting
To the yoke as in duty bound, like contented men.
It was these people—of that I am convinced—
Who bribed the guards and urged them on to do it.
290 Of all the institutions of mankind
The greatest curse is money. It destroys
Our cities, it takes men away from home,
Corrupts men's honest minds, and teaches them
To enter on disreputable courses.
It shows them how to lead immoral lives
And flout the gods in everything they do.
But every one of the bribers will be caught
Sooner or later, they may be sure of that.
But by the reverence I owe to Zeus,
300 I tell you this upon my solemn oath,
That if you do not find the author of
This burial, and produce him before my eyes,
Death alone will be too good for you; you will be
Left hanging, till you tell about this outrage.
Then, when you next go stealing, you will know
What you may take, and learn for once and all
Not to love money without asking where
It comes from. You will find ill-gotten gains
Have ruined many more than they have saved.

GUARD. May I speak? Or shall I just turn
310 round and go?

CREON. Do you still need telling that your voice annoys me?

GUARD. Where does it hurt? In your ears or in your heart?

CREON. Is there any call for you to define my pain?

GUARD. The criminal troubles your mind, and I your ears.

CREON. Oh, you were born with a loose tongue, I can see.

GUARD. Maybe I was, but this I didn't do.

CREON. You did, and worse. You sold your life for money.

GUARD. How dreadful to judge by appearances, then be wrong.

CREON. Moralize as you please; but if you do not show me
The men who did this thing, you will bear witness 320
That dishonest winnings bring you into trouble.

[*Exit* CREON *to the palace*]

GUARD. Well, I only hope he's caught; but whether he is
Or not—it's in the hands of fortune now—
You won't see me coming this way again.
I never thought I'd get away with this.
It's more than I hoped—the gods be praised for it.

[*Exit*]

CHORUS. The world is full of wonderful things
But none more so than man,
This prodigy who sails before the storm-winds,
Cutting a path across the sea's gray face 330
Beneath the towering menace of the waves.
And Earth, the oldest, the primeval god,
Immortal, inexhaustible Earth,
She too has felt the weight of his hand
As year after year the mules are harnessed
And plows go back and forwards in the fields.
Merry birds and forest beasts,
Fish that swim in the deep waters,
Are gathered into the woven nets
Of man the crafty hunter. 340
He conquers with his arts
The beasts that roam in the wild hill-country;
He tames the horses with their shaggy manes
Throwing a harness around their necks,
And the tireless mountain bull.

Speech he has made his own, and thought
That travels swift as the wind,

And how to live in harmony with others
In cities, and how to shelter himself
From the piercing frost, cold rain, when the open
350 Fields can offer but a poor night's lodging.
He is ever-resourceful; nothing that comes
Will find him unready, save Death alone.
Then he will call for help and call in vain,
Though often, where cure was despaired of, he has found one.

The wit of man surpasses belief,
It works for good and evil too;
When he honors his country's laws, and the right
He is pledged to uphold, then city
360 Hold up your head; but the man
Who yields to temptation and brings evil home
Is a man without a city; he has
No place in the circle of my hearth,
Nor any part in my counsels.

[*Enter* GUARD, *leading* ANTIGONE *prisoner*]

But what is this? The gods alone know.
Is it Antigone? She and no other.
Oh unhappy daughter of
Your wretched father Oedipus,
What is it? Have they arrested you?
370 Have you broken the royal commandment?
Has your foolishness brought you to this?

GUARD. Here she is! This is the girl who did it!
We caught her burying him. But where is Creon?

CHORUS. Here, coming from the palace, just in time.

[*Enter from the palace* CREON *with attendants*]

CREON. Coming in time for what? What is it now?

GUARD. My lord, a man should never swear to anything
Second thoughts belie the first. I could have sworn
I wouldn't have come back here again in a hurry
After the tongue-lashing you gave me last time.
380 But there's no pleasure like the one that comes
As a surprise, the last thing you expected.
So here I am, breaking my solemn oath,
Bringing this girl, who was caught performing
The final rites. We didn't draw lots this time.
This piece of luck belongs to me, and no-one else.
So now, my lord, she's yours, for you to examine
And question as you wish. I've done my duty;
It's someone else's problem from now on

CREON. This girl? Where did you take her? What was she doing?

GUARD. Burying the man. That's all there is to know. 390

CREON. Are you serious? Do you know what you are saying?

GUARD. I saw her burying the corpse, the thing
You had forbidden. What could be clearer than that?

CREON. You saw her? Captured her red-handed? How?

GUARD. It happened this way. When we returned to our posts
With your dreadful threats still ringing in our ears
We swept off every bit of dust that covered
The corpse, and left the rotting carcass bare,
Then sat down on the brow of a hill to windward
Where the stench couldn't reach us. We kept ourselves lively 400
By threatening each other with what would happen
If anyone were careless in his duty.
And so time passed, until the sun's bright disk
Stood midway in the heavens, and the heat
Began to burn us. Suddenly a whirlwind
Raised a dust storm, a black blot on the sky,
Which filled the plain, played havoc with the leaves
Of every tree in sight, and choked the air.
We shut our eyes and bore it; heaven sends
These things to try us. When it had gone at last 410
There was the girl; she gave a shrill sharp cry
Like a bird in distress when it sees its bed
Stripped of its young ones and the nest deserted.
So she cried, when she saw the corpse left bare,
Raising her voice in grief, and calling down
Curses on the men who had done this thing.
Then at once she brought handfuls of dry dust,
Lifted a handsome vase, and poured from it
The three drink-offerings to crown the dead.
When we see it, out we run and close around her 420

In a moment. She was not at all put out.
We taxed her with what she had done, both then
And earlier; she admitted everything,
Which made me glad, but miserable too.
Nothing makes you happier than to get yourself
Out of trouble; but it's quite another thing
To get friends into it. But there's nothing
I wouldn't do, to keep myself from harm.

CREON. You there; yes, you, who dare not look me in the face;
430 Do you admit this accusation or deny it?

ANT. Oh, I admit it. I make no denial.

CREON. [*to the* GUARD] Take yourself off, wherever you want to go,
A free man. You are cleared of a serious charge.
[*to* ANTIGONE] Now tell me, you, and keep your answers brief
Did you know there was an order forbidding this?

ANT. Yes. How could I help it? Everybody knew.

CREON. And yet you dared to go against the law?

ANT. Why not? It was not Zeus who gave the order.
And Justice living with the dead below
440 Has never given men a law like this
Nor did I think that your pronouncements were
So powerful that mere man could override
The unwritten and unfailing laws of heaven.
These live, not for today and yesterday
But for all time; they came, no man knows whence.
There is no man's resolve I fear enough
To answer to the gods for breaking these.
I knew that I must die—how could I help it?
Even without your edict; but if I die
450 Before my time is up, I count it gain.
For when a person lives as I do, in the midst
Of evils, what can death be but gain?
And so for me to happen on this fate
Is grief not worth a thought; but if I had left
My mother's son to lie a homeless corpse,
Then had I grieved. I do not grieve for this.
If what I do seems foolish in your sight
It may be that a fool condemns my folly.

CHORUS. This is her father's willful spirit in her,
460 Not knowing how to bend before the storm.

CREON. Come, you must learn that over-stubborn spirits
Are those most often humbled. Iron that has
Been hardened in the fire and cannot bend
You will find the first to snap and fly in pieces.
I have known high-mettled horses brought to order
By a touch on the bridle. Pride is not for those
Who live their lives at their neighbour's beck and call
This girl was already schooled in insolence
When she disobeyed the official proclamation.
And now she adds insult to injury 470
By boasting of it, glorying in her crime.
I swear, she is the man and I the woman
If she keeps her victory and goes unpunished.
No! Even though she be my sister's child,
If she were bound to me by ties more close
Than anyone who shares our household prayers
She and that sister of hers will not escape
The ultimate fate; for I accuse her too
Of equal guilt in plotting this burial.
So go and call her. I saw her indoors just now 480
Delirious, not knowing what she was saying.

[*Exeunt* Attendants *to the palace*]

A guilty mind betrays itself beforehand
When men go plotting mischiefs in the dark.
But no less do I hate the criminal
Who is caught, and tries to glorify his crime.

ANT. What more would you take from me than my life?

CREON. Not a thing. When I have that, I have all I want.

ANT. Then what are you waiting for? Your arguments
Fall on deaf ears; I pray they always will.
My loyalties are meaningless to you. 490
Yet, in the world's eyes, what could I have done
To earn me greater glory, than to give
My brother burial? Everybody here
Would cheer me, if they were not dumb with fear.
But royalty, among so many blessings,
Has power to say and do whatever it likes.

CREON. These Thebans take a different view from yours.

ANT. Not they. They only curb their tongues for your sake.

CREON. Then why be different? Are you not ashamed?

ANT. Ashamed? Of paying homage to a brother?

500

CREON. Was not the man he killed your brother too?

ANT. My brother, by one mother, by one father.

CREON. Then why pay honors hateful in his eyes?

ANT. The dead man will not say he finds them hateful.

CREON. When you honor him no higher than a traitor?

ANT. It was his brother died, and not his slave.

CREON. Destroying Thebes; while he died to protect it.

ANT. It makes no difference. Death asks these rites.

CREON. But a hero asks more honor than a traitor.

ANT. Who knows? The dead may find no harm in this.

510

CREON. Even death cannot change hatred into love.

ANT. But I was born for love, and not for hate!

CREON. Then if you have to love, go down and love
The dead; while I live, no woman shall rule me!

[*Enter* Attendants *from the palace with* ISMENE]

CHORUS. Look, the gates open and Ismene comes
Weeping for love and sisterhood.
Her brows are clouded, shadowing
Her face flushed red, and teardrops
Fall on her lovely cheek.

CREON. And you, a viper lurking in my house,

520

Were sucking my life's blood, while I, unknowing,
Raised a twin scourge to drive me from my throne.
Come, answer me. Will you confess your share
In this burial, or deny all knowledge of it?

ISM. I did it—if my sister will allow me.
Half the blame is mine. I take it on myself.

ANT. No! Justice will not let you! You refused,
And I denied you any part in it.

ISM. But now you are in trouble. I am not
Ashamed to ride the storm out at your side.

530

ANT. Who did it, Hades and the dead can witness.
I love not those who only talk of love.

ISM. No, sister, do not reject me. Let
Me die with you and sanctify the dead.

ANT. You shall not share my death. You had no hand in this.
Do not say you had. My death will be enough.

ISM. What joy have I in life when you are gone?

ANT. Ask Creon. All your care has been for him.

ISM. Why do you want to hurt me? It does no good.

ANT. You are right. If I mock you it is for my pain.

540

ISM. Then tell me how I can help you, even now.

ANT. Save yourself. I do not grudge you your escape.

ISM. Then is poor Ismene not to share your fate?

ANT. It was you who chose to live, and I to die.

ISM. At least I tried to move you from your choice.

ANT. One side approved your wisdom, the other mine.

ISM. And yet the offence is the same for both of us.

ANT. Be of good heart. You live; but I have been
Dead for a long time now, to serve the dead.

CREON. Here are two fools, one lately come to folly,

550

The other since the day that she was born.

ISM. Indeed, my lord, such sense as nature gives us
Is not for ever. It goes in time of trouble.

CREON. Like yours, when you chose bad friends and evil ways.

ISM. How can I bear to live without my sister?

CREON. Sister? You have no sister. She is dead.

ISM. But will you kill your son's appointed bride?

CREON. I will. My son has other fields to plow.

ISM. He will never love another as he loved her.

CREON. No son of mine will wed an evil woman. 560

ISM. Haemon, my dearest! How your father wrongs you!

CREON. Let us have no further talk of marriages.

CHORUS. You will do it, then? You will rob your son of his bride?

CREON. Not I, but Death; yes, Death will break the match.

CHORUS. The decision stands, then, that the girl must die?

CREON. For you, and me. Let us have no more delay.
Servants, take them inside. From this time on
They must be women, not let out alone.
Even the boldest of us turns and runs
The moment he can see death closing in. 570

[*Exeunt* Attendants *with* ANTIGONE *and* ISMENE]

CHORUS. Blessed are those whose days have not tasted evil,
For once the gods have set a house tottering
The curse will never fade, but continues
From generation unto generation,
Like a storm rolling over the dark waters
Driven by the howling Thracian gales,
Stirring black mud from the bottom of the sea;
And the wind-torn headlands answer back
In a sullen roar, as the storm breaks over them.

I look on the house of Labdacus 580
And see how, from time immemorial,
The sorrows of the living have been heaped upon
The sorrows of those that died before them.
One generation does not set another
Free, but some god strikes them down
And they have no means of deliverance.
Over the last root of the house of Oedipus
Shone a ray of hope; but now this too has been
Laid low by a handful of bloody dust
Demanded by the gods of the underworld, 590
By unthinking words, and the heart's delirium.

Zeus, what man's transgression can restrain your power,
When neither Sleep, that encompasses all things,
Nor the months' unwearied and god-ordered march
Can arrest it? You do not grow old with the years
But rule in shining splendor as Olympus' king.
As it was in the past, this law will hold
Tomorrow and until the end of time:
That mortal life has a limited capacity. 600
When it aims too high, then the curse will fall.

For Hope, whose territory is unbounded,
Brings comfort to many, but to many others
Insane desires and false encouragement.
A man may go blindly on his way
Then walk into the fire and burn himself,
And so disillusion comes.
In his wisdom, someone coined the famous saying
That when a god leads a man's mind on
To destruction, sooner or later he comes
To believe that evil is good, good evil, 610
And then his days of happiness are numbered.

[*Enter* HAEMON]

But here is Haemon, your youngest son.
Does he come to grieve for the doom that has fallen
Upon Antigone, his promised bride,
To complain of the marriage that is taken from him?

CREON. We shall not need second sight to tell us that.
My son, have you heard that sentence has been passed
On your betrothed? Are you here to storm at me?
Or have I your good will, whatever I do?

HAEMON. Father, I am in your hands. You in your wisdom
Lay down for me the paths I am to follow. 620
There is no marriage in the world
That I would put before my good advisor.

CREON. Yes, keep this always in your heart, my son:
Accept your father's word as law in all things.
For that is why men pray to have
Dutiful children growing up at home,
To repay their father's enemies in kind
And honor those he loves no less than he does.

561 **Haemon . . . wrongs you** it is uncertain whether this line is spoken by Antigone or Ismene

But a man is sowing troubles for himself
630 And enemies' delight—what else?—when he
Sires sons who bring no profit to their father.
So, my son, do not be led by passing fancy
To lose your head for a woman's sake. You know,
The warmth goes out of such embraces, when
An evil woman shares your home and bed.
False friends are deadlier than a festered wound.
So turn from her with loathing; ler her find
A husband for herself among the dead.
For now that I have caught her, the only one
640 Of all the city to disobey me openly,
My people shall not see me break my word.
I shall kill her. Let her plead the sacred ties
Of kinship! If I bring up my own family
To flout me, there will be no holding others.
A man who sees his family obey him
Will have authority in public matters.
But if anyone offends, or violates the laws,
No word of praise shall he ever have from me.
Whoever the state appoints must be obeyed,
650 In little things or great things, right or wrong.
I should have confidence that such a man
Would be as good a ruler as a subject
And in a hail of spears would stand his ground
Where he was put, a comrade you could trust.
But disobedience is the worst of evils;
It is this that ruins cities, it is this
That makes homes desolate, turns brothers in arms
To headlong rout. But those who are preserved
Owe their lives, the greater part of them, to discipline.
660 And so we must stand up for law and order,
Not let ourselves be worsted by a woman.
If yield we must, then let us yield to a man.
Let no-one call us woman's underlings.

CHORUS. Unless the years have robbed me of my wits
You seem to have sound sense in what you say.

HAEMON. Father, the gods endow mankind with reason,
The highest quality that we possess.
It is not for me to criticize your words.
I could not do it, and would hate to try.
And yet, two heads are sometimes better than
670 one;
At least, it is my place to watch, on your behalf,
All that men do and say and criticize.
Fear of your frown prevents the common man
From saying anything that would displease you,
But I can hear these murmurs in the dark,
The feeling in the city for this girl.
"No woman" they say "has ever deserved death less,
Or died so shamefully in a noble cause.
When her brother fell in the slaughter, she would not
Leave him unburied, to provide a meal 680
For carrion dogs or passing birds of prey.
Is she not, then, deserving golden honors?"
This is what men are whispering to each other.
Father, there is nothing dearer to my heart
Than your continuing prosperity.
What finer ornament could children have
Than a father's proud success—or he, than theirs?
So wear an open mind; do not suppose
That you are right, and everyone else is wrong.
A man who thinks he has monopoly 690
Of wisdom, no rival in speech or intellect,
Will turn out hollow when you look inside him.
However wise he is, it is no disgrace
To learn, and give way gracefully.
You see how trees that bend to winter floods
Preserve themselves, save every twig unbroken,
But those that stand rigid perish root and branch,
And also how the man who keeps his sails
Stretched taut, and never slackens them, overturns
And finishes his voyage upside down. 700
Let your anger rest; allow us to persuade you.
If a young man may be permitted his opinion
I should say it would be best for everyone
To be born omniscient; but otherwise—
And things have a habit of falling out differently—
It is also good to learn from good advice.

CHORUS. My lord, if he speaks to the point you ought to listen,
And Haemon, you to him. There is sense on both sides.

CREON. And is a man of my age to be taught
What I should think by one so young as this?

HAEMON. Nothing that is not right; young 710
though I may be,
You should judge by my behavior, not my age.

CREON. What sort of behavior is it to honor rebels?

HAEMON. I would never suggest that the guilty should be honored.

CREON. And is she not infected with this disease?

HAEMON. The people of Thebes unanimously deny it.

CREON. Will the city tell me how I am to rule?

HAEMON. Listen to that! Who is being childish now?

CREON. Is the state to listen to any voice but mine?

HAEMON. There is no state, when one man is its master. 720

CREON. Is not the state supposed to be the ruler's?

HAEMON. You would do well as the monarch of a desert.

CREON. It seems the woman has a champion here.

HAEMON. Then you are the woman! It is you I care about!

CREON. Insolent cub! Will you argue with your father?

HAEMON. I will, when I see you falling into error.

CREON. Am I wrong to respect my own prerogatives?

HAEMON. It is no respect, when you offend the gods.

CREON. How contemptible, to give way to a woman!

HAEMON. At least I do not give way to temptation. 730

CREON. But every word you say is a plea for her.

HAEMON. And for you, and for me, and for the gods below.

CREON. You will never marry her this side of the grave.

HAEMON. Then she will die—and take somebody with her.

CREON. So! Do you dare to go so far? Are you threatening me?

HAEMON. Is it threatening, to protest a wrong decision?

CREON. You shall pay for this. A fine one to teach wisdom!

HAEMON. If you were not my father, I should call you a fool.

CREON. You woman's slave; do not try to wheedle me!

HAEMON. Would you stop everyone from speaking but yourself? 740

CREON. Indeed! I tell you, by the gods above us,
You shall pay for using such language to your father.

[*to the* Attendants]

Bring this abomination out, and let her die
Here, in his presence, at her bridegroom's side.

HAEMON. No, she will never perish at my side,
So do not think it. From this moment on
Your eyes will never see my face again.
So rave away, to those who have more patience!

[*Exit*]

CHORUS. My lord, he has gone away in angry haste.
Young tempers are fierce when anything provokes them. 750

CREON. Let him do or dream all men can do and more.
He shall never save those girls from punishment.

CHORUS. Do you mean to put the two of them to death?

CREON. You are right to ask. Not her whose hands are clean.

CHORUS. And how do you intend to kill the other?

CREON. I shall take her where nobody ever comes.
And shut her in a rocky vault alive,
With the minimum of food that is permitted
To stop pollution falling on the city.
There she may pray to Death, the only god 760
She worships, and perhaps he may forgive her.
If not, she will learn—but when it is too late—
That honoring the dead is wasted effort.

[*Exit*]

CHORUS. Love, whom we fight but never conquer,
Love, the ravager of proud possessions

Who keep eternal vigilance
In the softness of a young girl's cheek,
You go wherever the wide seas go
And among the cottages of country-dwellers.
770 None of the immortal gods can escape you,
Nor man, whose life is as a single day,
And, to whoever takes you in, comes madness.

The minds of honest men you lead
Out of the paths of virtue to destruction.
Father is at odds with son
And it is you who set this quarrel in their hearts.
One glance from the eyes of a ready bride
Bright with desire, and a man is enslaved.
On the throne of the eternal laws
780 Love has a place, for there the goddess Aphrodite
Decides men's fates, and there is no withstanding her.

[*Enter* Attendants *with* ANTIGONE *bound*]

It is my turn now; at a sight like this
The voice of the laws cannot hold me back
Or stop the tears from pouring down my cheeks.
Here comes Antigone, on her way
To the bridal-chamber where all must go to rest.
790 ANT. See me, citizens of my fatherland, as I go out
On my last journey; as I look my last on the sunlight,
Never to see it again; Death, who puts all to sleep,
Takes me as I am,
With life still in me, to the shores of the midnight lake,
A bride with no choir to accompany her way,
With no serenade at the bedroom door;
I am to marry with the King of Darkness!
CHORUS. And so you go with honor and praise
Below to the caverns of the dead;
No sickness has wasted you away,
You do not pay the wages of the sword,
But will go to death a law unto yourself
As no human being has done before you. 800
ANT. I have heard of one, a stranger among us from Phrygia,
Tantalus' daughter, and her sad end on Mount Sipylus,
Growing slowly into stone as a tree is wrapped with ivy.
And the story goes
That her body pines in unceasing snow and rain
And tears from her streaming eyes pour upon her breast.
Her fate is mine; like her I go to rest.
CHORUS. But she was a goddess, born of gods,
And we are mortals, mortal born.
When a woman has to die, it is 810
A great distinction, for her to share
The lot of those who are one removed from gods,
Both here, and in the manner of her death.
ANT. Oh, you make fun of me! Gods of my fathers!
Must you laugh in my face? Can you not wait till I am gone?
Oh, my city; Thebans, proud in your possessions;
Chariot-thundering plain, you at least will bear witness
How no friends mourn for my passing, by what laws
I go to my rock-barred prison, my novel tomb.
Luckless Antigone, an alien in both worlds, 820
Among the living and among the dead!
CHORUS. You have driven yourself to the furthest limit of daring
And run, my child, against the high throne
Where justice sits; and great has been your fall.
Perhaps you are paying the price of your father's sin.
ANT. You have touched the memory bitterest in my mind,
The dirge for my father that is never finished,
For the fate of us all, the famous house of Labdacus.
Oh, the curse born
In a mother's bed; doomed mother, sleeping with her son, 830

780 **Aphrodite** goddess of love, or, more accurately, of sexual desire 792 **A bride . . . bedroom door** according to Greek custom bride and groom were accompanied home by singing friends, who also sang outside the wedding chamber in the evening

801 **Tantalus' daughter** Niobe, daughter of the King of Phrygia in Asia Minor, turned into stone as punishment for boasting herself superior to the gods

My father. Poor Antigone, what parents brought you
Into this world! Now I go to join them, accursed, unwed.
Oh, my brother, how ill-fated was your marriage.
Your dead hand has reached out to destroy the living.

CHORUS. Pious actions are a sort of piety.
But a man who has authority in his keeping
Can permit no offence against authority.
Your own willful temper has destroyed you.

ANT. Friendless, unwept, without a wedding song,
840 They call for me, and I must tread my road.
Eye of heaven, light of the holy sun,
I may look on you no longer.
There is no friend to lament my fate,
No-one to shed a tear for me.

[*Enter* CREON]

CREON. Let me tell you, if songs and dirges before dying
Did any good, we should never hear the end of them.
Take her, and be quick about it. Lock her up
In her cavern tomb, as I have ordered you,
And leave her alone—to die, if she prefers,
850 Or live in her tomb, for that will be her home.
Whatever becomes of her our hands are clean.
But in this world she has a place no longer.

ANT. Tomb, bridal-chamber, my eternal home
Hewn from the rock, where I must go to meet
My own, those many who have died, and been
Made welcome by Persephone in the shadow-world.
I am the last, my death the worst of all
Before my allotted span of years has run.
But as I go I have this hope in heart,
860 That my coming may be welcome to my father,
My mother; welcome, dearest brother, to you.
For when you died, with my own hands I washed
And robed your bodies, and poured offerings
Over your graves. Now this is my reward,
Polyneices, for rendering such services to you.
Yet wisdom would approve my honoring you.
If I were a mother; if my husband's corpse
Were left to rot, I never should have dared
Defy the state to do what I have done. 870
What principle can justify such words?
Why, if my husband died I could take another;
Someone else could give me a child if I lost the first;
But Death has hidden my mother and father from me.
No brother can be born to me again.
Such was the principle by which I chose
To honor you; and for this Creon judges me guilty
Of outrage and transgression, brother mine!
And now he seizes me to lead me off,
Robbed of my bride-bed and my marriage song. 880
I shall never marry, never be a mother.
And so, in misery, without a friend,
I go still living to the pit of death.
Which one of heaven's commandments have I broken?
Why should I look to the gods any longer
After this? To whom am I to turn for help
When doing right has branded me a sinner?
If the gods approve what is happening to me,
After the punishment I shall know my fault,
But if my judges are wrong, I wish them no worse 890
Than what they have unjustly done to me.

CHORUS. Still the same tempestuous spirit carrying her along.

CREON. Then those who are charged with taking her
Shall have cause to repent their slowness.

ANT. Oh, that word has brought me
Very near my death.

CREON. I can offer you no hope.
Your punishment stands unchanged.

ANT. City of my father in the land of Thebes, 900
The time has come, they take me away.
Look, princes of Thebes; this is the last
Daughter of the house of your kings.
See what I suffer, and at whose hands,
For doing no less than heaven bids us do.

833 **Oh, my brother** not Oedipus, but Polyneices, whose marriage with the daughter of the king of Argos had cemented the alliance against Thebes
856 **Persephone** queen of the dead

867 **If I were a mother born to me again** this passage is possibly spurious, and omitted by some editors

[*Exeunt* Attendants, *leading off* ANTIGONE]

CHORUS. So Danae in her beauty endured the change
From the bright sky to the brazen cell,
And there she was hidden, lost to the living world.
Yet she was of proud birth too, my daughter,
And the seed of Zeus was trusted to her keeping
910 That fell in golden rain.
But the power of fate is terrible.
Wealth cannot keep you from its reach, nor war,
Nor city walls, nor the dark sea-beaten ships.
And the king of the Edonians, the fiery-tempered
Son of Dryas, was held in bondage
For his savage taunts, at Dionysus' will,
Clapped in a rocky cell; and so the full
Flowering of his madness passed from him gradually
And he came to recognize
920 The god he had insulted in his frenzy.
He had sought to stop the women when the god was in them
And the Bacchic torches, and enraged the piping Muses.
And by the Dark Rocks at the meeting of two waters
Lie the shores of Bosporos and Thracian Salmydessos.
Here was a sight for the eyes
Of the city's neighbour, Ares—
The two sons of Phineus, blinded
By stepmother's fury, their sightless eyes
Appealing for vengeance, calling down a curse
On her bloody hands and the shuttle turned dagger.
930
Pining in grief they bewailed their cruel fate.
How sad their mother's marriage; but her line
Went back to the ancient family
Of Erechtheus—she was a child
Of the North Wind, nursed in distant caves,
Who played with her father's storms, a child of the gods
Running swift as a steed upon the high hills.
Yet on her too the gray Fates laid their hand, my daughter.

[*Enter* TEIRESIAS, *led by a boy*]

TEIRESIAS. Princes of Thebes, we have come here side by side,
One pair of eyes for both of us. That is how 940
Blind men must walk, supported by a guide.

CREON. What news have you for us, old Teiresias?

TEIR. I will tell you. Listen when the prophet speaks.

CREON. I have never yet disregarded your advice.

TEIR. And so have kept Thebes safely on her course.

CREON. I know my debt to you, and acknowledge it.

TEIR. Then listen. Once more you stand on the verge of doom.

CREON. What do you mean? I shudder at your words.

TEIR. You will know, when you hear the the warnings of my art.
As I took my place upon my ancient seat 950
Of augury, where all the birds come flocking,
I heard a noise I had never heard before,
Their cries distorted in a scream of fury,
And I knew that they were clawing, killing each other;
The whirring of wings told a tale too clear.
I was frightened, and went at once to light the altar
And offer sacrifices; but from my offerings
No flame sprang up. Fat melted on the thighs
And oozed in slow drops down to quench the embers

905 **Danae** the chorus adduce from mythology parallels to Antigone's plight. **Danae** was imprisoned by her father in a brazen tower to avert a prophecy that she would bear a son who would grow up to kill him. But Zeus, king of the gods, appeared to her in a shower of golden rain and fathered her son Perseus, who grew up to fulfil the prophecy. **Lycurgus** son of Dryas persecuted the worshippers of Dionysus, and as punishment for his insolence was driven mad by the god and died. **Cleopatra** married **Phineus,** King of Salmydessos in Thrace, and bore him two sons. Phineus later imprisoned her and took a new wife, who blinded the boys 923 **Dark Rocks** at the entrance to what is now the Black Sea 924 **Bosporos** narrow strip of water separating Greece from Asia Minor 926 **Ares** god of war, whose home was in the wild regions of Thrace

934 **Erechtheus** legendary king of Athens

And smoked and spluttered; and the gall was scattered
960
Into the air. The streaming thighs were raw,
Bare of the fat which once enfolded them.
And so my rites had failed. I asked a sign
And none was given, as I learnt from this boy here.
He is my guide, as I am guide to others.
Your counsels brought this sickness on our state.
The altars of our city and our homes
All are defiled by dogs and birds of prey
Who feed on Oedipus' unhappy son.
970 And so the gods no longer accept our prayers,
Our sacrifices, our burnt offerings.
The birds no longer warn us with their cries;
They have drunk the fat blood of a slaughtered man.
Think on these things, my son. To err is human,
But when we err, then happy is the man
Who is not stubborn, and has sense enough
To remedy the fault he has committed.
Give the dead his due, and do not stab a man
When he is down. What good to kill him twice?
980 I have your interests at heart, and speak
To help you. No advisor is more welcome
Than when you profit from his good advice.

CREON. You circle me like archers, all of you,
And I am made your target! Even the prophets
Conspire against me. They have long been using me
As merchandise, a thing to buy and sell!
If profit is what you seek, go look abroad!
There is silver in Sardis, gold in India.
But you will not bury this man in his grave,
990 No, not if the eagles of great Zeus himself
Should lay his flesh before their master's throne.
Not even that defilement frightens me
Enough to bury him, for well I know
No human being can defile the gods.
The wisest of us, old Teiresias,
Sink to the depths, when they hide their evil thoughts
In fair-phrased speeches for the sake of money.

TEIR. If men only knew, would only realize—

CREON. Knew what? Another pronouncement! Let us hear!

TEIR. Good counsel is worth more than worldly riches.
1000

CREON. Just as stupidity is the greatest harm.

TEIR. Yet that is the sickness that has tainted you.

CREON. I do not want to call a prophet names.

TEIR. But you do, when you say my prophecies are false.

CREON. Men of your tribe were always moneyseekers.

TEIR. And men of yours have always been dictators.

CREON. Have you forgotten you are speaking to your king?

TEIR. No. It was because of me that you saved Thebes.

CREON. You are a wise prophet but in love with evil.

TEIR. You will move me to tell the unutterable secret.
1010

CREON. Tell it—as long as there is no profit in it!

TEIR. I do not think so—as far as you are concerned.

CREON. You will make no money out of my decision.

TEIR. Then listen well. Before the sun's swift wheels
Have numbered many more days of your life,
You will surrender corpse for corpses, one
Begotten from the seed of your own loins,
Because you have sent this world to join the next
And cruelly lodged the living in the grave,
But keep Death's property on earth, unburied,
1020
Robbed of its honor, an unhallowed corpse.
This is not for you to say, nor for the gods
In heaven, but in doing this you wrong them.
And so the Avengers, Furies sent by Death
And by the gods, lie in waiting to destroy you
And snare you in the evils you have worked.
So watch, and you will see if I am bribed
To say these things. Before much time is out
The cries of men and womenfolk will fill your house.
And hatred rises against you in every city
1030
Whose mangled sons were left for burial

988 **Sardis** city of Asia Minor containing the royal treasury

1024 **Furies** supernatural pursuers of the wrong-doer

To dogs, or beasts, or birds of prey, who bore
Their stinking breath to every soldier's home.
Archer you call me; then these are the arrows
I send into your heart, since you provoke me,
Sure arrows; you will not escape their sting.
Boy, take me to my home again, and leave him
To vent his fury on some younger man,
And learn to moderate his tongue, and bear
1040 A better spirit in his breast than now.

[*Exit*]

CHORUS. He has gone, my lord; his prophecies were fearful.
As long as I remember, since my hair
Has turned from black to white, this man has never
Made one false prophecy about our city.

CREON. I know it as well as you. My mind is troubled.
To yield is fatal; but to resist and bring
A curse on my proud spirit—that too is hard.

CHORUS. Son of Menoeceus, you must listen to good advice.

CREON. What's to be done? Tell me and I will do it.

CHORUS. Go free the girl from her prison in
1050 the rocks
And give the corpse an honorable tomb.

CREON. Is this your advice? You think that I should yield?

CHORUS. Yes, lord, as quickly as you can. The gods
Move fast to cut short man's stupidity.

CREON. It is hard; but I resign my dear resolve.
We cannot fight against necessity.

CHORUS. Go do it now; do not leave it to another.

CREON. I will go as I am. Servants, be off with you,
Each and every one; take axes in your hands
1060 And go to the hill you can see over there.
Now that my judgment has been reversed
I shall be there to free her, as I imprisoned her.
Perhaps after all the gods' ways are the best
And we should keep them till our lives are done.

[*Exit*]

CHORUS. You who are known by many names,
Who blessed the union of Cadmus' daughter,
Begotten by Zeus the Thunderer, guarding
The land of Italy famed in story,
King of Eleusis, in the land-locked plain
Of Deo where the wanderer finds welcome, 1070
Bacchus whose home is Thebes, mother-city of Bacchanals,
By Ismenus' tranquil waters where the fierce dragon's teeth were sown.

The fitful gleam of the torchlight finds you
Amid the smoke on the slopes of the forked mountains
Where tread your worshippers, the nymphs
Of Corycia, by Castalia's stream.
From Nysa's ivy-mantled slopes,
From the green shore carpeted with vines
You come, and they are no human lips that cry
Your name, as you make your progress through the ways of Thebes. 1080

For it is she you honor above all other cities,
And your mother too, who died by a bolt from heaven.
And now the whole city labors under
This grievous malady, come with healing feet
Down from the slopes of Parnassus or the sounding sea.

Conductor of the stars, whose breath is made of fire,
Lord of the voices that cry aloud in the night,
Son born of Zeus, appeared to us, oh lord,
With the Thyiads your servants who in nightly abandon
Dance before you, Iacchus, the bringer of all blessings. 1090

1066 **Cadmus' daughter** Semele, mortal mother, by Zeus, of Dionysus 1069 **Eleusis** home of the mystery-cult devoted to Demeter, goddess of the crops, and her daughter Persephone. The worship of Dionysus had infiltrated into this rite 1070 **Deo** Demeter 1072 **By Ismenus'...were sown** Thebes was founded by Cadmus, who killed a dragon guarding the site, near the Ismenus River, and sowed the dragon's teeth in the ground. From them sprang up armed men who fought each other. All were killed but five, who became the ancestors of the Thebans. 1076 **Corycia** cave on Mt. Parnassus **Castalia** fountain on Mt. Parnassus sacred to the Muses 1077 **Nysa** legendary scene of the nursing of Dionysus

[*Enter* MESSENGER]

MESSENGER. You who live by Amphion's and Cadmus' walls,
No man's estate is ever so assured
That I would set it down as good or bad.
Fortune can raise us, fortune cast us down,
Depending on our luck, from day to day,
But for how long? No man can see the future.
For Creon was once blessed, as I count blessings;
He saved the land of Cadmus from its enemies,
Became its sole and undisputed king
1100 And ruled, proud father of a princely line.
Now everything is gone. A man who forfeits
All of life's pleasures I can count no longer
Among the living, but as dead in life.
So stack your house with treasures as you will
And live in royal pomp; when joy is absent
I would not give the shadow of a breath
For all the rest, compared with joy alone.

CHORUS. What is this new royal grief you come to tell us?

MESS. Death; and the living must answer to the dead.

1110 CHORUS. Who killed? And who has been killed? Tell us.

MESS. Haemon, and by a hand he knew too well.

CHORUS. By his father's hand? Or was it by his own?

MESS. His own, in anger for his father's murder.

CHORUS. Oh prophet, how much truth was in your words.

MESS. That is how things are. For the rest you must decide.

[*Enter* EURYDICE]

CHORUS. And here is Eurydice, the unhappy wife
Of Creon; she is coming from the palace.

EURYDICE. People of Thebes, I heard what you were saying
As I was going from my house to offer
1120 Devotions at the goddess Pallas' shrine.
I stood there with my hand about to draw
The bolt, and my ears were greeted by this tale
Of family disaster. Terrified,
I fell back swooning in my servants' arms.
But tell again what you were telling then.
The first grief is over. I shall listen now.

MESS. Dear lady, I shall tell you what I saw
Omitting nothing, exactly as it happened.
Why should I give false comfort? You would soon
1130 Know I was lying. Truth is always best.
I attended on your husband to direct his way
Across the plain, where Polyneices' corpse,
Mangled by dogs, still lay unburied.
We prayed the goddess of the roads, and Pluto.
To have mercy on us and restrain their wrath,
Performed the ritual washing of the corpse,
Cut branches and cremated what was left of him
And raised a hillock of his native soil
Above him; then made for the cavern, where the girl
1140 Waited for Death to share her rocky bed.
Far off, one of us heard a piercing cry
Coming from that unholy bridal chamber
And came to report it to our master Creon.
As he approached, a cry of anguish came
To greet him, half-heard words; he groaned aloud
And in his grief said "Creon, you are doomed;
Can my fear be true? Is the path I tread today
To be the bitterest path I ever trod?
The voice that greets me is my son's; men, run ahead,
1150 Make for the tomb; there is an opening
Where someone has wrenched the stones away. Squeeze inside
To the cell-mouth, see if it is Haemon's voice
I hear, or if the gods are mocking me."
And so, at our despairing master's bidding,
We made the search, and in the farthest corner
Of the tomb we saw her, hanged by the neck
In a noose of twisted linen, soft as silk,
While Haemon stood with his arms clasped round her waist
Weeping for his bride now with the dead,
1160 For his father's actions and his foredoomed marriage.
When he saw him his father gave a fearful cry

1091 **Amphion** legendary musician whose lyre-playing charmed the stones to build a wall around Thebes

1134 **Pluto** god of the underworld

And went to him and called to him through his tears
"Oh Haemon, what is this that you have done?
What has possessed you? Have you gone insane?
Come out, my son, I beg you, I implore you."
But the boy glared back at him wild-eyed,
Spat in his face, and without a word of answer
Drew his cross-hilted sword and thrust at him
But missed, as he jumped aside. Then in wild remorse
The poor wretch threw his weight upon the point 1170
And drove it half into his side. As long as sense
Was left him, he clasped the girl in a limp embrace
And as his breath came hard, a jet of blood
Spurted from his lips, and ran down her pallid cheek.
The bodies lie in each other arms. He has
Claimed his bride—in the next world, not in this—
And he has given proof to all mankind
That of all human ills, bad counsel is the worst.

[*Exit* EURYDICE *to the palace*]

CHORUS. What would you make of this? Eurydice
Has vanished without a word, good or bad. 1180

MESS. It alarms me too. Yet I nourish the hope
That now she knows her loss she does not think it proper
To mourn in public, but has gone inside
To set her maids to mourn for her bereavement.
She has learnt discretion and will not be foolish.

CHORUS. I am not so sure. To me this unnatural silence
Is as ominous as the wildest excess of grief.

MESS. Well, I shall go in and see, in case
She is keeping some dark purpose hidden from us
In her grief-torn heart. You are right to be concerned. 1190
It is just as dangerous to be too quiet.

[*Exit*]

CHORUS. But here is Creon coming himself
Bringing testimony all too plain,
The work of his and no other's madness,
If I may speak out, and his own wrongdoing.

[*Enter* CREON *with servants bearing the body of* HAEMON]

CREON. Oh deadly end of stubborn sins
Born in the blindness of understanding!
See here, a son dead, a father who killed him.
Oh the fatal workings of my mind;
My son, to die so young, 1200
So soon to be taken from me
By my folly, not by yours.

CHORUS. Perhaps you see now too late what was best.

CREON. Yes, I have learned my bitter lesson.
Some god must have chosen that moment
To crush me under his heavy hand
And hurl me into cruelty's ways,
Riding roughshod over all I held dear.
Oh, mankind, you were born to suffer!

[*Enter* SECOND MESSENGER *from the palace*]

MESSENGER. Master, you do not come empty-handed; but there is 1210
More in store for you. You bear one load of grief
But soon you will see another, in your home.

CREON. My grief is here; is any worse to come?

MESS. Your wife is dead—true mother to her son
To the last, poor lady—by a wound still fresh.

CREON. Oh Death, ever-open door,
Do you have no mercy on me?
You who bring this tale of death and sorrow
What is this you are saying to me?
What news is this, my boy? 1220
My wife is dead? One more
To add to the pile of corpses?

MESS. See for yourself. It is no longer hidden.

[*The body of* EURYDICE *is brought out*]

CREON. Oh, here is another, a second blow.
What has fate in store for me after this?
I have but this moment lifted
My child in my arms, and again
I see a corpse brought out to greet me.
Oh wretched mother; oh my child.

MESS. There she lies at the altar, knife-point in her heart. 1230

She mourned the noble fate of Megareus,
The first to die, then his; then closed her eyes
For ever, and with her dying breath called down
A curse on you for murdering her sons.

CREON. I am shaken with fear. Will nobody take
His two-edged sword and run me through?
For, oh, I am sick at heart.
Sorrow has made me his own.

MESS. Yes, she whose body you see lying here
1240 Laid the deaths of both sons at your door.

CREON. And what was the violent manner of her leaving?

MESS. Her own hand drove the knife into her heart
When she had heard them singing her son's dirge.

CREON. Nobody else can bear the guilt,
No-one can take the blame from me.
I killed you, I, your unhappy father,
This is the truth.
Servants, take me away from this place.
Let me stay not a moment longer.
1250 Creon has ceased to exist.

CHORUS. Good advice, if there can be any good in evil.
In present trouble the shortest way is best.

CREON. Let it come. What better fate could I ask
Than the fate which ushers in my life's last day?
Let it come, the best of all;
Let me never see tomorrow's dawn.

CHORUS. All in its proper time. We have things to see to
Here and now. The future is in other hands.

CREON. But everything I want was in that prayer.

CHORUS. Save your prayers. Whatever is going to happen 1260
Is already fated. Nobody can change it.

CREON. Come, take this hot-headed fool away,
A fool who killed you, my son, in my blindness,
And you too, who are lying here; poor fool.
I do not know
Which way I am to take, where to lean;
My hands can do nothing right;
I am crushed beneath my fate.

[*Exit*]

CHORUS. To be happy it is first of all necessary
To be wise, and always remember 1270
To give the gods their due.
The measure of a proud man's boasting
Shall be the measure of his punishment
And teach him late in life
The nature of true wisdom.

1231 **Megareus** a minor incident in the siege of Thebes, which Sophocles could expect his audience to know. Megareus, son of Creon, sacrificed himself in an attempt to appease the gods' wrath against the city.

Review Questions

1. Does *Antigone* follow the unities?
2. Outline the episodes of the play. What is the dramatic function of each episode?
3. How does Sophocles foreshadow the catastrophes?
4. What is the basic conflict?
5. What is the emotional impact of the denouement?
6. What does the Chorus contribute to the play?
7. What do we learn about Creon from the scene with Teiresias? With Haemon?
8. Does the denouement seem "necessary and probable?"
9. What Greek dramatic conventions are apparent in *Antigone?*
10. What is accomplished in the Parodus?
11. What are the dramatic functions of the scenes between Ismene and Antigone? Haemon and Creon?
12. Evaluate *Antigone* in terms of Aristotle's definition of tragedy.
13. What are the religious implications of the play? The political?
14. Evaluate Antigone and Creon in terms of Aristotle's concept of the "tragic flaw."
15. What is the meaning of the final speech by the Chorus?
16. What important discoveries are made?
17. Describe Creon's change during the play.
18. Who is at fault for the catastrophes?
19. What does Eurydice contribute to the play?
20. How has Sophocles made the Guard a human character?
21. Is Creon a sympathetic character? Antigone?
22. What does the play tell us about Greek culture?
23. What is the purpose of Creon's opening speech?
24. What is the Greek attitude toward man as expressed in the first Ode?
25. How does Sophocles expose the conflicts?
26. What is the setting?
27. Assuming that only three speaking characters appeared at once on stage, indicate how the parts might be assigned.

28. What does Sophocles contribute to Greek drama?
29. Discuss *Antigone* in terms of universality.
30. What rites are involved in *Antigone?*
31. What is the effect of having Antigone leave the stage so early?
32. What would the effect be if she were to die on stage?
33. What scene is left out that a modern playwright would include?
34. Using the same basic conflicts, outline a play with Haemon as the central character.

HAMLET

William Shakespeare (1564–1616)

EDITED BY R. C. BALD

Shakespeare's birthplace was Stratford-on-Avon, where he was given a grammar school education, shared his middle-class family's financial ups-and-downs, and married Ann Hathaway, who was eight years his senior. In the late 1580's Shakespeare went to London where he soon became connected with the theater, at first as an actor and then as a dramatist. The professional theaters were repertory companies consisting of small groups of men who were an acting and producing unit, and who usually had several playwrights creating new plays for them. Shakespeare was attached to the Lord Chamberlain's Company. He quickly won a reputation as a playwright and became a shareholder in the Globe Theater. His success in the theater made it possible for him to retire in 1611 to his native Stratford as a well-to-do gentleman.

Shakespeare's works are usually divided into four groups: (1) 1590–1594, a period of imitation and experimentation; (2) 1595–1600, tragedies and comedies; (3) 1601–1608, tragedies and satiric comedies; and (4) 1609–1611, dramatic romances. *Hamlet* belongs to the tragedy-of-blood, a popular form of drama at the end of the century, but differs markedly from those of Shakespeare's contemporaries in its depth of characterization and breadth of vision.

Shakespeare's theater was characterized by an open courtyard enclosed by roofed-over galleries three stories high. The main acting area was a large platform which projected into the center of the courtyard, placing the actor in intimate contact with his audience. There were seats in the galleries but the groundlings stood in the pit during the performance. Scenery was suggestive or absent altogether, and there was no drop curtain. In addition to the platform, two other playing areas were used by the actor—a curtained inner alcove at the rear of the platform and another curtained upper alcove at the second floor level. Physically, such a theater gave the playwright wonderful freedom and flexibility to move his characters around in time and space and to tell a complex and interesting story in which all of the essential action could be placed directly before the audience. All of the actors were males, the female roles being played by boys. Despite the paucity of scenery, the richness of costuming and the vigor of the action made the Elizabethan theater a spectacular one.

This reconstruction of the Globe Theater of London shows the many playing areas available to the Elizabethan playwright for use in staging complicated plots involving all manner of shifts in time and place and varieties of character groupings.

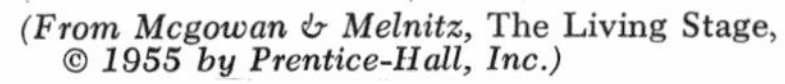

(From Mcgowan & Melnitz, The Living Stage, *© 1955 by Prentice-Hall, Inc.)*

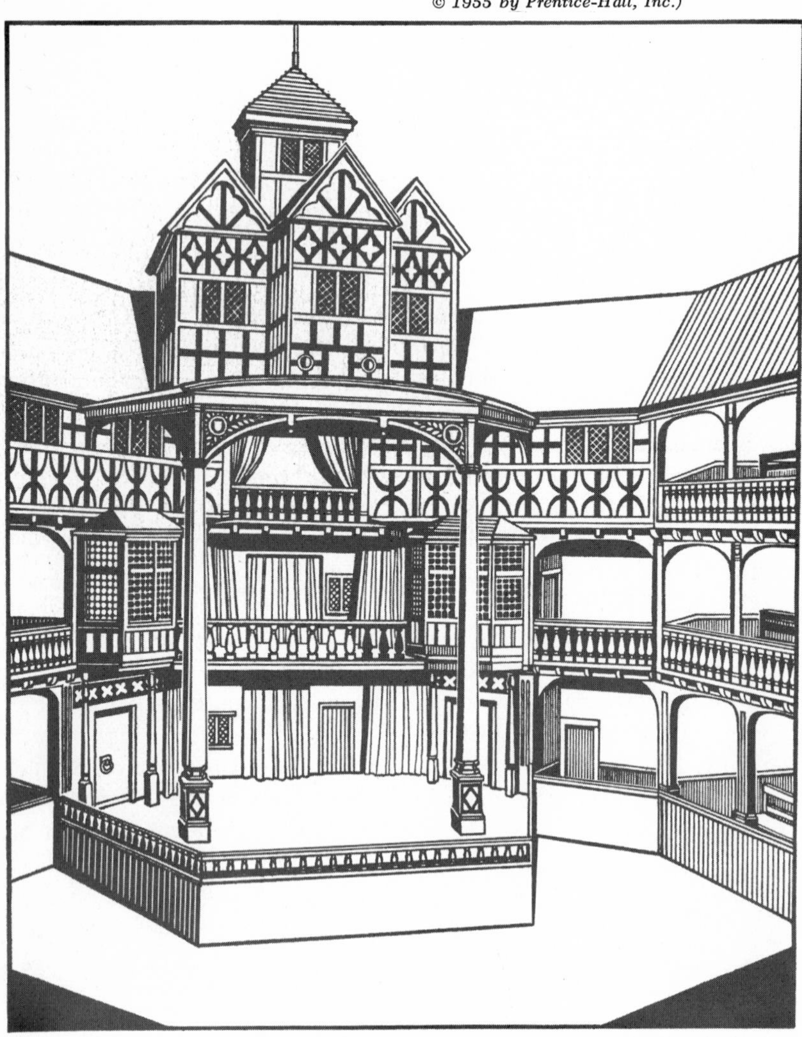

Drawing by Gerda Becker, after a reconstruction by John Crawford Adams

Hamlet in the open air, played on a modern reconstruction of a Shakespearian stage in Ashland, Oregon. The projection of the center stage into the audience gives the players the advantage of proximity in bringing out the nuances of Shakespeare's lines.

Dwaine Smith, Classic Studios

Peter Smith

Herb Nott & Co., Inc.

TOP LEFT. *Hamlet* performed on a platform stage with Edouardian costuming in the 1963 Minnesota Theater production, directed by Tyrone Guthrie. Left of center, Jessica Tandy and Lee Richardson play Gertrude and Claudius.

ABOVE. "Thoughts black, hands apt..." The play within the play in the 1957 Stratford Shakespeare Festival in Stratford, Ontario, Canada.

BOTTOM LEFT. Christopher Plummer as Hamlet in the 1957 Stratford, Ontario, Festival production.

Characters

CLAUDIUS, *King of Denmark*
HAMLET, *son to the former, and nephew to the present King*
POLONIUS, *lord chamberlain*
HORATIO, *friend to Hamlet*
LAERTES, *son to Polonius*
VOLTIMAND, CORNELIUS, ROSENCRANTZ, GUILDENSTERN, OSRIC, — *courtiers*
A Gentleman,
A Priest
MARCELLUS, BERNARDO, — *officers*
FRANCISCO, *a soldier*
REYNALDO, *servant to Polonius*
Players
Two Clowns, *gravediggers*
FORTINBRAS, *prince of Norway*
A Captain
English Ambassadors
GERTRUDE, *Queen of Denmark, and mother to Hamlet*
OPHELIA, *daughter to Polonius*

Lords, Ladies, Officers, Soldiers, Sailors, Messengers, and other Attendants

GHOST *of Hamlet's Father*

SCENE: *Denmark*

THE TRAGEDY OF HAMLET, PRINCE OF DENMARK

ACT ONE *Scene One*

Enter BERNARDO and FRANCISCO, *two Sentinels.*

BERNARDO. Who's there?
FRANCISCO. Nay, answer me. Stand and unfold yourself.
BER. Long live the king!
FRAN. Bernardo?
BER. He.
FRAN. You come most carefully upon your hour.
BER. 'Tis now struck twelve; get thee to bed, Francisco.
FRAN. For this relief much thanks: 'tis bitter cold,
And I am sick at heart.
BER. Have you had quiet guard?
FRAN. Not a mouse stirring. 10
BER. Well, good night:
If you do meet Horatio and Marcellus,
The rivals of my watch, bid them make haste.
FRAN. I think I hear them. Stand, ho! Who is there?

Enter HORATIO *and* MARCELLUS.

HORATIO. Friends to this ground.
MARCELLUS. And liegemen to the Dane.
FRAN. Give you good night.
MAR. O, farewell, honest soldier:
Who hath relieved you?
FRAN. Bernardo hath my place;
Give you good night. *Exit*

MAR. Holla, Bernardo!
BER. Say—
What, is Horatio there?
HOR. A piece of him.
BER. Welcome, Horatio: welcome, good Marcellus. 20
MAR. What, has this thing appeared again tonight?
BER. I have seen nothing.
MAR. Horatio says 'tis but our fantasy,
And will not let belief take hold of him
Touching this dreaded sight twice seen of us;
Therefore I have entreated him along
With us to watch the minutes of this night,
That, if again this apparition come,
He may approve our eyes and speak to it.
HOR. Tush, tush, 'twill not appear.
BER. Sit down awhile, 30
And let us once again assail your ears,
That are so fortified against our story,
What we have two nights seen.
HOR. Well, sit we down,
And let us hear Bernardo speak of this.
BER. Last night of all,
When yond same star that's westward from the pole
Had made his course to illume that part of heaven
Where now it burns, Marcellus and myself,
The bell then beating one—

13 **rivals** partners

29 **approve** corroborate

Enter GHOST.

40 MAR. Peace, break thee off, look where it comes again!

BER. In the same figure like the king that's dead.

MAR. Thou art a scholar, speak to it, Horatio.

BER. Looks a' not like the king? mark it, Horatio.

HOR. Most like; it harrows me with fear and wonder.

BER. It would be spoke to.

MAR. Question it, Horatio.

HOR. What art thou that usurp't this time of night,
Together with that fair and warlike form
In which the majesty of buried Denmark
Did sometimes march? by heaven I charge thee, speak!

MAR. It is offended.

50 BER. See, it stalks away.

HOR. Stay! speak, speak, I charge thee, speak! *Exit* GHOST.

MAR. 'Tis gone, and will not answer.

BER. How now, Horatio? you tremble and look pale.
Is not this something more than fantasy?
What think you on't?

HOR. Before my God, I might not this believe
Without the sensible and true avouch
Of mine own eyes.

MAR. Is it not like the king?

HOR. As thou art to thyself.
60 Such was the very armor he had on
When he the ambitious Norway combated;
So frowned he once, when in an angry parle
He smote the sledded Polacks on the ice.
'Tis strange.

MAR. Thus twice before, and jump at this dead hour,
With martial stalk hath he gone by our watch.

HOR. In what particular thought to work I know not,
But, in the gross and scope of my opinion,
This bodes some strange eruption to our state.

MAR. Good now, sit down, and tell me, he that knows, 70
Why this same strict and most observant watch
So nightly toils the subject of the land,
And why such daily cast of brazen cannon
And foreign mart for implements of war,
Why such impress of shipwrights, whose sore task
Does not divide the Sunday from the week,
What might be toward that this sweaty haste
Doth make the night joint laborer with the day;
Who is't that can inform me?

HOR. That can I;
At least the whisper goes so. Our last king, 80
Whose image even but now appeared to us,
Was as you know by Fortinbras of Norway,
Thereto pricked on by a most emulate pride,
Dared to the combat; in which our valiant Hamlet—
For so this side of our known world esteemed him—
Did slay this Fortinbras, who, by a sealed compact
Well ratified by law and heraldry,
Did forfeit, with his life, all those his lands
Which he stood seized of to the conqueror;
Against the which a moiety competent 90
Was gagéd by our king, which had returned
To the inheritance of Fortinbras,
Had he been vanquisher; as, by the same co-mart,
And carriage of the article designed,
His fell to Hamlet. Now sir, young Fortinbras,
Of unimprovéd mettle hot and full,
Hath in the skirts of Norway here and there
Sharked up a list of lawless resolutes,
For food and diet, to some enterprise
That hath a stomach in't; which is no other— 100
As it doth well appear unto our state—
But to recover of us, by strong hand
And terms compulsatory, those foresaid lands
So by his father lost; and this, I take it,
Is the main motive of our preparations,

48 **Denmark** King of Denmark 49 **sometimes** formerly 61 **Norway** King of Norway 65 **jump** just 68 **gross and scope** general range

72 **toils** makes toil 74 **mark** trading 75 **impress** conscription 77 **toward** imminent 83 **emulate** ambitious 87 **heraldry** law of arms 89 **seized** possessed 90 **moiety competent** sufficient quantity 91 **gagéd** pledged 93 **co-mart** joint bargain 94 **carriage** effect 96 **unimprovéd** unused 97 **skirts** outlying parts 98 **list** company 100 **stomach** show of daring

The source of this our watch, and the chief head
Of this posthaste and romage in the land.
BER. I think it be no other but e'en so;
Well may it sort that this portentous figure
Comes arméd through our watch so like the king
110 That was and is the question of these wars.
HOR. A mote it is to trouble the mind's eye.
In the most high and palmy state of Rome,
A little ere the mightiest Julius fell,
The graves stood tenantless and the sheeted dead
Did squeak and gibber in the Roman streets,
And even the like precurse of feared events,
As harbingers preceding still the fates
And prologue to the omen coming on,
120 Have heaven and earth together demonstrated
Unto our climatures and countrymen,
As stars with trains of fire, and dews of blood,
Disasters in the sun; and the moist star,
Upon whose influence Neptune's empire stands,
Was sick almost to doomsday with eclipse.
But soft, behold, lo where it comes again!

Enter GHOST.

I'll cross it though it blast me. Stay, illusion;
He spreads his arms.
If thou hast any sound or use of voice,
Speak to me.
If there be any good thing to be done
130 That may to thee do ease and grace to me,
Speak to me.
If thou art privy to thy country's fate,
Which, happily, foreknowing may avoid,
O speak!
Or if thou has uphoarded in thy life
Extorted treasure in the womb of earth,
For which they say you spirits oft walk in death,
The cock crows.
Speak of it. Stay and speak! Stop it, Marcellus.

MAR. Shall I strike at it with my partisan? 140
HOR. Do if it will not stand.
BER. 'Tis here!
HOR. 'Tis here!
MAR. 'Tis gone! [*Exit* GHOST.]
We do it wrong, being so majestical,
To offer it the show of violence,
For it is as the air invulnerable,
And our vain blows malicious mockery.
BER. It was about to speak when the cock crew.
HOR. And then it started like a guilty thing
Upon a fearful summons. I have heard,
The cock, that is the trumpet to the morn, 150
Doth with his lofty and shrill-sounding throat
Awake the god of day and at his warning,
Whether in sea or fire, in earth or air,
The extravagant and erring spirit hies
To his confine; and of the truth herein
This present object made probation.
MAR. It faded on the crowing of the cock.
Some say that ever 'gainst that season comes
Wherein our Savior's birth is celebrated
This bird of dawning singeth all night long, 160
And then they say no spirit dare stir abroad;
The nights are wholesome; then no planets strike,
No fairy takes, nor witch hath power to charm,
So hallowed and so gracious is the time.
HOR. So have I heard, and do in part believe it.
But look, the morn, in russet mantle clad,
Walks o'er the dew of yon high eastern hill.
Break we our watch up, and by my advice
Let us impart what we have seen tonight
Unto young Hamlet, for upon my life 170
This spirit, dumb to us, will speak to him:
Do you consent we shall acquaint him with it,
As needful in our loves, fitting our duty?
MAR. Let's do't, I pray; and I this morning know
Where we shall find him most conveniently.
Exeunt.

106 **head** cause 107 **romage** activity 109 **sort** happen 117 **precurse** foretokening 118 **harbingers** forerunners 119 **omen** dire event 121 **climatures** regions of the earth 123 **the moist star** the moon

140 **partisan** spear 154 **extravagant** wandering out of bounds 155 **confine** place of confinement 156 **probation** proof 162 **strike** exercise evil influence 163 **takes** enchant

Scene Two

Flourish. Enter CLAUDIUS, *King of Denmark,* GERTRUDE *the Queen, Councillors,* POLONIUS *and his son* LAERTES, HAMLET, *and others [including* VOLTIMAND *and* CORNELIUS*].*

KING. Though yet of Hamlet our dear brother's death
The memory be green, and that it us befitted
To bear our hearts in grief, and our whole kingdom
To be contracted in one brow of woe;
Yet so far hath discretion fought with nature,
That we with wisest sorrow think on him
Together with remembrance of ourselves:
Therefore our sometime sister, now our queen,
The imperial jointress to this warlike state,
10 Have we, as 'twere with a defeated joy,
With an auspicious and a dropping eye,
With mirth in funeral and with dirge in marriage,
In equal scale weighing delight and dole,
Taken to wife: nor have we herein barred
Your better wisdoms, which have freely gone
With this affair along. For all, our thanks.
Now follows that you know, young Fortinbras,
Holding a weak supposal of our worth,
Or thinking by our late dear brother's death
20 Our state to be disjoint and out of frame,
Colleaguéd with this dream of his advantage,
He hath not failed to pester us with message
Importing the surrender of those lands
Lost by his father, with all bonds of law,
To our most valiant brother. So much for him.
Now for ourself, and for this time of meeting.
Thus much the business is: we have here writ
To Norway, uncle of young Fortinbras—
Who, impotent and bedrid, scarcely hears
30 Of this his nephew's purpose—to suppress
His further gait herein, in that the levies,
The lists, and full proportions are all made
Out of his subject, and we here dispatch
You, good Cornelius, and you, Voltimand,
For bearers of this greeting to old Norway,
Giving to you no further personal power
To business with the king, more than the scope
Of these delated articles allow.
Farewell, and let your haste commend your duty.

COR., VOL. In that, and all things, will we show our duty.

40 KING. We doubt it nothing; heartily farewell.

Exeunt VOLTIMAND *and* CORNELIUS.

And now, Laertes, what's the news with you?
You told us of some suit, what is't, Laertes?
You cannot speak of reason to the Dane
And lose your voice; what wouldst thou beg, Laertes,
That shall not be my offer, not thy asking?
The head is not more native to the heart,
The hand more instrumental to the mouth,
Than is the throne of Denmark to thy father.
What wouldst thou have, Laertes?

50 LAERTES. My dread lord,
Your leave and favor to return to France,
From whence though willingly I came to Denmark,
To show my duty in your coronation;
Yet now, I must confess, that duty done,
My thoughts and wishes bend again toward France
And bow them to your gracious leave and pardon.

KING. Have you your father's leave? What says Polonius?

POL. He hath, my lord, wrung from me my slow leave
By laborsome petition, and at last

9 **jointress** a widow who holds a jointure, or life-interest in an estate 14 **barred** ignored 20 **disjoint** disorganized 21 **colleaguéd** combined 31 **gait** progress

32 **proportions** estimates of forces and supplies 38 **delated** extended 44 **Dane** King of Denmark 45 **lose your voice** speak in vain 47 **native** linked by nature to 48 **instrumental** serviceable

60 Upon his will I sealed my hard consent;
I do beseech you give him leave to go.
KING. Take thy fair hour, Laertes; time be thine,
And thy best graces spend it at thy will!
But now, my cousin Hamlet, and my son—
HAMLET. [*aside*] A little more than kin, and less than kind.
KING. How is it that the clouds still hang on you?
HAMLET. Not so, my lord; I am too much in the sun.
QUEEN. Good Hamlet, cast thy nightéd color off
And let thine eye look like a friend on Denmark,
70 Do not for ever with thy vailéd lids
Seek for thy noble father in the dust;
Thou know'st 'tis common; all that live must die,
Passing through nature to eternity.
HAMLET. Ay, madam, it is common.
QUEEN. If it be,
Why seems it so particular with thee?
HAMLET. Seems, madam, nay it is; I know not "seems."
'Tis not alone my inky cloak, good mother,
Nor customary suits of solemn black,
Nor windy suspiration of forced breath,
80 No, nor the fruitful river in the eye,
Nor the dejected havior of the visage,
Together with all forms, moods, shapes of grief,
That can denote me truly; these indeed seem,
For they are actions that a man might play,
But I have that within which passes show;
These but the trappings and the suits of woe.
KING. 'Tis sweet and commendable in your nature, Hamlet,
To give these mourning duties to your father
But you must know your father lost a father,
90 That father lost, lost his, and the survivor bound
In filial obligation for some term
To do obsequious sorrow; but to persever
In obstinate condolement is a course
Of impious stubbornness, 'tis unmanly grief;
It shows a will most incorrect to heaven,
A heart unfortified, a mind impatient,
An understanding simple and unschooled
For what we know must be, and is as common
As any the most vulgar thing to sense;
Why should we in our peevish opposition 100
Take it to heart? Fie, 'tis a fault to heaven,
A fault against the dead, a fault to nature,
To reason most absurd, whose common theme
Is death of fathers, and who still hath cried,
From the first corse till he that died today,
"This must be so." We pray you throw to earth
This prevailing woe, and think of us
As of a father, for let the world take note
You are the most immediate to our throne,
And with no less nobility of love 110
Than that which dearest father bears his son,
Do I impart toward you. For your intent
In going back to school in Wittenberg,
It is most retrograde to our desire,
And we beseech you bend you to remain
Here in the cheer and comfort of our eye,
Our chiefest courtier, cousin, and our son.
QUEEN. Let not thy mother lose her prayers, Hamlet;
I pray thee stay with us, go not to Wittenberg.
HAMLET. I shall in all my best obey you, madam. 120
KING. Why, 'tis a loving and a fair reply;
Be as ourself in Denmark. Madam, come;
This gentle and unforced accord of Hamlet
Sits smiling to my heart, in grace whereof,
No jocund health that Denmark drinks today
But the great cannon to the clouds shall tell,
And the king's rouse the heavens shall bruit again,
Re-speaking earthly thunder. Come away.
Flourish. Exeunt all except HAMLET.
HAMLET. O that this too too sullied flesh would melt,
Thaw and resolve itself into a dew, 130
Or that the Everlasting had not fixed
His canon 'gainst self slaughter! O God, O God,
How weary, stale, flat, and unprofitable
Seem to me all the uses of this world!
Fie on't, ah fie, 'tis an unweeded garden
That grows to seed, things rank and gross in nature
Possess it merely. That it should come to this—
But two months dead, nay not so much, not two—
So excellent a king, that was to this

67 **sun** *notice the pun with* son 69 **Denmark** King of Denmark 70 **vailéd** lowered 79 **suspiration** breathing 92 **obsequious** dutiful

114 **retrograde** opposed 127 **rouse** carousal **bruit again** echo 132 **canon** ordinance

140 Hyperion to a satyr, so loving to my mother,
That he might not beteem the winds of heaven
Visit her face too roughly. Heaven and earth,
Must I remember? why, she would hang on him
As if increase of appetite had grown
By what it fed on, and yet within a month—
Let me not think on't, frailty, thy name is woman—
A little month, or ere those shoes were old
With which she followed my poor father's body,
Like Niobe all tears, why she, even she—
150 O God, a beast, that wants discourse of reason,
Would have mourned longer—married with my uncle,
My father's brother, but no more like my father
Than I to Hercules, within a month,
Ere yet the salt of most unrighteous tears
Had left the flushing in her galléd eyes,
She married. O most wicked speed, to post
With such dexterity to incestuous sheets!
It is not, nor it cannot come to good;
But break, my heart, for I must hold my tongue.

Enter HORATIO, MARCELLUS, *and* BERNARDO.

HOR. Hail to your lordship!
160 HAMLET. I am glad to see you well;
Horatio—or I do forget myself.
HOR. The same, my lord, and your poor servant ever.
HAMLET. Sir, my good friend; I'll change that name with you;
And what make you from Wittenberg, Horatio?
Marcellus!
MAR. My good lord!
HAMLET. I am very glad to see you; good even, sir.
But what, in faith, make you from Wittenberg?
HOR. A truant disposition, good my lord.
HAMLET. I would not hear your enemy say so,
170 Nor shall you do my ear that violence
To make it truster of your own report
Against yourself; I know you are no truant.
But what is your affair in Elsinore?
We'll teach you to drink deep ere you depart.
HOR. My lord, I came to see your father's funeral.
HAMLET. I prithee do no mock me, fellow student;
I think it was to see my mother's wedding.
HOR. Indeed, my lord, it followed hard upon.
HAMLET. Thrift, thrift, Horatio, the funeral baked meats
Did coldly furnish forth the marriage tables. 180
Would I had met my dearest foe in heaven
Or ever I had seen that day, Horatio!
My father—methinks I see my father.
HOR. Where, my lord?
HAMLET. In my mind's eye, Horatio.
HOR. I saw him once, a' was a goodly king.
HAMLET. A' was a man, take him for all in all,
I shall not look upon his like again.
HOR. My lord, I think I saw him yesternight.
HAMLET. Saw who?
HOR. My lord, the king your father.
HAMLET. The king my father! 190
HOR. Season your admiration for a while
With an attent ear till I may deliver,
Upon the witness of these gentlemen,
This marvel to you.
HAMLET. For God's love let me hear.
HOR. Two nights together had these gentlemen,
Marcellus and Bernardo, on their watch
In the dead waste and middle of the night
Been thus encountered: a figure like your father,
Arméd at point exactly, cap-a-pe,
Apears before them, and with solemn march 200
Goes slow and stately by them; thrice he walked
By their oppressed and fear-surprisèd eyes,
Within his truncheon's length, whilst they, distilled
Almost to jelly with the act of fear,
Stand dumb and speak not to him; this to me
In dreadful secrecy impart they did,
And I with them the third night kept the watch,
Where as they had delivered both in time,
Form of the thing, each word made true and good,

140 **Hyperion** the sun-god 141 **beteem** permit 149 **Niobe** After the gods had killed all her children Niobe was turned into stone from which tears gushed continually 150 **discourse** process 155 **galléd** rubbed, inflamed

181 **dearest** bitterest 191 **season** moderate **admiration** astonishment 192 **attent** attentive 199 **at point** completely **cap-a-pe** from head to foot

210 The apparition comes: I knew your father;
These hands are not more like.

HAMLET. But where was this?

MAR. My lord, upon the platform where we watched.

HAMLET. Did you not speak to it?

HOR. My lord, I did,
But answer made it none; yet once methought
It lifted up its head, and did address
Itself to motion like as it would speak:
But even then the morning cock crew loud,
And at the sound it shrunk in haste away
And vanished from our sight.

HAMLET. 'Tis very strange.

220 HOR. As I do live, my honored lord, 'tis true,
And we did think it writ down in our duty
To let you know of it.

HAMLET. Indeed, indeed, sirs, but this troubles me.
Hold you the watch tonight?

ALL. We do, my lord.

HAMLET. Armed, say you?

ALL. Armed, my lord.

HAMLET. From top to toe?

ALL. My lord, from head to foot.

HAMLET. Then saw you not his face?

HOR. O yes, my lord, he wore his beaver up.

230 HAMLET. What, looked he frowningly?

HOR. A countenance more in sorrow than in anger.

HAMLET. Pale or red?

HOR. Nay, very pale.

HAMLET. And fixed his eyes upon you?

HOR. Most constantly.

HAMLET. I would I had been there.

HOR. It would have much amazed you.

HAMLET. Very like, very like. Stayed it long?

HOR. While one with moderate haste might tell a hundred.

BOTH. Longer, longer.

HOR. Not when I saw't.

HAMLET. His beard was grizzled, no?

HOR. It was as I have seen it in his life, 240
A sable silvered.

HAMLET. I will watch tonight,
Perchance 'twill walk again.

HOR. I warrant it will.

HAMLET. If it assume my noble father's person,
I'll speak to it though hell itself should gape
And bid me hold my peace; I pray you all,
If you have hitherto concealed this sight,
Let it be tenable in your silence still,
And whatsomever else shall hap tonight,
Give it an understanding but no tongue.
I will requite your loves; so fare you well: 250
Upon the platform 'twixt eleven and twelve
I'll visit you.

ALL. Our duty to your honor.

HAMLET. Your loves, as mine to you; farewell. *Exeunt.*
My father's spirit in arms! all is not well;
I doubt some foul play; would the night were come!
Till then sit still, my soul; foul deeds will rise,
Though all the earth o'erwhelm them, to men's eyes. *Exit.*

Scene Three

Enter LAERTES *and* OPHELIA *his sister.*

LAERTES. My necessaries are embarked; farewell.
And, sister, as the winds give benefit,
And convoy is assistant, do not sleep,
But let me hear from you.

OPHELIA. Do you doubt that?

LAERTES. For Hamlet and the trifling of his favor,
Hold it a fashion and a toy in blood,

215 **it** its 229 **beaver** visor 3 **convoy** means of conveyance

237 **tell** count 241 **sable** black 247 **tenable** held back 255 **doubt** suspect

A violet in the youth of primy nature,
Forward, not permanent, sweet, not lasting,
The perfume and suppliance of a minute,
No more.

OPH. No more but so?

10 LAERTES. Think it no more.
For nature crescent does not grow alone
In thews and bulk, but as this temple waxes
The inward service of the mind and soul
Grows wide withal. Perhaps he loves you now,
And now no soil nor cautel doth besmirch
The virtue of his will; but you must fear,
His greatness weighed, his will is not his own,
For he himself is subject to his birth.
He may not, as unvalued persons do,
20 Carve for himself, for on his choice depends
The safety and health of this whole state,
And therefore must his choice be circumscribed
Unto the voice and yielding of that body
Whereof he is the head. Then if he says he loves you,
It fits your wisdom so far to believe it
As he in his particular act and place
May give his saying deed, which is no further
Than the main voice of Denmark goes withal.
Then weigh what loss your honor may sustain
30 If with too credent ear you list his songs,
Or lose your heart, or your chaste treasure open
To his unmastered importunity.
Fear it, Ophelia, fear it, my dear sister,
And keep you in the rear of your affection,
Out of the shot and danger of desire.
The chariest maid is prodigal enough
If she unmask her beauty to the moon;
Virtue itself scapes not calumnious strokes;
The canker galls the infants of the spring
40 Too oft before their buttons be disclosed;
And in the morn and liquid dew of youth
Contagious blastments are most imminent.
Be wary, then best safety lies in fear;
Youth to itself rebels, though none else near.

OPH. I shall the effect of this good lesson keep
As watchman to my heart. But, good my brother,
Do not, as some ungracious pastors do,
Show me the steep and thorny way to heaven,
Whiles like a puffed and reckless libertine
Himself the primrose path of dalliance treads,
And recks not his own rede. 50

LAERTES. O fear me not.
I stay too long; but here my father comes.

Enter POLONIUS.

A double blessing is a double grace;
Occasion smiles upon a second leave.

POL. Yet here, Laertes! aboard, aboard, for shame!
The wind sits in the shoulder of your sail,
And you are stayed for. There, my blessing with thee!
And these few precepts in thy memory
Look thou character. Give thy thoughts no tongue,
Nor any unproportioned thought his act. 60
Be thou familiar, but by no means vulgar.
The friends thou hast, and their adoption tried,
Grapple them unto thy soul with hoops of steel,
But do not dull thy palm with entertainment
Of each new-hatched, unfledged comrade. Beware
Of entrance to a quarrel, but being in,
Bear't that th' oppos'd may beware of thee.
Give every man thy ear, but few thy voice;
Take each man's censure, but reserve thy judgment.
Costly thy habit as thy purse can buy, 70
But not expressed in fancy; rich, not gaudy;
For the apparel oft proclaims the man,
And they in France of the best rank and station
Are often most select and generous, chief in that.
Neither a borrower nor a lender be,
For loan oft loses both itself and friend,
And borrowing dulls the edge of husbandry.
This above all, to thine ownself be true
And it must follow, as the night the day,

7 **primy** early 11 **crescent** growing 12 **this temple** the body 15 **soil** blemish **cautel** deceit 23 **yielding** consent 30 **credent** trustful 34-35 **keep . . . desire** do not go as far forward as affection will lead you, but avoid danger by staying out of range 36 **charies** most sparing 39 **canker** grub, caterpillar **galls** injures **infants of the spring** young flowers 40 **buttons** buds 42 **blastments** blights

51 **recks** heed **rede** advice 59 **character** engrave 60 **unproportioned** unbalanced 69 **censure** opinion 77 **husbandry** economy

80 Thou canst not then be false to any man.
Farewell; my blessing season this in thee!

LAERTES. Most humbly do I take my leave, my lord.

POL. The time invites you; go, your servants tend.

LAERTES. Farewell, Ophelia, and remember well
What I have said to you.

OPH. 'Tis in my memory locked
And you yourself shall keep the key of it.

LAERTES. Farewell. *Exit* LAERTES.

POL. What is't, Ophelia, he hath said to you?

OPH. So please you, something touching the Lord Hamlet.

90 POL. Marry, well bethought.
'Tis told me he hath very oft of late
Given private time to you, and you yourself
Have of your audience been most free and bounteous;
If it be so—as so 'tis put on me,
And that in way of caution—I must tell you
You do not understand yourself so clearly
As it behoves my daughter and your honor.
What is between you? give me up the truth.

OPH. He hath, my lord, of late made many tenders
100 Of his affection to me.

POL. Affection, pooh! you speak like a green girl
Unsifted in such perilous circumstance.
Do you believe his tenders, as you call them?

OPH. I do not know, my lord, what I should think.

POL. Marry, I will teach you: think yourself a baby
That you have ta'en these tenders for true pay,
Which are not sterling. Tender yourself more dearly,
Or (not to crack the wind of the poor phrase,
Running it thus) you'll tender me a fool.

OPH. My lord, he hath importuned me with love 110
In honorable fashion.

POL. Ay, fashion you may call it; go to, go to.

OPH. And hath given countenance to his speech, my lord,
With almost all the holy vows of heaven.

POL. Ay, springes to catch woodcocks. I do know,
When the blood burns, how prodigal the soul
Lends the tongue vows; these blazes, daughter,
Giving more light than heat, extinct in both,
Even in their promise, as it is a-making,
You must not take for fire. From this time 120
Be something scanter of your maiden presence;
Set your entreatments at a higher rate
Than a command to parley. For Lord Hamlet,
Believe so much in him that he is young,
And with a larger tether may he walk
Than may be given you: in few, Ophelia,
Do not believe his vows, for they are brokers,
Not of that dye which their investments show,
But mere implorators of unholy suits,
Breathing like sanctified and pious bawds, 130
The better to beguile. This is for all:
I would not, in plain terms, from this time forth
Have you so slander any moment leisure
As to give words or talk with the Lord Hamlet.
Look to't, I charge you; come your ways.

OPH. I shall obey, my lord.

Exeunt.

83 **tend** attend 99 **tenders** offers 102 **unsifted** untired 113 **countenance** confirmation 115 **springes** snares

122 **entreatments** interviews 123 **parley** conference under a truce 127 **brokers** go-betweens 128 **investments** vestments, clothes 129 **implorators** solicitors 133 **slander** misuse **moment** monetary

Scene Four

Enter HAMLET, HORATIO, *and* MARCELLUS.

HAMLET. The air bites shrewdly, it is very cold.

HOR. It is a nipping and an eager air.

HAMLET. What hour now?

HOR. I think it lacks of twelve.

MAR. No, it is struck.

HOR. Indeed? I heard it not; it then draws near the season
Wherein the spirit held his wont to walk.

A flourish of trumpets, and two pieces go off.

What does this mean, my lord?

HAMLET. The king doth wake tonight and takes his rouse,
Keeps wassail, and the swaggering up-spring reels;
And as he drains his draughts of Rhenish down
10 The kettledrum and trumpet thus bray out
The triumph of his pledge.

HOR. Is it a custom?

HAMLET. Ay, marry, is't;
But to my mind, though I am native here
And to the manner born, it is a custom
More honored in the breach than the observance.
This heavy-headed revel east and west
Makes us traduced and taxed of other nations;
They clepe us drunkards, and with swinish phrase
Soil our addition, and indeed it takes
20 From our achievements, though performed at height,
The pith and marrow of our attribute.
So, oft it chances in particular men
That for some vicious mole of nature in them,
As in their birth, wherein they are not guilty,
(Since nature cannot choose his origin)
By the o'ergrowth of some complexion,
Oft breaking down the pales and forts of reason,
Or by some habit that too much o'er-leavens
The form of plausive manners—that these men, 30
Carrying, I say, the stamp of one defect,
Being nature's livery, or fortune's star,
His virtues else—be they as pure as grace,
As infinite as man may undergo—
Shall in the general censure take corruption
From that particular fault: the dram of evil
Doth all the noble substance often dout
To his own scandal.

HOR. Look, my lord, it comes!

Enter GHOST.

HAMLET. Angels and ministers of grace defend us!
Be thou a spirit of health or goblin damned, 40
Bring with thee airs from heaven or blasts from hell,
Be thy intents wicked or charitable,
Thou com'st in such a questionable shape,
That I will speak to thee; I'll call thee Hamlet,
King, father, royal Dane; O, answer me!
Let me not burst in ignorance, but tell
Why thy canonized bones hearsèd in death
Have burst their cerements; why the sepulchre,
Wherein we saw thee quietly inurned,
Hath oped his ponderous and marble jaws 50
To cast thee up again! What may this mean
That thou, dead corse, again in complete steel
Revisits thus the glimpses of the moon,
Making night hideous, and we fools of nature
So horridly to shake our disposition
With thoughts beyond the reaches of our souls?
Say, why it this? wherefore? what should we do?

GHOST *beckons* HAMLET.

HOR. It beckons you to go away with it
As if it some impartment did desire
To you alone.

2 **eager** shape 9 **up-spring** a dance 10 **Rhenish** Rhine wine 18 **taxed of** upbraided by 19 **clepe** call 20 **addition** title, honor 21 **at height** at the highest pitch of excellence 24 **mole of nature** natural defect 26 **his** its 27 **complexion** disposition 28 **pales** fences

29 **o'erleavens** modifies 30 **plausive** plausible 32 **livery** badge **fortune's star** accidental mark 35 **censure** opinion 36 **dram** particle 37 **dout** extinguish 38 **his** its **scandal** harm 48 **cerements** gravecloths 55 **disposition** normal habit of thought

60 MAR. Look with what courteous action
It waves you to a more removéd ground;
But do not go with it.
HOR. No, by no means.
HAMLET. It will not speak; then I will follow it.
HOR. Do not, my lord.
HAMLET. Why, what should be the fear?
I do not set my life at a pin's fee,
And for my soul, what can it do to that,
Being a thing immortal as itself?
It waves me forth again, I'll follow it.
HOR. What if it tempt you toward the flood, my lord,
70 Or to the dreadful summit of the cliff
That beetles o'er his base into the sea,
And there assume some other horrible form,
Which might deprive your sovereignty of reason,
And draw you into madness? think of it:
The very place puts toys of desperation,
Without more motive, into every brain
That looks so many fathoms to the sea
And hears it roar beneath.
HAMLET. It waves me still;
Go on, I'll follow thee.
MAR. You shall not go, my lord.
HAMLET. Hold off your hands. 80
HOR. Be ruled, you shall not go.
HAMLET. My fate cries out,
And makes each petty artere in this body
As hardy as the Nemean lion's nerve;
Still am I call'd; unhand me, gentlemen;
By heaven, I'll make a ghost of him that lets me;
I say, away! go on, I'll follow thee.

Exeunt GHOST *and* HAMLET.

HOR. He waxes desperate with imagination.
MAR. Let's follow; 'tis not fit thus to obey him.
HOR. Have after. To what issue will this come?
MAR. Something is rotten in the state of Denmark. 90
HOR. Heaven will direct it.
MAR. Nay, let's follow him.

Exeunt.

65 **fee** value 71 **beetles** projects 73 **sovereignty of reason** supreme control exercised by reason 75 **toys** trifles, fancies

82 **artere** artery 83 **Nemean lion** the lion slain by Hercules **nerve** sinew 85 **lets** hinders

Scene Five

Enter GHOST *and* HAMLET.

HAMLET. Whither wilt thou lead me? speak, I'll go no further.
GHOST. Mark me.
HAMLET. I will.
GHOST. My hour is almost come,
When I to sulphurous and tormenting flames
Must render up myself.
HAMLET. Alas, poor ghost!
GHOST. Pity me not, but lend thy serious hearing
To what I shall unfold.
HAMLET. Speak, I am bound to hear.
GHOST. So art thou to revenge, when thou shalt hear.
HAMLET. What?
GHOST. I am thy father's spirit,
Doomed for a certain term to walk the night, 10
And for the day confined to fast in fires,
Till the foul crimes done in my days of nature
Are burnt and purged away: but that I am forbid
To tell the secrets of my prison house,
I could a tale unfold whose lightest word
Would harrow up thy soul, freeze thy young blood,
Make thy two eyes like stars start from their spheres,
Thy knotted and combinéd locks to part,

And each particular hair to stand an end,
20 Like quills upon the fretful porpentine.
But this eternal blazon must not be
To ears of flesh and blood. List, list, O list!
If thou didst ever thy dear father love—

HAMLET. O God!

GHOST. Revenge his foul and most unnatural murder.

HAMLET. Murder!

GHOST. Murder most foul, as in the best it is,
But this most foul, strange and unnatural.

HAMLET. Haste me to know't, that I with wings as swift
30 As meditation or the thoughts of love
May sweep to my revenge.

GHOST. I find thee apt,
And duller shouldst thou be than the fat weed
That roots itself in ease on Lethe wharf,
Wouldst thou not stir in this. Now, Hamlet, hear:
'Tis given out that, sleeping in my orchard,
A serpent stung me; so the whole ear of Denmark
Is by a forgéd process of my death
Rankly abused: but know, thou noble youth,
The serpent that did sting thy father's life
Now wears his crown.

40 HAMLET. O my prophetic soul!
My uncle?

GHOST. Ay, that incestuous, that adulterate beast,
With witchcraft of his wit, with traitorous gifts—
O wicked wit and gifts, that have the power
So to seduce!—won to his shameful lust
The will of my most seeming-virtuous queen;
O Hamlet, what a falling-off was there!
From me, whose love was of that dignity
That it went hand in hand even with the vow
50 I made to her in marriage, and to decline
Upon a wretch whose natural gifts were poor
To those of mine;
But virtue, as it never will be moved,
Though lewdness court it in a shape of heaven,
So lust, though to a radiant angel linked,
Will sate itself in a celestial bed
And prey on garbage.
But soft, methinks I scent the morning air;
Brief let me be. Sleeping within my orchard,
60 My custom always of the afternoon,
Upon my secure hour thy uncle stole
With juice of curséd hebenon in a vial,
And in the porches of mine ears did pour
The leperous distilment, whose effect
Holds such an enmity with blood of man,
That swift as quicksilver it courses through
The natural gates and alleys of the body,
And with a sudden vigor it doth posset
And curd, like eager droppings into milk,
70 The thin and wholesome blood; so did it mine,
And a most instant tetter barked about,
Most lazar-like, with vile and loathsome crust
All my smooth body.
Thus was I sleeping by a brother's hand
Of life, of crown, of queen at once dispatched,
Cut off even in the blossoms of my sin,
Unhouseled, disappointed, unaneled,
No reckoning made, but sent to my account
With all my imperfections on my head;
80 O horrible, O horrible, most horrible!
If thou hast nature in thee, bear it not;
Let not the royal bed of Denmark be
A couch for luxury and damnéd incest.
But howsomever thou pursues this act,
Taint not thy mind, nor let thy soul contrive
Against thy mother aught; leave her to heaven,
And to those thorns that in her bosom lodge
To prick and sting her. Fare thee well at once;
The glowworm shows the matin to be near,
90 And gins to pale his uneffectual fire.
Adieu, adieu, adieu: remember me. *Exit*

HAMLET. O all you host of heaven! O earth! what else?
And shall I couple hell? O fie! Hold, hold my heart,
And you, my sinews, grow not instant old,
But bear me stiffly up. Remember thee?
Ay, thou poor ghost, whiles memory holds a seat
In this distracted globe. Remember thee?
Yea, from the table of my memory
I'll wipe away all trivial fond records,

19 **an end** on end 20 **porpentine** porcupine 21 **eternal blazon** proclamation of the secrets of eternity 33 **Lethe** the river of oblivion

68 **posset** curdle 69 **eager** bitter 71 **tetter** eruption of the skin **barked** crusted 72 **lazar-like** like a leper 77 **unhouseled** without sacrament **unaneled** without extreme unction 98 **table** writing tablet

100 All saws of books, all forms, all pressures past,
That youth and observation copied there;
And thy commandment all alone shall live
Within the book and volume of my brain
Unmixed with baser matter; yes by heaven!
O most pernicious woman!
O villain, villain, smiling, damnéd villain!
My tables—meet it is I set it down
That one may smile, and smile, and be a villain;
At least I'm sure it may be so in Denmark.
[*Writing.*]
110 So uncle, there you are. Now to my word;
It is "Adieu, adieu, remember me:"
I have sworn't.

HOR. } MAR. } [*within*] My lord, my lord!

Enter HORATIO *and* MARCELLUS.

MAR. Lord Hamlet!
HOR. Heavens secure him!
HAMLET. So be it!
HOR. Illo, ho, ho, my lord!
HAMLET. Hillo, ho, ho, boy! come, bird, come.
MAR. How is't, my noble lord?
HOR. What news, my lord?
HAMLET. O, wonderful.
HOR. Good my lord, tell it.
HAMLET. No, you will reveal it.
HOR. Not I, my lord, by heaven.
120 MAR. Nor I, my lord.
HAMLET. How say you then, would heart of man once think it?
But you'll be secret?
BOTH. Ay, by heaven, my lord.
HAMLET. There's never a villain dwelling in all Denmark
But he's an arrant knave.
HOR. There needs no ghost, my lord, come from the grave
To tell us this.
HAMLET. Why right, you are in the right;
And so, without more circumstance at all,
I hold it fit that we shake hands and part;
You, as your business and desire shall point you,
130 For every man hath business and desire,
Such as it is, and for my own poor part,
Look you, I will go pray.

HOR. These are but wild and whirling words, my lord.
HAMLET. I'm sorry they offend you, heartily;
Yes, faith, heartily.
HOR. There's no offence, my lord.
HAMLET. Yes, by Saint Patrick, but there is, Horatio,
And much offence too. Touching this vision here,
It is an honest ghost, that let me tell you;
For your desire to know what is between us
O'ermaster't as you may; and now, good friends, 140
As you are friends, scholars and soldiers,
Give me one poor request.
HOR. What is't, my lord? we will.
HAMLET. Never make known what you have seen tonight.
BOTH. My lord, we will not.
HAMLET. Nay, but swear't.
HOR. In faith,
My lord, not I.
MAR. Nor I, my lord, in faith.
HAMLET. Upon my sword.
MAR. We have sworn, my lord, already.
HAMLET. Indeed, upon my sword, indeed.

GHOST *cries under the stage*

GHOST. Swear.
HAMLET. Ha, ha, boy, say'st thou so? art thou there, truepenny? 150
Come on, you hear this fellow in the cellarage,
Consent to swear.
HOR. Propose the oath, my lord.
HAMLET. Never to speak of this that you have seen,
Swear by my sword.
GHOST. Swear.
HAMLET. *Hic et ubique?* then we'll shift our ground.
Come hither, gentlemen,
And lay your hands again upon my sword.
Swear by my sword
Never to speak of this that you have heard. 160
GHOST. Swear by his sword.
HAMLET. Well said, old mole, canst work i' the earth so fast?
A worthy pioner! Once more remove, good friends.

100 **saws** maxims **forms** sketches **pressures** impressions 115 **Illo, ho, ho** the falconer's call to his hawk 127 **circumstance** formality

156 **hic et ubique** here and everywhere 163 **pioner** miner

HOR. O day and night, but this is wondrous strange!

HAMLET. And therefore as a stranger give it welcome.
There are more things in heaven and earth, Horatio,
Than are dreamt of in your philosophy.
But come:
Here as before, never, so help you mercy,
170 How strange or odd some'er I bear myself—
As I perchance hereafter shall think meet
To put an antic disposition on—
That you, at such times seeing me, never shall
With arms encumbered thus, or this headshake,
Or by pronouncing of some doubtful phrase,
As "Well, well, we know," or "We could, an if we would,"
Or "If we list to speak," or "There be, an if they might,"
Or such ambiguous giving out, to note
That you know aught of me: this do swear,
So grace and mercy at your most need help you. 180

GHOST. Swear.

HAMLET. Rest, rest, perturbèd spirit: [*They swear.*] so, gentlemen,
With all my love I do commend me to you,
And what so poor a man as Hamlet is
May do to express his love and friending to you,
God willing, shall not lack. Let us go in together,
And still your fingers on your lips, I pray.
The time is out of joint; O cursed spite
That ever I was born to set it right!
Nay come, let's go together. 190

Exeunt.

ACT TWO *Scene One*

Enter old POLONIUS, *with his man* REYNALDO.

POL. Give him this money and these notes, Reynaldo.

REYNALDO. I will, my lord.

POL. You shall do marvellous wisely, good Reynaldo,
Before you visit him, to make inquire
Of his behavior.

REY. My lord, I did intend it.

POL. Marry, well said, very well said. Look you, sir,
Inquire me first what Danskers are in Paris,
And how, and who, what means, and where they keep,
What company, at what expense, and finding,
10 By this encompassment and drift of question,
That they do know my son, come you more nearer
Than your particular demands will touch it;
Take you as 'twere some distant knowledge of him,
As thus, "I know his father and his friends,
And in part him;" do you mark this Reynaldo?

REY. Ay, very well, my lord.

POL. "And in part him, but," you may say, "not well;
But if't be he I mean he's very wild,
Addicted so and so," and there put on him
What forgeries you please; marry, none so rank 20
As may dishonor him, take heed of that,
But, sir, such wanton, wild and usual slips
As are companions noted and most known
To youth and liberty.

REY. As gaming, my lord.

POL. Ay, or drinking, fencing, swearing, quarrelling,
Drabbing—you may go so far.

REY. My lord, that would dishonor him.

POL. Faith, no, as you may season it in the charge.
You must not put another scandal on him,
That he is open to incontinency— 30
That's not my meaning; but breathe his faults so quaintly

172 **antic** odd, strange 174 **encumbered** folded
7 **Danskers** Danes 8 **keep** resort 10 **encompassment** circuitous route

28 **season** modify **charge** accusation 31 **quaintly** skilfully

That they may seem the taints of liberty,
The flash and outbreak of a fiery mind,
A savageness in unreclaimèd blood,
Of general assault.

REY. But, my good lord—

POL. Wherefore should you do this?

REY. Ay, my lord,
I would know that.

POL. Marry, sir, here's my drift,
And I believe it is a fetch of warrant:
You laying these slight sullies on my son,
40 As 'twere a thing a little soiled i' the working,
Mark you,
Your party in converse, him you would sound,
Having ever seen in the prenominate crimes
The youth you breathe of guilty, be assured
He closes with you in this consequence,
"Good sir," or so, or "friend," or "gentleman,"
According to the phrase or the addition
Of man and country.

REY. Very good, my lord.

POL. And then, sir, does a' this—a' does—
50 What was I about to say? By the mass, I was
About to say something; where did I leave?

REY. At "closes in the consequence,"
At "friend or so, and gentleman."

POL. At "closes in the consequence," ay, marry;
He closes with you thus: "I know the gentleman,
I saw him yesterday, or th'other day,
Or then, or then, with such, or such, and, as you say,
There was a' gaming, there o'ertook in's rouse,
There falling out at tennis," or perchance
60 "I saw him enter such a house of sale,"
Videlicet, a brothel, or so forth. See you now,
Your bait of falsehood takes this carp of truth,
And thus do we of wisdom and of reach,
With windlasses and with assays of bias,
By indirections find directions out;
So by my former lecture and advice
Shall you my son. You have me, have you not?

REY. My lord, I have.

POL. God be wi' ye, fare ye well.

REY. Good my lord!

POL. Observe his inclination in yourself. 70

REY. I shall, my lord.

POL. And let him ply his music.

REY. Well, my lord.

POL. Farewell! *Exit* REYNALDO.

Enter OPHELIA.

How now, Ophelia, what's the matter?

OPH. O my lord, my lord, I have been so affrighted!

POL. With what, i' the name of God?

OPH. My lord, as I was sewing in my closet,
Lord Hamlet with his doublet all unbraced,
No hat upon his head, his stockings fouled,
Ungartered and down-gyvèd to his ankle,
Pale as his shirt, his knees knocking each other, 80
And with a look so piteous in purport
As if he had been loosèd out of hell
To speak of horrors—he comes before me.

POL. Mad for thy love?

OPH. My lord, I do not know,
But truly I do fear it.

POL. What said he?

OPH. He took me by the wrist and held me hard,
Then goes he to the length of all his arm,
And with his other hand thus o'er his brow
He falls to such perusal of my face
As a' would draw it. Long stayed he so; 90
At last, a little shaking of mine arm
And thrice his head thus waving up and down,
He raised a sigh so piteous and profound
As it did seem to shatter all his bulk
And end his being; that done, he lets me go:
And with his head over his shoulder turned
He seemed to find his way without his eyes,
For out o' doors he went without their helps,
And to the last bended their light on me.

POL. Come, go with me; I will go seek the king. 100
This is the very ecstasy of love,
Whose violent property fordoes itself,
And leads the will to desperate undertakings,

32 **taints** faults 34 **unreclaimèd** unrestrained 35 **of general assault** which attack everyone 38 **fetch** device **of warrant** justifiable 43 **prenominate** aforementioned 45 **in this consequence** to this effect 47 **additional** title 58 **o'ertook** overcome **rouse** carousal, cups 63 **reach** capacity 64 **windlasses** crafty devices **assays of bias** roundabout attempts 65 **indirections** indirect means

77 **doublet** jacket 79 **down-gyvèd** hanging down like gyves or fetters 101 **ecstasy** madness 102 **property** propensity **fordoes** ruins

As oft as any passion under heaven
That does afflict our natures. I am sorry.
What, have you given him any hard words of late?

OPH. No, my good lord, but as you did command
I did repel his letters, and denied
His access to me.

POL. That hath made him mad.
110 I am sorry that with better heed and judgment
I had not quoted him; I feared he did but trifle
And meant to wreck thee; but, beshrew my jealousy,
By heaven it is as proper to our age
To cast beyond ourselves in our opinions,
As it is common for the younger sort
To lack discretion. Come, go we to the king,
This must be known; which, being kept close, might move
More grief to hide than hate to utter love.
Come.

Exeunt.

Scene Two

Flourish. Enter KING *and* QUEEN, ROSENCRANTZ *and* GUILDENSTERN, *with others.*

KING. Welcome, dear Rosencrantz and Guildenstern.
Moreover that we much did long to see you,
The need we have to use you did provoke
Our hasty sending. Something have you heard
Of Hamlet's transformation—so I call it,
Sith nor the exterior nor the inward man
Resembles that it was. What it should be,
More than his father's death, that thus hath put him
So much from the understanding of himself
10 I cannot dream of: I entreat you both
That, being of so young days brought up with him
And sith so neighbored to his youth and havior,
That you vouchsafe your rest here in our court
Some little time; so by your companies
To draw him on to pleasures, and to gather
So much as from occasion you may glean,
Whether aught to us unknown afflicts him thus,
That opened lies within our remedy.

QUEEN. Good gentlemen, he hath much talked of you,
20 And sure I am two men there are not living
To whom he more adheres. If it will please you
To show us so much gentry and good will
As to expend your time with us awhile,
For the supply and profit of our hope,
Your visitation shall receive such thanks
As fits a king's remembrance.

ROSENCRANTZ. Both your majesties
Might, by the sovereign power you have of us,
Put your dread pleasures more into command
Than to entreaty.

GUILDENSTERN. But we both obey,
30 And here give up ourselves in the full bent
To lay our service freely at your feet,
To be commanded.

KING. Thanks, Rosencrantz and gentle Guildenstern.

QUEEN. Thanks, Guildenstern and gentle Rosencrantz,
And I beseech you instantly to visit
My too much changéd son. Go, some of you,
And bring these gentlemen where Hamlet is.

GUIL. Heavens make our presence and our practices
Pleasant and helpful to him!

QUEEN. Ay, amen!

Exeunt ROSENCRANTZ, GUILDENSTERN [*and some Attendants.*]

111 **quoted** observed 12 **havior** way to life 18 **opened** made known 21 **adheres** is attached

114 **cast beyond ourselves** go too far 117 **move** cause 118 **to hide** if hidden **to utter love** if love is told 22 **gentry** courtesy 30 **in the full bent** to the full

Enter POLONIUS.

POL. The ambassadors from Norway, my good lord, 40
Are joyfully returned.

KING. Thou still hast been the father of good news.

POL. Have I, my lord? Assure you, my good liege,
I hold my duty, as I hold my soul,
Both to my God and to my gracious king;
And I do think, or else this brain of mine
Hunts not the trail of policy so sure
As it hath used to do, that I have found
The very cause of Hamlet's lunacy.

KING. O speak of that, that do I long to hear. 50

POL. Give first admittance to the ambassadors;
My news shall be the fruit to that great feast.

KING. Thyself do grace to them, and bring them in. [*Exit* POLONIUS.]
He tells me, my dear Gertrude, he hath found
The head and source of all your son's distemper.

QUEEN. I doubt it is no other but the main,
His father's death and our o'erhasty marriage.

KING. Well, we shall sift him.

Enter POLONIUS, VOLTIMAND *and* CORNELIUS.

Welcome, my good friends.
Say, Voltimand, what from our brother Norway?

VOLTIMAND. Most fair return of greetings and desires. 60
Upon our first, he sent out to suppress
His nephew's levies, which to him appeared
To be a preparation 'gainst the Polack,
But better looked into, he truly found
It was against your highness; whereat grieved
That so his sickness, age, and impotence
Was falsely borne in hand, sends out arrests
On Fortinbras; which he in brief obeys,
Receives rebuke from Norway, and in fine
Makes vow before his uncle never more 70
To give the assay of arms against your majesty:
Whereon old Norway, overcome with joy,
Gives him threescore thousand crowns in annual fee,
And his commission to employ those soldiers,
So levied as before, against the Polack,
With an entreaty, herein further shown, [*Gives a paper.*]
That it might please you to give quiet pass
Through your dominions for this enterprise
On such regards of safety and allowance
As therein are set down.

KING. It likes us well; 80
And at our more considered time we'll read,
Answer, and think upon this business.
Meantime we thank you for your well-took labor.
Go to your rest; at night we'll feast together;
Most welcome home! *Exeunt* AMBASSADORS.

POL. This business is well ended.
My liege and madam, to expostulate
What majesty should be, what duty is,
Why day is day, night night, and time is time,
Were nothing but to waste night, day and time.
Therefore, since brevity is the soul of wit, 90
And tediousness the limbs and outward flourishes,
I will be brief. Your noble son is mad;
Mad call I it, for, to define true madness,
What is't but to be nothing else but mad?
But let that go.

QUEEN. More matter with less art.

POL. Madam, I swear I use no art at all.
That he is mad 'tis true; 'tis true 'tis pity,
And pity 'tis 'tis true; a foolish figure,
But farewell it, for I will use no art.
Mad let us grant him then, and now remains 100
That we find out the cause of this effect,
Or rather say, the cause of this defect,
For this effect defective comes by cause:
Thus it remains, and the remainder thus.
Perpend:
I have a daughter—have while she is mine—
Who in her duty and obedience, mark,
Hath given me this; now gather, and surmise.
[*Reads*] *the letter.*
"To the celestial and my soul's idol, the most beautified Ophelia,"— 110

47 **policy** conduct of public affairs 53 **grace** honor 61 **upon our first** on our first raising the issue 67 **falsely borne in hand** deceived **arrests** staying orders 69 **in fine** in conclusion

79 **regards** conditions 86 **expostulate** explain 98 **figure** trope, figure of speech

That's an ill phrase, a vile phrase, "beautified" is a vile phrase; but you shall hear. Thus: [*Reads.*]
"In her excellent white bosom, these," &c.—

QUEEN. Came this from Hamlet to her?

POL. Good madam, stay awhile; I will be faithful. [*Reads.*]

"Doubt thou the stars are fire,
Doubt that the sun doth move,
Doubt truth to be a liar,
But never doubt I love.

120 "Oh dear Ophelia, I am ill at these numbers, I have not art to reckon my groans; but that I love thee best, O most best, believe it. Adieu.
Thine evermore, most dear lady, whilst this machine is to him, HAMLET."
This in obedience hath my daughter shown me,
And more above, hath his solicitings,
As they fell out by time, by means and place,
All given to mine ear.

KING. But how hath she
Received his love?

POL. What do you think of me?

130 KING. As of a man faithful and honorable.

POL. I would fain prove so. But what might you think,
When I had seen this hot love on the wing—
As I perceived it, I must tell you that,
Before my daughter told me—what might you,
Or my dear majesty your queen here, think,
If I had played the desk or table-book,
Or given my heart a winking, mute and dumb,
Or looked upon this love with idle sight—
What might you think? No, I went round to work,
140 And my young mistress thus I did bespeak:
"Lord Hamlet is a prince, out of thy star;
This must not be:" and then I prescripts gave her
That she should lock herself from his resort,
Admit no messengers, receive no tokens.
Which done, she took the fruits of my advice;
And he repelled (a short tale to make)—
Fell into a sadness, then into a fast,
Thence to a watch, thence into a weakness,
Thence to a lightness, and by this declension
Into the madness wherein now he raves, 150
And all we mourn for.

KING. Do you think 'tis this?

QUEEN. It may be, very like.

POL. Hath there been such a time, I would fain know that,
That I have positively said " 'Tis so,"
When it proved otherwise?

KING. Not that I know.

POL. [*pointing to his head and shoulder*]
Take this from this, if this be otherwise;
If circumstances lead me, I will find
Where truth is hid, though it were hid indeed
Within the centre.

KING. How may we try it further?

POL. You know sometimes he walks four hours together 160
Here in the lobby.

QUEEN. So he does, indeed.

POL. At such a time I'll loose my daughter to him;
Be you and I behind an arras then;
Mark the encounter; if he love her not,
And be not from his reason fallen thereon,
Let me be no assistant for a state
But keep a farm and carters.

KING. We will try it.

Enter HAMLET *reading on a book.*

QUEEN. But look where sadly the poor wretch comes reading.

POL. Away, I do beseech you both, away;
I'll board him presently.

Exeunt KING *and* QUEEN.

O give me leave, 170
How does my good Lord Hamlet?

HAMLET. Well, God-a-mercy.

POL. Do you know me, my lord?

HAMLET. Excellent well, you are a fish-monger.

POL. Not I, my lord.

HAMLET. Then I would you were so honest a man.

POL. Honest, my lord!

HAMLET. Ay sir, to be honest, as this world goes, is to be one man picked out of ten thousand. 180

120 **numbers** verses 137 **given my heart a winking** shut the eyes of my heart 139 **round** directly 141 **star** sphere 142 **prescripts** orders 148 **watch** sleeplessness 149 **lightness** lightheadedness **declension** decline

159 **centre** centre of the earth 165 **thereon** for this reason 170 **board** accost **presently** at once 172 **God-a-mercy** thank-you

POL. That's very true, my lord.

HAMLET. For if the sun breed maggots in a dead dog, being a good kissing carrion—Have you a daughter?

POL. I have, my lord.

HAMLET. Let her not walk i' the sun; conception is a blessing, but as your daughter may conceive—friend, look to't.

POL. [*aside*] How say you by that? Still harping on my daughter. Yet he knew me not at first; a' said I was a fishmonger: A' is far gone, far gone, and truly in my youth I suffered much extremity for love, very near this. I'll speak to him again.—What do you read, my lord? 190

HAMLET. Words, words, words.

POL. What is the matter, my lord?

HAMLET. Between who?

POL. I mean the matter that you read, my lord. 200

HAMLET. Slanders, sir; for the satirical rogue says here, that old men have gray beards, that their faces are wrinkled, their eyes purging thick amber and plum-tree gum, and that they have a plentiful lack of wit, together with most weak hams; all which, sir, though I most powerfully and potently believe, yet I hold it not honesty to have it thus set down; for yourself, sir, shall grow old as I am, if, like a crab, you could go backward. 210

POL. [*aside*] Though this be madness, yet there is method in't.—Will you walk out of the air, my lord?

HAMLET. Into my grave?

POL. Indeed, that's out of the air.—[*Aside*] How pregnant sometimes his replies are! a happiness that often madness hits on, which reason and sanity could not so prosperously be delivered of. I will leave him, and suddenly contrive the means of meeting between him and my daughter.—My honorable lord, I will most humbly take my leave of you. 220

HAMLET. You cannot, sir, take from me any thing that I will more willingly part withal: except my life, except my life, except my life.

POL. Fare you well, my lord.

HAMLET. These tedious old fools!

Enter ROSENCRANTZ *and* GUILDENSTERN.

POL. You go to seek the Lord Hamlet; there he is.

ROS. [*to* POLONIUS] God save you, sir! [*Exit* POLONIUS.] 230

GUIL. My most honored lord!

ROS. My dear lord!

HAMLET. My excellent good friends! How dost thou, Guildenstern? Ah, Rosencrantz! Good lads, how do you both?

ROS. As the indifferent children of the earth.

GUIL. Happy, in that we are not overhappy; On Fortune's cap we are not the very button.

HAMLET. Nor the soles of her shoe? 240

ROS. Neither, my lord.

HAMLET. Then you live about her waist, or in the middle of her favors.

GUIL. Faith, her privates we.

HAMLET. In the secret parts of Fortune? O most true, she is a strumpet. What news?

ROS. None, my lord, but that the world's grown honest.

HAMLET. Then is doomsday near; but your news is not true. Let me question more in particular: what have you, my good friends, deserved at the hands of Fortune, that she sends you to prison hither? 250

GUIL. Prison, my lord?

HAMLET. Denmark's a prison.

ROS. Then is the world one.

HAMLET. A goodly one, in which there are many confines, wards and dungeons, Denmark being one o' the worst.

ROS. We think not so, my lord. 260

HAMLET. Why then tis none to you; for there is nothing either good or bad, but thinking makes it so: to me it is a prison.

ROS. Why then your ambition makes it one; 'tis too narrow for your mind.

HAMLET. O God, I could be bounded in a nutshell, and count myself a king of infinite space, were it not that I have bad dreams.

GUIL. Which dreams indeed are ambition; for the very substance of the ambitious is merely the shadow of a dream. 270

HAMLET. A dream itself is but a shadow.

ROS. Truly, and I hold ambition of so airy

183 **good kissing carion** flesh good for kissing 197 **matter** (1) subject matter (2) subject of a quarrel 203 **purging** oozing 216 **pregnant** apt 224 **withal** with

237 **indifferent** ordinary 239 **button** top 258 **confines** cell **wards** sections of a prison

and light a quality, that it is but a shadow's shadow.

HAMLET. Then are our beggars bodies, and our monarchs and outstretched heroes the beggars' shadows. Shall we to the court? for, by my fay, I cannot reason.

280 BOTH. We'll wait upon you.

HAMLET. No such matter; I will not sort you with the rest of my servants, for, to speak to you like an honest man, I am most dreadfully attended. But in the beaten way of friendship, what make you at Elsinore?

ROS. To visit you, my lord, no other occasion.

HAMLET. Beggar that I am, I am even poor in thanks, but I thank you; and sure, dear friends, my thanks are too dear a halfpenny.

290 Were you not sent for? Is it your own inclining? Is it a free visitation? Come, come, deal justly with me, come, come; nay, speak.

GUIL. What should we say, my lord?

HAMLET. Why, any thing but to the purpose. You were sent for, and there is a kind of confession in your looks, which your modesties have not craft enough to color; I know the good king and queen have sent for you.

ROS. To what end, my lord?

300 HAMLET. That you must teach me. But let me conjure you, by the rights of our fellowship, by the consonancy of our youth, by the obligation of our ever-preserved love, and by what more dear a better proposer can charge you withal, be even and direct with me whether you were sent for or no.

ROS. [*aside to* GUILDENSTERN] What say you?

HAMLET. [*aside*] Nay then, I have an eye of you.—If you love me, hold not off.

310 GUIL. My lord, we were sent for.

HAMLET. I will tell you why; so shall my anticipation prevent your discovery, and your secrecy to the king and queen molt no feather. I have of late—but wherefore I know not—lost all my mirth, foregone all custom of exercises; and indeed it goes so heavily with my disposition, that this goodly frame the earth seems to me a sterile promontory; this most excellent canopy the air, look you, this brave o'erhanging firmament, this majestical roof 320 fretted with golden fire, why, it appeareth no thing to me but a foul and pestilent congregation of vapors. What a piece of work is man, how noble in reason, how infinite in faculties, in form and moving, how express and admirable in action, how like an angel in apprehension, how like a god! the beauty of the world, the paragon of animals! And yet to me what is this quintessence of dust? man delights not me, no, nor woman neither, though by your smiling you 330 seem to say so.

ROS. My lord, there was no such stuff in my thoughts.

HAMLET. Why did you laugh then, when I said "man delights not me"?

ROS. To think, my lord, if you delight not in man, what lenten entertainment the players shall receive from you; we coted them on the way, and hither are they coming, to offer you service.

HAMLET. He that plays the king shall be wel- 340 come, his majesty shall have tribute of me; the adventurous knight shall use his foil and target, the lover shall not sigh gratis, the humorous man shall end his part in peace, the clown shall make those laugh whose lungs are tickle o' the sere, and the lady shall say her mind freely, or the blank verse shall halt for't. What players are they?

ROS. Even those you were wont to take such delight in, the tragedians of the city. 350

HAMLET. How chances it they travel? their residence, both in reputation and profit, was better both ways.

ROS. I think their inhibition comes by the means of the late innovation.

HAMLET. Do they hold the same estimation they did when I was in the city? are they so followed?

276 **beggars** *i.e.* the men without ambition 277 **monarchs and . . . heroes** *i.e.* ambitious men **outstretched** enlarged, *i.e.* larger than ordinary men 289 **too dear a halfpenny** of little worth 291 **free** unforced 302 **consonancy** accord 304 **proposer** questioner 305 **even** fair 312 **prevent** come before **discovery** disclosure 313 **molt no feather** suffer no loss

315 **foregone** given up 321 **fretted** adorned 325 **express** well-devised 328 **paragon** model of excellence 337 **lenten** meagre 338 **coted** overtook 334 **target** shield 343 **humorous** eccentric 345 **tickle o' the sere** ready to go off at any moment 354 **inhibition** prohibition

ROS. No indeed, are they not.

360 HAMLET. How comes it? do they grow rusty?

ROS. Nay, their endeavor keeps in the wonted pace; but there is, sir, an eyrie of children, little eyases, that cry out on the top of question, and are most tyrannically clapped for't: these are now the fashion, and so berattle the common stages (so they call them) that many wearing rapiers are afraid of goosequills, and dare scarce come thither.

HAMLET. What, are they children? who 370 maintains 'em? how are they escoted? Will they pursue the quality no longer than they can sing? will they not say afterwards, if they should grow themselves to common players (as it is most like, if their means are no better) their writers do them wrong, to make them exclaim against their own succession?

ROS. Faith, there has been much to do on both sides, and the nation holds it no sin to tarre them to controversy; there was for a while no 380 money bid for argument, unless the poet and the player went to cuffs in the question.

HAMLET. Is't possible?

GUIL. O, there has been much throwing about of brains.

HAMLET. Do the boys carry it away?

ROS. Ay, that they do, my lord—Hercules and his load too.

HAMLET. It is not very strange, for my uncle is king of Denmark, and those that would make 390 mows at him while my father lived, give twenty, forty, fifty, and hundred ducats apiece for his picture in little. 'Sblood, there is something in this more than natural, if philosophy could find it out. *Flourish for the players.*

GUIL. There are the players.

HAMLET. Gentlemen, you are welcome to Elsinore. Your hands, come then. The appurtenance of welcome is fashion and ceremony; let me comply with you in this garb, lest my extent 400 to the players which, I tell you, must show fairly outwards, should more appear like entertainment than yours. You are welcome: but my uncle-father and aunt-mother are deceived.

GUIL. In what, my dear lord?

HAMLET. I am but mad north-north-west; when the wind is southerly I know a hawk from a handsaw.

Enter POLONIUS.

POL. Well be with you, gentlemen.

HAMLET. Hark you, Guildenstern, and you too, at each ear a hearer; that great baby you see 410 there is not yet out of his swaddling-clouts.

ROS. Happily he is the second time come to them, for they say an old man is twice a child.

HAMLET. I will prophesy he comes to tell me of the players; mark it. You say right, sir; o' Monday morning, 'twas then indeed.

POL. My lord, I have news to tell you.

HAMLET. My lord, I have news to tell you. When Roscius was an actor in Rome—

POL. The actors are come hither, my lord. 420

HAMLET. Buz, buz!

POL. Upon my honor—

HAMLET. Then came each actor on his ass—

POL. The best actors in the world, either for tragedy, comedy, history, pastoral, pastoral-comical, historical-pastoral, tragical-historical, tragical-comical-historical-pastoral, scene individable, or poem unlimited; Seneca cannot be too heavy, nor Plautus too light for the law of writ and the liberty. These are the only men. 430

HAMLET. O Jephthah, judge of Israel, what a treasure hadst thou!

POL. What a treasure had he, my lord?

HAMLET. Why,

"One fair daughter and no more,
The which he lovéd passing well."

POL. [*aside*] Still on my daughter.

HAMLET. Am I not i' the right, old Jephthah?

POL. If you call me Jephthah, my lord, I have a daughter that I love passing well. 440

362 **eyrie** nest, brood 363 **eyases** young hawks 365 **berattle** berate 367 **goosequills** pens 370 **escoted** supported **quality** profession 376 **succession** feature 378 **tarre** incite 380 **argument** plot of a play 386 **Hercules and his load** the sign outside the Globe Theater 390 **mows** faces, grimaces 397 **appurtenance** accompaniment 399 **comply** observe the formalities

401 **outwards** on the outside **entertainment** welcome 406 **hawk** (1) falcon (2) plasterer's mortarboard 407 **handsaw** (1) heron (2) carpenter's tool 411 **clouts** clothes 427 **individable** unchanged **unlimited** *i.e.,* ignoring the unities 429 **writ** writing 430 **liberty** the area outside city jurisdiction, *i.e.*, those who do not heed the rules

HAMLET. Nay, that follows not.

POL. What follows then, my lord?

HAMLET. Why,

"As by lot, God wot,"

and then, you know,

"It came to pass, as most like it was";

the first row of the pious chanson will show you more, for look where my abridgment comes.

Enter four or five PLAYERS.

You are welcome, masters, welcome all; I am
450 glad to see thee well. Welcome, good friends. O my old friend, thy face is valanced since I saw thee last; comest thou to beard me in Denmark? What, my young lady and mistress! by'r lady, your ladyship is nearer to heaven than when I saw you last by the altitude of a chopine. Pray God your voice, like a piece of uncurrent gold, be not cracked within the ring. Masters, you are all welcome. We'll e'en to't like French falconers, fly at any thing we see; we'll have a
460 speech straight; come, give us a taste of your quality, come, a passionate speech.

FIRST PLAYER. What speech, my good lord?

HAMLET. I heard thee speak me a speech once, but it was never acted, or if it was, not above once, for the play, I remember, pleased not the million; 'twas caviary to the general, but it was—as I received it, and others whose judgments in such matters cried in the top of mine—an excellent play, well digested in the
470 scenes, set down with as much modesty as cunning. I remember one said there were no sallets in the lines to make the matter savory, nor no matter in the phrase that might indict the author of affection, but called it an honest method, as wholesome as sweet, and by very much more handsome than fine. One speech in't I chiefly loved; 'twas Æneas' tale to Dido, and thereabout of it especially where he speaks of Priam's slaughter. If it live in your memory, begin at this line—let me see, let me see:
480
"The rugged Pyrrhus, like the Hyrcanian beast,"

—'tis not so; it begins with Pyrrhus:

"The rugged Pyrrhus, he whose sable arms,
Black as his purpose, did the night resemble
When he lay couchéd in the ominous horse,
Hath now this dread and black complexion smeared
With heraldry more dismal; head to foot
Now is he total gules, horridly tricked
With blood of fathers, mothers, daughters, sons,
Baked and impasted with the parching streets
490
That lend a tyrannous and damnéd light
To their lord's murder; roasted in wrath and fire
And thus o'er-sizéd with coagulate gore,
With eyes like carbuncles, the hellish Pyrrhus
Old grandsire Priam seeks."—

So proceed you.

POL. 'Fore God, my lord, well spoken, with good accent and good discretion.

FIRST PL. "Anon he finds him
Striking too short at Greeks; his antique sword,
500
Rebellious to his arm, lies where it falls,
Repugnant to command; unequal matched,
Pyrrhus at Priam drives, in rage strikes wide,
But with the whiff and wind of his fell sword
The unnervéd father falls. Then senseless Ilium,
Seeming to feel this blow, with flaming top
Stoops to his base, and with a hideous crash
Takes prisoner Pyrrhus' ear, for lo! his sword,
Which was declining on the milky head
Of reverend Priam, seemed i' the air to stick;
510
So, as a painted tyrant, Pyrrhus stood

447 **chanson** song 448 **my abridgement** that which cuts me short 451 **valanced** fringed 453 **young lady and mistress** the boy who played the leading female parts 455 **chopine** high-heeled shoe 456 **uncurrent** not legal tender 457 **ring** (1) tone (2) outer ring round the design of a coin 466 **general** public 468 **cried in the top of** spoke with more authority than 469 **digested** arranged 470 **modesty** moderation 471 **sallets** salads 474 **affection** affectation 476 **handsome** stately 477 **Aeneas' tale to Dido** In the *Aeneid* Aeneas relates to Dido the story of the fall of Troy

481 **Hyrcanian beast** tiger 483 **sable** black 487 **heraldry** heraldic device 488 **gules** the heraldic word for 'red' **tricked** colored (another heraldic term) 493 **o'ersizéd** glued over **coagulate** clotted 494 **carbuncles** red semi-precious stones 504 **fell** fierce 505 **unnervéd** feeble in sinew **Ilium** the citadel of Troy 507 **stoops to his base** collapses to the ground

And, like a neutral to his will and matter,
Did nothing.
But as we often see against some storm
A silence in the heavens, the rack stand still,
The bold winds speechless, and the orb below
As hush as death, anon the dreadful thunder
Doth rend the region; so, after Pyrrhus' pause,
A rousèd vengeance sets him new a-work,
520 And never did the Cyclops' hammers fall
On Mars's armour, forged for proof eterne,
With less remorse than Pyrrhus' bleeding sword
Now falls on Priam.
Out, out, thou strumpet Fortune! All you gods
In general synod take away her power,
Break all the spokes and fellies from her wheel,
And bowl the round nave down the hill of heaven,
As low as to the fiends!"

POL. This is too long.

530 HAMLET. It shall to the barber's with your beard; prithee, say on, he's for a jig or a tale of bawdry, or he sleeps; say on, come to Hecuba.

FIRST PL. "But who, ah woe! had seen the mobled queen—"

HAMLET. "The mobled queen"?

POL. That's good, "mobled queen" is good.

FIRST PL. "Run barefoot up and down, threatening the flames
With bisson rheum, a clout upon that head
Where late the diadem stood, and for a robe
About her lank and all o'er-teemèd loins,
540 A blanket in the alarm of fear caught up;
Who this had seen, with tongue in venom steeped,
'Gainst Fortune's state would treason have pronounced;
But if the gods themselves did see her then,
When she saw Pyrrhus make malicious sport
In mincing with his sword her husband's limbs,
The instant burst of clamor that she made—
Unless things mortal move them not at all—
Would have made milch the burning eyes of heaven,
And passion in the gods."

550 POL. Look whether he has not turned his color, and has tears in's eyes. Prithee no more.

HAMLET. 'Tis well; I'll have thee speak out the rest soon. Good my lord, will you see the players well bestowed? Do you hear, let them be well used, for they are the abstract and brief chronicles of the time; after your death you were better have a bad epitaph than their ill report while you live.

POL. My lord, I will use them according to their desert. 560

HAMLET. God's bodkin, man, much better; use every man after his desert, and who shall scape whipping? Use them after your own honor and dignity; the less they deserve, the more merit is in your bounty. Take them in.

POL. Come, sirs.

HAMLET. Follow him, friends; we'll hear a play tomorrow.

Exit POLONIUS [*with all the* PLAYERS *except the First.*]

Dost thou hear me, old friend; can you play the Murder of Gonzago? 570

FIRST PL. Ay, my lord.

HAMLET. We'll ha't tomorrow night. You could for a need study a speech of some dozen or sixteen lines, which I would set down and insert in't, could you not?

FIRST PL. Ay, my lord.

HAMLET. Very well. Follow that lord, and look you mock him not. [*Exit* FIRST PLAYER.] My good friends, I'll leave you till night; you are welcome to Elsinore. 580

ROS. Good my lord! *Exeunt.*

HAMLET. Ay, so, God bye to you.
Now I am alone.
O what a rogue and peasant slave am I!
Is it not monstrous that this player here
But in a fiction, in a dream of passion,
Could force his soul so to his own conceit
That from her working all his visage wanned,
Tears in his eyes, distraction in his aspect,

514 **against** in expectation of 515 **rack** clouds 520 **Cyclops** the workmen of Vulcan 521 **proof** invulnerability 526 **fellies** rim 527 **nave** hub 531 **jig** comic dialogue in song 533 **mobled** muffled 537 **bisson** blinding **rheum** moisture, tears **clout** cloth 539 **o'erteemed** (because, it was said, Hecuba had had fifty children)

548 **milch** tearful **burning eyes of heaven** the stars 554 **bestowed** lodged 587 **conceit** feeling, imagination

590 A broken voice, and his whole function suiting
With forms to his conceit? and all for nothing,
For Hecuba.
What's Hecuba to him, or he to Hecuba,
That he should weep for her? What would he do
Had he the motive and the cue for passion
That I have? He would drown the stage with tears,
And cleave the general ear with horrid speech,
Make mad the guilty and appal the free,
Confound the ignorant, and amaze indeed
600 The very faculties of eyes and ears;
Yet I,
A dull and muddy-mettled rascal, peak
Like John-a-dreams, unpregnant of my cause,
And can say nothing; no, not for a king,
Upon whose property and most dear life
A damned defeat was made. Am I a coward?
Who calls me villain, breaks my pate across,
Plucks off my beard and blows it in my face,
Tweaks me by the nose, gives me the lie i' the throat
610 As deep as to the lungs? who does me this, ha?
'Swounds, I should take it: for it cannot be
But I am pigeon-livered, and lack gall
To make oppression bitter, or ere this
I should ha' fatted all the region kites
With this slave's offal. Bloody, bawdy villain!
Remorseless, treacherous, lecherous, kindless villain!
O, vengeance!
Why, what an ass am I! This is most brave,
That I, the son of a dear father murdered,
Prompted to my revenge by heaven and hell, 620
Must like a whore, unpack my heart with words,
And fall a-cursing, like a very drab,
A stallion!
Fie upon't, foh! About, my brains; hum, I have heard
That guilty creatures sitting at a play
Have by the very cunning of the scene
Been struck so to the soul, that presently
They have proclaimed their malefactions;
For murder, though it have no tongue, will speak
With most miraculous organ. I'll have these players 630
Play something like the murder of my father,
Before mine uncle; I'll observe his looks,
I'll tent him to the quick; if a' do blench
I know my course. The spirit that I have seen
May be a devil, and the devil hath power
To assume a pleasing shape; yea, and perhaps
Out of my weakness and my melancholy,
As he is very potent with such spirits,
Abuses me to damn me; I'll have grounds
More relative than this; the play's the thing 640
Wherein I'll catch the conscience of the king.
Exit.

590 **function** behavior 602 **muddy-mettled** poor-spirited **peak** mope 603 **John-a-dreams** a dreamy fellow **unpregnant** unproductive 606 **defeat** destruction 616 **kindless** unnatural

627 **presently** at once 633 **tent** probe 640 **relative** relevant

ACT THREE *Scene One*

Enter KING, QUEEN, POLONIUS, OPHELIA, ROSENCRANTZ, GUILDENSTERN, LORDS.

KING. And can you by no drift of circumstance
Get from him why he puts on this confusion,
Grating so harshly all his days of quiet
With turbulent and dangerous lunacy?
ROS. He does confess he feels himself distracted,
But from what cause a' will by no means speak.
GUIL. Nor do we find him forward to be sounded,
But with a crafty madness keeps aloof
When we would bring him on to some confession
Of his true state.
QUEEN. Did he receive you well? 10
ROS. Most like a gentleman.
GUIL. But with much forcing of his disposition.

ROS. Niggard of question, but of our demands
Most free in his reply.
QUEEN. Did you assay him
To any pastime?
ROS. Madam, it so fell out, that certain players
We o'er-raught on the way; of these we told him,
And there did seem in him a kind of joy
To hear of it: they are here about the court
20 And, as I think, they have already order
This night to play before him.
POL. 'Tis most true,
And he beseeched me to entreat your majesties
To hear and see the matter.
KING. With all my heart; and it doth much content me
To hear him so inclined.
Good gentlemen, give him a further edge,
And drive his purpose into these delights.
ROS. We shall, my lord.
Exeunt ROSENCRANTZ *and* GUILDENSTERN
KING. Sweet Gertrude, leave us too,
For we have closely sent for Hamlet hither,
30 That he, as 'twere by accident, may here
Affront Ophelia;
Her father and myself, lawful espials,
Will so bestow ourselves that, seeing unseen,
We may of their encounter frankly judge,
And gather by him, as he is behaved,
If't be the affliction of his love or no
That thus he suffers for.
QUEEN. I shall obey you;
And for your part, Ophelia, I do wish
That your good beauties be the happy cause
Of Hamlet's wildness; so shall I hope your virtues
40 Will bring him to his wonted way again,
To both your honors.
OPH. Madam, I wish it may. [*Exit* QUEEN.]
POL. Ophelia, walk you here. Gracious, so please you.
We will bestow ourselves. [*To* OPHELIA] Read on this book,
That show of such an exercise may color
Your loneliness. We are oft to blame in this—
'Tis too much proved—that with devotion's visage
And pious action we do sugar o'er
The devil himself.
KING. [*aside*] O 'tis too true;
How smart a lash that speech doth give my conscience! 50
The harlot's cheek, beautied with plastering art,
Is not more ugly to the thing that helps it
Than is my deed to my most painted word:
O heavy burden!
POL. I hear him coming; let's withdraw, my lord. *Exeunt.*

Enter HAMLET

HAMLET. To be or not to be, that is the question,
Whether 'tis nobler in the mind to suffer
The slings and arrows of outrageous fortune,
Or to take arms against a sea of troubles,
And by opposing end them? To die, to sleep— 60
No more; and by a sleep to say we end
The heartache and the thousand natural shocks
That flesh is heir to, 'tis a consummation
Devoutly to be wished. To die, to sleep;
To sleep, perchance to dream; ay, there's the rub,
For in that sleep of death what dreams may come
When we have shuffled off this mortal coil
Must give us pause; there's the respect
That makes calamity of so long life;
For who would bear the whips and scorns of time, 70
The oppressor's wrong, the proud man's contumely,
The pangs of despised love, the law's delay,
The insolence of office and the spurns
That patient merit of the unworthy takes,
When he himself might his quietus make
With a bare bodkin? who would fardels bear,
To grunt and sweat under a weary life,
But that the dread of something after death,
The undiscovered country, from whose bourn
No traveler returns, puzzles the will, 80
And makes us rather bear those ills we have
Than fly to others that we know not of?
Thus conscience does make cowards of us all,
And thus the native hue of resolution
Is sicklied o'er with the pale cast of thought,

17 **o'er-raught** overtook 31 **affront** confront 32 **espials** spies 45 **color** excuse

65 **rub** obstruction 71 **contumely** scorn 75 **quietus** settlement 76 **bodkin** dagger **fardels** burdens 79 **bourn** boundary

And enterprises of great pitch and moment
With this regard their currents turn awry,
And lose the name of action. Soft you now,
The fair Ophelia! Nymph, in thy orisons
Be all my sins remembered.

90 OPH. Good my lord,
How does your honor for this many a day?

HAMLET. I humbly thank you, well, well, well.

OPH. My lord, I have remembrances of yours
That I have longéd long to re-deliver;
I pray you now receive them.

HAMLET. No, not I,
I never gave you aught.

OPH. My honored lord, you know right well you did,
And with them words of so sweet breath composed
As made these things more rich; their perfume lost,
100 Take these again, for to the noble mind
Rich gifts wax poor when givers prove unkind.
There, my lord.

HAMLET. Ha, ha, are you honest?

OPH. My lord?

HAMLET. Are you fair?

OPH. What means your lordship?

HAMLET. That if you be honest and fair, your honesty should admit no discourse to your beauty.

OPH. Could beauty, my lord, have better com-
110 merce than with honesty?

HAMLET. Ay, truly, for the power of beauty will sooner transform honesty from what it is to a bawd than the force of honesty can translate beauty into his likeness; this was sometime a paradox, but now the time gives it proof. I did love you once.

OPH. Indeed, my lord, you made me believe so.

HAMLET. You should not have believed me,
120 for virtue cannot so inoculate our old stock, but we shall relish of it; I loved you not.

OPH. I was the more deceived.

HAMLET. Get thee to a nunnery; why wouldst thou be a breeder of sinners? I am myself indifferent honest, but yet I could accuse me of such things, that it were better my mother had not borne me: I am very proud, revengeful, ambitious, with more offences at my beck than I
130 have thoughts to put them in, imagination to give them shape, or time to act them in. What should such fellows as I do crawling between earth and heaven? We are arrant knaves, all; believe none of us; go thy ways to a nunnery. Where's your father?

OPH. At home, my lord.

HAMLET. Let the doors be shut upon him, that he may play the fool no where but in's own house. Farewell.

140 OPH. O help him, you sweet heavens!

HAMLET. If thou dost marry, I'll give thee this plague for thy dowry: be thou as chaste as ice, as pure as snow, thou shalt not escape calumny. Get thee to a nunnery, go: farewell. Or if thou wilt needs marry, marry a fool, for wise men know well enough what monsters you make of them. To a nunnery go, and quickly too. Farewell.

OPH. O heavenly powers restore him!

150 HAMLET. I have heard of your paintings too, well enough; God hath given you one face, and you make yourselves another; you jig, you amble, and you lisp; you nickname God's creatures, and make your wantonness your ignorance. Go to, I'll no more on't; it hath made me mad. I say we will have no more marriage; those that are married already, all but one, shall live; the rest shall keep as they are. To a nunnery, go.
Exit.

OPH. O what a noble mind is here o'erthrown!
The courtier's, soldier's, scholar's eye, tongue,
160 sword,
The expectancy and rose of the fair state,
The glass of fashion and the mould of form,
The observed of all observers, quite, quite down,
And I of ladies most deject and wretched,
That sucked the honey of his music vows,
Now see that noble and most sovereign reason
Like sweet bells jangled, out of tune and harsh,
That unmatched form and feature of blown youth
Blasted with ecstasy; O woe is me
170 To have seen what I have seen, see what I see!

86 **pitch** height 87 **awry** aside 89 **orisons** prayers 110 **commerce** association 120 **inoculate** engraft **relish of** smack of, have a trace of

162 **glass** mirror **mould** model **form** behavior 169 **ecstasy** madness

Re-enter KING *and* POLONIUS.

KING. Love! his affections do not that way tend,
Nor what he spake, though it lacked form a little,
Was not like madness. There's something in his soul
O'er which his melancholy sits on brood,
And I do doubt the hatch and the disclose
Will be some danger; which for to prevent
I have in quick determination
Thus set it down: he shall with speed to England,
For the demand of our neglected tribute.
180 Haply the seas, and countries different,
With variable objects, shall expel
This something-settled matter in his heart,
Whereon his brains still beating puts him thus
From fashion of himself. What think you on't?
POL. It shall do well; but yet do I believe
The origin and commencement of his grief
Sprung from neglected love. How now, Ophelia?
You need not tell us what Lord Hamlet said;
We heard it all. My lord, do as you please,
But, if you hold it fit, after the play 190
Let his queen mother all alone entreat him
To show his grief; let her be round with him,
And I'll be placed, so please you, in the ear
Of all their conference. If she find him not,
To England send him, or confine him where
Your wisdom best shall think.
KING. It shall be so;
Madness in great ones must not unwatch'd go.
Exeunt.

Scene Two

Enter HAMLET *and three of the* PLAYERS.

HAMLET. Speak the speech, I pray you, as I pronounced it to you, trippingly on the tongue; but if you mouth it, as many of our players do, I had as lief the town crier spoke my lines. Nor do not saw the air too much with your hand, thus, but use all gently, for in the very torrent, tempest, and as I may say whirlwind of your passion, you must acquire and beget a temperance that may give it smoothness. O, it offends 10 me to the soul to hear a robustious periwig-pated fellow tear a passion to tatters, to very rags, to split the ears of the groundlings, who for the most part are capable of nothing but inexplicable dumb shows and noise: I would have such a fellow whipped for o'erdoing Termagant; it out-herods Herod: pray you avoid it.

FIRST PL. I warrant your honor.

HAMLET. Be not too tame neither, but let your own discretion be your tutor; suit the action to the word, the word to the action, with 20 this special observance, that you o'erstep not the modesty of nature: for any thing so o'erdone is from the purpose of playing, whose end, both at the first and now, was and is, to hold as 'twere the mirror up to nature, to show virtue her own feature, scorn her own image, and the very age and body of the time his form and pressure. Now this overdone or come tardy off, though it make the unskillful laugh, cannot but make the judicious grieve; the censure of the which one 30 must in your allowance o'erweigh a whole theatre of others. O there be players that I have seen play—and heard others praise, and that highly—not to speak it profanely, that neither having the accent of Christians nor the gait of Christian, pagan, nor man, have so strutted and bellowed, that I have thought some of nature's journeymen had made men, and not made them

182 **something-settled** somewhat settled 4 **had as lief** would as soon 10 **robustious** burly **periwig-pated** bewigged 12 **groundlings** those who paid the cheapest rate of admission 15 **Termagant . . . Herod** characters in old scriptural plays, noted for their violence

192 **round** direct 22 **modesty** moderation 27 **pressure** shape 28 **tardy** imperfectly 38 **journeymen** laborers

well, they imitated humanity so abominably.

40 FIRST PL. I hope we have reformed that indifferently with us, sir.

HAMLET. O reform it altogether, and let those that play your clowns speak no more than is set down for them, for there be of them that will themselves laugh, to set on some quantity of barren spectators to laugh too, though in the mean time some necessary question of the play be then to be considered; that's villainous, and shows a most pitiful ambition in the fool that

50 uses it. Go, make you ready. *Exeunt* PLAYERS.

Enter POLONIUS, ROSENCRANTZ, *and* GUILDENSTERN.

How now, my lord? will the king hear this piece of work?

POL. And the queen too, and that presently.

HAMLET. Bid the players make haste.

Exit POLONIUS.

Will you two help to hasten them?

ROS., GUILDENSTERN. We will, my lord.

Exeunt they two.

HAMLET. What, ho, Horatio!

Enter HORATIO.

HOR. Here, sweet lord, at your service.

HAMLET. Horatio, thou art e'en as just a man

60 As e'er my conversation coped withal.

HOR. O my dear lord—

HAMLET. Nay, do not think I flatter,

For what advancement may I hope from thee

That no revenue hast but thy good spirits

To feed and clothe thee? Why should the poor be flattered?

No, let the candied tongue lick absurd pomp,

And crook the pregnant hinges of the knee

Where thrift may follow fawning. Dost thou hear?

Since my dear soul was mistress of her choice,

And could of men distinguish her election,

She hath sealed thee for herself, for thou hast

70 been

As one in suffering all that suffers nothing,

A man that fortune's buffets and rewards

Hast ta'en with equal thanks; and blessed are those

Whose blood and judgment are so well co-medled,

That they are not a pipe for fortune's finger

To sound what stop she please. Give me that man

That is not passion's slave, and I will wear him

In my heart's core, ay, in my heart of heart,

As I do thee. Something too much of this.

There is a play tonight before the king; 80

One scene of it comes near the circumstance

Which I have told thee of my father's death;

I prithee, when thou seest that act a-foot,

Even with the very comment of thy soul

Observe my uncle. If his occulted guilt

Do not itself unkennel in one speech,

It is a damnéd ghost that we have seen,

And my imaginations are as foul

As Vulcan's stithy. Give him heedful note,

For I mine eyes will rivet to his face, 90

And after we will both our judgments join

In censure of his seeming.

HOR. Well, my lord;

If he steal aught the whilst this play is playing,

And scape detecting, I will pay the theft.

HAMLET. They are coming to the play, I must be idle;

Get you a place.

Enter Trumpets and Kettledrums, KING, QUEEN, POLONIUS, OPHELIA, ROSENCRANTZ, GUILDENSTERN, *and other Lords attendant with his Guard carrying torches. Danish march. Sound a flourish.*

KING. How fares our cousin Hamlet?

HAMLET. Excellent, i' faith, of the chameleon's dish; I eat the air, promise-crammed: you cannot feed capons so. 100

KING. I have nothing with this answer, Hamlet; these words are not mine.

HAMLET. No, nor mine now. [*To* POLONIUS] My lord, you played once i' the university, you say?

POL. That did I, my lord, and was accounted a good actor.

HAMLET. What did you enact?

40 **indifferently** fairly well 43 **clowns** comic rustic 53 **presently** immediately 60 **withal** with 66 **pregnant** supple 67 **thrift** profit 69 **election** choice

74 **blood** passion **co-medled** blended 85 **occulted** hidden 89 **stithy** smithy 92 **censure** judging **seeming** behavior 95 **idle** insane 98 **the chameleon's dish** air, on which the chameleon was supposed to live 102 **are not mine** are not an answer to my question

POL. I did enact Julius Cæsar; I was killed i' the Capitol; Brutus killed me.

110

HAMLET. It was a brute part of him to kill so capital a calf there. Be the players ready?

ROS. Ay, my lord, they stay upon your patience.

QUEEN Come hither, my dear Hamlet, sit by me.

HAMLET. No, good mother, here's metal more attractive. [*Lying down at* OPHELIA'S *feet.*]

POL. [*to the* KING] O ho, do you mark that?

120

HAMLET. Lady, shall I lie in your lap?

OPH. No, my lord.

HAMLET. I mean, my head upon your lap?

OPH. Ay, my lord.

HAMLET. Do you think I meant country matters?

OPH. I think nothing, my lord.

HAMLET. That's a fair thought to lie between maids' legs.

OPH. What is, my lord?

130

HAMLET. Nothing.

OPH. You are merry, my lord.

HAMLET. Who, I?

OPH. Ay, my lord.

HAMLET. O God, your only jig-maker. What should a man do but be merry? for, look you, how cheerfully my mother looks, and my father died within's two hours.

OPH. Nay, 'tis twice two months, my lord.

HAMLET. So long? Nay then, let the devil wear black, for I'll have a suit of sables. O heavens, die two months ago, and not forgotten yet? Then there's hope a great man's memory may outlive his life half a year, but by'r lady a' must build churches then, or else shall a' suffer not thinking on, with the hobbyhorse, whose epitaph is, "For O, for O, the hobbyhorse is forgot."

140

Hautboys play. The dumb-show enters.

Enter a King *and a* Queen *very lovingly; the* Queen *embracing him, and he her. She kneels, and makes show of protestation unto him. He takes her up, and declines his head upon her neck: he lays him down upon a bank of flowers: she, seeing him asleep, leaves him. Anon comes in another man, takes off his crown, kisses it, pours poison in the sleeper's ears, and leaves him. The* Queen *returns; finds the* King *dead, and makes passionate action. The* Poisoner *with some three or four comes in again, seems to condole with her. The dead body is carried away. The* Poisoner *woos the* Queen *with gifts: she seems harsh awhile, but in the end accepts his love.*

Exeunt.

OPH. What means this, my lord?

HAMLET. Marry, this is miching mallecho, it means mischief.

150

OPH. Belike this show imports the argument of the play.

Enter PROLOGUE

HAMLET. We shall know by this fellow; the players cannot keep counsel, they'll tell all.

OPH. Will a' tell us what this show meant?

HAMLET. Ay, or any show that you'll show him; be not you ashamed to show, he'll not shame to tell you what it means.

OPH. You are naught, you are naught; I'll mark the play.

PRO. For us and for our tragedy,
Here stooping to your clemency,
We beg your hearing patiently.

160

[*Exit.*]

HAMLET. Is this a prologue, or the posy of a ring?

OPH. 'Tis brief, my lord.

HAMLET. As woman's love.

Enter [*two* PLAYERS *as*] King *and* Queen.

PLAYER KING. Full thirty times hath Phœbus' cart gone round
Neptune's salt wash and Tellus' orbéd ground,
And thirty dozen moons with borrowed sheen
About the world have times twelve thirties been
Since love our hearts, and Hymen did our hands
Unite commutual in most sacred bands.

170

113 **stay upon your patience** await your leisure 127 **sables** furs

149 **milching mallecho** skulking mischief 158 **naught** indecent 163 **posy** inscription 167 **Phoebus' cart** the sun 171 **commutual** mutally

PLAYER QUEEN. So many journeys may the sun and moon
Make us again count o'er ere love be done!
But woe is me, you are so sick of late,
So far from cheer and from your former state,
That I distrust you. Yet, though I distrust,
Discomfort you my lord, it nothing must,
For women fear too much, even as they love,
And women's fear and love hold quantity:
180 In neither aught, or in extremity.
Now what my love is proof hath made you know,
And as my love is sized, my fear is so;
Where love is great, the littlest doubts are fear;
Where little fears grow great, great love grows there.

P. KING. Faith, I must leave thee, love, and shortly too;
My operant powers their functions leave to do;
And thou shalt live in this fair world behind,
Honored, beloved, and haply one as kind
For husband shalt thou—

P. QUEEN. O confound the rest!
Such love must needs be treason in my
190 breast.
In second husband let me be accurst,
None wed the second but who killed the first.

HAMLET. [*aside*] Wormwood, wormwood.

P. QUEEN. The instances that second marriage move
Are base respects of thrift, but none of love;
A second time I kill my husband dead
When second husband kisses me in bed.

P. KING. I do believe you think what now you speak,
But what we do determine oft we break.
200 Purpose is but the slave to memory,
Of violent birth but poor validity,
Which now like fruit unripe sticks on the tree,
But fall unshaken when they mellow be.
Most necessary 'tis that we forget
To pay ourselves what to ourselves is debt;
What to ourselves in passion we propose,
The passion ending, doth the purpose lose.
The violence of either grief or joy
Their own enactures with themselves destroy;
Where joy most revels, grief doth most la-
ment; 210
Grief joys, joy grieves, on slender accident.
This world is not for aye, nor 'tis not strange
That even our loves should with our fortunes change;
For 'tis a question left us yet to prove,
Whether love lead fortune, or else fortune love.
The great man down, you mark his favorite flies;
The poor advanced makes friends of enemies.
And hitherto doth love on fortune tend,
For who not needs shall never lack a friend,
And who in want a hollow friend doth try, 220
Directly seasons him his enemy.
But, orderly to end where I begun,
Our wills and fates do so contrary run,
That our devices still are overthrown;
Our thoughts are ours, their ends none of our own;
So think thou wilt no second husband wed,
But die thy thoughts when thy first lord is dead.

P. QUEEN. Nor earth to me give food, nor heaven light,
Sport and repose lock from me day and night,
To desperation turn my trust and hope, 230
An anchor's cheer in prison be my scope,
Each opposite that blanks the face of joy,
Meet what I would have well, and it destroy,
Both here and hence pursue me lasting strife,
If once a widow ever I be wife!

HAMLET. If she should break it now!

P. KING. 'Tis deeply sworn. Sweet, leave me here a while;
My spirits grow dull, and fain I would beguile
The tedious day with sleep. *Sleeps.*

P. QUEEN. Sleep rock thy brain,
And never come mischance between us
twain! *Exit.* 240

HAMLET. Madam, how like you this play?

176 **distrust** fear for 186 **operant** active

209 **enactures** fulfilment, performances 221 **seasons** ripens 231 **anchor's** hermit's 232 **blanks** turns pale

QUEEN. The lady doth protest too much, methinks.

HAMLET. O, but she'll keep her word.

KING. Have you heard the argument? Is there no offence in't?

HAMLET. No, no, they do but jest, poison in jest; no offence i' the world.

KING. What do you call the play?

250 HAMLET. The Mousetrap. Marry, how? Tropically. This play is the image of a murder done in Vienna; Gonzago is the duke's name, his wife Baptista; you shall see anon 'tis a knavish piece of work, but what o' that? your majesty and we that have free souls, it touches us not; let the galled jade wince, our withers are unwrung.

Enter LUCIANUS.

This is one Lucianus, nephew to the king.

OPH. You are as good as a chorus, my lord.

260 HAMLET. I could interpret between you and your love, if I could see the puppets dallying.

OPH. You are keen, my lord, you are keen.

HAMLET. It would cost you a groaning to take off mine edge.

OPH. Still better and worse.

HAMLET. So you must take your husbands. Begin murderer, leave thy damnable faces, and begin. Come: "the croaking raven doth bellow for revenge."

LUCIANUS. Thoughts black, hands apt,
270 drugs fit, and time agreeing,
Confederate season, else no creature seeing,
Thou mixture rank, of midnight weeds collected,
With Hecate's ban thrice blasted, thrice infected,
Thy natural magic and dire property
On wholesome life usurps immediately.

Pours the poison in his ears.

HAMLET. A' poisons him i' the garden for his estate. His name's Gonzago; the story is extant, and written in very choice Italian; you shall see anon how the murderer gets the love of
280 Gonzago's wife.

OPH. The king rises.

HAMLET. What, frighted with false fire?

QUEEN. How fares my lord?

POL. Give o'er the play.

KING. Give me some light; away!

POL. Lights, lights, lights!

Exeunt all but HAMLET *and* HORATIO.

HAMLET. Why, let the stricken deer go weep,
The hart ungallèd play,
For some must watch while some must sleep;
Thus runs the world away. 290

Would not this, sir, and a forest of feathers—if the rest of my fortunes turn Turk with me—with two Provincial roses on my razed shoes, get me a fellowship in a cry of players, sir?

HOR. Half a share.

HAMLET. A whole one, I.
For thou dost know, O Damon dear,
This realm dismantled was
Of Jove himself, and now reigns here
A very, very—pajock. 300

HOR. You might have rhymed.

HAMLET. O good Horatio, I'll take the ghost's word for a thousand pound. Didst perceive?

HOR. Very well, my lord.

HAMLET. Upon the talk of the poisoning?

HOR. I did very well note him.

HAMLET. Ah, ha! Come, some music! come, the recorders!
For if the king like not the comedy,
Why then belike—he likes it not, perdy. 310
Come, some music!

Enter ROSENCRANTZ *and* GUILDENSTERN.

GUIL. Good my lord, vouchsafe me a word with you.

HAMLET. Sir, a whole history.

GUIL. The king, sir—

HAMLET. Ay, sir, what of him?

GUIL. Is in his retirement marvellous distempered.

HAMLET. With drink, sir?

GUIL. No, my lord, with choler. 320

HAMLET. Your wisdom should show itself more richer to signify this to the doctor, for for me to put him to his purgation would perhaps plunge him into more choler.

245 **argument** outline of the plot 251 **tropically** figuratively 256 **galled** chafed **jade** horse **withers** shoulders of horse 257 **unwrung** not irritated 273 **Hecate** goddess of witchcraft

291 **forest of feathers** bunch of feathers sometimes part of an actor's costume 293 **Provincial roses** large rosettes worn by actors **razed** slashed 294 **cry** pack 300 **pajock** peacock 308 **recorders** flageolets 317 **distempered** out of sorts

GUIL. Good my lord, put your discourse into some frame, and start not so wildly from my affair.

HAMLET. I am tame, sir; pronounce.

GUIL. The queen your mother, in most great affliction of spirit, hath sent me to you. 330

HAMLET. You are welcome.

GUIL. Nay, good my lord, this courtesy is not of the right breed. If it shall please you to make me a wholesome answer, I will do your mother's commandment; if not, your pardon and my return shall be the end of my business.

HAMLET. Sir, I cannot.

GUIL. What, my lord?

HAMLET. Make you a wholesome answer—my wit's diseased; but, sir, such answer as I can make, you shall command, or rather, as you say, my mother; therefore no more, but to the matter: my mother, you say,— 340

ROS. Then thus she says: your behavior hath struck her into amazement and admiration.

HAMLET. O wonderful son, that can so stonish a mother! But is there no sequel at the heels of this mother's admiration? impart.

ROS. She desires to speak with you in her closet ere you go to bed. 350

HAMLET. We shall obey, were she ten times our mother. Have you any further trade with us?

ROS. My lord, you once did love me.

HAMLET. And do still, by these pickers and stealers.

ROS. Good my lord, what is your cause of distemper? you do surely bar the door upon your own liberty, if you deny your griefs to your friend. 360

HAMLET. Sir, I lack advancement.

ROS. How can that be, when you have the voice of the king himself for your succession in Denmark?

HAMLET. Ay, sir, but "while the grass grows"—the proverb is something musty.

Enter the PLAYERS *with recorders.*

O, the recorders: let me see one. To withdraw with you—why do you go about to recover the wind of me, as if you would drive me into a toil? 370

GUIL. O, my lord, if my duty be too bold, my love is too unmannerly.

HAMLET. I do not well understand that. Will you play upon this pipe?

GUIL. My lord, I cannot.

HAMLET. I pray you.

GUIL. Believe me, I cannot.

HAMLET. I do beseech you.

GUIL. I know no touch of it, my lord.

HAMLET. 'Tis as easy as lying; govern these ventages with your fingers and thumb, give it breath with your mouth, and it will discourse most eloquent music. Look you, these are the stops. 380

GUIL. But these cannot I command to any utterance of harmony; I have not the skill.

HAMLET. Why, look you now, how unworthy a thing you make of me! You would play upon me, you would seem to know my stops, you would pluck out the heart of my mystery, you would sound me from my lowest note to the top of my compass; and there is much music, excellent voice, in this little organ, yet cannot you make it speak. 'Sblood, do you think I am easier to be played on than a pipe? Call me what instrument you will, though you can fret me, yet you cannot play upon me. 390

Enter POLONIUS

God bless you, sir!

POL. My lord, the queen would speak with you, and presently.

HAMLET. Do you see yonder cloud that's almost in shape of a camel? 400

POL. By the mass and 'tis, like a camel indeed.

HAMLET. Methinks it is like a weasel.

POL. It is backed like a weasel.

HAMLET. Or like a whale?

POL. Very like a whale.

HAMLET. Then I will come to my mother by and by. They fool me to the top of my bent. I will come by and by. 410

POL. I will say so. *Exit.*

HAMLET. By and by is easily said.
Leave me, friends. [*Exeunt all but* HAMLET.]

326 **frame** coherent form 334 **wholesome** reasonable 350 **closet** private room 355 **pickers and stealers** hands 365 **'while the grass grows'**—*the proverb continues* 'oft starves the silly steed' 368 **recover the wind** get to windward

370 **toil** trap 372 **unmannerly** extreme 381 **ventages** wind-holes, stops 393 **organ** instrument

'Tis now the very witching time of night,
When churchyards yawn, and hell itself breathes out
Contagion to this world: now could I drink hot blood,
And do such bitter business as the day
Would quake to look on. Soft, now to my mother.
O heart, lose not thy nature, let not ever
The soul of Nero enter this firm bosom; 420
Let me be cruel, not unnatural.
I will speak daggers to her, but use none;
My tongue and soul in this be hypocrites;
How in my words somever she be shent,
To give them seals never, my soul, consent!
Exit.

Scene Three

Enter KING, ROSENCRANTZ, *and* GUILDENSTERN.

KING. I like him not, nor stands it safe with us
To let his madness range. Therefore prepare you;
I your commission will forthwith dispatch,
And he to England shall along with you:
The terms of our estate may not endure
Hazard so near us as doth hourly grow
Out of his brawls.
GUIL. We will ourselves provide.
Most holy and religious fear it is
To keep those many many bodies safe
10 That live and feed upon your majesty.
ROS. The single and peculiar life is bound,
With all the strength and armor of the mind,
To keep itself from noyance, but much more
That spirit upon whose weal depends and rests
The lives of many. The cess of majesty
Dies not alone, but like a gulf doth draw
What's near it with it; or it is a massy wheel
Fixed on the summit of the highest mount,
To whose huge spokes ten thousand lesser things
Are mortised and adjoined; which, when it falls,
20 Each small annexment, petty consequence,
Attends the boisterous ruin. Never alone
Did the king sigh, but with a general groan.
KING. Arm you, I pray you, to this speedy voyage,
For we will fetters put upon this fear
Which now goes too free-footed.
ROS. We will haste us.
Exeunt ROSENCRANTZ *and* GUILDENSTERN.

Enter POLONIUS

POL. My lord, he's going to his mother's closet.
Behind the arras I'll convey myself
To hear the process; I'll warrant she'll tax him home,
And as you said, and wisely was it said, 30
'Tis meet that some more audience than a mother,
Since nature makes them partial, should o'er-hear
The speech, of vantage. Fare you well, my liege;
I'll call upon you ere you go to bed
And tell you what I know.
KING. Thanks, dear my lord.
Exit [POLONIUS.]
O, my offence is rank, it smells to heaven;
It hath the primal eldest curse upon't,
A brother's murder! Pray can I not,
Though inclination be as sharp as will;

421 **Nero** (who had his mother Agrippina put to death) 425 **shent** reproved 426 **give them seals** ratify by means of actions

5 **terms** conditions **estate** rank 7 **provide** prepare 11 **peculiar** individual 13 **noyance** harm 15 **cess** cessation 16 **gulf** whirlpool 20 **mortised** fitted 21 **annexment** attachment 22 **ruin** crash 29 **process** proceedings **tax** take to task 33 **of vantage** from a vantage point 37 **primal eldest curse** the curse of Cain

40 My stronger guilt defeats my strong intent,
And, like a man to double business bound,
I stand in pause where I shall first begin,
And both neglect. What if this curséd hand
Were thicker than itself with brother's blood,
Is there not rain enough in the sweet heavens
To wash it white as snow? Whereto serves mercy
But to confront the visage of offence?
And what's in prayer but this twofold force,
To be forestalléd ere we come to fall,
50 Or pardoned being down? Then I'll look up;
My fault is past. But O, what form of prayer
Can serve my turn? "Forgive me my foul murder"?
That cannot be, since I am still possess'd
Of those effects for which I did the murder,
My crown, mine own ambition, and my queen.
May one be pardoned, and retain the offence?
In the corrupted currents of this world
Offence's gilded hand may shove by justice,
And oft 'tis seen the wicked prize itself
60 Buys out the law, but 'tis not so above;
There is no shuffling, there the action lies
In his true nature, and we ourselves compelled,
Even to the teeth and forehead of our faults,
To give in evidence. What then? what rests?
Try what repentance can; what can it not?
Yet what can it when one can not repent?
O wretched state! O bosom black as death!
O liméd soul, that, struggling to be free,
Art more engaged! Help, angels! make assay;
Bow, stubborn knees, and, heart with strings of
70 steel,
Be soft as sinews of the new-born babe!
All may be well. [*Retires and kneels.*]

Enter HAMLET

HAMLET. Now might I do it pat, now a' is a-praying,
And now I'll do't, and so a' goes to heaven,
And so am I revenged. That would be scann'd:
A villain kills my father, and for that
I, his sole son, do this same villain send
To heaven.
Why, this is hire and salary, not revenge.
A' took my father grossly, full of bread, 80
With all his crimes broad blown, as flush as May,
And how his audit stands who knows save heaven?
But in our circumstance and course of thought
'Tis heavy with him: and am I then revenged
To take him in the purging of his soul,
When he is fit and seasoned for his passage?
No.
Up, sword, and know thou a more horrid hent:
When he is drunk, asleep, or in his rage,
Or in the incestuous pleasure of his bed, 90
At game a-swearing, or about some act
That has no relish of salvation in't;
Then trip him, that his heels may kick at heaven,
And that his soul may be as damned and black
As hell, whereto it goes. My mother stays;
This physic but prolongs thy sickly days. *Exit.*

KING. My words fly up, my thoughts remain below;
Words without thoughts never to heaven go.
Exit.

47 **offence** guilt 56 **offence** results of guilt 58 **gilded** furnished with bribes 61 **shuffling** trickry 68 **liméd** entrapped 69 **engaged** entangled

73 **pat** readily 80 **full of bread** in full enjoyment of pleasure 81 **broad blown** in full bloom **flush** vigorous 82 **audit** account 86 **seasoned** prepared 88 **hent** opportunity

Scene Four

Enter QUEEN *and* POLONIUS.

POL. A' will come straight. Look you lay home to him;
Tell him his pranks have been too broad to bear with,
And that your grace hath screened and stood between
Much heat and him. I'll silence me even here.
Pray you, be round with him.

HAMLET. [*within*] Mother, mother, mother!

QUEEN. I'll warrant you;
Fear me not: withdraw, I hear him coming.

[POLONIUS *goes behind the arras.*]

Enter HAMLET.

HAMLET. Now, mother, what's the matter?

QUEEN. Hamlet, thou hast thy father much offended.

HAMLET. Mother, you have my father much offended. 10

QUEEN. Come, come, you answer with an idle tongue.

HAMLET. Go, go, you question with a wicked tongue.

QUEEN. Why, how now, Hamlet?

HAMLET. What's the matter now?

QUEEN. Have you forgot me?

HAMLET. No, by the rood, not so!
You are the queen, your husband's brother's wife,
And—would it were not so!—you are my mother.

QUEEN. Nay, then I'll set those to you that can speak.

HAMLET. Come, come, and sit you down; you shall not budge;
You go not till I set you up a glass
Where you may see the inmost part of you. 20

QUEEN. What wilt thou do? thou wilt not murder me?
Help, help, ho!

POL. [*behind*] What, ho! help, help, help!

HAMLET. [*drawing*] How now? a rat? Dead for a ducat, dead!

[*Makes a pass through the arras and kills* POLONIUS.]

POL. [*behind*] O, I am slain!

QUEEN. O me, what hast thou done?

HAMLET. Nay, I know not;
Is it the king?

QUEEN. O, what a rash and bloody deed is this!

HAMLET. A bloody deed! almost as bad, good mother,
As kill a king, and marry with his brother.

QUEEN. As kill a king!

HAMLET. Ay, lady, it was my word. 30

[*Lifts up the arras, and sees* POLONIUS.]

Thou wretched, rash, intruding fool, farewell!
I took thee for thy better; take thy fortune;
Thou find'st to be too busy is some danger.
Leave wringing of your hands; peace sit you down
And let me wring your heart, for so I shall,
If it be made a penetrable stuff,
If damnéd custom have not brassed it so
That it be proof and bulwark against sense.

QUEEN. What have I done, that thou darest wag thy tongue
In noise so rude against me?

HAMLET. Such an act 40
That blurs the grace and blush of modesty,
Calls virtue hypocrite, takes off the rose
From the fair forehead of an innocent love,
And sets a blister there, makes marriage-vows
As false as dicers' oaths; O, such a deed
As from the body of contraction plucks
The very soul, and sweet religion makes
A rhapsody of words. Heaven's face does glow,
And this solidity and compound mass,

1 **lay home** speak severely 2 **broad** unrestrained 5 **round** downright 14 **rood** cross

33 **busy** prying, meddlesome 37 **custom** habit 38 **proof** armor **sense** feeling 46 **contraction** contract, obligation 48 **glow** redden, blush for shame

With heated visage as against the doom, 50
Is thought-sick at the act.

QUEEN. Ay me, what act,
That roars so loud and thunders in the index?

HAMLET. Look here upon this picture, and on this,
The counterfeit presentment of two brothers.
See what a grace was seated on this brow:
Hyperion's curls, the front of Jove himself,
An eye like Mars, to threaten and command,
A station like the herald Mercury
New-lighted on a heaven-kissing hill,
A combination and a form indeed, 60
Where every god did seem to set his seal,
To give the world assurance of a man;
This was your husband. Look you now what follows;
Here is your husband, like a mildewed ear
Blasting his wholesome brother. Have you eyes?
Could you on this fair mountain leave to feed,
And batten on this moor? Ha! have you eyes?
You cannot call it love, for at your age
The heyday in the blood is tame, it's humble,
And waits upon the judgment; and what judgment 70
Would step from this to this? Sense sure you have,
Else could you not have motion, but sure that sense
Is apoplexed, for madness would not err,
Nor sense to ecstasy was ne'er so thralled
But it reserved some quantity of choice
To serve in such a difference. What devil was't
That thus hath cozened you at hoodman-blind?
Eyes without feeling, feeling without sight,
Ears without hands or eyes, smelling sans all,
Or but a sickly part of one true sense 80
Could not so mope.
O shame, where is thy blush? Rebellious hell,
If thou canst mutine in a matron's bones,
To flaming youth let virtue be as wax
And melt in her own fire; proclaim no shame
When the compulsive ardor gives the charge,
Since frost itself as actively doth burn,
And reason panders will.

QUEEN. O Hamlet, speak no more;
Thou turn'st my eyes into my very soul,
And there I see such blank and grainéd spots 90
As will not leave their tinct.

HAMLET. Nay, but to live
In the rank sweat of an enseamèd bed,
Stewed in corruption, honeying and making love
Over the nasty sty—

QUEEN. O speak to me no more;
These words like daggers enter in mine ears;
No more, sweet Hamlet.

HAMLET. A murderer and a villain,
A slave that is not twentieth part the tithe
Of your precedent lord, a vice of kings,
A cutpurse of the empire and the rule,
That from a shelf the precious diadem stole 100
And put it in his pocket—

QUEEN. No more.

HAMLET. A king of shreds and patches—

Enter GHOST.

Save me, and hover o'er me with your wings,
You heavenly guards! What would your gracious figure?

QUEEN. Alas, he's mad.

HAMLET. Do you not come your tardy son to chide,
That, lapsed in time and passion, lets go by
The important acting of your dread command?
O, say!

GHOST. Do not forget; this visitation 110
Is but to whet thy almost blunted purpose.
But look, amazement on thy mother sits.
O step between her and her fighting soul;
Conceit in weakest bodies strongest works.
Speak to her, Hamlet.

HAMLET. How is it with you, lady?

QUEEN. Alas, how is't with you,
That you do bend your eye on vacancy,
And with the incorporal air do hold discourse?
Forth at your eyes your spirits wildly peep,

50 **against** at the approach of 52 **index** preliminaries, table of contents 54 **presentment** representation 56 **Hyperion** the sun god **front** forehead 58 **station** attitude 64 **ear** (of wheat) 67 **batten** gorge, pasture 69 **heyday** youth 70 **waits upon** defers to 73 **apoplexed** subject to aberrations or fits 74 **ecstasy** madness **thralled** in bondage 76 **serve** employ **difference** power of distinguishing 77 **cozened** deceived **hoodman-blind** blind-man's-buff 81 **so mope** be so uncertain 83 **mutine** mutiny, rebel

86 **compulsive** compelling **gives the charge** orders the attack 88 **panders** is subservient to 90 **grainéd** ingrained 91 **tinct** color, dye 92 **enseamèd** greasy 97 **tithe** tenth part 98 **precedent** previous **vice** clown 99 **cutpurse** pickpocket 113 **fighting** struggling 114 **conceit** imagination

120 And, as the sleeping soldiers in the alarm,
Your bedded hairs like life in excrements,
Start up and stand an end. O gentle son,
Upon the heat and flame of thy distemper
Sprinkle cool patience. Whereon do you look?

HAMLET. On him, on him! Look you, how pale he glares!
His form and cause conjoined, preaching to stones,
Would make them capable. Do not look upon me,
Lest with this piteous action you convert
My stern effects; then what I have to do
130 Will want true color—tears perchance for blood.

QUEEN. To whom do you speak this

HAMLET. Do you see nothing there?

QUEEN. Nothing at all; yet all that is I see.

HAMLET. Nor did you nothing hear?

QUEEN. No, nothing but ourselves.

HAMLET. Why, look you there! look, how it steals away!
My father, in his habit as he lived!
Look, where he goes, even now, out at the portal! *Exit* GHOST

QUEEN. This is the very coinage of your brain;
This bodiless creation ecstasy
Is very cunning in.

HAMLET. Ecstasy!
140 My pulse as yours doth temperately keep time
And makes as healthful music; it is not madness
That I have uttered. Bring me to the test,
And I the matter will reword, which madness
Would gambol from. Mother, for love of grace
Lay not that flattering unction to your soul,
That not your trespass but my madness speaks;
It will but skin and film the ulcerous place
Whiles rank corruption, mining all within,
Infects unseen. Confess yourself to heaven,
150 Repent what's past, avoid what is to come,
And do not spread the compost on the weeds
To make them ranker. Forgive me this my virtue,
For in the fatness of these pursy times
Virtue itself of vice must pardon beg,
Yea, curb and woo for leave to do him good.

QUEEN. O Hamlet, thou hast cleft my heart in twain.

HAMLET. O, throw away the worser part of it,
And live the purer with the other half.
Good night, but go not to my uncle's bed;
160 Assume a virtue, if you have it not.
That monster custom, who all sense doth eat
Of habits evil, is angel yet in this,
That to the use of actions fair and good
He likewise gives a frock or livery
That aptly is put on. Refrain tonight,
And that shall lend a kind of easiness
To the next abstinence; the next more easy,
For use almost can change the stamp of nature,
And either curb the devil, or throw him out
170 With wondrous potency. Once more, good night,
And when you are desirous to be blessed,
I'll blessing beg of you.—For this same lord,
[*Pointing to* POLONIUS.]
I do repent; but heaven hath pleased it so,
To punish me with this, and this with me,
That I must be their scourge and minister.
I will bestow him and will answer well
The death I gave him. So again, good night.
I must be cruel only to be kind;
Thus bad begins, and worse remains behind.
One word more, good lady.

180 QUEEN. What shall I do?

HAMLET. Not this, by no means, that I bid you do;
Let the bloat king tempt you again to bed,
Pinch wanton on your cheek, call you his mouse,
And let him for a pair of reechy kisses,
Or paddling in your neck with his damned fingers,
Make you to ravel all this matter out
That I essentially am not in madness,
But mad in craft. 'Twere good you let him know,
For who, that's but a queen, fair, sober, wise,

121 **excrements** outgrowths 122 **an** on 127 **capable** able to feel 129 **effects** deeds 130 **color** appearance **for** instead of 145 **unction** ointment 148 **mining** undermining 152 **virtue** apparent self-righteousness 153 **fatness** grossness **pursy** corpulent

155 **curb** bow 161 **sense** feeling sensitiveness 162 **of** from 164 **livery** uniform 165 **aptly** easily 168 **use** habit **stamp** form, impression 175 **scourge** instrument of punishment **minister** agent 176 **bestow** hide 182 **bloat** bloated 183 **wanton** wantonly 184 **reechy** reeking, dirty 186 **ravel . . . out** unravel 188 **in craft,** *i.e.,* pretendedly

190 Would from a paddock, from a bat, a gib,
Such dear concernings hide? who would do so?
No, in despite of sense and secrecy,
Unpeg the basket on the house's top,
Let the birds fly, and like the famous ape,
To try conclusions, in the basket creep
And break your own neck down.

QUEEN. Be thou assured, if words be made of breath
And breath of life, I have no life to breathe
What thou hast said to me.

HAMLET. I must to England; you know that?

200 QUEEN. Alack,
I had forgot; 'tis so concluded on.

HAMLET. There's letters sealed, and my two schoolfellows,
Whom I will trust as I will adders fanged,
They bear the mandate; they must sweep my way
And marshal me to knavery. Let it work,
For 'tis the sport to have the enginer
Hoist with his own petar, and't shall go hard
But I will delve one yard below their mines,
And blow them at the moon: O 'tis most sweet
When in one line two crafts directly meet. 210
This man shall set me packing;
I'll lug the guts into the neighbor room.
Mother, good night indeed. This counsellor
Is now most still, most secret, and most grave,
Who was in life a foolish prating knave.
Come, sir, to draw toward an end with you.
Good night, mother.

Exit HAMLET *tugging in* POLONIUS.

ACT FOUR *Scene One*

Enter KING, *and* QUEEN, *with* ROSENCRANTZ *and* GUILDENSTERN.

KING. There's matter in these sighs, these profound heaves,
You must translate; 'tis fit we understand them.
Where is your son?

QUEEN. Bestow this place on us a little while.

[*Exeunt* ROSENCRANTZ *and* GUILDENSTERN.]

Ah, mine own lord, what have I seen tonight!

KING. What, Gertrude, how does Hamlet?

QUEEN. Mad as the sea and wind when both contend
Which is the mightier; in his lawless fit,
Behind the arras hearing something stir,
Whips out his rapier, cries "a rat, a rat!" 10
And in this brainish apprehension kills
The unseen good old man.

KING. O heavy deed!
It had been so with us had we been there.
His liberty is full of threats to all—
To you yourself, to us, to every one.
Alas, how shall this bloody deed be answered?
It will be laid to us, whose providence
Should have kept short, restrained, and out of haunt
This mad young man; but so much was our love,
We would not understand what was most fit; 20
But like the owner of a foul disease,

190 **paddock** toad **gib** cat 191 **dear concernings** matters of personal importance

204 **mandate** orders **sweep** prepare 205 **marshal** lead 206 **enginer** engineer 207 **hoist** blown up **petar** mine, bomb 208 **delve** dig, tunnel 11 **brainish apprehension** imaginary fear 18 **out of haunt** out of the way

To keep it from divulging, let it feed
Even on the pith of life. Where is he gone?
QUEEN. To draw apart the body he hath killed,
O'er whom his very madness, like some ore
Among a mineral of metals base,
Shows itself pure; a' weeps for what is done.
KING. O Gertrude, come away!
The sun no sooner shall the mountains touch,
30 But we will ship him hence, and this vile deed
We must, with all our majesty and skill,
Both countenance and excuse. Ho, Guildenstern!

Enter ROSENCRANTZ *and* GUILDENSTERN.

Friends both, go join you with some further aid;
Hamlet in madness hath Polonius slain,
And from his mother's closet hath he dragged him.
Go seek him out; speak fair, and bring the body
Into the chapel. I pray you haste in this.
Exeunt ROSENCRANTZ *and* GUILDENSTERN.
Come, Gertrude, we'll call up our wisest friends,
And let them know both what we mean to do
And what's untimely done; [so haply slander—] 40
Whose whisper o'er the world's diameter,
As level as the cannon to his blank,
Transports his poisoned shot—may miss our name,
And hit the woundless air. O, come away!
My soul is full of discord and dismay. *Exeunt.*

Scene Two

Enter HAMLET.

HAMLET. Safely stowed.
GENTLEMEN. [*within*] Hamlet, Lord Hamlet!
HAMLET. What noise? who calls on Hamlet? O, here they come.

Enter ROSENCRANTZ *and* GUILDENSTERN.

ROS. What have you done, my lord, with the dead body?
HAMLET. Compounded it with dust, whereto 'tis kin.
ROS. Tell us where 'tis that we may take it
10 thence, and bear it to the chapel.
HAMLET. Do not believe it.
ROS. Believe what?
HAMLET. That I can keep your counsel and not mine own. Besides, to be demanded of a sponge! what replication should be made by the son of a king?
ROS. Take you me for a sponge, my lord?
HAMLET. Ay, sir, that soaks up the king's
20 countenance, his rewards, his authorities. But such officers do the king best service in the end: he keeps them, like an ape, in the corner of his jaw—first mouthed, to be last swallowed; when he needs what you have gleaned, it is but squeezing you, and sponge, you shall be dry again.
ROS. I understand you not, my lord.
HAMLET. I am glad of it; a knavish speech sleeps in a foolish ear.
30 ROS. My lord, you must tell us where the body is, and go with us to the king.
HAMLET. The body is with the king, but the king is not with the body. The king is a thing—
GUIL. A thing, my lord!
HAMLET. Of nothing; bring me to him. Hide fox, and all after. *Exeunt.*

25 **ore** precious metal 26 **mineral** vein 32 **countenance** acknowledge 8 **compounded** mixed

42 **blank** target 20 **countenance** favor 29 **sleeps** is not understood

Scene Three

Enter KING, *and two or three.*

KING. I have sent to seek him, and to find the body.
How dangerous is it that this man goes loose;
Yet must not we put the strong law on him;
He's loved of the distracted multitude,
Who like not in their judgment, but their eyes,
And where 'tis so, the offender's scourge is weighed,
But never the offence. To bear all smooth and even,
This sudden sending him away must seem
Deliberate pause; diseases desperate grown
10 By desperate appliance are relieved,
Or not at all.

Enter ROSENCRANTZ.

How now, what hath befallen?

ROS. Where the dead body is bestowed, my lord,
We cannot get from him.

KING. But where is he?

ROS. Without, my lord; guarded, to know your pleasure.

KING. Bring him before us.

ROS. Ho, Guildenstern! bring in my lord.

Enter HAMLET *and* GUILDENSTERN.

KING. Now, Hamlet, where's Polonius?

HAMLET. At supper.

KING. At supper! where?

20 HAMLET. Not where he eats, but where a' is eaten; a certain convocation of politic worms are e'en at him. Your worm is your only emperor for diet; we fat all creatures else to fat us, and we fat ourselves for maggots; your fat king and your lean beggar is but variable service—two dishes, but to one table; that's the end.

KING. Alas, alas!

HAMLET. A man may fish with the worm that hath eat of a king, and eat of the fish that 30 hath fed of that worm.

KING. What dost thou mean by this?

HAMLET. Nothing but to show you how a king may go a progress through the guts of a beggar.

KING. Where is Polonius?

HAMLET. In heaven. Send thither to see; if your messenger find him not there, seek him i' the other place yourself. But if indeed you find him not within this month, you shall nose him 40 as you go up the stairs into the lobby.

KING. Go seek him there. [*To some Attendants.*]

HAMLET. A' will stay till you come. [*Exeunt Attendants.*]

KING. Hamlet, this deed, for thine especial safety—
Which we do tender, as we dearly grieve
For that which thou hast done—must send thee hence
With fiery quickness; therefore prepare thyself;
The bark is ready, and the wind at help,
The associates tend, and every thing is bent
For England.

HAMLET. For England!

KING. Ay, Hamlet.

50 HAMLET. Good.

KING. So is it, if thou knew'st our purposes.

HAMLET. I see a cherub that sees them. But come; for England! Farewell, dear mother.

KING. Thy loving father, Hamlet.

HAMLET. My mother; father and mother is

4 **distracted** unstable 6 **scourge** punishment 10 **appliance** medical treatment 21 **convocation of politic worms . . . emperor for diet** (a punning allusion to the Diets of the Holy Roman Empire held at Worms)

25 **variable service** different courses 34 **progress** state journey made by a king 45 **tender** care for **dearly** deeply 49 **tend** wait

man and wife, man and wife is one flesh, and so my mother. Come, for England! [*Exit.*]

KING. Follow him at foot; tempt him with speed aboard.
Delay it not; I'll have him hence tonight.
Away! for every thing is sealed and done
60 That else leans on the affair; pray you, make haste.

[*Exeunt* ROSENCRANTZ *and* GUILDENSTERN.]

And, England, if my love thou hold'st at aught—
As my great power thereof may give thee sense,
Since yet thy cicatrice looks raw and red
After the Danish sword, and thy free awe
Pays homage to us—thou mayst not coldly set
Our sovereign process, which imports at full
By letters congruing to that effect
The present death of Hamlet. Do it, England;
For like the hectic in my blood he rages, 70
And thou must cure me; till I know 'tis done,
Howe'er my haps, my joys were ne'er begun.

Exit.

Scene Four

Enter FORTINBRAS, *with his Army over the stage.*

FORTINBRAS. Go, captain, from me greet the Danish king;
Tell him that by his licence Fortinbras
Claims the conveyance of a promised march
Over his kingdom. You know the rendezvous.
If that his majesty would aught with us,
We shall express our duty in his eye;
And let him know so.

CAPTAIN. I will do't, my lord.

FOR. Go softly on.

[*Exeunt* FORTINBRAS *and his Forces.*]

Enter HAMLET, ROSENCRANTZ, [GUILDENSTERN *and others.*]

HAMLET. Good sir, whose powers are these?

10 CAPTAIN. They are of Norway, sir.

HAMLET. How purposed, sir, I pray you?

CAPTAIN. Against some part of Poland.

HAMLET. Who commands them, sir?

CAPTAIN. The nephew to old Norway, Fortinbras.

HAMLET. Goes it against the main of Poland, sir,
Or for some frontier?

CAPTAIN. Truly to speak, and with no addition,
We go to gain a little patch of ground
That hath in it no profit but the name.
To pay five ducats, five, I would not farm it, 20
Nor will it yield to Norway or the Pole
A ranker rate, should it be sold in fee.

HAMLET. Why then, the Polack never will defend it.

CAPTAIN. Yes, it is already garrisoned.

HAMLET. Two thousand souls and twenty thousand ducats
Will not debate the question of this straw;
This is the imposthume of much wealth and peace,
That inward breaks, and shows no cause without
Why the man dies. I humbly thank you, sir.

CAPTAIN. God be wi' you, sir. [*Exit.*]

ROS. Will't please you go, my lord? 30

HAMLET. I'll be with you straight. Go a little before. [*Exeunt all except* HAMLET.]
How all occasions do inform against me,
And spur my dull revenge! What is a man

61 **leans on** concerns 62 **England** King of England **hold'st at aught** valuest at all 3 **conveyance** convoy 9 **powers** forces 15 **main** principal part

63 **give thee sense** make thee perceive 64 **cicatrice** scar 66 **coldly set** disregard 67 **process** command 68 **congruing** amounting 69 **present** immediate 70 **hectic** fever 72 **haps** fortunes 17 **addition** exaggeration 22 **ranker** higher **in fee** outright 27 **imposthume** ulcer 32 **inform against** denounce

If his chief good and market of his time
Be but to sleep and feed? a beast, no more.
Sure, he that made us with such large discourse
Looking before and after, gave us not
That capability and godlike reason
To fust in us unused. Now, whether it be
40 Bestial oblivion, or some craven scruple
Of thinking too precisely on the event—
A thought which, quartered, hath but one part wisdom,
And ever three parts coward—I do not know
Why yet I live to say "This thing's to do,"
Sith I have cause, and will, and strength, and means
To do't. Examples gross as earth exhort me:
Witness this army of such mass and charge,
Led by a delicate and tender prince,
Whose spirit, with divine ambition puffed,
Makes mouths at the invisible event, 50
Exposing what is mortal and unsure
To all that fortune, death and danger dare,
Even for an eggshell. Rightly to be great
Is not to stir without great argument,
But greatly to find quarrel in a straw
When honor's at the stake. How stand I then
That have a father killed, a mother stained,
Excitements of my reason and my blood,
And let all sleep? while to my shame I see
The imminent death of twenty thousand men, 60
That for a fantasy and trick of fame
Go to their graves like beds, fight for a plot
Whereon the numbers cannot try the cause,
Which is not tomb enough and continent
To hide the slain? O, from this time forth
My thoughts be bloody, or be nothing worth!
Exit.

Scene Five

Enter QUEEN, HORATIO, *and a* GENTLEMAN.

QUEEN. I will not speak with her.

GENTLEMAN. She is importunate, indeed distract;
Her mood will needs be pitied.

QUEEN. What would she have?

GENT. She speaks much of her father, says she hears
There's tricks i' the world, and hems, and beats her heart,
Spurns enviously at straws, speaks things in doubt
That carry but half sense; her speech is nothing,
Yet the unshapéd use of it doth move
The hearers to collection; they aim at it,
And botch the words up fit to their own thoughts, 10
Which, as her winks and nods and gestures yield them,
Indeed would make one think there might be thought,
Though nothing sure, yet much unhappily.

HOR. 'Twere good she were spoken with, for she may strew
Dangerous conjectures in ill-breeding minds;
Let her come in. [*Exit* GENTLEMAN.]

QUEEN. To my sick soul, as sin's true nature is,
Each toy seems prologue to some great amiss;
So full of artless jealousy is guilt, 20

34 **market** profit 36 **discourse** power of reasoning 39 **fust** grow mouldy 40 **oblivion** forgetfulness 41 **event** outcome 47 **charge** expense 2 **distract** distracted, unbalanced 5 **tricks** deceits 6 **spurns enviously at straws** takes offence at trifles 7 **nothing** nonsence 8 **unshapéd** incoherent

50 **makes mouths at** makes faces at, defies 58 **blood** passion, anger 61 **trick** whim 64 **continent** receptacle 9 **collection** attempt to collect some meaning from it 10 **botch** patch 15 **ill-breeding** liable to misinterpret 18 **toy** trifle **amiss** misfortune 19 **artless** uncontrolled **jealousy** suspicion

It spills itself in fearing to be spilt.

Enter OPHELIA *distracted.*

OPH. Where is the beauteous majesty of Denmark?

QUEEN. How now, Ophelia?

OPH. [*sings*] How should I your true love know
From another one?
By his cockle hat and staff,
And his sandal shoon.

QUEEN. Alas, sweet lady, what imports this song?

OPH. Say you? Nay, pray you, mark.

[*Sings.*] He is dead and gone, lady,
He is dead and gone;
30 At his head a grass-green turf,
At his heels a stone
O, ho!

QUEEN. Nay, but Ophelia—

OPH. Pray you, mark.

[*Sings.*] White his shroud as the mountain snow—

Enter KING.

QUEEN. Alas, look here, my lord.

OPH. [*sings*] Larded all with sweet flowers,
Which bewept to the grave did not go
With true-love showers.

40 KING. How do you, pretty lady?

OPH. Well, God 'ild you! They say the owl was a baker's daughter. Lord, we know what we are, but know not what we may be. God be at your table!

KING. Conceit upon her father.

OPH. Pray you, let's have no words of this; but when they ask you what it means, say you this:

[*Sings.*] To-morrow is Saint Valentine's day,
50 All in the morning betime,
And I a maid at your window,
To be your Valentine.
Then up he rose, and donned his clo'es,
And dupped the chamber door.
Let in the maid, that out a maid
Never departed more.

KING. Pretty Ophelia!

OPH. Indeed, la, without an oath I'll make an end on't:

[*Sings.*] By Gis and by Saint Charity, 60
Alack and fie for shame!
Young men will do't if they come to't,
By Cock, they are to blame.

Quoth she, "Before you tumbled me,
You promised me to wed."

He answers

So would I ha' done by yonder sun,
And thou hadst not come to my bed.

KING. How long hath she been thus?

OPH. I hope all will be well. We must be patient, but I cannot choose but weep to think they would lay him i' the cold ground. My brother shall know of it; and so I thank you for your good counsel. Come, my coach! Good 70 night, ladies; good night, sweet ladies; good night, good night. *Exit.*

KING. Follow her close; give her good watch, I pray you. [*Exit* HORATIO.]

O, this is the poison of deep grief; it springs
All from her father's death—and now behold!
O Gertrude, Gertrude,
When sorrows come, they come not single spies,
But in battalions: first, her father slain;
Next, your son gone, and he most violent author 80
Of his own just remove; the people muddied,
Thick and unwholesome in their thoughts and whispers
For good Polonius' death; and we have done but greenly
In hugger-mugger to inter him; poor Ophelia
Divided from herself and her fair judgment,
Without the which we are pictures, or mere beasts;
Last, and as much containing as all these,
Her brother is in secret come from France,
Feeds on his wonder, keeps himself in clouds,
And wants not buzzers to infect his ear 90
With pestilent speeches of his father's death,
Wherein necessity, of matter beggared,
Will nothing stick our person to arraign

25 **cockle hat and staff** the insignia of a pilgrim 26 **shoon** shoes 27 **imports** means 37 **larded** decked 41 **'ild yield,** *i.e.,* reward 45 **conceit** thought 50 **betime** early 54 **dupped** opened

60 **Gis** Jesus 81 **muddied** confused 83 **greenly** unskilfully **84 hugger-mugger** surreptitious haste 89 **wonder** uncertainly **in clouds** secluded 90 **buzzers** those who repeat rumors 93 **nothing stick** hesitate not at all **arraign** accuse

In ear and ear. O my dear Gertrude, this,
Like to a murdering-piece, in many places
Gives me superfluous death. *A noise within*

QUEEN. Alack, what noise is this?

KING. Where are my Switzers? Let them guard the door.

Enter a MESSENGER.

What is the matter?

GENTLEMAN. Save yourself, my lord;
The ocean, overpeering of his list,
100 Eats not the flats with more impiteous haste
Than young Laertes, in a riotous head,
O'erbears your officers. The rabble call him lord,
And, as the world were now but to begin,
Antiquity forgot, custom not known,
The ratifiers and props of every word,
They cry, "Choose we; Laertes shall be king!"
Caps, hands, and tongues applaud it to the clouds,
"Laertes shall be king, Laertes king!"
A noise within

QUEEN. How cheerfully on the false trail they cry!
110 O, this is counter, you false Danish dogs!

KING. The doors are broke.

Enter LAERTES *with others.*

LAERTES. Where is this king? Sirs, stand you all without.

DANES. No, let's come in.

LAERTES. I pray you, give me leave.

DANES. We will, we will.
[*They retire without the door.*]

LAERTES. I thank you; keep the door. O thou vile king,
Give me my father.

QUEEN. Calmly, good Laertes.

LAERTES. That drop of blood that's calm proclaims me bastard,
Cries cuckold to my father, brands the harlot
Even here between the chaste unsmirchéd brow
Of my true mother.

KING. What is the cause, Laertes, 120
That thy rebellion looks so giant-like?
Let him go, Gertrude, do not fear our person;
There's such divinity doth hedge a king,
That treason can but peep to what it would,
Acts little of his will. Tell me, Laetres,
Why thou art thus incensed. Let him go, Gertrude.
Speak, man.

LAERTES. Where is my father?

KING. Dead.

QUEEN. But not by him.

KING. Let him demand his fill.

LAERTES. How came he dead? I'll not be juggled with.
To hell allegiance, vows to the blackest devil, 130
Conscience and grace to the profoundest pit!
I dare damnation. To this point I stand,
That both the worlds I give to negligence,
Let come what comes, only I'll be revenged
Most throughly for my father.

KING. Who shall stay you?

LAERTES. My will, not all the world's:
And for my means, I'll husband them so well,
They shall go far with little.

KING. Good Laertes,
If you desire to know the certainty
Of your dear father's death, is't writ in your revenge 140
That swoopstake you will draw both friend and foe,
Winner and loser?

LAERTES. None but his enemies.

KING. Will you know them then?

LAERTES. To his good friends thus wide I'll ope my arms,
And, like the kind life-rendering pelican,
Repast them with my blood.

KING. Why, now you speak
Like a good child and a true gentleman.
That I am guiltless of your father's death,
And am most sensibly in grief for it,

95 **murdering-piece** piece of artillery loaded so as to scatter its shot 97 **Switzers** Swiss guards 99 **overpeering** pressing across **list** boundary 100 **impiteous** pitiless 101 **head** armed band 105 **word** pledge 110 **counter** following the scent backwards

122 **fear** fear for 124 **peep** have a glimpse of **would** desires 132 **to this point I stand** I stand firm on this one thing 133 **both the worlds** *i.e.*, this and the next **give to negligence** am indifferent to 135 **thoroughly** thoroughly 141 **swoopstake** at random 145 **life-rendering** *i.e.*, because it was supposed to feed its young on its own blood 146 **repast** feed 149 **sensibly** feelingly

150 It shall as level to your judgment 'pear
As day does to your eye.
[*A noise within*] Let her come in.
LAERTES. How now, what noise is that?

Enter OPHELIA.

O heat, dry up my brains; tears seven-times salt,
Burn out the sense and virtue of mine eye!
By heaven, thy madness shall be paid with weight,
Till our scale turn the beam. O rose of May,
Dead maid, kind sister, sweet Ophelia!
O heavens, is't possible a young maid's wits
Should be as mortal as an old man's life?
160 Nature is fine in love, and where 'tis fine,
It sends some precious instance of itself
After the thing it loves.
OPH. [*sings*] They bore him barefaced on the bier,
(Hey non nonny, nonny, hey nonny)
And in his grave rained many a tear—
Fare you well, my dove!
LAERTES. Hadst thou thy wits, and didst persuade revenge.
It could not move thus.
OPH. You must sing "A-down a-down,
170 an you call him a-down-a."
O, how the wheel becomes it! It is the false steward, that stole his master's daughter.
LAERTES. This nothing's more than matter.
OPH. There's rosemary, that's for remembrance—pray you, love, remember; and there is pansies, that's for thoughts.
LAERTES. A document in madness, thoughts and remembrance fitted.
OPH. There's fennel for you, and colum-
180 bines; there's rue for you, and here's some for me—we may call it herb of grace o' Sundays. O, you must wear your rue with a difference. There's a daisy; I would give you some violets, but they withered all when my father died. They say a' made a good end—
[*Sings.*] For bonny sweet Robin is all my joy.

LAERTES. Thought and afflictions, passion, hell itself,
She turns to favor and to prettiness.
OPH. [*sings*]
And will a' not come again?
190 And will a' not come again?
No, no, he is dead;
Go to thy death-bed;
He never will come again.
His beard was as white as snow,
All flaxen was his poll;
He is gone, he is gone,
And we cast away moan;
God ha' mercy on his soul!
And of all Christian souls, I pray God. God be
200 wi' you. *Exit.*
LAERTES. Do you see this, O God?
KING. Laertes, I must commune with your grief,
Or you deny me right. Go but apart,
Make choice of whom your wisest friends you will,
And they shall hear and judge 'twixt you and me.
If by direct or by collateral hand
They find us touched, we will our kingdom give,
Our crown, our life, and all that we call ours,
To you in satisfaction; but if not,
210 Be you content to lend your patience to us,
And we shall jointly labor with your soul
To give it due content.
LAERTES. Let this be so.
His means of death, his obscure funeral,
No trophy, sword, nor hatchment o'er his bones,
No noble rite nor formal ostentation,
Cry to be heard, as 'twere from heaven to earth,
That I must call't in question.
KING. So you shall,
And where the offence is let the great axe fall.
I pray you, go with me. *Exeunt.*

156 **beam** ballance 160 **fine** sensitive 161 **instance** token 173 **nothing** nonsense **matter** sense 177 **document** piece of instruction

188 **favor** beauty 195 **poll** head 202 **commune with** share 205 **collateral hand** indirect means 207 **touched** involved 214 **hatchment** coat of arms 215 **ostentation** ceremony 216 **cry to be heard** demand explanation 218 **axe** *i.e.,* of vengeance

Scene Six

Enter HORATIO *with an* ATTENDANT

HOR. What are they that would speak with me?

SERVANT. Seafaring men, sir; they say they have letters for you.

HOR. Let them come in. [*Exit* ATTENDANT.]
I do not know from what part of the world
I should be greeted, if not from Lord Hamlet.

Enter SAILORS.

SAILOR. God bless you, sir.

10 HOR. Let him bless thee too.

SAIL. A' shall, sir, an't please him. There's a letter for you, sir; it came from the ambassador that was bound for England; if your name be Horatio, as I am let to know it is.

HOR. [*reads*] "Horatio, when thou shalt have overlooked this, give these fellows some means to the king; they have letters for him. Ere we were two days old at sea, a pirate of very warlike appointment gave us chase. Finding ourselves too slow of sail, we put on a compelled valor, and in the grapple I boarded them; on the instant they got clear of our ship, 20 so I alone became their prisoner. They have dealt with me like thieves of mercy, but they knew what they did; I am to do a good turn for them. Let the king have the letters I have sent, and repair thou to me with as much speed as thou wouldest fly death. I have words to speak in thine ear will make thee dumb, yet are they much too light for the bore of the matter. These good fellows will bring thee 30 where I am. Rosencrantz and Guildenstern hold their course for England. Of them I have much to tell thee. Farewell.

'He that thou knowest thine, HAMLET.'

Come, I will give you way for these your letters,
And do't the speedier that you may direct me
To him from whom you brought them.

Exeunt.

Scene Seven

Enter KING *and* LAERTES.

KING. Now must your conscience my acquittance seal,
And you must put me in your heart for friend,
Sith you have heard, and with a knowing ear,
That he which hath your noble father slain
Pursued my life.

LAERTES. It well appears. But tell me
Why you proceeded not against these feats
So crimeful and so capital in nature,
As by your safety, wisdom, all things else,
You mainly were stirred up.

KING. O, for two special reasons,
Which may to you perhaps seem much unsinewed, 10
But yet to me they're strong. The queen his mother
Lives almost by his looks, and for myself—

23 **thieves of mercy** merciful robbers
29 **bore** caliber, *i.e.,* importance

My virtue or my plague, be it either which—
She is so conjunctive to my life and soul
That, as the star moves not but in his sphere,
I could not but by her. The other motive
Why to a public count I might not go
Is the great love the general gender bear him,
Who, dipping all his faults in their affection,
Would, like the spring that turneth wood to stone, 20
Convert his gyves to graces; so that my arrows,
Too slightly timbered far so loud a wind,
Would have reverted to my bow again,
And not where I had aimed them.

LAERTES. And so have I a noble father lost,
A sister driven into desp'rate terms,
Whose worth, if praises may go back again,
Stood challenger on mount of all the age
For her perfections; but my revenge will come.

KING. Break not your sleeps for that; you must not think 30
That we are made of stuff so flat and dull
That we can let our beard be shook with danger
And think it pastime. You shortly shall hear more;
I loved your father, and we love ourself,
And that, I hope, will teach you to imagine—

Enter a MESSENGER *with letters.*

How now! what news?

MESSENGER. Letters, my lord, from Hamlet;
This to your majesty, this to the queen.

KING. From Hamlet? who brought them?

MES. Sailors, my lord, they say; I saw them not.
They were given me by Claudio; he received them 40
Of him that brought them.

KING. Laertes, you shall hear them.
Leave us. *Exit* MESSENGER.

[*Reads.*]"High and mighty, You shall know I am set naked on your kingdom. Tomorrow shall I beg leave to see your kingly eyes, when I shall, first asking your pardon thereunto, recount the occasion of my sudden and more strange return.

HAMLET."

What should this mean? Are all the rest come back? 50
Or is it some abuse, and no such thing?

LAERTES. Know you the hand?

KING. 'Tis Hamlet's character. "Naked"—
And in a postscript here, he says "alone."
Can you devise me?

LAERTES. I am lost in it, my lord; but let him come.
It warms the very sickness in my heart
That I shall live and tell him to his teeth,
"Thus diddest thou.'

KING. If it be so, Laertes—
As how should it be so? how otherwise?— 60
Will you be ruled by me?

LAERTES. Ay, my lord;
So you will not o'errule me to a peace.

KING. To thine own peace. If he be now returned,
As checking at his voyage, and that he means
No more to undertake it, I will work him
To an exploit, now ripe in my device,
Under the which he shall not choose but fall:
And for his death no wind of blame shall breathe,
But even his mother shall uncharge the practice,
And call it accident.

LAERTES. My lord, I will be ruled; 70
The rather if you could devise it so
That I might be the organ.

KING. It falls right.
You have been talked of since your travel much,
And that in Hamlet's hearing, for a quality
Wherein they say you shine; your sum of parts
Did not together pluck such envy from him
As did that one, and that, in my regard,
Of the unworthiest siege.

LAERTES. What part is that, my lord?

KING. A very riband in the cap of youth,
Yet needful too, for youth no less becomes 80
The light and careless livery that it wears
Than settled age his sables and his weeds,
Importing health and graveness. Two months since,

27 **go back again** *i.e.,* to what she once was 28 **on mount** on high 29 **for** to defend

51 **abuse** deceit 53 **character** handwriting 64 **checking at** fighting shy of 69 **uncharge** fail to suspect **practice** plot 72 **organ** instrument 75 **parts** talents 78 **siege** rank 79 **riband** ornament 80 **becomes** is appropriately clad in 81 **livery** costume 82 **sables** blacks (or furs) **weeds** garments

Here was a gentleman of Normandy.
I have seen myself, and served against, the French,
And they can well on horseback, but this gallant
Had witchcraft in't; he grew unto his seat,
And to such wondrous doing brought his horse
As he had been incorpsed and demi-natured
With the brave beast, so far he topped my thought
90 That I, in forgery of shapes and tricks,
Come short of what he did.

LAERTES. A Norman was't?

KING. A Norman.

LAERTES. Upon my life, Lamord.

KING. The very same.

LAERTES. I know him well; he is the brooch indeed
And gem of all the nation.

KING. He made confession of you,
And gave you such a masterly report
For art and exercise in your defence,
100 And for your rapier most especial,
That he cried out 'twould be a sight indeed
If one could match you; the scrimers of their nation
He swore had neither motion, guard, nor eye,
If you opposed them. Sir, this report of his
Did Hamlet so envenom with his envy,
That he could nothing do but wish and beg
Your sudden coming o'er to play with him.
Now, out of this—

LAERTES. What out of this, my lord?

KING. Laertes, was your father dear to you?
110 Or are you like the painting of a sorrow,
A face without a heart?

LAERTES. Why ask you this?

KING. Not that I think you did not love your father,
But that I know love is begun by time,
And that I see, in passages of proof,
Time qualifies the spark and fire of it.
There lives within the very flame of love
A kind of wick or snuff that will abate it
And nothing is at a like goodness still,
For goodness, growing to a plurisy,
120 Dies in his own too-much; that we would do
We should do when we would, for this "would" changes
And hath abatements and delays as many
As there are tongues, are hands, are accidents,
And then this "should" is like a spendthrift sigh,
That hurts by easing. But, to the quick of the ulcer—
Hamlet comes back; what would you undertake
To show yourself in deed your father's son
More than in words?

LAERTES. To cut his throat i' the church.

KING. No place, indeed, should murder sanctuarize;
Revenge should have no bounds. But, good Laertes,
130 Will you do this, keep close within your chamber.
Hamlet returned shall know you are come home;
We'll put on those shall praise your excellence,
And set a double varnish on the fame
The Frenchman gave you, bring you in fine together
And wager on your heads. He, being remiss,
Most generous, and free from all contriving,
Will not peruse the foils, so that with ease,
Or with a little shuffling, you may choose
140 A sword unbated, and in a pass of practice
Requite him for your father.

LAERTES. I will do't,
And for that purpose I'll anoint my sword.
I bought an unction of a mountebank,
So mortal, that but dip a knife in it,
Where it draws blood no cataplasm so rare,
Collected from all simples that have virtue
Under the moon, can save the thing from death
With this contagion, that, if I gall him slightly,
That is but scratched withal. I'll touch my point

89 **incorpsed and demi-natured** united and made half 90 **topped** exceeded 91 **forgery** invention, imagination 95 **brooch** ornament 98 **masterly report** report of mastery or skill 99 **art** skill **exercise** agility 102 **scrimers** fencers 114 **passages of proof** incidents which test 115 **qualifies** weakens 117 **snuff** burnt part of the wick

118 **still** always 119 **plurisy** excess 120 **that** what 125 **hurts by easing** damages while it gives relief (because sighs were supposed to draw blood from the heart) **quick** sensitive part 135 **in fine** eventually 137 **contriving** plotting 138 **peruse** scan carefully 139 **unbated** not blunted 143 **unction** ointment **mountebank** pedlar of patent medicines 144 **mortal** deadly 145 **cataplasm** poultice 146 **simples** herbs 148 **withal** with 149 **gall** scratch

It may be death.

150 KING. Let's further think of this,
Weigh what convenience both of time and means
May fit us to our shape. If this should fail,
And that our drift look through our bad performance,
'Twere better not assayed; therefore this project
Should have a back or second that might hold
If this should blast in proof. Soft, let me see;
We'll make a solemn wager on your cunnings.
I ha't;
When in your motion you are hot and dry—
160 As make your bouts more violent to that end—
And that he calls for drink, I'll have preferred him
A chalice for the nonce, whereon but sipping,
If he by chance escape your venomed stuck,
Our purpose may hold there.

Enter QUEEN.

But stay, what noise?

QUEEN. One woe doth tread upon another's heel,
So fast they follow; your sister's drowned, Laertes.

LAERTES. Drowned! O where?

QUEEN. There is a willow grows askant the brook
That shows his hoary leaves in the glassy stream;
170 Therewith fantastic garlands did she make
Of crowflowers, nettles, daisies, and long purples
That liberal shepherds give a grosser name,
But our cold maids do dead men's fingers call them.
There, on the pendent boughs her crownet weeds
Clambering to hang, an envious sliver broke,
When down her weedy trophies and herself
Fell in the weeping brook. Her clothes spread wide,
And mermaid-like awhile they bore her up,
Which time she chanted snatches of old lauds,
As one incapable of her own distress, 180
Or like a creature native and indued
Unto that element; but long it could not be
Till that her garments, heavy with their drink,
Pulled the poor wretch from her melodious lay
To muddy death.

LAERTES. Alas then, she is drowned?

QUEEN. Drowned, drowned.

LAERTES. Too much of water hast thou, poor Ophelia,
And therefore I forbid my tears; but yet
It is our trick; nature her custom holds,
Let shame say what it will; when these are gone, 190
The woman will be out. Adieu, my lord;
I have a speech of fire, that fain would blaze,
But that this folly douts it. *Exit.*

KING. Let's follow, Gertrude.
How much I had to do to calm his rage!
Now fear I this will give it start again;
Therefore let's follow. *Exeunt.*

152 **shape** plan 153 **drift** purpose **look** become visible 155 **back** supporter 156 **blast** come to ruin **in proof** when put to the test 157 **cunnings** skills 159 **motion** activity 161 **preferred** offered 162 **chalice** cup **nonce** occasion 163 **stuck** thrust 168 **askant** alongside

174 **pendent** hanging 175 **crownet** coronet **sliver** bough 179 **lauds** hymns 180 **incapable** unconscious 181 **indued** accustomed 182 **that element** *i.e.,* water 193 **douts** puts out

ACT FIVE *Scene One*

Enter two CLOWNS [*with spades, etc.*]

FIRST CLOWN. Is she to be buried in Christian burial when she wilfully seeks her own salvation?

SECOND CLOWN. I tell thee she is; therefore make her grave straight. The crowner hath sat on her, and finds it Christian burial.

FIRST CL. How can that be, unless she drowned herself in her own defence?

SECOND CL. Why, 'tis found so.

10 FIRST CL. It must be *se offendendo;* it cannot be else. For here lies the point: if I drown myself wittingly, it argues an act, and an act hath three branches; it is, to act, to do, to perform: argal, she drowned herself wittingly.

SECOND CL. Nay, but hear you, goodman delver—

FIRST CL. Give me leave. Here lies the water—good; here stands the man—good; if the man go to this water and drown himself, it is, will

20 he nill he, he goes—mark you that; but if the water come to him and drown him, he drowns not himself; argal, he that is not guilty of his own death shortens not his own life.

SECOND CL. But is this law?

FIRST CL. Ay, marry, is't—crowner's quest law.

SECOND CL. Will you ha' the truth on't? If this had not been a gentlewoman, she should have been buried out o' Christian burial.

FIRST CL. Why, there thou say'st; and the

30 more pity that great folk should have countenance in this world to drown or hang themselves, more than their even Christian. Come, my spade; there is no ancient gentlemen but gardeners, ditchers, and gravemakers—they hold up Adam's profession.

SECOND CL. Was he a gentleman?

FIRST CL. A' was the first that ever bore arms.

SECOND CL. Why, he had none.

FIRST CL. What, art a heathen? How dost 40 thou understand the Scripture? The Scripture says Adam digged; could he dig without arms? I'll put another question to thee; if thou answerest me not to the purpose, confess thyself—

SECOND CL. Go to.

FIRST CL. What is he that builds stronger than either the mason, the shipwright, or the carpenter?

SECOND CL. The gallowsmaker, for that frame outlives a thousand tenants. 50

FIRST CL. I like thy wit well, in good faith; the gallows does well, but how does it well? it does well to those that do ill; now, thou dost ill to say the gallows is built stronger than the church; argal, the gallows may do well to thee. To't again, come.

SECOND CL. "Who builds stronger than a mason, a shipwright, or a carpenter?"

FIRST CL. Ay, tell me that and unyoke.

SECOND CL. Marry, now I can tell. 60

FIRST CL. To't.

SECOND CL. Mass, I cannot tell.

Enter HAMLET *and* HORATIO *afar off.*

FIRST CL. Cudgel thy brains no more about it, for your dull ass will not mend his pace with beating, and when you are asked this question next, say "a gravemaker;" the houses he makes lasts till doomsday. Go, get thee to Yaughan, and fetch me a stoup of liquor.

[*Exit* SECOND CLOWN.
He digs, and] *sings.*

5 **straight** immediately **crowner** coroner 10 **se offendendo** a blunder for 'se defendendo,' in self-defence 14 **argal** ergo, therefore 16 **delver** digger 19 **will he nill he** willy-nilly 25 **quest** inquest 29 **there thou say'st** there you're saying something 30 **countenance** permission 32 **even** fellow

37 **bore arms** (a pun) had a coat of arms, the sign of gentle birth 59 **unyoke** make an end to it 68 **stoup** mug

In youth when I did love, did love,
70 Methought it was very sweet
To contract—O—the time for—a—my behove,
O—methought there—a—was nothing—a—meet.

HAMLET. Has this fellow no feeling of his business, that a' sings in gravemaking?

HOR. Custom hath made it in him a property of easiness.

HAMLET. 'Tis e'en so; the hand of little employment hath the daintier sense.

FIRST CL. *Sings.*

But age with his stealing steps
80 Hath clawed me in his clutch,
And hath shipped me until the land,
As if I had never been such.

[*Throws up a skull.*]

HAMLET. That skull had a tongue in it, and could sing once; how the knave jowls it to the ground, as if it were Cain's jawbone, that did the first murder! This might be the pate of a politician, which this ass now o'er-reaches; one that would circumvent God, might it not?

HOR. It might, my lord.

90 HAMLET. Or of a courtier, which could say "Good morrow, sweet lord! How dost thou, good lord?" This might be my lord such-a-one, that praised my lord such-a-one's horse, when a' meant to beg it—might it not?

HOR. Ay, my lord.

HAMLET. Why, e'en so—and now my Lady Worm's, chapless, and knocked about the mazzard with a sexton's spade; here's fine revolution, and we had the trick to see't. Did these 100 bones cost no more the breeding, but to play at loggats with 'em? mine ache to think on't.

FIRST CL. *Sings.*

A pickaxe and a spade, a spade,
For and a shrouding-sheet;
O, a pit of clay for to be made
For such a guest is meet.

[*Throws up another skull.*]

HAMLET. There's another; why may not that be the skull of a lawyer? Where be his quiddities now, his quillets, his cases, his tenures, and his tricks? why does he suffer this mad 110 knave now to knock him about the sconce with a dirty shovel, and will not tell him of his action of battery? Hum! This fellow might be in't time a great buyer of land, with his statutes, his recognizances, his fines, his double vouchers, his recoveries; is this the fine of his fines, and the recovery of his recoveries, to have his fine pate full of fine dirt? will his vouchers vouch him no more of his purchases, and double ones too, than the length and breadth of a pair of inden- 120 tures? The very conveyances of his lands will scarcely lie in this box, and must the inheritor himself have no more, ha?

HOR. Not a jot more, my lord.

HAMLET. Is not parchment made of sheepskins?

HOR. Ay, my lord, and of calfskins too.

HAMLET. They are sheep and calves which seek out assurance in that. I will speak to this fellow. Whose grave's this, sirrah? 130

FIRST CL. Mine, sir.

O, a pit of clay for to be made [*Sings.*]
For such a guest is meet.

HAMLET. I think it be thine indeed, for thou liest in't.

FIRST CL. You lie out on't, sir, and therefore 'tis not yours; for my part, I do not lie in't, yet it is mine.

HAMLET. Thou dost lie in't, to be in't and say it is thine; 'tis for the dead, not for the 140 quick; therefore thou liest.

FIRST CL. 'Tis a quick lie, sir; 'twill away again from me to you.

HAMLET. What man dost thou dig it for?

FIRST CL. For no man, sir.

HAMLET. What woman, then?

FIRST CL. For none, neither.

HAMLET. Who is to be buried in't?

FIRST CL. One that was a woman, sir; but, rest her soul, she's dead. 150

HAMLET. How absolute the knave is! we

71 **behove** benefit 72 **meet** fitting 75 **custom** habit **property** characteristic 76 **easiness** indifference 78 **dantier sense** finer feeling 81 **intil** into 84 **jowls** flings 87 **o'erreaches** gets the better of 97 **chapless** without a jawbone **mazzard** pate 101 **loggats** a game like bowls 108 **quiddities** definitions **quillets** quibbles 109 **tenures** terms of holding land 111 **sconce** skull 113 **battery** assault 114 **statues and recognisances** two different kinds of bonds 116 **fines . . . double vouchers** various types of procedure for transferring land **fine** end 120 **indentures** legal documents on parchment 121 **conveyances** deeds 129 **seek out assurance** put their trust 136 **out on't** outside it 141 **quick** living 151 **absolute** positive

must speak by the card, or equivocation will undo us. By the Lord, Horatio, this three years I have took note of it, the age is grown so picked that the toe of the peasant comes so near the heel of the courtier he galls his kibe. How long hast thou been gravemaker?

FIRST CL. Of all the days i' the year, I came to't that day that our last king Hamlet over-
160 came Fortinbras.

HAMLET. How long is that since?

FIRST CL. Cannot you tell that? every fool can tell that; it was the very day that young Hamlet was born—he that is mad and sent into England.

HAMLET. Ay, marry, why was he sent into England?

FIRST CL. Why, because a' was mad: a' shall recover his wits there or, if a' do not, 'tis no
170 great matter there.

HAMLET. Why?

FIRST CL. 'Twill not be seen in him there; there the men are as mad as he.

HAMLET. How came he mad?

FIRST CL. Very strangely, they say.

HAMLET. How strangely?

FIRST CL. Faith, e'en with losing his wits.

HAMLET. Upon what ground?

FIRST CL. Why, here in Denmark: I have
180 been sexton here, man and boy, thirty years.

HAMLET. How long will a man lie i' the earth ere he rot?

FIRST CL. Faith, if a' be not rotten before a' die—as we have many pocky corses nowadays that will scarce hold the laying in—he will last you some eight year or nine year. A tanner will last you nine year.

HAMLET. Why he more than another?

FIRST CL. Why sir, his hide is so tanned with
190 his trade that a' will keep out water a great while; and your water is a sore decayer of your whoreson dead body. Here's a skull now; this skull hath lien yon i' the earth three-and-twenty years.

HAMLET. Whose was it?

FIRST CL. A whoreson mad fellow's it was; whose do you think it was?

HAMLET. Nay, I know not.

FIRST CL. A pestilence on him for a mad rogue! a' poured a flagon of Rhenish on my 200 head once. This same skull, sir, was Yorick's skull, the king's jester.

HAMLET. This?

FIRST CL. E'en that.

HAMLET. Let me see. [*Takes the skull.*] Alas, poor Yorick! I knew him, Horatio: a fellow of infinite jest, of most excellent fancy; he hath borne me on his back a thousand times, and now how abhorred in my imagination it is! my gorge rises at it. Here hung those lips 210 that I have kissed I know not how oft. Where be your gibes now? your gambols, your songs, your flashes of merriment that were wont to set the table on a roar? Not one now to mock your own grinning? quite chapfallen? Now get you to my lady's chamber, and tell her, let her paint an inch thick, to this favor she must come; make her laugh at that. Prithee, Horatio, tell me one thing.

HOR. What's that, my lord? 220

HAMLET. Dost thou think Alexander looked o' this fashion i' the earth?

HOR. E'en so.

HAMLET. And smelt so? pah!

[*Puts down the skull.*]

HOR. E'en so, my lord.

HAMLET. To what base uses we may return, Horatio! Why may not imagination trace the noble dust of Alexander till a' find it stopping a bunghole?

HOR. 'Twere to consider too curiously to 230 consider so.

HAMLET. No, faith, not a jot; but to follow him thither with modesty enough, and likelihood to lead it, as thus: Alexander died, Alexander was buried, Alexander returneth to dust; the dust is earth, of earth we make loam, and why of that loam whereto he was converted might they not stop a beer barrel?

Imperious Cæsar, dead and turned to clay,
Might stop a hole to keep the wind away. 240

152 **by the card** by the compass, precisely **equivocation** double meanings 155 **picked** fastidious 156 **galls his kibe** scrapes the chilblains on his heels 178 **upon what ground** for what cause 184 **pocky** diseased 185 **hold the laying in** last till burial

200 **Rhenish** Rhine wine 215 **chapfallen** (1) jawless (2) dejected 217 **favor** appearance 233 **modesty** moderation

O, that that earth which kept the world in awe
Should patch a wall to expel the winter's flaw!
But soft, but soft awhile; here comes the king,

Enter KING, QUEEN, LAERTES, *and a Coffin, with Lords Attendant,* [*a* DOCTOR OF DIVINITY *following.*]

The queen, the courtiers. Who is this they follow?
And with such maiméd rites? This doth betoken
The corse they follow did with desperate hand
Fordo its own life; 'twas of some estate.
Couch we awhile, and mark.
[*Retiring with* HORATIO.]

LAERTES. What ceremony else?

HAMLET. That is Laertes,
A very noble youth; mark. 250

LAERTES. What ceremony else?

DOCTOR. Her obsequies have been as far enlarged
As we have warranty. Her death was doubtful
And, but that great command o'ersways the order,
She should in ground unsanctified have lodged
Till the last trumpet; for charitable prayers,
Shards, flints and pebbles should be thrown on her:
Yet here she is allowed her virgin crants,
Her maiden strewments, and the bringing home
Of bell and burial. 260

LAERTES. Must there no more be done?

DOCTOR. No more be done.
We should profane the service of the dead
To sing a requiem and such rest to her
As to peace-parted souls.

LAERTES. Lay her i' the earth,
And from her fair and unpolluted flesh
May violets spring! I tell thee, churlish priest,
A ministering angel shall my sister be,
When thou liest howling.

HAMLET. What, the fair Ophelia!

QUEEN. Sweets to the sweet; farewell!
[*Scattering flowers*]
I hoped thou shouldst have been my Hamlet's wife; 270
I thought thy bride-bed to have decked, sweet maid,
And not have strewed thy grave.

LAERTES. O, treble woe
Fall ten times treble on that curséd head
Whose wicked deed thy most ingenious sense
Deprived thee of! Hold off the earth awhile,
Till I have caught her once more in mine arms; *Leaps in the grave.*
Now pile your dust upon the quick and dead,
Till of this flat a mountain you have made
To o'ertop old Pelion or the skyish head
Of blue Olympus.

HAMLET. [*advancing*] What is he whose grief 280
Bears such an emphasis, whose phrase of sorrow
Conjures the wandering stars and makes them stand
Like wonder-wounded hearers? This is I,
Hamlet the Dane. *Leaps in after* LAERTES.

LAERTES. The devil take thy soul!
[*Grappling with him.*]

HAMLET. Thou pray'st not well.
I prithee take thy fingers from my throat,
For, though I am not splenitive and rash,
Yet have I in me something dangerous,
Which let thy wisdom fear. Hold off thy hand!

KING. Pluck them asunder.

QUEEN. Hamlet, Hamlet! 290

ALL. Gentlemen—

HOR. Good my lord, be quiet.
[*The Attendants part them, and they come out of the grave.*]

HAMLET. Why, I will fight with him upon this theme
Until my eyelids will no longer wag.

QUEEN. O my son, what theme?

HAMLET. I loved Ophelia; forty thousand brothers

245 **maiméd rites** incomplete ceremonial 247 **fordo** destroy **estate** rank 248 **couch** hide 253 **have warranty** are permitted **doubtful** uncertain 254 **great command** *i.e.,* that of the King **o'ersways** overrules 256 **for** instead of 257 **shards** broken pottery 258 **crants** garland 259 **strewments** strewing of flowers on the grave **bringing home** laying to rest

274 **sense** senses 277 **quick** living 279 **Pelion . . . Olympus** (according to the Greek legend, the Titans piled Mt. Pelion on Mt. Ossa in their attempt to storm Mt. Olympus) 287 **splenitive** excitable

Could not with all their quantity of love
Make up my sum. What wilt thou do for her?
KING. O, he is mad, Laertes.
QUEEN. For love of God, forbear him.
HAMLET. 'Swounds, show me what thou'lt do:
300 Woo't weep? woo't fight? woo't fast? woo't tear thyself?
Woo't drink up eisel? eat a crocodile?
I'll do't. Dost thou come here to whine,
To outface me with leaping in her grave?
Be buried quick with her, and so will I:
And if thou prate of mountains, let them throw
Millions of acres on us, till our ground,
Singeing his pate against the burning zone,
Make Ossa like a wart! Nay, an thou'lt mouth,
I'll rant as well as thou.
310 QUEEN. This is mere madness:
And thus awhile the fit will work on him;
Anon, as patient as the female dove
When that her golden couplets are disclosed,
His silence will sit drooping.
HAMLET. Hear you, sir;
What is the reason that you use me thus?
I loved you ever: but it is no matter;
Let Hercules himself do what he may,
The cat will mew, and dog will have his day.
Exit.
KING. I pray you, good Horatio, wait upon him. *Exit* HORATIO.
[*To* LAERTES] Strengthen your patience in our last night's speech; 320
We'll put the matter to the present push.
Good Gertrude, set some watch over your son.
This grave shall have a living monument:
An hour of quiet shortly shall we see;
Till then, in patience our proceeding be.
Exeunt.

Scene Two

Enter HAMLET *and* HORATIO.

HAMLET. So much for this, sir; now shall you see the other.
You do remember all the circumstance?
HOR. Remember it, my lord!
HAMLET. Sir, in my heart there was a kind of fighting
That would not let me sleep; methought I lay
Worse than the mutines in the bilboes. Rashly,
And praised be rashness for it—let us know
Our indiscretion sometimes serves us well
When our deep plots do pall, and that should learn us
10 There's a divinity that shapes our ends,
Rough-hew them how we will—
HOR. That is most certain.
HAMLET. Up from my cabin,
My sea-gown scarfed about me, in the dark
Groped I to find out them, had my desire,
Fingered their packet, and in fine withdrew
To mine own room again, making so bold,
My fears forgetting manners, to unseal
Their grand commission; where I found, Horatio—
O royal knavery!—an exact command,
Larded with many several sorts of reasons, 20
Importing Denmark's health and England's too,
With, ho! such bugs and goblins in my life,
That on the supervise, no leisure bated,
No, not to stay the grinding of the axe,
My head should be struck off.
HOR. Is't possible?
HAMLET. Here's the commission; read it at more leisure.
But wilt thou hear now how I did proceed?
HOR. I beseech you.

299 **forbear him** leave him alone 302 **eisel** vinegar 304 **outface** outdo 6 **mutines** mutineers **bilboes** irons 9 **pall** fail

313 **couplets** twins **disclosed** hatched 321 **present push** immediate test 15 **fine** conclusion 20 **larded** adorned 21 **importing** concerning 22 **bugs** bugbears 23 **supervise** perusal **bated** subtracted

HAMLET. Being thus benetted round with vallanies—
Or I could make a prologue to my brains, 30
They had begun the play—I sat me down,
Devised a new commission, wrote it fair;
I once did hold it, as our statists do,
A baseness to write fair, and labored much
How to forget that learning, but, sir, now
It did me yeoman's service; wilt thou know
The effect of what I wrote?

HOR. Ay, good my lord.

HAMLET. An earnest conjuration from the king,
As England was his faithful tributary,
As love between them like the palm might flourish, 40
As peace should still her wheaten garland wear
And stand a comma 'tween their amities,
And many such-like "as'es" of great charge,
That, on the view and knowing of these contents,
Without debatement further, more or less,
He should the bearers put to sudden death,
Not shriving-time allowed.

HOR. How was this sealed?

HAMLET. Why, even in that was heaven ordinant.
I had my father's signet in my purse,
Which was the model of that Danish seal; 50
Folded the writ up in the form of the other,
Subscribed it, gave't the impression, placed it safely,
The changeling never known. Now, the next day
Was our seafight, and what to this was sequent
Thou know'st already.

HOR. So Guildenstern and Rosencrantz go to't.

HAMLET. Why, man, they did make love to this employment;
They are not near my conscience; their defeat
Does by their own insinuation grow;
'Tis dangerous when the baser nature comes 60
Between the pass and fell incenséd points
Of mighty opposites.

HOR. Why, what a king is this!

HAMLET. Does it not, think thee, stand me now upon—
He that hath killed my king, and whored my mother,
Popped in between the election and my hopes,
Thrown out his angle for my proper life,
And with such cozenage—is't not perfect conscience
To quit him with this arm? and is't not to be damned
To let this canker of our nature come
In further evil? 70

HOR. It must be shortly known to him from England
What is the issue of the business there.

HAMLET. It will be short; the interim is mine,
And a man's life's no more than to say "one."
But I am very sorry, good Horatio,
That to Laertes I forgot myself;
For, by the image of my cause, I see
The portraiture of his; I'll court his favors;
But sure the bravery of his grief did put me
Into a towering passion.

HOR. Peace, who comes here? 80

Enter young OSRIC, *a courtier.*

OSRIC. Your lordship is right welcome back to Denmark.

HAMLET. I humbly thank you, sir.
[*Aside to* HORATIO.]
Dost know this water-fly?

HOR. [*aside to* HAMLET] No, my good lord.

HAMLET. [*aside to* HORATIO] Thy state is the more gracious, for 'tis a vice to know him. He hath much land, and fertile: let a beast be lord of beasts, and his crib shall stand at the king's mess; 'tis a chough, as I say, spacious in the possession of dirt. 90

OSRIC. Sweet lord, if your lordship were at

30 **or** ere, before 33 **statists** statesmen 36 **yeoman's service** sturdy service 38 **conjuration** exhortation 39 **tributary** vassal 42 **comma** connecting link 43 **charge** force 47 **shriving-time** time for confession 48 **ordinant** propitious 52 **subscribed** signed **impression** (of the seal) 54 **sequent** subsequent 58 **defeat** destruction 59 **insinuation** intrusion 60 **baser** of lower rank

61 **pass** thrust **fell** fierce 63 **does it not . . . stand me now upon** am I not now obliged 66 **angle** fishing-line **proper** own 67 **cozenage** deceit **conscience** justice 68 **quit** repay 69 **canker** cancer 73 **interim** time between 78 **portraiture** picture, portrayal 79 **bravery** display, ostentation 89 **mess** table **chough** jackdaw

leisure, I should impart a thing to you from his majesty.

HAMLET. I will receive it, sir, with all diligence of spirit. Put your bonnet to his right use; 'tis for the head.

OSRIC. I thank your lordship, it is very hot.

HAMLET. No, believe me, 'tis very cold; the wind is northerly.

100 OSRIC. It is indifferent cold, my lord, indeed.

HAMLET. But yet methinks it is very sultry and hot, or my complexion—

OSRIC. Exceedingly, my lord; it is very sultry —as 'twere—I cannot tell how. But, my lord, his majesty bade me signify to you, that a' has laid a great wager on your head; sir, this is the matter—

HAMLET. I beseech you, remember—

[HAMLET *motions him to put on his hat.*]

OSRIC. Nay, good my lord; for my ease, in 110 good faith. Sir, here is newly come to court Laertes; believe me, an absolute gentleman, full of most excellent differences, of very soft society and great showing: indeed, to speak feelingly of him, he is the card or calendar of gentry, for you shall find in him the continent of what parts a gentleman would see.

HAMLET. Sir, his definement suffers no perdition in you, though I know to divide him inventorially would dizzy the arithmetic of 120 memory, and yet but yaw neither, in respect of his quick sail. But, in the verity of extolment, I take him to be a soul of great article, and his infusion of such dearth and rareness as, to make true diction of him, his semblable is his mirror, and who else would trace him, his umbrage, nothing more.

OSRIC. Your lordship speaks most infallibly of him.

HAMLET. The concernancy, sir? why do we wrap the gentleman in our more rawer breath? 130

OSRIC. Sir?

HOR. It's not possible to understand in another tongue? You will to't, sir, really.

HAMLET. What imports the nomination of this gentleman?

OSRIC. Of Laertes?

HOR. His purse is empty already; all's golden words are spent.

HAMLET. Of him, sir.

OSRIC. I know you are not ignorant— 140

HAMLET. I would you did, sir; yet, in faith, if you did, It would not much approve me; well, sir.

OSRIC. You are not ignorant of what excellence Laertes is—

HAMLET. I dare not confess that, lest I should compare with him in excellence; but to know a man well were to know himself.

OSRIC. I mean, sir, for his weapon; but in the imputation laid on him by them, in his meed 150 he's unfellowed.

HAMLET. What's his weapon?

OSRIC. Rapier and dagger.

HAMLET. That's two of his weapons: but, well.

OSRIC. The king, sir, hath wagered with him six Barbary horses, against the which he has impawned, as I take it, six French rapiers and poniards, with their assigns, as girdle, hangers, and so. Three of the carriages, in faith, are very 160 dear to fancy, very responsive to the hilts, most delicate carriages, and of very liberal conceit.

HAMLET. What call you the carriages?

HOR. I knew you must be edified by the margent ere you had done.

OSRIC. The carriages, sir, are the hangers.

HAMLET. The phrase would be more germane to the matter, if we could carry a cannon by our sides; I would it might be hangers till then. But, on: six Barbary horses against six 170

100 **indifferent** moderately 112 **differences** accomplishments **of very soft society** pleasant company **great showing** fine appearance 114 **card or calendar** pattern **gentry** gentlemanliness 115 **continent** sum total **parts** good qualities 117 **definement** description **perdition** loss 118 **divide him inventorially** make a list of his qualities 119 **arithmetic** reckoning power **but** only **yaw** fail to hold its course, *i.e.*, come short of the mark 121 **in the verility of extolment** to praise him accurately 122 **article** scope **infusion** character 123 **dearth** scarcity **make true diction** speak truly 124 **semblable** resemblance, equal 125 **trace** copy **umbrage** shadow 129 **concernancy** purport

130 **rawer** cruder 134 **nomination** mention 142 **approve me** be to my advantage 147 **compare with** rival 150 **imputation** reputation **meed** desert **unfellowed** unequalled 158 **impawned** staked 159 **assigns** appurtenances 160 **carriages** hangers 161 **dear** pleasing **fancy** taste **responsive** well-matched 162 **liberal conceit** elegant design 164 **edified** instructed 165 **margent** marginal note 167 **germane** suitable 168 **cannon** (Hamlet is referring to 'gun-carriages')

French swords, their assigns, and three liberal-conceited carriages; that's the French bet against the Danish. Why is this "impawned," as you call it?

OSRIC. The king, sir, hath laid, sir, that in a dozen passes between yourself and him, he shall not exceed you three hits; he hath laid on twelve for nine, and it would come to immediate trial, if your lordship would vouch-safe the answer.

180 HAMLET. How if I answer no?

OSRIC. I mean, my lord, the opposition of your person in trial.

HAMLET. Sir, I will walk here in the hall. If it please his majesty, it is the breathing time of day with me. Let the foils be brought, the gentleman willing, and the king hold his purpose, I will win for him an I can; if not, I will gain nothing but my shame and the odd hits.

OSRIC. Shall I redeliver you e'en so?

190 HAMLET. To this effect, sir; after what flourish your nature will.

OSRIC. I commend my duty to your lordship.

HAMLET. Yours, yours. [*Exit* OSRIC.] He does well to commend it himself; there are no tongues else for's turn.

HOR. This lapwing runs away with the shell on his head.

HAMLET. A' did comply with his dug before a' sucked it. Thus has he—and many more of

200 the same bevy that I know the drossy age dotes on—only got the tune of the time and, out of an habit of encounter, a kind of yesty collection, which carries them through and through the most fanned and winnowed opinions, and do but blow them to their trial, the bubbles are out.

Enter a LORD

LORD. My lord, his majesty commended him to you by young Osric, who brings back to him that you attend him in the hall; he sends to

210 know if your pleasure hold to play with Laertes, or that you will take longer time.

HAMLET. I am constant to my purposes; they follow the king's pleasure; if his fitness speaks, mine is ready, now or whensoever, provided I be so able as now.

LORD. The king and queen and all are coming down.

HAMLET. In happy time.

LORD. The queen desires you to use some gentle entertainment to Laertes before you fall 220 to play.

HAMLET. She well instructs me. [*Exit* LORD.]

HOR. You will lose this wager, my lord.

HAMLET. I do not think so; since he went into France, I have been in continual practice; I shall win at the odds. But thou wouldst not think how ill all's here about my heart—but it is no matter.

HOR. Nay, good my lord—

HAMLET. It is but foolery, but it is such a kind of gain-giving as would perhaps trouble a woman.

HOR. If your mind dislike anything, obey it; I will forestall their repair hither, and say you are not fit.

HAMLET. Not a whit, we defy augury. There is special providence in the fall of a sparrow. If it be now, 'tis not to come; if it be not to come, it will be now; if it be not now, yet it will come—the readiness is all. Since no man has 240 aught of what he leaves, what is't to leave betimes? Let be.

A table prepared with flagons of wine on it. Trumpets and drums. [*Enter*] *officers with cushions. Then enter* KING, QUEEN, [OSRIC] *and all the state. Foils and daggers* [*brought in*]. [*Then enter*] LAERTES.

KING. Come, Hamlet, come and take this hand from me.

[*The* KING *puts* LAERTES' *hand into* HAMLET'S.]

HAMLET. Give me your pardon, sir. I have done you wrong,
But pardon't, as you are a gentleman.
This presence knows,
And you must needs have heard, how I am punished 250
With sore distraction. What I have done
That might your nature, honor and exception

175 **laid** stipulated 178 **for** instead of 184 **breathing** exercise 189 **redeliver you** take back your reply 196 **lapwing** a bird said to be able to run as soon as it was hatched 198 **comply** compliment 200 **drossy** degenerate 202 **encounter** formal greeting **yesty** frothy 203 **carries them through** makes them impress 204 **fanned and winnowed** experienced

220 **entertainment** greeting, welcome 231 **gaingiving** misgiving 234 **repair** coming 241 **betimes** early 248 **this presence** those present 252 **exception** objection

Roughly awake, I here proclaim was madness.
Was't Hamlet wronged Laertes? never Hamlet.
If Hamlet from himself be ta'en away,
And when he's not himself does wrong Laertes,
Then Hamlet does it not, Hamlet denies it.
Who does it then? his madness. If't be so,
Hamlet is of the faction that is wronged;
260 His madness is poor Hamlet's enemy.
Sir, in this audience,
Let my disclaiming from a purposed evil
Free me so far in your most generous thoughts,
That I have shot my arrow o'er the house,
And hurt my brother.

LAERTES. I am satisfied in nature,
Whose motive, in this case, should stir me most
To my revenge; but in my terms of honor
I stand aloof, and will no reconcilement
Till by some elder masters of known honor
270 I have a voice and precedent of peace
To keep my name ungored. But till that time
I do receive your offered love like love,
And will not wrong it.

HAMLET. I embrace it freely,
And will this brother's wager frankly play.
Give us the foils. Come on.

LAERTES. Come, one for me.

HAMLET. I'll be your foil, Laertes; in mine ignorance
Your skill shall, like a star i' the darkest night,
Stick fiery off indeed.

LAERTES. You mock me, sir.

HAMLET. No, by this hand.

KING. Give them the foils, young Osric. Cousin Hamlet,
280 You know the wager?

HAMLET. Very well, my lord;
Your grace has laid the odds o' the weaker side.

KING. I do not fear it; I have seen you both;
But since he's bettered, we have therefore odds.

LAERTES. This is too heavy; let me see another.

HAMLET. This likes me well. These foils have all a length? *Prepare to play.*

OSRIC. Ay, my good lord.

KING. Set me the stoups of wine upon that table.
If Hamlet give the first or second hit,
290 Or quit in answer of the third exchange,
Let all the battlements their ordnance fire;
The king shall drink to Hamlet's better breath,
And in the cup an union shall he throw,
Richer than that which four successive kings
In Denmark's crown have worn. Give me the cups,
And let the kettle to the trumpet speak,
The trumpet to the cannoneer without,
The cannons to the heavens, the heaven to earth,
"Now the king drinks to Hamlet." Come, begin;
300 And you, the judges, bear a wary eye.
Trumpets the while.

HAMLET. Come on, sir.

LAERTES. Come, my lord.
They play.

HAMLET. One.

LAERTES. No.

HAMLET. Judgment.

OSRIC. A hit, a very palpable hit.

Drums; flourish of trumpets; a piece goes off.

LAERTES. Well; again.

KING. Stay, give me drink. Hamlet, this pearl is thine;
Here's to thy health. Give him the cup.

HAMLET. I'll play this bout first; set it by awhile.
Come. [*They play.*] Another hit; what say you?

LAERTES. A touch, a touch, I do confess't.

KING. Our son shall win.

QUEEN. He's fat, and scant of breath.
Here, Hamlet, take my napkin, rub thy brows;
310 The queen carouses to thy fortune, Hamlet.

HAMLET. Good madam!

KING. Gertrude, do not drink.

QUEEN. I will, my lord; I pray you, pardon me. [*Drinks.*]

KINGS. [*aside*] It is the poisoned cup; it is too late.

HAMLET. I dare not drink yet, madam; by and by.

QUEEN. Come, let me wipe thy face.

LAERTES. My lord, I'll hit him now.

KING. I do not think't.

259 **of the faction** on the side 265 **in nature** *i.e.*, as a son 271 **ungored** uninjured 276 **foil** something that sets off another by contrast 278 **stick fiery off** stand out brilliantly 288 **stoups** goblets

290 **quit in answer of** score a hit in 293 **union** pearl 296 **kettle** kettledrum 308 **fat** sweaty **scant** short

LAERTES. [*aside*] And yet it is almost against my conscience.

HAMLET. Come, for the third, Laertes, you but dally;
I pray you, pass with your best violence;
320 I am afeared you make a wanton of me.

LAERTES. Say you so? come on. *Play.*

OSRIC. Nothing, neither way.

LAERTES. Have at you now!

[LAERTES *wounds* HAMLET; *then*] *in scuffling, they change rapiers,* [*and* HAMLET *wounds* LAERTES.]

KING. Part them; they are incensed.

HAMLET. Nay, come, again.

The QUEEN *falls.*

OSRIC. Look to the queen there, ho!

HORATIO. They bleed on both sides. How is it, my lord?

OSRIC. How is't, Laertes?

LAERTES. Why, as a woodcock to mine own springe,
Osric; I am justly killed with mine own treachery.

HAMLET. How does the queen?

KING. She swoons to see them bleed.

330 QUEEN. No, no, the drink, the drink—O my dear Hamlet—
The drink, the drink!—I am poisoned. [*Dies.*]

HAMLET. O villany! Ho! let the door be locked;
Treachery! seek it out.

LAERTES. It is here, Hamlet; Hamlet, thou art slain;
No medicine in the world can do thee good,
In thee there is not half an hour of life;
The treacherous instrument is in thy hand,
Unbated and envenomed. The foul practice
Hath turned itself on me; lo, here I lie,
340 Never to rise again. Thy mother's poisoned.
I can no more; the king, the king's to blame.

HAMLET. The point envenomed too!
Then, venom, to thy work. *Hurts the* KING.

ALL. Treason! treason!

KING. O yet defend me, friends; I am but hurt.

HAMLET. Here, thou incestuous, murderous, damnéd Dane,
Drink off this potion; is thy union here?
Follow my mother. KING *dies.*

LAERTES. He is justly served;
It is a poison tempered by himself.
350 Exchange forgiveness with me, noble Hamlet;
Mine and my father's death come not upon thee,
Nor thine on me! *Dies.*

HAMLET. Heaven make thee free of it! I follow thee.
I am dead, Horatio. Wretched queen, adieu!
You that look pale and tremble at this chance,
That are but mutes or audience to this act,
Had I but time—as this fell sergeant, death,
Is strict in his arrest—O, I could tell you—
But let it be.—Horatio, I am dead,
360 Thou livest; report me and my cause aright
To the unsatisfied.

HOR. Never believe it;
I am more an antique Roman than a Dane.
Here's yet some liquor left.

HAMLET. As thou'rt a man,
Give me the cup. Let go; by heaven, I'll have't.
O good Horatio, what a wounded name,
Things standing thus unknown, shall live behind me!
If thou didst ever hold me in thy heart,
Absent thee from felicity awhile,
And in this harsh world draw thy breath in pain
To tell my story.

March afar off, and shout within.

370 What warlike noise is this?

OSRIC. Young Fortinbras, with conquest come from Poland,
To the ambassadors of England gives
This warlike volley.

HAMLET. O, I die, Horatio;
The potent poison quite o'er-crows my spirit;
I cannot live to hear the news from England,
But I do prophesy the election lights
On Fortinbras; he has my dying voice;
So tell him, with the occurrents, more and less,
Which have solicited—the rest is silence. *Dies.*

HOR. Now cracks a noble heart, good night, sweet prince,
380 And flights of angels sing thee to thy rest!
Why does the drum come hither?

320 **wanton** spoilt child 327 **woodcock** the silliest of all birds **springe** snare 338 **unbated** unblunted **practice** plot

357 **sergeant** a sheriff's officer 374 **o'ercrows** overcomes 377 **voice** vote 378 **occurrents** occurrences 378 **solicited** prompted (this)

Enter FORTINBRAS, *the* ENGLISH AMBASSADORS *with drum, colors, and Attendants.*

FOR. Where is this sight?
HOR. What is it you would see?
If aught of woe or wonder, cease your search.
FOR. This quarry cries on havoc. O proud Death,
What feast is toward in thin eternal cell,
That thou so many princes at a shot
So bloodily hast struck?
FIRST AMBASSADOR. The sight is dismal,
And our affairs from England come too late;
The ears are senseless that should give us hearing,
390 To tell him his commandment is fulfilled,
That Rosencrantz and Guildenstern are dead;
Where should we have our thanks?
HOR. Not from his mouth,
Had it the ability of life to thank you;
He never gave commandment for their death.
But since, so jump upon this bloody question,
You from the Polack wars, and you from England,
Are here arrived, give order that these bodies
High on a stage be placéd to the view,
And let me speak to the yet unknowing world
400 How these things came about; so shall you hear
Of carnal, bloody and unnatural acts,
Of accidental judgments, casual slaughters,
Of deaths put on by cunning and forced cause,
And, in this upshot, purposes mistook
Fall'n on the inventors' heads: all this can I
Truly deliver.
FOR. Let us haste to hear it,
And call the noblest to the audience.
For me, with sorrow I embrace my fortune; 410
I have some rights of memory in this kingdom,
Which now to claim my vantage doth invite me.
HOR. Of that I shall have also cause to speak,
And from his mouth whose voice will draw no more;
But let this same be presently performed,
Even while men's minds are wild; lest more mischance
On plots and errors happen.
FOR. Let four captains
Bear Hamlet like a soldier to the stage,
For he was likely, had he been put on,
To have proved most royally; and for his passage 420
The soldiers' music and the rites of war
Speak loudly for him.
Take up the bodies; such a sight as this
Becomes the field, but here shows much amiss.
Go bid the soldiers shoot.

Exeunt marching; after the which, a peal of ordnance are shot off.

385 **quarry** heap of dead **cries** proclaims **havoc** slaughter 396 **jump** exactly **question** affair 399 **stage** platform 403 **casual** chance

404 **put on** brought about 411 **of memory** not forgotten 412 **vantage** opportunity 415 **presently** immediately 416 **wild** disturbed 417 **on** over and above

Review Questions

1. What is the dramatic function of the first scene?
2. Contrast the atmosphere of Act I, Scenes 1 and 2.
3. What kind of an impression does Claudius make in his first long speech? Comment on his treatment of Hamlet in this scene.
4. What is the effect of Hamlet's first soliloquy?
5. What kind of a man was Hamlet's father? How does he compare with Claudius?
6. What is Polonius' view of the world? Does his advice to his children relate to his actions?
7. Comment on Hamlet's description of the tragic flaw in his fourth speech in Act I, Scene 4. Is Hamlet flawed?
8. Describe the tactics of Claudius and Polonius in dealing with Hamlet.
9. How does Hamlet deal with these tactics?
10. What kinds of characters are Rosencrantz and Guildenstern?
11. Is Hamlet mad?
12. What does the play within the play have to say about the nature of man?
13. Why is Gertrude unable to see the Ghost?
14. What do you make of the King's inability to pray for forgiveness?
15. Why doesn't Hamlet slay the King when he is praying?
16. What does Ophelia contribute to the play?
17. How does the effect of the death of Polonius on Laertes parallel Hamlet's plight?
18. What changes take place within Hamlet during the course of the play? How do you account for them?
19. Comment on Claudius' connection with poison.
20. Is Hamlet's death in vain? Does he accomplish his objective?
21. What is the essential difference in attitude toward life between Hamlet and Claudius?
22. How do you account for Gertrude's behavior?
23. Compare the conventions of the Greek stage with the Elizabethan. How did they affect playwriting?
24. What does Shakespeare gain in the use of a freer form?
25. What part do religious beliefs play in *Hamlet?*
26. Contrast the structure of *Hamlet* with that of *Antigone*.

THE MISER

Molière (1622-1673)

TRANSLATED BY
LLOYD C. PARKS

Jean Baptiste Poquelin, later Molière, one of the outstanding comic writers of the theater, was born in Paris, the son of an upholsterer who was in the service of the king. Molière was well educated but turned his back on a legal career to join a theatrical company, which suffered great economic hardships. For twelve years "The Theater Illustrious" toured the provinces playing under all kinds of conditions. During these years, Molière perfected his skill as an actor and began writing original plays for the company. When the troupe returned to Paris in 1658 and he was invited to play before the court, Molière won the favor of Louis XIV with one of his comedies, enabling the company to establish itself on a permanent basis in Paris.

Molière wrote some thirty plays, freely borrowing from Latin comedy and the devices and characters of the Italian improvised comedy. *The Miser,* for example, is an adaptation of Aristophanes' *The Pot of Gold*. He was especially successful with his satires of the foibles and follies of his contemporaries —avarice, hypocrisy, arrogance, sanctimoniousness and all manner of pretensiousness. His shafts of wit struck home so that he was constantly at odds with the church and the professions. Among the important plays of Molière are *Tartuffe, Don Juan, The Misanthrope, The Imaginary Invalid, The Would-Be-Gentleman* and *The School for Wives*.

In seventeenth-century France, plays were staged in a rectangular hall, partially as the result of following the shape of the Hotel de Bourgogne, the most prominent place for producing plays during the previous century, and partially because of the practice of converting roofed-over tennis courts into playhouses. The Palais Royal Theater, which Cardinal Richelieu built in 1637, was a rectangular hall that accommodated about 1500 people. Some spectators sat in seats on the ground floor level and others in the galleries along the sides of the hall placed at right angles to the stage. The acting area was behind the proscenium arch, the first such arch to appear in a French theater. Molière's troupe used the Palais Royal from 1660 to 1673. Although the theater was equipped with elaborate stage scenery for spectacular effects, Molière made little use of it in his comedies. *The Miser,* which was first produced in this theater in 1668, calls simply for a hall with a garden scene in the background.

Frosine, in the 1967 Roundabout Theater production.

Richard B. Kline

"I give him the same authority over you that God gave me, and I expect you to do everything he tells you," Elise, Valère, and Harpagon from Act I of the 1965 Comedie Francaise production.

Photo Fred Fehl

Ronald Berger

ABOVE. John Lacy and Elizabeth Owens of the 1967 Roundabout Theater Company.

Two portrayals of Harpagon and Frosine:

BELOW. Hume Cronyn and Zoe Caldwell of the 1965 Minnesota Theater Company.

Harpagon and his money box:
RIGHT TOP, Michel Aumont in the Comedie Francaise production, and RIGHT BOTTOM, Hume Cronyn in the Minnesota Theater production.

Drawing by Gerda Becker, after an engraving by Van Lochen (From Macgowan & Melnitz, The Living Stage, *©1955 by Prentice-Hall, Inc.)*

In the Petit-Bourbon Theater, a room in the palace of the Duke of Bourbon where Molière's company first performed, the audience occupied the main floor and surrounding balconies while the play took place within the frame of the proscenium arch, seen here in the background. It was during this period that the proscenium arch, with its closeable curtain and changeable backdrop scenery, came into use.

Photo Fred Fehl

Characters

HARPAGON, *father of* CLEANTH *and* ELISE, *and in love with* MARIANNE
CLEANTH, HARPAGON'S *son, and in love with* MARIANNE
ELISE, HARPAGON'S *daughter, and in love with* VALÈRE
VALÈRE, ANSELM'S *son, and in love with* ELISE
MARIANNE, ANSELM'S *daughter, and in love with* CLEANTH
ANSELM, *father of* VALÈRE *and* MARIANNE
FROSINE, *a woman of intrigue*
MASTER SIMON, *a broker*
MASTER JACQUES, HARPAGON'S *coachman and cook*
LA FLÈCHE, CLEANTH'S *valet*
DAME CLAUDE, HARPAGON'S *maid*
BRINDAVOINE, HARPAGON'S *lackey*
LA MERLUCHE, HARPAGON'S *lackey*
A COMMISSARY AND HIS CLERK

SCENE: *Paris, Harpagon's house.*

THE MISER

ACT ONE

(*Enter* VALÈRE *and* ELISE.)

VALÈRE. What is it, charming Elise? Are you melancholy? After all the obliging assurances you so kindly gave of faith in me? Alas! I see you sighing in the midst of my joy! Tell me, do you regret our engagement—to which my ardor has perhaps constrained you?

ELISE. No, Valère, I could not regret what I have done for you. I feel myself drawn by pow- 10 ers far too sweet, and I lack strength to wish that things were not as they are. But to tell the truth, I fear to think of the consequences. I am much afraid that I love you a little more than I ought.

VALÈRE. Ah! Elise, what can you have to fear from the kindness you have shown me?

ELISE. Alas! a hundred things: my father's wrath, reproaches from my family, the censure of the world—but most of all, Valère, a change 20 in your heart and that criminal coldness with which those of your sex most often repay the over-ardent testimonies of innocent love.

VALÈRE. Oh! do not do me the wrong of judging me by others. Suspect me of anything, Elise, but not that I should fail in my duty to you. I love you too much for that, and I will love you as long as I live.

ELISE. Ah! that is the way you all talk. All men are alike in their speech; their actions 30 alone reveal their differences.

VALÈRE. If our actions alone reveal what we are, then at least wait and judge my heart by mine; and do not invent crimes for me simply because unhappy apprehension has bred unjust fear. I beg you, do not kill me with mortal blows of outrageous suspicion. Give me time to convince you, by a thousand and one proofs, that my intentions are honorable.

ELISE. Alas! how easily we are persuaded by those we love! Yes, Valère, I think you have no 40 room in your heart for deceit. I am convinced that you love me truly, and will always be faithful to me. I have no wish to doubt you; I am sad only because I fear I may be blamed by others.

VALÈRE. What is it that worries you?

ELISE. I would have nothing to fear if everyone saw you as I do. For in your very person I see enough to justify what I have done. My heart has all your merit for its defense, reinforced by 50 that gratitude which Heaven has bade me owe you. Not an hour passes but I picture to myself the terrible catastrophe which brought us into one another's sight; your amazing generosity, which made you risk your life to preserve mine from the fury of the waves; the great pains you took, how tenderly you cared for me after lifting me from the water; and the assiduous homage of your ardent love, which neither time nor difficulty has discouraged; which causes you to 60 neglect both family and fatherland; which detains you in this place, and makes you hide your rank for my sake; and which has reduced you to wearing my father's livery. All of this has certainly made a wonderful impression on me, and in my eyes is justification enough for the engagement I have consented to. But perhaps that is not enough to justify it to the world, nor am I sure that every one feels as I do.

70 VALÈRE. For all that you have said, it is only through my love that I pretend to merit your esteem, and as for your scruples, a father like yours is justification enough for anything you might do. His excessive avarice and the austere manner in which he lives with his children might well authorize far stranger things than this. Pardon me, charming Elise, for talking this way in front of you, but you know there is no good to be said on that score. But, if, as I 80 hope, I can finally find my parents again, it will not be hard to win him over. I am waiting impatiently for news of them, and I will go and inquire if it is much longer in coming.

ELISE. Oh! Valère, do not go away, I beg you. Think only of winning my father's confidence.

VALÈRE. You have seen how I go about it; you saw how artfully compliant I was obliged to be in order to introduce myself into his ser- 90 vice—under what mask of sympathy and agreement I disguise my feelings to please him—what role I play to gain his affection. And I am making admirable progress. I have discovered that, to win men over, there is no better way than to trick yourself out in their inclinations, fall in with their maxims, burn incense to their faults, and applaud everything they do. One need have no fear of overdoing complaisance. No matter how obviously you play on their feel- 100 ings, the shrewdest men are always the greatest dupes when it comes to flattery. There is nothing so impertinent or so ridiculous that you can't make them swallow it—if you season it well with praise. Sincerity, of course, suffers a little by this trade. But if you need certain men, you must adapt yourself to them. And, since there is no other way of winning them over, it is not the flatterers who are at fault, but those who wish to be flattered.

110 ELISE. Why don't you try to gain my brother's support too—in the event my maid should decide to tell our secret?

VALÈRE. I cannot manage both of them at the same time. The father's temperament and the son's are so opposed, it would be hard to accommodate the confidings of both at once. But you, for your part, could approach your brother, and avail yourself of his friendship to get him to act on our behalf. There he comes now. I'll withdraw. Use the occasion to sound 120 him out, but don't disclose our affair unless you think the time is ripe. *(Exit.)*

ELISE. I don't know if I will have the courage to confide in him.

(Enter CLEANTH.*)*

CLEANTH. I am very happy to find you alone, Elise. I have been burning to unburden a secret to you.

ELISE. Here I am, ready to listen, Cleanth. What do you wish to tell me? 130

CLEANTH. A thousand things, Elise—all bound up in three words: I'm in love.

ELISE. You are in love?

CLEANTH. I am in love. But before I say more, I know I am dependent on my father; that the name of son subjects me to his wishes; that we should not commit ourselves without the consent of those who brought us into the world; that Heaven has made them the masters of our troth; that we are enjoined not to pledge 140 it except by their direction; that having never been affected by foolish passions, they are in a condition to be deceived much less often than we are, and can see more clearly what is best for us. I know that we ought to trust the light of their prudence rather than the blindness of our passion and that the extravagance of youth most often lures us toward the precipice of sorrow. I am telling all this to you, Elise, so that you won't take the trouble to tell it to *me*. For, 150 to tell the truth, my love will not listen. So, please do not make objections.

ELISE. Are you engaged, Cleanth, to her whom you love?

CLEANTH. No, but I am resolved to be. And again I beg you not to offer any reasons to dissuade me.

ELISE. Am I such a stranger, Cleanth?

CLEANTH. No, Elise; but you are not in love. You do not know the violence that tender love 160 does to our hearts. I mistrust your prudence.

ELISE. Alas! Cleanth, let us not talk of my prudence. There is no one who is not deficient in that at least once in a lifetime; and if I opened my heart to you, perhaps in your eyes I should seem far less prudent than you are.

CLEANTH. Ah! I wish to Heaven, that your heart, like mine . . .

ELISE. First of all, let us finish with your affair. Tell me, who is she. . . .

CLEANTH. A young lady who has lived but a short time in this neighborhood, and who seems to have been made to inspire love in all who see her. Nature never shaped anything more lovable. I felt transported the moment I saw her. Her name is Marianne and she lives under the protection of her mother—a good woman who is almost always ill, and whom her daughter holds in such loving regard, it is unbelievable. She waits on her, takes pity on her, and consoles her so tenderly that it touches your heart. She has the most charming way in the world of going about her business. A thousand graces shine through her every action. Such alluring sweetness, such engaging goodness, such adorable civility! such . . . Oh! Elise, if you could only see her!

ELISE. I see a great deal of her, Cleanth, through what you have told me. And to understand her, it is enough for me that you love her.

CLEANTH. I have discovered, in a roundabout way, that they are not very well provided for, and that even with frugal management, they can hardly stretch their income far enough to cover all their needs. Imagine, Elise, what a pleasure it would be to be able to raise the fortunes of the person one loves, adroitly to supply a little help for the modest needs of a virtuous family. And think how unpleasant it must be for me to be powerless to taste that pleasure because of my father's stinginess, to be powerless to surprise this beautiful girl with some proof of my love for her.

ELISE. Oh! Cleanth, I can easily conceive how exasperated you must feel.

CLEANTH. Ah! Elise, much more so than you can imagine. Really, have you ever seen anything more cruel than the rigorous economy he imposes on us, than this queer stinginess under which we languish? What good will wealth do us, if it comes only when we are past the age when we can most enjoy it, if even to maintain myself I am now obliged to go into debt on every side, and if I am reduced with you to seeking help from tradesmen to find the means to wear decent clothes? I really wanted to ask you to help me find out father's attitude toward my present feelings. If I find him contrary, I am resolved to go away, in the company of that wonderful creature, to enjoy whatever fortune Providence may offer us. I am having somebody look everywhere for money to borrow for this purpose; and, if your affairs are in the same state as mine, if father insists on opposing our desires, we will both leave him, and free ourselves of this tyranny, to which his insupportable avarice has so long subjected us.

ELISE. It is only too true that he gives us more reason every day to regret our mother's death, and that . . .

CLEANTH. I can hear his voice. Let us go somewhere else to conclude our confidences. Later we will join forces and assault his hard heart together. (*Exeunt.*)

(*Enter* HARPAGON *and* LA FLÈCHE.)

HARPAGON. Get out of here at once, and don't answer back! Go on, leave my house! You master-mind of crime! You born gallows bait!

FLÈCHE (*aside*). I have never seen anything so wicked as this cursèd old man, and I believe, begging your pardon, he has a devil in his flesh.

HARPAGON. Are you muttering between your teeth?

FLÈCHE. Why chase me out of the house?

HARPAGON. As though you didn't know why! Scoundrel! Go quickly before I beat you!

FLÈCHE. What have I done?

HARPAGON. You have done enough to make me want you to leave.

FLÈCHE. My master your son gave me orders to wait for him.

HARPAGON. Go and wait for him in the street, not here in my house, standing there as stiff and straight as a post to watch what goes on and profit from everything. . . . I will not have someone continually spying on my business, a traitor whose cursèd eyes besiege all my actions, devour all I possess, and ferret about in every corner for something to steal.

FLÈCHE. How the deuce do you expect anyone to steal from you? Can you rob a man when he keeps everything under lock and key, and stands guard day and night?

HARPAGON. I will lock up whatever I think

should be locked up, and I will stand guard as I please. (*to audience*) There, isn't that the talk of a spy who watches everything you do? I tremble lest he suspect something about my money. (*to* LA FLÈCHE) Are you the kind of man who would go about spreading the story that I have money hidden away? 270

FLÈCHE. *Do* you have money hidden away?

HARPAGON. No, you rascal, I didn't say that. (*aside*) I'm losing my temper. (*to* LA FLÈCHE) I mean, would you go around spreading the story that I do have some—out of malice?

FLÈCHE. Hoho! what difference does it make to us, if you have or have not? Things are always the same for us anyway.

HARPAGON. Ha! you play the reasoner! I'll teach you how to reason with your ears. (*lifting his hand to give* LA FLÈCHE *a box on the ear*) One last time—get out of here! 280

FLÈCHE. All right, I'm going.

HARPAGON. Wait. You're not taking anything of mine with you?

FLÈCHE. What could I take of yours?

HARPAGON. Come here, so I can see. Show me your hands.

FLÈCHE. There they are.

HARPAGON (*sarcastically*). Your other hands. 290

FLÈCHE. My other hands?

HARPAGON. Yes.

FLÈCHE (*good-humoredly*). There they are.

HARPAGON (*pointing to* LA FLÈCHE's *breeches*). Have you put anything inside there?

FLÈCHE. See for yourself.

HARPAGON (*feeling the knees of* LA FLÈCHE's *breeches*). These breeches are just right for hiding stolen goods, and I wish somebody had been hanged for it. . . . 300

FLÈCHE. Ah! how well a man like that deserves what he fears, and what pleasure it would give me to steal from him.

HARPAGON. Eh?

FLÈCHE. What?

HARPAGON. What did you say about stealing?

FLÈCHE. I said that you are poking everywhere to see if I have stolen anything from you. 310

HARPAGON. That's what I intend to do.

FLÈCHE (*aside*). A pox on avarice and the avaricious!

HARPAGON. How's that? What did you say?

FLÈCHE. What did I say?

HARPAGON. Yes. What did you say about avarice and the avaricious?

FLÈCHE. I said, a pox on avarice and the avaricious.

HARPAGON. Who are you talking about? 320

FLÈCHE. About avaricious men.

HARPAGON. And who are they, these avaricious men?

FLÈCHE. They are misers and villains.

HARPAGON. But who do you mean by that?

FLÈCHE. What are you so upset about?

HARPAGON. I am upset about what I ought to be upset about.

FLÈCHE. Do you think I mean you?

HARPAGON. I think what I think. But I want you to tell me who you were speaking to when you said that. 330

FLÈCHE. I . . . I was speaking to my beret.

HARPAGON. And I might well knock it off.

FLÈCHE. Would you stop me from cursing avaricious men?

HARPAGON. No, but I'll stop you from chattering and being insolent. Keep quiet.

FLÈCHE. I haven't named anybody.

HARPAGON. I'll thrash you if you talk. 340

FLÈCHE. If your nose feels snotty, blow it.

HARPAGON. Will you be quiet?

FLÈCHE. Yes, in spite of myself.

HARPAGON. Ah! ah!

FLÈCHE (*showing him one of his waist-coat pockets*). Look, here's another pocket. Are you satisfied?

HARPAGON. Come now, give it back to me without any more searching.

FLÈCHE. What? 350

HARPAGON. What you took from me.

FLÈCHE. I took nothing from you.

HARPAGON. Are you sure?

FLÈCHE. Positive.

HARPAGON. Goodbye! Go to the devil!

FLÈCHE. Well, I must say, I have been very handsomely dismissed!

HARPAGON. At least I have laid something to your conscience.

(*Exit* LA FLÈCHE.) 360

That rascal of a valet makes me uneasy, and I don't care to see the limping cur around here. (*alone*) It's certainly no small worry having a large sum of money in this house, and it's a lucky man who has his fortune well invested, and can carry what he needs for expenses on his own person. It's no little problem to find, in an entire house, a safe hiding place for it. Because, to my way of thinking, your strong-boxes are suspect; I'd never trust my money to one. In my opinion they are nothing but bait for thieves, they are what a thief always goes after first.

(*Enter* CLEANTH *and* ELISE *unnoticed.*)

Still, I don't know if it was wise to bury the ten thousand écus I was paid yesterday in the garden. Ten thousand gold écus is a rather large sum to have about the house. (*noticing* CLEANTH *and* ELISE) Oh! Heavens! I must have given myself away! I must have been carried away by anxiety—and I think I spoke out loud while I was reasoning with myself all alone here. . . . What's the matter?

CLEANTH. Nothing, father.

HARPAGON. Have you been there very long?

ELISE. We have just come.

HARPAGON. You heard . . .

CLEANTH. What, father?

HARPAGON. There . . .

ELISE. What?

HARPAGON. What I just said.

CLEANTH. No.

HARPAGON. Yes, you did, you did.

ELISE. I beg your pardon, but we didn't.

HARPAGON. I can plainly see you heard something. I was talking to myself about how hard it is to find money these days, and I said that anyone who happens to have ten thousand écus about the house is a very lucky man.

CLEANTH. We held back for fear of interrupting you.

HARPAGON. I am only too glad to let you know what I said. So you won't get it all wrong and think it is I who have the ten thousand écus.

CLEANTH. We don't concern ourselves with your affairs.

HARPAGON. Would to God I had that much money, ten thousand écus!

CLEANTH. I don't believe it.

HARPAGON. It would be a fine thing for me.

ELISE. These are matters . . .

374 **écus** The monetary units mentioned in the play had the following values: twelve **deniers** = one **sol;** twenty sols = one **franc;** three francs = one **écu;** ten francs = one **pistole;** twenty francs = one **gold louis**

HARPAGON. I could certainly use it.

CLEANTH. I think that . . .

HARPAGON. It would set me up very comfortably.

ELISE. You are . . .

HARPAGON. I wouldn't complain then, as I do now, about how hard the times are!

CLEANTH. My God, father, you have no room to complain: everyone knows you are well-off.

HARPAGON. What! I am well-off? Those who say so are liars. Nothing could be more untrue. And those who go around spreading such a story are all villains.

ELISE. Don't be angry.

HARPAGON. It is very strange that my own children should betray me and become my enemies.

CLEANTH. Am I your enemy because I say you are well-off?

HARPAGON. Yes. That kind of talk and your extravagant spending will one day cause somebody to come here and to cut my throat, under the impression that my clothes are lined with money.

CLEANTH. What extravagant spending have I done?

HARPAGON. What? Is there anything more scandalous than the sumptuous clothes that you parade all over the city? Yesterday I was criticizing your sister, but this is far worse. This cries out to Heaven for vengeance; and, taking you from head to foot, there is enough on you to buy a good piece of property. I have told you twenty times, son, that your ways displease me very much. You are breaking your neck to look like a marquis, and in order to go about dressed as you are, I am sure you must be stealing from me.

CLEANTH. Ha! how could I steal from you?

HARPAGON. How should I know? Then where do you get the means to keep up your fashionable appearance?

CLEANTH. I, father? Why, I gamble, and, since I am very lucky, I put all the money I win on my back.

HARPAGON. That is very ill-advised. If you are lucky at cards you ought to profit by it, and invest your money at an honest interest, so that one day you will find it has . . . I should like very much to know, not to mention the rest, what good are all those ribbons you are garnished with from head to foot, as if half a dozen laces would not be enough to hold up your breeches? Is it really necessary to spend your money on wigs, when you can wear the hair that grows on your head, which doesn't cost a sou? I'll wager your wigs and ribbons alone are worth at least twenty pistoles. And twenty pistoles bring in eight francs, six sols, and eight deniers a year, even at eight per cent interest.

CLEANTH. You are quite right.

HARPAGON. Enough of that; let us talk about something else. Eh? (*aside, seeing* CLEANTH *and* ELISE *making signs to one another*) I think they are signalling one another to pick my pockets. (*to* CLEANTH *and* ELISE) What do those signs mean?

ELISE. We were bargaining as to who should speak first, my brother or myself. Both of us have something to tell you.

HARPAGON. And I, too, have something to tell both of you.

CLEANTH. It is about marriage, father, that we wish to speak with you.

HARPAGON. And it is marriage also that I want to discuss with you.

ELISE. Oh! father!

HARPAGON. Why "Oh! father!"? Is it the word, daughter, or the thing that frightens you?

CLEANTH. Marriage could be frightening in both respects, depending on how you mean it. And we are afraid that our inclinations might not agree with your choice.

HARPAGON. Have a little patience. Don't get alarmed. I know what is best for you both, and neither one of you will have reason to complain of anything I intend to do. Now, to begin at the beginning, tell me, have you ever seen a girl named Marianne, who lives not far from here?

CLEANTH. Yes, father.

HARPAGON (*to* ELISE). And you?

ELISE. I have heard of her.

HARPAGON. What do you think of this girl, Cleanth?

CLEANTH. An extremely charming person.

HARPAGON. Her physiognomy?

CLEANTH. Very honest and intelligent.

HARPAGON. Her air and manner?

CLEANTH. Exquisite, to be sure.

HARPAGON. Don't you think a girl like that is worth some consideration?

CLEANTH. Yes, father.

HARPAGON. That she might be a very desirable match?

CLEANTH. Very desirable.

HARPAGON. That she looks very much as though she would make a good housewife?

CLEANTH. No doubt.

HARPAGON. And that a husband would be completely satisfied with her?

CLEANTH. Surely.

HARPAGON. There is one slight obstacle. I am afraid she may not have as much money as one might reasonably expect.

CLEANTH. Ah! father, money is no consideration when it is a question of marrying an honest woman.

HARPAGON. Pardon me. if I disagree! But there is always this to be said: if a fortune does not measure up to one's expectations, one can always try to make it up some other way.

CLEANTH. Of course.

HARPAGON. Well—I am happy to find that you agree with me, because her maidenly conduct and sweet disposition have won my heart, and I am resolved to marry her. Provided she has some kind of property.

CLEANTH. Eh?

HARPAGON. What?

CLEANTH. You say you have resolved . . .

HARPAGON. To marry Marianne.

CLEANTH. Who? you, you?

HARPAGON. Yes. I, I, I! What do you mean by that?

CLEANTH. I feel dizzy all of a sudden. I think I'll go. (*Exit* CLEANTH.)

HARPAGON. It will pass. Quick, go into the kitchen and drink a large glass of plain water. (*to* ELISE) There's one of your lily-livered dandies—no more constitution than a chicken! Well, daughter, that's what I have decided for myself. As for your brother, I have a certain widow in mind that someone spoke to me about this very morning. And as for you, I am going to give you to Signor Anselm.

ELISE. To Signor Anselm?

HARPAGON. Yes. A man who is mature, pru-

465 **laces** ties lacing the breeches to the doublet. Men of fashion often ornamented their laces with ribbons

dent and wise, who is not over fifty, and who is famous for his great wealth.

ELISE. I would rather not get married at all, father, if you please.

HARPAGON. And I, my little girl, my pet, would rather you did get married, if you please.

ELISE. I beg your pardon, father.

HARPAGON. I beg your pardon, daughter.

ELISE. I am Signor Anselm's most humble servant, but, with your permission, I will not marry him.

HARPAGON. I am your very humble valet, but, with your permission, you shall marry him—this very evening.

ELISE. This very evening?

HARPAGON. This very evening.

ELISE. That shall never be, father.

HARPAGON. That shall be, daughter.

ELISE. No.

HARPAGON. Yes.

ELISE. I tell you, no.

HARPAGON. I tell you, yes.

ELISE. You shall never force me to do such a thing.

HARPAGON. I shall force you to do such a thing.

ELISE. I would kill myself sooner than marry such a husband.

HARPAGON. You will not kill yourself, and you shall marry him. Such audacity! Did you ever hear of a daughter talking to her father that way?

ELISE. Did you ever hear of a father marrying off his daughter that way?

HARPAGON. It is a match which will admit of no objection. And I wih wager that everyone will approve my choice.

ELISE. And I will wager that no reasonable person could possibly approve it.

HARPAGON. Here is Valère. Would you be willing to let him be the judge of this matter for both of us?

ELISE. I'll consent to that.

HARPAGON. Will you abide by his decision?

ELISE. Yes. I will stand by whatever he says.

HARPAGON. It's settled then.

(*Enter* VALÈRE.)

Here, Valère. We have elected you to decide who is in the right, my daughter or myself.

VALÈRE. You, sir, there's no contradicting that.

HARPAGON. You know, of course, what we are talking about.

VALÈRE. No, but you couldn't be wrong; you are reason itself.

HARPAGON. Tonight I want to give her a husband who is as rich as he is wise, and the hussy tells me to my face she will have no part of him. What do you say to that?

VALÈRE. What do I say to that?

HARPAGON. Yes.

VALÈRE. Hoho!

HARPAGON. What?

VALÈRE. I say that fundamentally I am of your opinion; and that you couldn't possibly be wrong; but on the other hand, she is not absolutely in the wrong either, and . . .

HARPAGON. How so! Signor Anselm is a considerable match. He is a gentleman: noble, cultured, poised, intelligent and very rich; and he has no children left from his first marriage. Could she do better?

VALÈRE. True, but she might tell you that you are hurrying things somewhat, and that she ought to have a little time at least to find out whether she can adapt her temperament to . . .

HARPAGON. This is an opportunity that must be grasped by the forelock. This match offers me an advantage which I would find in no other. He has agreed to take her without a dowry and . . .

VALÈRE. Without a dowry?

HARPAGON. Yes.

VALÈRE. Ah! I have nothing more to say. You see, here is a reason that is entirely convincing; one can only defer to it. . . .

HARPAGON. To me it represents a considerable saving.

VALÈRE. Certainly. There's no denying it. It's true your daughter may suggest to you that marriage is a more important step than you are inclined to think; that it is a question of being happy or unhappy for the rest of one's life; and that a partnership which will last till death should never be entered on without great precaution.

HARPAGON. Without a dowry!

VALÈRE. You are right. That decides everything, naturally. Though there are those who might tell you that in such matters you certainly ought to have some regard for your daughter's inclinations, and that the great difference in age, in temperament, and in sensibility would render such a marriage liable to very unhappy accidents.

HARPAGON. Without a dowry!

VALÈRE. Oh! there's no gainsaying that, as everyone knows. Who the deuce would argue the point? Not that there aren't many fathers who are more interested in their daughters' happiness than in the money they give with them; who would never sacrifice them to their own interest; and who seek, above all else, to insure that sweet conformity in marriage which is a continuous source of honor, tranquillity and joy, and which . . .

HARPAGON. Without a dowry!

VALÈRE. Very true. That closes every mouth. Without a dowry! An irrefutable argument!

HARPAGON. Wait! I think I hear a dog barking. (*aside*) Is someone trying to get at my money? (*to* VALÈRE) Don't move; I'll be back in a minute. (*Exit* HARPAGON.)

ELISE. Are you joking, Valère, talking to him this way?

VALÈRE. I don't want to sour him. This way I can better accomplish my own ends. Opposing his ideas to his face is a sure way to spoil everything. There are certain minds you have to take by the bias. Some temperaments are inimical to any kind of resistance: they stiffen themselves against the truth, and always balk when they confront the straight road of reason. You can guide them where you want to take them only by leading them in a roundabout way. Pretend that you consent to what he wants; you will be more certain to get your way in the end. . . .

ELISE. But this marriage, Valère?

VALÈRE. We'll break it on the bias.

ELISE. What can we contrive if it is to be concluded tonight?

VALÈRE. You must ask them to delay it. Feign a sickness.

ELISE. But they will discover the pretense—if they call in the doctor.

VALÈRE. Are you joking? Do doctors know anything about sickness? Come now, with doctors you can have any sickness you please, and they will find reasons for your having it, and tell you where it comes from.

(*Enter* HARPAGON.)

HARPAGON (*aside*). It was nothing, thank God!

VALÈRE. As a last resort we could run away and leave all this behind. And if your love, Elise, is capable of firmness . . . (*seeing* HARPAGON) Yes, a daughter should obey her father. She should have no concern for what her husband is like; and, when such a powerful argument as *without a dowry* intervenes, she should be ready to accept whatever is given her.

HARPAGON. Good! That was well said, that!

VALÈRE. Sir, I beg pardon if I have been too forward, and for having made so bold as to talk to her this way.

HARPAGON. What do you mean? I am delighted. And I want to give you absolute power over her. (*to* ELISE) There's no good running away. (ELISE *moves to the end of the stage.*) I give him the same authority over you that God gave me, and I expect you to do everything he tells you.

VALÈRE (*to* ELISE). After that how can you resist my remonstrances! Sir, I will follow her and continue the lessons I have been giving her.

HARPAGON. Yes, you will oblige me. Truly . . .

VALÈRE. I think it is good to pull in the reins with her.

HARPAGON. That's right, you should. . . .

VALÈRE. Don't worry about a thing; I am sure I can manage this.

HARPAGON. Do, do as you like. I am going to take a little walk through the city. I'll be back shortly.

VALÈRE. Yes, money is the most precious thing in the world, and you ought to thank God for the honest father He has given you. He knows what it takes to live. When someone offers to take a girl without a dowry, she ought not to look any further. Everything is included in *without a dowry;* it takes the place of beauty, youth, birth, honor, intelligence and probity. (*Exeunt* VALÈRE *and* ELISE.)

HARPAGON. Ah! bravo, bravo! Spoken like an oracle. Lucky the man with such a servant!

690 **by the bias** by indirection

ACT TWO

(CLEANTH *is on stage. Enter* LA FLÈCHE.)

CLEANTH. Ah! you traitor! What new mischief have you been getting into? Didn't I give you orders? . . .

FLÈCHE. Yes sir! I came here with every intention of waiting for you, but your father, the most ungracious man in the world, chased me out of the house, in spite of myself, and I came close to getting a beating.

CLEANTH. How goes our business? Things are more pressing now than ever. Since I last saw you, I have discovered that my own father is my rival.

FLÈCHE. Your father is in love?

CLEANTH. Yes; and I had all the trouble in the world to keep him from seeing how much this news distressed me.

FLÈCHE. Him, dabbling in love? What the devil can he be thinking of? Does public opinion mean nothing to him? Was love made for men built like that?

CLEANTH. It must be for my sins that he has got this idea into his head.

FLÈCHE. For what reason do you keep your love a secret from him?

CLEANTH. So that he will be less suspicious. So that he won't suspect my actions should it become necessary to try and prevent his marriage. What answer did they give you?

FLÈCHE. By Heaven, sir, those that have to borrow are in a very bad way! A man has to put up with strange things when he is reduced, as you are, to putting himself into the hands of sharks.

CLEANTH. You couldn't get the money?

FLÈCHE. Not exactly. Our Master Simon, the broker, who was recommended to us as an energetic, determined man, assures me he has left no stone unturned to serve you—and that your face alone has won his heart.

CLEANTH. Will I get the fifteen thousand francs I asked for?

FLÈCHE. Yes, but there are some trifling conditions attached—which you must accept, if you expect anything to be done.

CLEANTH. Did he let you speak to the man who is supposed to lend the money?

FLÈCHE. Oh, really, it is not so simple as all that. He took more pains to hide himself than you do yourself; it is all much more mysterious than you might think. They will by no means tell his name, and they are going to bring you together today in a private house, so that he can learn from your own lips who your family is and what your expectations are. But I don't have the slightest doubt that your father's name alone will make things easy for you.

CLEANTH. And especially the fact that our mother is dead, whose property no one can take from me.

FLÈCHE. Here are a few articles which he himself dictated to our go-between, to be shown to you before any action will be taken.

"Supposing that the lender is satisfied with the collateral offered, and that the borrower has reached his majority and is from a family whose estate is large, solid, assured and free from all encumbrance, a valid and precise contract will be drawn up in the presence of a notary, the most honest man available, who, for that reason, must be chosen by the lender, to whom it is of the utmost importance that the contract be properly drawn up."

CLEANTH. I have no objection to that.

FLÈCHE. "The lender, in order not to burden his conscience with any scruples, intends to charge no more than six per cent interest."

CLEANTH. Six per cent interest? By Jove, an honest fellow indeed! There is no reason to complain about that.

FLÈCHE. Indeed not!

"But, since the said lender does not have the sum required in his own house, and because, in order to oblige the borrower, he is forced to borrow himself at the rate of twenty per cent, it is only fair that the said, first borrower should pay this interest without prejudice to the other, considering that it is only to oblige him that the said lender will borrow the sum requested."

90 CLEANTH. What the devil! What Jew, what Arab am I dealing with? That's more than twenty-five per cent interest!

FLÈCHE. That's right. That's what I told him. You had better look into it yourself.

CLEANTH. What is there to look into? I need money. I will have to agree to anything.

FLÈCHE. That's what I told him.

CLEANTH. Is there something else?

FLÈCHE. Only a small item.

100 "Of the fifteen thousand francs that are requested, the lender can count on only twelve thousand francs in cash. As for the remaining thousand écus, the borrower must take them in furniture, clothing, and jewelry, a list of which follows this note, and which the said lender has, in all good faith, priced as moderately as he possibly can."

CLEANTH. What does he mean by that?

FLÈCHE. Listen to the list.

110 "First: one four-poster bed, with Hungarian point lace handsomely sewn on olive-colored cloth, with six chairs, and a counterpane of the same material; all in good condition and lined with changeable red and blue taffeta.

"In addition: one bedstead canopy of good, dry rose-colored serge, with silk fringes."

CLEANTH. What does he expect me to do with that?

FLÈCHE. Hold on.

120 "In addition: a set of tapestries; the subject of which is *The Amours of Gombaut and Macaea.*

"In addition: one large walnut table, with twelve columns, or turned pillars, pulling out at either end, and fitted with half-a-dozen joint stools under it."

CLEANTH. My God! What good will that do me?

FLÈCHE. Be patient.

"In addition: three large muskets inlaid with 130 mother-of-pearl, with three matching tripods.

"In addition: one brick furnace with two retorts and three recipients, very useful for anyone interested in distilling.

"In addition: a Bologna lute with all its strings, or few lacking.

"In addition: a troll-madam table and a chess board, with a goose game restored from the Greeks; all very fine to pass away the time when one has nothing to do.

140 "In addition: a lizard skin, three feet long, and half-filled with straw—a very agreeable curiosity to hang from a bedroom ceiling.

"The total mentioned above, easily worth more than four thousand, five hundred francs, is reduced in price to one thousand écus by the moderation of the lender."

CLEANTH. May the plague choke him and his moderation, the traitor! Cut-throat that he is! Have you ever heard of such usury? Can't he 150 be satisfied with the furious interest he demands, without making me take all the junk he has heaped up, for three thousand francs? I won't get more than two hundred écus for the lot! And yet I must resign myself and consent to whatever he wants. He is in a position to make me accept anything. The dog has me by the throat.

FLÈCHE. Sir, I see you taking the very same road, no offense intended, that Panurge followed 160 to his ruin: taking money in advance, buying dear and selling cheap, and eating your wheat in the blade.

CLEANTH. What would you have me do? You see what young men are reduced to by the cursèd avarice of their fathers! Is it any wonder, after this, that the sons should wish their fathers' death?

FLÈCHE. I must confess, the stinginess of yours would infuriate the calmest man in the 170 world. I am not strongly inclined toward the gallows, thank God, and when I am with my colleagues, seeing them taking big chances for small gains, I always know when to pull my iron out of the fire, and when it is prudent to drop out of any adventure that smells ever so little of the gallows. But, to tell the truth, the way your father acts tempts me very much to

121 **The Amours . . . Macaea** a popular rustic romance of the time

136 **troll-madam** game played with ivory balls rolled into numbered holes or compartments 159 **Panurge** the improvident rascal in Rabelais' *Gargantua and Pantagruel*

steal from him. And I think, if I did rob him, I would be doing a good deed.

180 CLEANTH. Give me the note; I want to look it over again.

(*Enter* MASTER SIMON *and* HARPAGON.)

SIMON. Yes sir, he is a young man in need of money. The state of his affairs obliges him to find some, and he will agree to anything you prescribe.

HARPAGON. But are you convinced, Master Simon, that I will run no risk? Are you acquainted with the name, the fortune and the
190 family of the party for whom you are speaking?

SIMON. No, I cannot give you any definite information about him; and it was only by chance that he was directed to me; but he himself will enlighten you about everything. And his man assures me that you will be satisfied when you meet him. All I can tell you is that his family is very rich, that his mother is already dead, and that he will guarantee, if you wish it, that his father will die before eight
200 months are out.

HARPAGON. That is something, indeed. Charity, Master Simon, obliges us to make others happy when it is in our power to do so.

SIMON. To be sure.

FLÈCHE (*low to* CLEANTH). What does this mean? Our Master Simon talking to your father!

CLEANTH (*low to* LA FLÈCHE). Could they have told him who I am? or have you betrayed
210 me?

SIMON (*noticing* CLEANTH *and* LA FLÈCHE). Aha! you are in a hurry! Who told you this was the house? (*to* HARPAGON) In any event, sir, it was not I who revealed your name and lodgings. But, in my opinion, no great harm has been done: they are discreet fellows, and now you can discuss your business together.

HARPAGON. What?

SIMON. This is the gentleman who wants to
220 borrow the fifteen thousand francs, the one I was telling you about.

HARPAGON. What! you rascal! It is you who abandon yourself to such culpable extremities!

CLEANTH. What! father, it is you who carry on this shameful business!

(*Exit* MASTER SIMON *and* LA FLÈCHE.)

HARPAGON. It is you who want to ruin yourself by such deplorable borrowing!

CLEANTH. It is you who seek to enrich yourself by this criminal usury! 230

HARPAGON. Do you dare, after that, to show your face to me?

CLEANTH. Do you dare, after that, to show your face to the world?

HARPAGON. Tell me, aren't you ashamed to descend to such debauchery, to hurl yourself into horrible expenditure, and shamefully to squander the wealth that your ancestors have amassed for you by the sweat of their brows? 240

CLEANTH. How can you help but blush for disgracing your class this way with this trade you practise, sacrificing your honor and reputation to your insatiable desire to pile écu on écu and outdoing, in point of interest, the most infamous subtleties ever invented by the most notorious usurers?

HARPAGON. Get out of my sight, scoundrel, get out of my sight!

CLEANTH. Who is the greater criminal in 250 your opinion: the man who buys money because he needs it, or the man who steals money but has no use for it?

HARPAGON. Leave the room I tell you, and stop chafing my ears.

(*Exit* CLEANTH.)

I am not a bit sorry that this has happened; it is a warning to me to watch everything he does more closely than ever.

(*Enter* FROSINE.) 260

FROSINE. Sir . . .

HARPAGON. Wait a moment. I'll be back to talk with you. (*aside*) It's about time I take a peek at my money. (*Exit.*)

(*Enter* LA FLÈCHE.)

FLÈCHE. The whole thing is very amusing. He must surely have a large store of supplies somewhere in the house, because we couldn't find a thing that's listed in the inventory he gave us. 270

FROSINE. Ah! it's you, my poor La Flèche! To what do we owe this meeting?

FLÈCHE. Aha! it's you, Frosine! What are *you* doing here?

FROSINE. What I do everywhere else: play the go-between in negotiations, make myself useful to others, and profit as much as I possibly can by whatever slight talent I may have. You know that in this world one is obliged to live by one's wits. And for women like myself
280 Heaven has provided no other source of income than intrigue and persistency.

FLÈCHE. Do you have some business with the master of the house?

FROSINE. Yes, I am transacting some small business for him—for which I hope to be compensated.

FLÈCHE. By him? Ah! in faith, you'll have to be pretty sharp to get anything out of *him;* I warn you, money costs very dearly in this
290 house.

FROSINE. There are certain services that are wonderfully effective.

FLÈCHE. I am your humble servant. But you don't know Signor Harpagon, yet. Signor Harpagon is of all humans the least human, the hardest and tightest mortal of all mortals. No service can push his gratitude far enough to make him unclench his fists. Of praise, esteem, benevolent words and friendship as much as
300 you like, but money?—nothing doing. There is nothing more dry and withered than his favors and caresses, and "give" is a word for which he has such an aversion that he never says "I give," but "I lend, you good-day."

FROSINE. Mercy me! I know the art of milking a man. I have the secret for bringing out his tenderness, for tickling his heart, for finding his soft spot.

FLÈCHE. Useless here! If money is involved,
310 I defy you to touch the man in question. On that score he is a Turk; and his turkery is the despair of all who know him; you could be dying, and he wouldn't turn a hair. In a word, he loves money more than reputation, honor or virtue, and the sight of anyone who expects to be paid throws him into convulsions. It wounds him mortally. It pierces his heart. It tears out his entrails. And if . . . He's coming back; I must be going. *(Exit.)*

(Enter HARPAGON.)
320

HARPAGON *(aside)*. All is as it should be. *(to* FROSINE) How now! What is it, Frosine?

FROSINE. Ah! Mercy me, how well you are looking! You are the very picture of health!

HARPAGON. Who? I?

FROSINE. Never have I seen your color so fresh and jovial.

HARPAGON. Really?

FROSINE. Never in your life were you as young as you are now; I see men of twenty-five who are older than you. 330

HARPAGON. Nevertheless, Frosine, I'm a good sixty years old.

FROSINE. Well, what is that, sixty years old? A worry indeed! It's the bloom of life, that is. And now you are entering on a man's prime season.

HARPAGON. That's true. However, twenty years less wouldn't do me any harm, as I see it.

FROSINE. Are you joking? You have no need 340 of them. You bid fair to live to be a hundred.

HARPAGON. Do you think so?

FROSINE. Of course. You show every indication. Hold still a bit. Oh, there it is! There it is! Between your two eyes!—a sign of long life!

HARPAGON. Do you know something about these things?

FROSINE. Certainly. Show me your hand. Ah! Mercy me, what a life line!

HARPAGON. How's that? 350

FROSINE. Don't you see how far that line goes?

HARPAGON. Well, yes. What does it mean?

FROSINE. By my faith, I said a hundred years, but you will pass the one hundred and twenty mark.

HARPAGON. Is it possible?

FROSINE. You deserve a beating. I tell you, you will bury your children and your children's children. 360

HARPAGON. So much the better! How goes our little transaction?

FROSINE. Need you ask? Did anyone ever see me start anything I couldn't finish? I have an especially wonderful talent for marriages. There aren't two people in the world that I couldn't find a way to couple in no time at all. If I had the notion, I believe I could marry the Grand Turk to the Republic of Venice. 370 But, to be sure, there wasn't any such great

370 **Grand Turk** the Sultan. Turkey and Venice were conventional instances of irreconcilable hostility.

difficulty involved in this affair. Since I have business at their house, I have already discussed you at length with both of them; and I told the mother what plans you had conceived for Marianne, on seeing her pass through the street and take the air at her window.

HARPAGON. She answered . . .

FROSINE. She received the proposition with joy! And when I informed her that you are very desirous her daughter should be present tonight at the signing of the marriage contract which is to take place here, she readily consented. And she has entrusted her daughter to me for the evening.

HARPAGON. I am obliged, Frosine, to give a supper for Signor Anselm, and I would like her to attend this feast.

FROSINE. A good idea. After dinner, she is to pay your daughter a visit; from here she plans to go and see the fair; and afterwards she can come back for supper.

HARPAGON. Fine! They can go together in my carriage. Which I will lend them.

FROSINE. That will suit her perfectly.

HARPAGON. But, Frosine, have you talked to the mother about the money she can give her daughter? Did you tell her she ought to help a little, herself? That she should make some special effort? That she should bleed herself for an occasion like this? For, I tell you again, no one marries a girl unless she brings something in.

FROSINE. What! This is a girl who will bring you twelve thousand francs a year.

HARPAGON. Twelve thousand francs a year?

FROSINE. Yes. First of all: those who raised and nurtured her were very sparing on food. She is a girl used to living on salad, milk, cheese, and apples, and consequently doesn't require a richly set table, or fancy jellies or barley syrup all the time, or all the other delicacies that most women must have. And this is no trifling matter. It will make a difference of at least three thousand francs a year. Besides, she feels that true elegance lies in simplicity, and she doesn't care for magnificent clothes, or rich jewelry, or sumptuous furniture—things which young ladies are usually so passionately addicted to. And that little item is worth more than four thousand francs a year. What's more, she has a tremendous aversion to cards—a thing not common in women nowadays. I know of one in our neighborhood who, at thirties and forties, mind you, lost twenty thousand francs this year! But suppose we take only a quarter of that. Five thousand francs a year for cards, and four thousand francs for clothes and jewelry, make nine thousand francs. And we will figure one thousand écus for food. Isn't that your twelve thousand francs a year—every sou of it?

HARPAGON. Yes, not bad: but this account has nothing real in it.

FROSINE. I beg your pardon. Is the great sobriety that she will bring to your marriage nothing real? Or her inheritance of a great love for simplicity in dress? Or the acquisition of a great fund of hatred for cards?

HARPAGON. It is a mockery to try and make up a dowry out of the expenses that she won't put me to. I won't give a receipt for something I don't receive. I must be able to touch something.

FROSINE. Mercy me! you will touch enough. They spoke to me about a certain country where they have some property. You shall be the master of it.

HARPAGON. That remains to be seen. But Frosine, there is something else that bothers me. The girl is young, as you can see, and young people usually like only their own kind, and seek only their company. I am afraid that a man of my age might not be to her taste, and that this might cause some little disorder in my house, which would not suit me at all!

FROSINE. Ah! how little you know her! This is another thing about her that I was going to mention. She has a frightful aversion to all young men, and feels no love except for the old.

HARPAGON. Her?

FROSINE. Yes, her. I wish you could hear her on that subject. She can't so much as stand the sight of a young fellow; but she is in ecstasy, she tells me, when she can look at a handsome old man with a majestic beard. For her, the oldest are the most charming. And I warn you not to go and make yourself look younger than you are. She likes a man to be sixty at the very least. It wasn't four months

424 **thirties and forties** the card game *trent et quarante* or *rouge et noir,* distantly related to blackjack

ago, that, all set to be married, she broke off the marriage on the spot because her lover let it be known he was only fifty-six years old—and didn't use spectacles to sign the contract.

HARPAGON. Just for that?

FROSINE. Yes. She says she simply couldn't be satisfied with a man of fifty-six, and above all, she is for the nose that wears spectacles.

480 HARPAGON. Really, this is something altogether new!

FROSINE. It goes much deeper than most people know. Like most young girls she has a few paintings and a few prints in her room, but what do you think the subjects are? Adonises? Cephaluses? Parises? or Apollos? No. They are handsome portraits of Saturn, of King Priam, of old Nestor, and good father Anchises on his son's shoulders!

490 HARPAGON. That is admirable! I should never have suspected it. And I am very happy to learn she has that kind of disposition. In fact, had *I* been a woman, I wouldn't have liked young men at all.

FROSINE. I can well believe you. What are they but fancy drugs? And to love them, ha! They are nothing but handsome idiots, good-looking fops that make you envy their complexions. I'd really like to know what there is

500 to them!

HARPAGON. As for me, I can't understand it. I don't know why some women are so fond of them.

FROSINE. They must be stark mad. To find youth amiable! Is there any common sense in it? Are they men, these young dandies? Can you become attached to one of those animals?

HARPAGON. That's what I have always said—with their effeminate, milk-fed voices, and their

510 three little wisps of beard turned up like cat's whiskers, with their mouse-colored wigs, and their sloppy breeches, and their puffed-out stomachs!

FROSINE. They are well-built, indeed, compared with a person like you! (*to the audience*) There's a man for you! There is someone who is a pleasure to look at! This is how a man should be made and dressed to inspire love.

HARPAGON. You like the way I look?

FROSINE. I should say! You are ravishing, 520 you ought to have your portrait painted. Turn round a bit, if you please. You couldn't be better. Let me see you walk. (*to the audience*) Here is a body that is trim, supple and tall as it ought to be. And not marked by any infirmity.

HARPAGON. None to speak of, thank God! (*coughs*) Except my catarrh that bothers me from time to time.

FROSINE. That is nothing. Your catarrh is 530 not unbecoming to you. You cough gracefully.

HARPAGON. But tell me, hasn't Marianne seen me yet? Hasn't she noticed me at all, passing by her house?

FROSINE. No. But we have talked about you a great deal. I sketched a portrait of your person for her. And I did not fail to boast of your merits and the advantage it would be for her to have a husband like you.

HARPAGON. You have done well. And I 540 thank you.

FROSINE. I would like, sir, to ask a small favor of you. I have a lawsuit that I am on the point of losing for want of a little money; and you could easily assure my winning this suit if you would show me some little kindness. (HARPAGON *frowns.*) Ah! how well you will please her! What a marvellous impression your old-fashioned ruff will make! But she will be especially charmed by your breeches, attached to 550 your doublet with laces; they'll make her go wild over you. A laced-up lover will seem to her a wonderful treat.

HARPAGON. Really, it delights me to hear you say it.

FROSINE. To tell the truth, sir, this suit is of the utmost importance to me. I am ruined if I lose it, and the least bit of help would set everything right for me. (HARPAGON *frowns.*) I wish you could have seen the rapture in her 560 face when she heard me speak of you. Her eyes sparkled with joy as I recited your qualities. In short, I left her in a state of extreme impatience to see this marriage entirely concluded.

HARPAGON. You have given me great pleasure, Frosine. And I must confess, I am under all the obligation in the world to you.

FROSINE. I beg you, sir, to give me the slight help I need. It will put me on my feet again. And I will be eternally indebted to you. 570

485 **Adonises . . . Anchises** types of youthful beauty contrasted with types of elderly worth

HARPAGON. Goodbye! I must get my mail ready.

FROSINE. I assure you, sir, you couldn't relieve me in a greater need.

HARPAGON. I will leave orders, so my coach will be ready to take you to the fair.

FROSINE. I would not importune you, were I not forced to do so—out of necessity.

HARPAGON. And I'll see to it that supper is ready early so that you won't get sick. 580

FROSINE. Do not refuse me this favor, I beg of you.

HARPAGON. I am going. There, someone is calling me. I'll see you by and by.

(*Exit* HARPAGON.)

FROSINE. May the fever rack you! Cur! Villain! The devil take you! The miser was deaf to all my attacks. Nevertheless I must not drop his suit: for in any case, there is the other party. I am sure of a good reward from them! 590

ACT THREE

(*On stage:* HARPAGON, CLEANTH, ELISE, VALÈRE, DAME CLAUDE, MASTER JACQUES, BRINDAVOINE *and* LA MERLUCHE.)

HARPAGON. Here, all of you come here. I want to give you orders for this evening, and assign everyone a job. Step forward, Dame Claude. Let's begin with you. Good, I see you are already armed. I consign to you the task of cleaning up the house; but be especially careful not to rub the furniture too hard, or 10 you'll wear it out. Furthermore, I assign you to see to the bottles during supper. And if any of them are carried off, or if anything is broken, you will be responsible, and I'll deduct it from your wages.

JACQUES (*aside*). A convenient punishment.

HARPAGON (*to* DAME CLAUDE). Go. . . .

(*Exit* DAME CLAUDE.)

You, Brindavoine, and you, La Merluche, are 20 appointed to rinse the glasses, and to serve the wine—but only when someone is thirsty. And don't follow the example of those impudent lackies who go and *incite* people to drink and put the notion in their heads when they aren't even thinking about it. Wait until they have asked you more than once, and remember always to bring a lot of water.

JACQUES (*aside*). Yes, pure wine goes to the head.

MERLUCHE. Shall we take our canvas smocks 30 off, sir?

HARPAGON. Yes, when you see the guests coming, and be careful not to spoil your clothes.

BRINDAVOINE. You know very well, sir, that one side of my doublet is covered with a big spot of lamp-oil.

MERLUCHE. And I, sir, have a big hole in the back of my breeches, and I can be seen, begging your pardon . . .

HARPAGON. Peace! Keep that side discreetly 40 turned toward the wall, and always show your front side to the world. And you, always hold your hat like this (*holds his hat over his chest*) when you serve.

(*Exeunt* LA MERLUCHE *and* BRINDAVOINE.)

And as for you, my daughter, keep an eye open when they clear away the table, and see to it that nothing goes to waste. That's a proper job for a young girl. But meanwhile, prepare yourself to receive my fiancée, who is coming 50 to pay you a visit, and take you to the fair with her. Did you hear what I said?

ELISE. Yes, father.

HARPAGON. And you, my son, the dandy whose latest escapade I was so good as to forgive, don't you go getting any ideas either and make sour faces at her.

CLEANTH. I, father? Sour faces? And for what reason?

60 HARPAGON. By God, we know the drift of children whose fathers remarry, and how they feel toward what is called a stepmother. But, if you would like me to forget your last prank, I especially recommend that you treat this person to some of your most cheerful looks and give her the best reception you possibly can.

CLEANTH. To tell you the truth, father, I cannot promise you to be very glad she is to become my stepmother. I should be lying if I 70 told you I would. But as for receiving her well and showing her a pleasant face, I promise to obey you punctually on that score.

HARPAGON. At least take care you do.

CLEANTH. You will see you will have no reason to complain.

HARPAGON. You will do wisely.

(*Exeunt* CLEANTH *and* ELISE.)

Valère, help me with this. Oh, there you are, Master Jacques! Come here. I have saved you 80 for the last.

JACQUES. Is it to your coachman, sir, or is it to your cook you wish to speak? For I am one and the other.

HARPAGON. To the two of you.

JACQUES. But to which of us first?

HARPAGON. To the cook.

JACQUES. One moment then if you please. (*Takes off his coachman's coat and appears dressed as a cook.*)

90 HARPAGON. What the deuce kind of ceremony is this?

JACQUES. You have only to speak.

HARPAGON. I have committed myself, Master Jacques, to give a supper tonight.

JACQUES (*aside*). This is miraculous!

HARPAGON. Tell me now, will you give us a fine feast?

JACQUES. Yes, if you will give me a good deal of money.

100 HARPAGON. What the devil! always money! It seems they have nothing else to say: money, money, money! That's the sword they keep by their bed, money!

VALÈRE. I have never heard a more impertinent answer. How miraculous it is to be able to set out a fine feast when you have a lot of money! It is the easiest thing in the world to do, and there is no man so poor in wit that he couldn't do as much. But it is a clever man who can talk about providing a fine feast for 110 little money!

JACQUES. A fine feast for little money?

VALÈRE. Yes.

JACQUES. By my faith, Mr. Steward, you would oblige us if you would let us in on your secret—and if you will take my place as cook! You meddle so much in this house already, you might as well be the factotum.

HARPAGON. Be quiet. What will we need?

JACQUES. There is your steward who will 120 provide a fine feast at small cost.

HARPAGON. Ha! I want you to answer me.

JACQUES. How many will you be at table?

HARPAGON. We will be eight or ten. When there is enough for eight, there is plenty for ten.

VALÈRE. Naturally.

JACQUES. Very well, we will need four kinds of soup and five other dishes. Soups, entrées . . .

HARPAGON. What the devil! That's enough 130 to feed a whole city.

JACQUES. Roast . . .

HARPAGON (*putting his hand over* MASTER JACQUES' *mouth*). Ah! traitor, you are eating up all my money!

JACQUES. Side dishes . . .

HARPAGON (*putting his hand over* MASTER JACQUES' *mouth again*). More?

VALÈRE. Do you want to make everybody split open? Do you think our master invites 140 people in order to *murder* them with food? Go and read the rules of health a while—and ask the doctors if there is anything more prejudicial to man than excessive eating.

HARPAGON. He is right.

VALÈRE. Learn, Master Jacques, you and the like of you, that a table overloaded with food is a cut-throat; that if you want to prove yourself a friend to those you invite, frugality should reign at the meals you serve; and that, accord- 150 ing to the saying of the ancients, we should eat to live, and not live to eat.

HARPAGON. Oh! but that was well said! Come here, I want to embrace you for that saying. It is the most beautiful sentence I have ever heard in my life. We should live to eat, and not eat to li . . . No, that isn't it. How was it you said it?

VALÈRE. We should eat to live, and not live to eat. 160

HARPAGON. Yes, do you hear that? Who was the great man who said it?

VALÈRE. At the moment I can't recall his name.

HARPAGON. Remember to write it down for me. I want to have it carved in gold letters above the mantelpiece in my dining room.

VALÈRE. I won't forget. And as for your supper, you have only to leave it to me. I will order things to be done as they should be.

HARPAGON. Take care of it then.

JACQUES. So much the better; it will mean less trouble for me.

HARPAGON. We should have those things that people don't eat much of, that satisfy the appetite quickly: a nice mutton stew, rather fat, with some kind of a meat-pie well garnished and chestnuts to go with it. Yes, that! And let there be a lot of it.

VALÈRE. Leave everything to me.

HARPAGON. Now, Master Jacques, my coach must be cleaned up.

JACQUES. One moment. That was addressed to the coachman. (*Exit, and reappears in his coachman's coat.*) You said . . . ?

HARPAGON. That you should clean up my coach, and have my horses ready to drive to the fair.

JACQUES. Your horses, sir? Faith, they are in no condition to walk. I won't say they are down on their litters. The poor beasts don't have any, so I'd be speaking very improperly. But you make them observe such strict fasts that they are now no more than ideas or ghosts or appearances of horses.

HARPAGON. No wonder they are sick; they do nothing.

JACQUES. And because they do nothing, sir, must they eat nothing? It would be much better for them, poor animals, to work a lot, and to eat accordingly. It breaks my heart to see them so weak, because, to tell the truth, I have so much affection for my horses, that when I see them suffer, it's just as though it were myself. Every day I take food out of my own mouth to feed them; it is a very hard nature, sir, that feels no pity for the next one.

HARPAGON. It won't be much work for them to go as far as the fair.

JACQUES. No, sir, I haven't the courage to drive them, and it would lie on my conscience if I hit them with the whip, in the condition they're in. How do you expect them to pull a carriage?—they can't even pull themselves.

VALÈRE. Sir, I will ask our neighbor Picard if he will be good enough to drive them. Besides, we shall need him here to help prepare the supper.

JACQUES. Very well! I'd still rather they died under someone else's hands and not mine.

VALÈRE. Master Jacques is intent on cavilling.

JACQUES. Mister Steward is intent on seeming indispensable.

HARPAGON. Peace!

JACQUES. Sir, I can't stand flatterers, and I see what he is doing. He continually restricts the bread, the wine, the wood, the salt, and the candles just to scratch your ear, to win your favor. It makes me angry. And it grieves me to hear what people say about you every day. Because I feel a real affection for you, in spite of myself; and after my horses, you are the person I like most.

HARPAGON. Could I learn from you, Master Jacques, what people say about me?

JACQUES. Yes, sir, if I could be sure it wouldn't make you angry.

HARPAGON. No, not in the least.

JACQUES. Pardon me, but I know very well you'd fly into a rage.

HARPAGON. Not at all. On the contrary, it will give me great pleasure to learn what is said about me.

JACQUES. Sir, since it is your wish, I tell you frankly: people everywhere are laughing at you. They taunt us with a thousand jokes about you on all sides, and they are never so happy as when tearing you to ribbons or making up countless stories about your stinginess. One says that you have special almanacs printed, in which you have doubled the quarter-days and vigils, so you can take advantage of the fasts you impose on your household. Another says you always have a quarrel ready to pick with your valets when it is time for holiday gifts, or when they are leaving, so you'll have a reason for not giving them anything. This one tells the story that you once tried to bring your neighbor's cat to court for eating up the remainder of a leg of

252 **quarter-days . . . vigils** periods of fasting

mutton. Somebody else says that you yourself were caught coming to steal your horses' oats, and that in the dark your coachman, the one before me, gave you I don't know how many blows with his stick, which you didn't care to say anything about. Shall I go on? We can't go anywhere without hearing people pull you apart. You are the talk of the town, the laughing-stock of the world. And they never refer to you except by the name of miser, cut-throat, villain, or shark.

HARPAGON. You are a fool, a scoundrel, a rascal, an insolent knave! (*Beats him.*)

JACQUES. There! Didn't I say it would be that way? You wouldn't believe me. I warned you that you would get angry if I told you the truth.

HARPAGON. Then learn how to talk.

(*Exit* HARPAGON.)

VALÈRE. As far as I can see, Master Jacques, you are poorly paid for your frankness.

JACQUES. By God! Mister Upstart, playing the man of importance, it is none of your business. Save your laughs for your own beating when you get it, and don't come laughing at mine.

VALÈRE. Ah! good Master Jacques, please don't be angry.

JACQUES (*aside*). He's backing down. I'll pretend to be tough, and if he is fool enough to be afraid of me, I'll give him a little thrashing. Did you know, Mister Comedian, that I myself never laugh?—and that if you get my temper up you are likely to be laughing out of the other side of your mouth?

VALÈRE. Gently now!

JACQUES. Why gently? What if I don't feel like being gentle?

VALÈRE. Please!

JACQUES. You are an impertinent fellow.

VALÈRE. Good Master Jacques!

JACQUES. There is no such person as good Master Jacques. If I get a stick, I'll beat the importance out of you.

VALÈRE. (*picking up the stick on the table*). What did you say? a stick?

JACQUES. Oh! I wasn't talking about that one.

VALÈRE. Did you know, Mister Fool, that I am man enough to thrash you?

JACQUES. I don't doubt it.

VALÈRE. That you are, by any standard, nothing but a miserable cook?

JACQUES. I know very well.

VALÈRE. And that you don't know me yet?

JACQUES. I beg your pardon.

VALÈRE. You'll beat me, you say?

JACQUES. I was joking.

VALÈRE. And your joking is not to my taste. This will teach you that you're a scurvy joker. (*Beats him.*) (*Exit* VALÈRE.)

JACQUES. A pox on sincerity! It's a wretched practice. Here and now I renounce it, and I will never tell the truth again. As for my master, I'll let that go—he has some right to beat me. But, as for this steward, I'll take my revenge if I can.

(*Enter* FROSINE *and* MARIANNE.)

FROSINE. Do you know, Master Jacques, if your master is at home?

JACQUES. Yes, he certainly is. I know it all too well!

FROSINE. Tell him, pray, that we are here.

(*Exit* MASTER JACQUES.)

MARIANNE. Ah! Frosine, I am in such a strange state! If I must tell what I feel: I am very much afraid of this interview.

FROSINE. But why? What is it that worries you?

MARIANNE. Alas! Need you ask? Can't you imagine the alarm of a person just about to see the rack she is to be tortured on?

FROSINE. I can plainly see that Harpagon is not the rack you would choose to embrace if you're thinking of an agreeable death. And I know by your expression that the dandy you were telling me about is somewhere in your thoughts.

MARIANNE. Yes, Frosine. That I do not wish to deny. The respectful visits he paid at our house have had, I must confess, some effect on my heart.

FROSINE. But have you learned *who* he is?

MARIANNE. No, I don't in the least know *who* he is, but I do know he is fashioned in a way that inspires love and that, if the choice were left at my disposal, I would take him sooner than any other, and that he contributes not a little to make me find the husband you would give me a horrible torment.

FROSINE. Mercy me! all those dandies are

agreeable enough, and they play their parts very well, but most of them are poor as churchmice. You would do much better to take an old husband who will leave you a lot of money. I will admit that the senses will not find full measure on the side which I am speaking for, and there are some slightly distasteful details to be endured with such a husband—but it won't be for 370 long. His death, believe me, will soon put you in a position to pick a more attractive one, who will make up for everything.

MARIANNE. Bless me, Frosine, it seems a very strange business when, to be happy, one must hope or wait for the demise of someone. And death does not always lend itself to the plans we make.

FROSINE. Are you joking? You are marrying him only on the understanding that he will 380 soon leave you a widow. That ought to be one of the articles in the contract. It would be very impertinent in him not to die before three months are out.

(*Enter* HARPAGON.)

Speak of the devil . . .

MARIANNE. Ah! Frosine, what a face!

HARPAGON. Do not be offended, my beauty, if I come to you wearing spectacles. I know that your charms are striking enough—are visible 390 enough by themselves—that there is no need of glasses to perceive them. But after all, it is through glasses we observe the stars, and I maintain and guarantee that you are a star. And what a star! The most beautiful star in the realm of stars. Frosine, she doesn't say a word, and she doesn't show, so it seems to me, that she is at all pleased to see me.

FROSINE. That is because she is still all surprise. And then, the girls nowadays are always 400 shy about showing straightway what is in their hearts.

(*Enter* ELISE.)

HARPAGON. You are right. (*to* MARIANNE) Here, darling beauty, is my daughter, who has come to greet you.

MARIANNE. I acquit myself, madam, much too tardily of this visit.

ELISE. You have done that, madam, which I ought to have done. It was my place to antici- 410 pate you.

HARPAGON. You see how tall she is; but weeds grow fast.

MARIANNE (*aside to* FROSINE). Oh, what an unpleasant man!

HARPAGON. What does the beauty say?

FROSINE. That she thinks you are wonderful.

HARPAGON. You do me too much honor, adorable darling.

MARIANNE (*aside to* FROSINE). Such an animal! 420

HARPAGON. I am obliged for your sentiments.

MARIANNE (*aside to* FROSINE). I can't stand any more of this.

(*Enter* CLEANTH.)

HARPAGON. Here is my son, who also comes to pay you his respects.

MARIANNE (*aside to* FROSINE). Ah! Frosine, what a coincidence! This is the very person I spoke to you about.

FROSINE. The adventure is fantastic. 430

HARPAGON. I see you are astonished to find that I have such big children; but I shall soon be rid of them both.

CLEANTH. Madam, to tell the truth, this is an encounter which I by no means expected; and my father surprised me not a little when he told me a while ago of his intentions.

MARIANNE. I can say the same for myself. This is an unforeseen meeting, which has surprised me as much as it has you. I too was not 440 at all prepared for such an encounter.

CLEANTH. It is true that my father, madam, could not make a handsomer choice, and the honor of seeing you is a real joy for me; but for all that, I will not assure you that I rejoice over the design you may have to become my stepmother. That compliment, I confess, is too much for me; it is a title, if you please, that I do not want for you. This speech may seem brutal in the eyes of some, but I am sure you 450 are a person who will take it in the right sense. You can easily imagine, madam, that this is a marriage which is bound to be somewhat repugnant to me; for you know what kind of man I am and how much it clashes with my interests. In short, you will not be offended if I tell you, with my father's permission, that if things depended on me, these nuptials would never take place.

HARPAGON. Your compliment is very imper- 460

tinent! What a nice confession to make to her!

MARIANNE. And I, in answer to you, have this to say: our feelings are quite mutual. If it is true that you would find it repugnant to have me for a stepmother, it would be no less so for me, I assure you, to have you for a stepson. Do not think, pray, that it is I who seek to be the source of your uneasiness. I should be very sorry to cause you any displeasure; and if I did not see myself forced to it by an absolute power, I give you my word, I would never consent to a marriage that pains you.

HARPAGON. She is right. A stupid compliment like that deserves a stupid answer. I beg pardon, my beauty, for my son's impertinence. He is a young ass who doesn't yet know the weight of his own words.

MARIANNE. I assure you that what he said has not offended me in the least. On the contrary, it has been a pleasure to hear him express his true sentiments. I like that kind of confession from him. If he had spoken in any other way, I would have far less esteem for him.

HARPAGON. It is very kind of you to forgive his faults this way. Time will make him wiser, and you will see that he will have a change of heart.

CLEANTH. No, father, it is not capable of change; and I earnestly entreat madam to believe that.

HARPAGON. Just see how extravagant he is! He goes on more rashly than ever.

CLEANTH. Would you have me belie my heart?

HARPAGON. Again! Would you mind changing the subject?

CLEANTH. Very well, since you wish me to speak in a different manner . . . Permit me, madam, to put myself in my father's place, to confess that I have never seen anything in the world as lovely as you; that I can conceive nothing to equal the happiness of pleasing you; and that the title of your husband is a glory, a felicity, that I would prefer to the destiny of the greatest prince on earth. Yes, madam, the happiness of possessing you, is in my estimation, the fairest of all fortunes; it is the goal of my whole ambition. I would do anything to make such a conquest; and the most powerful obstacles . . .

HARPAGON. Moderation, son, if you please.

CLEANTH. This is a compliment I am paying the lady, for you.

HARPAGON. By God! I have a tongue to express myself, and I have no need of a proxy the likes of you. Here, bring chairs.

FROSINE. No. It will be better for us to go directly to the fair. Then we'll be back early and have the whole time afterward to talk with you.

HARPAGON. Then tell them to hitch up the horses to the carriage. I beg you to excuse me, my beauty, for not having thought to give you a little refreshment before you start out.

CLEANTH. I have provided for that, father. I had them bring a few plates of Chinese oranges, some lemons, and some preserves; which I sent for in your name.

HARPAGON (*aside to* VALÈRE). Valère!

VALÈRE. He's out of his head.

CLEANTH. Do you think, father, that it isn't enough? Madam will please have the kindness to excuse it.

MARIANNE. It was not at all necessary.

CLEANTH. Have you ever, madam, seen more fire in a diamond than in this one you see on my father's finger? (*Takes ring off* HARPAGON'S *finger.*)

MARIANNE. It is true that it shines quite brightly.

CLEANTH. You must see it from close up. (*Puts ring on* MARIANNE'S *hand.*)

MARIANNE. It is very handsome, I must say, and it sparkles a great deal. (*Begins to take ring off her finger.*)

CLEANTH. No, no, madam; it is on hands much too lovely. My father makes you a present of it.

HARPAGON. I?

CLEANTH. Isn't it true, father, that you want the lady to keep it for love of you?

HARPAGON (*aside to* CLEANTH). What is this?

CLEANTH. Foolish question. He makes a sign to me that I should make you accept it.

MARIANNE. I don't at all want . . .

CLEANTH. Are you joking? He has no intention of taking it back.

HARPAGON (*aside*). I'm losing my temper.

MARIANNE. It would be . . .

CLEANTH. No, I tell you, you will offend him.

MARIANNE. Please . . .

CLEANTH. Out of the question.

HARPAGON (*aside*). A pox . . .

CLEANTH. Your refusal is making him angry.

HARPAGON (*aside to* CLEANTH). Ah! you traitor!

CLEANTH. You see he's getting desperate.

HARPAGON (*aside to* CLEANTH). You murderer, you!

570

CLEANTH. Father, it's not my fault. I am doing what I can to oblige her to keep it, but she is determined.

HARPAGON (*aside to* CLEANTH). Scoundrel!

CLEANTH. You are the cause, madam, of my father's quarreling with me.

HARPAGON (*aside to* CLEANTH). Knave!

CLEANTH. You will make him ill. Please, madam, do not resist any longer.

580

FROSINE. Mercy me! what a fuss! Keep the ring if the gentleman wants you to have it.

MARIANNE. So that you won't fly into a rage, I will keep it for the time being; and I will find another opportunity to return it.

(*Enter* BRINDAVOINE.)

BRINDAVOINE. Sir, there's a man here who wants to talk to you.

HARPAGON.. Tell him I am busy, and to come back some other time.

590

BRINDAVOINE. He says he has money for you.

HARPAGON (*to* MARIANNE). Please excuse me. I'll be back presently.

(*Enter* LA MERLUCHE *running; collides with* HARPAGON *and knocks him down.*)

MERLUCHE. Sir . . .

HARPAGON. Ah! I am dying!

CLEANTH. What is it, father, are you hurt?

HARPAGON. The traitor must surely have been paid by my debtors to make me break my neck.

600

VALÈRE (*to* HARPAGON). There's no harm done.

MERLUCHE. I beg your pardon, sir, I thought I did right to come running.

HARPAGON. What are you here for, murderer?

MERLUCHE. To tell you that neither of your horses has any shoes.

HARPAGON. Take them to the blacksmith, right away.

610

CLEANTH. While waiting for the horses to be shod, father, I will do the honors of the house for you, and conduct madam into the garden, where I shall have the refreshments served.

(*Exeunt* FROSINE, ELISE, MARIANNE *and* CLEANTH.)

HARPAGON. Valère, keep an eye on all that; and take care, pray, to save me as much as you can, so that we can send it back to the dealer.

620

VALÈRE. Rest assured. (*Exit* VALÈRE.)

HARPAGON. Oh, impertinent son! You are trying to ruin me!

ACT FOUR

(*Enter* CLEANTH, MARIANNE, ELISE *and* FROSINE.)

CLEANTH. Let us go in again; we shall be much better off in here. There is no longer anyone suspect around, and we can speak freely.

ELISE. Yes, madam, my brother has confided to me the love he bears you. I know what pain and frustration such obstacles can cause; and it is a most kindly sympathy, I assure you, that provokes my interest in your adventure.

10

MARIANNE. It is a sweet consolation to see a person like you interested in oneself, and I implore you, madam, always to cherish your generous friendship for me—so capable of softening the cruel blows of misfortune.

FROSINE. By my faith, you are unlucky people, both of you, for not having told me about your affair before all this happened. I could, no doubt, have warded off these troubles. I wouldn't have brought matters to such a pass as this.

20

CLEANTH. What can you expect? It is my

evil destiny has willed it so. But, dear Marianne, what have you resolved to do?

MARIANNE. Alas! am I in a position to resolve anything? Dependent as I am, can I do more than hope?

CLEANTH. Is there nothing in your heart to encourage me but barren hope? No benevolent pity? No helpful kindness? No lively affection at all?

MARIANNE. What can I tell you? Put yourself in my place, and see what I can do. Advise me. Order me. I put myself in your hands. And I believe you are too reasonable to demand more of me than is allowed by honor and decorum.

CLEANTH. Alas! to what am I reduced if you limit me to the pallid sentiments that rigorous honor and scrupulous decorum will allow?

MARIANNE. But what would you have me do? Even though I could ignore many of the niceties which our sex is obliged to observe, I have too much consideration for my mother. She has reared me with extreme tenderness. I could never resolve to do anything that would cause her displeasure. Go and speak to her. Do everything in your power to win her over. You may do and say whatever you please; I give you my permission. And if it is only a question of declaring in your favor, I readily consent to make a confession to her of all that I feel for you.

CLEANTH. Frosine, my poor Frosine, would you help us?

FROSINE. By my faith, is there any need to ask? I will with all my heart. You know that by nature I am human enough. Heaven didn't give me a heart of bronze, and I am only too eager to do little services for people when I see they love one another sincerely and honorably. What can we do about this?

CLEANTH. Think a little, I beg you.

MARIANNE. Show us a way.

ELISE. Invent something that will undo what you have done.

FROSINE. That is rather difficult. (*to* MARIANNE) As to your mother, she is not altogether unreasonable: perhaps you could win her over, and make her decide to transfer the gift she intends for the father to the son. (*to* CLEANTH) But the worst part of this is that your father is—your father.

CLEANTH. That's understood.

FROSINE. I mean he will bear a grudge if she refuses him openly, and he will be in no humor afterward to give his consent to your marriage. It will be necessary, to do it well, that the refusal come from himself. We must try by some means to make her distasteful to him.

CLEANTH. You are right.

FROSINE. Yes, I am right. I know it very well. That is what has to be done. But the deuce of it is to find a way. Wait; if we had a woman, getting on in years, with my talent, and who could act well enough to counterfeit a lady of quality, with the help of a train made up in a hurry and some bizarre name of marchioness or viscountess, who we could pretend comes from Brittany, I could be clever enough to convince him that she was a rich person who, besides her houses, had a hundred thousand écus in solid silver, that she was hopelessly in love with him, and wanted to be his wife so badly that she would sign over all her property to him in a marriage contract. I don't in the least doubt that he would lend an ear to the proposition. For, in short, although he loves you very much, he loves money a little more. And, once blinded by this illusion, once he has consented to what concerns you most, it will matter little afterward if he is undeceived when he looks more closely into the estate of our marchioness.

CLEANTH. This is all very well thought out.

FROSINE. Leave it to me. I just thought of a friend of mine who is the very woman we want.

CLEANTH. Rest assured, Frosine, of my gratitude if you succeed in this. But dear Marianne, let us begin by persuading your mother; there is still much to be done to break off this marriage. For your part, I beseech you, make every effort you possibly can. Use all the power that her love for you gives you over her. Unfold your eloquent graces without reserve—those all-powerful charms that Heaven has located in your eyes and lips. And forget none, please, of those tender expressions, or those soft entreaties, or those touching caresses to which, I am persuaded, no one could refuse anything.

(*Enter* HARPAGON.)

MARIANNE. I will do all in my power, and I won't forget a thing.

HARPAGON (*aside*). Hey! what's this? My son kisses the hand of his future stepmother; and his future stepmother does not offer much resistance. Could there be more to this than meets the eye?

ELISE. Here is my father.

HARPAGON. The carriage is ready. You can leave when you please. 130

CLEANTH. Since you are not going, father, I will drive them myself.

HARPAGON. No, stay. They can go just as well by themselves. I need you here.

(*Exeunt* FROSINE, ELISE *and* MARIANNE.)

HARPAGON. Oh! by the way, apart from the question of her becoming your stepmother, what do you think of this person?

CLEANTH. What do I think of her?

140 HARPAGON. Yes—of her manner, her figure, her beauty, and her wit?

CLEANTH. So so.

HARPAGON. What do you mean?

CLEANTH. To tell you frankly, I did not find her what I thought her to be. She has the manner of an out-and-out coquette, her figure is rather awkward, here beauty is mediocre, and she has a very common kind of wit. But don't think, father, that I am trying to set you against 150 her. Because, stepmother for stepmother, I like this one as much as I would any other.

HARPAGON. Nevertheless you were telling her a while ago . . .

CLEANTH. I did say a few nice things to her in your name—but that was to please you.

HARPAGON. So then, you don't feel the slightest inclination for her?

CLEANTH. I? None at all.

HARPAGON. That's too bad, for it puts an end 160 to an idea that came into my head. Seeing her here made me reflect on my age, and I thought to myself that people might find fault with me for marrying such a young girl. This consideration made me abandon my plans; but, since I have already asked her to marry and am bound by my word, I would have given her to you—if you had not shown such an aversion.

CLEANTH. To me?

HARPAGON. To you.

170 CLEANTH. In marriage?

HARPAGON. In marriage.

CLEANTH. Listen. It is true she is not much to my taste. But to make you happy, father, I will resign myself to marrying her—since it is your wish.

HARPAGON. Mine? I am more reasonable than you think. I would not force your inclination.

CLEANTH. Pardon me, I will do myself this violence out of love for you.

HARPAGON. No, no. A marriage can never be 180 happy where there is no affection.

CLEANTH. Affection is something, father, that will come afterwards, perhaps. They say that love is often the fruit of marriage.

HARPAGON. No, the venture ought not to be risked on the man's side. There may be painful consequences to which I would not care to expose myself. If you had felt some inclination for her earlier, I would have had you marry her in my place. But since that is not the case, I will 190 carry out my first plan, and marry her myself.

CLEANTH. Very well, father, since this is the way things are, I am obliged to bare my heart to you: I must reveal our secret. The truth is that I have loved her since the first time I saw her out walking, that my intention up to a while ago was to ask you if I could have her for my wife, and that nothing has held me back but your declaration of your own sentiments and fear of displeasing you. 200

HARPAGON. Have you visited her?

CLEANTH. Yes, father.

HARPAGON. Very often?

CLEANTH. Often enough—for the time I had.

HARPAGON. Were you well received?

CLEANTH. Very well. But they did not know who I was. That is why Marianne was so surprised a while ago.

HARPAGON. Did you declare your passion to her, and your intention of marrying her? 210

CLEANTH. Certainly, and I have even broached the subject a little to her mother.

HARPAGON. Did she give your proposal a hearing?

CLEANTH. Yes, a very civil one.

HARPAGON. And does her daughter return your love appreciably?

CLEANTH. If appearances are to be trusted, I am persuaded, father, that she feels some affection for me. 220

HARPAGON. I am happy to learn such a secret. It is exactly what I wanted to know. And now, son, do you know what you will have to do? You will have to think, if you please, about getting over your love, about giving up your pursuit of this person whom I intend for myself, and about marrying, in a short time, the woman I have chosen for you!

CLEANTH. So, father, you have tricked me! Very well! Since things have come to this pass, I declare to you that I will never cease loving Marianne, that I will go to any limit to dispute the conquest with you, and though you have the mother's consent on your side, I will perhaps find others who will fight for me.

HARPAGON. What? You scoundrel! You have the audacity to stalk my game?

CLEANTH. It is you who are stalking mine: I knew her first.

HARPAGON. Am I not your father? Don't you owe me your respect?

CLEANTH. These are not matters in which the children are obliged to defer to their fathers. Love knows no master.

HARPAGON. I'll teach you to know me—by the mastery of a good stick.

CLEANTH. All your threats will do no good.

HARPAGON. Will you renounce Marianne?

CLEANTH. On no account.

HARPAGON. Bring me a stick, quickly.

(*Enter* MASTER JACQUES.)

JACQUES. Now, now, now! gentlemen, what is this? What can you be thinking of?

CLEANTH. I laugh at it all.

JACQUES. Ah! gently, sir.

HARPAGON. To talk with such impudence!

JACQUES. Oh! sir, please.

CLEANTH. I won't yield an inch.

JACQUES. Eh, what? to your father?

HARPAGON. Leave him to me. (*Menaces* CLEANTH *with his stick.*)

JACQUES. Eh, what? to your son? Once more, leave off, for my sake.

HARPAGON. I want to make *you,* Master Jacques, judge of this affair—to prove I am right.

JACQUES. I am willing. (*to* CLEANTH) Go a little farther off.

HARPAGON. I am in love with a girl I want to marry, and that scoundrel has the impudence to be in love with the same girl at the same time, and intends, despite my orders, to marry her.

JACQUES. Ah! he is in the wrong.

HARPAGON. Isn't it a shocking thing for a son to enter into competition with his father? Shouldn't he, out of respect, refrain from meddling where my affections are involved?

JACQUES. You are right. Let me talk to him. Stay here. (*Goes to* CLEANTH.)

CLEANTH. Yes, of course, since he has chosen you for judge, I'll not back out. It isn't important to me who it is, and I too am willing to refer myself to you, Master Jacques, in this matter of our difference.

JACQUES. You do me great honor.

CLEANTH. I am very much taken with a young lady who returns all my interest, and who has tenderly received the offer of my heart; and my father has taken it into his head to trouble our love by making her an offer of marriage.

JACQUES. He is in the wrong, surely.

CLEANTH. Isn't he ashamed, at his age, to dream of marrying? Is it becoming in him to be amorous? Wouldn't he do better to leave that business to young fellows?

JACQUES. You are right; he is making a fool of himself. Let me say a few words to him. (*Returns to* HARPAGON.) Well, your son is not so strange as you make him out to be; he has submitted to reason. He says he knows that he owes you respect, that he was carried away by the heat of the argument, and that he will not refuse to submit to anything that pleases you, provided you intend to treat him better than you have done, and that you give him someone in marriage with whom he will have reason to be satisfied.

HARPAGON. Ah, tell him, Master Jacques, that with this provision, he may expect anything he *wants* from me; and that, Marianne excepted, he is at liberty to choose any girl he pleases.

JACQUES. Leave it to me. (*to* CLEANTH) Well, your father is not as unreasonable as you make him out to be, and he admitted to me that it was only your rage that roused his temper, that he is angry only about the way you conducted yourself, and that he will be very much disposed to grant all your wishes provided you will go about it gently, and show him the deference, respect, and submission that a son owes his father.

CLEANTH. Ah! Master Jacques, you can assure him that if he grants me Marianne, he will see that I will always be the most submissive man in the world, and that I will never do anything except by his wish.

JACQUES (*going to* HARPAGON). It's done. He consents to what you ask.

330 HARPAGON. It's the happiest conclusion in the world.

JACQUES (*going to* CLEANTH). It's all decided. He is satisfied with your promises.

CLEANTH. Heaven be praised!

JACQUES (*in the middle of the stage*). Gentlemen, you have only to talk together. Here you are in agreement now, and you were about to fall out because of a misunderstanding!

CLEANTH. My poor Master Jacques, I will be

340 obliged to you for life.

JACQUES. It was nothing, sir.

HARPAGON. You have made me happy, Master Jacques, and you deserve a reward. (MASTER JACQUES *puts out his hand.*) Go—I shall remember it, I assure you.

JACQUES. I kiss your hand.

(*Exit* MASTER JACQUES.)

CLEANTH. I beg your pardon, father, for showing my temper in that way.

350 HARPAGON. It was nothing.

CLEANTH. I assure you, it gives me all the concern in the world.

HARPAGON. As for myself, it gives me all the joy in the world to see you reasonable.

CLEANTH. How good of you to forget my fault so quickly!

HARPAGON. One easily forgets his child's faults when one sees him return to the path of duty.

360 CLEANTH. What! you harbor no resentment for all my extravagance?

HARPAGON. You oblige me not to by the submission and respect you show.

CLEANTH. And I, I promise you, father, will bear the memory of your kindness to the grave.

HARPAGON. And I, I promise you that there is nothing you shall not have from me.

CLEANTH. Ah! father, I have nothing more to ask: you gave me all when you gave me

370 Marianne.

HARPAGON. What?

CLEANTH. I say, father, that you have made me too happy. You gave me all when you agreed to give me Marianne.

HARPAGON. Who said anything about giving you Marianne?

CLEANTH. You, father.

HARPAGON. I?

CLEANTH. Certainly.

HARPAGON. What! You are the one who 380 promised to renounce her.

CLEANTH. I renounce her?

HARPAGON. Yes.

CLEANTH. Not in the least.

HARPAGON. You haven't abandoned your pretensions to her?

CLEANTH. On the contrary, I am more determined than ever.

HARPAGON. What! you rascal, again?

CLEANTH. Nothing can change my mind. 390

HARPAGON. Let me at you, traitor!

CLEANTH. Do whatever you please.

HARPAGON. I forbid you ever to see me again.

CLEANTH. It's all the same to me.

HARPAGON. I abandon you.

CLEANTH. Abandon me.

HARPAGON. I disown you as my son.

CLEANTH. So be it.

HARPAGON. I disinherit you.

CLEANTH. Anything you like. 400

HARPAGON. And I give you my curse.

CLEANTH. I have no need of your gifts.

(*Exit* HARPAGON.)

(*Enter* LA FLÈCHE.)

FLÈCHE. Ah! sir! I have found you just in time! Follow me quickly.

CLEANTH. What's the matter?

FLÈCHE. Follow me, I tell you—our troubles are over.

CLEANTH. What?

FLÈCHE (*shows him the chest*). Here's your 410 way out.

CLEANTH. How?

FLÈCHE. Your father's treasure. I dug it up!

CLEANTH. Where was it?

FLÈCHE. You shall know everything. Run. I hear him screaming.

(*Exeunt* LA FLÈCHE *and* CLEANTH.)

(*Enter* HARPAGON.)

HARPAGON. Stop thief! Stop thief! Stop assassin! Stop murderer! Justice, Divine Justice! I 420 am ruined! I've been murdered! He cut my throat, he stole my money! Who can it be? What's become of him? Where is he? Where is he hiding? What shall I do to find him? Where shall I run? Where shan't I run? Isn't that he there? Isn't this he here? Who's this? (*Sees his own shadow and grabs his own arm.*) Stop! Give me back my money, you rogue. . . . Ah! it is myself. My mind is unhinged, and I don't know where I am, who I am, or what I am doing. (*Falls to his knees.*) Alas! my poor money, my poor money, my dear friend, they have taken you from me. And since they carried you off, I've lost my support, my consolation, my joy. Everything is at an end for me; I have no more to do in this world! I cannot live without you! It's finished. I can no more. (*Lies down.*) I am dying. I am dead. I am buried! Isn't there anybody who would like to bring me back to life by returning my dear money or by telling me who took it? (*rising to his knees*) What did you say? It was nobody. (*Stands.*) Whoever did the job must have watched very closely for his chance; for he chose exactly the time when I was talking to my treacherous son. (*Takes his hat and cane.*) I'll go out. I'll go and demand justice. I'll order them to torture everyone in my house for a confession: the maids, the valets, my son, my daughter—and myself too! What a crowd of people! Everybody I cast my eyes on arouses my suspicion, and everything seems to be my thief. Eh! what are you talking about there? About the man that robbed me? Why are you making that noise up there? Is my thief there? (*Kneels and addresses the audience.*) Please, if anyone has any information about my thief, I beg you to tell me. Are you sure he isn't hidden there among you? They all look at me and laugh. (*Rises.*) You will probably see that they all had a part in this robbery. Here, quick, commissaries, archers, provosts, judges, tortures, scaffolds, and executioners! I want to have everybody hanged. And if I don't recover my money, I'll hang myself afterward!

ACT FIVE

(*On stage:* HARPAGON, *the* COMMISSARY *and his clerk.*)

COMMISSARY. Leave me alone. I know my business, thank God! I didn't start investigating robberies yesterday. I wish I had a sack of francs for every man I've sent to the gallows!

HARPAGON. All the magistrates are interested in taking this case in hand. What's more, if no one sees to it that I recover my money, I shall demand justice from Justice herself!

COMMISSARY. We must follow the prescribed procedure. How much was it you said was in this moneybox?

HARPAGON. Ten thousand écus, to the sou.

COMMISSARY. Ten thousand écus?

HARPAGON. Ten thousand écus.

COMMISSARY. It was a considerable theft.

HARPAGON. No penalty would be too great for the enormity of the crime. If it goes unpunished, nothing is too sacred to be safe.

COMMISSARY. In what coin was the sum?

HARPAGON. In good gold louis and solid pistoles.

COMMISSARY. Whom do you suspect of this theft?

HARPAGON. Everybody! I want you to arrest the whole city and the suburbs!

COMMISSARY. We mustn't frighten anyone, take my word for it. We must try and obtain some evidence quietly. Then afterward we can proceed more rigorously in recovering the deniers that were taken from you.

(*Enter* MASTER JACQUES *from the kitchen.*)

JACQUES. I'll be back in a little while. First I want you to cut his throat. Then I want you to singe his feet. Then I want you to put him in boiling water. Then I want you to hang him from the ceiling.

HARPAGON. Who? The man who robbed me?

40 JACQUES. I was talking about the suckling pig your steward just sent me. I want to dress him for you according to my fancy.

HARPAGON. That is not the question. You must talk to this gentleman about something else.

COMMISSARY. Don't be frightened. I am not a man who would cause you scandal. Everything will be done quietly.

JACQUES. Is the gentleman one of your sup-
50 per guests?

COMMISSARY. Now, my dear friend, you must hide nothing from your master.

JACQUES. Faith, sir, I will show you all I know: I will treat you the best I possibly can.

HARPAGON. We aren't talking about that.

JACQUES. If I can't give you as fine a feast as I want to, it's the fault of a certain gentleman, a certain steward, who has clipped my wings with the scissors of his economy.

60 HARPAGON. Traitor! We are investigating something more important than supper. I want you to give me information about the money that was stolen from me.

JACQUES. Did someone steal your money?

HARPAGON. Yes, you rascal! And I'll have you hanged if you don't give it back.

COMMISSARY. For Heaven's sake, don't bully him! I can see by his face he's an honest man. Without making us send him to jail, he will tell
70 you everything you want to know. Yes, my friend, if you tell us what you know, no harm will come to you. You will be rewarded by your master, as you deserve to be. Just this morning someone took his money. Is it possible you don't have some information about this matter?

JACQUES (*aside*). Exactly what I need to get my revenge on our steward! Ever since he came into this house he has been the favorite—only *his* advice is listened to. Then, too, the beating
80 he gave me sticks in my craw.

HARPAGON. What are you mumbling about?

COMMISSARY. Leave him alone. He is preparing to give you satisfaction. I told you he is an honest man.

JACQUES. Sir, since you want me to tell you something about this business, I think it was a certain gentleman, a certain steward, who did the job.

HARPAGON. Valère?

90 JACQUES. Yes.

HARPAGON. He? Who seemed to be so trustworthy?

JACQUES. Himself. I think he is the one who robbed you.

HARPAGON. On what grounds do you think so?

JACQUES. On what grounds?

HARPAGON. Yes.

JACQUES. I think so . . . on the grounds that . . . I think so. 100

COMMISSARY. But it is necessary that you tell us what proof you have.

HARPAGON. Did you see him sneaking around the place where I kept my money?

JACQUES. Yes, certainly. Where did you keep your money?

HARPAGON. In the garden.

JACQUES. Exactly. I saw him sneaking through the garden. What was this money in?

HARPAGON. A moneybox. 110

JACQUES. That's it. I saw him with a moneybox.

HARPAGON. This moneybox . . . What did it look like? I'll soon see if it was mine.

JACQUES. What did it look like?

HARPAGON. Yes.

JACQUES. It looked like . . . it looked like a moneybox.

COMMISSARY. Of course. But describe it a little, so we can see . . . 120

JACQUES. It was a large moneybox.

HARPAGON. The one that was stolen from me was small.

JACQUES. Oh, yes—it was small if you want to look at it that way. I call it large on account of what it contained.

COMMISSARY. What color was it?

JACQUES. What color?

COMMISSARY. Yes.

JACQUES. It was the color of . . . yes, the 130 color of it was . . . Can't you help me out a bit?

HARPAGON. Eh!

JACQUES. Wasn't it red?

HARPAGON. No, gray.

JACQUES. Oh! yes, grayish-red. That's what I meant to say.

HARPAGON. There isn't the slightest doubt. That is definitely it. Write, sir, write down his testimony. Heavens! who's to be trusted nowa- 140 days? You can't put your faith in anything!

After this, I fear I am a man who might rob himself.

JACQUES. Sir, he is coming back. At least don't go and tell him it was I who told you this.

(*Enter* VALÈRE.)

HARPAGON. Advance. Come. Confess the darkest deed, the most horrible atrocity ever committed.

150 VALÈRE. What do you mean, sir?

HARPAGON. What! traitor, you do not even blush for your crime?

VALÈRE. What crime can you be talking of?

HARPAGON. What crime am I talking of? Infamous! As though you didn't know what I mean! It is useless for you to try and cover up. The deed has been discovered. Someone has just told me all. Really! How could you abuse my kindness that way—insinuate yourself into 160 my house to betray me—to play a trick of that kind on me!

VALÈRE. Sir, since someone has told you all, I shall not try to find a way out. I deny nothing.

JACQUES (*aside*). Hoho! Could I have guessed right without thinking?

VALÈRE. It was my intention to speak to you about it, and I wanted to wait for more favorable conditions to do so. But since things are the way they are, I beg you not to be angry. Be 170 good enough to hear my reasons.

HARPAGON. And what wonderful reasons can you give me, infamous thief?

VALÈRE. Ah! sir, I have not deserved those names. It is true I am guilty of an offense against you. But, after all, my fault is pardonable.

HARPAGON. How, pardonable? A premeditated crime? An assassination of this sort?

VALÈRE. Please don't lose your temper. When 180 you have heard me, you will see that the evil done is not so great as you make it out.

HARPAGON. The evil is not so great as I make it out! What? My blood! My entrails!—You scoundrel!

VALÈRE. Your blood, sir, has not fallen into evil hands. I belong to a class which is not beneath it, and there is nothing in all this for which I cannot make full reparation.

HARPAGON. That is my intention precisely— 190 that you shall make full restitution of what you have ravished from me.

VALÈRE. Your honor, sir, shall be fully satisfied.

HARPAGON. It has nothing to do with honor. But, tell me, what ever possessed you to do it?

VALÈRE. Alas! You are asking me?

HARPAGON. Yes I really am.

VALÈRE. A god who is his own excuse for everything he does: Love.

HARPAGON. Love? 200

VALÈRE. Yes.

HARPAGON. A beautiful love, a beautiful love indeed! Love of my gold louis.

VALÈRE. No, sir, it was not in the least your wealth that tempted me. That wasn't what dazzled me. And I swear I will make no claims whatsoever on your property, provided you let me keep what I have.

HARPAGON. I will do no such thing, by God! See how insolent he is! He wants to keep the 210 proceeds of his theft.

VALÈRE. Do you call it a theft?

HARPAGON. Do I call it a theft! A treasure like that!

VALÈRE. A treasure indeed! The most precious you have, without a doubt! But your giving me such a treasure would be no real loss to you. I ask you on bended knee to give me this enchanting treasure. If you want to do right you will grant my request. 220

HARPAGON. I will do nothing of the kind. What is he saying?

VALÈRE. We have promised to be faithful to one another. We have vowed never to separate.

HARPAGON. Your vow is admirable. Your promise is amusing.

VALÈRE. We are engaged to an eternal union.

HARPAGON. I shall forbid the banns, I assure you.

VALÈRE. Naught but death can part us. 230

HARPAGON. You are certainly bewitched by my money.

VALÈRE. I have told you, sir, it was not selfish interest that drove me to do what I have done. My heart was not impelled by the motives you suspect. A nobler idea was my inspiration.

HARPAGON. You'll see: it is out of Christian charity he wants to keep my money! But I'll set all to rights. The law, you brazen scoundrel, will make me amends for everything! 240

VALÈRE. You may proceed as you like in the matter. I am ready to suffer any violence that will please you. But at least believe, I beg, that if any harm is done, I am the only one to accuse. Your daughter is in no way to blame for any of this.

HARPAGON. Certainly I believe that. It would be very strange, indeed, if my daughter had a part in this crime. But I want to get my treasure back. I want you to confess where you have carried it off to!

VALÈRE. I? Your treasure has not been carried off at all, but is here—at home.

HARPAGON (*aside*). Oh, my dear moneybox! (*to* VALÈRE) My treasure has not left the house?

VALÈRE. No, sir.

HARPAGON. Well. Tell me now, haven't you even . . . tampered a bit?

VALÈRE. I, tamper? Ah! you do us both a great wrong. The love that consumes me is wholly pure and respectful.

HARPAGON (*aside*). He's consumed with love for my moneybox?

VALÈRE. I would have died rather than reveal to your treasure a single offensive thought. It would have been an insult to so much honor and virtue.

HARPAGON (*aside*). My moneybox honorable and virtuous?

VALÈRE. I limited my desires to the pleasure of merely seeing. No criminal act has profaned the passion that is inspired by those lovely eyes.

HARPAGON (*aside*). My moneybox's lovely eyes? He talks like a lover discussing his mistress.

VALÈRE. Dame Claude, sir, knows the truth of this adventure. She can bear witness . . .

HARPAGON. What! my maid is an accomplice in this business?

VALÈRE. Yes, sir, she stood as a witness at our engagement. But it was not until she had learned how honorable were my intentions that she helped me to persuade your daughter to pledge her fidelity to me and accept my pledge in return.

HARPAGON (*aside*). Ha? Is his fear of the law making his mind wander? (*to* VALÈRE) Why confuse us by bringing my daughter into this?

VALÈRE. I tell you, sir, I had all the trouble in the world to persuade modesty to grant what love desired.

HARPAGON. Whose modesty?

VALÈRE. Your daughter's. And it wasn't until yesterday that she was able to make up her mind and sign a mutual promise of marriage with me.

HARPAGON. My daughter signed a promise of marriage with you?

VALÈRE. Just as I, on my part, signed one with her.

HARPAGON. O Heavens! Another disgrace!

JACQUES (*to the* COMMISSARY). Write, sir, write.

HARPAGON. Aggravation of misfortune! Excess of despair! Come, sir, do the duty of your office. Draw me up an indictment against him as a thief and an instigator.

VALÈRE. Those are names which do not belong to me. When it is known who I am . . .

(*Enter* ELISE, MARIANNE *and* FROSINE.)

HARPAGON. Ah! profligate daughter! Unworthy of a father like me! This is how you put into practice the lessons I gave you! You let yourself become infatuated with an infamous thief! You promise him your hand without my consent! But you will be undone, both of you. (*to* ELISE) Four good, strong walls will answer for your conduct. (*to* VALÈRE) A good, tall gallows will give me satisfaction for your audacity.

VALÈRE. It is not your passion that will judge the matter. I will at least be heard before I am condemned.

HARPAGON. I was mistaken to say the gallows. You will be broken alive on the wheel.

ELISE. Ah! father, be a little more human in your sentiments, I beseech you. Do not push things to the violent extreme of paternal power. Do not let yourself be carried away by the first impulse of passion. Give yourself time. Consider what you wish to do. Take pains. Look more closely at the person who has roused your wrath. He is not what your eyes have judged him to be. You will find it far less strange that I should have given myself to him when you learn that, were it not for him, you would have lost me long ago, and forever. Yes, father, he is the man who saved me from the great peril, the peril you know I was so close to in the water—the man to whom you owe the life of the same daughter who . . .

HARPAGON. All that is nothing. It would have been better for me had he let you drown and not do what he has done.

ELISE. Father, out of paternal love for me . . .

HARPAGON. No, no! I won't hear another word. The law must do its duty.

JACQUES (*aside*). You'll pay for the beating you gave me.

350 FROSINE (*aside*). This is a queer mix-up.

(*Enter* ANSELM.)

ANSELM. What is it, Signor Harpagon? I see you are very much disturbed.

HARPAGON. Ah! Signor Anselm, you now behold the most unfortunate of men. Here is I don't know how much trouble and disorder to complicate the contract you came to sign! My money has been attacked! My honor has been attacked! And there stands a traitor, a profligate 360 who has violated all that is most sacred to man —who has insinuated himself into my house under the name of servant in order to steal my money and seduce my daughter!

VALÈRE. Who cares about this money that you make so much noise about?

HARPAGON. Yes, they have made each other a promise of marriage. This outrage is your concern, Signor Anselm. You are the man who ought to take action against him. Have him 370 prosecuted by the law! Revenge yourself for his insolence!

ANSELM. I have no intention of forcing myself on anybody or of making any claims to a heart that has already given itself to another. But of course I am ready to fight for your interests. As if the cause were my own.

HARPAGON. This gentleman here is an honest commissary, who assures me that he will neglect no part of his official duty. (*to the* COMMISSARY) 380 Indict him, sir, in due form! And make everything sound very criminal!

VALÈRE. I don't see what sort of crime you can make out of my passion for your daughter or what punishment you think I can be condemned to for our engagement. When it is known who I am . . .

HARPAGON. I don't give a damn for all those tales. Nowadays the world is only too full of thieves of nobility, of impostors who take ad- 390 vantage of their insignificance and impudently bedeck themselves with the first illustrious name they take a fancy to.

VALÈRE. I'll have you know I am too honest to adorn myself with aught that is not mine. All Naples can testify to my birth.

ANSELM. Careful. Watch what you say. You run a greater risk here than you think. You have before you a man to whom all Naples is known and who can easily see through a trumped-up story. 400

VALÈRE. I am a man with nothing to fear. If you know Naples, you know who Don Thomas d'Alburcy was.

ANSELM. Of course I know who he was. Few people were better acquainted with him than I.

HARPAGON. I don't give a damn for Don Thomas or Don Smith.

ANSELM. Please, let him talk. We will see what he has to say about him.

VALÈRE. I have this to say: it was he who 410 brought me into the world.

ANSELM. He?

VALÈRE. Yes.

ANSELM. Come now. You deceive yourself. Try some other story that might be more successful. Don't expect to save yourself by this imposture.

VALÈRE. Watch what you say. This is no imposture. I advance no claim that I cannot easily justify. 420

ANSELM. What! You dare to call yourself the son of Thomas d'Alburcy?

VALÈRE. I dare. And I am ready to defend that truth against no matter whom.

ANSELM. Fantastic audacity! Learn to your confusion that it was sixteen years ago, at the very least, that the man you speak of perished at sea with his wife and children while trying to save their lives from the cruel persecutions that accompanied the disorder at Naples and 430 which precipitated the exile of more than one noble family.

VALÈRE. Yes, but learn to your own confusion, that his seven-year-old son, with a single servant, was saved from the shipwreck by a Spanish vessel—and that the son then saved now speaks to you. Learn that the captain of that vessel, touched by my misfortune, took a liking to me and brought me up as his own son—that arms have been my occupation since 440 the time I was able to hold them—that I learned a short time ago that my father is not dead, as I had always thought—that while passing through this city in search of him an adventure planned by Heaven gave me a glimpse of charming Elise—that the sight of her made me a slave to her beauty—and that the violence of my love and her father's severity made me resolve to enter into his house and send another in search of my parents.

ANSELM. What proof do you have beyond your bare word that this is not a fable you have constructed on a foundation of truth?

VALÈRE. The Spanish captain, a ruby signet that belonged to my father, an agate bracelet that my mother placed upon my arm, and old Pedro, the servant who with me was saved from the shipwreck.

MARIANNE. Alas! I myself can answer for what you have said. You are not deceiving us. Your account has made clear to me that you are my brother!

VALÈRE. You, my sister?

MARIANNE. Yes. My heart was moved the moment you opened your mouth. Our mother, whom you will see again, has diverted me a thousand times with the misfortunes of our family. Heaven did not suffer us either to perish in that unhappy shipwreck—but our lives were saved only at the expense of our liberty. They were pirates who took us, my mother and me, off the wreckage of our vessel. After ten years of slavery, we regained our liberty through a happy accident, and returned to Naples. There we found that all our property had been sold and were not able to uncover any news of my father. We sailed for Genoa, where my mother went to gather up the sad remains of our dissipated family fortune. From there, fleeing the barbarous injustice of her kinsmen, she came to these parts, where she has lived scarcely more than a languishing life.

ANSELM. O Heaven—such are the signs of Thy power! How clearly Thou hast shown us that Thou alone canst work miracles! Embrace me, children both! Mingle your joy with that of your father!

VALÈRE. You are our father?

MARIANNE. Is it for you my mother has shed so many tears?

ANSELM. Yes, my daughter, yes, my son, I am Don Thomas d'Alburcy, whom Heaven saved from the waves with all the money he had with him—and who, believing for more than sixteen years you all were dead, was preparing, after long voyages, to seek the consolation of a new family through marriage with a good and gentle young lady. When I saw how much my life would be in danger should I return to Naples, I abandoned the idea forever. Having found a way to sell what I had there, I established my residence here. Under the name of Anselm I sought to leave behind the sorrows of the name which has caused me so many reverses.

HARPAGON. Is that your son?

ANSELM. Yes.

HARPAGON. I hold you responsible for the ten thousand écus he stole from me.

ANSELM. He? He stole from you?

HARPAGON. He himself.

VALÈRE. Who told you?

HARPAGON. Master Jacques.

VALÈRE. It is you that say so?

JACQUES. Look, I'm not saying a thing.

HARPAGON. Yes. This gentleman is the commissary who took down his testimony.

VALÈRE. Can you believe me capable of such a villainous deed?

HARPAGON. Capable or not capable, I want my money back.

(*Enter* CLEANTH *and* LA FLÈCHE.)

CLEANTH. Torment yourself no longer, father. Accuse no one. I have uncovered some information about your affair, and I have come to tell you that, if you will resign yourself to letting me marry Marianne, your money will be returned to you.

HARPAGON. Where is it?

CLEANTH. Don't worry. It's in a place that I will answer for. Everything depends on me. It only remains for you to tell me your decision. You can choose whether to give me Marianne or lose your moneybox.

HARPAGON. Nothing has been removed from it?

CLEANTH. Nothing. Let us see if it is your intention to subscribe to this marriage and join your consent to that of her mother—who has given her the liberty to choose between us two.

MARIANNE. But you do not realize that his consent is not enough, or that Heaven, along with my brother, whom you now behold (*Points to* VALÈRE.) has restored my father to me. You must win me from *him*.

ANSELM. Heaven, my children, did not restore me to you in order that I should oppose your desires. Signor Harpagon, you very well know that the choice of a young lady falls to the son and not to the father. Come now, don't make people say what is too obvious to need expression. Give your consent to this double ceremony as I have.

HARPAGON. Before I can make up my mind, I must see my moneybox.

CLEANTH. You shall see it safe and sound.

HARPAGON. I have no money to give my children for their marriages.

ANSELM. Oh well, I have some for both of them. Don't let that bother you.

HARPAGON. You will commit yourself to stand the cost of both these marriages?

ANSELM. Yes, I will commit myself. Are you satisfied?

HARPAGON. Yes, provided that you have me a suit made for the wedding.

ANSELM. Agreed. Come, let us indulge the happiness which this joyous day bestows upon us.

COMMISSARY. Hold, gentlemen! Hold on, one moment, if you please! Who is going to pay for all the writing I've done?

HARPAGON. We have no need of your writing.

COMMISSARY. No? But I, on the other hand, can't pretend to have done it for nothing.

HARPAGON (*points to* MASTER JACQUES). As payment I give you this man. Take him and hang him.

JACQUES. Alas! what is a man supposed to do? They beat me before for telling the truth. Now they want to hang me for lying.

ANSELM. Signor Harpagon, you ought to pardon him his trickery.

HARPAGON. You'll pay the commissary then.

ANSELM. So be it. Let us go at once and share our joy with your mother.

HARPAGON. And I, to see my dear, dear moneybox.

Review Questions

1. In what respects is *The Miser* neoclassical?
2. How does Moliére use exaggeration for comic effect? Cite specific instances.
3. How does Molière delineate Harpagon as an antisocial character?
4. Why does Cleanth need to borrow money?
5. What is the source of comedy in the negotiation of a loan? See Act II, Scene 1.
6. What are the conflicts between Harpagon and Cleanth?
7. Describe Molière's use of teasing as a comic device in Act II, Scene 6.
8. To what extent do the comic effects rely on performance?
9. Describe Molière's use of comic violence in the scene between Harpagon and Mr. James.
10. What discoveries are used for comic effect?
11. How is the diamond ring used for comic effect?
12. Discuss Molière's use of misunderstanding.
13. How does Harpagon fit into Bergson's theory of comedy?
14. How does Molière make use of stichomythia? Of soliloquy?
15. Contrast Anselm and Harpagon.
16. What is the significance of Harpagon's repetition of "without a dowry?" See Act I, Scene 7.
17. Is the recognition scene comic?
18. How is Valère disguised? Why?
19. How is Harpagon's character delineated before he appears?
20. Describe Harpagon's initial appearance.
21. How is Cleanth dressed?
22. What is the basis of the matrimonial arrangements which Harpagon makes for his children?
23. Cite examples of comic business.
24. Describe Frosina, the match-maker.
25. Does the comedy serve a social purpose?

26. What farcical aspects are used by Molière?
27. Compare the use of ridicule with *The School for Scandal.*
28. Molière is known as a playwright of common sense. How does *The Miser* illustrate this?
29. Is the play unified?
30. How does Molière prevent the play from becoming too savage?

THE SCHOOL FOR SCANDAL

Richard Brinsley Sheridan (1751-1816)

EDITED BY JOHN LOFTIS

Sheridan was preeminently a theater man who, although he spent only six years in writing plays (1773–1779), contributed to the English stage two plays second in popularity only to Shakespeare. He was born in Dublin, the son of an actor father and a dramatist mother. His romantic marriage had all the aspects of drama including a flight to France and two duels.

He was an actor who turned to playwriting, winning his first success with *The Rivals,* which was produced at Covent Garden in 1775. A year later he became manager of the Drury Lane Theater, where he scored a dazzling success with *The School for Scandal,* first performed in 1777. Two years later Sheridan retired from the theater to enter politics. As a member of Parliament he found a new arena for his considerable theatrical gifts.

NOTE ON THE TEXT

Professor Loftis has, in his edition of the play, preserved Sheridan's stylistic and typographical peculiarities, emending and correcting only as necessary for clarity and setting off his alterations with brackets. One specific peculiarity: the stage direction "(*Aside.*)" most often follows rather than precedes the intended line or phrase. In the original this stage direction was in some places left off altogether, and Professor Loftis has here inserted it, in brackets, in places where its absence would cause confusion.

Photo Fred Fehl

Photo Fred Fehl

ABOVE. Lady Sneerwell and Mrs. Candour of the 1962 Tennent Production Company play, directed by Sir John Gielgud.

LEFT. Sir Oliver Surface, played by Sir John Gielgud, with the profligate nephew, Charles Surface.

RIGHT. The famous screen episode, a masterpiece of discovery and reversal, as seen, ABOVE, in an engraving contemporary with the play, and BELOW, in the 1966 APA-Phoenix Repertory Company production.

BELOW. From R. to L., Sir Oliver, Sir Peter Teazle, Maria, and Lady Teazle during the final scene.

Photo Fred Fehl

Mrs. Abingdon, Mr. King, Mr. Smith, and Mr. Palmer, in the Characters of Lady Teazle Sir Peter Teazle, Charles and Joseph Surface.

Harvard College Library Theater Collection

Maurice Manson

Characters

MEN

SIR PETER TEAZLE	*Mr. King*
SIR OLIVER SURFACE	*Mr. Yates*
JOSEPH SURFACE	*Mr. Palmer*
CHARLES SURFACE	*Mr. Smith*
CRABTREE	*Mr. Parsons*
SIR BENJAMIN BACKBITE	*Mr. Dodd*
ROWLEY	*Mr. Aickin*
TRIP	*Mr. LaMash*
MOSES	*Mr. Baddeley*
SNAKE	*Mr. Packer*
CARELESS	*Mr. Farren*

and other Companions to CHARLES [SURFACE],
Servants, etc.

WOMEN

LADY TEAZLE	*Mrs. Abington*
MARIA	*Miss P. Hopkins*
LADY SNEERWELL	*Miss Sherry*
MRS. CANDOUR	*Miss Pope*

SCENE: *London*

Note: *The names at the right are those of the original players.*

THE SCHOOL FOR SCANDAL

Prologue

Spoken by Mr. King

Written by D. Garrick, Esq.

A School for Scandal! tell me, I beseech you,
Needs there a school this modish art to teach you?
No need of lessons now, the knowing think—
We might as well be taught to eat and drink.
Caused by a dearth of scandal, should the vapors
Distress our fair ones—let 'em read the papers;
Their pow'rful mixtures such disorders hit;
Crave what they will, there's *quantum sufficit.*
'Lord!' cries my Lady Wormwood (who loves tattle,
10 And puts much salt and pepper in her prattle),
Just ris'n at noon, all night at cards when threshing
Strong tea and scandal—'Bless me, how refreshing!
Give me the papers, Lisp—how bold and free! (*Sips.*)
Last night Lord L—— (*sips*) *was caught with Lady D——*
For aching heads what charming sal volatile! (*Sips.*)
If Mrs. B.——will still continue flirting,
We hope she'll DRAW, *or we'll* UNDRAW *the curtain.*
Fine satire, poz—in public all abuse it,
But, by ourselves (*sips*), our praise we can't refuse it.
20 Now, Lisp, read *you*—there, at that dash and star.'
'Yes, ma'am.—*A certain Lord had best beware,*
Who lives not twenty miles from Grosv'nor Square;
For should he Lady W——find willing,
WORMWOOD *is bitter*'——'Oh! that's me! the villain!
Throw it behind the fire, and never more
Let that vile paper come within my door.'—
Thus at our friends we laugh, who feel the dart;
To reach our feelings, we ourselves must smart.
Is our young bard so young, to think that he

30 Can stop the full spring-tide of calumny?
Knows he the world so little, and its trade?
Alas! the devil is sooner raised than laid.
So strong, so swift, the monster there's no gagging:
Cut Scandal's head off—still the tongue is wagging.
Proud of your smiles once lavishly bestow'd,
Again your young Don Quixote takes the road:
To show his gratitude, he draws his pen,
And seeks this hydra, Scandal, in his den.
For your applause all perils he would through—
40 He'll fight—that's *write*—a cavalliero true,
Till every drop of blood—that's *ink*—is spilt for you.

ACT ONE *Scene One*

[LADY SNEERWELL's *house.*]

LADY SNEERWELL *at the dressing-table—* SNAKE *drinking chocolate.*

LADY SNEER. The paragraphs, you say, Mr. Snake, were all inserted?

SNAKE. They were, madam, and as I copied them myself in a feigned hand, there can be no suspicion whence they came.

LADY SNEER. Did you circulate the reports of Lady *Brittle's* intrigue with Captain *Boastall?*

SNAKE. That is in as fine a train as your ladyship could wish,—in the common course of things, I think it must reach Mrs. *Clackit's* ears within four-and-twenty hours; and then, you know, the business is as good as done.

LADY SNEER. Why, truly, Mrs. *Clackit* has a very pretty talent, and a great deal of industry.

SNAKE. True, madam, and has been tolerably successful in her day:—to my knowledge, she has been the cause of six matches being broken off, and three sons being disinherited, of four forced elopements, as many close confinements, nine separate maintenances, and two divorces;—nay, I have more than once traced her causing a *Tête-à-Tête* in the *Town and Country Magazine,* when the parties perhaps had never seen each other's faces before in the course of their lives.

LADY SNEER. She certainly has talents, but her manner is gross.

SNAKE. 'Tis very true,—she generally designs well, has a free tongue, and a bold invention; but her coloring is too dark, and her outline often extravagant. She wants that *delicacy* of *hint,* and *mellowness* of *sneer,* which distinguish your ladyship's scandal.

LADY SNEER. Ah! you are partial, Snake.

SNAKE. Not in the least; everybody allows that Lady *Sneerwell* can do more with a *word* or a *look* than many can with the most labored detail, even when they happen to have a little truth on their side to support it.

LADY SNEER. Yes, my dear Snake; and I am no hypocrite to deny the satisfaction I reap from the success of my efforts. Wounded myself, in the early part of my life, by the envenomed tongue of slander, I confess I have since known no pleasure equal to the reducing of others to the level of my own injured reputation.

SNAKE. Nothing can be more natural. But, Lady Sneerwell, there is one affair in which you have lately employed me, wherein, I confess, I am at a loss to guess your motives.

LADY SNEER. I conceive you mean with respect to my neighbor, Sir Peter Teazle, and his family?

SNAKE. I do; here are two young men, to whom Sir Peter has acted as a kind of guardian since their father's death; the elder possessing the most amiable character, and universally well spoken of; the youngest, the most dissipated and extravagant young fellow in the kingdom, without friends or character,—the former an avowed admirer of your ladyship, and apparently your favorite; the latter attached to Maria, Sir Peter's ward, and confessedly beloved by her. Now, on the face of these circumstances, it is utterly unaccountable to me, why you, the widow of a city knight, with a good jointure, should not close with the passion of a man of such character and expectations as Mr. *Surface;* and more so why you should be so uncommonly earnest to destroy the mutual attachment subsisting between his brother *Charles* and *Maria.*

LADY SNEER. Then, at once to unravel this mystery, I must inform you that love has no share whatever in the intercourse between Mr. *Surface* and me.

24 **the Town and Country Magazine** specialized in reporting the intrigues of prominent persons

SNAKE. No!

LADY SNEER. His real attachment is to *Maria,* or her fortune; but, finding in his brother a favored rival, he has been obliged to mask his pretensions, and profit by my assistance.

SNAKE. Yet still I am more puzzled why you should interest yourself in his success.

LADY SNEER. Heav'ns! how dull you are! Cannot you surmise the weakness which I hitherto, through shame, have concealed even from *you?* Must I confess that *Charles*—that libertine, that extravagant, that bankrupt in fortune and reputation—that he it is for whom I am thus anxious and malicious, and to gain whom I would sacrifice everything?

SNAKE. Now, indeed, your conduct appears consistent; but how came you and Mr. *Surface* so confidential?

LADY SNEER. For our mutual interest. I have found him out a long time since—I know him to be artful, selfish, and malicious—in short, a sentimental knave.

SNAKE. Yet, Sir Peter vows he has not his equal in England—and, above all, he praises him as a man of sentiment.

LADY SNEER. True; and with the assistance of his sentiment and hypocrisy he has brought him [Sir Peter] entirely into his interest with regard to *Maria.*

Enter Servant.

SERV. Mr. Surface.

LADY SNEER. Show him up. *Exit Servant.* He generally calls about this time. I don't wonder at people's giving him to me for a lover.

Enter JOSEPH SURFACE.

JOS. SURF. My dear Lady Sneerwell, how do you do to-day? Mr. Snake, your most obedient.

LADY SNEER. Snake has just been arraigning me on our mutual attachment, but I have informed him of our real views; you know how useful he has been to us; and, believe me, the confidence is not ill placed.

JOS. SURF. Madam, it is impossible for me to suspect a man of Mr. *Snake*'s sensibility and discernment.

LADY SNEER. Well, well, no compliments now;—but tell me when you saw your mistress, *Maria*—or, what is more material to me, your brother.

JOS. SURF. I have not seen either since I left you; but I can inform you that they never meet. Some of your stories have taken a good effect on Maria.

LADY SNEER. Ah, my dear Snake! the merit of this belongs to you. But do your brother's distresses increase?

JOS. SURF. Every hour;—I am told he has had another execution in the house yesterday; in short, his dissipation and extravagance exceed any thing I ever heard of.

LADY SNEER. Poor Charles!

JOS. SURF. True, madam;—notwithstanding his vices, one can't help feeling for him.—Aye, poor Charles! I'm sure I wish it was in *my* power to be of any essential service to him.—For the man who does not share in the distresses of a brother, even though merited by his own misconduct, deserves—

LADY SNEER. O lud! you are going to be moral, and forget that you are among friends.

JOS. SURF. Egad, that's true!—I'll keep that sentiment till I see Sir Peter. However, it is certainly a charity to rescue Maria from such a libertine, who, if he is to be reclaimed, can be so only by a person of your ladyship's superior accomplishments and understanding.

SNAKE. I believe, Lady Sneerwell, here's company coming,—I'll go and copy the letter I mentioned to you.—Mr. Surface, your most obedient. *Exit* SNAKE.

JOS. SURF. Sir, your very devoted.—Lady Sneerwell, I am very sorry you have put any further confidence in that fellow.

LADY SNEER. Why so?

JOS. SURF. I have lately detected him in frequent conference with old *Rowley,* who was formerly my father's steward, and has never, you know, been a friend of mine.

LADY SNEER. And do you think he would betray us?

JOS. SURF. Nothing more likely: take my word for't, Lady Sneerwell, that fellow hasn't virtue enough to be faithful even to his own villainy.—Hah! Maria!

Enter MARIA.

LADY SNEER. Maria, my dear, how do you do?—What's the matter?

MARIA. Oh! there is that disagreeable lover of mine, Sir *Benjamin Backbite,* has just called at my guardian's, with his odious uncle, *Crabtree;* so I slipped out, and run hither to avoid them.

180 LADY SNEER. Is that all?

JOS. SURF. If my brother *Charles* had been of the party, ma'am, perhaps you would not have been so much alarmed.

LADY SNEER. Nay, now you are severe; for I dare swear the truth of the matter is, Maria heard *you* were here;—but, my dear, what has Sir Benjamin done, that you should avoid him so?

MARIA. Oh, he has done nothing—but 'tis 190 for what he has said,—his conversation is a perpetual libel on all his acquaintance.

JOS. SURF. Aye, and the worst of it is, there is no advantage in not knowing him; for he'll abuse a stranger just as soon as his best friend—and his uncle's as bad.

LADY SNEER. Nay, but we should make allowance; Sir Benjamin is a wit and a poet.

MARIA. For my part, I own, madam, wit loses its respect with me, when I see it in com- 200 pany with malice.—What do you think, Mr. Surface?

JOS. SURF. Certainly, madam; to smile at the jest which plants a thorn in another's breast is to become a principal in the mischief.

LADY SNEER. Pshaw! there's no possibility of being witty without a little ill nature: the malice of a good thing is the barb that makes it stick.—What's your opinion, Mr. Surface?

JOS. SURF. To be sure, madam, that conver- 210 sation, where the spirit of raillery is suppressed, will ever appear tedious and insipid.

MARIA. Well, I'll not debate how far scandal may be allowable; but in a man, I am sure, it is always contemptible.—We have pride, envy, rivalship, and a thousand motives to depreciate each other; but the male slanderer must have the cowardice of a woman before he can traduce one.

Enter Servant.

220 SERV. Madam, Mrs. Candour is below, and, if your ladyship's at leisure, will leave her carriage.

LADY SNEER. Beg her to walk in.

[*Exit Servant.*]

Now Maria, however here is a character to your taste; for, though Mrs. Candour is a little talkative, everybody allows her to be the best-natured and best sort of woman.

MARIA. Yes, with a very gross affectation of good nature and benevolence, she does more 230 mischief than the direct malice of old Crabtree.

JOS. SURF. I'faith 'tis very true, Lady Sneerwell; whenever I hear the current running against the characters of my friends, I never think them in such danger as when Candour undertakes their defence.

LADY SNEER. Hush!—here she is!

Enter MRS. CANDOUR.

MRS. CAN. My dear Lady Sneerwell, how have you been this century?—Mr. Surface, what 240 news do you hear?—though indeed it is no matter, for I think one hears nothing else but scandal.

JOS. SURF. Just so, indeed, madam.

MRS. CAN. Ah, Maria! child,—what, is the whole affair off between you and Charles? His extravagance, I presume—the town talks of nothing else.

MARIA. I am very sorry, ma'am, the town has so little to do. 250

MRS. CAN. True, true, child: but there is no stopping people's tongues.—I own I was hurt to hear it, as indeed I was to learn, from the same quarter, that your guardian, Sir Peter, and Lady Teazle have not agreed lately so well as could be wished.

MARIA. 'Tis strangely impertinent for people to busy themselves so.

MRS. CAN. Very true, child, but what's to be done? People will talk—there's no preventing 260 it.—Why, it was but yesterday I was told that Miss Gadabout had eloped with Sir Filigree Flirt.—But, Lord! there's no minding what one hears—though, to be sure, I had this from very good authority.

MARIA. Such reports are highly scandalous.

MRS. CAN. So they are, child—shameful, shameful! But the world is so censorious, no character escapes.—Lord, now who would have suspected your friend, Miss Prim, of an indis- 270 cretion? Yet such is the ill-nature of people, that they say her uncle stopped her last week, just as she was stepping into the York Diligence with her dancing-master.

MARIA. I'll answer for't there are no grounds for the report.

MRS. CAN. Oh, no foundation in the world, I dare swear; no more, probably, than for the story circulated last month, of Mrs. Festino's
280 affair with Colonel Cassino;—though, to be sure, that matter was never rightly cleared up.

JOS. SURF. The license of invention some people take is monstrous indeed.

MARIA. 'Tis so.—But, in my opinion, those who report such things are equally culpable.

MRS. CAN. To be sure they are; tale-bearers are as bad as the tale-makers—'tis an old observation, and a very true one—but what's to be done, as I said before? how will you prevent
290 people from talking?—To-day, Mrs. Clackit assured me Mr. and Mrs. Honeymoon were at last become mere man and wife, like the rest of their acquaintances.—She likewise hinted that a certain widow, in the next street, had got rid of her dropsy and recovered her shape in a most surprising manner. And at the same time Miss Tattle, who was by, affirmed that Lord Buffalo had discovered his lady at a house of no extraordinary fame—and that Sir Harry Bou-
300 quet and Tom Saunter were to measure swords on a similar provocation. But, Lord, do you think I would report these things! No, no! tale-bearers, as I said before, are just as bad as tale-makers.

JOS. SURF. Ah! Mrs. Candour, if everybody had your forbearance and good nature!

MRS. CAN. I confess, Mr. Surface, I cannot bear to hear people attacked behind their backs, and when ugly circumstances come out against
310 one's acquaintance I own I always love to think the best.—By the bye, I hope it is not true that your brother is absolutely ruined?

JOS. SURF. I am afraid his circumstances are very bad indeed, ma'am.

MRS. CAN. Ah!—I heard so—but you must tell him to keep up his spirits—everybody almost is in the same way! Lord Spindle, Sir Thomas Splint, Captain Quinze, and Mr. Nickit —all up, I hear, within this week; so, if
320 Charles is undone, he'll find half his acquaintances ruined too—and that, you know, is a consolation.

JOS. SURF. Doubtless, ma'am—a very great one.

Enter Servant.

SERV. Mr. Crabtree and Sir Benjamin Backbite. *Exit Servant.*

LADY SNEER. So, Maria, you see your lover pursues you; positively you shan't escape.

Enter CRABTREE *and* SIR BENJAMIN BACKBITE.

330

CRAB. Lady Sneerwell, I kiss your hands. Mrs. Candour, I don't believe you are acquainted with my nephew, Sir Benjamin Backbite? Egad, ma'am, he has a pretty wit, and is a pretty poet too; isn't he, Lady Sneerwell?

SIR BEN. O fie, uncle!

CRAB. Nay, egad it's true—I'll back him at a rebus or a charade against the best rhymer in the kingdom. Has your ladyship heard the epigram he wrote last week on Lady Frizzle's 340 feather catching fire?—Do, Benjamin, repeat it —or the charade you made last night extempore at Mrs. Drowzie's conversazione.—Come now; your *first* is the name of a fish, your *second* a great naval commander, and——

SIR BEN. Uncle, now—prithee——

CRAB. I'faith, ma'am, 'twould surprise you to hear how ready he is at these things.

LADY SNEER. I wonder, Sir Benjamin, you never publish anything. 350

SIR BEN. To say truth, ma'am, 'tis very vulgar to print; and, as my little productions are mostly satires and lampoons on particular people, I find they circulate more by giving copies in confidence to the friends of the parties—however, I have some love elegies, which, when favored with this lady's smiles, I mean to give to the public.

CRAB. 'Fore heav'n, ma'am, they'll immortalize you!—you'll be handed down to posterity 360 like Petrarch's Laura, or Waller's Sacharissa.

SIR BEN. Yes, madam, I think you will like them, when you shall see them on a beautiful quarto page, where a neat rivulet of text shall murmur through a meadow of margin. 'Fore gad, they will be the most elegant things of their kind!

CRAB. But, ladies, that's true—have you heard the news?

MRS. CAN. What, sir, do you mean the report of— 370

CRAB. No, ma'am, that's not it.—Miss Nicely is going to be married to her own footman.

MRS. CAN. Impossible!

CRAB. Ask Sir Benjamin.

SIR BEN. 'Tis very true, ma'am—everything

is fixed, and the wedding liveries bespoke.

CRAB. Yes—and they *do* say there were pressing reasons for it.

LADY SNEER. Why, I *have* heard something of this before.

MRS. CAN. It can't be—and I wonder any one should believe such a story of so prudent a lady as Miss Nicely.

SIR BEN. O lud! ma'am, that's the very reason 'twas believed at once. She has always been so *cautious* and so *reserved,* that everybody was sure there was some reason for it at bottom.

MRS. CAN. Why, to be sure, a tale of scandal is as fatal to the credit of a prudent lady of her stamp as a fever is generally to those of the strongest constitutions; but there is a sort of puny, sickly reputation that is always ailing, yet will outlive the robuster characters of a hundred prudes.

SIR BEN. True, madam, there are valetudinarians in reputation as well as constitution, who, being conscious of their weak part, avoid the least breath of air, and supply their want of stamina by care and circumspection.

MRS. CAN. Well, but this may be all a mistake. You know, Sir Benjamin, very trifling circumstances often give rise to the most injurious tales.

CRAB. That they do, I'll be sworn, ma'am. Did you ever hear how Miss Piper came to lose her lover and her character last summer at Tunbridge?—Sir Benjamin, you remember it?

SIR BEN. Oh, to be sure!—the most whimsical circumstance—

LADY SNEER. How was it, pray?

CRAB. Why, one evening, at Mrs. Ponto's assembly, the conversation happened to turn on the difficulty of breeding Nova Scotia sheep in this country. Says a young lady in company, 'I have known instances of it; for Miss Letitia Piper, a first cousin of mine, had a Nova Scotia sheep that produced her twins.' 'What!' cries the old Dowager Lady Dundizzy (who you know is as deaf as a post), 'has Miss Piper had twins?' This mistake, as you may imagine, threw the whole company into a fit of laughing. However, 'twas the next morning everywhere reported, and in a few days believed by the whole town, that Miss Letitia Piper had actually been brought to bed of a fine boy and a girl—and in less than a week there were people who could name the father, and the farm-house where the babies were put out to nurse!

LADY SNEER. Strange, indeed!

CRAB. Matter of fact, I assure you.—O lud! Mr. Surface, pray is it true that your uncle, Sir Oliver, is coming home?

JOS. SURF. Not that I know of, indeed, sir.

CRAB. He has been in the East Indias a long time. You can scarcely remember him, I believe.—Sad comfort, whenever he returns, to hear how your brother has gone on!

JOS. SURF. Charles has been imprudent, sir, to be sure; but I hope no busy people have already prejudiced Sir Oliver against him,—he may reform.

SIR BEN. To be sure he may—for my part I never believed him to be so utterly void of principle as people say—and though he has lost all his friends, I am told nobody is better spoken of by the Jews.

CRAB. That's true, egad, nephew. If the old Jewry were a ward, I believe Charles would be an alderman; no man more popular there, 'fore gad! I hear he pays as many annuities as the Irish tontine; and that, whenever he's sick, they have prayers for the recovery of his health in the Synagogue.

SIR BEN. Yet no man lives in greater splendor.—They tell me, when he entertains his friends, he can sit down to dinner with a dozen of his own securities; have a score [of] tradesmen waiting in the antechamber, and an officer behind every guest's chair.

JOS. SURF. This may be entertainment to you, gentlemen, but you pay very little regard to the feelings of a brother.

MARIA [*Aside.*]. Their malice is intolerable!—Lady Sneerwell, I must wish you a good morning—I'm not very well. *Exit* MARIA.

MRS. CAN. O dear! she changes color very much!

LADY SNEER. Do, Mrs. Candour, follow her—she may want assistance.

MRS. CAN. That I will, with all my soul, ma'am.—Poor dear girl! who knows what her situation may be! *Exit* MRS. CANDOUR.

LADY SNEER. 'Twas nothing but that she could not bear to hear Charles reflected on, notwithstanding their difference.

452 **Irish tontine** a life annuity scheme sponsored by the Irish parliament

SIR BEN. The young lady's *penchant* is obvious.

CRAB. But, Benjamin, you mustn't give up the pursuit for that; follow her, and put her into good humor. Repeat her some of your own verses.—Come, I'll assist you.

SIR BEN. Mr. Surface, I did not mean to hurt you; but depend upon't your brother is utterly undone. (*Going.*)

CRAB. O lud, aye! undone as ever man was —can't raise a guinea. (*Going.*)

SIR BEN. And everything sold, I'm told, that was movable. (*Going.*)

CRAB. I have seen one that was at his house —not a thing left but some empty bottles that were overlooked, and the family pictures, which I believe are framed in the wainscot. (*Going.*)

SIR BEN. And I am very sorry to hear also some bad stories against him. (*Going.*)

CRAB. Oh, he has done many mean things, that's certain. (*Going.*)

SIR BEN. But, however, as he's your brother— (*Going.*)

CRAB. We'll tell you all, another opportunity.

Exeunt CRABTREE *and* SIR BENJAMIN.

LADY SNEER. Ha, ha! ha! 'tis very hard for them to leave a subject they have not quite run down.

JOS. SURF. And I believe the abuse was no more acceptable to your ladyship than to Maria.

LADY SNEER. I doubt her affections are farther engaged than we imagined; but the family are to be here this evening, so you may as well dine where you are, and we shall have an opportunity of observing farther;—in the meantime, I'll go and plot mischief, and you shall study sentiments.

Exeunt.

Scene Two

SIR PETER TEAZLE'S *house.*

Enter SIR PETER.

SIR PETER. When an old bachelor takes a young wife, what is he to expect?—'Tis now six months since Lady Teazle made me the happiest of men—and I have been the miserablest dog ever since that ever committed wedlock! We tift a little going to church, and came to a quarrel before the bells were done ringing. I was more than once nearly choked with gall during the honeymoon, and had lost all comfort in life before my friends had done wishing me joy! Yet I chose with caution—a girl bred wholly in the country, who never knew luxury beyond one silk gown, nor dissipation above the annual gala of a race ball. Yet now she plays her part in all the extravagant fopperies of the fashion and the town, with as ready a grace as if she had never seen a bush nor a grass-plat out of Grosvenor Square! I am sneered at by my old acquaintance—paragraphed in the newspapers. She dissipates my fortune, and contradicts all my humors; yet the worst of it is, I doubt I love her, or I should never bear all this. However, I'll never be weak enough to own it.

Enter ROWLEY.

ROW. Oh! Sir Peter, your servant,—how is it with you, sir?

SIR PET. Very bad, Master Rowley, very bad; —I meet with nothing but crosses and vexations.

ROW. What can have happened to trouble you since yesterday?

SIR PET. A good question to a married man!

ROW. Nay, I'm sure your lady, Sir Peter, can't be the cause of your uneasiness.

507 **doubt** fear

SIR PET. Why, has anyone told you she was dead?

ROW. Come, come, Sir Peter, you love her, notwithstanding your tempers don't exactly agree.

SIR PET. But the fault is entirely hers, Master Rowley. I am, myself, the sweetest-tempered man alive, and hate a teasing temper—and so I tell her a hundred times a day.

ROW. Indeed!

SIR PET. Aye; and what is very extraordinary, in all our disputes she is always in the wrong! But Lady Sneerwell, and the set she meets at her house, encourage the perverseness of her disposition. Then, to complete my vexations, Maria, my ward, whom I ought to have the power of a father over, is determined to turn rebel too, and absolutely refuses the man whom I have long resolved on for her husband; —meaning, I suppose, to bestow herself on his profligate brother.

ROW. You know, Sir Peter, I have always taken the liberty to differ with you on the subject of these two young gentlemen. I only wish you may not be deceived in your opinion of the elder. For Charles, my life on't! he will retrieve his errors yet. Their worthy father, once my honored master, was, at his years, nearly as wild a spark; yet, when he died, he did not leave a more benevolent heart to lament his loss.

SIR PET. You are wrong, Master Rowley. On their father's death, you know, I acted as a kind of guardian to them both, till their uncle Sir Oliver's Eastern liberality gave them an early independence; of course, no person could have more opportunities of judging of their hearts, and I was never mistaken in my life. Joseph is indeed a model for the young men of the age. He is a man of sentiment, and acts up to the sentiments he professes; but, for the other, take my word for't, if he had any grains of virtue by descent, he has dissipated them with the rest of his inheritance. Ah! my old friend, Sir Oliver, will be deeply mortified when he finds how part of his bounty has been misapplied.

ROW. I am sorry to find you so violent against the young man, because this may be the most critical period of his fortune. I came hither with news that will surprise you.

SIR PET. What! let me hear.

ROW. Sir Oliver *is* arrived, and at this moment in town.

SIR PET. How! you astonish me! I thought you did not expect him this month.

ROW. I did not; but his passage has been remarkably quick.

SIR PET. Egad, I shall rejoice to see my old friend,—'tis sixteen years since we met—we have had many a day together; but does he still enjoin us not to inform his nephews of his arrival?

ROW. Most strictly. He means, before it is known, to make some trial of their dispositions.

SIR PET. Ah! There needs no art to discover their merits—however, he shall have his way; but, pray, does he know I am married?

ROW. Yes, and will soon wish you joy.

SIR PET. What, as we drink health to a friend in a consumption! Ah, Oliver will laugh at me—we used to rail at matrimony together—but he has been steady to his text. Well, he must be at my house, though—I'll instantly give orders for his reception. But, Master Rowley, don't drop a word that Lady Teazle and I ever disagree.

ROW. By no means.

SIR PET. For I should never be able to stand Noll's jokes; so I'd have him think, Lord forgive me! that we are a very happy couple.

ROW. I understand you—but then you must be very careful not to differ while he's in the house with you.

SIR PET. Egad, and so we must—and that's impossible. Ah! Master Rowley, when an old bachelor marries a young wife, he deserves—no —the crime carries the punishment along with it. *Exeunt.*

End of Act Ist.

ACT TWO *Scene One*

SIR PETER TEAZLE'S *house.*

Enter SIR PETER *and* LADY TEAZLE.

SIR PET. Lady Teazle, Lady Teazle, I'll not bear it!

LADY TEAZ. Sir Peter, Sir Peter, you may bear it or not, as you please; but I ought to have my own way in everything, and what's more, I *will* too.—What! though I was educated in the country, I know very well that women of fashion in London are accountable to nobody after they are married. 10

SIR PET. Very well, ma'am, very well,—so a husband is to have no influence, no authority?

LADY TEAZ. Authority! No, to be sure—if you wanted authority over me, you should have adopted me, and not married me; I am sure you were old enough.

SIR PET. Old enough!—aye, there it is!—Well, well, Lady Teazle, though my life may be made unhappy by your temper, I'll not be ruined by your extravagance. 20

LADY TEAZ. My extravagance! I'm sure I'm not more extravagant than a woman of fashion ought to be.

SIR PET. No, no, madam, you shall throw away no more sums on such unmeaning luxury. 'Slife! to spend as much to furnish your dressing-room with flowers in winter as would suffice to turn the Pantheon into a greenhouse, and give a *fête champêtre* at Christmas!

30 LADY TEAZ. Lord, Sir Peter, am I to blame because flowers are dear in cold weather? You should find fault with the climate, and not with me. For my part, I am sure I wish it was spring all the year round, and that roses grew under one's feet!

SIR PET. Oons! madam—if you had been born to this, I shouldn't wonder at your talking thus.—But you forget what your situation was when I married you.

LADY TEAZ. No, no, I don't; 'twas a very disagreeable one, or I should never have married *you.* 40

SIR PET. Yes, yes, madam, you were then in somewhat an humbler style—the daughter of a plain country squire. Recollect, Lady Teazle, when I saw you first, sitting at your tambour, in a pretty figured linen gown, with a bunch of keys by your side, your hair combed smooth over a roll, and your apartment hung round with fruits in worsted, of your own working. 50

LADY TEAZ. O, yes! I remember it very well, and a curious life I led—my daily occupation to inspect the dairy, superintend the poultry, make extracts from the family receipt-book, and comb my aunt Deborah's lapdog.

SIR PET. Yes, yes, ma'am, 'twas so indeed.

LADY TEAZ. And then, you know, my evening amusements! To draw patterns for ruffles, which I had not the materials to make; to play Pope Joan with the curate; to read a novel to my aunt; or to be stuck down to an old spinet to strum my father to sleep after a fox-chase. 60

SIR PET. I am glad you have so good a memory. Yes, madam, these were the recreations I took you from; but now you must have your coach—*vis-à-vis*—and three powdered footmen

28 **the Pantheon** a large concert hall in London, so called because it had a dome like that of the Pantheon in Rome 29 **fête champêtre** outdoor entertainment

46 **tambour** a circular frame used for embroidering
60 **Pope Joan** a card game 68 **cats** horses

before your chair and, in summer, a pair of white cats to draw you to Kensington Gardens.—No recollection, I suppose, when you were content to ride double, behind the butler, on a docked coach-horse?

LADY TEAZ. No—I swear I never did that—I deny the butler and the coach-horse.

SIR PET. This, madam, was your situation—and what have I not done for you? I have made you a woman of fashion, of fortune, of rank—in short, I have made you my wife.

LADY TEAZ. Well, then, and there is but one thing more you can make me to add to the obligation—and that is——

SIR PET. My widow, I suppose?

LADY TEAZ. Hem! hem!

SIR PET. Thank you, madam—but don't flatter yourself; for though your ill-conduct may disturb my peace, it shall never break my heart, I promise you: however, I am equally obliged to you for the hint.

LADY TEAZ. Then why will you endeavor to make yourself so disagreeable to me, and thwart me in every little elegant expense?

SIR PET. 'Slife, madam, I say, had you any of these elegant expenses when you married me?

LADY TEAZ. Lud, Sir Peter! would you have me be out of the fashion?

SIR PET. 'Slife, madam, I say, had you any of these elegant expenses when you married me?

LADY TEAZ. For my part, I should think you would like to have your wife thought a woman of taste.

SIR PET. Aye—there again—taste! Zounds! madam, you had no taste when you married *me!*

LADY TEAZ. That's very true, indeed, Sir Peter! and, *after* having married you, I am sure I should never pretend to taste again! But now, Sir Peter, if we have finished our daily jangle, I presume I may go to my engagement of [at] Lady Sneerwell's?

SIR PET. Aye—there's another precious circumstance!—a charming set of acquaintance you have made there!

LADY TEAZ. Nay, Sir Peter, they are people of rank and fortune, and remarkably tenacious of reputation.

SIR PET. Yes, egad, they are tenacious of reputation with a vengeance; for they don't choose anybody should have a character but themselves! Such a crew! Ah! many a wretch has rid on a hurdle who has done less mischief than those utterers of forged tales, coiners of scandal,—and clippers of reputation.

LADY TEAZ. What! would you restrain the freedom of speech?

SIR PET. Oh! they have made you just as bad as any one of the society.

LADY TEAZ. Why, I believe I do bear a part with a tolerable grace. But I vow I have no malice against the people I abuse; when I say an ill-natured thing, 'tis out of pure good humor—and I take it for granted they deal exactly in the same manner with me. But, Sir Peter, you know you promised to come to Lady Sneerwell's too.

SIR PET. Well, well, I'll call in just to look after my own character.

LADY TEAZ. Then, indeed, you must make haste after me or you'll be too late.—So goodbye to ye. *Exit* LADY TEAZLE.

SIR PET. So—I have gained much by my intended expostulations! Yet with what a charming air she contradicts everything I say, and how pleasingly she shows her contempt of my authority. Well, though I can't make her love me, there is a great satisfaction in quarreling with her; and I think she never appears to such advantage as when she's doing everything in her power to plague me. *Exit.*

118 **hurdle** sledge on which traitors were taken to the place of execution

Scene Two

LADY SNEERWELL'S.

LADY SNEERWELL, MRS. CANDOUR, CRABTREE, SIR BENJAMIN BACKBITE, *and* JOSEPH SURFACE.

LADY SNEER. Nay, positively, we will hear it.

JOS. SURF. Yes, yes, the epigram, by all means.

SIR BEN. Plague on't, uncle! 'tis mere nonsense.

CRAB. No, no; 'fore gad, very clever for an extempore!

10 SIR BEN. But, ladies, you should be acquainted with the circumstance,—you must know, that one day last week, as Lady Betty Curricle was taking the dust in Hyde Park, in a sort of duodecimo phaëton, she desired me to write some verses on her ponies; upon which, I took out my pocket-book, and in one moment produced the following:

'Sure never were seen two such beautiful ponies!
Other horses are clowns, and these macaronies!
Nay, to give 'em this title I'm sure isn't wrong—
20 Their legs are so slim, and their tails are so long.'

CRAB. There, ladies—done in the smack of a whip, and on horseback too!

JOS. SURF. A very Phœbus, mounted—indeed, Sir Benjamin.

SIR BEN. O dear sir—trifles—trifles.

Enter LADY TEAZLE *and* MARIA.

MRS. CAN. I must have a copy.

LADY SNEER. Lady Teazle, I hope we shall see Sir Peter.

30 LADY TEAZ. I believe he'll wait on your ladyship presently.

LADY SNEER. Maria, my love, you look grave. Come, you shall sit down to cards with Mr. Surface.

14 **duodecimo** very small (a bibliographical term)

MARIA. I take very little pleasure in cards—however, I'll do as your ladyship pleases.

LADY TEAZ [*Aside.*]. I am surprised Mr. Surface should sit down with *her.*—I thought he would have embraced this opportunity of speaking to me before Sir Peter came. 40

MRS. CAN. Now, I'll die but you are so scandalous, I'll forswear your society.

LADY TEAZ. What's the matter, Mrs. Candour?

MRS. CAN. They'll not allow our friend Miss Vermilion to be handsome.

LADY SNEER. Oh, surely, she's a pretty woman.

CRAB. I am very glad you think so, ma'am.

MRS. CAN. She has a charming fresh color. 50

LADY TEAZ. Yes, when it is fresh put on.

MRS. CAN. O fie! I'll swear her color is natural—I have seen it come and go.

LADY TEAZ. I dare swear you have, ma'am—it goes of a night, and comes again in the morning.

MRS. CAN. Ha! ha! ha! how I hate to hear you talk so! But surely, now, her sister *is,* or *was,* very handsome.

CRAB. Who? Mrs. Evergreen?—O Lord! she's six-and-fifty if she's an hour! 60

MRS. CAN. Now positively you wrong her; fifty-two or fifty-three is the utmost—and I don't think she looks more.

SIR BEN. Ah! there is no judging by her looks, unless one could see her face.

LADY SNEER. Well, well, if Mrs. Evergreen *does* take some pains to repair the ravages of time, you must allow she effects it with great ingenuity; and surely that's better than the careless manner in which the widow Ochre caulks her wrinkles. 70

SIR BEN. Nay, now, Lady Sneerwell, you are severe upon the widow. Come, come, it is not that she paints so ill—but, when she has finished her face, she joins it on so badly to her neck, that she looks like a mended statue, in which the connoisseur may see at once that the head's modern, though the trunk's antique!

80 CRAB. Ha! ha! ha! Well said, nephew!

MRS. CAN. Ha! ha! ha! Well, you make me laugh, but I vow I hate you for't.—What do you think of Miss Simper?

SIR BEN. Why, she has very pretty teeth.

LADY TEAZ. Yes; and on that account, when she is neither speaking nor laughing (which very seldom happens), she never absolutely shuts her mouth, but leaves it always on a jar, as it were.

90 MRS. CAN. How can you be so ill-natured?

LADY TEAZ. Nay, I allow even that's better than the pains Mrs. Prim takes to conceal her losses in front. She draws her mouth till it positively resembles the aperture of a poor's-box, and all her words appear to slide out edgeways.

LADY SNEER. Very well, Lady Teazle; I see you can be a little severe.

LADY TEAZ. In defence of a friend it is but justice;—but here comes Sir Peter to spoil our

100 pleasantry.

Enter SIR PETER TEAZLE.

SIR PET. Ladies, your most obedient—Mercy on me, here is the whole set! a character dead at every word, I suppose. (*Aside.*)

MRS. CAN. I am rejoiced you are come, Sir Peter. They have been *so* censorious. They will allow good qualities to nobody—not even good nature to our friend Mrs. Pursy.

LADY TEAZ. What, the fat dowager who was

110 at Mrs. Codille's last night?

MRS. CAN. Nay, her bulk is her misfortune; and, when she takes such pains to get rid of it, you ought not to reflect on her.

LADY SNEER. That's very true, indeed.

LADY TEAZ. Yes, I know she almost lives on acids and small whey; laces herself by pulleys; and often, in the hottest noon of summer, you may see her on a little squat pony, with her hair platted up behind like a drummer's, and

120 puffing round the Ring on a full trot.

MRS. CAN. I thank you, Lady Teazle, for defending her.

SIR PET. Yes, a good defence, truly.

MRS. CAN. But Sir Benjamin is as censorious as Miss Sallow.

CRAB. Yes, and she is a curious being to pretend to be censorious!—an awkward gawky, without any one good point under heaven.

MRS. CAN. Positively you shall not be so very severe. Miss Sallow is a relation of mine by 130 marriage, and, as for her person, great allowance is to be made; for, let me tell you, a woman labors under many disadvantages who tries to pass for a girl at six-and-thirty.

LADY SNEER. Though, surely, she is handsome still—and for the weakness in her eyes, considering how much she reads by candlelight, it is not to be wondered at.

MRS. CAN. True; and then as to her manner, upon my word I think it is particularly grace- 140 ful, considering she never had the least education; for you know her mother was a Welch milliner, and her father a sugar-baker at Bristol.

SIR BEN. Ah! you are both of you too good-natured!

SIR PET. Yes, damned good-natured! This their own relation! mercy on me! (*Aside.*)

SIR BEN. And Mrs. Candour is of so moral a turn she can sit for an hour to hear Lady Stucco talk sentiment. 150

LADY TEAZ. Nay, I vow Lady Stucco is very well with the dessert after dinner; for she's just like the French fruit one cracks for mottoes—made up of paint and proverb.

MRS. CAN. Well, I never will join in ridiculing a friend; and so I constantly tell my cousin Ogle, and you all know what pretensions she has to be critical in beauty.

CRAB. Oh, to be sure! she has herself the oddest countenance that ever was seen; 'tis a col- 160 lection of features from all the different countries of the globe.

SIR BEN. So she has, indeed—an Irish front!

CRAB. Caledonian locks!

SIR BEN. Dutch nose!

CRAB. Austrian lip!

SIR BEN. Complexion of a Spaniard!

CRAB. And teeth *à la Chinoise!*

SIR BEN. In short, her face resembles a *table d'hôte* at Spa—where no two guests are of a 170 nation——

CRAB. Or a congress at the close of a general war—wherein all the members, even to her eyes,

120 **Ring** a drive and promenade in Hyde Park

appear to have a different interest, and her nose and chin are the only parties likely to join issue.

MRS. CAN. Ha! ha! ha!

SIR PET. Mercy on my life!—a person they dine with twice a week! (*Aside.*)

[LADY SNEER. Go—go—you are a couple of provoking toads.]

MRS. CAN. Nay, but I vow you shall not carry the laugh off so—for give me leave to say, that Mrs. Ogle—

SIR PET. Madam, madam, I beg your pardon—there's no stopping these good gentlemen's tongues. But when I tell *you,* Mrs. Candour, that the lady they are abusing is a particular friend of mine—I hope you'll not take her part.

LADY SNEER. Well said, Sir Peter! but you are a cruel creature—too phlegmatic yourself for a jest, and too peevish to allow wit on others.

SIR PET. Ah, madam, true wit is more nearly allied to good nature than your ladyship is aware of.

LADY TEAZ. True, Sir Peter; I believe they are so near akin that they can never be united.

SIR BEN. Or rather, madam, suppose them man and wife, because one so seldom sees them together.

LADY TEAZ. But Sir Peter is such an enemy to scandal, I believe he would have it put down by parliament.

SIR PET. 'Fore heaven, madam, if they were to consider the sporting with reputation of as much importance as poaching on manors, and pass *An Act for the Preservation of Fame,* I believe many would thank them for the bill.

LADY SNEER. O lud! Sir Peter; would you deprive us of our privileges?

SIR PET. Aye, madam; and then no person should be permitted to kill characters or run down reputations, but qualified old maids and disappointed widows.

LADY SNEER. Go, you monster!

MRS. CAN. But sure you would not be quite so severe on those who only report what they hear.

SIR PET. Yes, madam, I would have law merchant for them too; and in all cases of slander currency, whenever the drawer of the lie was not to be found, the injured parties should have a right to come on any of the indorsers.

219 **law merchant** system of laws for the regulation of commerce

CRAB. Well, for my part, I believe there never was a scandalous tale without some foundation.

LADY SNEER. Come, ladies, shall we sit down to cards in the next room?

Enter Servant and whispers SIR PETER.

SIR PET. I'll be with them directly.
—[*Exit Servant.*]

[*Aside.*] I'll get away . . .

LADY SNEER. Sir Peter, you are not leaving us?

SIR PET. Your ladyship must excuse me; I'm called away by particular business—but I leave my character behind me. *Exit* SIR PETER.

SIR BEN. Well certainly, Lady Teazle, that lord of yours is a strange being; I could tell you some stories of him would make you laugh heartily, if he wasn't your husband.

LADY TEAZ. O pray don't mind that—come, do let's hear them.

(*They join the rest of the company, all talking as they are going into the next room.*)

JOS. SURF (*Rising with* MARIA.). Maria, I see you have no satisfaction in this society.

MARIA. How is it possible I should? If to raise malicious smiles at the infirmities and misfortunes of those who have never injured us be the province of wit or humor, heaven grant me a double portion of dulness!

JOS. SURF. Yet they appear more ill-natured than they are; they have no malice at heart.

MARIA. Then is their conduct still more contemptible; for, in my opinion, nothing could excuse the intemperance of their tongues but a natural and ungovernable bitterness of mind.

JOS. SURF. But can you, Maria, feel thus for others, and be unkind to me alone? Is hope to be denied the tenderest passion?

MARIA. Why will you distress me by renewing this subject?

JOS. SURF. Ah, Maria! you would not treat me thus, and oppose your guardian, Sir Peter's will, but that I see that profligate *Charles* is still a favored rival.

MARIA. Ungenerously urged! But, whatever my sentiments of that unfortunate young man are, be assured I shall not feel more bound to give him up, because his distresses have lost him the regard even of a brother.

(LADY TEAZLE *returns.*)

JOS. SURF. Nay, but, Maria, do not leave me with a frown—by all that's honest, I swear—Gad's life, here's Lady Teazle. (*Aside.*)—You must not—no, you shall not—for, though I have the greatest regard for Lady Teazle——

MARIA. Lady Teazle!

JOS. SURF. Yet were Sir Peter to suspect——

LADY TEAZ (*Coming forward.*). What's this, pray? Do you take her for me?—Child, you are wanted in the next room.— *Exit* MARIA. What is all this, pray?

JOS. SURF. Oh, the most unlucky circumstance in nature! Maria has somehow suspected the tender concern I have for your happiness, and threatened to acquaint Sir Peter with her suspicions, and I was just endeavoring to reason with her when you came.

LADY TEAZ. Indeed! but you seemed to adopt a very tender mode of reasoning—do you *usually* argue on your knees?

JOS. SURF. Oh, she's a child—and I thought a little bombast——but, Lady Teazle, when are you to give me your judgment on my library, as you promised?

LADY TEAZ. No, no,—I begin to think it would be imprudent, and you know I admit you as a lover no further than *fashion* requires.

JOS. SURF. True—a mere Platonic cicisbeo, what every London wife is *entitled* to.

LADY TEAZ. Certainly, one must not be out of the fashion; however, I have so many of my country prejudices left, that, though Sir Peter's ill humor may vex me ever so, it never shall provoke me to——

JOS. SURF. The only revenge in your power. Well, I applaud your moderation.

LADY TEAZ. Go—you are an insinuating wretch! But we shall be missed—let us join the company.

JOS. SURF. But we had best not return together.

LADY TEAZ. Well, don't stay—for Maria shan't come to hear any more of your *reasoning,* I promise you. *Exit* LADY TEAZLE.

JOS. SURF. A curious dilemma, truly, my politics have run me into! I wanted, at first, only to ingratiate myself with Lady Teazle, that she might not be my enemy with Maria; and I have, I don't know how, become her serious lover. Sincerely I begin to wish I had never made such a point of gaining so *very good* a character, for it has led me into so many cursed rogueries that I doubt I shall be exposed at last. *Exit.*

Scene Three

SIR PETER'S.

Enter SIR OLIVER SURFACE *and* ROWLEY.

SIR OLIV. Ha! ha! ha! and so my old friend is married, hey?—a young wife out of the country.—Ha! ha! ha!—that he should have stood bluff to old bachelor so long, and sink into a husband at last!

ROW. But you must not rally him on the subject, Sir Oliver; 'tis a tender point, I assure you, though he has been married only seven months.

SIR OLIV. Then he has been just half a year on the stool of repentance!—Poor Peter! But you say he has entirely given up Charles—never sees him, hey?

ROW. His prejudice against him is astonishing, and I am sure greatly increased by a jealousy of him with Lady Teazle, which he has

299 **cicisbeo** recognized gallant of a married woman

5 **bluff** firm

been industriously led into by a scandalous society in the neighborhood, who have contributed not a little to Charles's ill name; whereas the truth is, I believe, if the lady is partial to either of them, his brother is the favorite.

SIR OLIV. Aye,—I know there are a set of malicious, prating, prudent gossips, both male and female, who murder characters to kill time, and will rob a young fellow of his good name before he has years to know the value of it,—but I am not to be prejudiced against my nephew by such, I promise you! No, no;—if Charles has done nothing false or mean, I shall compound for his extravagance.

ROW. Then, my life on't, you will reclaim him.—Ah, sir, it gives me new life to find that *your* heart is not turned against him, and that the son of my good old master has one friend, however, left.

SIR OLIV. What! shall I forget, Master Rowley, when I was at his years myself? Egad, my brother and I were neither of us very *prudent* youths—and yet, I believe, you have not seen many better men than your old master was?

ROW. Sir, 'tis this reflection gives me assurance that Charles may yet be a credit to his family.—But here comes Sir Peter.

SIR OLIV. Egad, so he does!—Mercy on me, he's greatly altered, and seems to have a settled married look! One may read husband in his face at this distance!

Enter SIR PETER TEAZLE.

SIR PET. Hah! Sir Oliver—my old friend! Welcome to England a thousand times!

SIR OLIV. Thank you, thank you, Sir Peter! and i'faith I am glad to find you well, believe me!

SIR PET. Ah! 'tis a long time since we met—sixteen years, I doubt, Sir Oliver, and many a cross accident in the time.

SIR OLIV. Aye, I have had my share—but, what! I find you are married, hey, my old boy?—Well, well, it can't be helped—and so I wish you joy with all my heart!

SIR PET. Thank you, thank you, Sir Oliver.—Yes, I have entered into the happy state—but we'll not talk of that now.

SIR OLIV. True, true, Sir Peter; old friends should not begin on grievances at first meeting. No, no, no.

ROW (*to* SIR OLIVER.). Take care, pray, sir.

SIR OLIV. Well, so one of my nephews is a wild rogue, hey?

SIR PET. Wild! Ah! my old friend, I grieve for your disappointment there—he's a lost young man, indeed; however, his brother will make you amends; *Joseph* is, indeed, what a youth should be—everybody in the world speaks well of him.

SIR OLIV. I am sorry to hear it—he has too good a character to be an honest fellow.—Everybody speaks well of him! Psha! then he has bowed as low to knaves and fools as to the honest dignity of genius or virtue.

SIR PET. What, Sir Oliver! do you blame him for not making enemies?

SIR OLIV. Yes, if he has merit enough to deserve them.

SIR PET. Well, well—you'll be convinced when you know him. 'Tis edification to hear him converse—he professes the noblest sentiments.

SIR OLIV. Ah, plague of his sentiments! If he salutes me with a scrap of morality in his mouth, I shall be sick directly. But, however, don't mistake me, Sir Peter; I don't mean to defend Charles's errors—but, before I form my judgment of either of them, I intend to make a trial of their hearts—and my friend Rowley and I have planned something for the purpose.

ROW. And Sir Peter shall own for once he has been mistaken.

SIR PET. Oh, my life on Joseph's honor!

SIR OLIV. Well, come, give us a bottle of good wine, and we'll drink the lad's health, and tell you our scheme.

SIR PET. *Allons,* then!

SIR OLIV. And don't, Sir Peter, be so severe against your old friend's son. Odds my life! I am not sorry that he has run out of the course a little; for my part, I hate to see prudence clinging to the green succors of youth; 'tis like ivy round a sapling, and spoils the growth of the tree. *Exeunt.*

End of Act the Second.

ACT THREE *Scene One*

SIR PETER'S.

SIR PETER TEAZLE, SIR OLIVER SURFACE, *and* ROWLEY.

SIR PET. Well, then—we will see this fellow first, and have our wine afterwards. But how is this, Master Rowley? I don't see the jet of your scheme.

ROW. Why, sir, this Mr. Stanley, whom I was speaking of, is nearly related to them, by their mother; he was once a merchant in Dublin, but has been ruined by a series of undeserved misfortunes. He has applied, by letter, since his confinement, both to Mr. *Surface* and *Charles*—from the former he has received nothing but evasive promises of future service, while Charles has done all that his extravagance has left him power to do; and he is, at this time, endeavoring to raise a sum of money, part of which, in the midst of his own distresses, I know he intends for the service of poor Stanley.

SIR OLIV. Ah! he is my brother's son.

SIR PET. Well, but how is Sir Oliver personally to——

ROW. Why, sir, I will inform Charles and his brother that Stanley has obtained permission to apply in person to his friends, and, as they have neither of them ever seen him, let Sir Oliver assume his character, and he will have a fair opportunity of judging at least of the benevolence of their dispositions; and believe me, sir, you will find in the youngest brother one who, in the midst of folly and dissipation, has still, as our immortal bard expresses it,—

> 'a tear for pity, and a hand
> Open as day, for melting charity.'

5 **jet** point 33 **a tear...charity.'** *Henry IV, Part II,* IV.iv.31–32

SIR PET. Psha! What signifies his having an open hand or purse either, when he has nothing left to give? Well, well, make a trial, if you please; but where is the fellow whom you brought for Sir Oliver to examine, relative to Charles's affairs?

ROW. Below, waiting his commands, and no one can give him better intelligence.—This, Sir Oliver, is a friendly Jew, who, to do him justice, has done everything in his power to bring your nephew to a proper sense of his extravagance.

SIR PET. Pray let us have him in.

ROW. Desire Mr. Moses to walk upstairs.

SIR PET. But why should you suppose he will speak the truth?

ROW. Oh, I have convinced him that he has no chance of recovering certain sums advanced to Charles but through the bounty of Sir Oliver, who he knows is arrived; so that you may depend on his fidelity to his [own] interest. I have also another evidence in my power, one Snake, whom I have detected in a matter little short of forgery, and shall shortly produce to remove some of *your* prejudices, Sir Peter, relative to Charles and Lady Teazle.

SIR PET. I have heard too much on that subject.

ROW. Here comes the honest Israelite.

Enter MOSES.

—This is Sir Oliver.

SIR OLIV. Sir, I understand you have lately had great dealings with my nephew Charles.

MOS. Yes, Sir Oliver—I have done all I could for him, but he was ruined before he came to me for assistance.

SIR OLIV. That was unlucky, truly—for you

have had no opportunity of showing your talents.

MOS. None at all—I hadn't the pleasure of knowing his distresses—till he was some thousands worse than nothing.

SIR OLIV. Unfortunate, indeed! But I suppose you have done all in your power for him, honest Moses?

MOS. Yes, he knows that. This very evening I was to have brought him a gentleman from the city, who doesn't know him, and will, I believe, advance him some money.

SIR PET. What, one Charles has never had money from before?

MOS. Yes; Mr. Premium, of Crutched Friars—formerly a broker.

SIR PET. Egad, Sir Oliver, a thought strikes me!—Charles, you say, doesn't know Mr. Premium?

MOS. Not at all.

SIR PET. Now then, Sir Oliver, you may have a better opportunity of satisfying yourself than by an old romancing tale of a poor relation;—go with my friend Moses, and represent Mr. *Premium,* and then, I'll answer for't, you will see your nephew in all his glory.

SIR OLIV. Egad, I like this idea better than the other, and I may visit *Joseph* afterwards, as old *Stanley*.

SIR PET. True—so you may.

ROW. Well, this is taking Charles rather at a disadvantage, to be sure. However, Moses—you understand Sir Peter, and will be faithful?

MOS. You may depend upon me,—this is near the time I was to have gone.

SIR OLIV. I'll accompany you as soon as you please, Moses; but hold! I have forgot one thing—how the plague shall I be able to pass for a Jew?

MOS. There's no need—the principal is Christian.

SIR OLIV. Is he?—I'm sorry to hear it—but, then again, an't I rather too smartly dressed to look like a money-lender?

SIR PET. Not at all; 'twould not be out of character, if you went in your own carriage—would it, Moses?

MOS. Not in the least.

SIR OLIV. Well, but how must I talk? there's certainly some cant of usury, and mode of treating, that I ought to know.

SIR PET. Oh, there's not much to learn—the great point, as I take it, is to be exorbitant enough in your demands—hey, Moses?

MOS. Yes, that's a very great point.

SIR OLIV. I'll answer for't I'll not be wanting in that. I'll ask him eight or ten per cent on the loan, at least.

MOS. If you ask him no more than that, you'll be discovered immediately.

SIR OLIV. Hey! what the plague! how much then?

MOS. That depends upon the circumstances. If he appears not very anxious for the supply, you should require only forty or fifty per cent; but if you find him in great distress, and want the moneys very bad—you may ask double.

SIR PET. A good honest trade you're learning, Sir Oliver!

SIR OLIV. Truly I think so—and not unprofitable.

MOS. Then, you know, you haven't the moneys yourself, but are forced to borrow them for him of a friend.

SIR OLIV. Oh! I borrow it of a friend, do I?

MOS. Yes, and your friend is an unconscionable dog, but you can't help it.

SIR OLIV. My friend is an unconscionable dog, is he?

MOS. Yes, and he himself has not the moneys by him—but is forced to sell stock at a great loss.

SIR OLIV. He is forced to sell stock, is he, at a great loss, is he? Well, that's very kind of him.

SIR PET. I'faith, Sir Oliver—Mr. Premium, I mean—you'll soon be master of the trade. But, Moses! wouldn't you have him run out a little against the Annuity Bill? That would be in character, I should think.

MOS. Very much.

ROW. And lament that a young man now must be at years of discretion before he is suffered to ruin himself?

MOS. Aye, great pity!

SIR PET. And abuse the public for allowing merit to an act whose only object is to snatch

86 **Crutched Friars** street near the Tower of London

159 **Annuity Bill** measure to protect the estates of minors which became law during the initial run of the play

misfortune and imprudence from the rapacious relief of usury, and give the minor a chance of inheriting his estate without being undone by coming into possession.

SIR OLIV. So, so—Moses shall give me further instructions as we go together.

SIR PET. You will not have much time, for your nephew lives hard by.

SIR OLIV. Oh, never fear! my tutor appears so able, that though Charles lived in the next street, it must be my own fault if I am not a complete rogue before I turn the corner.

Exeunt SIR OLIVER *and* MOSES.

SIR PET. So now I think Sir Oliver will be convinced;—you are partial, Rowley, and would have prepared Charles for the other plot.

ROW. No, upon my word, Sir Peter.

SIR PET. Well, go bring me this Snake, and I'll hear what he has to say presently.—I see Maria, and want to speak with her.—*Exit* ROWLEY. I should be glad to be convinced my suspicions of Lady Teazle and Charles were unjust. I have never yet opened my mind on this subject to my friend *Joseph*—I'm determined I will do it—*he* will give me his opinion sincerely.

Enter MARIA.

So, child, has Mr. Surface returned with you?

MARIA. No, sir—he was engaged.

SIR PET. Well, Maria, do you not reflect, the more you converse with that amiable young man, what return his partiality for you deserves?

MARIA. Indeed, Sir Peter, your frequent importunity on this subject distresses me extremely —you compel me to declare, that I know no man who has ever paid me a particular attention whom I would not prefer to Mr. Surface.

SIR PET. So—here's perverseness! No, no, Maria, 'tis Charles only whom you would prefer —'tis evident his vices and follies have won your heart.

MARIA. This is unkind, sir—you know I have obeyed you in neither seeing nor corresponding with him; I have heard enough to convince me that he is unworthy my regard. Yet I cannot think it culpable, if, while my understanding severely condemns his vices, my heart suggests some pity for his distresses.

SIR PET. Well, well, pity him as much as you please, but give your heart and hand to a worthier object.

MARIA. Never to his brother!

SIR PET. Go, perverse and obstinate! But take care, madam; you have never yet known what the authority of a guardian is—don't compel me to inform you of it.

MARIA. I can only say, you shall not have *just* reason. 'Tis true, by my father's will, I am for a short period bound to regard you as his substitute, but must cease to think you so, when you would compel me to be miserable.

Exit MARIA.

SIR PET. Was ever man so crossed as I am! everything conspiring to fret me!—I had not been involved in matrimony a fortnight, before her father, a hale and hearty man, died—on purpose, I believe, for the pleasure of plaguing me with the care of his daughter. But here comes my helpmate! She appears in great good humor. How happy I should be if I could tease her into loving me, though but a little!

Enter LADY TEAZLE.

LADY TEAZ. Lud! Sir Peter, I hope you haven't been quarreling with Maria—it isn't using me well to be ill humored when I am not by.

SIR PET. Ah, Lady Teazle, you might have the power to make me good humored at all times.

LADY TEAZ. I am sure I wish I had—for I want you to be in charming sweet temper at this moment. Do be good humored now, and let me have two hundred pounds, will you?

SIR PET. Two hundred pounds! what, an't I to be in a good humor without paying for it! But speak to me thus, and i'faith there's nothing I could refuse you. You shall have it; but seal me a bond for the repayment.

LADY TEAZ. O, no—there—my note of hand will do as well.

SIR PET (*Kissing her hand.*). And you shall no longer reproach me with not giving you an independent settlement,—I mean shortly to surprise you; but shall we always live thus, hey?

LADY TEAZ. If you please. I'm sure I don't care how soon we leave off quarrelling, provided you'll own *you* were tired first.

SIR PET. Well—then let our future contest be, who shall be most obliging.

LADY TEAZ. I assure you, Sir Peter, good nature becomes you. You look now as you did before we were married!—when you used to walk with me under the elms, and tell me stories of what a gallant you were in your youth, and chuck me under the chin, you would, and ask me if I thought I could love an old fellow, who would deny me nothing—didn't you?

SIR PET. Yes, yes, and you were as kind and attentive.

LADY TEAZ. Aye, so I was, and would always take your part, when my acquaintance used to abuse you, and turn you into ridicule.

SIR PET. Indeed!

LADY TEAZ. Aye, and when my cousin Sophy has called you a stiff, peevish old bachelor, and laughed at me for thinking of marrying one who might be my father, I have always defended you—and said, I didn't think you so ugly by any means, and that I dared say you'd make a very good sort of a husband.

SIR PET. And you prophesied right—and we shall certainly now be the happiest couple——

LADY TEAZ. And never differ again!

SIR PET. No, never!—though at the same time, indeed, my dear Lady Teazle, you must watch your temper very narrowly; for in all our little quarrels, my dear, if you recollect, my love, you always began first.

LADY TEAZ. I beg your pardon, my dear Sir Peter: indeed, you always gave the provocation.

SIR PET. Now, see, my angel! take care—*contradicting* isn't the way to keep friends.

LADY TEAZ. Then, don't *you* begin it, my love!

SIR PET. There, now! you—you are going on—you don't perceive, my life, that you are just doing the very thing which you know always makes me angry.

LADY TEAZ. Nay, you know if you will be angry without any reason——

SIR PET. There now! you want to quarrel again.

LADY TEAZ. No, I am sure I don't—but, if you will be so peevish——

SIR PET. There now! who begins first?

LADY TEAZ. Why, you, to be sure. I said nothing—but there's no bearing your temper.

SIR PET. No, no, madam, the fault's in your own temper.

LADY TEAZ. Aye, you are just what my cousin Sophy said you would be.

SIR PET. Your cousin Sophy is a forward, impertinent gipsy.

LADY TEAZ. You are a great bear, I'm sure, to abuse my relations.

SIR PET. Now may all the plagues of marriage be doubled on me, if ever I try to be friends with you any more!

LADY TEAZ. So much the better.

SIR PET. No, no, madam; 'tis evident you never cared a pin for me, and I was a madman to marry you—a pert, rural coquette, that had refused half the honest squires in the neighborhood!

LADY TEAZ. And I am sure I was a fool to marry you—an old dangling bachelor, who was single at fifty, only because he never could meet with any one who would have him.

SIR PET. Aye, aye, madam; but you were pleased enough to listen to me—*you* never had such an offer before.

LADY TEAZ. No! didn't I refuse Sir Twivy Tarrier, who everybody said would have been a better match—for his estate is just as good as yours—and he has broke his neck since we have been married.

SIR PET. I have done with you, madam! You are an unfeeling, ungrateful—but there's an end of everything. I believe you capable of anything that's bad. Yes, madam, I now believe the reports relative to you and Charles, madam—yes, madam, you and Charles—are not without grounds——

LADY TEAZ. Take care, Sir Peter! you had better not insinuate any such thing! I'll not be suspected with*out cause,* I promise you.

SIR PET. Very well, madam! very well! a separate maintenance as soon as you please. Yes, madam, or a divorce! I'll make an example of myself for the benefit of all old bachelors. Let us separate, madam.

LADY TEAZ. Agreed! agreed! And now, my dear Sir Peter, we are of a mind once more, we may be the *happiest couple,* and *never differ again,* you know: ha! ha! Well, you are going to be in a passion, I see, and I shall only interrupt you—so, bye! bye! *Exit.*

SIR PET. Plagues and tortures! can't I make her angry neither? Oh, I am the miserablest fellow! But I'll not bear her presuming to keep her temper—no! she may break my heart, but she shan't keep her temper. *Exit.*

Scene Two

CHARLES's *house.*

Enter TRIP, MOSES, *and* SIR OLIVER SURFACE.

TRIP. Here, Master Moses! if you'll stay a moment, I'll try whether—what's the gentleman's name?

SIR OLIV. Mr. Moses, what *is* my name? (*Aside.*)

MOS. Mr. Premium.

TRIP. Premium—very well.

Exit TRIP, *taking snuff.*

10 SIR OLIV. To judge by the servants one wouldn't believe the master was ruined. But what!—sure, this was my brother's house?

MOS. Yes, sir; Mr. Charles bought it of Mr. Joseph, with the furniture, pictures, &c., just as the old gentleman left it—Sir Peter thought it a great piece of extravagance in him.

SIR OLIV. In my mind, the other's economy in *selling* it to him was more reprehensible by half.

20 *Re-enter* TRIP.

TRIP. My master says you must wait, gentlemen; he has company, and can't speak with you yet.

SIR OLIV. If he knew *who* it was wanted to see him, perhaps he wouldn't have sent such a message?

TRIP. Yes, yes, sir; he knows *you* are here—I didn't forget little Premium—no, no, no.

SIR OLIV. Very well—and I pray, sir, what 30 may be your name?

TRIP. Trip, sir—my name is Trip, at your service.

SIR OLIV. Well, then, Mr. Trip, you have a pleasant sort of a place here, I guess.

TRIP. Why, yes—here are three or four of us pass our time agreeably enough; but then our wages are sometimes a little in arrear—and not very great either—but fifty pounds a year, and find our own bags and bouquets.

SIR OLIV [*Aside.*]. Bags and bouquets! halters 40 and bastinadoes!

TRIP. But *à propos,* Moses, have you been able to get me that little bill discounted?

SIR OLIV [*Aside.*]. Wants to raise money, too! —mercy on me! Has his distresses, I warrant, like a lord,—and affects creditors and duns.

MOS. 'Twas not to be done, indeed, Mr. Trip. (*Gives the note.*)

TRIP. Good lack, you surprise me! My friend *Brush* has indorsed it, and I thought when he 50 put his mark on the back of a bill 'twas as good as cash.

MOS. No, 'twouldn't do.

TRIP. A small sum—but twenty pounds. Hark'ee, Moses, do you think you couldn't get it me by way of annuity?

SIR OLIV [*Aside.*]. An annuity! ha! ha! ha! a footman raise money by way of annuity! Well done, luxury, egad!

MOS. But you must insure your place. 60

TRIP. Oh, with all my heart! I'll insure my place, and my life too, if you please.

SIR OLIV [*Aside.*]. It's more than I would your neck.

TRIP. But then, Moses, it must be done before this d—d register takes place—one wouldn't like to have one's name made public, you know.

MOS. No, certainly. But is there nothing you could deposit? 70

TRIP. Why, nothing capital of my master's wardrobe has dropped lately; but I could give you a mortgage on some of his winter clothes,

39 **bags and bouquets** referring to the dress of footmen 66 **d—d register** referring to the provision in the Annuity Bill for registering life annuities

with equity of redemption before November—or you shall have the reversion of the French velvet, or a post-obit on the blue and silver;—these, I should think, Moses, with a few pair of point ruffles, as a collateral security—hey, my little fellow?

80 MOS. Well, well. (*Bell rings.*)

TRIP. Gad, I heard the bell! I believe, gentlemen, I can now introduce you. Don't forget the annuity, little Moses! This way, gentlemen, insure my place, you know.

SIR OLIV [*Aside.*]. If the man be a shadow of his master, this is the temple of dissipation indeed! *Exeunt.*

Scene Three

CHARLES [SURFACE], CARELESS, &C., &C.
at a table with wine, &c.

CHAS. SURF. 'Fore heaven, 'tis true!—there's the great degeneracy of the age. Many of our acquaintance have taste, spirit, and politeness; but, plague on't, they won't drink.

CARE. It is so, indeed, Charles! they give in to all the substantial luxuries of the table, and abstain from nothing but wine and wit.

CHAS. SURF. Oh, certainly society suffers by it intolerably! for now, instead of the social 10 spirit of raillery that used to mantle over a glass of bright Burgundy, their conversation is become just like the Spa-water they drink, which has all the pertness and flatulence of champagne, without its spirit or flavor.

I GENT. But what are *they* to do who love play better than wine?

CARE. True! there's Harry diets himself for gaming, and is now under a hazard regimen.

CHAS. SURF. Then he'll have the worst of it. 20 What! you wouldn't train a horse for the course by keeping him from corn! For my part, egad, I am now never so successful as when I am a little merry—let me throw on a bottle of champagne, and I never lose—at least I never feel my losses, which is exactly the same thing.

2 GENT. Aye, that I believe.

CHAS. SURF. And, then, what man can pretend to be a believer in love, who is an abjurer of wine? 'Tis the test by which the lover knows 30 his own heart. Fill a dozen bumpers to a dozen beauties, and she that floats at top is the maid that has bewitched you.

CARE. Now then, Charles, be honest, and give us your real favorite.

CHAS. SURF. Why, I have withheld her only in compassion to you. If I toast her, you must give a round of her peers—which is impossible—on earth.

CARE. Oh, then we'll find some canonised vestals or heathen goddesses that will do, I war- 40 rant!

CHAS. SURF. Here then, bumpers, you rogues! bumpers! Maria! Maria— (*Drink.*)

I GENT. Maria who?

CHAS. SURF. O, damn the surname!—'tis too formal to be registered in Love's calendar—but now, Sir Toby Bumper, beware—we must have beauty superlative.

CARE. Nay, never study, Sir Toby: we'll stand to the toast, though your mistress should 50 want an eye—and you know you have a song will excuse you.

SIR TOBY. Egad, so I have! and I'll give him the song instead of the lady. [*Sings.*]

SONG AND CHORUS

Here's to the maiden of bashful fifteen;
 Here's to the widow of fifty;
Here's to the flaunting extravagant quean,
 And here's to the housewife that's thrifty.
Chorus. Let the toast pass— 60
 Drink to the lass—
I'll warrant she'll prove an excuse for the glass.

Here's to the charmer whose dimples we prize;
 Now to the maid who has none, sir;

76 **post-obit** claim to be satisfied after the death of the original owner

Here's to the girl with a pair of blue eyes,
And here's to the nymph with but one, sir.
Chorus. Let the toast pass, &c.

Here's to the maid with a bosom of snow:
Now to *her* that's as brown as a berry:
70 Here's to the wife with a face full of woe,
And now for the damsel that's merry.
Chorus. Let the toast pass, &c.

For let 'em be clumsy, or let 'em be slim,
Young or ancient, I care not a feather:
So fill a pint bumper quite up to the brim,
—And let us e'en toast 'em together.
Chorus. Let the toast pass, &c.

ALL. Bravo! Bravo!

Enter TRIP, *and whispers* CHARLES SURFACE.

80 CHAS. SURF. Gentlemen, you must excuse me a little.—Careless, take the chair, will you?

CARE. Nay, prithee, Charles, what now? This is one of your peerless beauties, I suppose, has dropped in by chance?

CHAS. SURF. No, faith! To tell you the truth, 'tis a Jew and a broker, who are come by appointment.

CARE. Oh, damn it! let's have the Jew in—

I GENT. Aye, and the broker too, by all
90 means.

2 GENT. Yes, yes, the Jew and the broker.

CHAS. SURF. Egad, with all my heart!—Trip bid the gentlemen walk in.— [*Exit* TRIP.] Though there's one of them a stranger, I can tell you.

CARE. Charles, let us give them some generous Burgundy, and perhaps they'll grow conscientious.

CHAS. SURF. Oh, hang 'em, no! wine does
100 but draw forth a man's *natural* qualities; and to make *them* drink would only be to whet their knavery.

Enter TRIP, SIR OLIVER SURFACE, *and* MOSES.

CHAS. SURF. So, honest Moses; walk in, pray, Mr. Premium—that's the gentleman's name, isn't it, Moses?

MOS. Yes, sir.

CHAS. SURF. Set chairs, Trip.—Sit down, Mr. Premium.—Glasses, Trip.—Sit down, Moses.—
110 Come, Mr. Premium, I'll give you a sentiment; here's 'Success to usury!'—Moses, fill the gentleman a bumper.

MOS. Success to usury!

CARE. Right, Moses—usury is prudence and industry, and deserves to succeed.

SIR OLIV. Then here's—All the success it deserves!

CARE. No, no, that won't do! Mr. Premium, you have demurred to the toast, and must drink it in a pint bumper. 120

I GENT. A pint bumper, at least.

MOS. Oh, pray, sir, consider—Mr. Premium's a gentleman.

CARE. And therefore loves good wine.

2 GENT. Give Moses a quart glass—this is mutiny, and a high contempt of the chair.

CARE. Here, now for't! I'll see justice done, to the last drop of my bottle.

SIR OLIV. Nay, pray, gentlemen—I did not expect this usage. 130

CHAS. SURF. No, hang it, Careless, you shan't; Mr. Premium's a stranger.

SIR OLIV [*Aside.*]. Odd! I wish I was well out of this company.

CARE. Plague on 'em then! if they won't drink, we'll not sit down with 'em. Come, Harry, the dice are in the next room.—Charles, you'll join us—when you have finished your business with these gentlemen?

CHAS. SURF. I will! I will!—*Exeunt* [*Gentlemen*]. Careless! 140

CARE. Well!

CHAS. SURF. Perhaps I may want *you*.

CARE. Oh, you know I am always ready—word, note, or bond, 'tis all the same to me.

Exit.

MOS. Sir, this is Mr. Premium, a gentleman of the strictest honor and secrecy; and always performs what he undertakes. Mr. Premium, this is—— 150

CHAS. SURF. Pshaw! have done! Sir, my friend Moses is a very honest fellow, but a little slow at expression; he'll be an hour giving us our titles. Mr. Premium, the plain state of the matter is this—I am an extravagant young fellow who want[s] money to borrow; you I take to be a prudent old fellow, who ha[s] got money to lend. I am blockhead enough to give fifty per cent sooner than not have it; and you, I presume, are rogue enough to take a hundred 160 if you could get it. Now, sir, you see we are acquainted at once, and may proceed to business without farther ceremony.

SIR OLIV. Exceeding frank, upon my word. I see, sir, you are not a man of many compliments.

CHAS. SURF. Oh, no, sir! plain dealing in business I always think best.

SIR OLIV. Sir, I like you the better for't. However, you are mistaken in one thing—I have no money to lend, but I believe I could procure some of a friend; but then he's an unconscionable dog—isn't he, Moses? And must sell stock to accommodate you—mustn't he, Moses?

MOS. Yes, indeed! You know I always speak the truth, and scorn to tell a lie!

CHAS. SURF. Right! People that expect truth generally do. But these are trifles, Mr. Premium. What! I know money isn't to be bought without paying for't!

SIR OLIV. Well, but what security could you give? You have no land, I suppose?

CHAS. SURF. Not a mole-hill, nor a twig, but what's in beau-pots out at the window!

SIR OLIV. Nor any stock, I presume?

CHAS. SURF. Nothing but live stock—and that's only a few pointers and ponies. But pray, Mr. Premium, are you acquainted at all with any of my connections?

SIR OLIV. Why, to say truth, I am.

CHAS. SURF. Then you must know that I have a devilish rich uncle in the East Indies, Sir *Oliver Surface,* from whom I have the greatest expectations.

SIR OLIV. That you have a wealthy uncle, I have heard—but how your expectations will turn out is more, I believe, than you can tell.

CHAS. SURF. Oh, no!—there can be no doubt—they tell me I'm a prodigious favorite—and that he talks of leaving me everything.

SIR OLIV. Indeed! this is the first I've heard on't.

CHAS. SURF. Yes, yes, 'tis just so.—Moses knows 'tis true; don't you, Moses?

MOS. Oh, yes! I'll swear to't.

SIR OLIV [*Aside.*]. Egad, they'll persuade me presently I'm at Bengal.

CHAS. SURF. Now I propose, Mr. Premium, if it's agreeable to you, a post-obit on Sir Oliver's life; though at the same time the old fellow has been so liberal to me that I give you my word I should be very sorry to hear anything had happened to him.

SIR OLIV. Not more than *I* should, I assure you. But the bond you mention happens to be just the worst security you could offer me—for I might live to a hundred and never recover the principal.

CHAS. SURF. Oh, yes, you would!—the moment Sir Oliver dies, you know, you'd come on me for the money.

SIR OLIV. Then I believe I should be the most unwelcome dun you ever had in your life.

CHAS. SURF. What! I suppose you are afraid now that Sir Oliver is too good a life?

SIR OLIV. No, indeed I am not—though I have heard he is as hale and healthy as any man of his years in Christendom.

CHAS. SURF. There again you are misinformed. No, no, the climate has hurt him considerably, poor uncle Oliver. Yes, he breaks apace, I'm told—and so much altered lately that his nearest relations don't know him.

SIR OLIV. No! Ha! ha! ha! so much altered lately that his relations don't know him! Ha! ha! ha! that's droll, egad—ha! ha! ha!

CHAS. SURF. Ha! ha!—you're glad to hear that, little Premium.

SIR OLIV. No, no, I'm not.

CHAS. SURF. Yes, yes, you are—ha! ha! ha!—you know that mends your chance.

SIR OLIV. But I'm told Sir Oliver is coming over—nay, some say he is actually arrived.

CHAS. SURF. Pshaw! sure I must know better than you whether he's come or not. No, no, rely on't, he is at this moment at Calcutta, isn't he, Moses?

MOS. Oh, yes, certainly.

SIR OLIV. Very true, as you say, you must know better than I, though I have it from pretty good authority—haven't I, Moses?

MOS. Yes, most undoubted!

SIR OLIV. But, sir, as I understand you want a few hundreds immediately, is there nothing you would dispose of?

CHAS. SURF. How do you mean?

SIR OLIV. For instance, now—I have heard—that your father left behind him a great quantity of massy old plate.

CHAS. SURF. O lud! that's gone long ago—Moses can tell you how better than I can.

SIR OLIV. Good lack! all the family race-cups and corporation-bowls! (*Aside.*)—Then it was also supposed that his library was one of the most valuable and complete.

184 **beau-pots** ornamental vases for flowers

CHAS. SURF. Yes, yes, so it was—vastly too much so for a private gentleman—for my part, I was always of a communicative disposition, so I thought it a shame to keep so much knowl- 270 edge to myself.

SIR OLIV [*Aside.*]. Mercy on me! learning that had run in the family like an heirloom!—[*Aloud.*] Pray, what are become of the books?

CHAS. SURF. You must inquire of the auctioneer, Master Premium, for I don't believe even Moses can direct you there.

MOS. I never meddle with books.

SIR OLIV. So, so, nothing of the family property left, I suppose?

280 CHAS. SURF. Not much, indeed; unless you have a mind to the family pictures. I have got a room full of ancestors above—and if you have a taste for old paintings, egad, you shall have 'em a bargain!

SIR OLIV. Hey! and the devil! sure, you wouldn't sell your forefathers, would you?

CHAS. SURF. Every man of 'em, to the best bidder.

SIR OLIV. What! your great-uncles and aunts?

290 CHAS. SURF. Aye, and my great-grandfathers and grandmothers too.

SIR OLIV. Now I give him up!—(*Aside.*)—What the plague, have you no bowels for your own kindred? Odd's life! do you take me for Shylock in the play, that you would raise money of me on your own flesh and blood?

CHAS. SURF. Nay, my little broker, don't be angry: what need *you* care, if you have your money's worth?

SIR OLIV. Well, I'll be the purchaser—I think 300 I can dispose of the family.—[*Aside.*] Oh, I'll never forgive him this! never!

Enter CARELESS.

CARE. Come, Charles, what keeps you?

CHAS. SURF. I can't come yet. I'faith! we are going to have a sale above—here's little Premium will buy all my ancestors!

CARE. Oh, burn your ancestors!

CHAS. SURF. No, he may do that afterwards, if he pleases. Stay, Careless, we want you; egad, 310 you shall be auctioneer—so come along with us.

CARE. Oh, have with you, if that's the case. —I can handle a hammer as well as a dice box!

SIR OLIV [*Aside.*]. Oh, the profligates!

CHAS. SURF. Come, Moses, you shall be appraiser, if we want one.—Gad's life, little Premium, you don't seem to like the business.

SIR OLIV. Oh, yes, I do, vastly! Ha! ha! yes, yes, I think it a rare joke to sell one's family by auction—ha! ha!—[*Aside.*] Oh, the prodigal! 320

CHAS. SURF. To be sure! when a man wants money, where the plague should he get assistance, if he can't make free with his own relations? *Exeunt.*

End of the third Act.

ACT FOUR *Scene One*

Picture-room at CHARLES'S.

Enter CHARLES SURFACE, SIR OLIVER SURFACE, MOSES, *and* CARELESS.

CHAS. SURF. Walk in, gentlemen, pray walk in!—here they are, the family of the Surfaces, up to the Conquest.

SIR OLIV. And, in my opinion, a goodly collection.

CHAS. SURF. Aye, aye, these are done in true spirit of portrait-painting—no volunteer grace or expression—not like the works of your mod- 10 ern Raphael, who gives you the strongest resemblance, yet contrives to make your own portrait independent of you; so that you may sink the original and not hurt the picture. No, no; the merit of these is the inveterate likeness—all stiff and awkward as the originals, and like nothing in human nature beside!

SIR OLIV. Ah! we shall never see such figures of men again.

20 CHAS. SURF. I hope not. Well, you see, Master Premium, what a domestic character I am—here I sit of an evening surrounded by my family. But come, get to your pulpit, Mr. Auctioneer—here's an old gouty chair of my grandfather's will answer the purpose.

CARE. Aye, aye, this will do. But, Charles, I have ne'er a hammer; and what's an auctioneer without his hammer?

CHAS. SURF. Egad, that's true. What parch-

30 ment have we here? (*Takes down a roll.*) *'Richard, heir to Thomas'*—our genealogy in full. Here, Careless, you shall have no common bit of mahogany—here's the family tree for you, you rogue—this shall be your hammer, and now you may knock down my ancestors with their own pedigree.

SIR OLIV [*Aside.*]. What an unnatural rogue! —an *ex post facto* parricide!

CARE. Yes, yes, here's a list of your genera-

40 tion indeed;—faith, Charles, this is the most convenient thing you could have found for the business, for 'twill serve not only as a hammer, but a catalogue into the bargain.—But come, begin—A-going, a-going, a-going!

CHAS. SURF. Bravo, Careless! Well, here's my great-uncle, Sir Richard Raviline, a marvellous good general in his day, I assure you. He served in all the Duke of Marlborough's wars, and got that cut over his eye at the battle of Malplaquet.

50 What say you, Mr. Premium? look at him—there's a hero for you! not cut out of his feathers, as your modern clipped captains are, but enveloped in wig and regimentals, as a general should be. What do you bid?

MOS. Mr. Premium would have you speak.

CHAS. SURF. Why, then, he shall have him for ten pounds, and I am sure that's not dear for a staff-officer.

SIR OLIV [*Aside.*]. Heaven deliver me! his

60 famous uncle Richard for ten pounds!—Very well, sir, I take him at that.

CHAS. SURF. Careless, knock down my uncle Richard.—Here, now, is a maiden sister of his, my great-aunt Deborah, done by Kneller, thought to be in his best manner, and a very formidable likeness. There she is, you see, a shepherdess feeding her flock. You shall have her for five pounds ten—the sheep are worth the money.

SIR OLIV [*Aside.*]. Ah! poor Deborah! a 70 woman who set such a value on herself!—Five pound ten—she's mine.

CHAS. SURF. Knock down my aunt Deborah! Here, now, are two that were a sort of cousins of theirs.—You see, Moses, these pictures were done some time ago, when beaux wore wigs, and the ladies wore their own hair.

SIR OLIV. Yes, truly, head-dresses appear to have been a little lower in those days.

CHAS. SURF. Well, take that couple for the 80 same.

MOS. 'Tis [a] good bargain.

CHAS. SURF. Careless!—This, now, is a grandfather of my mother's, a learned judge, well known on the western circuit.—What do you rate him at, Moses?

MOS. Four guineas.

CHAS. SURF. Four guineas! Gad's life, you don't bid me the price of his wig.—Mr. Premium, *you* have more respect for the woolsack; 90 do let us knock his lordship down at fifteen.

SIR OLIV. By all means.

CARE. Gone!

CHAS. SURF. And there are two brothers of his, William and Walter Blunt, Esquires, both members of Parliament, and noted speakers; and, what's very extraordinary, I believe this is the first time they were ever bought and sold.

SIR OLIV. That's very extraordinary, indeed! I'll take them at your own price, for the honor 100 of Parliament.

CARE. Well said, little Premium! I'll knock 'em down at forty.

CHAS. SURF. Here's a jolly fellow—I don't know what relation, but he was mayor of Manchester; take him at eight pounds.

SIR OLIV. No, no—six will do for the mayor.

CHAS. SURF. Come, make it guineas, and I'll throw you the two aldermen there into the bargain. 110

SIR OLIV. They're mine.

CHAS. SURF. Careless, knock down the mayor and aldermen. But, plague on't! we shall be all

49 **battle of Malplaquet** victory over the French, September 11, 1709 64 **Kneller** Sir Godfrey Kneller (1646–1723), a famous portrait painter

90 **respect for the woolsack** respect for judges (who sat on seats made of bags of wool when they attended the House of Lords)

day retailing in this manner; do let us deal wholesale—what say you, little Premium? Give me three hundred pounds for the rest of the family in the lump.

CARE. Aye, aye, that will be the best way.

SIR OLIV. Well, well, anything to accommodate you; they are mine. But there is one portrait which you have always passed over. 120

CARE. What, that ill-looking little fellow over the settee?

SIR OLIV. Yes, sir, I mean that; though I don't think him so ill-looking a little fellow, by any means.

CHAS. SURF. What, that? Oh, that's my uncle Oliver! 'Twas done before he went to India.

CARE. Your uncle Oliver! Gad, then you'll never be friends, Charles. That, now, to me, is as stern a looking rogue as ever I saw—an unforgiving eye, and a damned disinheriting countenance! an inveterate knave, depend on't. Don't you think so, little Premium? 130

SIR OLIV. Upon my soul, sir, I do not; I think it is as honest a looking face as any in the room, dead or alive. But I suppose your uncle Oliver goes with the rest of the lumber?

CHAS. SURF. No, hang it! I'll not part with poor Noll. The old fellow has been very good to me, and, egad, I'll keep his picture while I've a room to put it in. 140

SIR OLIV. The rogue's my nephew after all! (*Aside.*)—But, sir, I have somehow taken a fancy to that picture.

CHAS. SURF. I'm sorry for't, for you certainly will not have it. Oons! haven't you got enough of 'em?

SIR OLIV. I forgive him everything! (*Aside.*) —But, sir, when I take a whim in my head, I don't value money. I'll give you as much for that as for all the rest. 150

CHAS. SURF. Don't tease me, master broker; I tell you I'll not part with it, and there's an end on't.

SIR OLIV. How like his father the dog is!—(*Aloud.*) Well, well, I have done.—I did not perceive it before, but I think I never saw such a resemblance.—Well, sir—here is a draught for your sum. 160

CHAS. SURF. Why, 'tis for eight hundred pounds!

SIR OLIV. You will not let Sir Oliver go?

CHAS. SURF. Zounds! no! I tell you, once more.

SIR OLIV. Then never mind the difference; we'll balance another time. But give me your hand on the bargain; you are an honest fellow, Charles—I beg pardon, sir, for being so free.—Come, Moses. 170

CHAS. SURF. Egad, this is a whimsical old fellow!—but hark'ee, Premium, you'll prepare lodgings for these gentlemen.

SIR OLIV. Yes, yes, I'll send for them in a day or two.

CHAS. SURF. But hold—do now—send a genteel conveyance for them, for, I assure you, they were most of them used to ride in their own carriages.

SIR OLIV. I will, I will, for all but—Oliver. 180

CHAS. SURF. Aye, all but the little honest nabob.

SIR OLIV. You're fixed on that?

CHAS. SURF. Peremptorily.

SIR OLIV. A dear extravagant rogue!—Good day!—Come, Moses,—Let me hear now who dares call him profligate!

Exeunt SIR OLIVER *and* MOSES.

CARE. Why, this is the oddest genius of the sort I ever saw! 190

CHAS. SURF. Egad, he's the prince of brokers, I think. I wonder how the devil Moses got acquainted with so honest a fellow.—Ha! here's Rowley.—Do, Careless, say I'll join the company in a moment.

CARE. I will—but don't let that old blockhead persuade you to squander any of that money on old musty debts, or any such nonsense; for tradesmen, Charles, are the most exorbitant fellows! 200

CHAS. SURF. Very true, and paying them is only encouraging them.

CARE. Nothing else.

CHAS. SURF. Aye, aye, never fear.—*Exit* CARELESS. So! this was an odd old fellow, indeed! Let me see, two-thirds of this is mine by right—five hundred and thirty pounds. 'Fore heaven! I find one's ancestors are more valuable relations than I took 'em for!—Ladies and gentlemen, your most obedient and very grateful humble servant. 210

Enter ROWLEY.

Ha! old Rowley! egad, you are just come in time to take leave of your old acquaintance.

ROW. Yes, I heard they were going. But I

wonder you can have such spirits under so many distresses.

CHAS. SURF. Why, there's the point—my distresses are so many, that I can't afford to part with my spirits; but I shall be rich and splenetic, all in good time. However, I suppose you are surprised that I am not more sorrowful at parting with so many near relations; to be sure, 'tis very affecting; but, rot 'em, you see they never move a muscle, so why should I?

ROW. There's no making you serious a moment.

CHAS. SURF. Yes, faith: I am so now. Here, my honest Rowley, here, get me this changed, and take a hundred pounds of it immediately to old Stanley.

ROW. A hundred pounds! Consider only——

CHAS. SURF. Gad's life, don't talk about it! poor Stanley's wants are pressing, and, if you don't make haste, we shall have some one call that has a better right to the money.

ROW. Ah! there's the point! I never will cease dunning you with the old proverb——

CHAS. SURF. 'Be *just* before you're *generous,*' hey!—Why, so I would if I could; but Justice is an old lame hobbling beldame, and I can't get her to keep pace with Generosity, for the soul of me.

ROW. Yet, Charles, believe me, one hour's reflection——

CHAS. SURF. Aye, aye, it's all very true; but, hark'ee, Rowley, while I have, by heaven I'll give—so, damn your economy! and now for hazard.

Exit.

Scene Two

The parlor.

Enter SIR OLIVER SURFACE *and* MOSES.

MOS. Well, sir, I think, as Sir Peter said, you have seen Mr. Charles in high glory; 'tis great pity he's so extravagant.

SIR OLIV. True, but he wouldn't sell my picture.

MOS. And loves wine and women so much.

SIR OLIV. But he wouldn't sell my picture!

MOS. And game[s] so deep.

SIR OLIV. But he wouldn't sell my picture. Oh, here's Rowley.

Enter ROWLEY.

ROW. So, Sir Oliver, I find you have made a purchase——

SIR OLIV. Yes, yes, our young rake has parted with his ancestors like old tapestry.

ROW. And here has he commissioned me to redeliver you part of the purchase-money—I mean, though, in your necessitous character of old *Stanley*.

MOS. Ah! there is the pity of all: he is so damned charitable.

ROW. And I left a hosier and two tailors in the hall, who, I'm sure, won't be paid, and this hundred would satisfy 'em.

SIR OLIV. Well, well, I'll pay his debts—and his benevolence too; but now I am no more a broker, and you shall introduce me to the elder brother as old Stanley.

ROW. Not yet awhile; Sir Peter, I know, means to call there about this time.

Enter TRIP.

TRIP. O gentlemen, I beg pardon for not showing you out; this way—Moses, a word.

Exeunt TRIP *and* MOSES.

SIR OLIV. There's a fellow for you! Would

you believe it, that puppy intercepted the Jew on our coming, and wanted to raise money before he got to his master!

40 ROW. Indeed!

SIR OLIV. Yes, they are now planning an annuity business. Ah, Master Rowley, in my days, servants were content with the follies of their masters, when they were worn a little threadbare—but now they have their vices, like their birthday clothes, with the gloss on. *Exeunt.*

Scene Three

A library [*in* JOSEPH SURFACE'S *house.*]

JOSEPH SURFACE *and Servant.*

JOS. SURF. No letter from Lady Teazle?

SERV. No, sir.

JOS. SURF [*Aside.*]. I am surprised she hasn't sent, if she is prevented from coming. Sir Peter certainly does not suspect me. Yet I wish I may not lose the heiress, through the scrape I have drawn myself in with the wife; however, Charles's imprudence and bad character are 10 great points in my favor. (*Knocking.*)

SERV. Sir, I believe that must be Lady Teazle.

JOS. SURF. Hold! See whether it is or not, before you go to the door—I have a particular message for you, if it should be my brother.

SERV. 'Tis her ladyship, sir; she always leaves her chair at the milliner's in the next street.

JOS. SURF. Stay, stay—draw that screen before the window—that will do;—my opposite neighbor is a maiden lady of so curious a tem- 20 per.—(*Servant draws the screen, and exit.*) I have a difficult hand to play in this affair. Lady Teazle has lately suspected my views on Maria; but she must by no means be let into that secret, —at least, not till I have her more in my power.

Enter LADY TEAZLE.

LADY TEAZ. What, sentiment in soliloquy! Have you been very impatient now? O lud! don't pretend to look grave. I vow I couldn't 30 come before.

JOS. SURF. O madam, punctuality is a species of constancy, a very unfashionable quality in a lady.

LADY TEAZ. Upon my word, you ought to pity me. Do you know that Sir Peter is grown so ill-tempered to me of late, and so jealous of *Charles* too—that's the best of the story, isn't it?

JOS. SURF (*Aside.*). I am glad my scandalous friends keep that up.

LADY TEAZ. I am sure I wish he would let Maria marry him, and then perhaps he would 40 be convinced; don't you, Mr. Surface?

JOS. SURF (*Aside.*). Indeed I do not.—Oh, certainly I do! for then my dear Lady Teazle would also be convinced how wrong her suspicions were of my having any design on the silly girl.

LADY TEAZ. Well, well, I'm inclined to believe you. But isn't it provoking, to have the most ill-natured things said to one? And there's my friend Lady Sneerwell has circulated I don't 50 know how many scandalous tales of me! and all without any foundation, too—that's what vexes me.

JOS. SURF. Aye, madam, to be sure, that *is* the provoking circumstance—without foundation! yes, yes, there's the mortification, indeed; for, when a scandalous story is believed against one, there certainly is no comfort like the consciousness of having deserved it.

LADY TEAZ. No, to be sure—then I'd forgive 60 their malice; but to attack me, who am really so innocent, and who never say an ill-natured thing of anybody—that is, of any friend—and then Sir Peter, too, to have him so peevish, and so suspicious, when I know the integrity of my own heart—indeed 'tis monstrous!

46 **birthday clothes** worn on the king's birthday

JOS. SURF. But, my dear Lady Teazle, 'tis your own fault if you suffer it. When a husband entertains a groundless suspicion of his wife, and withdraws his confidence from her, the original compact is broke, and she owes it to the honor of her sex to endeavor to outwit him.

LADY TEAZ. Indeed! So that, if he suspects me without cause, it follows that the best way of curing his jealousy is to give him reason for't?

JOS. SURF. Undoubtedly—for your husband should never be deceived in you: and in that case it becomes *you* to be frail in compliment to *his* discernment.

LADY TEAZ. To be sure, what you say is very reasonable, and when the consciousness of my own innocence——

JOS. SURF. Ah, my dear madam, there is the great mistake; 'tis this very conscious innocence that is of the greatest prejudice to you. What is it makes you negligent of forms, and careless of the world's opinion? why, the *consciousness* of your innocence. What makes you thoughtless in your conduct, and apt to run into a thousand little imprudences? why, the *consciousness* of your innocence. What makes you impatient of Sir Peter's temper and outrageous at his suspicions? why, the *consciousness* of your own innocence!

LADY TEAZ. 'Tis very true!

JOS. SURF. Now, my dear Lady Teazle, if you would but once make a trifling *faux pas,* you can't conceive how cautious you would grow—and how ready to humor and agree with your husband.

LADY TEAZ. Do you think so?

JOS. SURF. Oh, I'm sure on't; and then you would find all scandal would cease at once, for—in short, your character at present is like a person in a plethora, absolutely dying of too much health.

LADY TEAZ. So, so; then I perceive your prescription is, that I must sin in my own defence, and part with my virtue to preserve my reputation?

JOS. SURF. Exactly so, upon my credit, ma'am.

LADY TEAZ. Well, certainly this is the oddest doctrine, and the newest receipt for avoiding calumny?

JOS. SURF. An infallible one, believe me. *Prudence,* like *experience,* must be paid for.

LADY TEAZ. Why, if my understanding were once convinced——

JOS. SURF. Oh, certainly, madam, your understanding *should* be convinced. Yes, yes—heaven forbid I should persuade you to do anything you *thought* wrong. No, no, I have too much honor to desire it.

LADY TEAZ. Don't you think we may as well leave honor out of the argument?

JOS. SURF. Ah, the ill effects of your country education, I see, still remain with you.

LADY TEAZ. I doubt they do, indeed; and I will fairly own to you, that if I could be persuaded to do wrong, it would be by Sir Peter's ill-usage sooner than your honorable logic, after all.

JOS. SURF. Then, by this hand, which he is unworthy of—— [*Taking her hand.*]

Re-enter Servant.

'Sdeath, you blockhead—what do you want?

SERV. I beg pardon, sir, but I thought you wouldn't choose Sir Peter to come up without announcing him.

JOS. SURF. Sir Peter!—Oons—the devil!

LADY TEAZ. Sir Peter! O lud! I'm ruined! I'm ruined!

SERV. Sir, 'twasn't I let him in.

LADY TEAZ. Oh! I'm undone! What will become of me, now, Mr. Logic?—Oh! mercy, he's on the stairs—I'll get behind here—and if ever I'm so imprudent again——

(*Goes behind the screen.*)

JOS. SURF. Give me that book.

(*Sits down. Servant pretends to adjust his hair.*)

Enter SIR PETER TEAZLE.

SIR PET. Aye, ever improving himself!—Mr. Surface, Mr. Surface——

JOS. SURF. Oh, my dear Sir Peter, I beg your pardon. (*Gaping, and throws away the book.*) I have been dozing over a stupid book. Well, I am much obliged to you for this call. You haven't been here, I believe, since I fitted up this room. Books, you know, are the only things I am a coxcomb in.

SIR PET. 'Tis very neat indeed. Well, well, that's proper; and you make even your screen a source of knowledge—hung, I perceive, with maps.

JOS. SURF. Oh, yes, I find great use in that screen.

SIR PET. I dare say you must—certainly—when you want to find anything in a hurry.

JOS. SURF [*Aside.*]. Aye, or to hide anything in a hurry either.

SIR PET. Well, I have a little private business——

JOS. SURF. You needn't stay. (*To Servant.*)

SERV. No, sir. *Exit.*

JOS. SURF. Here's a chair, Sir Peter—I beg——

SIR PET. Well, now we are alone, there is a subject, my dear friend, on which I wish to unburden my mind to you—a point of the greatest moment to my peace: in short, my good friend, Lady Teazle's conduct of late has made me extremely unhappy.

JOS. SURF. Indeed! I am very sorry to hear it.

SIR PET. Yes, 'tis but too plain she has not the least regard for me; but, what's worse, I have pretty good authority to suspect she must have formed an attachment to another.

JOS. SURF. You astonish me!

SIR PET. Yes! and, between ourselves, I think I have discovered the person.

JOS. SURF. How! you alarm me exceedingly.

SIR PET. Aye, my dear friend, I knew you would sympathize with me!

JOS. SURF. Yes, believe me, Sir Peter, such a discovery would hurt me just as much as it would you.

SIR PET. I am convinced of it.—Ah! it is a happiness to have a friend whom one can trust even with one's family secrets. But have you no guess who I mean?

JOS. SURF. I haven't the most distant idea. It can't be Sir Benjamin Backbite!

SIR PET. O, no! What say you to Charles?

JOS. SURF. My brother! impossible!

SIR PET. Ah, my dear friend, the goodness of your own heart misleads you—you judge of others by yourself.

JOS. SURF. Certainly, Sir Peter, the heart that is conscious of its own integrity is ever slow to credit another's treachery.

SIR PET. True; but your brother has no sentiment—you never hear him talk so.

JOS. SURF. Yet I can't but think Lady Teazle herself has too much principle——

SIR PET. Aye; but what's her principle against the flattery of a handsome, lively young fellow?

JOS. SURF. That's very true.

SIR PET. And then, you know, the difference of our ages makes it very improbable that she should have any great affection for me; and if she were to be frail, and I were to make it public, why the town would only laugh at me, the foolish old bachelor who had married a girl.

JOS. SURF. That's true, to be sure—they *would* laugh.

SIR PET. Laugh! aye, and make ballads, and paragraphs, and the devil knows what of me.

JOS. SURF. No, you must never make it public.

SIR PET. But then again—that the nephew of my old friend, Sir Oliver, should be the person to attempt such a wrong, hurts me more nearly.

JOS. SURF. Aye, there's the point. When ingratitude barbs the dart of injury, the wound has double danger in it.

SIR PET. Aye—I, that was, in a manner, left his guardian—in whose house he had been so often entertained—who never in my life denied him—my advice!

JOS. SURF. Oh, 'tis not to be credited! There *may* be a man capable of such baseness, to be sure; but, for my part, till you can give me positive proofs, I cannot but doubt it. However, if it should be proved on him, he is no longer a brother of mine! I disclaim kindred with him —for the man who can break through the laws of hospitality, and attempt the wife of his friend, deserves to be branded as the pest of society.

SIR PET. What a difference there is between you! What noble sentiments!

JOS. SURF. Yet I cannot suspect Lady Teazle's honor.

SIR PET. I am sure I wish to think well of her, and to remove all ground of quarrel between us. She has lately reproached me more than once with having made no settlement on her; and, in our last quarrel, she almost hinted that she should not break her heart if I was dead. Now, as we seem to differ in our ideas of expense, I have resolved she shall be her own mistress in that respect for the future; and, if I *were* to die, she shall find that I have not been inattentive to her interest while living. Here, my friend, are the drafts of two deeds, which I wish to have your opinion on. By one, she will enjoy eight hundred a year independent while I live; and, by the other, the bulk of my fortune after my death.

270

JOS. SURF. This conduct, Sir Peter, is indeed truly generous.— (*Aside.*) I wish it may not corrupt my pupil.

SIR PET. Yes, I am determined she shall have no cause to complain, though I would not have her acquainted with the latter instance of my affection yet awhile.

JOS. SURF. Nor I, if I could help it. (*Aside.*)

SIR PET. And now, my dear friend, if you please, we will talk over the situation of your hopes with *Maria.*

280

JOS. SURF (*Softly.*). No, no, Sir Peter; another time, if you please.

SIR PET. I am sensibly chagrined at the little progress you seem to make in her affection.

JOS. SURF. I beg you will not mention it. What are my disappointments when your happiness is in debate! (*Softly.*)—'Sdeath, I shall be ruined every way! (*Aside.*)

SIR PET. And though you are so averse to my acquainting Lady Teazle with your passion, I am sure she's not your enemy in the affair.

290

JOS. SURF. Pray, Sir Peter, now oblige me. I am really too much affected by the subject we have been speaking on to bestow a thought on my own concerns. The man who is entrusted with his friend's distresses can never——

Enter Servant.

Well, sir?

SERV. Your brother, sir, is speaking to a gentleman in the street, and says he knows you are within.

300

JOS. SURF. 'Sdeath, blockhead—I'm not within—I'm out for the day.

SIR PET. Stay—hold—a thought has struck me—you shall be at home.

JOS. SURF. Well, well, let him up.— [*Exit Servant.*]
He'll interrupt Sir Peter—however—

SIR PET. Now, my good friend, oblige me, I entreat you. Before Charles comes, let me conceal myself somewhere; then do you tax him on the point we have been talking on, and his answers may satisfy me at once.

310

JOS. SURF. O, fie, Sir Peter! would you have me join in so mean a trick?—to trepan my brother too?

SIR PET. Nay, you tell me you are *sure* he is innocent; if so, you do him the greatest service by giving him an opportunity to clear himself, and you will set my heart at rest. Come, you shall not refuse me; here, behind the screen will be (*Goes to the screen.*)—Hey! what the devil! there seems to be *one* listener here already—I'll swear I saw a petticoat!

320

JOS. SURF. Ha! ha! ha! Well, this is ridiculous enough. I'll tell you, Sir Peter, though I hold a man of intrigue to be a most despicable character, yet you know, it doesn't follow that one is to be an absolute Joseph either! Hark'ee! 'tis a little French milliner, a silly rogue that plagues me—and having some character—on your coming, she ran behind the screen.

330

SIR PET. Ah, you rogue!—But, egad, she has overheard all I have been saying of my wife.

JOS. SURF. Oh, 'twill never go any further, you may depend on't!

SIR PET. No! then, i'faith, let her hear it out.—Here's a closet will do as well.

JOS. SURF. Well, go in then.

340

SIR PET. Sly rogue! sly rogue! (*Goes into the closet.*)

JOS. SURF. A very narrow escape, indeed! and a curious situation I'm in, to part man and wife in this manner.

LADY TEAZ (*Peeping from the screen.*). Couldn't I steal off?

JOS. SURF. Keep close, my angel!

SIR PET (*Peeping out.*). Joseph, tax him home.

350

JOS. SURF. Back, my dear friend!

LADY TEAZ (*Peeping.*). Couldn't you lock Sir Peter in?

JOS. SURF. Be still, my life!

SIR PET (*Peeping.*). You're sure the little milliner won't blab?

JOS. SURF. In, in, my dear Sir Peter!—'Fore gad, I wish I had a key to the door.

Enter CHARLES SURFACE.

CHAS. SURF. Hollo! brother, what has been the matter? Your fellow would not let me up at first. What! have you had a Jew or a wench with you?

360

JOS. SURF. Neither, brother, I assure you.

CHAS. SURF. But what has made Sir Peter steal off? I thought he had been with you.

JOS. SURF. He was, brother; but, hearing *you* were coming, he did not choose to stay.

CHAS. SURF. What! was the old gentleman afraid I wanted to borrow money of him! 370

JOS. SURF. No, sir, but I am sorry to find, Charles, that you have lately given that worthy man grounds for great uneasiness.

CHAS. SURF. Yes, they tell me I do that to a great many worthy men. But how so, pray?

JOS. SURF. To be plain with you, brother, he thinks you are endeavoring to gain Lady Teazle's affections from him.

CHAS. SURF. Who, I? O lud! not I, upon my word.—Ha! ha! ha! so the old fellow has found out that he has got a young wife, has he?—or, what's worse, has her ladyship discovered that she has an old husband? 380

JOS. SURF. This is no subject to jest on, brother.—He who can laugh——

CHAS. SURF. True, true, as you were going to say—then, seriously, I never had the least idea of what you charge me with, upon my honor.

JOS. SURF. Well, it will give Sir Peter great satisfaction to hear this. (*Aloud.*) 390

CHAS. SURF. To be sure, I once thought the lady seemed to have taken a fancy to me; but, upon my soul, I never gave her the least encouragement. Besides, you know my attachment to Maria.

JOS. SURF. But sure, brother, even if Lady Teazle had betrayed the fondest partiality for you——

CHAS. SURF. Why, look'ee, Joseph, I hope I shall never deliberately do a dishonorable action—but if a pretty woman were purposely to throw herself in my way—and that pretty woman married to a man old enough to be her father—— 400

JOS. SURF. Well!

CHAS. SURF. Why, I believe I should be obliged to borrow a little of your morality, that's all.—But, brother, do you know now that you surprise me exceedingly, by naming *me* with Lady Teazle; for, faith, I alway[s] understood *you* were her favorite. 410

JOS. SURF. Oh, for shame, Charles! This retort is foolish.

CHAS. SURF. Nay, I swear I have seen you exchange such significant glances——

JOS. SURF. Nay, nay, sir, this is no jest——

CHAS. SURF. Egad, I'm serious! Don't you remember—one day, when I called here——

JOS. SURF. Nay, prithee, Charles—— 420

CHAS. SURF. And found you together——

JOS. SURF. Zounds, sir, I insist——

CHAS. SURF. And another time, when your servant——

JOS. SURF. Brother, brother, a word with you!—(*Aside.*) Gad, I must stop him.

CHAS. SURF. Informed me, I say, that——

JOS. SURF. Hush! I beg your pardon, but Sir Peter has overheard all we have been saying—I knew you would clear yourself, or I should not have consented. 430

CHAS. SURF. How, Sir Peter! Where is he?

JOS. SURF. Softly, there! (*Points to the closet.*)

CHAS. SURF. Oh, 'fore heaven, I'll have him out.—Sir Peter, come forth!

JOS. SURF. No, no——

CHAS. SURF. I say, Sir Peter, come into court. —(*Pulls in* SIR PETER.) What! my old guardian! —What—turn inquisitor, and take evidence, incog.? 440

SIR PET. Give me your hand, Charles—I believe I have suspected you wrongfully—but you mustn't be angry with Joseph—'twas my plan!

CHAS. SURF. Indeed!

SIR PET. But I acquit you. I promise you I don't think near so ill of you as I did. What I have heard has given me great satisfaction.

CHAS. SURF. Egad, then, 'twas lucky you didn't hear any more. Wasn't it, Joseph? (*Half aside.*) 450

SIR PET. Ah! you would have retorted on him.

CHAS. SURF. Aye, aye, that was a joke.

SIR PET. Yes, yes, I know his honor too well.

CHAS. SURF. But you might as well have suspected him as me in this matter, for all that. Mightn't he, Joseph? (*Half aside.*)

SIR PET. Well, well, I believe you.

JOS. SURF [*Aside.*]. Would they were both out of the room! 460

SIR PET. And in future, perhaps, we may not be such strangers.

Enter Servant who whispers JOSEPH SURFACE.

JOS. SURF. Lady Sneerwell!—stop her by all means—[*Exit Servant.*] Gentlemen—I beg pardon—I must wait on you downstairs—here's a person come on particular business.

CHAS. SURF. Well, you can see him in another room. Sir Peter and I haven't met a long time, and I have something to say to him.

JOS. SURF. They must not be left together.—I'll send Lady Sneerwell away, and return directly.—(*Aside.*) Sir Peter, not a word of the French milliner.

Exit JOSEPH SURFACE.

SIR PET. Oh! not for the world!—Ah, Charles, if you associated more with your brother, one might indeed hope for your reformation. He is a man of sentiment.—Well, there is nothing in the world so noble as a man of sentiment!

CHAS. SURF. Pshaw! he is too moral by half, and so apprehensive of his good name, as he calls it, that I suppose he would as soon let a priest into his house as a girl.

SIR PET. No, no,—come, come,—you wrong him. No, no, Joseph is no rake, but he is not such a saint in that respect either,—I have a great mind to tell him—we should have a laugh! (*Aside.*)

CHAS. SURF. Oh, hang him! he's a very anchorite, a young hermit!

SIR PET. Hark'ee—you must not abuse him; he may chance to hear of it again, I promise you.

CHAS. SURF. Why, you won't tell him?

SIR PET. No—but—this way.—[*Aside.*] Egad, I'll tell him.—Hark'ee, have you a mind to have a good laugh at Joseph?

CHAS. SURF. I should like it of all things.

SIR PET. Then, i'faith, we will!—I'll be quit with him for discovering me. (*Aside.*)—He had a girl with him when I called.

CHAS. SURF. What! Joseph? you jest.

SIR PET. Hush!—a little—French milliner—and the best of the jest is—she's in the room now.

CHAS. SURF. The devil she is!

SIR PET. Hush! I tell you. (*Points* [*to the screen*].)

CHAS. SURF. Behind the screen! 'Slife, let's unveil her!

SIR PET. No, no, he's coming:—you shan't, indeed!

CHAS. SURF. Oh, egad, we'll have a peep at the little milliner!

SIR PET. Not for the world!—Joseph will never forgive me.

CHAS. SURF. I'll stand by you——

SIR PET (*Struggling with Charles.*). Odds, here he is!

JOSEPH SURFACE *enters just as* CHARLES *throws down the screen.*

CHAS. SURF. Lady Teazle, by all that's wonderful!

SIR PET. Lady Teazle, by all that's horrible!

CHAS. SURF. Sir Peter, this is one of the smartest French milliners I ever saw. Egad, you seem all to have been diverting yourselves here at hide and seek—and I don't see who is out of the secret. Shall I beg your ladyship to inform me?—Not a word!—Brother, will you please to explain this matter? What! Morality dumb too!—Sir Peter, though I *found* you in the dark, perhaps you are not so now! All mute! Well—though *I* can make nothing of the affair, I suppose you perfectly understand one another; so I'll leave you to yourselves.—(*Going.*) Brother, I'm sorry to find you *have given that worthy man so much uneasiness,*—Sir Peter! there's nothing *in the world so noble as a man of sentiment!*

Exit CHARLES.

([*They*] *stand for some time looking at each other.*)

JOS. SURF. Sir Peter—notwithstanding I confess that appearances are against me—if you will afford me your patience—I make no doubt but I shall explain everything to your satisfaction.

SIR PET. If you please—

JOS. SURF. The fact is, sir, Lady Teazle, knowing my pretensions to your ward Maria—I say, sir, Lady Teazle, being apprehensive of the jealousy of your temper—and knowing my friendship to the family—she, sir, I say—called here—in order that—I might explain those pretensions—but on your coming—being apprehensive—as I said—of your jealousy—she withdrew—and this, you may depend on't is the whole truth of the matter.

SIR PET. A very clear account, upon my word; and I dare swear the lady will vouch for every article of it.

LADY TEAZ (*Coming forward.*). For not one word of it, Sir Peter!

SIR PET. How! don't you think it worth while to agree in the lie?

LADY TEAZ. There is not one syllable of truth in what that gentleman has told you. 570

SIR PET. I believe you, upon my soul, ma'am!

JOS. SURF (*Aside.*). 'Sdeath, madam, will you betray me?

LADY TEAZ. Good Mr. Hypocrite, by your leave, I will speak for myself.

SIR PET. Aye, let her alone, sir; you'll find she'll make out a better story than *you,* without prompting.

LADY TEAZ. Hear me, Sir Peter!—I came here on no matter relating to your ward, and 580 even ignorant of this gentleman's pretensions to her—but I came, seduced by his insidious arguments, at least to listen to his pretended passion, if not to sacrifice *your* honor to his baseness.

SIR PET. Now, I believe, the truth *is* coming, indeed!

JOS. SURF. The woman's mad!

LADY TEAZ. No, sir; she has recovered her senses, and your own arts have furnished her 590 with the means.—Sir Peter, I do not expect you to credit me—but the tenderness you expressed for me, when I am sure you could not think I was a witness to it, has penetrated to my heart, and had I left the place without the shame of this discovery, my future life should have spoke[n] the sincerity of my gratitude. As for that smooth-tongue hypocrite, who would have seduced the wife of his too credulous friend, while he affected honorable addresses to his 600 ward—I behold him now in a light so truly despicable, that I shall never again respect myself for having listened to him. *Exit.*

JOS. SURF. Notwithstanding all this, Sir Peter, heaven knows——

SIR PET. That you are a villain!—and so I leave you to your conscience.

JOS. SURF. You are too rash, Sir Peter; you shall hear me. The man who shuts out conviction by refusing to—— 610

SIR PET. Oh!—

Exeunt, JOSEPH SURFACE *following and speaking.*

End of Act 4th.

ACT FIVE *Scene One*

The library [*in* JOSEPH SURFACE'S *house.*]

Enter JOSEPH SURFACE *and Servant.*

JOS. SURF. Mr. Stanley! why should you think I would see him? you *must* know he comes to ask something.

SERV. Sir, I should not have let him in, but that Mr. Rowley came to the door with him.

JOS. SURF. Pshaw! blockhead! to suppose that I should *now* be in a temper to receive visits from poor relations!—Well, why don't you show the fellow up?

10 SERV. I will, sir.—Why, sir, it was not my fault that Sir Peter discovered my lady——

JOS. SURF. Go, fool! [*Exit Servant.*] Sure, Fortune never played a man of my policy such a trick before! My character with Sir Peter, my hopes with Maria, destroyed in a moment! I'm in a rare humor to listen to other people's distresses! I shan't be able to bestow even a benevolent sentiment on Stanley.—So! here he comes, and Rowley with him. I must try to recover myself—and put a little charity into my 20 face, however. *Exit.*

Enter SIR OLIVER SURFACE *and* ROWLEY.

SIR OLIV. What! does he avoid us? That was he, was it not?

ROW. It was, sir—but I doubt you are come

a little too abruptly—his nerves are so weak, that the sight of a poor relation may be too much for him.—I should have gone first to break you to him.

30 SIR OLIV. A plague of his nerves!—Yet this is he whom Sir Peter extols as a man of the most benevolent way of thinking!

ROW. As to his way of thinking, I cannot pretend to decide; for, to do him justice, he appears to have as much speculative benevolence as any private gentleman in the kingdom, though he is seldom so sensual as to indulge himself in the exercise of it.

SIR OLIV. Yet has a string of charitable sentiments, I suppose, at his fingers' ends!

40 ROW. Or, rather, at his tongue's end, Sir Oliver; for I believe there is no sentiment he has more faith in than that 'Charity begins at home.'

SIR OLIV. And his, I presume, is of that domestic sort which never stirs abroad at all.

ROW. I doubt you'll find it so;—but he's coming—I mustn't seem to interrupt you; and you know, immediately as you leave him, I

50 come in to announce your arrival in your real character.

SIR OLIV. True; and afterwards you'll meet me at Sir Peter's.

ROW. Without losing a moment.

Exit ROWLEY.

SIR OLIV. So! I don't like the complaisance of his features.

Re-enter JOSEPH SURFACE.

JOS. SURF. Sir, I beg you ten thousand par-

60 dons for keeping you a moment waiting—Mr. Stanley, I presume.

SIR OLIV. At your service.

JOS. SURF. Sir, I beg you will do me the honor to sit down—I entreat you, sir.

SIR OLIV. Dear sir—there's no occasion.—Too civil by half! (*Aside.*)

JOS. SURF. I have not the pleasure of knowing you, Mr. Stanley; but I am extremely happy to see you look so well. You were nearly related

70 to my mother, I think, Mr. Stanley?

SIR OLIV. I was, sir—so nearly that my present poverty, I fear, may do discredit to her wealthy children—else I should not have presumed to trouble you.

JOS. SURF. Dear sir, there needs no apology: he that is in distress, though a stranger, has a right to claim kindred with the wealthy;—I am sure I wish *I* was one of that class, and had it in my power to offer you even a small relief.

SIR OLIV. If your uncle, Sir Oliver, were 80 here, I should have a friend.

JOS. SURF. I wish he were, sir, with all my heart: you should not want an advocate with him, believe me, sir.

SIR OLIV. I should not *need* one—my distresses would recommend me; but I imagined his bounty had enabled *you* to become the agent of his charity.

JOS. SURF. My dear sir, you were strangely misinformed. Sir Oliver is a worthy man, a very 90 worthy sort of man; but—avarice, Mr. Stanley, is the vice of age. I will tell you, my good sir, in confidence, what he has done for me has been a mere nothing; though people, I know, have thought otherwise, and, for my part, I never chose to contradict the report.

SIR OLIV. What! has he never transmitted you bullion! rupees! pagodas!

JOS. SURF. O dear sir, nothing of the kind! No, no; a few presents now and then—china— 100 shawls—Congo tea—avadavats and India[n] crackers—little more, believe me.

SIR OLIV [*Aside.*]. Here's gratitude for twelve thousand pounds!—Avadavats and Indian crackers!

JOS. SURF. Then, my dear sir, you have heard, I doubt not, of the extravagance of my brother; there are very few would credit what I have done for that unfortunate young man.

SIR OLIV. Not I, for one! (*Aside.*) 110

JOS. SURF. The sums I have lent him! Indeed I have been exceedingly to blame—it was an amiable weakness: however, I don't pretend to defend it—and now I feel it doubly culpable, since it has deprived me of the pleasure of serving *you,* Mr. Stanley, as my heart dictates.

SIR OLIV [*Aside.*]. Dissembler!—Then, sir, you cannot assist me?

JOS. SURF. At present, it grieves me to say, I cannot; but, whenever I have the ability, you 120 may depend upon hearing from me.

SIR OLIV. I am extremely sorry——

98 **rupees** Indian coins, then worth about two shillings **pagodas** Indian coins, then worth about eight shillings 101 **avadavats** very small Indian songbirds 102 **India crackers** fire crackers

JOS. SURF. Not more than I am, believe me; to pity, without the power to relieve, is still more painful than to ask and be denied.

SIR OLIV. Kind sir, your most obedient humble servant.

JOS. SURF. You leave me deeply affected, Mr. Stanley.—William, be ready to open the door.

130 SIR OLIV. O dear sir, no ceremony.

JOS. SURF. Your very obedient.

SIR OLIV. Sir, your most obsequious.

JOS. SURF. You may depend upon hearing from me, whenever I can be of service.

SIR OLIV. Sweet sir, you are too good.

JOS. SURF. In the meantime I wish you health and spirits.

SIR OLIV. Your ever grateful and perpetual humble servant.

140 JOS. SURF. Sir, yours as sincerely.

SIR OLIV. Now I am satisfied! *Exit.*

JOS. SURF (*Solus.*). This is one bad effect of a good character; it invites applications from the unfortunate, and there needs no small degree of address to gain the reputation of benevolence without incurring the expense. The silver ore of pure charity is an expensive article in the catalogue of a man's good qualities; whereas the sentimental French plate I use instead of it

150 makes just as good a show, and pays no tax.

Enter ROWLEY.

ROW. Mr. Surface, your servant—I was apprehensive of interrupting you—though my business demands immediate attention—as this note will inform you.

JOS. SURF. Always happy to see Mr. Rowley. —(*Reads.*) How! *'Oliver—Surface!'*—My uncle arrived!

ROW. He is, indeed—we have just parted—quite well, after a speedy voyage, and impatient 160 to embrace his worthy nephew.

JOS. SURF. I am astonished!—William! stop Mr. Stanley, if he's not gone.

ROW. Oh! he's out of reach, I believe.

JOS. SURF. Why didn't you let me know this when you came in together?

ROW. I thought you had particular business. But I must be gone to inform your brother, and appoint him here to meet his uncle. He will be with you in a quarter of an hour. 170

JOS. SURF. So he says. Well, I am strangely overjoyed at his coming.—(*Aside.*) Never, to be sure, was anything so damned unlucky!

ROW. You will be delighted to see how well he looks.

JOS. SURF. Oh! I'm rejoiced to hear it.—(*Aside.*) Just at this time!

ROW. I'll tell him how impatiently you expect him.

JOS. SURF. Do, do; pray give my best duty 180 and affection. Indeed, I cannot express the sensations I feel at the thought of seeing him.—[*Exit* ROWLEY.] Certainly his coming just at this time is the cruellest piece of ill fortune. *Exit.*

Scene Two

At SIR PETER'S.

Enter MRS. CANDOUR *and Maid.*

MAID. Indeed, ma'am, my lady will see nobody at present.

MRS. CAN. Did you tell her it was her friend Mrs. Candour?

MAID. Yes, madam; but she begs you will excuse her.

MRS. CAN. Do go again; I shall be glad to see her, if it be only for a moment, for I am sure she must be in great distress.— *Exit Maid.* Dear heart, how provoking; I'm not mistress 10 of half the circumstances! We shall have the whole affair in the newspapers, with the names of the parties at length, before I have dropped the story at a dozen houses.

Enter SIR BENJAMIN BACKBITE.

O dear Sir Benjamin! you have heard, I suppose——

SIR BEN. Of Lady Teazle and Mr. Surface——

MRS. CAN. And Sir Peter's discovery——

SIR BEN. Oh, the strangest piece of business, to be sure!

MRS. CAN. Well, I never was so surprised in my life. I am so sorry for all parties, indeed I am.

SIR BEN. Now, I don't pity Sir Peter at all—he was so extravagantly partial to Mr. Surface.

MRS. CAN. Mr. Surface! Why, 'twas with Charles Lady Teazle was detected.

SIR BEN. No such thing—Mr. Surface is the gallant.

MRS. CAN. No, no—Charles is the man. 'Twas Mr. Surface brought Sir Peter on purpose to discover them.

SIR BEN. I tell you I have it from one——

MRS. CAN. And I have it from one——

SIR BEN. Who had it from one, who had it——

MRS. CAN. From one immediately—— But here's Lady Sneerwell; perhaps she knows the whole affair.

Enter LADY SNEERWELL.

LADY SNEER. So, my dear Mrs. Candour, here's a sad affair of our friend Lady Teazle!

MRS. CAN. Aye, my dear friend, who could have thought it——

LADY SNEER. Well, there's no trusting appearances; though, indeed, she was always too lively for me.

MRS. CAN. To be sure, her manners were a little too free—but she was very young!

LADY SNEER. And had, indeed, some good qualities.

MRS. CAN. So she had, indeed. But have you heard the particulars?

LADY SNEER. No; but everybody says that Mr. Surface——

SIR BEN. Aye, there, I told you—Mr. Surface was the man.

MRS. CAN. No, no, indeed—the assignation was with Charles.

LADY SNEER. With Charles! You alarm me, Mrs. Candour.

MRS. CAN. Yes, yes, he was the lover. Mr. Surface—do him justice—was only the informer.

SIR BEN. Well, I'll not dispute with you, Mrs. Candour; but, be it which it may, I hope that Sir Peter's wound will not——

MRS. CAN. Sir Peter's wound! Oh, mercy! I didn't hear a word of their fighting.

LADY SNEER. Nor I, a syllable.

SIR BEN. No! what, no mention of the duel?

MRS. CAN. Not a word.

SIR BEN. O Lord—yes, yes—they fought before they left the room.

LADY SNEER. Pray let us hear.

MRS. CAN. Aye, do oblige us with the duel.

SIR BEN. 'Sir,' says Sir Peter—immediately after the discovery—'you are a most ungrateful fellow.'

MRS. CAN. Aye, to Charles——

SIR BEN. No, no—to Mr. Surface—a most ungrateful fellow; and old as I am, sir,' says he, 'I insist on immediate satisfaction.'

MRS. CAN. Aye, that must have been to Charles; for 'tis very unlikely Mr. Surface should go to fight in his house.

SIR BEN. 'Gad's life, ma'am, not at all—'giving me immediate satisfaction.'—On this, madam, Lady Teazle, seeing Sir Peter in such danger, ran out of the room in strong hysterics, and Charles after her, calling out for hartshorn and water! Then, madam, they began to fight with swords——

Enter CRABTREE.

CRAB. With pistols, nephew—I have it from undoubted authority.

MRS. CAN. O Mr. Crabtree, then it is all true!

CRAB. Too true, indeed, ma'am, and Sir Peter's dangerously wounded——

SIR BEN. By a thrust of *in seconde* quite through his left side——

CRAB. By a bullet lodged in the thorax.

MRS. CAN. Mercy on me! Poor Sir Peter!

CRAB. Yes, ma'am—though Charles would have avoided the matter, if he could.

MRS. CAN. I knew Charles was the person.

SIR BEN. Oh, my uncle, I see, knows nothing of the matter.

CRAB. But Sir Peter taxed him with the basest ingratitude——

SIR BEN. That I told you, you know.

102 **in seconde** a fencing term

CRAB. Do, nephew, let me speak!—and insisted on an immediate——

SIR BEN. Just as I said.

CRAB. Odds life, nephew, allow others to know something too! A pair of pistols lay on the bureau (for Mr. Surface, it seems, had come
120 the night before late from Salt-Hill, where he had been to see the Montem with a friend, who has a son at Eton), so, unluckily, the pistols were left charged.

SIR BEN. I heard nothing of this.

CRAB. Sir Peter forced Charles to take one, and they fired, it seems, pretty nearly together. Charles's shot took place, as I told you, and Sir Peter's missed; but, what is very extraordinary, the ball struck against a little bronze Pliny that
130 stood over the chimney-piece, grazed out of the window at a right angle, and wounded the postman, who was just coming to the door with a double letter from Northamptonshire.

SIR BEN. My uncle's account is more circumstantial, I must confess; but I believe mine is the true one, for all that.

LADY SNEER [*Aside.*]. I am more interested in this affair than they imagine, and must have better information. *Exit* LADY SNEERWELL.

140 SIR BEN (*After a pause looking at each other.*). Ah! Lady Sneerwell's alarm is very easily accounted for.

CRAB. Yes, yes, they certainly *do* say—but that's neither here nor there.

MRS. CAN. But, pray, where is Sir Peter at present?

CRAB. Oh! they brought him home, and he is now in the house, though the servants are ordered to deny it.

150 MRS. CAN. I believe so, and Lady Teazle, I suppose, attending him.

CRAB. Yes, yes; I saw one of the faculty enter just before me.

SIR BEN. Hey! who comes here?

CRAB. Oh, this is he—the physician, depend on't.

MRS. CAN. Oh, certainly! it must be the physician; and now we shall know.

Enter SIR OLIVER SURFACE.

CRAB. Well, doctor, what hopes?

160 MRS. CAN. Aye, doctor, how's your patient?

121 **Montem** a festival celebrated by the students of Eton at Salt Hill

SIR BEN. Now, doctor, isn't it a wound with a small-sword?

CRAB. A bullet lodged in the thorax, for a hundred!

SIR OLIV. Doctor! a wound with a small-sword! and a bullet in the thorax?—Oons! are you mad, good people?

SIR BEN. Perhaps, sir, you are not a doctor?

SIR OLIV. Truly, I am to thank you for my degree, if I am. 170

CRAB. Only a friend of Sir Peter's, then, I presume. But, sir, you must have heard of this accident?

SIR OLIV. Not a word!

CRAB. Not of his being dangerously wounded?

SIR OLIV. The devil he is!

SIR BEN. Run through the body——

CRAB. Shot in the breast——

SIR BEN. By one Mr. Surface—— 180

CRAB. Aye, the younger.

SIR OLIV. Hey! what the plague! you seem to differ strangely in your accounts—however, you agree that Sir Peter is dangerously wounded.

SIR BEN. Oh, yes, we agree there.

CRAB. Yes, yes, I believe there can be no doubt of that.

SIR OLIV. Then, upon my word, for a person in that situation, he is the most imprudent man 190 alive—for here he comes, walking as if nothing at all were the matter.

Enter SIR PETER TEAZLE.

Odds heart, Sir Peter! you are come in good time, I promise you; for we had just *given you over*.

SIR BEN. Egad, uncle, this is the most sudden recovery!

SIR OLIV. Why, man! what do you do out of bed with a small-sword through your body, and 200 a bullet lodged in your thorax?

SIR PET. A small-sword and a bullet?

SIR OLIV. Aye; these gentlemen would have killed you without law or physic, and wanted to dub me a doctor—to make me an accomplice.

SIR PET. Why, what is all this?

SIR BEN. We rejoice, Sir Peter, that the story of the duel is not true, and are sincerely sorry for your other misfortunes. 210

SIR PET. So, so; all over the town already. (*Aside.*)

CRAB. Though, Sir Peter, you were certainly vastly to blame to marry at all, at your years.

SIR PET. Sir, what business is that of yours?

MRS. CAN. Though, indeed, as Sir Peter made so good a husband, he's very much to be pitied.

SIR PET. Plague on your pity, ma'am! I de-
220 sire none of it.

SIR BEN. However, Sir Peter, you must not mind the laughing and jests you will meet with on this occasion.

SIR PET. Sir, I desire to be master in my own house.

CRAB. 'Tis no uncommon case, that's one comfort.

SIR PET. I insist on being left to myself: without ceremony, I insist on your leaving my
230 house directly!

MRS. CAN. Well, well, we are going; and depend on't, we'll make the best report of you we can.

SIR PET. Leave my house!

CRAB. And tell how hardly you have been treated.

SIR PET. Leave my house!

SIR BEN. And how patiently you bear it.

SIR PET. Fiends! vipers! furies! Oh! that
240 their own venom would choke them!

Exeunt MRS. CANDOUR, SIR BENJAMIN BACKBITE, CRABTREE, &C.

SIR OLIV. They are very provoking indeed, Sir Peter.

Enter ROWLEY.

ROW. I heard high words—what has ruffled you, Sir Peter?

SIR PET. Pshaw! what signifies asking? Do I ever pass a day without my vexations?

250 SIR OLIV. Well, I'm not inquisitive—I come only to tell you that I have seen both my nephews in the manner we proposed.

SIR PET. A precious couple they are!

ROW. Yes, and Sir Oliver is convinced that your judgment was right, Sir Peter.

SIR OLIV. Yes, I find *Joseph* is indeed the man, after all.

ROW. Yes, as Sir Peter says, he's a man of sentiment.

SIR OLIV. And acts up to the sentiments he professes. 260

ROW. It certainly is edification to hear him talk.

SIR OLIV. Oh, he's a model for the young men of the age! But how's this, Sir Peter? you don't join in your friend Joseph's praise, as I expected.

SIR PET. Sir Oliver, we live in a damned wicked world, and the fewer we praise the better.

ROW. What! do *you* say so, Sir Peter, who were never mistaken in your life? 270

SIR PET. Pshaw! plague on you both! I see by your sneering you have heard the whole affair. I shall go mad among you!

ROW. Then, to fret you no longer, Sir Peter, we are indeed acquainted with it all. I met Lady Teazle coming from Mr. Surface's, so humbled that she deigned to request me to be her advocate with you.

SIR PET. And does Sir Oliver know all too? 280

SIR OLIV. Every circumstance.

SIR PET. What, of the closet—and the screen, hey?

SIR OLIV. Yes, yes, and the little French milliner. Oh, I have been vastly diverted with the story! ha! ha!

SIR PET. 'Twas very pleasant.

SIR OLIV. I never laughed more in my life, I assure you: ha! ha!

SIR PET. O, vastly diverting! ha! ha! 290

ROW. To be sure, Joseph with his sentiments! ha! ha!

SIR PET. Yes, yes, his sentiments! ha! ha! A hypocritical villain!

SIR OLIV. Aye, and that rogue Charles to pull Sir Peter out of the closet: ha! ha!

SIR PET. Ha! ha! 'twas devilish entertaining, to be sure!

SIR OLIV. Ha! ha! Egad, Sir Peter, I should like to have seen your face when the screen was thrown down: ha! ha! 300

SIR PET. Yes, yes, my face when the screen was thrown down: ha! ha! Oh, I must never show my head again!

SIR OLIV. But come, come, it isn't fair to laugh at you neither, my old friend—though, upon my soul, I can't help it.

SIR PET. Oh, pray don't restrain your mirth on my account—it does not hurt me at all! I

310 laugh at the whole affair myself. Yes, yes, I think being a standing jest for all one's acquaintances a very happy situation. O yes, and then of a morning to read the paragraphs about Mr. S——, Lady T——, and Sir P——, will be so entertaining!

ROW. Without affectation, Sir Peter, you may despise the ridicule of fools. But I see Lady Teazle going towards the next room; I am sure you must desire a reconciliation as earnestly as she
320 does.

SIR OLIV. Perhaps my being here prevents her coming to you. Well, I'll leave honest Rowley to mediate between you; but he must bring you all presently to Mr. Surface's, where I am now returning, if not to reclaim a libertine, at least to expose hypocrisy.

SIR PET. Ah! I'll be present at your discovering yourself there with all my heart—though 'tis a vile unlucky place for discoveries!

330 ROW. We'll follow.

[*Exit* SIR OLIVER SURFACE.]

SIR PET. She is not coming here, you see, Rowley.

ROW. No, but she has left the door of that room open, you perceive. See, she is in tears!

SIR PET. Certainly a little mortification appears very becoming in a wife! Don't you think it will do her good to let her pine a little?

ROW. Oh, this is ungenerous in you!

SIR PET. Well, I know not what to think. 340 You remember, Rowley, the letter I found of hers, evidently intended for Charles!

ROW. A mere forgery, Sir Peter! laid in your way on purpose. This is one of the points which I intend *Snake* shall give you conviction on.

SIR PET. I wish I were once satisfied of that. She looks this way. What a remarkably elegant turn of the head she has! Rowley, I'll go to her.

ROW. Certainly.

SIR PET. Though, when it is known that we 350 are reconciled, people will laugh at me ten times more!

ROW. Let them laugh, and retort their malice only by showing them you are happy in spite of it.

SIR PET. I'faith, so I will! and, if I'm not mistaken, we may yet be the happiest couple in the country.

ROW. Nay, Sir Peter—he who once lays aside suspicion—— 360

SIR PET. Hold, my dear Rowley! if you have any regard for me, never let me hear you utter anything like a sentiment—I have had enough of them to serve me the rest of my life. *Exeunt.*

Scene Three

The library [*in* JOSEPH SURFACE'S *house*].

JOSEPH SURFACE *and* LADY SNEERWELL.

LADY SNEER. Impossible! Will not Sir Peter immediately be reconciled to Charles, and of consequence no longer oppose his union with Maria? The thought is distraction to me!

JOS. SURF. Can passion furnish a remedy?

LADY SNEER. No, nor cunning either. Oh, I was a fool, an idiot, to league with such a blunderer!

10 JOS. SURF. Sure, Lady Sneerwell, *I* am the greatest sufferer; yet you see I bear the accident with calmness.

LADY SNEER. Because the disappointment doesn't reach your *heart;* your *interest* only attached you to Maria. Had you felt for *her* what *I* have for that ungrateful libertine, neither your temper nor hypocrisy could prevent your showing the sharpness of your vexation.

JOS SURF. But why should your reproaches fall on *me* for this disappointment? 20

LADY SNEER. Are you not the cause of it? What had you to do to bate in your pursuit of Maria to pervert Lady Teazle by the way? Had you not a sufficient field for your roguery in blinding Sir Peter, and supplanting your brother? I hate such an avarice of crimes; 'tis an unfair monopoly, and never prospers.

JOS. SURF. Well, I admit I have been to blame. I confess I deviated from the direct road of wrong, but I don't think we're so totally defeated neither.

LADY SNEER. No!

JOS. SURF. You tell me you have made a trial of Snake since we met, and that you still believe him faithful to us—

LADY SNEER. I do believe so.

JOS. SURF. And that he has undertaken, should it be necessary, to swear and prove that Charles is at this time contracted by vows and honor to your ladyship—which some of his former letters to you will serve to support?

LADY SNEER. This, indeed, might have assisted.

JOS. SURF. Come, come; it is not too late yet.—[*Knocking at the door.*] But hark! this is probably my uncle, Sir Oliver: retire to that room; we'll consult farther when he's gone.

LADY SNEER. Well! but if *he* should find you out too—

JOS. SURF. Oh, I have no fear of that. Sir Peter will hold his tongue for his own credit['s] sake—and you may depend on't I shall soon discover Sir Oliver's weak side!

LADY SNEER. I have no diffidence of your abilities—only be constant to one roguery at a time. *Exit.*

JOS. SURF. I will, I will! So! 'tis confounded hard, after such bad fortune, to be baited by one's confederate in evil. Well, at all events, my character is so much better than Charles's, that I certainly—hey!—what!—this is not *Sir Oliver,* but old *Stanley* again! Plague on't! that he should return to tease me just now! We shall have Sir Oliver come and find him here—and——

Enter SIR OLIVER SURFACE

Gad's life, Mr. Stanley, why have you come back to plague me just at this time? You must not stay now, upon my word.

SIR OLIV. Sir, I hear your uncle Oliver is expected here, and though he has been so penurious to *you,* I'll try what he'll do for *me.*

JOS. SURF. Sir, 'tis impossible for you to stay now, so I must beg—— Come any other time, and I promise you, you shall be assisted.

SIR OLIV. No: Sir Oliver and I must be acquainted.

JOS. SURF. Zounds, sir! then I insist on your quitting the room directly.

SIR OLIV. Nay, sir!

JOS. SURF. Sir, I insist on't!—Here, William! show this gentleman out. Since you compel me, sir—not one moment—this is such insolence! (*Going to push him out.*)

Enter CHARLES SURFACE

CHAS. SURF. Heyday! what's the matter now? What the devil, have you got hold of my little broker here? Zounds, brother, don't hurt little Premium. What's the matter, my little fellow?

JOS. SURF. So! he has been with you, too, has he?

CHAS. SURF. To be sure he has! Why, 'tis as honest a little—— But sure, Joseph, you have not been borrowing money too, have you?

JOS. SURF. Borrowing! no! But, brother, you know here we expect Sir Oliver every——

CHAS. SURF. O gad, that's true! Noll mustn't find the little broker here, to be sure.

JOS. SURF. Yet, Mr. *Stanley* insists——

CHAS. SURF. Stanley! why his name is *Premium.*

JOS. SURF. No, no, *Stanley.*

CHAS. SURF. No, no, *Premium.*

JOS. SURF. Well, no matter which—but——

CHAS. SURF. Aye, aye, Stanley or Premium, 'tis the same thing, as you say; for I suppose he goes by half [a] hundred names, besides A.B.'s at the coffee-houses.

JOS. SURF. Death! here's Sir Oliver at the door. (*Knocking again.*) Now I beg, Mr. Stanley——

CHAS. SURF. Aye, and I beg, Mr. Premium——

SIR OLIV. Gentlemen——

JOS. SURF. Sir, by heaven you shall go!

CHAS. SURF. Aye, out with him, certainly.

SIR OLIV. This violence——

JOS. SURF. 'Tis your own fault.

CHAS. SURF. Out with him, to be sure. (*Both forcing* SIR OLIVER *out.*)

Enter SIR PETER *and* LADY TEAZLE, MARIA, *and* ROWLEY.

SIR PET. My old friend, Sir Oliver—hey! What in the name of wonder!—Here are dutiful nephews!—assault their uncle at the first visit!

LADY TEAZ. Indeed, Sir Oliver, 'twas well we came in to rescue you.

ROW. Truly it was; for I perceive, Sir Oliver, the character of old Stanley was no protection to you.

130 SIR OLIV. Nor of Premium either: the necessities of the *former* could not extort a shilling from *that* benevolent gentleman; and now, egad, I stood a chance of faring worse than my ancestors, and being knocked down without being bid for.

(*After a pause,* JOSEPH *and* CHARLES *turning to each other.*)

JOS. SURF. Charles!

CHAS. SURF. Joseph!

140 JOS. SURF. 'Tis now complete!

CHAS. SURF. Very!

SIR OLIV. Sir Peter, my friend, and Rowley too—look on that elder nephew of mine. You know what he has already received from my bounty; and you know also how gladly I would have regarded half my fortune as held in trust for him—judge, then, my disappointment in discovering him to be destitute of truth—charity—and gratitude!

150 SIR PET. Sir Oliver, I should be more surprised at this declaration, if I had not myself found him selfish, treacherous, and hypocritical!

LADY TEAZ. And if the gentleman pleads not guilty to these, pray let him call *me* to his character.

SIR PET. Then, I believe, we need add no more.—if he knows himself, he will consider it as the most perfect punishment that he is known to the world.

160 CHAS. SURF (*Aside.*). If they talk this way to *Honesty,* what will they say to *me,* by and by?

(SIR PETER, LADY TEAZLE, *and* MARIA *retire.*)

SIR OLIV. As for that prodigal, his brother, there——

CHAS. SURF (*Aside.*). Aye, now comes my turn: the damned family pictures will ruin me!

JOS. SURF. Sir Oliver!—uncle!—will you honor me with a hearing?

CHAS. SURF (*Aside.*). Now if Joseph would 170 make one of his long speeches, I might recollect myself a little.

SIR OLIV [*to* JOSEPH SURFACE.]. I suppose you would undertake to justify yourself entirely?

JOS. SURF. I trust I could.

SIR OLIV. Pshaw!—Well, sir! and *you* (*to* CHARLES) could justify yourself too, I suppose?

CHAS. SURF. Not that I know of, Sir Oliver.

SIR OLIV. What!—Little Premium has been let too much into the secret, I presume?

CHAS. SURF. True, sir; but they were family 180 secrets, and should never be mentioned again, you know.

ROW. Come, Sir Oliver, I know you cannot speak of Charles's follies with anger.

SIR OLIV. Odd's heart, no more I can—nor with gravity either. Sir Peter, do you know the rogue bargained with me for all his ancestors—sold me judges and generals by the foot—and maiden aunts as cheap as broken china.

CHAS. SURF. To be sure, Sir Oliver, I did 190 make a little free with the family canvas, that's the truth on't. My ancestors may certainly rise in evidence against me, there's no denying it; but believe me sincere when I tell you—and upon my soul I would not say it if I was not—that if I do not appear mortified at the exposure of my follies, it is because I feel at this moment the warmest satisfaction in seeing you, my liberal benefactor.

SIR OLIV. Charles, I believe you. Give me 200 your hand again; the ill-looking little fellow over the settee has made your peace.

CHAS. SURF. Then, sir, my gratitude to the original is still increased.

LADY TEAZ (*Pointing to* MARIA.). Yet, I believe, Sir Oliver, here is one whom Charles is still more anxious to be reconciled to.

SIR OLIV. Oh, I have heard of his attachment there; and, with the young lady's pardon, if I construe right—that blush—— 210

SIR PET. Well, child, speak your sentiments.

MARIA. Sir, I have little to say, but that I shall rejoice to hear that he is happy; for me, whatever claim I had to his affection, I willingly resign it to one who has a better title.

CHAS. SURF. How, Maria!

SIR PET. Heyday! what's the mystery now? While he appeared an incorrigible rake, you would give your hand to no one else; and now that he is likely to reform, I warrant 220 you won't have him.

MARIA. His own heart—and Lady Sneerwell know the cause.

CHAS. SURF. Lady Sneerwell!

JOS. SURF. Brother, it is with great concern I am obliged to speak on this point, but my regard to justice compels me, and Lady Sneerwell's injuries can no longer be concealed.

(*Goes to the door.*)

230 *Enter* LADY SNEERWELL.

SIR PET. So! another French milliner!—Egad, he has one in every room in the house, I suppose!

LADY SNEER. Ungrateful Charles! Well may you be surprised, and feel for the indelicate situation which your perfidy has forced me into.

CHAS. SURF. Pray, uncle, is this another plot of yours? For, as I have life, I don't understand it.

240 JOS SURF. I believe, sir, there is but the evidence of one person more necessary to make it extremely clear.

SIR PET. And that person, I imagine, is Mr. Snake.—Rowley, you were perfectly right to bring him with us, and pray let him appear.

ROW. Walk in, Mr. Snake.

Enter SNAKE.

I thought his testimony might be wanted; however, it happens unluckily, that he comes to 250 confront Lady Sneerwell, and not to support her.

LADY SNEER. Villain! Treacherous to me at last! (*Aside.*)—Speak, fellow, have *you* too conspired against me?

SNAKE. I beg your ladyship ten thousand pardons: you paid me extremely liberally for the lie in question; but I have unfortunately been offered double to speak the truth.

SIR PET. Plot and counterplot, egad—I wish 260 your ladyship joy of the success of your negotiation.

LADY SNEER. The torments of shame and disappointment on you all!

LADY TEAZ. Hold, Lady Sneerwell—before you go, let me thank you for the trouble you and that gentleman have taken, in writing letters to me from Charles, and answering them yourself; and let me also request you to make my respects to the Scandalous College, of which 270 you are president, and inform them, that Lady Teazle, licentiate, begs leave to return the diploma they granted her, as she leaves off practice, and kills characters no longer.

LADY SNEER. You too, madam!—provoking —insolent! May your husband live these fifty years! *Exit.*

SIR PET. Oons! what a fury!

LADY TEAZ. A malicious creature, indeed!

SIR PET. Hey! not for her last wish?

LADY TEAZ. Oh, no! 280

SIR OLIV. Well, sir, and what have you to say now?

JOS. SURF. Sir, I am so confounded, to find that Lady *Sneerwell* could be guilty of suborning Mr. *Snake* in this manner, to impose on us all, that I know not what to say; however, lest her revengeful spirit should prompt her to injure my brother, I had certainly better follow her directly. *Exit.*

SIR PET. Moral to the last drop! 290

SIR OLIV. Aye, and marry her, Joseph, if you can.—Oil and vinegar, egad! you'll do very well together.

ROW. I believe we have no more occasion for Mr. Snake at present.

SNAKE. Before I go, I beg pardon once for all, for whatever uneasiness I have been the humble instrument of causing to the parties present.

SIR PET. Well, well, you have made atonement by a good deed at last. 300

SNAKE. But I must request of the company, that it shall never be known.

SIR PET. Hey! what the plague! are you ashamed of having done a right thing once in your life?

SNAKE. Ah, sir,—consider I live by the badness of my character—I have nothing but my infamy to depend on! and, if it were once known that I had been betrayed into an honest action, I should lose every friend I have in the world. 310

SIR OLIV. Well, well—we'll not traduce you by saying anything in your praise, never fear. *Exit* SNAKE.

SIR PET. There's a precious rogue! yet that fellow is a writer and a critic!

LADY TEAZ. See, Sir Oliver, there needs no persuasion now to reconcile your nephew and Maria. 320

(CHARLES *and* MARIA *apart.*)

SIR OLIV. Aye, aye, that's as it should be, and, egad, we'll have the wedding to-morrow morning.

CHAS. SURF. Thank you, my dear uncle.

SIR PET. What, you rogue! don't you ask the girl's consent first?

CHAS. SURF. Oh, I have done that a long time—above a minute ago—and she has looked yes. 330

MARIA. For shame, Charles!—I protest, Sir Peter, there has not been a word——

SIR OLIV. Well, then, the fewer the better—may your love for each other never know abatement.

SIR PET. And may you live as happily together as Lady Teazle and I—intend to do!

CHAS. SURF. Rowley, my old friend, I am sure you congratulate me; and I suspect that I owe you much. 340

SIR OLIV. You do, indeed, Charles.

ROW. If my efforts to serve you had not succeeded you would have been in my debt for the attempt—but deserve to be happy—and you overpay me.

SIR PET. Aye, honest Rowley always said you would reform.

CHAS SURF. Why as to reforming, Sir Peter, I'll make no promises, and that I take to be a proof that I intend to set about it.— 350
But here shall be my monitor—my gentle guide.—Ah! can I leave the virtuous path those
eyes illumine?
Though thou, dear maid, shouldst wa[i]ve thy
beauty's sway,
Thou still must rule, because I *will* obey:
An humbled fugitive from Folly view,
No sanctuary near but *Love* and—You;
(*To the audience.*)
You can, indeed, each anxious fear remove, 360
For even *Scandal* dies, if *you* approve.

Finis.

Epilogue

WRITTEN BY G. COLMAN, ESQ.[1]

SPOKEN BY MRS. ABINGTON [2]

I, who was late so volatile and gay,
Like a trade-wind must now blow all one way,
Bend all my cares, my studies, and my vows,
To one old rusty weathercock—my spouse!
So wills our virtuous bard—the motley Bayes
Of crying epilogues and laughing plays!
Old bachelors, who marry smart young wives,
Learn from our play to regulate your lives:
Each bring his dear to town, all faults upon her—
10 London will prove the very source of honor.
Plunged fairly in, like a cold bath it serves,
When principles relax, to brace the nerves.
Such is my case;—and yet I might deplore
That the gay dream of dissipation's o'er;
And say, ye fair, was ever lively wife,

[1] **G. Colman, Esq.** the dramatist, George Colman the elder (1732–1794) [2] **Mrs. Abington** Frances Abington, who had the role of Lady Teazle

5 **Bayes** alluding to the dramatist burlesqued in the Duke of Buckingham's *The Rehearsal*

Born with a genius for the highest life,
Like me untimely blasted in her bloom,
Like me condemned to such a dismal doom?
Save money—when I just knew how to waste it!
20 Leave London—just as I began to taste it!
Must I then watch the early crowing cock,
The melancholy ticking of a clock;
In the lone rustic hall for ever pounded,
With dogs, cats, rats, and squalling brats surrounded?
With humble curates can I now retire,
(While good Sir Peter boozes with the squire,)
And at backgammon mortify my soul,
That pants for loo, or flutters at a vole?
Seven's the main! Dear sound!—that must expire,
30 Lost at hot cockles, round a Christmas fire!
The transient hour of fashion too soon spent,
Farewell the tranquil mind, farewell content!
Farewell the plumèd head, the cushioned tête,
That takes the cushion from its proper seat!
That spirit-stirring drum!—card drums I mean,
Spadille—odd trick—pam—basto—king and queen!
And you, ye knockers, that, with brazen throat,
The welcome visitors' approach denote;
Farewell! all quality of high renown,
40 Pride, pomp, and circumstance of glorious town!
Farewell! your revels I partake no more,
And Lady Teazle's occupation's o'er!
All this I told our bard—he smiled, and said 'twas clear,
I ought to play deep tragedy next year.
Meanwhile he drew wise morals from his play,
And in these solemn periods stalked away:—
'Blest were the fair like you; her faults who stopped,
And closed her follies when the curtain dropped!
No more in vice or error to engage,
50 Or play the fool at large on life's great stage.'

28 **loo** a card game **vole** the winning of all the tricks 29 **Seven's the main** a term in the game of hazard 30 **hot cockles** a country game 32 **Farewell . . . occupation's o'er!** these lines parody a soliloquy of Othello, III.iii.347–357 35 **drum** an evening party at a private house 36 **Spadille** ace of spades **pam** jack of clubs **basto** ace of clubs

Review Questions

1. What is satirized?
2. Where does the action take place?
3. Is the plot unified?
4. How are names used as a means of characterization?
5. Describe the art of gossiping.
6. What is Lady Sneerwell's objective?
7. Comment on Sheridan's skill in character revelation.
8. What characters are sympathetic? Unsympathetic?
9. What are the dramatic functions of the picture auction scene?
10. Evaluate the "screen scene" as a comic incident.
11. What other function does the scene serve?
12. What does the play tell us about the social milieu?
13. What is Sheridan's point of view?
14. What is the social level of the characters?
15. Is Sheridan primarily interested in ridiculing folly or is his focus on the rewards of good nature?
16. Cite examples of comic irony.
17. How is Charles characterized in Scene 1?
18. What is the nature and function of the disagreement between the Teazles in Act II, Scene 1?
19. How does Sheridan use exaggeration as a technique of satire?
20. Is the "screen scene" on the level of comedy or farce?
21. How is the screen an embodiment of Joseph's character?
22. What melodramatic elements are found in the play?
23. Comment on Sir Oliver as the *deus ex machina.*
24. In sentimental comedy we are asked to admire good rather than laugh at the bad. Evaluate *School for Scandal* on these terms.
25. Are feelings a reliable guide for conduct? What is Sheridan's point of view?
26. Contrast Charles and Joseph.

AN ENEMY OF THE PEOPLE

Henrik Ibsen (1828-1906)

ADAPTED BY
Arthur Miller

The father of modern drama, Ibsen, was born in Skien, Norway. He felt the frustrations and restraints of the provincial life that he later was to protest against so vigorously in his plays. He struggled for recognition as a romantic poet and dramatist but attracted little attention. In 1851 he became associated with the national theater at Bergen as a playwright and director. Twelve years later he left Norway to live in Germany and Italy, where for more than a quarter of a century he continued to write plays.

His realistic period began with *Pillars of Society* in 1877, was followed by *A Doll's House* and *Ghosts*. The public indignation aroused by Ibsen's forthright treatment of social problems led him to write a scathing indictment of society in *An Enemy of the People*. Other notable plays of Ibsen are *Peer Gynt, The Master Builder, Rosmersholm, The Wild Duck* and *Hedda Gabler*.

Arthur Miller (1915–   )

Born a New Yorker, Miller attended the University of Michigan, where his aptitude for playwriting was so marked that he won three cash awards. After graduation he worked in the Federal Theater before becoming a script writer for the Columbia Broadcasting Company. His first professional production on Broadway was *The Man Who Had All the Luck*, in 1944, which did little to bring him recognition. Three years later, however, *All My Sons* won the Drama Critics Circle Award. His most successful play, *The Death of A Salesman,* appeared in

1949 to establish him as one of the foremost of contemporary playwrights. Other notable Miller plays are *The Crucible, A View from the Bridge,* and *After the Fall.*

Miller was attracted to Ibsen's *An Enemy of the People* because of its frontal attack on the hypocrisy of vested interests. In preparing his version of the play, he set out to transform the original dialogue into contemporary English while retaining the central theme. Miller's statement of his objective indicates his point of view:

> Throughout the play I tried to peel away the trappings of the moment, its relatively accidental details which ring the dull green tones of Victorianism, and to show that beneath there still lives the terrible wrath of Henrik Ibsen, who could make a play as men make watches, precisely, intelligently, and telling not merely the minute and the hour but the age."

RIGHT. Schematic diagrams of the sets for Miller's adaptation.

Morten Kiil and Dr. Stockmann, from Gene Frankel's 1959 off-Broadway production.

Photo by permission of Gene Frankel

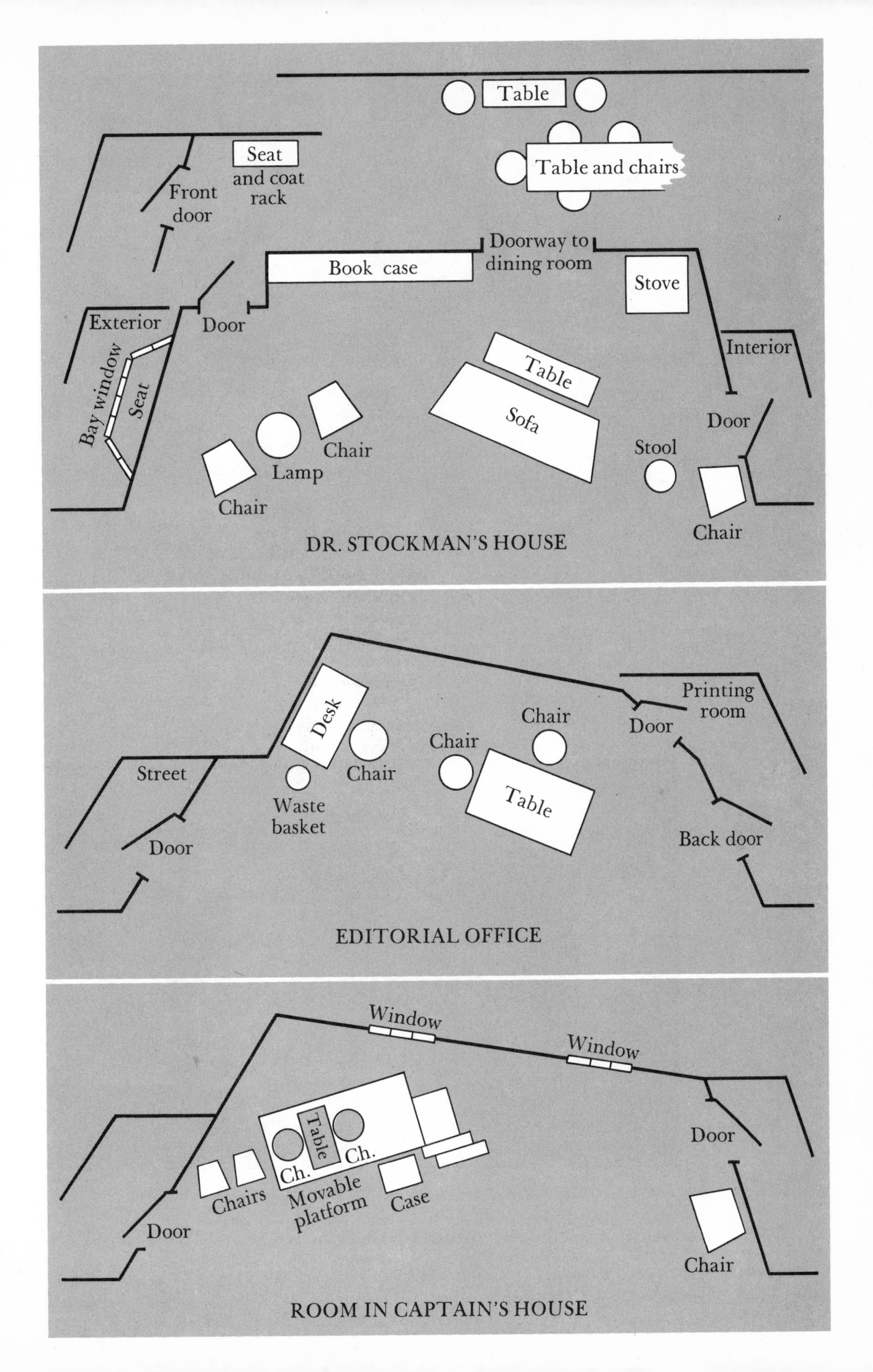
Table
Seat
and coat
rack
Table and chairs
Front
door
Doorway to
dining room
Book case
Stove
Exterior
Door
Interior
Bay window
Seat
Table
Sofa
Door
Stool
Chair
Lamp
Chair
Chair
DR. STOCKMAN'S HOUSE
Desk
Chair
Printing
room
Door
Chair
Street
Chair
Waste
basket
Table
Door
Back door
EDITORIAL OFFICE
Window
Window
Table
Ch.
Ch.
Door
Chairs
Movable
platform
Case
Door
Chair
ROOM IN CAPTAIN'S HOUSE

NET-TV

A prelude of comfort and prosperity: from L. to R., Catherine, Hovstad, Billing, Dr. Stockmann, Captain Horster, and the two sons, Morten and Ejlif, in the 1966 National Educational Television production, starring James Daley as Stockmann.

NET-TV

Stockmann becomes the "enemy." His brother, Peter, mayor of the town, steps forward as the voice of the "majority."

NET-TV

Isolated by the townspeople, the Stockmann family draws together.

"And the strong must learn to be lonely."

NET-TV

Characters

MORTEN KIIL, *Mrs. Stockmann's father*
BILLING, *a junior newspaper editor*
MRS. STOCKMANN, *wife of* DR. STOCKMANN
PETER STOCKMANN, DR. STOCKMANN'S *brother, the Mayor*
HOVSTAD, *Editor of the People's Daily Messenger*
DR. STOCKMANN, *medical officer of the Baths*
MORTEN } *sons of* DR. *and* MRS. STOCKMANN
EJLIF }
CAPTAIN HORSTER, *a ship's captain*
PETRA, *daughter of* DR. *and* MRS. STOCKMANN, *a teacher*
ASLAKSEN, *a publisher*
THE DRUNK
TOWNSPEOPLE

The action takes place in a Norwegian town.

AN ENEMY OF THE PEOPLE

ACT ONE *Scene One*

It is evening. DR. STOCKMANN'S *living-room is simply but cheerfully furnished. A doorway* U. R. *leads into the entrance hall, which extends from the front door to the dining-room. Only a small part of the hallway is seen* U. R., *but there is a passageway extending back-stage from the front door to the dining-room. This dining-room will be described below. The point is that the passage-way is practical for actors, but unseen by the audience. There is a doorway or archway* U. L. *which leads into the dining-room. Just inside this doorway we see the* R. *end of a dining-room table. There is one dining-room chair downstage, one at* R. *of the table and two just above. A short distance up-stage of the end of the table that is visible to the audience is a sideboard or table with one chair on each side of it. The* R. *end of the dining-room table, the one visible to the audience, stands about halfway between* R. *and* L. *side of the sideboard or table. Down* L., *about two-thirds of the way to the curtain-line, is another door which leads into* STOCKMANN'S *study and other rooms of the house.* U. L., *fitting into the corner of the room, is a tiled stove. Somewhat below this and to* R., *is a sofa with a table behind it.* D. L. *below door is an armchair, and near it another small chair. In* R. *foreground, somewhat to* R. *of* C., *are two chairs, a small table between them, on which stand a lamp and a bowl of apples. A bay window is in* R. *wall about halfway down-stage, and immediately below this is a bench or window seat.*

As the curtain rises KIIL *is busily eating in the dining room.* BILLING *is watching him.* KIIL *quickly rises and goes around* BILLING *to his coat and hat which are lying on upstage end of sofa.*

BILLING (*Following him.*). You sure eat fast, Mr. Kiil!

KIIL. Eating don't get you anywhere, boy. (BILLING *helps him with his coat.*) Tell my daughter I went home.

10

BILLING. All right. (*He returns to dining-room and begins to eat.* KIIL *crosses to* D. R. *of* R. C. *table, sees apple, stops, takes it, bites it, likes it, takes another, which he puts into his pocket. Starts toward door* U. R. *but circles back to table and takes a third apple, which he puts into his pocket. He notices tobacco humidor on table, looks slyly up at dining-room, comes* D. *to* L. *of table and covertly fills his coat pocket with tobacco. As he sets the humidor down,* CATHERINE *enters* D. L. KIIL *starts off* U. R. CATHERINE *starts to put on apron.*)

20

CATHERINE (*Crosses* D. C.). Father! You're not going, are you?

KIIL. Got all kinds of business to tend to.

CATHERINE. Oh, you're only going to sit alone in your room and you know it! Stay—

Mr. Billing's here, and Mr. Hovstad's coming; it'll be interesting for you.

30 KIIL. No, I got all kinds of business. Only reason I come over was the butcher told me you bought roast beef today. And it was very tasty, dear.

CATHERINE. Why don't you wait for Tom? He only went for a little walk.

KIIL (*Points to tobacco can on table.*). You suppose he'd mind if I filled my pipe?

CATHERINE. Oh, help yourself! (*He does so.*) And why don't you take some apples? (*Offering* 40 *him bowl of apples.*) You should always have some fruit in your room, go ahead.

KIIL. No, no, wouldn't think of it.

CATHERINE. Why don't you move in with us, Father? I often wonder if you're eating.

KIIL. I'm eating. Well . . . (*Doorbell rings* U. R.) See you soon, Catherine.

CATHERINE (*Crosses* U. C. *to door* U. R.). That must be Hovstad.

(KIIL *steps* R. *and lights his pipe.*)

50 PETER (*Entering hall.*). Good evening, Catherine. How are you tonight? (*Sees* KIIL.) Mr. Kiil!

KIIL. Your Honor! (*Takes big bite out of apple and goes out* U. R.)

CATHERINE. You mustn't mind him, Peter. He's getting terribly old. Wouldn't you like some supper?

PETER STOCKMANN (*Sees* BILLING *who has stepped into dining-room archway and given a* 60 *suggestion of a salute.*). No . . . no, thanks.

CATHERINE (*Nervously, quietly.*). He just sort of dropped by, Peter.

PETER (CATHERINE *has taken his coat and hangs it up in* U. R. *hall.*). That's all right. I can't take hot food in the evening, anyway. I stick to my tea and toast. Much healthier and more economical.

CATHERINE (*Smiling.*). You sound as though Tom and I threw money out the window.

70 PETER (*Crossing* D. C., *looks* U. *and then to* D. L. *door.*). Not you, Catherine. He wouldn't be home, would he?

CATHERINE (*Following him.*). He went for a little walk with the boys.

PETER. You don't think that's dangerous—right after dinner? (*Loud knocking on door.* CATHERINE *crosses* U. R. *to door.*) *That* sounds like my brother. (PETER *crosses* R. C.)

CATHERINE. Tom? He hasn't knocked on the door for ten years. (HOVSTAD *enters* U. R., *coat* 80 *and hat in hand.*) Mr. Hovstad! Come in, please.

HOVSTAD (*Handing her hat and coat, then crossing* D. R. *to* R. *of* PETER. CATHERINE *hangs up clothes in hallway* U. R.). Sorry I'm late. I was held up at the printing shop. (*A little surprised.*) Good evening, Your Honor. (CATHERINE *crosses* U. *around* R. *table to* L. *of* PETER.)

PETER (*Sitting in* R. C. *chair.*). Hovstad. On business, no doubt. 90

HOVSTAD. Partly. It's about an article for the paper . . .

PETER. Ha! I didn't doubt it. I understand my brother has become a very prolific contributor to—what do you call it—(*Sarcastically.*) *The People's Daily Liberator?*

HOVSTAD (*Holding his ground. Crosses* PETER.). *The People's Daily Messenger,* sir? (*Turning to* PETER.) The Doctor sometimes honors the *Messenger* when he wants to uncover the real truth 100 of some subject.

PETER. The truth. Oh, yes, I see . . .

CATHERINE (*Nervously crossing* D. *to* HOVSTAD.). Would you like to . . . (*Points to dining-room.*)

HOVSTAD. No, thanks.

PETER. I don't want you to think I blame the Doctor for using your columns. After all, every performer goes for the audience that applauds him most. It's really not your paper I 110 have anything against, Mr. Hovstad. (CATHERINE *busies herself with little housework things on sofa table, crossing from* D. *end of sofa to* U. *end.*)

HOVSTAD. I really didn't think so, Your Honor.

PETER. As a matter of fact, I happen to admire the spirit of tolerance in our town—it's magnificent. Just don't forget that we have it because we all believe in the same thing; it 120 brings us together.

HOVSTAD. Kirsten Springs, you mean?

PETER. The Springs, Mr. Hovstad, our wonderful new Springs. They've changed the soul of this town. Mark my words, Kirsten Springs are going to put us on the map, and there's no question about it.

CATHERINE (*Moving* U. C. *of sofa table.*). That's what Tom says, too.

PETER. Everything is shooting ahead; real estate going up, money changing hands every hour, business humming . . .

HOVSTAD. And no more unemployment.

PETER. Right. Give us a really good summer and sick people will be coming here in carloads, the Springs will turn into a regular fad, a new Carlsbad. And for once, the well-to-do people won't be the only ones paying taxes in this town.

HOVSTAD. I hear reservations are really starting to come in?

PETER. Coming in every day. Looks very promising, very promising.

HOVSTAD. That's fine. (*To* CATHERINE.) Then the Doctor's article will come in handy.

PETER. He's written something again?

HOVSTAD. No, it's a piece he wrote during the winter recommending the water. But at the time, I let the article lie . . .

PETER. Why, some hitch in it?

HOVSTAD. Oh, no, I just thought it would have a bigger effect in the spring, when people start planning for the summer.

PETER. That's smart, Mr. Hovstad, very smart.

CATHERINE (*Crossing* D. *to* L. *of* HOVSTAD.). Tom is always so full of ideas about the Springs; every day he . . .

PETER. Well, he ought to be, he gets his salary from the Springs, my dear.

HOVSTAD. Oh, I think it's more than that, don't you? Doctor Stockmann *created* Kirsten Springs.

PETER (*Looks at* HOVSTAD.). You don't say! I've been hearing that lately, but I did think I had a certain modest part . . .

CATHERINE. Oh, Tom always says . . .

HOVSTAD. I only meant the original idea was . . .

PETER (*Rises, crosses* D. L.). My good brother is never at a loss for ideas. All sorts of ideas. But when it comes to putting them into action you need another kind of man, and I did think that at least people in this house would . . .

CATHERINE. But, Peter, dear . . . we didn't mean to . . . (*To* HOVSTAD, *helping him off stage toward dining-room a little.*) Go get yourself a bite, Mr. Hovstad, my husband will be here any minute.

HOVSTAD (*Overlapping a little.*). Thank you, maybe just a little something . . . (*Enters dining-room through* U. L. *doorway, sits in* D. *chair.*)

PETER (*Lowering his voice.*). Isn't it remarkable . . . Why is it that people without background can never learn tact?

CATHERINE. Why upset yourself, Peter? Can't you and Thomas share the honor, like good brothers?

PETER. The trouble is that certain men are never satisfied to share, Catherine.

CATHERINE. Nonsense. You've always gotten along beautifully with Tom . . . (DOCTOR THOMAS STOCKMANN, MORTEN, EJLIF *and* CAPTAIN HORSTER *are heard approaching.* CATHERINE *crosses up to hall* U. R.) That must be him now. (STOCKMANN, HORSTER *and the boys,* EJLIF *and* MORTEN, *enter* U. R. *joking and laughing, about racing each other home.*)

STOCKMANN (*Taking off coat, revealing smoking-jacket underneath.*). Hey, Catherine! Here's another guest for you! Here's a hanger for your coat, Captain. (*During following,* CATHERINE *is trying to tell* STOCKMANN *about* PETER.)

HORSTER. I don't need . . .

STOCKMANN. Oh, that's right, you don't wear overcoats! (*Claps* MORTEN *on the behind.* MORTEN *spars a moment.*) Go on in, boys. You kids must be hungry all over again. (*Boys exit* U. R. *and appear in dining-room.*) Come here, Captain Horster, I want you to get a look at this roast. (HORSTER *crosses* L. *to dining-room, sits in* U. *chair.*)

CATH. Tom, dear . . . (*Motions toward* PETER.)

STOCKMANN (*Turns, sees* PETER.). Oh, Peter . . . (*Crosses above* R. *chairs to* PETER, C., *holding out his hand.*) Say, now, this is really nice. (CATHERINE *crosses* D. R. *in front of table.*)

PETER. I'll have to go in a minute.

STOCKMANN (*Crossing* R. *to* CATHERINE.). Oh, nonsense, not with the toddy on the table. You haven't forgotten the toddy, have you, Catherine? (*Kisses* CATHERINE.)

CATHERINE (*Crossing* U. *to dining-room.*). Of course, not, I've got the water boiling. (*Goes into dining-room, closes portieres.*)

PETER. Toddy, too?!

STOCKMANN (*Crosses to* PETER, *takes his arm, seats him in* R. C. *chair.*). Sure, just sit down and make yourself at home.

PETER (*Resisting a little, but sitting.*). No, thanks, I don't go in for drinking parties.

STOCKMANN (*At* L. *of* PETER.). But this is no party.

PETER. What else do you call it? (*Looks toward dining-room.*) It's extraordinary how you people can consume all this food and live.

STOCKMANN. Why? What's finer than to watch young people eat! (*Nudging* PETER.) Peter, those are the fellows who are going to stir up the whole future.

PETER. Is that so?! What's there to stir up?

STOCKMANN. Don't worry, they'll let us know when the time comes. Old idiots like you and me, we'll be left behind like . . .

PETER. I've never been called *that* before.

STOCKMANN (*Fixing book in bookcase.*). Oh, Peter, don't jump on me every minute, will you? You know your trouble, Peter—your impressions are blunted. You ought to sit up there in that crooked corner of the North for five years like I did and then come back here. It's like watching the first seven days of Creation.

PETER. Here?!

STOCKMANN. Things to work and fight for, Peter! Without that, you're dead. (*Calling.*) Catherine, are you sure the mailman came today?

CATHERINE (*From dining-room.*). There wasn't any mail today.

STOCKMANN (*Crossing to* L. *of* PETER.). And another thing, Peter, a good income; *that's* something you learn to value after you've lived on a starvation diet.

PETER. When did you starve?

STOCKMANN. Damned near! It was pretty tough going a lot of the time up there. And now, to be able to live like a prince—tonight, for instance, we had roast beef for dinner and, by God, there was enough left for supper, too! (*Takes* PETER's *arm, tries to push him to dining-room.*) Please have a piece—come here.

PETER (*At* C.). Oh, no, no—please, certainly not.

STOCKMANN. At least, let me show it to you! Come in here, we even have a table-cloth.

PETER. I saw it.

STOCKMANN (*Offering fruit to* PETER.). Live to the hilt! That's my motto. Anyway, Catherine says I'm earning almost as much as we spend.

PETER (*Declining fruit.*). Well, you're improving.

STOCKMANN (*Crossing* PETER U. *to dining-room.*). Why can't I give myself the pleasure of having young interesting people around me? You'll see—when Hovstad comes in, we'll talk and . . .

PETER (*Sitting in* R. C. *chair.*). Oh, yes, Hovstad. That reminds me—he told me he was going to print one of your articles.

STOCKMANN. One of my articles?

PETER. Yes, about the Springs—an article you wrote during the winter.

STOCKMANN (*Checking his appointment book in front of sofa.*). Oh, that one—in the first place, I don't want that one printed right now.

PETER. No? It sounded to me as though it would be very timely.

STOCKMANN. Under normal conditions maybe so.

PETER. Well, what's abnormal about the conditions now?

STOCKMANN (*In front of sofa, turns.*). I can't say that for the moment, Peter—at least not tonight. There could be a great deal abnormal about conditions—then again, there could be nothing at all.

PETER. Well, you've managed to sound mysterious. Is there anything wrong? Something you are keeping from me? Because I wish once in a while you'd remind yourself that I am chairman of the board for the Springs, as well as Mayor.

STOCKMANN. And I'd like you to remember that, Peter. (*Crosses* D. *behind sofa.*) Look, let's not get into each other's hair.

PETER. For God's sake, no—I don't make a habit of getting into people's *hair*. But I'd like to underline that everything concerning Kirsten Springs must be treated in a businesslike manner, through the proper channels and dealt with by the legally constituted authorities. I can't allow anything done behind my back in a roundabout way.

STOCKMANN (*Crossing back to* PETER *with bowl of nuts, offering him some.*). When did I ever go behind your back, Peter?

PETER (*Declining nuts, but* STOCKMANN *takes some.*). You have an ingrained tendency to go *your own way,* Thomas, and that simply can't go on in a well-organized society. The individual really must subordinate himself to the overall—or more accurately (*Indicating self.*) to the authorities who are in charge of the general welfare.

STOCKMANN (*Crossing back behind sofa.*). Well, that's probably so, (*Cracks nut.*) but how the hell does that concern me, Peter?

PETER (*Rises, crosses* U. *a step.*). My dear Thomas, this is exactly what you will never learn—but you had better watch out because some day you might pay dearly for it. (*Crosses* U. R. *to coat in hall* U. R.) Now I've said it—good-bye.

STOCKMANN. Are you out of your mind? (*Follows* PETER U. R. C. *behind table, carrying bowl.*) You're absolutely on the wrong track.

PETER. I am usually not—anyway, may I be excused? (*Nods into dining-room.*) Good-bye, Catherine. Good evening, gentlemen. (*He leaves* U. R. *The men mumble farewells.*)

CATHERINE (*Entering from dining-room.*). He left?

STOCKMANN (*Surprised at* PETER'S *behavior. Above* R. *chair.*) Yes, he did, and thoroughly burned up.

CATHERINE (*At* U. C.). What'd you do to him now?

STOCKMANN. What does he want from me? He can't expect me to give him an accounting of every move I make—every thought I think, until I'm ready to do it.

CATHERINE. Why? What should you give him an accounting of?

STOCKMANN. Just leave that to me, Catherine. (*Crosses to bay window* R., *looking out, setting bowl on window seat.*) It is peculiar that the mailman didn't come today. (CATHERINE *goes to dining-room. Men enter downstage from dining-room, opening portieres:* HORSTER L. *of* HOVSTAD; HOVSTAD *crosses* D. *to* L. *of* R. C. *chair;* BILLING *in front of* D. *end of sofa;* EJLIF *and* MORTEN R. *of* L. *chair.*)

BILLING (*Stretching out his arms.*). After a meal like that, by God, I feel like a new man. This house is so . . .

HOVSTAD (*Cutting him off.*). The Mayor certainly wasn't in a glowing mood tonight.

STOCKMANN. It's his stomach—he has a lousy digestion.

HOVSTAD (*Indicating* BILLING *and self.*). I think two editors from the *People's Daily Messenger* didn't help, either.

STOCKMANN. No, it's just that Peter is a lonely man—poor fellow, all he knows is official business and duties and then all that damn weak tea that he pours into himself. Catherine, may we have the toddy?

CATHERINE (*From dining-room.*). I'm just getting it.

STOCKMANN (*Takes* HORSTER *to sofa, crossing* HOVSTAD *and* BILLING.). Sit down here on the couch with me, Captain Horster—a rare guest like you—sit here. Sit down, friends. (HORSTER *sits on* D. *end of sofa.*)

HORSTER. This used to be such an ugly house; suddenly it's beautiful!

BILLING (*To* HORSTER, *intimately, indicating* STOCKMANN.). Great man. (STOCKMANN, *embarrassed, turns to see to whom* BILLING *refers, sits;* BILLING *crosses* U. *around to* R. *chair, sits. The men rise as* CATHERINE *brings in from dining-room tray with pot, glasses, three bottles and sets it on table behind sofa, then crosses and sits in* L. *chair.*)

CATHERINE (*Entering.*). Here you are. Help yourselves.

STOCKMANN (*Fixing toddy.*). We sure will. (EJLIF *is tucking in* MORTEN'S *sweater.*) And the cigars, Ejlif—you know where the box is—and, Morten, get my pipe. (MORTEN *and* EJLIF *exit* L. *and* EJLIF *just overhears* STOCKMANN'S *suspicions about cigars.*) I have a sneaking suspicion that Ejlif is snitching a cigar now and then, but I don't pay any attention. (MORTEN *re-enters* L. *and stands on* STOCKMANN'S R. *with his pipe.*) Catherine, you know where I put it? Oh, he's got it. Good boys! (EJLIF *re-enters* L. *with cigars, offers them to* HORSTER, HOVSTAD *and* BILLING *then sits* U. *of* MORTEN *on window seat* R. *eating nuts from bowl.* STOCKMANN *gives toddy to* HOVSTAD, BILLING *and* HORSTER *then returns to* U. *of sofa.*) Help yourselves, fellows. I'll stick to the pipe—this one's gone through plenty of blizzards with me up in the north. (*Sits* U. *end of sofa.*) Skol! (BILLING *and* HOVSTAD *clink glasses,* HORSTER *and* STOCKMANN *clink glasses. All drink.* STOCKMANN *looks around.*) Home! (*All look at* STOCKMANN.) What an invention, heh!

CATHERINE (*After a moment.*). Are you sailing soon, Captain Horster?

HORSTER. I expect to be ready next week.

CATHERINE. And then to America, Captain?

HORSTER. Yes, that's the plan.

BILLING. Oh, then you won't be home for the new election?

HORSTER. Is there going to be another election?

BILLING. Don't you know? (STOCKMANN *lights pipe.*)

HORSTER. No, I don't get mixed up in those things.

BILLING. But you are interested in public affairs, aren't you?

HORSTER. Frankly, I don't understand a thing about it.

CATHERINE (*Sympathetically.*). Neither do I, Captain; maybe that's why I'm always so glad to see you.

BILLING. Just the same, you ought to vote, Captain.

HORSTER. Even if I don't understand anything about it?

BILLING. Understand? What do you mean by that? Society, Captain, is like a ship—every man should do something to help navigate the ship.

HORSTER. That may be all right on shore, but on board a ship it doesn't work out so well. (PETRA, *carrying hat and coat with textbooks and notepads under her arm, enters from hall* U. R.)

PETRA. Good evening. (*Men rise.* PETRA *removes her coat and hat and places books on hall chair* U. R. *There are mutual greetings.*)

STOCKMANN (*Warmly.*). Good evening, Petra.

PETRA (*Crosses* C. *to* STOCKMANN, *throwing kiss to* CATHERINE, *which she throws back.*) And here you are lying around like lizards while I'm out slaving.

STOCKMANN (*Embracing* PETRA *at* C.). Well, you come and be a lizard, too. (*To company.*) I look at her and I say to myself—how did I do it!

BILLING (*Close to* HOVSTAD.). Great young woman. (*Crosses to* PETRA.) Shall I mix a toddy for you?

PETRA. Thank you, I had better do it myself—you always mix it too strong. Oh, Father, I forgot—I have a letter for you. (*Goes to hall* U. R., *brings down book with letter in it.*)

STOCKMANN (*Crosses after her. Alerted, sets drink on table, returns to* C.). Who's it from?

PETRA (*Takes letter, backs* D. R. *then* C., STOCKMANN *follows her.*). I met the mailman on the way to school this morning and he gave me your mail, too, and I just didn't have time to run back.

STOCKMANN. And you don't give it to me until now!

PETRA. I really didn't have time to run back, Father.

CATHERINE (*Standing.*). If she didn't have time . . .

STOCKMANN. Let's see it—come on, child . . . (*Slaps* PETRA's *fanny, takes letter, looks at envelope, recognizes it, crosses* D. R. C.) Yes, indeed.

CATHERINE. Is that the one you've been waiting for?

STOCKMANN (*Crossing* L. *to study.*). I'll be right back. There wouldn't be a light on in my room, would there? (CATHERINE *takes his glasses out of his pocket as he goes out.*)

CATHERINE. The lamp is on the desk burning away. (*Turns* C.)

STOCKMANN (*Re-entering* L.). Please excuse me for a moment. (CATHERINE *puts his glasses in his hand as he goes back out* L. *Closes door.* CATHERINE *turns.*)

PETRA. What's that, Mother? (PETRA *crosses slowly to table, fixes drink.*)

CATHERINE. I don't know. The last couple of days he has been asking again and again about the mailman.

BILLING. Probably an out-of-town patient of his. (CATHERINE *sits.*)

PETRA. Poor Father, he's got much too much to do. (*She mixes her drink, comes around sofa.*) This ought to taste good.

HOVSTAD (*Crossing to* PETRA.). By the way, what happened to that English novel you were going to translate for us?

PETRA. I started to, but I got so busy . . .

HOVSTAD. Oh, have you been teaching evening school again?

PETRA. Two hours a night.

BILLING. Plus the high school every day?

PETRA. Yes, five hours, and every night a pile of lessons to correct . . .

CATHERINE. She never stops going.

HOVSTAD. Maybe that's why I always think of you as kind of breathless, and . . . well, breathless.

PETRA. I love it. I get so wonderfully tired. (PETRA *sits.*)

BILLING (*To* HORSTER.). She looks tired. (BILLING *crosses* R. *to* R. *chair, all sit.*)

MORTEN (*Crossing to in front of* BILLING.). 540 You must be a wicked woman, Petra. (BILLING *beckons* MORTEN, *who approaches;* EJLIF *follows with nut bowl.*)

PETRA (*Laughing.*). Wicked?

MORTEN. You work so much. My teacher says that work is a punishment for our sins.

EJLIF. And you believe that?

CATHERINE. Ejlif! Of course he believes his teacher.

BILLING (*Smiling.*). Don't stop him . . .

550 HOVSTAD. Don't you like to work, Morten?

MORTEN. Work? No.

HOVSTAD. Then what will you ever amount to in this world?

MORTEN. Me? I'm going to be a Viking.

EJLIF. You can't! You'd have to be a heathen!

MORTEN. So I'll be a heathen.

CATHERINE (*Rising, crossing* R.; *men rise.*). I think it's getting late, boys . . .

BILLING. I agree with you, Morten; I 560 think . . .

CATHERINE (*Interrupting* BILLING.). You certainly don't, Mr. Billing.

BILLING. Yes, by God, I do. I'm a real heathen and proud of it. (*Lifts* MORTEN. CATHERINE *tries to stop this violent exercise.*) You'll see, pretty soon we are all going to be heathens.

MORTEN. And then we can do anything we want——

BILLING. *Right!* You see, Morten . . .

570 CATHERINE (*Interrupting.*). Don't you have any homework for tomorrow, boys? Better go in and do it.

EJLIF. Oh, can't we stay in here awhile?

CATHERINE (*Takes bowl.*). No, neither of you—now run along.

EJLIF. Good night.

MORTEN. Good night. But I don't have any homework . . . (*Boys exit into hall* U. R. HOVSTAD *edges over to* PETRA. CATHERINE *picks up nut* 580 *bowl, sets it on* R. *table.*)

HOVSTAD. You don't really think it hurts them to listen to such talk, do you? (*Enter* STOCKMANN L.)

CATHERINE. I don't know, but I don't like it. (*As* STOCKMANN *breaks for door* L.) Tom!

STOCKMANN (*Crossing* C., *open letter in his hand.*) Boys, there is going to be news in this town!

BILLING. News?
CATHERINE (*Crossing to* STOCKMANN *at* C.). What kind of news? } (*Together.*) 590

STOCKMANN. Hunh?—A terrific discovery, Catherine.

HOVSTAD. Really?
CATHERINE. That you made? } (*Together.*)

STOCKMANN (*At* C. *of table.*). That I made. (*Walks back and forth.*) Now let the baboons running this town call me a lunatic! Now they'd better watch out. Oh, how the mighty have fallen! (U. *above* R. *table.*) 600

PETRA. What is it, Father?

STOCKMANN. Oh, if Peter were only here! Now you'll see how human beings can walk around and make judgments like blind rats.

HOVSTAD. What in the world's happened, Doctor?

STOCKMANN (*Above table.*). It is the general opinion, isn't it, that our town is a sound and healthy spot?

HOVSTAD. Of course. 610

CATHERINE. What happened?

STOCKMANN. Even a rather unusually healthy spot——Oh, God . . . (*Throws his arms up, holding glasses in* L. *hand,* CATHERINE *takes glasses from him, puts them in his pocket.*) a place that can be recommended, not only to all people but sick people.

CATHERINE. But, Tom, what are you——?

STOCKMANN. And we certainly have recommended it. I myself have written and written 620 about it, in the *People's Messenger,* pamphlets . . .

HOVSTAD. Yes, yes, but, Doctor, what are you trying to say?

STOCKMANN. The miraculous Springs that cost such a fortune to build. The whole Health Institute is a pest hole.

PETRA. Father! The Springs?
CATHERINE. Our Springs?
BILLING. That's unbelievable! } (*Together.*) 630

STOCKMANN (*Crossing* R. *to* D. R., *then* L. *to*

HORSTER.). You know the filth up in Windmill Valley—that stuff that has such a stinking smell? It comes down from the tannery up there and the same damn poisonous mess comes right out into (*To* HORSTER.) the blessed, miraculous water we're supposed to *cure* people with!

HORSTER. You mean actually where our beaches are?

640 STOCKMANN (*At* D. L.). Exactly.

HOVSTAD. How are you so sure about this, Doctor?

STOCKMANN (*Crossing* C. *to* R. *of* HOVSTAD.). I had a suspicion about it a long time ago—last year there were too many sick cases among the visitors; typhoid and gastric disturbances.

CATHERINE. That *did* happen. (*To* BILLING.) I remember Mrs. Svensen's niece . . .

STOCKMANN (*Crossing to* CATHERINE.). Yes, 650 dear. At the time we thought that the visitors brought the bug, but later this winter I got a new idea and I started investigating the water.

CATHERINE. So that's what you've been working on!

STOCKMANN. I sent samples of the water to the University for an exact chemical analysis.

HOVSTAD. And that's what you have received?

STOCKMANN (*Showing letter.*). This is it. It 660 proves the existence of infectious organic matter in the water. (*A little pause.* HOVSTAD *is looking at* BILLING.)

CATHERINE. Well, thank God you discovered it in time.

STOCKMANN. I think we can say that, Catherine.

CATHERINE. Isn't it wonderful!

HOVSTAD. And what do you intend to do now, Doctor?

670 STOCKMAN. Put the thing right, of course.

HOVSTAD. Do you think that can be done?

STOCKMANN. If not, the whole Institute is useless—but there's nothing to worry about—I am quite clear on what has to be done.

CATHERINE. But, Tom, why'd you keep it so secret?

STOCKMANN. What'd you want me to do?—go out and shoot my mouth off before I really knew? No, thanks, I'm not that crazy. (*He* 680 *walks around, rubbing his hands.*) You don't realize what this means, Catherine—(*Crosses to* BILLING.) the whole water system has got to be changed.

CATHERINE. The *whole* water system?! (*Fades to* L. *above sofa table.*)

STOCKMANN. The whole water system. The intake is too low, it's got to be raised to a much higher spot. The whole construction's got to be ripped out!

PETRA. Well, Dad, at least you can prove they 690 should have listened to you!

STOCKMANN. Ha, she remembers!

CATHERINE. That's right, you did warn them . . .

STOCKMANN. Of course I warned them! When they started the damned thing I told them not to build it down there. But who am I, a mere scientist to tell politicians where to build a health institute! Well, now they're going to get it both barrels! 700

BILLING. This is tremendous . . . (*To* HORSTER.) He's a great man!

STOCKMANN (*Turns.*). It's bigger than tremendous. Wait'll they see this. (*Crosses to* PETRA.) Petra, my report is on my desk . . . (PETRA *sets glass down, runs out* L.) And envelopes, Catherine! (CATHERINE *goes into dining-room;* PETRA *returns with report, gives it to* STOCKMANN.) Gentlemen, this final proof from the University and my report . . . (*Flicks* 710 *pages.*) five solid, explosive pages . . .

CATHERINE (*Returns, hands him envelopes.*). Is that big enough?

STOCKMANN. Fine. Right to the Board of Directors! (*Hands report, letter to* CATHERINE.) Will you give this to the maid . . . what's her name again?

CATHERINE. Randine, dear, Randine . . .

STOCKMANN. Tell our darling Randine to wipe her nose and run over to the Mayor right 720 now. (CATHERINE *stands looking at him as though she'd had a little pain.*) What's the matter, dear?

CATHERINE. I don't know . . .

PETRA. What's Uncle Peter going to say to this?

CATHERINE. That's what I'm wondering.

STOCKMANN. What can he say! He ought to be damn glad that such an important fact is brought out before we start an epidemic. Hurry, 730 dear! (CATHERINE *goes into dining-room.*)

HOVSTAD (*Crossing* R. *from behind sofa between* STOCKMANN *and* PETRA.) I would like to put a brief item about this discovery in the *Messenger.*

STOCKMANN. Yes, now I'd really be grateful for it.

HOVSTAD. Because the public ought to know soon.

740

STOCKMANN. Right away.

BILLING. By God, you'll be the leading man in this town, Doctor.

STOCKMANN (*Crossing* BILLING *to* D. R.). Oh, there was nothing to it. Every detective gets a lucky break once in his life. But just the same, I . . .

BILLING. Hovstad, don't you think the town ought to pay Dr. Stockmann some tribute?

750

STOCKMANN. Oh, no, no . . .

HOVSTAD. Let's all put in a word for . . .

BILLING (*Crossing* D. R. PETRA *takes drink from sofa table.*). I'll talk to Aslaksen about it. (CATHERINE *enters, crosses* C. HOVSTAD *picks up drink from* R. *table.*)

STOCKMANN (*Crossing* C.). No, no, fellows, no fooling around. I won't put up with any commotion. Even if the Board of Directors want to give me an increase, I won't take it . . . (*To* CATHERINE.) I just won't take it, Catherine.

760

CATHERINE. That's right, Tom.

PETRA (*Lifting glass.*). Skol, Father!

ALL. Skol, Doctor. (*They drink.*)

HORSTER. Doctor, I hope this will bring you great honor and pleasure.

STOCKMANN. Thanks, friends, thanks. There's one blessing above all others: to have earned the respect of one's neighbors is . . . is . . . Catherine, I'm going to dance! (*He grabs* CATHERINE, *starts singing and whirls her around. On second phrase,* PETRA *joins the circle. Boys enter* L., *go* R. *and stand on window seat.* HORSTER, HOVSTAD *and* BILLING *join the dancing circle. All are singing.*)

770

CATHERINE (*Seeing boys, screams.*). Children! (*Boys run out* L.)

FAST CURTAIN

Scene Two

SCENE: *The same. The following morning.*

CATHERINE (*Entering from dining-room with sealed letter, crosses above sofa to* D. L. *door.*). Are you there, Tom?

STOCKMANN (*Off* L.). I just got in. (*Entering* D. L.; *his coat is buttoned wrong. Closes door.*) What's up?

CATHERINE (*Giving him letter.*). From Peter. It just came.

STOCKMANN (*Taking letter.*). Peter! Oh, let's see. (*Opens envelope, reads letter, crosses* C., *holding up letter to catch* R. *sunlight.*) "I am returning herewith the report you submitted . . ."

10

CATHERINE (*Following him.*). Well, what does he say? Don't stand there!

STOCKMANN (*Putting letter in his pocket.*). He just says he'll come around this afternoon.

CATHERINE (*Buttoning his coat correctly.*). Oh. Well, maybe you ought to try to remember to be home then.

STOCKMANN. Oh, I sure will. I'm through with my morning visits, anyway.

20

CATHERINE. I'm dying to see how he's going to take it.

STOCKMANN. Why, is there any doubt? He'll probably make it look like he made the discovery, not me.

CATHERINE. But aren't you a little bit afraid of that?

STOCKMANN. Oh, underneath he'll be happy, Catherine. (*Kisses her. One arm is around her.*) It's just that Peter is so damn afraid that somebody else is going to do something good for this town.

30

CATHERINE. I wish you'd go out of your way

and share the honors with him. Couldn't we say that he put you on the right track or something? (KIIL *enters hallway* U. R.)

STOCKMANN (*Embracing* CATHERINE.). Oh, I don't mind—as long as it makes everybody happy.

40

KIIL (*Pokes head into room from hall* U. R., *chuckling.*). Is it really true? (*Crosses* D. R. C.)

CATHERINE (*Crosses* U. *of* R. C. *table.*). Father! Come on in.

STOCKMANN (*A step to* KIIL.). Well, good morning!

KIIL. It better be true, or I'm going.

STOCKMANN. What had better be true?

KIIL (*Crossing to* D. *of* R. *table.*). This crazy story about the water system. Is it true?

50

CATHERINE. Of course it's true.

STOCKMANN. How did you find out about it?

KIIL. Petra came flying by on her way to school this morning.

STOCKMANN. Oh, she did?

KIIL. Yes. I thought she was trying to make a fool out of me . . .

CATHERINE. Now, Father, why would she do that?

60

KIIL. Nothing pleases young people more than to make fools out of old people. But this is true, eh?

STOCKMANN. Of course it's true——(*Seating* KIIL *in* R. C. *chair.* CATHERINE *is above* R. *table.*) Sit down here. It's pretty lucky for the town, eh?

KIIL (*Fighting his laughter.*). Lucky for the town?!

STOCKMANN. I mean that I made the discovery before it was too late.

70

KIIL. Tom, I never thought you had the imagination to pull your own brother's leg like this.

STOCKMANN. Pull his leg?

CATHERINE. But, Father, he's not . . .

KIIL. How does it go now? Let me get it straight. There's some kind of . . . like cockroaches in the waterpipes . . . ?

STOCKMANN (*Laughing.*). No, not cockroaches . . .

80

KIIL. Well, some kind of little animals . . .

CATHERINE. Bacteria, Father . . .

KIIL. Ah, but a whole mess of them, eh?

STOCKMANN. Oh, there'd be millions and millions . . .

KIIL. And nobody can see them but you, is that it?

STOCKMANN. Yes, that's . . . well, of course, anybody with a micro . . . (*Breaks off.*) What are you laughing at?

90

CATHERINE (*Smiling at* KIIL.). You don't understand, Father, nobody can actually see bacteria, but that doesn't mean they're not there . . .

KIIL (*Chuckling.*). Good girl, you stick with him. By God, this is the best thing I ever heard in my life!

STOCKMANN (*Smiling.*). What do you mean?

KIIL. But tell me, you think you are going to get your brother to actually believe this?

100

STOCKMANN. Well, we'll see soon enough!

KIIL. You really think he's that crazy?

STOCKMANN. I hope the whole town will be that "crazy," Morten.

KIIL. Ya, they probably are, and it'll serve them right, too—they think they're so much smarter than us old-timers. Your good brother ordered them to bounce me out of the council, so they chased me out like a dog. (*Rising.*) Make jackasses out of all of them, Stockmann.

110

STOCKMANN (*Interrupting.*). Yes, but Morten . . .

KIIL. Long-eared, short-tailed jackasses . . . Stockmann, if you can make the Mayor and his elegant friends grab at this bait, I will give a couple hundred crowns to charity, and right now, right on the spot.

STOCKMANN (*Interrupting,* KIIL *crosses* L. C.). Well, that would be very kind of you, but I'm . . .

120

KIIL. I haven't got much to play around with, but if you can pull the rug out from under him with this cockroach business, I'll give at least fifty crowns to charity. (HOVSTAD *enters the hall* U. R.) Maybe this'll teach them to put some brains back in City Hall!

HOVSTAD (*Crossing* D. R.). Good morning! Oh, pardon me——

STOCKMANN. Come on in.

130

KIIL (*Crossing to below table.*). Oh, this one is in on it, too?

HOVSTAD. What's that, sir?

STOCKMANN. Of course, he's in on it.

KIIL. Couldn't I have guessed that—and it's going to be in the papers, I suppose. You're sure tying down the corners, aren't you? Well, lay it on thick. I've got to go.

STOCKMANN. Oh, no, stay a while, let me explain it to you!

KIIL (*Crossing* STOCKMANN *to* L. *of* HOVSTAD.).
140 Oh, I get it, don't worry! Only, you can see them, heh? That's the best idea I've ever heard in my life. (*He goes out* U. R. CATHERINE *then goes off* R. *through dining-room, appears in hall* U. R. *closing portieres tightly*.)

CATHERINE (*Laughing*.). But, Father, you don't understand about bacteria . . .

STOCKMANN (*Laughing*.). The old badger doesn't believe a word of it.

HOVSTAD. What does he think you're doing?

150 STOCKMANN. Making an idiot out of my brother, imagine that?

HOVSTAD (*Crossing* STOCKMANN *to* C.). You got a few minutes?

STOCKMANN. Sure, as long as you like.

HOVSTAD. Have you heard from the Mayor?

STOCKMANN. Only that he's coming over later.

HOVSTAD. I've been thinking about this since last night . . . (*Crosses to* STOCKMANN.)

160 STOCKMANN. Don't say?

HOVSTAD. For you as a medical man, a scientist, this is a really rare opportunity. But I've been wondering if you realize that it ties in with a lot of other things.

STOCKMANN. How do you mean? Sit down ——(*They sit*, STOCKMANN *in* R. *chair*, HOVSTAD *in* R. C. *chair*.) What are you driving at?

HOVSTAD. You said last night that the water comes from impurities in the ground——

170 STOCKMANN. It comes from the poisonous dump in Windmill Valley.

HOVSTAD. Doctor, I think it comes from an entirely different dump—the same dump that is poisoning and polluting our whole social life in this town.

STOCKMANN. For God's sake, Hovstad, what are you babbling about?

HOVSTAD. Everything that matters in this town has fallen into the hands of a few bureau-
180 crats.

STOCKMANN. Well, they're not all bureaucrats——

HOVSTAD. They're all rich—all with old reputable names and they've got everything in the palm of their hands.

STOCKMANN. Yes, but they happen to have ability and knowledge.

HOVSTAD. Did they show ability and knowledge when they built the water system where
190 they did?

STOCKMANN. No, of course not, but that happened to be a blunder and we'll clear it up now.

HOVSTAD. You really imagine it's going to be as easy as all that?

STOCKMANN. Easy or not easy, it's got to be done.

HOVSTAD. Doctor, I've made up my mind to give this whole scandal very special treatment.

STOCKMANN. Now wait—you can't call it a scandal yet. 200

HOVSTAD. Doctor, when I took over the *People's Messenger*, I swore I'd blow that smug cabal of old, stubborn, self-satisfied fogies to bits. This is the story that can do it.

STOCKMANN. But I still think we owe them a deep debt of gratitude for building the Springs.

HOVSTAD. The Mayor being your brother, I wouldn't ordinarily want to touch it, but I know you'd never let that kind of thing obstruct the truth. 210

STOCKMANN. Of course not, but . . .

HOVSTAD. I want you to understand me. I don't have to tell you I come from a simple family. I know in my bones what the underdog needs—he's got to have a say in the government of society—that's what brings out ability, intelligence, and self-respect in people.

STOCKMANN. I understand that, but . . .

HOVSTAD. I think a newspaper man who turns down any chance to give the underdog a lift is 220 taking on a responsibility that I don't want. (*Rises, paces* C. *and back to table*.) I know perfectly well that in fancy circles they call it agitation, and they can call it anything they like if it makes them happy—but I have my own conscience!

STOCKMANN (*Interrupting*.). I agree with you, Hovstad . . . (ASLAKSEN *knocks, then enters* U. R.) but this is just the water supply and . . . (STOCKMANN *rises, crosses* R. *and* U.) Damn 230 it, come in.

ASLAKSEN (*Entering from* U. R.). I beg your pardon, Doctor, if I intrude . . . (STOCKMANN *takes him by* R. *arm and brings him* D. C.)

HOVSTAD (*Crossing* D. R.). Are you looking for me, Aslaksen?

ASLAKSEN. No, I didn't know you were here. I want to see the Doctor.

STOCKMANN. What can I do for you?

ASLAKSEN. Is it true, Doctor, what I hear 240 from Mr. Billing that you intend to campaign for a better water system?

STOCKMANN (*Offers chair.*). Yes, for the Institute—but it's not a campaign.

ASLAKSEN. I just wanted to call and tell you that we are behind you one hundred percent.

HOVSTAD (*To* STOCKMANN.). There, you see . . .

STOCKMANN. Mr. Aslaksen, I thank you with all my heart, but, you see . . .

ASLAKSEN. We can be important, Doctor. When the little businessman wants to push something through, he turns out to be the majority, you know, and it's always good to have the majority on your side.

STOCKMANN. That's certainly true, but I don't understand what this is all about. It seems to me it's a simple, straightforward business. The water . . .

ASLAKSEN. Of course, we intend to behave with moderation, Doctor. I always try to be a moderate and careful man.

STOCKMANN. You are known for that, Mr. Aslaksen, but . . .

ASLAKSEN. Kirsten Springs are becoming a gold mine for this town. Especially for the little businessmen, and that's why, in my capacity as Chairman of the Property Owners' Association . . .

STOCKMANN. Yes . . .

ASLAKSEN. And furthermore, as a representative of the Temperance Society—you probably know, Doctor, that I am active for prohibition.

STOCKMANN. So I've heard.

ASLAKSEN. As a result, I come into contact with all kinds of people, and since I'm known to be a law-abiding and solid citizen, I have a certain influence in this town—(*Advancing a little to* HOVSTAD.) you might even call it a little power.

STOCKMANN. I know that very well, Mr. Aslaksen.

ASLAKSEN. That's why you can see that it would be practically nothing for me to arrange a demonstration.

STOCKMANN. Demonstration? What are you going to demonstrate about?

ASLAKSEN. The citizens of the town complimenting you for bringing this important matter to everybody's attention. Obviously it would have to be done with the utmost moderation so as not to hurt the authorities . . .

HOVSTAD. This could knock the big-bellies right into the garbage can!

ASLAKSEN (*Crossing to* HOVSTAD.). No indiscretion or extreme aggressiveness toward the authorities, Mr. Hovstad! (HOVSTAD *crosses to window seat* R., *sits, takes notes.*) I don't want any wild-eyed radicalism on this thing. (ASLAKSEN *to* STOCKMANN.) I've had enough of that in my time, and no good ever comes of it, but for a good solid citizen to express his calm, frank and free opinion is something nobody can deny.

STOCKMANN (*Shaking his hand.*). My dear Aslaksen, I can't tell you how it heartens me to hear this kind of support. I'm happy—I really am—I'm happy. Listen! Wouldn't you like a glass of sherry?

ASLAKSEN. I am a member of the Temperance Society, I——

STOCKMANN. Well, how about a glass of beer?

ASLAKSEN. I don't think I can go quite that far, Doctor. Well, good day, and I want you to remember that the little man is behind you like a wall. You have the solid majority on your side, because when the little man takes over . . .

STOCKMANN (*Takes his arm, crosses* ASLAKSEN *in front and starts out* U. R.). Thanks for that, Mr. Aslaksen—and good day.

ASLAKSEN. Are you going to the printing shop, Mr. Hovstad?

HOVSTAD. I just have a thing or two to attend to here.

ASLAKSEN. Very well. (*He leaves* U. R.; STOCKMANN *follows him into hall, then returns* D. R.)

HOVSTAD (*Rising, puts notes in pocket, crosses* C.). Well, what do you say to a little hypodermic for these fence-sitting deadheads? Everybody's afraid—afraid—they know perfectly well what's right, but they're afraid.

STOCKMANN. Why? I think that Aslaksen is a very sincere man.

HOVSTAD. Isn't it time we pumped some guts into these well-intentioned men of good-will? Under all their liberal talk, they still idolize authority and that's got to be rooted out of this town. This blunder of the water system has to be made clear to every voter. Let me print your report.

STOCKMANN (*Turning away a little.*). Not until I talk to my brother.

HOVSTAD. I'll write an editorial in the meantime, and if the Mayor won't go along with us——

STOCKMANN. I don't see how you can imagine such a thing!

HOVSTAD. Believe me, Doctor, it's entirely possible . . .

STOCKMANN. Listen. I promise you: he will go along and then you can print my report, every word of it.

HOVSTAD. On your word of honor?

STOCKMANN (*Giving him manuscript.*). Here it is, take it. It can't do any harm for you to read it. Return it to me later.

HOVSTAD (*Takes manuscript, puts it in his pocket, starts out* U. R.). Good day, Doctor.

STOCKMANN. Good day. You will see it's going to be easier than you think.

HOVSTAD (*Stops.*). I hope so, Doctor, sincerely. Let me know as soon as you hear from His Honor. (*Goes out* U. R.)

STOCKMANN (*Crosses and looks in dining-room.*). Catherine! Oh, you're home already, Petra.

PETRA (*Entering dining-room from* L. *with glass of milk.*). I just got back from school. (*Comes into room, kisses* STOCKMANN, *crosses to stove to warm back.* CATHERINE *enters from dining-room.*)

CATHERINE. Hasn't he been here yet?

STOCKMANN. Peter? No, but I just had a long chat with Hovstad. (*Leading* CATHERINE D. C.) He's really fascinated with my discovery and, you know, it has more implications than I thought at first. Do you know what I have backing me up?

CATHERINE. What, in heaven's name, have you got backing you up?

STOCKMANN. The solid majority.

CATHERINE. Is that good? (PETRA *crosses* D., *sits on* D. *arm of sofa.*)

STOCKMANN. Good? It's wonderful. You can't imagine the feeling, Catherine, to know that your own town feels like a brother to you. I haven't felt so at home in this town since I was a boy. (*Doorbell.*)

CATHERINE. That's the front door. (*She crosses* U. *around table to hall* U. R.; *lets* PETER *in.*)

STOCKMANN. Oh, it's Peter, then. Come in. (PETER *enters from hall* U. R. PETRA *rises.*)

PETER (*Crossing* D. R.). Good morning!

CATHERINE. Good morning.

STOCKMANN. It's nice to see you, Peter.

CATHERINE. How are you today?

PETER. Well, so-so . . . (CATHERINE *crosses* U. *to* R. *of* PETRA; PETER *to* STOCKMANN.) I received your thesis about the condition of the Springs yesterday. (*Crosses* L., *puts hat on* R. C. *table, crosses* C., *turns to face* STOCKMANN.)

STOCKMANN. I got your note. Did you read it?

PETER. I read it.

STOCKMANN. Well, what do you have to say? (PETER *clears his throat, glances aside.*)

CATHERINE. Come on, Petra. (*She and* PETRA *exit* L., *closing door.*)

PETER (*After a moment.*). Thomas, was it really necessary to go into this investigation behind my back?

STOCKMANN. Yes, until I was convinced myself, there was no point in . . .

PETER. And now you are convinced?

STOCKMANN. Well, certainly—aren't you, too, Peter? (*Pause.*) The University chemists corroborated . . .

PETER. You intend to present this document to the Board of Directors, officially, as the Medical Officer of the Springs?

STOCKMANN. Of course, something's got to be done, and quick.

PETER. You always use such strong expressions, Thomas. (*Sits* C. *of sofa.*) Among other things, in your report, you say that we *guarantee* our guests and visitors a permanent case of poisoning.

STOCKMANN. Yes, but, Peter, how can you describe it any other way? Imagine! Poisoned internally and externally!

PETER. So you merrily conclude that we must build a waste disposal plant—and reconstruct a brand new water system from the bottom up?

STOCKMANN (*Taking* R. C. *chair, moves it* C. *as though to sit.*). Well, do you know some other way out? I don't.

PETER. I took a little walk over to the City Engineer this morning and in the course of conversation I sort of jokingly mentioned these changes—as something we might consider for the future, you know.

STOCKMANN. The future won't be soon enough, Peter.

PETER. The Engineer kind of smiled at my extravagance and gave me a few facts. I don't suppose you've taken the trouble to consider what your proposed changes would cost?

STOCKMANN. No, I never thought of that . . .

PETER. Naturally. Your little project would come to at least three hundred thousand crowns.

STOCKMANN (*Sitting.*). That expensive?

PETER. Oh, don't look so upset—it's only money. The worst thing is that it would take some two years.

STOCKMANN. Two years?

PETER. At the least, and what do you propose we do about the Springs in the meantime—shut them up, no doubt! Because we'd have to, you know. As soon as the rumor gets around
460 that the water is dangerous, we won't have a visitor left. And that's the picture, Thomas—you have it in your power to literally ruin your own town.

STOCKMANN (*Rises.*). Now look, Peter! I don't want to ruin anything.

PETER. Thomas, your report has not convinced me that the conditions are as dangerous as you try to make them.

STOCKMANN. Now, listen, they are even worse
470 than the report makes them out to be. Remember, summer is coming, and the warm weather.

PETER. *I* think you're exaggerating. A capable physician ought to know what precautions to take.

STOCKMANN. And then what?

PETER. The existing water supplies for the Springs are a fact, Thomas, and they've got to be treated as a fact. If you are reasonable and act with discretion, the Directors of the Institute
480 will be inclined to take under consideration any means to reasonably and without financial sacrifices make possible improvements.

STOCKMANN. Dear God, do you think for one minute that I would ever agree to such trickery?

PETER. Trickery?

STOCKMANN. Yes, a trick, a fraud, a lie, a treachery—a downright crime against the public and against the whole community.

PETER. I said before that I'm not convinced
490 that there is any actual danger.

STOCKMANN. Oh, you aren't? Anything else is impossible! My report is an absolute fact. (*Turns, violently replaces chair, steps* D.) The only trouble is that you and your administration were the ones who insisted that the water supply be built where it is, and now you're afraid to admit the blunder you committed. Damn it! Don't you think I can see through it all?

PETER (*Rises, crosses* D. C.). All right, let's
500 suppose that is true. Maybe I do care a little about my reputation. I still say I do it for the good of the town; without moral authority there can be no government. *And that is why, Thomas, it is my duty to prevent your report from reaching the Board.* Some time later I will bring up the matter for discussion. In the meantime, not a single word is to reach the public.

STOCKMANN. Oh, my dear Peter, do you imagine you can prevent that!

PETER. It will be prevented. 510

STOCKMANN. It can't be. There are too many people who already know about it.

PETER. Who? (*Angered.*) It can't possibly be those people from the *Daily Messenger* who . . .

STOCKMANN. Exactly. The liberal, free and independent press will stand up and do its duty!

PETER. You are an unbelievably irresponsible man, Thomas. Can't you imagine what consequences that is going to have for you?

STOCKMANN. For me? 520

PETER. Yes, for you and your family.

STOCKMANN (*Turning away.*). What the hell are you saying now?

PETER. I believe I have the right to think of myself as a helpful brother, Thomas.

STOCKMANN. You have been and I thank you deeply for it.

PETER. Don't mention it. I often couldn't help myself. I had hoped that by improving your finances I would be able to keep you from run- 530 ning *completely* hog-wild.

STOCKMANN. You mean it was only for your own sake?

PETER. Partly yes. What do you imagine people think of an official whose closest relatives get themselves into trouble time and time again?

STOCKMANN. And that's what I've done?

PETER. You do it without knowing it—you're like a man with an automatic brain—as soon as an idea breaks into your head, no matter how 540 idiotic it may be—you get up like a sleep-walker and start writing a pamphlet.

STOCKMANN (*Steps to* PETER.). Peter, don't you think it's a citizen's duty to share a new idea with the public?

PETER (*Crossing* D. L. C.). The public doesn't need new ideas—the public is much better off with old ideas.

STOCKMANN. You're not even embarrassed to say that? 550

PETER (*Crossing to* STOCKMANN.). Now look, I am going to lay this out once and for all.

You're always barking about authority. If a man gives you an order, he's persecuting you. Nothing is important enough to respect, once you decide to revolt against your superiors. All right, then, I give up. I'm not going to try to change you any more. I told you the stakes you are playing for here, and now I'm going to give you an order and I warn you, you'd better obey it if you value your career.

STOCKMANN. What kind of an order?

PETER. You are going to deny these rumors officially.

STOCKMANN. How?

PETER. You simply say that you went into the examination of the water more thoroughly and you find that you overestimated the danger.

STOCKMANN. I see!

PETER. And that you have complete confidence that whatever improvements are needed, the management will certainly take care of them.

STOCKMANN. My convictions come from the conditions of the water. My convictions will change when the water changes, and for no other reason.

PETER. What are you talking about convictions? You're an official, you keep your convictions to yourself!

STOCKMANN. To myself?!

PETER. As an official, I said. God knows as a private person that is something else, but as a subordinate employee of the Institute, you have no right to express any convictions or personal opinions about anything connected with policy!

STOCKMANN. Now you listen to me! I am a doctor and a scientist!!

PETER. What's this got to do with science?

STOCKMANN. And I have the right to express my opinion on anything in the world!

PETER. Not about the Institute—that I forbid.

STOCKMANN. You forbid!

PETER. I forbid you as your superior, and when I give orders you obey.

STOCKMANN (*Turning away from* PETER.). Peter, if you weren't my brother . . .

PETRA (*Throws* L. *door open, flies in,* CATHERINE *tries to restrain her,* PETRA *crosses to* L. *of* PETER.). Father! You aren't going to stand for this!

CATHERINE (*Following* PETRA.). Petra, Petra . . .

PETER. What have you two been doing, eavesdropping?

CATHERINE. You were talking so loud we couldn't help . . .

PETRA (*Interrupting.*). Yes, I was eavesdropping.

PETER (*Crossing below* STOCKMANN *to his* R.). That makes me very happy.

STOCKMANN (*Moving* L.). You said something to me about forbidding——

PETER. You forced me to.

STOCKMANN. So, you want me to spit in my own face officially, is that it?

PETER. Why must you always be so colorful?

STOCKMANN. And if I don't obey?

PETER. Then we will publish our own statement, to calm the public.

STOCKMANN. Good enough! And I will write against you. I will stick to what I said, and I will prove that I am right and that you are wrong, and what will you do then?

PETER. Then I simply won't be able to prevent your dismissal.

STOCKMANN (*Steps back.*). What!
PETRA (*Steps to* C.). Father! } (*Together.*)

PETER. Dismissed from the Institute is what I said. If you want to make war on Kirsten Springs, you have no right to be on the Board of Directors.

STOCKMANN. You'd dare to do that?

PETER. Oh, no, you're the daring man.

PETRA (*Crossing to* PETER, *below* STOCKMANN, *who crosses* D. C., *head in hands.*). Uncle, this is a rotten way to treat a man like Father.

CATHERINE (*Crossing below* STOCKMANN, *to* PETRA.). Will you be quiet, Petra.

PETER. So young and you've got opinions already—but that's natural. (*To* CATHERINE.) Catherine, dear, you're probably the only sane person in this house. Knock some sense into his head, will you? Make him realize what he's driving his whole family into.

STOCKMANN (*Crossing below to* PETER, *puts family behind him.*). My family concerns nobody but myself.

PETER. His family and his own town!

STOCKMANN. I'm going to show you who loves his town. The people are going to get the full stink of this corruption, Peter, and then we will see who loves his town.

PETER. You love your town when you blindly,

spitefully, stubbornly go ahead trying to cut off our most important industry?

STOCKMANN. That source is poisoned, man. We are getting fat by peddling filth and corruption to innocent people!

660 PETER. I think this has gone beyond opinions and convictions, Thomas. A man who can throw that kind of insinuation around is nothing but a traitor to society!

STOCKMANN (*Striving to control self.*). How dare you to . . . ?

CATHERINE (*Running in front of* STOCKMANN; PETRA *pulls* STOCKMANN *back.*). Tom!

PETRA (*Grabbing* STOCKMANN'S *arm.*). Be careful, Father!

670 PETER (*Taking hat, starting out* U. R., *with dignity.*). I won't expose myself to violence. You have been warned. Consider what you owe yourself and your family. Good day! (*He exits* U. R., *leaving front door open.*)

STOCKMANN (*Pacing* D. R., *then back to* D. L.). He's insulted! *He's* insulted!

CATHERINE (*Crossing* U. C., D. R., *then* L.). It's shameful, Thomas.

PETRA (*Crossing* U. L. C., *to stove, then* R. *to* 680 *look after* PETER, *back to* C. *at* R. *of* CATHERINE.). Oh, I would love to give him a piece of my mind.

STOCKMANN (*Still pacing.*). It was my own fault—I should have shown my teeth right from the beginning. He called me a traitor to society. Me! Damn it all, that is not going to stick.

CATHERINE. Please, think; he's got all the power on his side.

STOCKMANN. Yes, but I have the truth on 690 mine.

CATHERINE. Without power, what good is the truth? (*All turn and look at her.*)

STOCKMANN (*Crosses to* CATHERINE.). That's ridiculous, Catherine. I have the liberal press with me and the majority, the solid majority. If that isn't power, what is?

CATHERINE. But for Heaven's sake, Tom, you aren't going to . . . ?

STOCKMANN. What am I not going to do——?

700 CATHERINE. You aren't going to fight it out in public with your brother!

STOCKMANN. What the hell else do you want me to do?

CATHERINE. But it won't do you any earthly good—if they won't do it, they won't. All you'll get out of it is a notice that you're fired.

STOCKMANN. I am going to do my duty, Catherine. Me, the man he calls a traitor to society!

CATHERINE. And how about your duty to 710 your family—the people you're supposed to provide for?

PETRA. Don't always think of us first, Mother.

CATHERINE. You can talk—if worst comes to worst, you can manage for yourself, but what about the boys, Tom, and you and me?

STOCKMANN. What about you? You want me to be the miserable animal who'd crawl up the boots of that damn gang? Will you be happy if I can't face *myself* the rest of my life? 720

CATHERINE. Tom, Tom, there's so much injustice in the world—you've simply got to learn to live with it. If you go on this way, God help us, we'll have no money again. Is it so long since the North that you have forgotten what it was to live like we lived? (MORTEN *and* EJLIF *enter hall* U. R. *with school-books.* CATHERINE *sees them.*) Haven't we had enough of that for one lifetime? What will happen to them? We've got nothing if you are fired . . . ! (*The boys have* 730 *entered heartily; they cross* D. R., *then to* R. *of family.*)

STOCKMANN (*After seeing boys enter.*). Stop it! (*To boys, who are frightened by this scene.*) Well, boys, did you learn anything in school today?

MORTEN. We learned what an insect is . . .

STOCKMANN. You don't say!

MORTEN (*To* STOCKMANN.). What happened here? (*Crosses to* L. *of* STOCKMANN; *to* CATHERINE.) Why is everybody . . . ? 740

STOCKMANN (*Calming boys.*). Nothing, nothing! You know what I'm going to do, boys? From now on, I'm going to *teach you what a man is!* (CATHERINE *cries.*)

MEDIUM FAST CURTAIN

ACT TWO *Scene One*

The Editorial Office of "The People's Daily Messenger." The front door of the office is D. R. U. R. *is* BILLING'S *desk and chair. A wastebasket is downstage of desk. A large table, covered with newspapers, measures, etc., is* C. *with two chairs,* U. *and* R. *A door leading to printing shop is* U. L. D. L. *is a door to a small room. The room is dingy and cheerless, the furniture shabby, the chairs dirty.*

BILLING *is sitting at his desk* U. R., *reading* STOCKMANN'S *manuscript. After a moment,* HOVSTAD *enters* U. L., *carrying a ruler.* BILLING *looks up.*

BILLING. Doctor not come yet?

HOVSTAD (*Crossing to* BILLING, *looks over his shoulder.*). No, not yet. You finish it. (BILLING *holds up a hand to signal "just a moment." He reads on. After a moment he closes manuscript with a bang, glances up at* HOVSTAD *with some trepidation, then looks off.* HOVSTAD, *looking at* BILLING, *walks a few steps to* C. D. *table, sets ruler down, puts on coat.*) Well? What do you think of it?

BILLING (*As though with some hesitation.*). It's devastating. The Doctor is a brilliant man. I swear I myself never really understood how incompetent those fat fellows are, on top. (*Holding manuscript, rises, waves it a little.*) I hear the rumble of revolution in this.

HOVSTAD (*Glances at* U. L. *door, takes* BILLING D. R. C.). Sssh! Aslaksen's inside.

BILLING. Aslaksen's a coward. With all that moderation talk, all he's saying is, he's yellow. You're going to print this, aren't you?

HOVSTAD. Sure, I'm just waiting for the Doctor to give the word. And if his brother hasn't given in, we put it on the press anyway.

BILLING. Yes, but if the Mayor is against this it's going to get pretty rough. You know that, don't you?

HOVSTAD. Just let him try to block that reconstruction—the little businessmen and the whole town'll be screaming for his head. Aslaksen'll see to that.

BILLING (*Holding up manuscript.*). But the stockholders'll have to lay out a fortune of money if this goes through.

HOVSTAD. My boy, I think it's going to bust them! And when the Springs go busted, the people are finally going to understand the level of genius that's been running this town. Those five sheets of paper are going to put in a liberal administration once and for all.

BILLING. It's a revolution. You know that? (*With hope and fear.*) I mean it, we're on the edge of a real revolution! (STOCKMANN *enters* D. R., *takes manuscript from* BILLING, *holds it out to* HOVSTAD, *but doesn't give it to him.*)

STOCKMANN. Put it on the press!

BILLING (*Over* STOCKMANN'S *lines, crossing* U. L., *calling into shop.*). Mr. Aslaksen! The Doctor's here! (*Crosses* D. *to* L. C.)

HOVSTAD. Wonderful! What'd the Mayor say?

STOCKMANN. The Mayor has declared war, so war is what it's going to be. (*Crosses back in front of* HOVSTAD.) And this is only the beginning! You know what he tried to do? . . . He actually tried to blackmail me! He's got the nerve to tell me that I'm not allowed to speak my mind without his permission. Imagine the shameless effrontery!

HOVSTAD. He actually said it right out!?

STOCKMANN. Right to my face! The trouble with me was I kept giving them credit for being our kind of people, but they're *dictators!* (ASLAKSEN *enters* U. L., *crosses* U. *to* R. *of* STOCKMANN.) They're people who'll try to hold power even if they have to poison the town to do it!

ASLAKSEN. Now take it easy, Doctor, you

. . . mustn't always be throwing accusations. I'm with you, you understand, but—moderation.

STOCKMANN (*Cutting him off.*). What'd you think of the article, Hovstad?

HOVSTAD. It's a masterpiece. In one blow you've managed to prove beyond any doubt what kind of men are running us.

ASLAKSEN. May we print it now, then?

STOCKMANN. I should say *so!*

HOVSTAD (*Reaching for manuscript.*). We'll have it ready for tomorrow's paper.

STOCKMANN. And, listen, Mr. Aslaksen, do me a favor, will you? You run a fine paper, but supervise the printing personally, heh? I'd hate to see the weather report stuck into the middle of my article.

ASLAKSEN (*Laughs.*). Don't worry, there won't be a mistake this time!

STOCKMANN. Make it perfect, heh? Like you were printing money. You can't imagine how I'm dying to see it in print. After all the lies in the papers, the half lies, the quarter lies—to finally see the absolute, unvarnished truth about something important . . . ! And this is only the beginning. We'll go on to other subjects, and blow up every lie we live by! What do you say, Aslaksen?

ASLAKSEN (*Nods in agreement, but.*). Just remember . . .

BILLING and HOVSTAD (*Together with* ASLAKSEN.). "Moderation!" (BILLING *and* HOVSTAD *are greatly amused.*)

ASLAKSEN (*To* BILLING *and* HOVSTAD.). I don't see what's so funny about that!

BILLING (*Crossing above table to* STOCKMANN, *enthralled.* HOVSTAD *gives* L.). Doctor Stockmann . . . I feel as though I were standing in some historic painting. Goddammit, this is a historic day! Some day this scene'll be in a museum. Entitled, "The Day the Truth Was Born." (*All are embarrassed by this.* ASLAKSEN *and* HOVSTAD *look away.*)

STOCKMANN (*Suddenly.*). Oh! I've got a patient half-bandaged down the road. (*Crosses to door* D. R., *returns and exclaims "Oh," gives* BILLING *manuscript.* BILLING *follows, takes manuscript from* STOCKMANN, *who exits* D. R.)

HOVSTAD (*Moving to* ASLAKSEN.). I hope you realize how useful he could be to us.

ASLAKSEN (*Crossing* HOVSTAD *to* D. L. C.). I don't like that business about "this is only the beginning." Let him stick to the Springs.

BILLING (*Crossing* HOVSTAD *to* ASLAKSEN. HOVSTAD *takes manuscript from* BILLING, *studies it.*) What makes you so scared all the time?

ASLAKSEN. I have to live here. It'd be different if he were attacking the national Government or something, but if he thinks I'm going to start going after the whole town administration . . .

BILLING. What's the difference, bad is bad!

ASLAKSEN. Yes, but there is a difference. You attack the national Government, what's going to happen? Nothing. They go right on. But a town administration—they're liable to be overthrown or something! I represent the small property owners in this town . . .

BILLING. Ha! It's always the same. Give a man a little property and the truth can go to hell!

ASLAKSEN. Mr. Billing, I'm older than you are; I've seen fire-eaters before. (*Points to* BILLING's *desk.*) You know who used to work at your desk before you? Councilman Stensford—*Councilman!*

BILLING. Just because I work at a renegade's desk, does that mean . . . ?

ASLAKSEN. You're a politician; a politician never knows where he's going to end up. And, besides, you applied for a job as secretary to the Magistrate, didn't you?

HOVSTAD. Billing!

BILLING (*To* HOVSTAD.). Well, why not? If I get it I'll have a chance to put across some good things——(*Turns back to* ASLAKSEN.) I could put plenty of big boys on the spot with a job like that!

ASLAKSEN. All right, I'm just saying . . . People change. Just remember, when you call me a coward—I may not have made the hot speeches, but I never went back on my beliefs, either. Unlike some of the big radicals around here, I didn't change. Of course, I *am* a little more moderate . . .

HOVSTAD. Oh, God!

ASLAKSEN (*Glaring at* HOVSTAD.). I don't see what's so funny about that! (*He goes out* D. L.)

BILLING (*After watching him off.*). If we could get rid of him, we . . .

HOVSTAD. Take it easy, he pays the printing

bill, he's not that bad. (*Crosses to* BILLING, *with manuscript.*) I'll get the printer on this . . . (*Starts out to* U. L. *door.*)

BILLING. Say, Hovstad, how about asking Stockmann to back us? Then we could really put out a paper!

HOVSTAD. What would he do for money?

BILLING. His father-in-law.

HOVSTAD. Kiil? Since when has he got money?

180

BILLING. I think he's loaded with it.

HOVSTAD. No! Really, as long as I've known him, he's worn the same overcoat, the same suit . . .

BILLING. Yeah, and the same ring on his right hand. You ever get a look at that boulder? (*Points to his finger.*)

HOVSTAD. No, I never . . .

BILLING. All year he wears the diamond inside. But on New Year's Eve, he turns it around.

190

Figure it out, when a man has no visible means of support, what's he living on?—Money, right? Now, my idea is . . . (PETRA *enters* D. R., *carrying a book.*)

PETRA. Hello.

HOVSTAD (*Stepping down a little.*). Well, fancy seeing you here! Sit down, what . . . ?

PETRA (*Tossing book on* BILLING'S *desk with a certain peeve.*). I want to ask you something.

BILLING (*Crossing* U. *to desk.*). What's that?

200

PETRA. That English novel you wanted translated.

HOVSTAD. Aren't you going to do it?

PETRA (*Crossing to* HOVSTAD *at* C.). I don't get this?

HOVSTAD. You don't get what?

PETRA. This book is absolutely against everything you people believe.

HOVSTAD. Oh, it isn't that bad . . . (*Looks at* BILLING; *neither has read it.*)

210

PETRA. But, Mr. Hovstad, it says if you're good there's a super-natural force that'll fix it so you end up happy. And if you're bad, you'll be punished. Since when does the world work that way?

HOVSTAD. Yeah, but, Petra, this is a newspaper; people like to read that kind of thing. They buy the paper for that and then we slip in our political stuff. A newspaper can't buck the public . . .

220

PETRA. You don't say! (*She starts to go out* D. R. HOVSTAD *hurries to her, grabs her arm at door, holds her.*)

HOVSTAD. Now, wait a minute. I don't want you to go feeling that way. (*Holds out manuscript to* BILLING.) Here, take this to the printer, will you?

BILLING (*Taking it.*). Sure. (*He exits* U. L.)

HOVSTAD (*Leading her back to* C.). I just want you to understand something: I never even read that book. It was Billing's idea.

230

PETRA. I thought he was a radical.

HOVSTAD. He is. But he's also a . . .

PETRA. A newspaper man.

HOVSTAD. Well, that, too. But I was going to say that Billing is trying to get the job as secretary to the Magistrate.

PETRA. What?

HOVSTAD. People are people, Miss Stockmann.

PETRA. But, the Magistrate! He's been fighting everything progressive in this town for thirty years.

240

HOVSTAD. Let's not argue about it, I just didn't want you to go out of here with a wrong idea of me. I guess you know that I . . . happen to admire women like you. I've never had a chance to tell you, but I . . . well, I want you to know it. Do you mind? (*He smiles.*)

PETRA. No, I don't mind, but reading that book upset me. I really don't understand. . . . Will you tell me why you're supporting my father?

250

HOVSTAD. What's the mystery? It's a matter of principle.

PETRA. But a paper that'll print a book like that has no principle.

HOVSTAD. Why do you jump to such extremes! You're just like . . .

PETRA. Like what?

HOVSTAD. I simply meant that . . .

260

PETRA. Like my father, you meant. You really have no use for him, do you?

HOVSTAD (*Chiding a little, takes her arms, guides her back.*). Now wait a minute!

PETRA. What's behind this? Are you just trying to hold my hand or something?

HOVSTAD. I happen to agree with your father, and that's why I'm printing his stuff! Nothing would please me more than to hold your hand, Miss Stockmann, but I assure you this . . .

270

PETRA. You're trying to put something over, I think. Why are you in this?

HOVSTAD. Who are you accusing? Billing gave you that book, not me!

PETRA. But you don't mind printing it, do you? What're you trying to do with my father?—you have no principles, what are you up to here?! (ASLAKSEN, *manuscript in his hand, hurriedly enters from* D. L. *door, looking off. He closes door.*)

280

ASLAKSEN. My God! Hovstad! (*Sees* PETRA, *stops.* PETRA, *frightened, jumps to* R. *of* HOVSTAD.) Miss Stockmann!

PETRA. I don't think I've been so frightened in my life. (*She goes out* D. R. HOVSTAD *starts after her.*)

HOVSTAD (*Following her.*). Please, you mustn't think I . . .

ASLAKSEN (*As* HOVSTAD *starts to move, following and stopping him.*). Where are you going? The Mayor's out there.

290

HOVSTAD. The Mayor!

ASLAKSEN. He wants to speak to you. He came in the back door. He doesn't want to be seen.

HOVSTAD (*Crossing to* D. L. *door.*). What does he want?

ASLAKSEN. I'll watch for anyone coming in here.

300

HOVSTAD (*Opening* D. L. *door.*). Come in, Your Honor!

PETER (*Entering* D. L. *and looking the place over.*). Thank you. (*He crosses* HOVSTAD. HOVSTAD *carefully closes* D. L. *door.*) It's clean! I always imagined this place would look dirty. But it's clean. (*Sets hat on* BILLING'S *desk.*) Very nice, Mr. Aslaksen.

ASLAKSEN. Not at all, Your Honor. I mean to say I always . . .

310

HOVSTAD (*Crossing to* L. *of table.*). What can I do for you, Your Honor? (*Offers him* U. L. *chair, but* PETER *is sitting in* L. C. *chair.*) Sit down?

PETER. I had a very annoying thing happen today, Mr. Hovstad.

HOVSTAD. That so?

PETER. It seems my brother has written some sort of . . . memorandum. About the Springs.

320

HOVSTAD. You don't say! (ASLAKSEN *starts to fade to* U. L. *door.*)

PETER (*Looking at* HOVSTAD *now.*). Ah . . . he mentioned it . . . to you?

HOVSTAD. Ah . . . yes. I think he said something about it.

PETER (*Points to manuscript, stopping* ASLAKSEN *at* U. L. *door.*) That's it, isn't it?

ASLAKSEN. This? (*Crosses to* R. *of* PETER.) I don't know, I haven't had a chance to look at it, the printer just handed it to me . . .

330

HOVSTAD (*Crossing* U. *a little, speaking behind* PETER.). Isn't that the thing the printer wanted the spelling checked?

ASLAKSEN. That's it, it's only a question of spelling. I'll be right back . . .

PETER. I'm very good at spelling. (*Holds out his hand.*) Maybe I can help you?

HOVSTAD. No, Your Honor, there's some Latin in it . . . you wouldn't know Latin, would you?

340

PETER. Oh, yes. I used to help my brother with his Latin all the time. Let me have it. (ASLAKSEN *gives him manuscript.* PETER *looks at title on first page, then glances up at* HOVSTAD, *who avoids his eyes.*) You're going to print this?

HOVSTAD. I can't very well refuse a signed article. A signed article is the author's responsibility.

PETER (*Holding up manuscript.*). Mr. Aslaksen, you're going to allow this?

350

ASLAKSEN. I'm the publisher, not the editor, Your Honor. My policy is, freedom for the editor.

PETER. You have a point; I can see that.

ASLAKSEN (*Reaching for manuscript.*). So if you don't mind . . .

PETER. Not at all. (*But he holds on to manuscript.*) This reconstruction of the Springs . . .

ASLAKSEN. I realize, Your Honor, it does mean tremendous sacrifices for the stockholders . . .

360

PETER. Don't upset yourself. The first thing a Mayor learns is that the less wealthy can always be prevailed upon to demand a spirit of sacrifice for the public good.

ASLAKSEN. I'm glad you see that.

PETER. Oh, yes. Especially when it's the wealthy who are going to do the sacrificing. What you don't seem to understand, Mr. Aslaksen, is that so long as I am Mayor, any changes in those baths are going to be paid for by a municipal loan.

370

ASLAKSEN. A municipal . . . You mean you're going to tax the people for this?

PETER. Exactly.

HOVSTAD. But the Springs are a private corporation . . .

PETER (*Sets cane on table.*). The corporation built Kirsten Springs out of its own money. If the people want them changed, the people naturally must pay the bill. The corporation is in no position to put out any more money. It simply can't do it.

ASLAKSEN. That's impossible. People will never stand for another tax. (*To* PETER.) Is this a fact, or your opinion?

PETER. It happens to be a fact. Plus another fact—you'll forgive me for talking about facts in a newspaper office—but don't forget that the Springs will take two years to make over. Two years without income for your small businessmen, Mr. Aslaksen, and a heavy new tax, besides. And all because . . . (*Throttling manuscript in his hand.*) because of this dream, this hallucination that we live in a pest-hole . . .

HOVSTAD. That's based on science . . .

PETER (*Throwing manuscript on table.*). This is based on vindictiveness, on his hatred of authority, and nothing else. (*Pounds fist on manuscript.*) This is the mad dream of a man who is trying to blow up our way of life! It has nothing to do with reform or science or anything else but pure and simple destruction! And I intend to see to it that the people understand it exactly so!

ASLAKSEN (*Hit by this.*). My God! Maybe . . . (*Crosses* PETER *to* R. *of* HOVSTAD, *takes* HOVSTAD D. L.) You sure you want to support this thing, Hovstad?

HOVSTAD (*Nervously.*). Frankly, I'd never thought of it in quite that way. I mean . . . (*Crosses above* ASLAKSEN; *to* PETER.) When you think of it psychologically it's completely possible, of course, that the man is simply out to . . . I don't know what to say, Your Honor. I'd hate to hurt the town in any way . . . I never imagined we'd have to have a new tax.

PETER. You should have imagined it, because you're going to have to advocate it. Unless, of course, liberal and radical newspaper readers enjoy high taxes. . . . (*Takes own manuscript out of inside coat pocket.*) You'd know that better than I, of course. I happen to have here a brief story of the actual facts. It proves that with a little care, nobody need be harmed at all by the water. Of course, in time we'd have to make a few minor structural changes, and we'd pay for those.

HOVSTAD. May I see that?

PETER. I want you to *study* it, Mr. Hovstad, and see if you don't agree that . . . (BILLING *hurries in quickly from* U. L., *closing door, comes* D. *around back of table.*)

BILLING. Are you expecting the Doctor?

PETER (*Alarmed, rising quickly, replacing manuscript in pocket.*). He's here?

BILLING (*Motioning to street at* R.). He's just crossing the street. (ASLAKSEN *crosses quickly to* D. R. *door.*)

PETER. I'd rather not run into him here. How can I . . . ?

BILLING (*Taking* PETER *to* D. L. *door.*). Right this way, sir. Hurry up. . . .

ASLAKSEN (*At* R. *door, peeking.*). Hurry up!

PETER (*Going out* D. L. *door with* BILLING.). Get him out of here right away!

HOVSTAD (*Covering* STOCKMANN's *manuscript with papers on table, sitting in* D. C. *chair.*). Do something, do something! (ASLAKSEN *rushes to* BILLING's *desk, turns chair up, sits and becomes very, very busy, seating himself to cover hat.*)

STOCKMANN (*Entering* D. R. *and crossing* C.). Any proofs yet? (*Looks at* HOVSTAD, *then at* ASLAKSEN.) I guess not, heh?

ASLAKSEN (*Without turning.*). No, you can't expect them for some time.

STOCKMANN. You mind if I wait?

HOVSTAD (*Trying to smile.*). No sense in that, Doctor; it'll be quite a while yet.

STOCKMANN (*Laughing, places his hand on* HOVSTAD's *back.*). Bear with me, Hovstad, I just can't wait to see it in print.

HOVSTAD. We're pretty busy, Doctor, so . . .

STOCKMANN (*Starting for* D. R. *door.*). Don't let me hold you up. That's the way to be, busy, busy. We'll make this town shine like a jewel! (*Exits* D. R. *After a moment he returns.*) Just one thing, I . . .

HOVSTAD. Couldn't we talk some other time? We're very . . .

STOCKMANN. Two words. Just walking down the street now, I looked at the people, in the stores, driving the wagons, and suddenly I was . . . well, touched, you know? By their innocence, I mean. What I'm driving at is when this exposé breaks, they're liable to start making a saint out of me or something, and I . . . (*Moves to* ASLAKSEN.) Aslaksen, I want you to promise me that you're not going to try to get up any dinner for me, or . . .

480

ASLAKSEN (*Rising.*). Doctor, there's no use concealing . . .

STOCKMANN. I knew it! Now look, I will simply not attend a dinner in my honor.

HOVSTAD (*Rising.*). Doctor, I think it's time we . . . (CATHERINE *enters* D. R. *and crosses to* STOCKMANN.)

CATHERINE. I thought so! Thomas, I want you home. Now come. I want you to talk to Petra. (*She returns to* D. R. *door.*)

490

STOCKMANN. What happened? What are you doing here?

HOVSTAD. Something wrong, Mrs. Stockmann?

CATHERINE (*Crossing to* HOVSTAD.). Doctor Stockmann is the father of three children, Mr. Hovstad!

STOCKMANN. Now look, dear, everybody knows that, what's the . . .

500

CATHERINE (*Restraining an outburst at* STOCKMANN.). Nobody would believe it from the way you're dragging us into this disaster!

HOVSTAD. Oh, now, Mrs. Stockmann . . .

STOCKMANN. What disaster?

CATHERINE (*To* HOVSTAD.). He treats you like a son and you want to make a fool of him.

HOVSTAD (*Gives way,* CATHERINE *follows.*). *I'm* not making a . . .

STOCKMANN. Catherine, how can you accuse . . .

510

CATHERINE (*To* HOVSTAD, *backs him to below table.*). He'll lose his job at the Springs, do you realize that? You print the article and they'll grind him up like a piece of flesh!

STOCKMANN (*Putting hat on table.*). Catherine, you're embarrassing me! I beg your pardon, gentlemen . . .

CATHERINE. Mr. Hovstad, what are you up to?

STOCKMANN. I won't have you jumping at Hovstad, Catherine!

520

CATHERINE (*To* STOCKMANN.). I want you home! This man is not your friend!

STOCKMANN. He is my friend—any man who shares my risk is my friend! You simply don't understand that as soon as this breaks, everybody in this town is going to come out in the streets . . . (*Picks up cane from table.*) and drive that gang of . . . (*He notices cane, recognizes it, looks at* HOVSTAD, *then* ASLAKSEN.) What's this? (*No reply. He looks from* ASLAKSEN *to desk, sees hat and picks it up on cane, comes* D. *As he goes to desk,* ASLAKSEN *crosses to* D. *of table,* CATHERINE *goes around* L. *and* U. *of table.*) What the hell is he doing here?

530

ASLAKSEN. All right, Doctor, now let's be calm and . . .

STOCKMANN (*Crossing* D. L., ASLAKSEN *and* HOVSTAD *give up,* CATHERINE *backs to* D. R. *end of table, looking at door.*). Where is he? What'd he do, talk you out of it? Hovstad! (*No reply.*) He won't get away with it; where'd you hide him? (*Opens door* D. L.)

540

ASLAKSEN. Be careful, Doctor! (PETER *enters* D. L. *and crosses* D. R. C. BILLING *enters* D. L. *and stands* D. L., *closes door.* PETER *is trying to hide his embarrassment.*)

STOCKMANN (*Crossing to* PETER *at* R. C.). Well, Peter! Poisoning the water wasn't enough, you're working on the press now, eh?

550

PETER. My hat, please. And my stick. (STOCKMANN *puts on* PETER's *hat.*) Now what's *this* nonsense? Take that off, that's official insignia!

STOCKMANN. I just wanted you to realize, Peter . . . (*Takes off hat.*) that anyone may wear this hat in a democracy, and . . . (*Handing him hat.*) that a free citizen is not afraid to touch it. And as for the baton of command, Your Honor, it can pass from hand to hand. So don't gloat yet. (*Hands stick to* PETER.) The people haven't spoken. (*Turning to* HOVSTAD *and* ASLAKSEN.) And I have the people because I have the truth, my friends.

560

ASLAKSEN (*Moving down.*). Doctor, we're not scientists; we can't judge whether your article is really true.

STOCKMANN. Then print it under my name; let *me* defend it!

HOVSTAD (*Moving down.*). I'm not printing it. I'm not going to sacrifice this newspaper. When the whole story gets out the public is not going to stand for any changes in the Springs.

570

ASLAKSEN. His Honor just told us, Doctor. You see, there will have to be a new tax . . .

STOCKMANN. Ahhh! Yes. I see! That's why

you're not scientists suddenly and can't decide if I'm telling the truth. Well, so.

HOVSTAD. Don't take that attitude. The point is . . .

STOCKMANN (*Crossing to* ASLAKSEN; CATHERINE *gives* R.). The point, the point, oh, the point is going to fly through this town like an arrow, and I'm going to fire it! Will you print this article as a pamphlet? I'll pay for it.

ASLAKSEN. I'm not going to ruin this paper or this town. Doctor, for the sake of your family . . .

CATHERINE (*Picking up hat from table, moving* D. *to* L. *of* STOCKMANN.). You can leave his family out of this, Mr. Aslaksen. God help me, I think you people are horrible!

STOCKMANN. My article, if you don't mind!

ASLAKSEN (*Giving it to him.*). Doctor, you won't get it printed in this town.

PETER. Can't you forget it? (*Indicating* HOVSTAD *and* ASLAKSEN.) Can't you see now that everybody . . . ?

STOCKMANN. Your Honor, I can't forget it, and you will never forget it as long as you live. I'm going to call a mass meeting and I . . .

PETER. And who is going to rent you a hall?

STOCKMANN. Then I will take a drum and go from—(*Crosses to* PETER.) street to street proclaiming that the springs are befouled and poison is rotting the body politic!

PETER. And I believe you really are that mad!

STOCKMANN (*Waving manuscript in his hand.*). Mad? Oh, my brother, you haven't even heard me raise my voice yet. Catherine? (*He holds out his* L. *arm, she takes it. They cross* PETER *and go stiffly out* D. R. PETER *shakes his head regretfully, reaches into pocket, takes out his own manuscript, looks at* ASLAKSEN, *who crosses and takes it.* ASLAKSEN *quickly looks at* HOVSTAD, *who crosses and takes it.* HOVSTAD *looks at* BILLING, *who crosses and takes it, gestures a salute and exits* U. L. PETER *acknowledges* BILLING'S *salute as*)

FAST CURTAIN

Scene Two

A room in CAPTAIN HORSTER'S *house. The room is bare, as though unused for a long time. There is a platform* R. *of* C. *with a chair and a small table on it.* R. *of platform are two small chairs.* D. L. *is a highbacked chair. Two windows with shutters are in back wall. A shelf is between them. There is a doorway* D. R. *and an archway in* L. *wall, which leads to a doorway.*

At rise, the stage is empty. CAPTAIN HORSTER *enters from* R., *carrying a pitcher of water on a tray with two glasses. As he is putting these on the table,* BILLING *enters* L.

BILLING. Captain Horster?

HORSTER (*Tidying up platform table; doesn't see* BILLING.). Oh, come in. I don't have enough chairs for a lot of people, so I decided not to have chairs at all.

BILLING. My name is Billing. Don't you remember, at the Doctor's house?

HORSTER (*A little coldly.*). Oh, yes, sure—I've been so busy I didn't recognize you. (*Crosses* BILLING *to* U. L. C. *window, looks out.*) Why don't those people come inside?

BILLING. I don't know. I guess they're waiting for the Mayor or somebody important so they can be sure it's respectable in here. I wanted to ask you a question before it begins, Captain. (HORSTER *crosses to* BILLING.) Why are you lending your house for this? I never heard of you connected with anything political.

HORSTER. I'll answer that. I travel most of the year . . . Did you ever travel?

BILLING. Not abroad, no.

HORSTER. Well, I've been in a lot of places where people aren't allowed to say unpopular things. Did you know that?

40 BILLING. Sure, I've read about it.

HORSTER (*Simply.*). Well, I don't like it. (*Starts to go out* D. R.)

BILLING (*Dutifully writes down "doesn't like it."*). One more question. (HORSTER *stops.*) What's your opinion about the Doctor's proposition to rebuild the Springs?

HORSTER (*After a moment.*). Don't understand a thing about it. (HORSTER *sees some people in room* U. L., *through door.*) Come in.

50 Come in. (NANSEN, HENRIK *and* EDVARD *enter* L. *and cross* U. C. BILLING *crosses* D. L.) I don't have enough chairs, so you'll just have to stand. (HORSTER *goes out* D. R.)

HENRIK (*As soon as* HORSTER *is off.*). Try the horn.

EDVARD. No, let him start to talk first.

NANSEN (*Taking out horn.*). Wait'll they hear this! I could blow your moustache off with this! (HORSTER *has re-entered* R., *carrying two*

60 *more glasses. Stops on seeing horn.*)

HORSTER (*Setting things on table.*). I don't want any rough-house, you hear me? (CATHERINE *and* PETRA *enter* L.) Come in. I've got chairs just for you. (*As the women move to* HORSTER *at* C. PETRA *crosses* U. *of* CATHERINE *and reaches* HORSTER *first.*)

CATHERINE (*Nervously.*). There's quite a crowd on the sidewalk. Why don't they come in?

HORSTER. I suppose they're waiting for the

70 Mayor.

PETRA. Are all those people on his side?

HORSTER. Who knows? People are bashful . . . (BILLING *crosses to ladies at* C.) and it's so unusual to come to a meeting like this, I suppose they . . .

BILLING (*Taking off hat.*). Good evening, ladies. (CATHERINE *and* PETRA *don't look at him.*) I don't blame you for not speaking. I just wanted to say I don't think this is going to be a place

80 for ladies tonight.

CATHERINE. I don't remember asking your advice, Mr. Billing.

BILLING. I'm not as bad as you think, Mrs. Stockmann.

CATHERINE. Then why did you print the Mayor's statement and not a word about my husband's report? Nobody's had a chance to find out what he really stands for. Why, everybody on the street there is against him already!

BILLING. If we printed his report it only 90 would have hurt your husband.

CATHERINE. Mr. Billing, I've never said this to anyone in my life, but I think you're a liar. (*Suddenly* NANSEN, *who is directly behind* CATHERINE, *lets out a blast on his horn. The women jump.* HORSTER *moves the women* D. L. C., *then goes* U. *to the three men who have moved* U. L. C.)

HORSTER. You do that once more and I'll throw you out of here! (PETER *enters* L., *briskly* 100 *and crosses to women. Behind him are* HEDVIG, GEORG, *and* GUNNAR, *who cross* D. R. *in front of chair.* BILLING *crosses to the men.*)

PETER (*Nodding.*). Catherine? Petra? (HORSTER *crosses* D. *to* R. *of* PETER. GUNNAR *tries to get* EDVARD'S *attention.*)

PETRA. Good evening.

PETER. Why so coldly? He wanted a meeting and he's got it. (*To* HORSTER.) Isn't he here? (*A* DRUNK *crosses to* U. L. *group.* HEDVIG *and* 110 GUNNAR *watch him.*)

HORSTER. The Doctor is going around town to be sure that there's a good attendance. (*He crosses* U. C. *and watches* DRUNK.)

PETER. Fair enough. By the way, Petra, did you paint that poster—the one somebody stuck on the town hall?

PETRA. If you can call it a painting, yes.

PETER. You know I could arrest you, it's against the law to deface the Town Hall. 120

PETRA (*Holding out hands for handcuffs.*). Well, here I am.

CATHERINE. If you arrest her, Peter, I'll never speak to you!

PETER (*Crossing* D. L., *laughing.*). Catherine, you have no sense of humor! (*He sees* HEDVIG, GUNNAR *and* GEORG *in front of his chair. They dart* U. *and he sits.* DRUNK, *egged on by the* U. L. *group, crosses* D. *to* HORSTER.)

DRUNK. Say, friend, who's runnin'! Who's 130 the candidate?!

HORSTER. You're drunk, Mister. Now get out of here.

DRUNK. There's no law says a man who's drunk can't vote!

HORSTER (*Crossing* DRUNK *in front of him, pushes* DRUNK *to* L. *door as crowd laughs.*). Get out of here, get out . . .

DRUNK. I wanna vote! I got a right to vote! (ASLAKSEN *has entered* L. *and* HORSTER *pushes* DRUNK *into him.* ASLAKSEN *recoils upstage;* HORSTER *pushes* DRUNK *out door* L.)

ASLAKSEN (*Hurriedly and covertly crossing* D. *to* PETER.). Your Honor, (*Indicates* L. *door.*) he's . . .

STOCKMANN (*Offstage.*). Right this way, gentlemen! (HOVSTAD *enters* L., *looks around, sees* PETER, *comes* D. *to* L. *of* ASLAKSEN.) In you go, come on, fellows . . . (PAUL *and* KNUT *enter* L., *followed by* STOCKMANN. *Then* TORA, PETER *and* FINN *enter* L. GUNNAR *crosses to* R. *of* HEDVIG *and* HANS, *who are in front of platform.*) Sorry no chairs, gentlemen, but we couldn't get a hall, y'know, so just relax, it won't take long. (STOCKMANN *crosses* C., *sees* PETER.) Glad you're here, Peter!

PETER. Wouldn't miss it for the world.

STOCKMANN (*Crossing to* CATHERINE *and* PETRA, *taking off hat and coat, giving them to* PETRA.). How do you feel, Catherine?

CATHERINE. Just promise me, don't lose your temper . . . (STOCKMANN *helps them to chairs.* CATHERINE *sits in* R. *chair,* PETRA *in* R. *chair. While* HORSTER *is looking* R. DRUNK *enters* L. *and crosses* D. R. C.)

DRUNK. Look, if you ain't votin', what the hell's going on here!

HORSTER (*Starting after him.*). Did I tell you to get out of here?

DRUNK (*Imperiously.*). Don't push.

PETER (*Rising.*). I order you to get out of here and stay out!

DRUNK (*Imperiously.*). I don't like the tone of your voice! And if you don't watch your step I'm gonna tell the *Mayor* right now and he'll throw yiz all in the jug! (*Crowd is laughing,* DRUNK *turns to them.*) What're you, revolution here?! (*Amidst loud laughter,* DRUNK *turns and walks out* L., *immensely pleased with himself.*)

STOCKMANN (*Mounting platform, quieting crowd.*). All right, gentlemen, we might as well begin. Quiet down, please. (*Crowd moves in* L. STOCKMANN *looks at* CATHERINE, *then at crowd.*) The issue is very simple . . .

ASLAKSEN. We haven't elected a chairman, Doctor.

STOCKMANN. I'm sorry, Mr. Aslaksen, this isn't a meeting; I advertised a lecture and I . . .

HENRIK (*Raising hand.*). I came to a meeting, Doctor, there's got to be some kind of control here.

STOCKMANN. What do you mean, control . . . what is there to control?

HEDVIG. Sure, let him speak, this is no meeting!

EDVARD (*Stepping to* PETER.). Your Honor, why don't you take charge of this . . . ?

STOCKMANN. Just a minute now . . .

EDVARD (*Crossing* L. *to in front of* HEDVIG.). Somebody responsible has got to take charge . . . (*To* HEDVIG.) There's a big difference of opinion here . . . (*Returning* L. *of* GUNNAR.)

STOCKMANN. What makes you so sure? You don't even know yet what I'm going to say.

NANSEN. I've got a pretty good idea what you're going to say and I don't like it! If a man doesn't like it here let him go where it suits him better, we don't want any trouble-makers here! (*A low grunt of assent from crowd.* STOCKMANN *looks at them.*)

STOCKMANN. Now look, friend, you don't know anything about me . . .

NANSEN. We know plenty about you, Stockmann.

STOCKMANN. From what, from the newspapers? How do you know I don't like this town? (*Holds up notes.*) I'm here to save the life of this town.

PETER (*Rising quickly.*). Now just a minute, Doctor. (*Crowd quickly becomes silent from* L. *to* R.) I think the democratic thing to do is to elect a chairman.

EDVARD (*Quickly raising his hand.*). I nominate the Mayor!

NANSEN (*Quickly raising his hand.*). Second the Mayor!

PETER. No, no, no. That wouldn't be fair. We want a neutral person. I suggest Mr. Aslaksen who has always . . .

HEDVIG. I came to a lecture, I didn't . . .

NANSEN (*To* HEDVIG.). What're you afraid of a fair fight? (*To* PETER.) Second Mr. Aslaksen! (*Crowd assents: "Very good choice," etc.*)

STOCKMANN. All right, if that's your pleasure. I just want to remind you that the reason I arranged for this lecture was that I have a very important message for you people and . . . (ASLAKSEN *crosses* D. C.; STOCKMANN *gets off platform.*) I couldn't get it into the press and nobody would rent me a hall. (*To* PETER.) I just hope I'll be given time to speak here. (*To* ASLAKSEN.) Mr. Aslaksen? (*The crowd applauds* ASLAKSEN, *who mounts platform.* STOCKMANN *crosses to between* PETRA *and* CATHERINE. KNUT *crosses to* R. *of platform.* NANSEN *crosses and talks to* BILLING. HOVSTAD *crosses* R. *and talks to* PETER. FINN *crosses* D. *to* L. *of* EDVARD. KIIL *enters* L. *and stands just* R. *of* GABRIEL.)

ASLAKSEN. I have just one word before we start. Whatever is said tonight, please remember, the highest civic virtue is moderation. (*He can't help turning to* STOCKMANN, *then looks over to* PETER.) Now if anybody wants to speak . . . (DRUNK *enters* L. *suddenly and crosses* C.)

DRUNK. I heard that! Since when you allowed to electioneer at the polls? (*Crowd pushes him back to door* L. *amid laughter.*) I'm gonna report this to the Mayor, goddammit! (STOCKMANN *crosses* D. L., *looks after* DRUNK.)

ASLAKSEN. Quiet, please, quiet. (*Complete quiet.*) Does anybody want the floor? (STOCKMANN *raises his hand but* PETER *also raises his, almost imperceptibly.*)

PETER. Mr. Chairman!

ASLAKSEN (*Quickly.*). His Honor the Mayor will address the meeting. (*Great applause.* STOCKMANN *returns to his position* L. *of* PETRA. PETER *rises and crosses to platform, which he mounts.* EDVARD *pulls* GUNNAR *to get better view of* PETER. BILLING *crosses to* D. C. *edge of platform as* HENRIK *goes* U. L. C. *to talk to* NANSEN. KIIL *sits in the Mayor's chair,* D. R. HOVSTAD *crosses to behind* BILLING.)

PETER. Gentlemen, there's no reason to take very long to settle this tonight and return to our ordinary calm and peaceful life. Here's the issue: Doctor Stockmann, my brother—and believe me, it's not easy to say this—has decided to destroy Kirsten Springs, our Health Institute . . . (*Crowd is dead quiet.*)

STOCKMANN. Peter!

ASLAKSEN. Let the Mayor continue, please. There mustn't be any interruptions.

PETER. He has a long and very involved way of going about it, but that's the brunt of it, believe me.

NANSEN (*Rather quietly.*). Then what're we wasting time for? Run him out of town! (HENRIK *"plots" with* NANSEN. *Others agree;* HEDVIG *disagrees.*)

PETER. Now wait a minute. I want no violence here. I want you to understand his motives. He is a man, always has been, who is never happy unless he is badgering authority, ridiculing authority, destroying authority. He wants to attack the Springs so he can prove that the Administration blundered in the construction.

STOCKMANN (*To* ASLAKSEN.). May I speak, I . . . ?

ASLAKSEN. The Mayor's not finished. (STOCKMANN *turns and steps* D. *distractedly.*)

PETER. Thank you. Now there are a number of people here who seem to feel that the Doctor has a right to say anything he pleases. After all, we are a democratic country. Now God knows, in ordinary times, I'd agree a hundred percent with anybody's right to say anything. But these are not ordinary times. Nations have crises and so do towns. There are ruins of nations and there are ruins of towns all over the world, and they were wrecked by people who in the guise of reform and pleading for justice and so on, broke down all authority and left only revolution and chaos.

STOCKMANN (*Crossing* D. L. *of platform.*). What the hell are you talking about!

ASLAKSEN (*As crowd begins to murmur.*). I'll have to insist, Doctor . . .

STOCKMANN. I called a lecture, I didn't invite him to attack me. (*Crosses to crowd.*) He's got the press and every hall in town to attack me and I've got nothing but this room tonight. (*Crowd snarls and advances on* STOCKMANN.)

ASLAKSEN. I don't think you're making a very good impression, Doctor. (*Assenting laughter and catcalls.* DRUNK *whistles loudly from arch* L. HORSTER *quiets him.* HOVSTAD *crosses* D. *then* U. *to* BILLING. GUNNAR *and* EDVARD *cross to* GABRIEL *to deplore situation.* STOCKMANN *backs away from crowd, dismayed, goes up to confer with family.* ASLAKSEN *rings and calls for quiet, finally gets it.*) Please continue, Your Honor.

PETER. Now this is our crisis. We know what this town was without our Institute. We could barely afford to keep the streets in condition; it was a dead, third-rate hamlet. Today we're just on the verge of becoming internationally known as a resort. I predict that within five years the income of every man in this room will be immensely greater. (HENRIK *chuckles at this prospect.*) I predict that our schools will be bigger and better; and in time this town will be crowded with fine carriages; (GABRIEL *beams at* KIIL, *who glowers back.*) great homes will be built here, first-class stores will open all along Main Street. (*Crowd murmurs in appreciation.*) I predict that if we were not defamed and maliciously attacked we will some day be one of the richest and most beautiful resort towns in the world. (*General applause.*) There are your choices. Now all you've got to do is ask yourselves a simple question—has any one of us the right, the "democratic" right as they like to call it, to pick at minor flaws in the Springs, to exaggerate the most picayune faults . . . (*Cries of "No, no!"*) and to attempt to publish these defamations for the whole world to see? We live or die on what the outside world thinks of us! I believe there is a line that must be drawn, and if a man decides to cross that line, we the people must finally take him by the collar and declare, "You cannot say that." (*An uproar of assent.* HENRIK *and* NANSEN *cross* D. *after* STOCKMANN. BILLING *and* HOVSTAD *forcibly stop them and they return* U. R. C. EDVARD *reaches and pulls* GUNNAR *back* L. *out of danger.* GABRIEL *crosses to* FINN, *takes him* U. L. C. HORSTER *crosses* D. L.) All right, then. I think we all understand each other. Mr. Aslaksen, I move that Doctor Stockmann be prohibited from reading his report at this meeting. (*Ovation.* PETER *returns to his chair* D. R., *accepting the handshakes and plaudits of crowd. He finds* KIIL *sitting in his chair;* KIIL *disgustedly rises and scornfully gives* PETER *his place.* STOCKMANN *is behind his family at* L., *talking to them.* ASLAKSEN *is ringing bell and finally quiets the enthusiasm.*)

ASLAKSEN. Quiet, please! Please, now! I think we can proceed to the vote. (PETRA *claps* STOCKMANN *on the back.*)

STOCKMANN. Well, aren't you going to let me speak at all?

ASLAKSEN. Doctor, we are just about to vote on that question.

STOCKMANN. But damn it, man, I've got a right to . . .

PETRA (*Moving behind* STOCKMANN.). Point of order, Father!

STOCKMANN (*Remembering.*). Yes, point of order!

ASLAKSEN. Yes, Doctor? (STOCKMANN, *at a loss, turns to* PETRA *for further instruction.*)

PETRA. You want to discuss the motion.

STOCKMANN. That's right, damn it. I want to discuss the motion!

ASLAKSEN. Ah . . . (*Glances at* PETER, *who nods.*) All right, go ahead. (PETRA *sits.*)

STOCKMANN (*Moving to* D. *of platform.*). Now listen. (*Pointing to* PETER.) He talks and he talks and he talks, but not a word about the facts. (*Holding up papers.*)

HENRIK (*Snarling.*). We don't want to hear any more about the water!

NANSEN. You're just trying to blow up everything!

STOCKMANN. Well, judge for yourselves. Let me read . . . (*Crowd calls, "No, no, no." This rapidly builds into the biggest, noisiest reaction: shouting, horns blowing, bell ringing. Crutches and canes are waved in the air.* PETRA *and* CATHERINE *rise.*)

ASLAKSEN (*Ringing for quiet.*). Please, please now, quiet. We can't have this uproar! (*Quiet finally comes.*) I think, Doctor, that the majority wants to take the vote before you start to speak. If they so will, you can speak, otherwise . . . majority rules, you won't deny that.

STOCKMANN (*Turns and tosses notes to* PETRA.). Don't bother voting. I understand everything now. Can I have a few minutes?

PETER (*Rising.*). Mr. Chairman . . .

STOCKMANN (*Crossing* D. C.; *to* PETER.). I won't mention the Institute. (*Crowd recoils before him.*) I have a new discovery that's a thousand times more important than all the institutes in the world. (*To* ASLAKSEN.) May I have the platform?

ASLAKSEN (*Looking over crowd to* PETER.). I don't see how we can deny him that as long as he confines himself to . . . (*Crowd discusses* ASLAKSEN'S *decision.* HOVSTAD *fades* D. R. C.)

STOCKMANN. The Springs are not the subject. (*He mounts platform.* ASLAKSEN, CATHERINE, *and* PETRA *sit.* TORA *crosses to* U. *of* PETER; FINN *crosses* U. R.; BILLING *and* HOVSTAD *are* D. R. C.; HORSTER *crosses* L. C.; GABRIEL *crosses to in front of* PETER; EDVARD and GUNNAR *cross* U. R. C.; PAUL *crosses* D. C.; GEORG *puts bag of raisins in pocket.*) Before I go into my subject, I want to congratulate the "liberals" and "radicals" among us—like Mr. Hovstad . . . (BILLING *takes notes during* STOCKMANN'S *speech.*)

HOVSTAD. What do you mean, radical!

Where's your evidence to call me a radical! (DRUNK *enters* L. *and leans against the arch.*)

STOCKMANN. You got me there. There isn't any evidence. I guess there never really was. I just wanted to congratulate you on your self-control tonight—you who have fought in every parlor for the principle of free speech these many years.

HOVSTAD. I believe in democracy. When my readers are overwhelmingly against something, I'm not going to impose my will on the majority.

STOCKMANN. You have begun my remarks, Mr. Hovstad. (*Turns to crowd.*) Gentlemen, Mrs. Stockmann, Miss Stockmann, tonight I was struck by a sudden flash of light, a discovery second to none. But before I tell it to you, a little story. (*Slight improvisation of exasperation.*) I put in a good many years in the North of our country. Up there the rulers of the world are the great seal and the gigantic squadrons of duck. Man lives on ice, huddled together in a little pile of stone. His whole life consists of grubbing for food. Nothing more. He can barely speak his own language. And it came to me one day that it was romantic and sentimental for a man of my education to be tending these people. They had not yet reached the stage where they needed a doctor. If the truth were to be told, a veterinary would be more in order. (*A murmur of displeasure works through crowd.*)

BILLING. Is that the way you refer to decent, hard-working people!

STOCKMANN. I expected that, my friend, but don't think you can fog up my brain with that magic word, the People! Not any more! Just because there is a mass of organisms with the human shape . . . (*Crowd reacts to this insult.*) they do not automatically become a People. That *honor* has to be *earned!* Nor does one automatically become "A Man" by having human shape, and living in a house, and feeding one's face—and agreeing with one's neighbors. (*Slight reaction to this insult.*) That name *also* has to be earned. (*Crowd becomes quiet by the force of his words.*) Now, when I came to my conclusions about the Springs . . .

PETER (*Rising.*). You have no right to . . .

STOCKMANN. That's a picayune thing to catch me on a word, Peter, I'm not going into the Springs. (*To crowd.*) When I became convinced of my theory about the water, the authorities moved in at once, and I said to myself, I will fight them to the death because . . .

NANSEN (*Quietly.*). What're you trying to make, a revolution here? (*To* GUNNAR.) He's a revolutionist!

STOCKMANN (*Almost pleading to* NANSEN.). Let me finish! (*To crowd.*) I thought to myself—the majority, I have the majority! And let me tell you, friends, it was a grand feeling. Because the reason I came back to this place of my birth was that I wanted to give my education to this town, I loved it, so I spent months without pay or encouragement and dreamed up the whole project of the Springs. And why? Not as my brother says, so that fine carriages could crowd our streets, but so that we might cure the sick, so that we might meet people from all over the world and learn from them, and become broader and more civilized—in other words, more like Men, more like A People.

EDVARD. You don't like anything about this town, do you?

NANSEN. Admit it, you're a revolutionist, aren't you? Admit it!

STOCKMANN. I don't admit it! I proclaim it now! I am in revolt against the age-old lie that the majority is *always* right! (*Crowd's reaction is astonished, stunned.*)

HOVSTAD. He's an aristocrat all of a sudden!

STOCKMANN. And more! I tell you now, that the majority is always wrong, and in this way!

PETER. Have you lost your mind! Stop talking before . . .

STOCKMANN. Was the majority right when they stood by while Jesus was crucified? (*Silence.*) Was the majority right when they refused to believe that the earth moved round the sun, and let Galileo be driven to his knees like a dog? It takes fifty years for the majority to be right. The majority is never right until it *does* right.

HOVSTAD. I want to state right now, that although I've been this man's friend and I've eaten at his table many times, I now cut myself off from him absolutely. (*Starts to leave* U. R.; GABRIEL, BILLING *and* FINN *restrain him.* EDVARD *and* GUNNAR *start off;* STOCKMANN'S *pleas bring them back.*)

STOCKMANN. Answer me this! Please, one more moment! A platoon of soldiers is walking down a road toward the enemy. Every one of them is convinced he is on the right road, the safe road. But two miles ahead stands one lonely man, the outpost. He sees that this road is dangerous, that his comrades are walking into a trap. He runs back, he finds the platoon. Isn't it clear that this man must have the right to warn the majority, to argue with the majority, to fight with the majority if he believes he has the truth? Before many can know something, *one* must know it! (*His passion has made a silence.*) It's always the same. Rights are sacred until it hurts for somebody to use them. I beg you now —I realize the cost is great, the inconvenience is great, the risk is great that other towns will get the jump on us while we're rebuilding . . .

PETER. Aslaksen, he's not allowed to . . .

STOCKMANN. Let me prove it to you! The water is poisoned!

NANSEN (*Crosses to below platform, waving fist in air;* PETRA *rises and crosses to give* STOCKMANN *his report, but bumps into* NANSEN.). One more word about poison and I'm gonna take you outside! (*Crowd surges forward.* CATHERINE *pulls* PETRA *back* D. L. *Bell is ringing; crowd is roaring. Canes and crutches are waved in the air. Even the* DRUNK, *who has dozed off while leaning in archway* L., *starts to fight an imaginary opponent. All are violent "for the good of the town."* KIIL *takes this all in, then darts away off* L. HENRIK *has crossed, and is arguing with the women.* HEDVIG *screams when crowd moves forward, then runs* R. C. *with* HANS; GUNNAR *crosses to her.* HORSTER, *who has been pulling men out of the crowd, sees* HENRIK *with the two women and crosses to get him away, then stays* D. L. *to protect the women.* PETER *is standing* R. C., *watching all this.*)

PETER. That's enough! Now stop it! Quiet! There is not going to be any violence here!! (*People in the crowd look at* PETER *and become quiet. After a moment.*) Doctor, come down and give Mr. Aslaksen the platform.

STOCKMANN. I'm not through yet.

PETER. Come down or I will not be responsible for what happens.

CATHERINE. I'd like to go home; come on, Tom.

PETER. I move the Chairman order the speaker to leave the platform.

EDVARD. Sit down!
NANSEN. Get off that platform! } (*Together.*)
(*Others join in.*)

STOCKMANN. All right. Then I'll take this to out-of-town newspapers until the whole country is warned . . .

PETER. You wouldn't dare!

HOVSTAD (*Breaking away* R. C.). You're trying to ruin this town, that's all, trying to ruin it.

STOCKMANN. You are trying to build a town on a morality so rotten that it will infect the country and the world! If the only way you can prosper is this murder of freedom and truth, then I say with all my heart—let it be destroyed, let the people perish! (*He jumps down from rear of platform and crosses to his family* D. R. HORSTER *helps him with his hat and coat. Crowd turns to* PETER *for action.*)

NANSEN. Arrest him!
HENRIK and FINN. He's a traitor! Traitor! }
GABRIEL. Revolution!

ASLAKSEN (*Ringing for quiet.*). I would like to submit the following resolution: The people assembled here tonight, decent and patriotic citizens, in defense of their town and their country, declare, that Doctor Stockmann, Medical Officer of the Springs, is an enemy of the people and of his community.

CATHERINE. That's not true! He loves this town!

STOCKMANN. You damned fools, you fools! (*Crowd advances on* STOCKMANN.)

ASLAKSEN (*Shouting over the din.*). Is there anyone against this motion? Anyone against? (*Crowd becomes quiet. After a moment.*)

HORSTER (*Raises hand.*). I am (*Crowd backs away.*)

ASLAKSEN. One?

DRUNK (*Raises his hand, sleepily.*). Me, too! You can't do without a Doctor . . . (*Everyone looks back at* ASLAKSEN.) Anybody'll tell you . . .

ASLAKSEN. Anyone else? With all votes against two, this assembly formally declares Doctor Thomas Stockmann to be the people's enemy. In the future, all dealings with him by decent, patriotic citizens will be on that basis. The meeting is adjourned. (*Applause.* ASLAKSEN *and* BILLING *and* HOVSTAD *cross* D. R. *to* PETER;

HOVSTAD *helps him on with coat.* HEDVIG *and* GEORG *cross* C.)

STOCKMANN (*Stepping to* HORSTER.). Captain, do you have room for us on your ship to America?

HORSTER. Any time you say, Doctor. (NANSEN *steps* D., *looks at* HORSTER, *then crosses* U. R.) 650

STOCKMANN. Catherine! (*She takes his* R. *arm.*) Petra? (*She takes his* L. *arm. They start for door* U. L. *Crowd falls silent; a gauntlet is formed.* HEDVIG *looks at the three, then hides her boy's head, ashamed, and turns away herself. As the three start to move:*)

NANSEN. Doctor! (*Slight pause.*) You'd better get on that ship soon.

CATHERINE (*Quickly.*). Let's go out the back door . . . 660

HORSTER. Right this way . . .

STOCKMANN. No, no! No back doors! (*To crowd.*) I don't want to mislead anybody—the enemy of the people is not finished in this town—not quite yet! And if anybody thinks . . .

HENRIK (*Suddenly.*). Traitor! (*Quickly the noise builds.*)

EDVARD. Enemy! Enemy! } (*Together.*)
NANSEN. Throw him in the river! Come on, throw him in the river! } (*Together.*) 670

(*Out of the noise, a chant emerges; soon the whole crowd is calling, "Enemy! Enemy!" stamping their feet on last syllable. Through the two lines the* STOCKMANNS, *erect, move. Crowd is snapping at them like animals.* STOCKMANN, PETER, BILLING, ASLAKSEN *and* HOVSTAD *are seen watching* D. L. *The whole stage throbs with the chant, "Enemy, enemy, enemy."*)

CURTAIN 680

ACT THREE

SCENE: *Same as* ACT I, SCENE I.

The following morning. Windows at R. *are broken. Disorder. There are small rocks around the room:* D. C., *under* C. *chair, under the* R. C. *chair, and in front of bay window.*

STOCKMANN *enters* D. L. *with robe over shirt and trousers; closes door. It's cold in the house. He picks up a stone from* D. C., *sets it on table where there is a little pile of rocks.*

STOCKMANN. Catherine! Tell what's-her-name there's still some rocks to pick up in here!

CATHERINE (*Off* U. L.). She's not finished sweeping up the glass! (STOCKMANN *bends down to get another stone under a chair when a rock is thrown through one of the last remaining panes.* 10 *He whirls around and rushes to* U. *of window, looks out.* CATHERINE *runs in from dining-room door and crosses to* STOCKMANN. *They put their arms round each other.*) You all right?!

STOCKMANN (*Looking out window.*). A little boy. Look at him run. (*Picking up stone in front of window.*) How fast the poison spreads—even to the children. (*Crosses and sets rock on* R. C. *table.*)

CATHERINE (*Looking out window, has chill.*). 20 It's hard to believe this is the same town . . .

STOCKMANN. I'm going to keep these like sacred relics. I'll put them in my will. I want the boys to have these in their homes to look at every day. (*Shudders.*) Cold in here. Why hasn't what's-her-name got the glazier here?

CATHERINE (*Turns to him, steps* D.). She's getting him . . .

STOCKMANN. She's been getting him for two hours. We'll freeze to death in here. (*Pulls muffler around neck.*) 30

CATHERINE (*Unwillingly.*). He won't come here, Tom.

STOCKMANN. No! The glazier's afraid to fix my windows?

CATHERINE. You don't realize . . . people don't like to be pointed out. He's got neighbors, I suppose, and . . . (*A knock on* U. R. *door.*) Is that someone at the door? (*She goes to* U. R. *door.* STOCKMANN *picks up stone under* R. *chair.* CATHERINE *returns.*) Letter for you.

40

STOCKMANN (*Taking and opening it.*). What's this now?

CATHERINE (*Picking up stone under* C. *chair.*). I don't know how we're going to do any shopping with everybody ready to bite my head off . . .

STOCKMANN. Well, what do you know! We're evicted!

50

CATHERINE. Oh, no!

STOCKMANN. He hates to do it, but with public opinion what it is . . .

CATHERINE (*Frightened, crosses* U. C.). Maybe we shouldn't have let the boys go to school today?

STOCKMANN (*Crosses* U. R. *around table to* U. C.). Now don't get all frazzled again . . .

CATHERINE. But the landlord is such a nice man. If he's got to throw us out the town must be ready to murder us!

60

STOCKMANN. Just calm down, will you? (*Leads her to* C. *chair, sits, pulls her down on his* L. *knee.*) We'll go to America and the whole thing'll be like a dream . . .

CATHERINE. But I don't want to go to America. . . . (*Noticing his pants.*) When did this get torn?

STOCKMANN. Must've been last night . . .

CATHERINE. Your best pants!

70

STOCKMANN. Well, it shows you, that's all. Man goes out to fight for the truth should never wear his best pants. (*She half-laughs.*) Stop worrying, will you? You'll sew them up and in no time at all we'll be three thousand miles away . . .

CATHERINE. But how do you know it'll be any different there?

STOCKMANN. I don't know, it just seems to me in a big country like that, the spirit must be bigger. Still, I suppose they must have the solid majority there, too? I don't know, at least there must be more room to hide there.

80

CATHERINE. Think about it more, will you? I'd hate to go half around the world and find out we're in the same place.

STOCKMANN. You know, Catherine, I don't think I'm ever going to forget the face of that crowd last night.

CATHERINE (*Puts shawl around him.*). Don't think about it . . .

90

STOCKMANN. Some of them had their teeth bared, like animals in a pack. And who leads them? Men who call themselves liberals! Radicals! (*She looks around at furniture, figuring.*) The crowd lets out one roar and where are they —my liberal friends! I bet if I walked down the street now not one of them would admit he ever met me! It's hard to believe, it's . . . Are you listening to me?

CATHERINE. I was just wondering what we'll ever do with this furniture if we go to America?

100

STOCKMANN. Don't you ever listen when I talk, dear?

CATHERINE. Why must I listen? *I* know you're right. (PETRA *enters* U. R. CATHERINE *sees her, rises.*) Petra! Why aren't you in school?

STOCKMANN (*Rises, as* PETRA *crosses, steps back a little.*). What's the matter? (PETRA *crosses* D., *then* L. *to* STOCKMANN *at* C.; CATHERINE *comes* D. *a step and watches.* PETRA *kisses* STOCKMANN.)

110

PETRA. I'm fired.

CATHERINE. They wouldn't!

PETRA. As of two weeks from now. But I couldn't bear to stay there.

STOCKMANN (*Shocked.*). Mrs. Busk fired you?

CATHERINE. Who'd ever imagine she could do such a thing?

PETRA. It hurt her. I could see it, because we've always agreed so about things. But she didn't dare do anything else . . .

120

STOCKMANN. The glazier doesn't dare fix the windows, the landlord doesn't dare let us stay on . . .

PETRA. The landlord!

STOCKMANN. Evicted, darling! Oh, God, on the wreckage of all the civilizations in the world there ought to be a big sign—"They Didn't Dare!"

130

PETRA. I really can't blame her, Father, she showed me three letters she got this morning . . .

STOCKMANN. From whom?

PETRA. They weren't signed . . .

STOCKMANN. Oh, naturally. The big patriots with their anonymous indignation, scrawling out the darkness of their minds onto dirty little slips of paper—that's morality, and *I'm* the traitor! What'd the letters say?

PETRA. Well, one of them was from somebody who said that he'd heard at the club that somebody who visits this house said I had radical opinions about certain things.

STOCKMANN. Oh, wonderful! Somebody heard that somebody heard that *she* heard that *he* heard!—Catherine, pack as soon as you can. I feel as though vermin were crawling all over me. (*He starts to door* D. L. HORSTER *enters* U. R. *immediately and crosses* D. R.)

HORSTER. Good morning!

STOCKMANN (*Crossing to* HORSTER D. R. C.). Captain! You're just the man I want to see.

HORSTER. I thought I'd see how you all were . . .

CATHERINE. That's awfully nice of you, Captain . . . (*Stepping down and crossing to* L. *of* STOCKMANN.) and I want to thank you for seeing us through the crowd last night.

PETRA. Did you get home all right? We hated to leave you alone with that mob.

HORSTER. Oh, nothing to it. In a storm, there's just one thing to remember—it will pass.

STOCKMANN. Unless it kills you.

HORSTER (*After a moment.*). You mustn't let yourself get too bitter.

STOCKMANN. I'm trying, I'm trying. But I don't guarantee how I'll feel when I try to walk down the street with "Traitor" branded on my forehead.

CATHERINE. Don't think about it. } (*Together*)
HORSTER. Ah, what's a word? }

STOCKMANN. A word can be like a needle sticking in your heart, Captain. It can dig and corrode like an acid, until you become what they want you to be—really an enemy of the people.

HORSTER. You mustn't ever let that happen, Doctor.

STOCKMANN. Frankly, I don't give a damn any more. Let summer come, let an epidemic break out, then they'll know who they drove into exile. When are you sailing?

PETRA (*Stepping* D. C.). You really decided to go, Father?

STOCKMANN. Absolutely. When do you sail, Captain?

HORSTER (*Crossing* D. L. C. *to* L. *of* PETRA.). That's really what I came to talk to you about.

STOCKMANN. Why, something happen to the ship?

CATHERINE (*Happily to* STOCKMANN.). You see! We can't go!

HORSTER. No, the ship will sail. But I won't be aboard.

STOCKMANN. No!

PETRA. You fired, too? 'Cause I was this morning!

CATHERINE. Oh, Captain, you shouldn't have given us your house . . .

HORSTER. Oh, I'll get another ship. It's just that the owner, Mr. Vik, happens to belong to the same party as the Mayor, and I suppose when you belong to a party and the party takes a certain position . . . Because Mr. Vik himself is a very decent man . . .

STOCKMANN. Oh, they're all decent men!

HORSTER. No, really, he's not like the others . . .

STOCKMANN. He doesn't have to be. A party is like a sausage grinder—it mashes up clear heads, longheads, fatheads, blockheads, and what comes out?—meatheads! (*Bell at* U. R. *door.* PETRA *goes to answer it.*)

CATHERINE (*Crossing to* U. *of* R. C. *table.*). Maybe that's the glazier . . .

STOCKMANN (*Stepping to* HORSTER.). Imagine, Captain . . . (*Pointing to door.*) He refused to come all morning. (PETER *enters* U. R. *and stands just below arch.* PETRA *stays in hall.*)

PETER. If you're busy . . .

STOCKMANN (*Crossing to* D. *of* R. C. *table.* HORSTER *crosses* D. L. C.). Just picking up rocks and broken glass. Come in, Peter. What can I do for you this fine, brisk morning? (*He demonstratively pulls his robe tighter around his throat.*)

CATHERINE (*Indicating dining-room.*). Come inside, won't you, Captain?

HORSTER (*Crossing* U.). Yes. I'd like to finish our talk, Doctor.

STOCKMANN (*Stepping* L. *a little.*). Be with you in a minute, Captain. (HORSTER *exits into dining-room, preceded by* CATHERINE *and* PETRA. PETER *says nothing, looking at the damage; he is standing* D. R.) Keep your hat on if you like, it's a little draughty in here today.

PETER. Thanks, I believe I will. (*Puts his*

hat on.) I think I caught cold last night—that house was freezing.

STOCKMANN. I thought it was kind of warm —suffocating, as a matter of fact. What do you want?

PETER. May I sit down? (*Starts to sit in* R. C. *chair.*)

STOCKMANN. Not there, a piece of the solid majority . . . (*Refers to window.*) is liable to open your skull! There. (*Indicates* D. L. *chair.* PETER *crosses to* D. L. *chair, sits, while taking a large envelope out of his breast pocket.*) Now don't tell me!

PETER. Yes. (*Hands him envelope.*)

STOCKMANN (*Gets it and sets it on table, returns, sits on* R. C. *chair.*). I'm fired.

PETER. The Board met this morning. There was nothing else to do, considering the state of public opinion. (*Pause.*)

STOCKMANN. You look scared, Peter.

PETER. I . . . haven't completely forgotten that you're still my brother.

STOCKMANN. I doubt that.

PETER. You have no practice left in this town, Thomas.

STOCKMANN. People always need a doctor.

PETER. A petition is going from house to house. Everybody is signing it. A pledge not to call you any more. I don't think a single family will dare refuse to sign it.

STOCKMANN. You started that, didn't you?

PETER. No. As a matter of fact, I think it's all gone a little too far. I never wanted to see you ruined, Thomas. This will ruin you.

STOCKMANN. No, it won't . . .

PETER. For once in your life, will you act like a responsible man?

STOCKMANN. Why don't you say it, Peter? You're afraid I'm going out of town to start publishing things about the Springs, aren't you?

PETER. I don't deny that. (*Takes off hat.*) Thomas, if you really have the good of the town at heart you can accomplish everything without damaging anybody, including yourself. (*Pause.*)

STOCKMANN. What's this now?

PETER. Let me have a signed statement saying that in your zeal to help the town, you went overboard and exaggerated—put it any way you like, just so you calm anybody who might feel nervous about the water. If you'll give me that, you've got your job, and I give you my word you can gradually make all the improvements you feel are necessary. Now that gives you what you want . . .

STOCKMANN. You're nervous, Peter.

PETER (*He is; steps back to sofa.*). I am not nervous!

STOCKMANN (*Rises, stands* U. C. *of* PETER.). You expect me to remain in charge while people are being poisoned?

PETER. In time you can make your changes . . .

STOCKMANN. When—five years, ten years? You know your trouble, Peter? You just don't grasp, even now, that there are certain men you can't buy.

PETER. I'm quite capable of understanding that; but you don't happen to be one of those men. (*Slight pause.*)

STOCKMANN. What do you mean by that now?

PETER. You know damned well what I mean by that. Morten Kiil is what I mean by that.

STOCKMANN. Morten Kiil?

PETER (*Rising.*). Your father-in-law, Morten Kiil.

STOCKMANN. I swear, Peter, one of us is out of his mind; what are you talking about?

PETER. Now don't try to charm me with that professional innocence . . .

STOCKMANN. What are you talking about?

PETER. You don't know that your father-in-law has been running around all morning buying up stock in Kirsten Springs?

STOCKMANN (*Perplexed.*). Buying up stock?

PETER. Buying up stock, every share he can lay his hands on!

STOCKMANN. Well, I don't understand, Peter, what's that got to do with . . . ?

PETER (*Crossing* STOCKMANN *to* D. *of* R. C. *chair in agitation; takes off hat.*). Oh, come now, come now, come now . . .

STOCKMANN (*Crossing to* D. *of sofa.*). I hate you when you do that! Don't just walk around gabbling "Come now, come now"—what the hell are you talking about?

PETER. Very well, if you insist on being dense. A man wages a relentless campaign to destroy confidence in a corporation. He even goes so far as to call a mass meeting against it. The very next morning, when people are still in a state of shock about it all, his father-in-law runs all over town picking up shares at half their value.

STOCKMANN (*After a pause.*). My God!

PETER. And you have the nerve to speak to me about principles?

STOCKMANN. You mean you actually believe that I . . . ?

PETER. I'm not interested in psychology! I believe what I see! And what I see is nothing but a man doing a dirty, filthy job for Morten Kiil, and let me tell you, by tonight every man in this town'll see the same thing!

350

STOCKMANN. Peter, you, you . . . !

PETER (*Pointing to study door* L.). Now go to your desk and write me a statement denying everything you've been saying or . . .

STOCKMANN. Peter, you're a low creature!

PETER. All right, then, you'd better get this one straight, Thomas. If you're figuring on opening another attack from out of town, keep this in mind: the morning it's published I will send out a subpoena for you and begin a prosecution for conspiracy. I've been trying to make you respectable all my life; now if you want to make the big jump there'll be nobody there to hold you back. Now do we understand each other?

360

STOCKMANN. Oh, we do, Peter! (KIIL *enters hall* U. R. PETER *starts for door and almost bumps into him.* STOCKMANN *crosses* U. *to* R. *of dining-room arch.*) Get the girl—what the hell is her name?—scrub the floors, wash down the walls, a pestilence has been here!

370

PETER (*Turning to* STOCKMANN, *pointing to* KIIL.). Hah! (*He exits* U. R. KIIL *crosses* D. *to* R. *table; sits in* R. *chair.*)

STOCKMANN (*Crossing* D. *to* L. *of* KIIL.). Morten, now what have you done? What's the matter with you? Do you realize what this makes me look like?! (KIIL *simply sits there, grinning up at him; takes some stock shares out of his inside coat pocket and sets them on table.* STOCKMANN *breaks off on seeing them.*) Is that . . . them?

380

KIIL. That's them, yes. Kirsten Springs shares. And very easy to get this morning.

STOCKMANN. Morten, don't play with me, what's this all about?

KIIL. What are you so nervous about? Can't a man buy some stock without . . . ?

390

STOCKMANN (*Moves to* KIIL.). I want an explanation, Morten.

KIIL. Thomas, they hated you last night.

STOCKMANN. You don't have to tell me that.

KIIL. But they also believed you. They'd love to murder you, but they believe you. (*Slight pause.*) The way they say it, the pollution is coming down the river from Windmill Valley.

STOCKMANN. That's exactly where it's coming from.

400

KIIL. Yes. And that's exactly where my tannery is.

STOCKMANN (*Sitting, slowly.*). Well, Morten, I never made a secret to you that the pollution was tannery waste.

KIIL. I'm not blaming you. It's my fault. I didn't take you seriously. But it's very serious now. Thomas, I got that tannery from my father, he got it from his father; and his father got it from my great-grandfather. I do not intend to allow my family's name to stand for the three generations of murdering angels who poisoned this town.

410

STOCKMANN. I've waited a long time for this talk, Morten. I don't think you can stop that from happening.

KIIL. No, but you can.

STOCKMANN. I?

KIIL (*Nudging the shares.*). I've bought these shares because . . .

420

STOCKMANN. Morten, you've thrown your money away: the Springs are doomed.

KIIL. I never throw my money away, Thomas. These were bought with your money.

STOCKMANN. My money? What . . . ?

KIIL. You've probably suspected that I might leave a little something for Catherine and the boys?

STOCKMANN. Well, naturally, I'd hoped you'd . . .

430

KILL (*Touches shares.*). I decided this morning to invest that money in some stock, Thomas.

STOCKMANN (*Slowly getting up. Slight indication of* CATHERINE *off* L.). You bought that junk with Catherine's money . . . !

KIIL. People call me badger, and that's an animal that roots out things, but it's also some kind of a pig, I understand. I've lived a clean man and I'm going to die clean. You're going to clean my name for me.

440

STOCKMANN. Morten . . .

KIIL. Now I want to see if you really belong in a strait-jacket.

STOCKMANN. How could you dare do such a thing? What's the matter with you?

KIIL. Now don't get excited, it's very simple. If you should make another investigation of the water . . .

450 STOCKMANN. I don't *need* another investigation, I . . .

KIIL. If you think it over and decide that you ought to change your opinion about the water . . .

STOCKMANN. But the water is poisoned, it's poisoned!

KIIL. If you simply go on insisting the water is poisoned, (*Holds up shares.*) with these in your house, then there's only one explanation

460 for you—you are absolutely crazy!

STOCKMANN. You're right! I'm mad! I'm insane!

KIIL (*Rising.*). You must be! You're stripping the skin off your family's back—only a madman would do a thing like that!

STOCKMANN. Morten, Morten, I'm a penniless man, why didn't you tell me before you bought this junk?

KIIL (*Crossing to* STOCKMANN.). Because you

470 would understand it better if I told you after. (*Holds him by lapels with terrific force.* STOCKMANN *turns his face away.*) And Goddammit, I think you do understand it now! Don't you! Millions of tons of water come down that river. How do you know the day you made your tests there wasn't something unusual about the water?

STOCKMANN (*Breaking* D. L. C.). No, I took too many samples.

KIIL. How do you know? (*Following him.*)

480 Why couldn't those little animals have clotted up only in the patch of water you souped out of the river? How do you know the rest of it wasn't pure?

STOCKMANN (*Crossing* KIIL *to* C. KIIL *follows.*). It's not probable . . . people were getting sick last summer . . .

KIIL. They were sick when they came here, or they wouldn't have come!

STOCKMANN. Not intestinal diseases, skin dis-

490 eases . . .

KIIL. The only place anybody gets a bellyache is here?! There are no carbuncles in Norway? Maybe the food was bad! Did you even think of the food?

STOCKMANN (*With desire to agree with him.*). No . . . I didn't look into the food . . .

KIIL. Then what the hell makes you so sure it's the water?

STOCKMANN. Because I tested the water and . . . 500

KIIL (*Turning to* STOCKMANN.). Admit it. We're all alone here . . . you have some doubt . . .

STOCKMANN (*Crossing,* U. *around table, then* L. C.). Well, nothing is a hundred percent on this earth, but . . .

KIIL. Then you have a perfect right to doubt the other way! You have a scientific right! And did you ever think of some disinfectant? I bet you never even thought of that! 510

STOCKMANN. Not for a mass of water like that, you can't . . .

KIIL. Everything can be killed. That's science! (*Crosses to* STOCKMANN, *turning him around.*) Thomas, I never liked your brother, you have a perfect right to hate him . . .

STOCKMANN. I didn't do it because I hate my brother!

KIIL (*During this speech,* STOCKMANN *slowly turns to face* KIIL.). Part of it, part of it, don't 520 deny it! You admit there's some doubt in your mind about the water, you admit there may be ways to disinfect it, and yet you went after your brother as though the only way to cure the thing was to blow up the whole Institute! There's hatred in that, boy, don't forget it. (*Crosses to* R. *table, picks up shares in* R. *hand, stands in front of* C. *chair.*) These can belong to you now, so be sure, be sure; tear the hatred out of your heart, stand naked in front of your- 530 self—*are you sure?!*

STOCKMANN. What right have you to gamble my family's future on the strength of my convictions?

KIIL. Ah ha! Then the convictions are not really that strong!

STOCKMANN. I am ready to hang for my convictions! (*Crosses* R. *to* KIIL.)But no man has a right to make martyrs of others; my family is innocent. Sell back those shares, give her what 540 belongs to her, I'm a penniless man!

KIIL. Nobody is going to say Morten Kiil wrecked this town. (*Crosses* R. *of* R. *chair, turns.*) You retract your "convictions," or these go to charity.

STOCKMANN. Everything?

KIIL. There'll be a little something for Catherine, but not much. I want my good name. It's exceedingly important to me.

550 STOCKMANN (*Bitterly.*). And charity . . .

KIIL. Charity will do it, or you will do it. It's a serious thing to destroy a town.

STOCKMANN. Morten, when I look at you I swear to God I see the devil! (HOVSTAD *and* ASLAKSEN *enter* U. R. STOCKMANN *starts after* KIIL, *who retreats* U. R.) You . . . (KIIL *almost bumps into* ASLAKSEN. STOCKMANN, U. R. C., *crosses* D. *below table, then* C.)

ASLAKSEN (*Holds up hand defensively.*).

560 Now don't get excited, please! (HOVSTAD *and* ASLAKSEN *smile a little at* KIIL.)

KIIL. Too many intellectuals here! (*He is standing below archway* U. R.)

ASLAKSEN (*Apologetically.*). Doctor, can we have five minutes of . . . ?

STOCKMANN. I've got nothing to say to you . . .

KIIL. I want an answer right away. You hear? I'm waiting. (*Exits* U. R.)

570 STOCKMANN. All right, say it quick. What do you want?

HOVSTAD (*Crossing* D. *to* L. *of* R. C. *table,* ASLAKSEN *crossing* D. *to* R. *of* R. C. *table.*). We don't expect you to forgive our attitude at the meeting, but . . .

STOCKMANN (*Grasping for the word.*). Your attitude was prone . . . prostrated . . . prostituted!

HOVSTAD. All right, call it whatever you

580 want . . .

STOCKMANN. I've got a lot on my mind, so get to the point. What do you want?

ASLAKSEN (*Crossing to* D. *of* R. C. *table.*). Doctor, you should have told us what was in back of it all. You could have had the *Messenger* behind you all the way.

HOVSTAD. You'd have had public opinion with you now. Why didn't you tell us?

STOCKMANN. Look, I'm very tired. Let's not

590 beat around the bush . . .

HOVSTAD (*Gestures toward door where* KIIL *went out.*). He's been all over town buying up stock in the Springs. It's no secret any more.

STOCKMANN (*Slight pause.*). Well, what about it?

HOVSTAD (*In a friendly way.*). You don't want me to spell it out, do you?

STOCKMANN. I certainly wish you would, I . . .

HOVSTAD. All right, let's lay it on the table. 600 Aslaksen, you want to . . . ?

ASLAKSEN. No—no, go ahead.

HOVSTAD. Doctor, in the beginning we supported you. (*Slowly, to drive it into his head.*) We couldn't go on supporting you because, in simple language, we didn't have the money to withstand the loss in circulation. You're boycotted now? Well, the paper would have been boycotted, too, if we'd stuck with you.

ASLAKSEN. You can see that, Doctor . . . 610

STOCKMANN. Oh, yes, but what do you want?

HOVSTAD. *The People's Messenger* can put on such a campaign that in two months you'll be hailed a hero in this town.

ASLAKSEN (*Crossing to* R. *of* HOVSTAD.). We're ready to go.

HOVSTAD. We will prove to the public that you had to buy up the stock because the management would not make the changes required for the public health. In other words, you did it 620 for absolutely scientific, public-spirited reasons. (*Steps to* STOCKMANN.) Now, what do you say, Doctor?

STOCKMANN. You want money from me, is that it?

ASLAKSEN. Well, now, Doctor . . .

HOVSTAD (*To* ASLAKSEN.). No, don't walk around it. (*To* STOCKMANN.) If we started to support you again, Doctor, we'd lose circulation for a while. We'd like you—or Mr. Kiil, 630 rather—to make up the deficit. (*Quickly, stepping to* STOCKMANN.) Now that's open and above-board and I don't see anything wrong with it. Do you? (*Pause.* STOCKMANN *looks at him, then crosses him and* ASLAKSEN *to window* R. *in thought.*)

ASLAKSEN. Remember, Doctor, you need the paper, you need it desperately.

STOCKMANN (*Returns to* D. R. *of* R. *chair.*). No, there's nothing wrong with it at all. I . . . 640 I'm not at all averse to cleaning up my name, although for myself it never was dirty. I don't *enjoy* being hated, if you know what I mean.

ASLAKSEN. Exactly.

HOVSTAD. Aslaksen, will you show him the budget? (ASLAKSEN *reaches into his pocket.*)

STOCKMANN. Just a minute. There is one point. I hate to keep repeating the same thing, but the water is poisoned.

650 HOVSTAD (*Crossing* ASLAKSEN.). Now, Doctor . . .

STOCKMANN. Just a minute. The Mayor says that he will levy a tax on everybody to pay for the reconstruction. I assume you are ready to support that tax at the same time you're supporting me?

ASLAKSEN. That tax would be extremely unpopular.

HOVSTAD. Doctor, with you back in charge of

660 the baths as Medical Officer, I have absolutely no fear that anything can go wrong . . .

STOCKMANN. In other words, you will clean up my name so that I can be in charge of the Corruption.

HOVSTAD. But we can't tackle everything at once. A new tax, there'd be an uproar!

ASLAKSEN. It would ruin the paper!

STOCKMANN. Then you don't intend to do anything about the water?

670 HOVSTAD. We have faith you won't let anyone get sick!

STOCKMANN. In other words, gentlemen, you are looking for someone to blackmail into paying your printing bill.

HOVSTAD (*Indignantly.*). We are trying to clear your name, Doctor Stockmann! And if you refuse to cooperate, if that's going to be your attitude . . .

STOCKMANN. Yes? Go on. What will you do?

680 HOVSTAD (*Taking* ASLAKSEN'S R. *arm, starts to cross* STOCKMANN.). I think we'd better go.

STOCKMANN (*Steps* D. *into their way.*). What will you do? I would like you to tell me! Me, the man two minutes ago you were going to make into a hero—what will you do now that I won't pay you!

ASLAKSEN. Doctor, the public is almost hysterical!

STOCKMANN. To my face, tell me what you

690 are going to do!

HOVSTAD. The Mayor will prosecute you for conspiracy to destroy a corporation, and without a paper behind you, you will end up in prison!

STOCKMANN. And you'll support him, won't you?! I want it from your mouth, Hovstad! This little victory you will not deny me. (HOVSTAD *crosses* STOCKMANN, *starts for* U. R. *door.* STOCKMANN *takes his* R. *arm, stops him.*) Tell the hero, Hovstad; you're going to go on crucifying the hero, are you not? Say it to me . . . you will 700 not leave here until I get this from your mouth!

HOVSTAD (*Stepping back, looking directly at him.*). You are a madman. You are insane with egotism, and don't excuse it with humanitarian slogans, because a man who'll drag his family through a lifetime of disgrace is a demon in his heart! (*Advances on* STOCKMANN.) You hear me? A demon who cares more for the purity of a public bath than the lives of his wife and children. Doctor Stockmann, you deserve every- 710 thing you're going to get! (HOVSTAD *starts to go* U. R. STOCKMANN *is struck by his ferocious conviction.* ASLAKSEN *comes toward him, taking budget out of his pocket.*)

EJLIF (*Off* R.). Mother!

ASLAKSEN (*Nervously.*). Doctor, please, consider it; it won't take much money and in two months' time I promise you your whole life will change and . . .

EJLIF (*Entering hall* U. R.). Mother! Mother! 720

CATHERINE (*Without shawl, running to front door* U. R. *from dining-room behind bookcase.*). What happened? My God, what's the matter? (STOCKMANN, *alarmed, crosses* U. *as* CATHERINE *brings* MORTEN *down, followed by* EJLIF. PETRA *and* HORSTER *enter* U. R.; *she crosses* D. C.; *he crosses* D. L. C.; HOVSTAD *with* ASLAKSEN *on his* R. *give to* L. C.) Something happened! Look at him!

MORTEN. I'm all right. It's nothin'. 730

STOCKMANN (*Very much the doctor.*). What happened here?

MORTEN. Nothin', Papa, I swear . . .

STOCKMANN (*To* EJLIF.). What happened? Why aren't you in school?

EJLIF. The teacher said we better stay home the rest of the week.

STOCKMANN. The boys hit him?

EJLIF. They started calling you names so he got sore and began to fight with one kid and 740 all of a sudden the whole bunch of them jumped on him.

CATHERINE (*To* MORTEN.). Why did you answer?

MORTEN (*Indignantly, to* STOCKMANN.). They

called him a traitor! (*To* EJLIF.) My father is no traitor!

EJLIF. But you didn't have to answer!

CATHERINE (*Pushing* EJLIF *away a little.*). You should've known they'd all jump on you! They could have killed you!

MORTEN. I don't care!

STOCKMANN (*To quiet him—and his own heart.*). Morten . . .

MORTEN (*Pulls away from* STOCKMANN.). I'll kill them! I'll take a rock and the next time I see one of them I'll kill him! (STOCKMANN *reaches for* MORTEN *who, thinking he will be chastised, starts to pull away.* STOCKMANN *catches him and starts gripping him against his chest.*) Let me go! Let me . . .

STOCKMANN. Morten . . . Morten . . . (MORTEN *cries in his arms.*)

MORTEN. They called you traitor, an enemy . . . (*He sobs.*)

STOCKMANN. Sssh. That's all. Wash your face. (*Turns to* ASLAKSEN *and* HOVSTAD.) Good day, gentlemen.

HOVSTAD. Let us know what you decide, and we'll . . .

STOCKMANN. I've decided. I am an enemy of the people . . .

CATHERINE. Tom, what are you saying?

STOCKMANN. To such people who teach their own children to think with their fists—to them I'm an enemy! And my boy . . . my boys . . . my family . . . I think you can count us all enemies!

ASLAKSEN. Doctor, you could have everything you want . . .

STOCKMANN. Except the truth. I could have everything but that. The water is poisoned.

HOVSTAD. But you'll be in charge . . .

STOCKMANN. But the children are poisoned, the people are poisoned! If the only way I can be a friend of the people is to take charge of that corruption, then I am an enemy! The water is poisoned, poisoned, poisoned, that's the beginning of it and that's the end of it! Now get out of here!

HOVSTAD. You know where you're going to end?

STOCKMANN (*Taking umbrella from* ASLAKSEN.). I said get out of here! (HOVSTAD *and* ASLAKSEN *cross* STOCKMANN *and the boys.* CATHERINE *and the boys cross* U. C. *around* R. *table.* PETRA *crosses* R. *to* STOCKMANN. HOVSTAD *crosses* D. L. C.)

CATHERINE. What are you doing?

ASLAKSEN. You're a fanatic! You're out of your mind!

CATHERINE. What are you doing?

STOCKMANN. They want me to buy the paper, the public, the pollution of the Springs, buy the whole pollution of this town. They'll make a hero out of me for that! (*Furiously to* ASLAKSEN *and* HOVSTAD.) But I am not a hero, I am the enemy and now you're first going to find out what kind of enemy I am! I will sharpen my pen like a dagger—you, all you "friends" of the people are going to bleed before I'm done! Go, tell them to sign the petitions, warn them not to call me when they're sick; beat up my children; and never let her . . . (*Points to* PETRA.) in the school again or she'll destroy the immaculate purity of the vacuum there! See to the barricades, the truth is coming, ring the bells, sound the alarm! The truth, the truth is out, and soon it will be prowling like a lion in the streets!

HOVSTAD. Doctor, you're out of your mind. (*He and* ASLAKSEN *turn* U. R. *to go quickly.* STOCKMANN *runs after them.*)

STOCKMANN. Out of here, out of here!

EJLIF (*Rushing at them.*). Don't you say that to him!

STOCKMANN (*At hall.*). Out of here! (*He throws umbrella after them, slams the door* U. R. *behind them, crosses* C. *with* EJLIF *on his* R. *After a moment:*) I've had all the ambassadors of hell today, but there'll be no more. Now, now listen, Catherine. Children, listen. We are besieged. They'll call for blood now, they'll whip the people like oxen . . . (*A rock comes through remaining pane of* R. *window.* MORTEN *starts for window.* STOCKMANN *stops him.* HORSTER *turns to face* STOCKMANN.) Stay away from there!

CATHERINE. The Captain knows where we can get a ship . . .

STOCKMANN. No ships!

PETRA. We're staying?

CATHERINE. But they can't go back to school, I won't let them out of the house!

STOCKMANN. We're staying.

PETRA. Good!

STOCKMANN. We must be careful now. We must live through this. Boys, no more school.

I'm going to teach you. And Petra will. Do you know any kids, street louts, hookey-
850 players . . . ?

EJLIF. Oh, sure!

STOCKMANN. We'll want about twelve of them to start. But I want them good and ignorant, absolutely uncivilized. Can we use your house, Captain!

HORSTER. Sure, I'm never there.

STOCKMANN. Fine! We'll begin, Petra, and we'll turn out not taxpayers and newspaper subscribers, but free and independent people, hun-
860 gry for the truth. Oh, I forgot! Petra, run to Grandpa and tell him . . . tell him . . . as follows . . . NO!

CATHERINE (*Puzzled.*). What do you mean?

STOCKMANN. It means, my dear, that we are all alone. And there'll be a long night before it's day . . . (*A rock smashes through another window.* PETRA *starts for window;* STOCKMANN *holds her back.* HORSTER *crosses to* D. *of window, crouches low and looks out.*)

HORSTER. Half the town is out. (STOCKMANN 870
pulls family down low. All are crouching a little.)

CATHERINE. What's going to happen? Tom! What's going to happen? (HORSTER *crosses* D. R. C., *looks* U. *at family.*)

STOCKMANN. I don't know. But remember now, everybody. You are fighting for the truth, and that's why you're alone. And that makes you strong—we're the strongest people in the world . . . (*Crowd noises build.*) And the 880
strong must learn to be lonely.

CURTAIN

Review Questions

1. What is Miller's importance in this version of the play?
2. What is Ibsen's point of view as expressed in this play?
3. Explain the basis for the line: "The strongest man is he who stands alone."
4. Do the Kirsten Springs have symbolic meaning?
5. Discuss the irony involved in Dr. Stockmann's expectations and the actual results.
6. When does tension begin in the action?
7. Contrast the characters of Peter and Dr. Stockmann.
8. Discuss Peter Stockmann's view that "The individual must subordinate himself to the over-all authorities."
9. Cite specific examples of Ibsen's skill in foreshadowing.
10. What effect does the letter have on Dr. Stockmann?
11. What is Kiil's dramatic function?
12. Summarize and evaluate Peter Stockmann's arguments in Act I, scene 2.
13. What are the basic conflicts? Do they have universality?
14. How does Ibsen portray the authorities who run the town?
15. Is Dr. Stockmann wise to remain at the end?
16. Describe the character of Aslaksen. What point of view does he represent?
17. What does Petra's book have to do with the play?
18. With which characters do you sympathize?
19. Comment on the political implications of Dr. Stockmann's statement: "Rights are sacred until it hurts somebody to use them."
20. What do Dr. Stockmann and Petra learn from their experience?
21. How do the playwrights treat the press?
22. What is the total effect of the play?
23. What is the general application of the play's meaning?
24. Was Dr. Stockmann free from blame?

MISS JULIE

August Strindberg (1849-1912)

TRANSLATED BY
E. M. SPRINCHORN

Sweden's outstanding playwright was born in Stockholm. He had a difficult and traumatic childhood and his adult years were filled with domestic torment and agonizing self-doubt. The experiences of his personal life are sharply revealed in many of his plays. He was a man of great imagination both in his plays and in his innovations in theatrical production.

Strindberg's plays fall into three periods. He first wrote romantic, historical plays before turning to realistic character studies in the late 1880's, such as *The Father* and *Miss Julie*. His final plays were experiments in expressionism, in which he probed into psychotic behavior in dream-like sequences, as in *The Spook Sonata* and *The Dream Play*.

Among the theatrical innovations suggested by Strindberg were an intimate theater, the abolition of footlights, and less make-up for the actors. "To make a real room of the stage, with the fourth wall missing, and a part of the furniture placed towards the audience, would probably produce a disturbing effect at present." The real wall of the set for *Miss Julie* was slanted diagonally across the stage to give it a more natural effect. "Having only a single setting, one may demand to have it real," Strindberg said. He objected to painted properties on the wall, and to the act divisions and intermissions in a play because they disrupted continuity. He filled in the pauses of the action by dance, pantomime and monologue. All of these indications suggest that Strindberg wished to stage his plays such as *Miss Julie* and *The Father* in an untheatrical fashion in order to give the impression of authenticity to match that of the characters in his plays.

Drawing by Cleon Throckmorton, from the Provincetown Playbill

(From Macgowan & Melnitz, The Living Stage, *©1955 by Prentice-Hall, Inc.)*

With his "little theater," Strindberg tried to create the atmosphere on intimacy that he considered necessary for naturalism.

Angus McBean

The foreshadowing of the end.

Characters

MISS JULIE, *twenty-five years old*
JEAN, *valet, thirty years old*
CHRISTINE, *the cook, thirty-five years old*

The action of the play takes place in the kitchen of the Count's manor house on Midsummer Eve in Sweden in the 1880's.

MISS JULIE

The scene is a large kitchen. The walls and ceiling are covered with draperies and hangings. The rear wall runs obliquely upstage from the left. On this wall to the left are two shelves with pots and pans of copper, iron, and pewter. The shelves are decorated with goffered paper. A little to the right can be seen three-fourths of a deep arched doorway with two glass doors, and through them can be seen a fountain with a statue of Cupid, lilac bushes in bloom, and the tops of some Lombardy poplars. From the left of the stage the corner of a large, Dutch-tile kitchen stove protrudes with part of the hood showing. Projecting from the right side of the stage is one end of the servants' dining table of white pine, with a few chairs around it. The stove is decorated with branches of birch leaves; the floor is strewn with juniper twigs. On the end of the table is a large Japanese spice jar filled with lilacs. An icebox, a sink, a wash basin. Over the door a big, old-fashioned bell; and to the left of the door the gaping mouth of a speaking tube.

CHRISTINE *is standing at the stove, frying something. She is wearing a light-colored cotton dress and an apron.* JEAN *enters, dressed in livery and carrying a pair of high-top boots with spurs. He sets them where they are clearly visible.*

JEAN. Tonight she's wild again. Miss Julie's absolutely wild!

CHRISTINE. You took your time getting back!

10 JEAN. I took the Count down to the station, and on my way back as I passed the barn I went in for a dance. And there was Miss Julie leading the dance with the game warden. But then she noticed me. And she came right up and chose me for the ladies' waltz. And she's been dancing ever since like—like I don't know what. She's absolutely wild!

CHRISTINE. That's nothing new. But she's been worse than ever during the last two weeks,
20 ever since her engagement was broken off.

JEAN. Yes, I never did hear all there was to that. He was a good man, too, even if he wasn't rich. Well, that's a woman for you.

(He sits down at the end of the table)

But, tell me, isn't it strange that a young girl like her—all right, young woman—prefers to stay home here with the servants rather than go with her father to visit her relatives?

CHRISTINE. I suppose she's ashamed to face them after that fiasco with her young man. 30

JEAN. No doubt. He wouldn't take any nonsense from her. Do you know what happened, Christine? I do. I saw the whole thing, even though I didn't let on.

CHRISTINE. Don't tell me you were there?

JEAN. Well, I was. They were in the barnyard one evening—and she was training him, as she called it. Do you know what she was doing? She was making him jump over her riding whip—training him like a dog. He jumped 40 over twice, and she whipped him both times. But the third time, he grabbed the whip from her, broke it in a thousand pieces—and walked off.

CHRISTINE. So that's what happened. Well, what do you know.

JEAN. Yes, that put an end to that affair.—Now have you got something good for me, Christine?

CHRISTINE (*Serving him from the frying pan*). Just a little bit of kidney. I cut it especially for you.

JEAN (*Smelling it*). Wonderful! My special *délice* (*Feeling the plate*) Hey, you didn't warm the plate!

CHRISTINE. You're more fussy than the Count himself when you set your mind to it. (*She rumples his hair gently*)

JEAN (*Irritated*). Cut it out! Don't muss up my hair. You know I don't like that!

CHRISTINE. Oh, now don't get mad. Can I help it if I like you?

(JEAN *eats.* CHRISTINE *gets out a bottle of beer*)

JEAN. Beer on Midsummer Eve! No thank you! I've got something much better than that. (*He opens a drawer in the table and takes out a bottle of red wine with a gold seal*) Do you see that? Gold Seal. Now give me a glass.—No, a wine glass of course. I'm drinking it straight.

CHRISTINE (*Goes back to the stove and puts on a small saucepan*). Lord help the woman who gets you for a husband. You're an old fussbudget!

JEAN. Talk, talk! You'd consider yourself lucky if you got yourself a man as good as me. It hasn't done you any harm to have people think I'm your fiancé. (*He tastes the wine*) Very good. Excellent. But warmed just a little too little. (*Warming the glass in his hands*) We bought this in Dijon. Four francs a liter, unbottled—and the tax on top of that. . . . What on earth are you cooking? It smells awful!

CHRISTINE. Some damn mess that Miss Julie wants for her dog.

JEAN. You should watch your language, Christine. . . . Why do you have to stand in front of the stove on a holiday, cooking for that mutt? Is it sick?

CHRISTINE. Oh, she's sick, all right! She sneaked out to the gatekeeper's mongrel and—got herself in a fix. And Miss Julie, you know, can't stand anything like that.

JEAN. She's too stuck-up in some ways and not proud enough in others. Just like her mother. The Countess felt right at home in the kitchen or down in the barn with the cows, but when she went driving, *one* horse wasn't enough for her; she had to have a pair. Her sleeves were always dirty, but her buttons had the royal crown on them. As for Miss Julie, she doesn't seem to care how she looks and acts. I mean, she's not really refined. Just now, down at the barn, she grabbed the game warden away from Anna and asked him to dance. You wouldn't see anybody in our class doing a thing like that. But that's what happens when the gentry try to act like the common people—they become common! . . . But she *is* beautiful! Magnificent! Ah, those shoulders—those——and so forth, and so forth!

CHRISTINE. Oh, don't exaggerate. Clara tells me all about her, and Clara dresses her.

JEAN. Clara, pooh! You women are always jealous of each other. *I've* been out riding with her. . . . And how she can dance!

CHRISTINE. Listen, Jean, you *are* going to dance with me, aren't you, when I am finished here?

JEAN. Certainly! Of course I am.

CHRISTINE. Promise?

JEAN. Promise! Listen if I say I'm going to do a thing, I do it. . . . Christine, I thank you for a delicious meal. (*He shoves the cork back into the bottle*)

(MISS JULIE *appears in the doorway, talking to someone outside*)

MISS JULIE. I'll be right back. Don't wait for me.

(JEAN *slips the bottle into the table drawer quickly and rises respectfully.* MISS JULIE *comes in and crosses over to* CHRISTINE, *who is at the mirror*)

MISS JULIE. Did you get it ready?

(CHRISTINE *signals that* JEAN *is present*)

JEAN (*Polite and charming*). Are you ladies sharing secrets?

MISS JULIE (*Flipping her handkerchief in his face*). Don't be nosey!

JEAN. Oh, that smells good! Violets.

MISS JULIE (*Flirting with him*). Don't be impudent! And don't tell me you're an expert on perfumes, too. I know you're an expert dancer.—No, don't look! Go away!

JEAN (*Inquisitive, but deferential*). What are you cooking? A witch's brew for Midsummer Eve? Something that reveals what the stars have in store for you, so you can see the face of your future husband?

MISS JULIE (*Curtly*). You'd have to have good eyes to see that. (*To* CHRISTINE) Pour it into a small bottle, and seal it tight. . . . Jean, come and dance a schottische with me.

JEAN (*Hesitating*). I hope you don't think I'm being rude, but I've already promised this dance to Christine.

MISS JULIE. She can always find someone else. Isn't that so, Christine? You don't mind if I borrow Jean for a minute, do you?

CHRISTINE. It isn't up to me. If Miss Julie is gracious enough to invite you, it isn't right for you to say no, Jean. You go on, and thank her for the honor.

JEAN. Frankly, Miss Julie, I don't want to hurt your feelings, but I wonder if it is wise—I mean for you to dance twice in a row with the same partner. Especially since the people around here are so quick to spread gossip.

MISS JULIE (*Bridling.*). What do you mean? What kind of gossip? What are you trying to say?

JEAN (*Retreating*). If you insist on misunderstanding me, I'll have to speak more plainly. It just doesn't look right for you to prefer one of your servants to the others who are hoping for the same unusual honor.

MISS JULIE. Prefer! What an idea! I'm really surprised. I, the mistress of the house, am good enough to come to their dance, and when I feel like dancing, I want to dance with someone who knows how to lead. After all I don't want to look ridiculous.

JEAN. As you wish. I am at your orders.

MISS JULIE (*Gently*). Don't take it as an order. Tonight we're all just happy people at a party. There's no question of rank. Now give me your arm.—Don't worry, Christine. I won't run off with your boy friend.

(JEAN *gives her his arm and leads her out*)

PANTOMIME SCENE. *This should be played as if the actress were actually alone. She turns her back on the audience when she feels like it; she does not look out into the auditorium; she does not hurry as if she were afraid the audience would grow impatient.* CHRISTINE *alone. In the distance the sound of the violins playing the schottische.* CHRISTINE, *humming in time with the music, cleans up after* JEAN, *washes the dishes, dries them, and puts them away in a cupboard. Then she takes off her apron, takes a little mirror from one of the table drawers, and leans it against the jar of lilacs on the table. She lights a tallow candle, heats a curling iron, and curls the bangs on her forehead. Then she goes to the doorway and stands listening to the music. She comes back to the table and finds the handkerchief that* MISS JULIE *left behind. She smells it, spreads it out, and then, as if lost in thought, stretches it, smooths it out, folds it in four, and so on.*

(JEAN *enters alone*)

JEAN. I told you she was wild! You should have seen the way she was dancing. They were peeking at her from behind the doors and laughing at her. Can you figure her out, Christine?

CHRISTINE. You might know it's her monthlies, Jean. She always acts peculiar then. . . . Well, are you going to dance with me?

JEAN. You're not mad at me because I broke my promise?

CHRISTINE. Of course not. Not for a little thing like that, you know that. And I know my place.

JEAN (*Grabs her around the waist*). You're a sensible girl, Christine. You're going to make somebody a good wife——

(MISS JULIE, *coming in, sees them together. She is unpleasantly surprised*)

MISS JULIE (*With forced gaiety*). Well, aren't you the gallant beau—running away from your partner!

JEAN. On the contrary, Miss Julie. As you can see, I've hurried back to the partner I deserted.

MISS JULIE (*Changing tack*). You know, you're the best dancer I've met.—But why are you wearing livery on a holiday. Take it off at once.

JEAN. I'd have to ask you to leave for a minute. My black coat is hanging right here—(*He moves to the right and points*)

MISS JULIE. You're not embarrassed because I'm here, are you? Just to change your coat? Go in your room and come right back again. Or else you can stay here and I'll turn my back.

JEAN. If you'll excuse me, Miss Julie. (*He goes off to the right. His arm can be seen as he changes his coat*)

MISS JULIE (*To* CHRISTINE). Tell me something, Christine. Is Jean your fiancé? He seems so intimate with you. 250

CHRISTINE. Fiancé? I suppose so. At least that's what we say.

MISS JULIE. What do you mean?

CHRISTINE. Well, Miss Julie, you have had fiancés yourself, and you know—

MISS JULIE. But we were properly engaged—!

CHRISTINE. I know, but did anything come of it?

260 (JEAN *comes back, wearing a cutaway coat and derby*)

MISS JULIE. *Très gentil, monsieur Jean! Très gentil!*

JEAN. *Vous voulez plaisanter, madame.*

MISS JULIE. *Et vous voulez parler français!* Where did you learn to speak French?

JEAN. In Switzerland. I was *sommelier* in one of the biggest hotels in Lucerne.

MISS JULIE. But you look quite the gentleman in that coat! *Charmant!* (*She sits down at the table*) 270

JEAN. Flatterer!

MISS JULIE (*Stiffening*). Who said I was flattering you?

JEAN. My natural modesty would not allow me to presume that you were paying sincere compliments to someone like me, and therefore I assumed that you were exaggerating, or, in other words, flattering me.

MISS JULIE. Where on earth did you learn to talk like that? Do you go to the theater often? 280

JEAN. And oher places. I get around.

262 **Très gentil . . .**
. . . parler française!
MISS JULIE. Very elegant, Mr. Jean! Very elegant.
JEAN. You wish to joke, my lady.
MISS JULIE. And you wish to speak French!

MISS JULIE. But weren't you born in this district?

JEAN. My father worked as a farm hand on the county attorney's estate, next door to yours. I used to see you when you were little. But of course you didn't notice me.

MISS JULIE. Did you really? 290

JEAN. Yes. I remember one time in particular—. But I can't tell you about that!

MISS JULIE. Of course you can. Oh, come on, tell me. Just this once—for me.

JEAN. No. No, I really couldn't. Not now. Some other time maybe.

MISS JULIE. Some other time? That means never. What's the harm in telling me now?

JEAN. There's no harm. I just don't feel like it.—Look at her. (*He nods at* CHRISTINE, *who has fallen asleep in a chair by the stove*) 300

MISS JULIE. Won't she make somebody a pretty wife! I'll bet she snores, too.

JEAN. No, she doesn't. But she talks in her sleep.

MISS JULIE (*Cynically*). Now how would you know she talks in her sleep?

JEAN (*Coolly*). I've heard her. . . .

(*Pause. They look at each other*)

MISS JULIE. Why don't you sit down? 310

JEAN. I wouldn't take the liberty in your presence.

MISS JULIE. But if I were to order you—?

JEAN. I'd obey.

MISS JULIE. Well then, sit down.—Wait a minute. Could you get me something to drink first?

JEAN. I don't know what there is in the icebox. Only beer, I suppose.

MISS JULIE. *Only* beer?! I have simple tastes. I prefer beer to wine. 320

(JEAN *takes a bottle of beer from the icebox and opens it. He looks in the cupboard for a glass and a saucer, and serves her*)

JEAN. At your service.

MISS JULIE. Thank you. Don't you want to drink, too?

JEAN. I'm not much of a beer-drinker, but if it's your wish—

MISS JULIE. My wish! I should think a gen- 330

tleman would want to keep his lady company.

JEAN. That's a point well taken! (*He opens another bottle and takes a glass*)

MISS JULIE. Now drink a toast to me! (JEAN *hesitates*) You're not shy, are you? A big, strong man like you? (*Playfully,* JEAN *kneels and raises his glass in mock gallantry*)

JEAN. To my lady's health!

MISS JULIE. Bravo! Now if you would kiss my shoe, you will have hit it off perfectly. (JEAN *hesitates, then boldly grasps her foot and touches it lightly with his lips*) Superb! You should have been an actor.

JEAN (*Rising*). This has got to stop, Miss Julie! Someone might come and see us.

MISS JULIE. What difference would that make?

JEAN. People would talk, that's what! If you knew how their tongues were wagging out there just a few minutes ago, you wouldn't—

MISS JULIE. What sort of things did they say? Tell me. Sit down and tell me.

JEAN (*Sitting down*). I don't want to hurt your feelings, but they used expressions that—that hinted at certain—you know what I mean. After all, you're not a child. And when they see a woman drinking, alone with a man—and a servant at that—in the middle of the night—well . . .

MISS JULIE. Well what?! Besides, we're not alone. Christine is here.

JEAN. Yes, asleep!

MISS JULIE. I'll wake her up then. (*She goes over to* CHRISTINE) Christine! Are you asleep? (CHRISTINE *babbles in her sleep*) Christine!—How sound she sleeps!

CHRISTINE (*Talking in her sleep*). Count's boots are brushed . . . put on the coffee . . . right away, right away, right . . . mm—mm . . . poofff . . . (MISS JULIE *grabs* CHRISTINE'S *nose*)

MISS JULIE. Wake up, will you!

JEAN (*Sternly*). Let her alone!

MISS JULIE (*Sharply*). What!

JEAN. She's been standing over the stove all day. She's worn out when evening comes. Anyone asleep is entitled to some respect.

MISS JULIE (*Changing tack*). That's a very kind thought. It does you credit. Thank you. (*She offers* JEAN *her hand*) Now come on out and pick some lilacs for me.

(*During the following,* CHRISTINE *wakes up and, drunk with sleep, shuffles off to the right to go to bed*)

JEAN. With you, Miss Julie?

MISS JULIE. Yes, with me.

JEAN. That's no good. Absolutely not.

MISS JULIE. I don't know what you're thinking. Maybe you're letting your imagination run away with you.

JEAN. I'm not. The other people are.

MISS JULIE. In what way? Imagining that I'm—*verliebt* in a servant?

JEAN. I'm not conceited, but it's been known to happen. And to these people nothing's sacred.

MISS JULIE. Why, I believe you're an aristocrat!

JEAN. Yes, I am.

MISS JULIE. I'm climbing down—

JEAN. Don't climb down, Miss Julie! Take my advice. No one will ever believe that you climbed down deliberately. They'll say that you fell.

MISS JULIE. I think more highly of these people than you do. Let's see who's right! Come on! (*She looks him over, challenging him*)

JEAN. You know, you're very strange.

MISS JULIE. Perhaps. But then so are you. . . . Besides, everything is strange. Life, people, everything. It's all scum, drifting and drifting on the water until it sinks—sinks. There's a dream I have every now and then. It's coming back to me now. I'm sitting on top of a pillar that I've climbed up somehow and I don't know how to get back down. When I look down I get dizzy. I have to get down but I don't have the courage to jump. I can't hold on much longer and I want to fall; but I don't fall. I know I won't have any peace until I get down; no rest until I get down, down on the ground. And if I ever got down on the ground, I'd want to go farther down, right down into the earth. . . . Have you ever felt anything like that?

JEAN. Never! I used to dream that I'm lying under a tall tree in a dark woods. I want to get up, up to the very top, to look out over the bright landscape with the sun shining on it, to rob the bird's nest up there with the golden eggs in it. I climb and I climb, but the trunk is so thick, and so smooth, and it's such a long way

393 **verliebt in a servant?** in love with a servant?

to that first branch. But I know that if I could just reach that first branch, I'd go right to the top as if on a ladder. I've never reached it yet, but some day I will—even if only in my dreams.

MISS JULIE. Here I am talking about dreams with you. Come out with me. Only into the park a way. (*She offers him her arm, and they start to go*)

JEAN. Let's sleep on nine midsummer flowers, Miss Julie, and then our dreams will come true!

(MISS JULIE *and* JEAN *suddenly turn around in the doorway.* JEAN *is holding his hand over one eye*)

MISS JULIE. You've caught something in your eye. Let me see.

JEAN. It's nothing. Just a bit of dust. It'll go away.

MISS JULIE. The sleeve of my dress must have grazed your eye. Sit down and I'll help you. (*She takes him by the arm and sits him down. She takes his head and leans it back. With the corner of her handkerchief she tries to get out the bit of dust*) Now sit still, absolutely still. (*She slaps his hand*) Do as you're told. Why, I believe you're trembling—a big, strong man like you. (*She feels his biceps*) With such big arms!

JEAN (*Warmingly*). Miss Julie!

MISS JULIE. Yes, *monsieur Jean?*

JEAN. *Attention! Je ne suis qu'un homme!*

MISS JULIE. Sit still, I tell you! . . . There now! It's out. Kiss my hand and thank me!

JEAN (*Rising to his feet*). Listen to me, Miss Julie!—Christine has gone to bed!—Listen to me, I tell you!

MISS JULIE. Kiss my hand first!

JEAN. Listen to me!

MISS JULIE. Kiss my hand first!

JEAN. All right. But you'll have no one to blame but yourself.

MISS JULIE. For what?

JEAN. For what! Are you twenty-five years old and still a child? Don't you know it's dangerous to play with fire?

MISS JULIE. Not for me. I'm insured!

JEAN (*Boldly*). Oh, no you're not! And even if you are, there's inflammable stuff next door.

MISS JULIE. Meaning you?

JEAN. Yes. Not just because it's me, but because I'm a young man—

MISS JULIE. And irresistibly handsome? What incredible conceit! A Don Juan, maybe! Or a Joseph! Yes, bless my soul, that's it: you're a Joseph!

JEAN. You think so?!

MISS JULIE. I'm almost afraid so! (JEAN *boldly steps up to her, grabs her around the waist, kisses her. She slaps his face*) None of that!

JEAN. Are you still playing games or are you serious?

MISS JULIE. I'm serious.

JEAN. Then you must have been serious just a moment ago, too! You take your games too seriously and that's dangerous. Well, I'm tired of your games, and if you'll excuse me, I'll return to my work. The Count will be wanting his boots on time, and it's long past midnight.

MISS JULIE. Put those boots down.

JEAN. No! This is my job. It's what I'm here for. But I never undertook to be a playmate for you. That's something I could never be. I consider myself too good for that.

MISS JULIE. You are proud.

JEAN. In some ways. Not in others.

MISS JULIE. Have you ever been in love?

JEAN. We don't use that word around here. But I've been interested in a lot of girls, if that's what you mean. . . . I even got sick once because I couldn't have the one I wanted—really sick, like the princes in the *Arabian Nights*—who couldn't eat or drink for love.

MISS JULIE. Who was the girl? (JEAN *does not reply*) Who was she?

JEAN. You can't make me tell you that.

MISS JULIE. Even if I ask you as an equal—ask you—as a friend? . . . Who was she?

JEAN. You.

MISS JULIE (*Sitting down*). How—amusing. . . .

JEAN. Yes, maybe so. Ridiculous. . . . That's why I didn't want to tell you about it before. But now I'll tell you the whole story. . . . Have you any idea what the world looks like from below? Of course you haven't. No more than a hawk or eagle has. You hardly ever see their backs because they're always soaring above us. I lived with seven brothers and sisters—and a

461 **Attention! . . . homme!** Be careful! I'm only a man!

pig—out on the waste land where there wasn't even a tree growing. But from my window I could see the wall of the Count's garden with the apple trees sticking up over it. That was the Garden of Eden for me, and there were many angry angels with flaming swords standing guard over it. But in spite of them, I and the other boys found a way to the Tree of Life. . . . I'll bet you despise me.

MISS JULIE. All boys steal apples.

JEAN. That's what you say now. But you still despise me. Never mind. One day I went with my mother into this paradise to weed the onion beds. Next to the vegetable garden stood a Turkish pavilion, shaded by jasmine and hung all over with honeysuckle. I couldn't imagine what it was used for. I only knew I had never seen such a beautiful building. People went in, and came out again. And one day the door was left open. I sneaked in. The walls were covered with portraits of kings and emperors, and the windows had red curtains with tassels on them. —You do know what kind of place I'm talking about, don't you? . . . I—(*He breaks off a lilac and holds it under* MISS JULIE'S *nose*) I had never been inside a castle, never seen anything besides the church. But this was more beautiful. And no matter what I tried to think about, my thoughts always came back—to that little pavilion. And little by little there arose in me a desire to experience just for once the whole pleasure of . . . *Enfin,* I sneaked in, looked about, and marveled. Then I heard someone coming! There was only one way out—for the upper-class people. But for me there was one more—a lower one. And I had no other choice but to take it. (MISS JULIE, *who has taken the lilac from* JEAN, *lets it fall to the table*) Then I began to run like mad, plunging through the raspberry bushes, ploughing through the strawberry patches, and came up on the rose terrace. And there I caught sight of a pink dress and a pair of white stockings. That was you. I crawled under a pile of weeds, under—well, you can imagine what it was like—under thistles that pricked me and wet dirt that stank to high heaven. And all the while I could see you walking among the roses. I said to myself, "If it's true that a thief can enter heaven and be with the angels, isn't it strange that a poor man's child here on God's green earth can't enter the Count's park and play with the Count's daughter."

MISS JULIE (*Sentimentally*). Do you think all poor children have felt that way?

JEAN (*Hesitatingly at first, then with mounting conviction*). If all poor ch—? Yes—yes, naturally. Of course!

MISS JULIE. It must be terrible to be poor.

JEAN (*With exaggerated pain and poignancy*). Oh, Miss Julie! You don't know! A dog can lie on the sofa with its mistress; a horse can have its nose stroked by the hand of a countess; but a servant—! (*Changing his tone*) Of course, now and then you meet somebody with guts enough to work his way up in the world, but how often?—Anyway, you know what I did afterwards? I threw myself into the millstream with all my clothes on. Got fished out and spanked. But the following Sunday, when Pa and everybody else in the house went to visit Grandma, I arranged things so I'd be left behind. Then I washed myself all over with soap and warm water, put on my best clothes, and went off to church—just to see you there once more. I saw you, and then I went home determined to die. But I wanted to die beautifully and comfortably, without pain. I remembered that it was fatal to sleep under an alder bush. And we had a big one that had just blossomed out. I stripped it of every leaf and blossom it had and made a bed of them in a bin of oats. Have you ever noticed how smooth oats are? As smooth to the touch as human skin. . . . So I pulled the lid of the bin shut and closed my eyes—fell asleep. And when they woke me I was really very sick. But I didn't die, as you can see.——What was I trying to prove? I don't know. There was no hope of winning you. But you were a symbol of the absolute hopelessness of my ever getting out of the circle I was born in.

MISS JULIE. You know, you have a real gift for telling stories. Did you go to school?

JEAN. A little. But I've read a lot of novels and gone to the theater. And I've also listened to educated people talk. That's how I've learned the most.

MISS JULIE. You mean to tell me you stand around listening to what we're saying!

JEAN. Certainly! And I've heard an awful lot, I can tell you—sitting on the coachman's seat

544 **pavilion** a privy 561 **Enfin** Finally

or rowing the boat. One time I heard you and a girl friend talking——

MISS JULIE. Really? . . . And just what did you hear?

JEAN. Well, now, I don't know if I could repeat it. I can tell you I was a little amazed. I couldn't imagine where you had learned such words. Maybe at bottom there isn't such a big difference as you might think, between people and people. 640

MISS JULIE. How vulgar! At least people in my class don't behave like you when we're engaged.

JEAN (*Looking her in the eye*). Are you sure?—Come on now, it's no use playing the innocent with me.

MISS JULIE. He was a beast. The man I offered my love was a beast.

JEAN. That's what you all say—afterwards.

650 MISS JULIE. All?

JEAN. I'd say so, since I've heard the same expression used several times before in similar circumstances.

MISS JULIE. What kind of circumstances?

JEAN. The kind we're talking about. I remember the last time I—

MISS JULIE (*Rising*). That's enough! I don't want to hear any more.

JEAN. How strange! Neither did she! . . . 660 Well, now if you'll excuse me, I'll go to bed.

MISS JULIE (*Softly*). Go to bed on Midsummer Eve?

JEAN. That's right. Dancing with that crowd up there really doesn't amuse me.

MISS JULIE. Jean, get the key to the boathouse and row me out on the lake. I want to see the sun come up.

JEAN. Do you think that's wise?

MISS JULIE. You sound as if you were wor- 670 ried about your reputation.

JEAN. Why not? I don't particularly care to be made ridiculous, or to be kicked out without a recommendation just when I'm trying to establish myself. Besides, I have a certain obligation to Christine.

MISS JULIE. Oh, I see. It's Christine now.

JEAN. Yes, but I'm thinking of you, too. Take my advice, Miss Julie, and go up to your room.

MISS JULIE. When did you start giving me orders? 680

JEAN. Just this once. For your own sake! Please! It's very late. You're so tired, you're drunk. You don't know what you're doing. Go to bed, Miss Julie.——Besides, if my ears aren't deceiving me, they're coming this way, looking for me. If they find us here together, you're done for!

(THE CHORUS *is heard coming nearer, singing*)

Two ladies came from out the clover, 690
Tri-di-ri-di-ralla, tri-di-ri-di-ra.
And one of them was green all over,
Tri-di-ri-di-ralla-la.
They told us they had gold aplenty,
Tri-di-ri-di-ralla, tri-di-ri-di-ra.
But neither of them owned a penny.
Tri-di-ri-di-ralla-la.
This wreath for you I may be plaiting,
Tri-di-ri-di-ralla, tri-di-ri-di-ra.
But it's for another I am waiting, 700
Tri-di-ri-ralla-la!

MISS JULIE. I know these people. I love them just as they love me. Let them come. You'll find out.

JEAN. No, Miss Julie, they don't love you! They take the food you give them, but they spit on it as soon as your back is turned. Believe me! Just listen to them. Listen to what they're singing.——No, you'd better not listen.

MISS JULIE (*Listening*). What are they sing- 710 ing?

JEAN. A dirty song—about you and me!

MISS JULIE. How disgusting! Oh, what cowardly, sneaking—

JEAN. That's what the mob always is—cowards! You can't fight them; you can only run away.

MISS JULIE. Run away? Where? There's no way out of here. And we can't go in to Christine. 720

JEAN. What about my room? What do you say? The rules don't count in a situation like this. You can trust me. I'm your friend, remember? Your true, devoted, and respectful friend.

MISS JULIE. But suppose—suppose they looked for you there?

661 **Midsummer Eve** A festive occasion, especially in northern lands. It is a festival ultimately of pagan origin which still retains some of its original license.

JEAN. I'll bolt the door. If they try to break it down, I'll shoot. Come, Miss Julie! (*On his knees*) Please, Miss Julie!

730 MISS JULIE (*Meaningfully*). You promise me that you—?

JEAN. I swear to you!

(MISS JULIE *goes out quickly to the right.* JEAN *follows her impetuously*)

THE BALLET. *The country people enter in festive costumes, with flowers in their hats. The fiddler is in the lead. A keg of small beer and a little keg of liquor, decorated with greenery, are set up on the table. Glasses are brought out.* 740 *They all drink, after which they form a circle and sing and dance the round dance, "Two ladies came from out the clover." At the end of the dance they all leave singing.*

(MISS JULIE *comes in alone; looks at the devastated kitchen; clasps her hands together; then takes out a powder puff and powders her face.* JEAN *enters. He is in high spirits*)

JEAN. You see! You heard them, didn't you? You've got to admit it's impossible to stay here.

750 MISS JULIE. No, I don't. But even if I did, what could we do?

JEAN. Go away, travel, get away from here!

MISS JULIE. Travel? Yes—but where?

JEAN. Switzerland, the Italian lakes. You've never been there?

MISS JULIE. No. Is it beautiful?

JEAN. Eternal summer, oranges, laurel trees, ah . . . !

MISS JULIE. But what are we going to do 760 there?

JEAN. I'll set up a hotel—a first-class hotel with a first-class clientele.

MISS JULIE. Hotel?

JEAN. I tell you that's the life! Always new faces, new languages. Not a minute to think about yourself or worry about your nerves. No looking for something to do. The work keeps you busy. Day and night the bells ring, the trains whistle, the busses come and go. And 770 all the while the money comes rolling in. I tell you it's the life!

MISS JULIE. Yes, that's the life. But what about me?

JEAN. The mistress of the whole place, the star of the establishment! With your looks—and your personality—it can't fail. It's perfect! You'll sit in the office like a queen, setting your slaves in motion by pressing an electric button. The guests will file before your throne and timidly lay their treasures on your table. You 780 can't imagine how people tremble when you shove a bill in their face! I'll salt the bills and you'll sugar them with your prettiest smile. Come on, let's get away from here—(*He takes a timetable from his pocket*)—right away—the next train! We'll be in Malmo at 6:30; Hamburg 8:40 in the morning; Frankfurt to Basle in one day; and to Como by way of the Gotthard tunnel in—let me see—three days! Three days!

MISS JULIE. You make it sound so wonder- 790 ful. But, Jean, you have to give me strength. Tell me you love me. Come and put your arms around me.

JEAN (*Hesitates*). I want to . . . but I don't dare. Not any more, not in this house. I do love you—without a shadow of a doubt. How can you doubt that, Miss Julie?

MISS JULIE (*Shyly, very becomingly*). You don't have to be formal with me, Jean. You can call me Julie. There aren't any barriers between 800 us now. Call me Julie.

JEAN (*Agonized*). I can't! There are still barriers between us, Miss Julie, as long as we stay in this house! There's the past, there's the Count. I've never met anyone I feel so much respect for. I've only got to see his gloves lying on a table and I shrivel up. I only have to hear that bell ring and I shy like a frightened horse. I only have to look at his boots standing there so stiff and proud and I feel my spine bending. (*He* 810 *kicks the boots*) Superstitions, prejudices that they've drilled into us since we were children! But they can be forgotten just as easily! Just we get to another country where they have a republic! They'll crawl on their hands and knees when they see my uniform. On their hands and knees, I tell you! But not me! Oh, no. I'm not made for crawling. I've got guts, backbone. And once I grab that first branch, you just watch me climb. I may be a valet now, but next year I'll be owning property; in ten years, I'll be living off 820 my investments. Then I'll go to Rumania, get myself some decorations, and maybe—notice I only say maybe—end up as a count!

788 **Como** in northern Italy

MISS JULIE. How wonderful, wonderful.

JEAN. Listen, in Rumania you can buy titles. You'll be a countess after all. *My* countess.

MISS JULIE. But I'm not interested in that. I'm leaving all that behind. Tell me you love
830 me, Jean, or else—or else what difference does it make what I am?

JEAN. I'll tell you a thousand times—but later! Not now. And not here. Above all, let's keep our feelings out of this or we'll make a mess of everything. We have to look at this thing calmly and coolly, like sensible people. (*He takes out a cigar, clips the end, and lights it*) Now you sit there and I'll sit here, and we'll talk as if nothing had happened.

840 MISS JULIE (*In anguish*). My God, what are you? Don't you have any feelings?

JEAN. Feelings? Nobody's got more feelings than I have. But I've learned how to control them.

MISS JULIE. A few minutes ago you were kissing my shoe—and now—!

JEAN (*Harshly*). That was a few minutes ago. We've got other things to think about now!

850 MISS JULIE. Don't speak to me like that, Jean!

JEAN. I'm just trying to be sensible. We've been stupid once; let's not be stupid again. Your father might be back at any moment, and we've got to decide our future before then.—Now what do you think about my plans? Do you approve or don't you?

MISS JULIE. I don't see anything wrong with them. Except one thing. For a big undertaking
860 like that, you'd need a lot of capital. Have you got it?

JEAN (*Chewing on his cigar*). Have I got it? Of course I have. I've got my knowledge of the business, my vast experience, my familiarity with languages. That's capital that counts for something, let me tell you.

MISS JULIE. You can't even buy the railway tickets with it.

JEAN. That's true. That's why I need a
870 backer—someone to put up the money.

MISS JULIE. Where can you find him on a moment's notice?

JEAN. You'll find him—if you want to be my partner.

MISS JULIE. I can't. And I don't have a penny to my name.

(*Pause*)

JEAN. Then you can forget the whole thing.

MISS JULIE. Forget—?

JEAN. And things will stay just the way they 880 are.

MISS JULIE. Do you think I'm going to live under the same roof with you, as your mistress? Do you think I'm going to have people sneering at me behind my back? How do you think I'll ever be able to look my father in the face after this? No, no! Take me away from here, Jean —the shame, the humiliation. . . . What have I done? Oh, my God, my God! What have I done? (*She bursts into tears*) 890

JEAN. Now don't start singing that tune. It won't work. What have you done that's so awful? You're not the first.

MISS JULIE (*Crying hysterically*). Now you despise me!—I'm falling, I'm falling!

JEAN. Fall down to me, and I'll lift you up again!

MISS JULIE. What awful hold did you have over me? What drove me to you? The weak to the strong? The falling to the rising! Or maybe 900 it was love? Love? This? You don't know what love is!

JEAN. Want to bet? Did you think I was a virgin?

MISS JULIE. You're vulgar! The things you say, the things you think!

JEAN. That's the way I was brought up and that's the way I am! Now don't get hysterical and don't play the fine lady with me. We're eating off the same platter now. . . . That's 910 better. Come over here and be a good girl and I'll treat you to something special. (*He opens the table drawer and takes out the wine bottle. He pours the wine into two used glasses*)

MISS JULIE. Where did you get that wine?

JEAN. From the wine cellar.

MISS JULIE. My father's burgundy!

JEAN. Should be good enough for his son-in-law.

MISS JULIE. I was drinking beer and you—! 920

JEAN. That shows that I have better taste than you.

MISS JULIE. Thief!

JEAN. You going to squeal on me?

MISS JULIE. Oh, God! Partner in crime with a petty house thief! I must have been drunk; I must have been walking in my sleep. Midsummer Night! Night of innocent games—

JEAN. Yes, very innocent!

930 MISS JULIE (*Pacing up and down*). Is there anyone here on earth as miserable as I am?

JEAN. Why be miserable? After such a conquest! Think of poor Christine in there. Don't you think she's got any feelings?

MISS JULIE. I thought so a while ago, but I don't now. A servant's a servant—

JEAN. And a whore's a whore!

MISS JULIE (*Falls to her knees and clasps her hands together*). Oh, God in heaven, put an 940 end to my worthless life! Lift me out of this awful filth I'm sinking in! Save me! Save me!

JEAN. I feel sorry for you, I have to admit it. When I was lying in the onion beds, looking up at you on the rose terrace, I—I'm telling you the truth now—I had the same dirty thoughts that all boys have.

MISS JULIE. And you said you wanted to die for me!

JEAN. In the oat bin? That was only a story.

950 MISS JULIE. A lie, you mean.

JEAN (*Beginning to get sleepy*). Practically. I think I read it in a paper about a chimney sweep who curled up in a wood-bin with some lilacs because they were going to arrest him for nonsupport of his child.

MISS JULIE. Now I see you for what you are.

JEAN. What did you expect me to do? It's always the fancy talk that gets the women.

MISS JULIE. You dog!

960 JEAN. You bitch!

MISS JULIE. Well, now you've seen the eagle's back—

JEAN. Wasn't exactly its back—!

MISS JULIE. I was going to be your first branch—!

JEAN. A rotten branch—

MISS JULIE. I was going to be the window dressing for your hotel—!

JEAN. And I the hotel—!

970 MISS JULIE. Sitting at the desk, attracting your customers, padding your bills—!

JEAN. I could manage that myself—!

MISS JULIE. How can a human soul be so dirty and filthy?

JEAN. Then why don't you clean it up?

MISS JULIE. You lackey! You shoeshine boy! Stand up when I talk to you!

JEAN. You lackey lover! You bootblack's tramp! Shut your mouth and get out of here! Who do you think you are telling me I'm 980 coarse? I've never seen anybody in my class behave as crudely as you did tonight. Have you ever seen any of the girls around here grab at a man like you did? Do you think any of the girls of my class would throw themselves at a man like that? I've never seen the like of it except in animals and prostitutes!

MISS JULIE (*Crushed*). That's right! Hit me! Walk all over me! It's all I deserve. I'm rotten. But help me! Help me to get out of this—if 990 there is any way out for me!

JEAN (*Less harsh*). I'd be doing myself an injustice if I didn't admit that part of the credit for this seduction belongs to me. But do you think a person in my position would have dared to look twice at you if you hadn't asked for it? I'm still amazed—

MISS JULIE. And still proud.

JEAN. Why not? But I've got to confess the victory was a little too easy to give me any real 1000 thrill.

MISS JULIE. Go on, hit me more!

JEAN (*Standing up*). No. . . . I'm sorry for what I said. I never hit a person who's down, especially a woman. I can't deny that, in one way, it was good to find out that what I saw glittering up above was only fool's gold, to have seen that the eagle's back was as gray as its belly, that the smooth cheek was just powder, and that there could be dirt under the manicured nails, 1010 that the handkerchief was soiled even though it smelled of perfume. But, in another way, it hurt me to find that everything I was striving for wasn't very high above me after all, wasn't even real. It hurts me to see you sink far lower than your own cook. Hurts, like seeing the last flowers cut to pieces by the autumn rains and turned to muck.

MISS JULIE. You talk as if you already stood high above me. 1020

JEAN. Well, don't I? Don't forget I could

make you a countess but you can never make me a count.

MISS JULIE. But I have a father for a count. You can never have that!

JEAN. True. But I might father my own counts—that is, if—

MISS JULIE. You're a thief! I'm not!

JEAN. There are worse things than being a thief. A lot worse. And besides, when I take a position in a house, I consider myself a member of the family—in a way, like a child in the house. It's no crime for a child to steal a few ripe cherries when they're falling off the trees, is it? (*He begins to feel passionate again*) Miss Julie, you're a beautiful woman, much too good for the likes of me. You got carried away by your emotions and now you want to cover up your mistake by telling yourself that you love me. You don't love me. You might possibly have been attracted by my looks—in which case your kind of love is no better than mine. But I could never be satisfied to be just an animal for you, and I could never make you love me.

MISS JULIE. Are you so sure of that?

JEAN. You mean there's a chance? I could love you, there's no doubt about that. You're beautiful, you're refined—(*He goes up to her and takes her hand*)—educated, lovable when you want to be, and once you set a man's heart on fire, I'll bet it burns forever. (*He puts his arm around her waist*) You're like hot wine with strong spices. One of your kisses is enough to—(*He attempts to lead her out, but she rather reluctantly breaks away from him*)

MISS JULIE. Let me go. You don't get me that way.

JEAN. Then how? Not by petting you and not with pretty words, not by planning for the future, not by saving you from humiliation! Then how, tell me how?

MISS JULIE. How? How? I don't know how! I don't know at all!—I hate you like I hate rats, but I can't get away from you.

JEAN. Then come away *with* me!

MISS JULIE (*Pulling herself together*). Away? Yes, we'll go away!——But I'm so tired. Pour me a glass of wine, will you? (JEAN *pours the wine.* MISS JULIE *looks at her watch*) Let's talk first. We still have a little time. (*She empties the glass of wine and holds it out for more*)

JEAN. Don't overdo it. You'll get drunk.

MISS JULIE. What difference does it make?

JEAN. What difference? It looks cheap.——What did you want to say to me?

MISS JULIE. We're going to run away together, right? But we'll talk first—that is, I'll talk. So far you've done all the talking. You've told me your life, now I'll tell you mine. That way we'll know each other through and through before we become traveling companions.

JEAN. Wait a minute. Excuse me, but are you sure you won't regret this afterwards, when you've surrendered your secrets?

MISS JULIE. I thought you were my friend.

JEAN. I am—sometimes. But don't count on me.

MISS JULIE. You don't mean that. Anyway, everybody knows my secrets.—My mother's parents were very ordinary people, just commoners. She was brought up, according to the theories of her time, to believe in equality, the independence of women, and all that. And she had a strong aversion to marriage. When my father proposed to her, she swore she would never become his wife. . . . But she did anyway. I was born—against my mother's wishes, as far as I can make out. My mother decided to bring me up as a nature child. And on top of that I had to learn everything a boy learns, so I could be living proof that women were just as good as men. I had to wear boy's clothes, learn to handle horses—but not to milk the cows. I was made to groom the horses and handle them, and go out hunting—and even had to try and learn farming! And on the estate all the men were set to doing the work of women, and the women to doing men's work—with the result that the whole place threatened to fall to pieces, and we became the local laughing-stock. Finally my father must have come out of his trance. He rebelled, and everything was changed according to his wishes. Then my mother got sick. I don't know what kind of sickness it was, but she often had convulsions, and she would hide herself in the attic or in the garden, and sometimes she would stay out all night. Then there occurred that big fire you've heard about. The house, the stables, the cowsheds, all burned down—and under very peculiar circumstances that led one to suspect arson. You see, the accident occurred the day after the insurance expired, and the premiums on the new policy, which my father had sent in, were delayed through the messenger's carelessness, and didn't arrive on time. (*She refills her glass and drinks*)

JEAN. You've had enough.

MISS JULIE. Who cares!——We were left without a penny to our name. We had to sleep in the carriages. My father didn't know where to turn for money to rebuild the house. Then Mother suggested to him that he might try to borrow money from an old friend of hers, who owned a brick factory, not far from here. Father takes out a loan, but there's no interest charged, which surprises him. So the place was rebuilt. (*She drinks some more*) Do you know who set fire to the place?

JEAN. Your honorable mother!

MISS JULIE. Do you know who the brick manufacturer was?

JEAN. Your mother's lover?

MISS JULIE. Do you know whose money it was?

JEAN. Let me think a minute. . . . No, I give up.

MISS JULIE. It was my mother's!

JEAN. The Count's, you mean. Or was there a marriage settlement?

MISS JULIE. There wasn't a settlement. My mother had a little money of her own which she didn't want under my father's control, so she invested it with her—friend.

JEAN. Who grabbed it!

MISS JULIE. Precisely. He appropriated it. Well, my father finds out what happened. But he can't go to court, can't pay his wife's lover, can't prove that it's his wife's money. That was how my mother got her revenge because he had taken control of the house. He was on the verge of shooting himself. There was even a rumor that he tried and failed. But he took a new lease on life and he forced my mother to pay for her mistakes. Can you imagine what those five years were like for me? I felt sorry for my father, but I took my mother's side because I didn't know the whole story. She had taught me to distrust and hate all men—you've heard how she hated men—and I swore to her that I'd never be slave to any man.

JEAN. But you got engaged to the attorney.

MISS JULIE. Only to make him slave to me.

JEAN. But he didn't want any of that?

MISS JULIE. Oh, he wanted to well enough, but I didn't give him the chance. I got bored with him.

JEAN. Yes, so I noticed—in the barnyard.

MISS JULIE. What did you notice?

JEAN. I saw what I saw. *He* broke off the engagement.

MISS JULIE. That's a lie! It was I who broke it off. Did he tell you that? He's beneath contempt!

JEAN. Come on now, he isn't as bad as that. So you hate men, Miss Julie?

MISS JULIE. Yes, I do. . . . Most of the time. But sometimes, when I can't help myself—oh. . . . (*She shudders in disgust*)

JEAN. Then you hate me, too?

MISS JULIE. You have no idea how much! I'd like to see you killed like an animal—

JEAN. Like a mad dog, without a moment's hesitation, right?

MISS JULIE. Right!

JEAN. But we don't have anything to shoot him with—and no dog! What are we going to do?

MISS JULIE. Go away from here.

JEAN. To torture ourselves to death?

MISS JULIE. No. To enjoy ourselves for a day or two, or a week, for as long as we can—and then—to die—

JEAN. Die? How stupid! I've got a better idea: start a hotel!

MISS JULIE (*Continuing without hearing* JEAN). —on the shores of Lake Como, where the sun is always shining, where the laurels bloom at Christmas, and the golden oranges glow on the trees.

JEAN. Lake Como is a stinking hole, and the only oranges I saw there were on the fruit stands. But it's a good tourist spot with a lot of villas and cottages that are rented out to lovers. Now there's a profitable business. You know why? They rent the villa for the whole season, but they leave after three weeks.

MISS JULIE (*Innocently*). Why after only three weeks?

JEAN. Because they can't stand each other any longer. Why else? But they still have to pay the rent. Then you rent it out again to another couple, and so on. There's no shortage of love—even if it doesn't last very long.

MISS JULIE. Then you don't want to die with me?

JEAN. I don't want to die at all! I enjoy life too much. And moreover, I consider taking your own life a sin against the Providence that gave us life.

MISS JULIE. You believe in God? You?

JEAN. Yes, certainly I do! I go to church every other Sunday.—Honestly, I've had enough of this talk. I'm going to bed.
to get off that easy? Don't you know that a man

MISS JULIE. Really? You think you're going owes something to the woman he's dishonored?

JEAN (*Takes out his purse and throws a silver coin on the table*). There you are. I don't want to owe anybody anything.

MISS JULIE (*Ignoring the insult*). Do you know what the law says—?

JEAN. Aren't you lucky the law says nothing about the women who seduce men!

MISS JULIE. What else can we do but go away from here, get married, and get divorced?

JEAN. Suppose I refuse to enter into this *mésalliance?*

MISS JULIE. *Mésalliance?*

JEAN. For me! I've got better ancestors than you. I don't have any female arsonist in my family.

MISS JULIE. How can you know?

JEAN. You can't prove the opposite because we don't have any family records—except in the police courts. But I've read the whole history of your family in that book on the drawing-room table. Do you know who the founder of your family line was? A miller—who let his wife sleep with the king one night during the Danish war. I don't have any ancestors like that. I don't have any ancestors at all! But I can become an ancestor myself.

MISS JULIE. This is what I get for baring my heart and soul to someone too low to understand, for sacrificing the honor of my family—

JEAN. Dishonor!—I warned you, remember? Drinking makes one talk, and talking's bad.

MISS JULIE. Oh, how sorry I am! . . . If only it had never happened! . . . If only you at least loved me!

JEAN. For the last time—What do you expect of me? Do you want me to cry? Jump over your whip? Kiss you? Do you want me to lure you to Lake Como for three weeks and then—? What am I supposed to do? What do you want? I've had more than I can take. This is what I get for involving myself with women. . . . Miss Julie, I can see that you're unhappy; I know that you're suffering; but I simply cannot understand you. My people don't behave like this. We don't hate each other. We make love for the fun of it, when we can get any time off from our work. But we don't have time for it all day and all night like you do. If you ask me, you're sick, Miss Julie. I'm sure that's it, Miss Julie.

MISS JULIE. You can be understanding, Jean. You're talking to me like a human being now.

JEAN. Well, be human yourself. You spit on me but you don't let me wipe it off—on you!

MISS JULIE. Help me, Jean. Help me. Tell me what I should do, that's all—which way to go.

JEAN. For Christ's sake, if only I knew myself!

MISS JULIE. I've been crazy—I've been out of my mind—but does that mean there's no way out for me?

JEAN. Stay here as if nothing had happened. Nobody knows anything.

MISS JULIE. Impossible! Everybody who works here knows. Christine knows.

JEAN. They don't know a thing. And anyhow they'd never believe it.

MISS JULIE (*Slowly, significantly*). But . . . it might happen again.

JEAN. That's true!

MISS JULIE. And there might be consequences.

JEAN (*Stunned*). Consequences!! What on earth have I been thinking of! You're right! There's only one thing to do: get away from here! Immediately! I can't go with you—that would give the whole game away. You'll have to go by yourself. Somewhere—I don't care where!

MISS JULIE. By myself? Where?—Oh, no, Jean, I can't. I can't!

JEAN. You've got to! Before the Count comes back. You know as well as I do what will happen if you stay here. After one mistake, you figure you might as well go on, since the damage is already done. Then you get more and more careless until—finally you're exposed. I tell you, you've got to get out of the country. Afterwards you can write to the Count and tell him

1247 **mesalliance** misalliance

everything—leaving me out, of course. He'd never be able to guess it was me. Anyway, I don't think he'd exactly like to find that out.

1330 MISS JULIE. I'll go—if you'll come with me!

JEAN. Lady, are you out of your mind!? "Miss Julie elopes with her footman." The day after tomorrow it would be in all the papers. The Count would never live it down.

MISS JULIE. I can't go away. I can't stay. Help me. I'm so tired, so awfully tired. . . . Tell me what to do. Order me. Start me going. I can't think any more, can't move any more. . . .

JEAN. Now do you realize how weak you all

1340 are? What gives you the right to go strutting around with your noses in the air as if you owned the world? All right, I'll give you your orders. Go up and get dressed. Get some traveling money. And come back down here.

MISS JULIE (*Almost in a whisper*). Come up with me!

JEAN. To your room? . . . You're going crazy again! (*He hesitates a moment*) No! No! Go! Right now! (*He takes her hand and leads*

1350 *her out*)

MISS JULIE (*As she is leaving*). Don't be so harsh, Jean.

JEAN. Orders always sound harsh. You've never had to take them.

(JEAN, *left alone, heaves a sigh of relief and sits down at the table. He takes out a notebook and a pencil and begins to calculate, counting aloud now and then. The pantomime continues until* CHRISTINE *enters, dressed for church, and carry-*

1360 *ing* JEAN'S *white tie and shirt front in her hand*)

CHRISTINE. Lord in Heaven, what a mess! What on earth have you been doing?

JEAN. It was Miss Julie. She dragged the whole crowd in here. You must have been sleeping awfully sound if you didn't hear anything.

CHRISTINE. I slept like a log.

JEAN. You already dressed for church?

CHRISTINE. Yes, indeed. Don't you remember you promised to go to Communion with me to-

1370 day?

JEAN. Oh, yes, of course. I remember. I see you've brought my things. All right. Come on, put it on me. (*He sits down, and* CHRISTINE *starts to put the white tie and shirt front on him. Pause*)

JEAN (*Yawning*). What's the lesson for today?

CHRISTINE. The beheading of John the Baptist, I suppose.

JEAN. My God, that will go on forever.— 1380

Hey, you're choking me! . . . Oh, I'm so sleepy, so sleepy.

CHRISTINE. What were you doing up all night? You look green in the face.

JEAN. I've been sitting here talking with Miss Julie.

CHRISTINE. That girl! She doesn't know how to behave herself!

(*Pause*)

1390

JEAN. Tell me something, Christine. . . .

CHRISTINE. Well, what?

JEAN. Isn't it strange when you think about it? Her, I mean.

CHRISTINE. What's so strange?

JEAN. Everything!

(*Pause.* CHRISTINE *looks at the half-empty glasses on the table*)

CHRISTINE. Have you been drinking with her?

1400

JEAN. Yes!

CHRISTINE. Shame on you!—Look me in the eyes! You haven't . . . ?

JEAN. Yes!

CHRISTINE. Is it possible? Is it really possible?

JEAN (*After a moment's consideration*). Yes. It is.

CHRISTINE. Oh, how disgusting! I could never have believed anything like this would happen! No. No. This is too much! 1410

JEAN. Don't tell me you're jealous of her?

CHRISTINE. No, not of her. If it had been Clara—or Sophie—I would have scratched your eyes out! But her—? That's different. I don't know why. . . . But it's still disgusting!

JEAN. Then you're mad at her?

CHRISTINE. No. Mad at you. You were mean and cruel to do a thing like that, very mean. The poor girl! . . . But let me tell you, I'm not going to stay in this house a moment longer, not 1420

when I can't have any respect for my employers.

JEAN. Why do you want to respect them?

CHRISTINE. Don't try to be smart. You don't

want to work for people who behave immorally, do you? Well, do you? If you ask me, you'd be lowering yourself by doing that.

JEAN. Oh, I don't know. I think it's rather comforting to find out that they're not one bit better than we are.

1430 CHRISTINE. Well, I don't. If they're not any better, there's no point in us trying to be like them.—And think of the Count. Think of all the sorrows he's been through in his time. No, sir, I won't stay in this house any longer. . . . Imagine! You, of all people! If it had been the attorney fellow; if it had been somebody respectable—

JEAN. Now just a minute—!

CHRISTINE. Oh, you're all right in your own 1440 way. But there's a big difference between one class and another. You can't deny that.——No, this is something I can never get over. She was so proud, and so sarcastic about men, you'd never believe she'd go and throw herself at one. And at someone like you! And *she* was going to have Diana shot, because the poor thing ran after the gatekeeper's mongrel!—Well, I tell you, I've had enough! I'm not going to stay here any longer. On the twenty-fourth of October, 1450 I'm leaving.

JEAN. Then what'll you do?

CHRISTINE. Well, since you brought it up, it's about time that you got yourself a decent place, if we're going to get married.

JEAN. Why should I go looking for another place? I could never get a place like this if I'm married.

CHRISTINE. Well, of course not! But you could get a job as a doorkeeper, or maybe try 1460 to get a government job as a caretaker somewhere. The government don't pay much, but they pay regular. And there's a pension for the wife and children.

JEAN (*Wryly*). Fine, fine! But I'm not the kind of fellow who thinks about dying for his wife and children this early in the game. I hate to say it, but I've got slightly bigger plans than that.

CHRISTINE. Plans! Hah! What about your ob- 1470 ligations? You'd better start giving them a little thought!

JEAN. Don't start nagging me about obligations! I know what I have to do without you telling me. (*He hears a sound upstairs*) Anyhow, we'll have plenty of chance to talk about this later. You just go and get yourself ready, and we'll be off to church.

CHRISTINE. Who is that walking around up there?

JEAN. I don't know. Clara, I suppose. Who else? 1480

CHRISTINE (*Starting to leave*). It can't be the Count, can it? Could he have come back without anybody hearing him?

JEAN (*Frightened*). The Count? No, it can't be. He would have rung.

CHRISTINE (*Leaving*). God help us! I've never heard of the like of this.

(*The sun has now risen and strikes the tops of the trees in the park. The light shifts gradually until it is shining very obliquely through the* 1490 *windows.* JEAN *goes to the door and signals.* MISS JULIE *enters, dressed for travel, and carrying a small bird cage, covered with a towel. She sets the cage down on a chair*)

MISS JULIE. I'm ready now.

JEAN. Shh! Christine's awake.

MISS JULIE (*She is extremely tense and nervous during the following*). Did she suspect anything?

JEAN. She doesn't know a thing.——My 1500 God, what happened to you?

MISS JULIE. What do you mean? Do I look so strange?

JEAN. You're white as a ghost, and you've—excuse me—but you've got dirt on your face.

MISS JULIE. Let me wash it off. (*She goes over to the wash basin and washes her face and hands*) There! Do you have a towel? . . . Oh, look the sun's coming up!

JEAN. That breaks the magic spell! 1510

MISS JULIE. Yes, we were spellbound last night, weren't we? Midsummer madness . . . Jean, listen to me! Come with me. I've got the money!

JEAN (*Suspiciously*). Enough?

MISS JULIE. Enough for a start. Come with me, Jean. I can't travel alone today. Midsummer Day on a stifling hot train, packed in with crowds of people, all staring at me—stopping at every station when I want to be flying. I can't 1520 Jean, I can't! . . . And everything will remind me of the past. Midsummer Day when I was a child and the church was decorated with leaves —birch leaves and lilacs . . . the table spread for dinner with friends and relatives . . . and after dinner, dancing in the park, with flowers and games. Oh, no matter how far you travel, the memories tag right along in the baggage car . . . and the regrets and the remorse.

JEAN. All right, I'll go with you! But it's got to be now—before it's too late! This very instant!

MISS JULIE. Hurry and get dressed! (*She picks up the bird cage*)

JEAN. But no baggage! It would give us away.

MISS JULIE. Nothing. Only what we can take to our seats.

JEAN (*As he gets his hat*). What in the devil have you got there? What is that?

MISS JULIE. It's only my canary. I can't leave it behind.

JEAN. A canary! My God, do you expect us to carry a bird cage around with us? You're crazy. Put that cage down!

MISS JULIE. It's the only thing I'm taking with me from my home—the only living thing who loves me since Diana was unfaithful to me! Don't be cruel, Jean. Let me take it with me.

JEAN. I told you to put that cage down!—— And don't talk so loud. Christine can hear us.

MISS JULIE. No, I won't leave it with a stranger. I won't. I'd rather have you kill it.

JEAN. Let me have the little pest, and I'll wring its neck.

MISS JULIE. Yes, but don't hurt it. Don't—. No, I can't do it!

JEAN. Don't worry, I can. Give it here.

(MISS JULIE *takes the bird out of the cage and kisses it*)

MISS JULIE. Oh, my little Serena, must you die and leave your mistress?

JEAN. You don't have to make a scene of it. It's a question of your whole life and future. You're wasting time! (JEAN *grabs the canary from her, carries it to the chopping block, and picks up a meat cleaver.* MISS JULIE *turns away*) You should have learned how to kill chickens instead of shooting revolvers—(*He brings the cleaver down*)—then a drop of blood wouldn't make you faint.

MISS JULIE (*Screaming*). Kill me too! Kill me! You can kill an innocent creature without turning a hair—then kill me. Oh, how I hate you! I loathe you! There's blood between us. I curse the moment I first laid eyes on you! I curse the moment I was conceived in my mother's womb.

JEAN. What good does your cursing do? Let's get out of here!

MISS JULIE (*Approaches the chopping block as if drawn to it against her will*). No, I don't want to go yet. I can't.—I have to see.—Shh! I hear a carriage coming! (*She listens but keeps her eyes fastened on the chopping block and cleaver*) You don't think I can stand the sight of blood, do you? You think I'm so weak! Oh, I'd love to see your blood and your brains on that chopping block. I'd love to see the whole of your sex swimming in a sea of blood just like that. I think I could drink out of your skull. I'd like to bathe my feet in your ribs! I could eat your heart roasted whole!——You think I'm weak! You think I loved you because my womb hungered for your seed. You think I want to carry your brood under my heart and nourish it with my blood! Bear your child and take your name!—Come to think of it, what is your name anyway? I've never heard your last name. You probably don't even have one. I'd be Mrs. Doorkeeper or Madame Floorsweeper. You dog with my name on your collar—you lackey with my initials on your buttons! Do you think I'm going to share you with my cook and fight over you with my maid?! Ohhh!— You think I'm a coward who wants to run away. No, I'm going to stay. Come hell or high water, I don't care! My father comes home—finds his bureau broken into—his money gone. Then he rings—on that bell—two rings for the valet. And then he sends for the sheriff—and I tell him everything. Everything! Oh, it'll be wonderful to have it all over . . . If only it will be over. . . . He'll have a stroke and die. Then there'll be an end to all of us. There'll be peace . . . and quiet . . . forever. . . . His coat of arms will be broken on the coffin; the Count's line dies out. But the valet's line will continue in an orphanage, win triumphs in the gutter, and end in jail! *

* Most editions of *Miss Julie* have a speech by Jean at this point: "Now there speaks the royal blood! Brava, Miss Julie. Only you mustn't let the cat out of the bag about the miller and his wife." Strindberg wanted this speech expunged as not in keeping with Jean's character [Professor Sprinchorn's note].

(CHRISTINE *enters, dressed for church and with a hymn-book in her hand.* MISS JULIE *rushes over to her and throws herself into her arms as if seeking protection*)

MISS JULIE. Help me, Christine! Help me against this man!

CHRISTINE (*Cold and unmoved*). This is a fine way to behave on a holy day! (*She sees the* 1630 *chopping block*) Just look at the mess you've made there! How do you explain that? And what's all this shouting and screaming about?

MISS JULIE. Christine, you're a woman, you're my friend! I warn you, watch out for this—this monster!

JEAN (*Ill at ease and a little embarrassed*). If you ladies are going to talk, I think I'll go and shave. (*He slips out to the right*)

MISS JULIE. You've got to understand, Chris- 1640 tine! You've got to listen to me!

CHRISTINE. No, I don't. I don't understand this kind of shenanigans at all. Where do you think you're going dressed like that? And Jean with his hat on?—Well?—Well?

MISS JULIE. Listen to me, Christine! If you'll just listen to me, I'll tell you everything.

CHRISTINE. I don't want to know anything.

MISS JULIE. You've got to listen to me—!

CHRISTINE. What about? About your stupid 1650 behavior with Jean? I tell you that doesn't bother me at all, because it's none of my business. But if you have any silly idea about talking him into skipping out with you, I'll soon put a stop to that.

MISS JULIE (*Extremely tense*). Christine, please don't get upset. Listen to me. I can't stay here, and Jean can't stay here. So you see, we have to go away.

CHRISTINE. Hm, hm, hm.

1660 MISS JULIE (*Suddenly brightening up*). Wait! I've got an idea! Why couldn't all three of us go away together?—out of the country—to Switzerland—and start a hotel. I've got the money, you see. Jean and I would be responsible for the whole affair—and Christine, you could run the kitchen, I thought. Doesn't that sound wonderful! Say yes! Say you'll come, Christine, then everything will be settled. Say you will! Please! (*She throws her arms around* 1670 CHRISTINE *and pats her*)

CHRISTINE (*Remaining aloof and unmoved*). Hm. Hm.

MISS JULIE (*Presto tempo*). You've never been traveling, Christine. You have to get out and see the world. You can't imagine how wonderful it is to travel by train—constantly new faces—new countries. We'll go to Hamburg, and stop over to look at the zoo—you'll love that. And we'll go to the theater and the opera. And then when we get to Munich, we'll go to 1680 the museums, Christine. They have Rubenses and Raphaels there—those great painters, you know. Of course you've heard about Munich where King Ludwig lived—you know, the king who went mad. And then we can go and see his castles—they're built just like the ones you read about in fairy tales. And from there it's just a short trip to Switzerland—with the Alps. Think of the Alps, Christine, covered with snow in the middle of summer. And oranges grow 1690 there, and laurel trees that are green the whole year round.—(JEAN *can be seen in the wings at the right, sharpening his straight razor on a strap held between his teeth and his left hand. He listens to* MISS JULIE *with a satisfied expression on his face, now and then nodding approvingly.* MISS JULIE *continues tempo prestissimo*) —And that's where we'll get a hotel. I'll sit at the desk while Jean stands at the door and receives the guests, goes out shopping, writes the 1700 letters. What a life that will be! The train whistle blowing, then the bus arriving, then a bell ringing upstairs, then the bell in the restaurant rings—and I'll be making out the bills—and I know just how much to salt them—you can't imagine how timid tourists are when you shove a bill in their face!—And you, Christine, you'll run the whole kitchen—there'll be no standing at the stove for you—of course not. If you're going to talk to the people, you'll have to dress 1710 neatly and elegantly. And with your looks—I'm not trying to flatter you, Christine—you'll run off with some man one fine day—a rich Englishman, that's who it'll be, they're so easy to—(*slowing down*)—to catch.—Then we'll all be rich.—We'll build a villa on Lake Como.—Maybe it does rain there sometimes, but—(*more and more lifelessly*)—the sun has to shine sometimes, too—even if it looks cloudy.—And—then . . . Or else we can always travel some more— 1720 and come back . . . (*pause*)—here . . . or somewhere else. . . .

CHRISTINE. Do you really believe a word of that yourself, Miss Julie?

MISS JULIE (*Completely beaten*). Do I believe a word of it myself?

CHRISTINE. Do you?

MISS JULIE (*Exhausted*). I don't know. I don't believe anything any more. (*She sinks* 1730 *down on the bench and lays her head between her arms on the table*) Nothing. Nothing at all.

CHRISTINE (*Turns to the right and faces* JEAN). So! You were planning to run away, were you?

JEAN (*Nonplused, lays his razor down on the table*). We weren't exactly going to run away! Don't exaggerate. You heard Miss Julie's plans. Even if she's tired now after being up all night, her plans are perfectly practical.

1740 CHRISTINE. Well, just listen to you! Did you really think you could get me to cook for that little—

JEAN (*Sharply*). You keep a respectful tongue in your mouth when you talk to your mistress! Understand?

CHRISTINE. Mistress!

JEAN. Yes, mistress!

CHRISTINE. Well of all the—! I don't have to listen—

1750 JEAN. Yes, you do! You need to listen more and talk less. Miss Julie is your mistress. Don't forget that! And if you're going to despise her for what she did, you ought to despise yourself for the same reason.

CHRISTINE. I've always held myself high enough to—

JEAN. High enough to make you look down on others!

CHRISTINE. —enough to keep from lowering 1760 myself beneath my position. No one can say that the Count's cook has ever had anything to do with the stable groom or the swineherd. No one can say that!

JEAN. Yes, aren't you lucky you got involved with a decent man!

CHRISTINE. What kind of a decent man is it who sells the oats from the Count's stables?

JEAN. Listen to who's talking! You get a commission on the groceries and take bribes 1770 from the butcher!

CRISTINE. How can you say a thing like that!

JEAN. And you tell me you can't respect your employers any more! You! You!

CHRISTINE. Are you going to church or aren't you? I should think you'd need a good sermon after your exploits.

JEAN. No, I'm not going to church! You can go alone and confess your own sins.

CHRISTINE. Yes, I'll do just that. And I'll come back with enough forgiveness to cover 1780 yours, too. Our Redeemer suffered and died on the cross for all our sins, and if we come to Him in faith and with a penitent heart, He will take all our sins upon Himself.

JEAN. Grocery sins included?

MISS JULIE. Do you really believe that, Christine?

CHRISTINE. With all my heart, as sure as I'm standing here. It was the faith I was born into, and I've held on to it since I was a little girl, 1790 Miss Julie. Where sin aboundeth, there grace aboundeth also.

MISS JULIE. If I had your faith, Christine, if only—

CHRISTINE. But you see, that's something you can't have without God's special grace. And it is not granted to everyone to receive it.

MISS JULIE. Then who receives it?

CHRISTINE. That's the secret of the workings of grace, Miss Julie, and God is no respecter of 1800 persons. With him the last shall be the first—

MISS JULIE. In that case, he does have respect for the last, doesn't he?

CHRISTINE (*Continuing*). —and it is easier for a camel to go through the eye of a needle than for a rich man to enter the kingdom of God. That's how things are, Miss Julie. I'm going to leave now—alone. And on my way out I'm going to tell the stable boy not to let any horses out, in case anyone has any ideas about 1810 leaving before the Count comes home. Goodbye. (*She leaves*)

JEAN. She's a devil in skirts!—And all because of a canary!

MISS JULIE (*Listlessly*). Never mind the canary. . . . Do you see any way out of this, any end to it?

JEAN (*After thinking for a moment*). No.

MISS JULIE. What would you do if you were in my place? 1820

JEAN. In your place? Let me think. . . . An aristocrat, a woman, and—fallen. . . . I don't know.——Or maybe I do.

MISS JULIE (*Picks up the razor and makes a gesture with it*). Like this?

JEAN. Yes. But *I* wouldn't do it, you understand. That's the difference between us.

MISS JULIE. Because you're a man and I'm a woman? What difference does that make?

JEAN. Just the difference that there is—between a man and a woman.

MISS JULIE (*Holding the razor in her hand*). I want to! But I can't do it. My father couldn't do it either, that time he should have done it.

JEAN. No, he was right not to do it. He had to get his revenge first.

MISS JULIE. And now my mother is getting her revenge again through me.

JEAN. Haven't you ever loved your father, Miss Julie?

MISS JULIE. Yes, enormously. But I must have hated him too. I must have hated him without knowing it. It was he who brought me up to despise my own sex, to be half woman and half man. Who's to blame for what has happened? My father, my mother, myself? Myself? I don't have a self that's my own. I don't have a single thought I didn't get from my father, not an emotion I didn't get from my mother. And that last idea—about all people being equal—I got that from him, my betrothed. That's why I say he's beneath contempt. How can it be my own fault? Put the blame on Jesus, like Christine does? I'm too proud to do that—and too intelligent, thanks to what my father taught me. . . . A rich man can't get into heaven? That's a lie. But at least Christine, who's got money in the savings bank, won't get in. . . . Who's to blame? What difference does it make who's to blame? I'm still the one who has to bear the guilt, suffer the consequences—

JEAN. Yes, but—

(*The bell rings sharply twice.* MISS JULIE *jumps up.* JEAN *changes his coat*)

JEAN. The Count's back! What if Christine—? (*He goes to the speaking tube, taps on it, and listens*)

MISS JULIE. Has he looked in his bureau yet?

JEAN. This is Jean, sir! (*Listens. The audience cannot hear what the* COUNT *says*) Yes, sir! (*Listens*) Yes, sir! Yes, as soon as I can. (*Listens*) Yes, at once, sir! (*Listens*) Very good, sir! In half an hour.

MISS JULIE (*Trembling with anxiety*). What did he say? For God's sake, what did he say?

JEAN. He ordered his boots and his coffee in half an hour.

MISS JULIE. Half an hour then! . . . Oh, I'm so tired. I can't bring myself to do anything. Can't repent, can't run away, can't stay, can't live . . . can't die. Help me, Jean. Command me, and I'll obey like a dog. Do me this last favor. Save my honor, save his name. You know what I ought to do but can't force myself to do. Let me use your will power. You command me and I'll obey.

JEAN. I don't know—I can't either, not now. I don't know why. It's as if this coat made me—. I can't give you orders in this. And now, after the Count has spoken to me, I—I can't really explain it—but—I've got the backbone of a damned lackey! If the Count came down here now and ordered me to cut my throat, I'd do it on the spot.

MISS JULIE. Pretend that you're him, and that I'm you. You were such a good actor just a while ago, when you were kneeling before me. You were the aristocrat then. Or else—have you ever been to the theater and seen a hypnotist? (JEAN *nods*) He says to his subject, "Take this broom!" and he takes it. He says, "Now sweep!" and he sweeps.

JEAN. But the person has to be asleep!

MISS JULIE (*Ecstatic*). I'm already asleep. The whole room has turned to smoke. You seem like an iron stove, a stove that looks like a man in black with a high hat. Your eyes are glowing like coals when the fire dies out. Your face is a white smudge, like ashes. (*The sun is now shining in on the floor and falls on* JEAN) It's so good and warm—(*She rubs her hands together as if warming them at a fire*) —and so bright—and so peaceful.

JEAN (*Takes the razor and puts it in her hand*) There's the broom. Go now, when the sun is up—out into the barn—and—(*He whispers in her ear*)

MISS JULIE (*Waking up*). Thanks! I'm going to get my rest. But tell me one thing. Tell me that the first can also receive the gift of grace. Tell me that, even if you don't believe it.

JEAN. The first? I can't tell you that.——But wait a moment, Miss Julie. I know what I can tell you. You're no longer among the first. You're among—the last.

MISS JULIE. That's true! I'm among the very last. I am the last!—Oh! Now I can't go! Tell me just once more, tell me to go!

1930 JEAN. Now I can't either. I can't!

MISS JULIE. And the first shall be the last. . . .

JEAN. Don't think—don't think! You're taking all my strength away. You're making me a coward. . . . What! I thought I saw the bell move. No. . . . Let me stuff some paper in it.—Afraid of a bell! But it isn't just a bell. There's somebody behind it. A hand that makes it move. And there's something that makes the hand move.——Stop your ears, that's it, stop your 1940 ears! But it only rings louder. Rings louder and louder until you answer it. And then it's too late. Then the sheriff comes—and then—(*There are two sharp rings on the bell.* JEAN *gives a start, then straightens himself up*) It's horrible! But there's no other way for it to end.—Go! (MISS JULIE *walks resolutely out through the door*)

THE END

Review Questions

1. Discuss the play as a "battle of the sexes."
2. What draws Julie and Jean together?
3. Describe Julie's family background.
4. Describe Jean's background.
5. How do their past lives influence their present actions?
6. What does the Master's bell symbolize?
7. What effect does the seduction have on the play?
8. Is Julie's suicide inevitable?
9. Why is Julie disdainful of men?
10. What is the point of the canary?
11. What purpose does the peasants' dance serve in the play?
12. How does the play indicate Strindberg's interest in hypnotic suggestion?
13. Who controls the action?
14. What does the reader learn about Julie before she appears?
15. What is Christine's opinion of Julie?
16. Compare Jean's treatment of Christine and Julie.
17. What style of performance does the play require?
18. What is the meaning of Miss Julie's dream? of Jean's dream?
19. What is Jean's objective?
20. Does Julie deserve her fate?
21. What do you make of Miss Julie's chopping block speech?
22. What is the emotional impact of the play?
23. Are the changes that take place during the action made credible?

MAJOR BARBARA

Bernard Shaw (1856-1950)

Shaw, like so many other English dramatists, was born in Dublin. He began his writing career as a novelist, but soon found himself a journalist-critic of music, painting and literature. He became one of the leaders of the Fabian Society and was an outspoken champion of Socialism. Responding to his admiration for Ibsen and the need for striking new plays for the Independent Theater, Shaw turned his attention in 1892 to the theater, where he found a congenial outlet for his theatrical flair and dramatic talent.

His first two plays were forthright attacks on contemporary social problems—slum landlordism in *Widowers' Houses* and prostitution and sweatshop labor in *Mrs. Warren's Profession*. His *Major Barbara* (1905) was another indictment of social ills.

Although Shaw departed from realistic problem plays, he continued to deal in his uncompromising fashion with the pervasive issues of modern society. While critical evaluation at first suggested that he was merely a clever showman, the impact of his work ultimately was acknowledged, until he was recognized as the creator of the most significant collection of dramatic literature in the twentieth century. Among the other notable plays of Shaw are *Heartbreak House, Man and Superman, Candida, Pygmalion, Caesar and Cleopatra, Arms and the Man,* and *Saint Joan*.

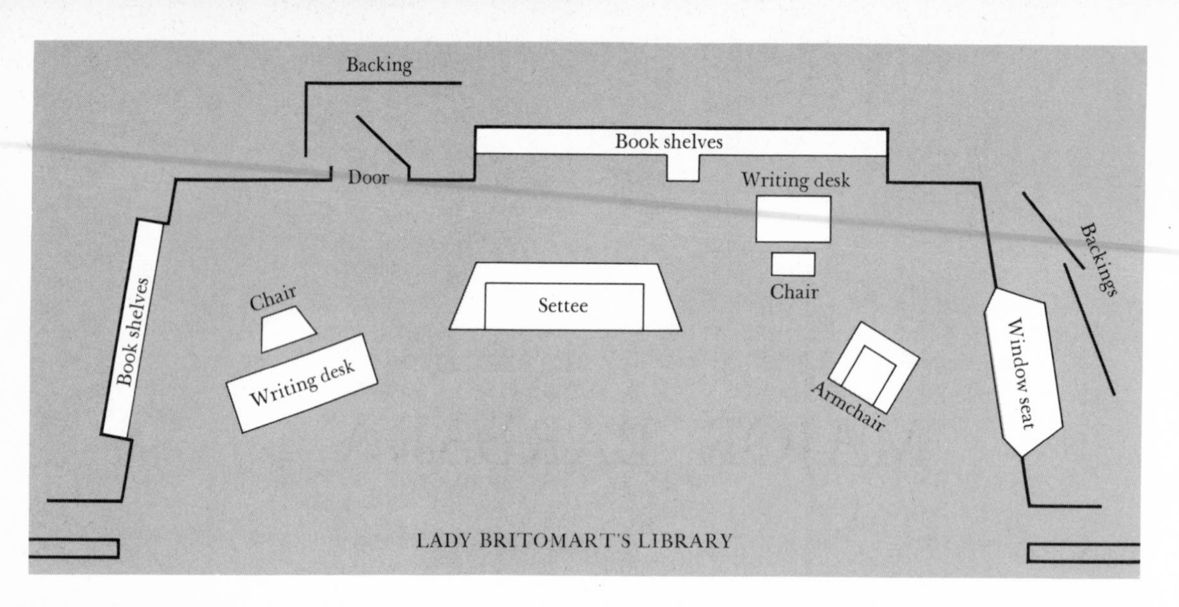

LADY BRITOMART'S LIBRARY

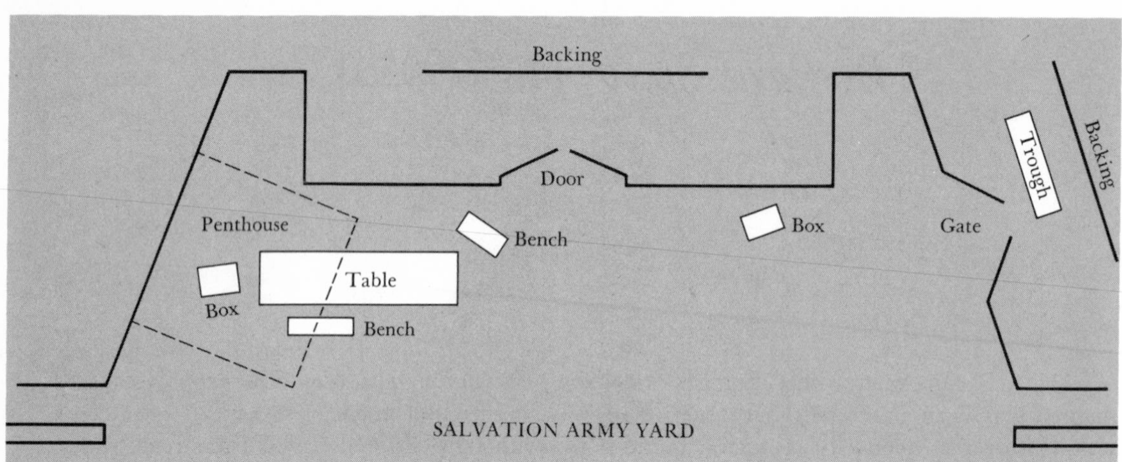

SALVATION ARMY YARD

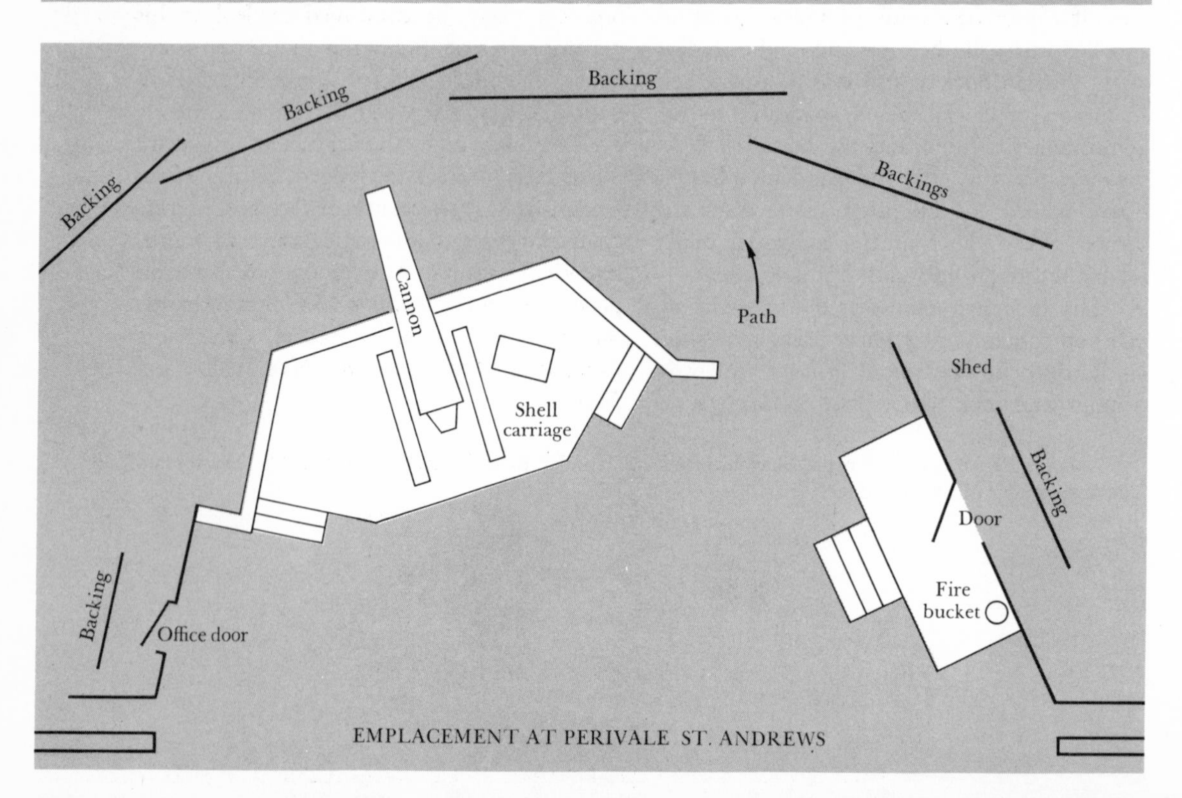

EMPLACEMENT AT PERIVALE ST. ANDREWS

RIGHT. Charles Laughton, Glynis Johns, Burgess Meredith, and Eli Wallach star in the 1956 Morosco Theater production. *(Photos by Friedman-Abeles.)*

LEFT. Schematic layouts for the Major Barbara sets.

Characters

STEPHEN UNDERSHAFT, *son of* ANDREW UNDERSHAFT *and* LADY BRITOMART

LADY BRITOMART, *daughter of the* EARL OF STEVENAGE *and wife of* ANDREW UNDERSHAFT

BARBARA UNDERSHAFT, *daughter of* ANDREW UNDERSHAFT *and* LADY BRITOMART; *a Major in the Salvation Army*

SARAH UNDERSHAFT, *daughter of* ANDREW UNDERSHAFT *and* LADY BRITOMART

ADOLPHUS CUSINS, *fiancé of* BARBARA UNDERSHAFT

CHARLES LOMAX, *fiancé of* SARAH UNDERSHAFT

MORRISON, LADY BRITOMART'S *butler*

ANDREW UNDERSHAFT, *husband of* LADY BRITOMART; *head of Undershaft and Lazarus, munitions makers*

RUMMY (ROMOLA) MITCHENS,
SNOBBY (BRONTERRE O'BRIEN) PRICE, } *Regulars at the West Ham Salvation Army shelter*

PETER SHIRLEY, *a discharged workman, poor but honest*

JENNY HILL, *a Salvation Army lass*

BILL WALKER, *a young tough*

MRS. BAINES, *a Salvation Army Commissioner*

BILTON, *a foreman in Undershaft and Lazarus*

MAJOR BARBARA

ACT ONE

It is after dinner in January 1906, in the library in Lady Britomart Undershaft's house in Wilton Crescent. A large and comfortable settee is in the middle of the room, upholstered in dark leather. A person sitting on it (it is vacant at present) would have, on his right, Lady Britomart's writing table, with the lady herself busy at it; a smaller writing table behind him on his left; the door behind him on Lady Britomart's side; and a window with a window seat directly on his left. Near the window is an armchair.

Lady Britomart is a woman of fifty or thereabouts, well dressed and yet careless of her dress, well bred and quite reckless of her breeding, well mannered and yet appallingly outspoken and indifferent to the opinion of her interlocutors, amiable and yet peremptory, arbitrary, and high-tempered to the last bearable degree, and withal a very typical managing matron of the upper class, treated as a naughty child until she grew into a scolding mother, and finally settling down with plenty of practical ability and worldly experience, limited in the oddest way with domestic and class limitations, conceiving the universe exactly as if it were a large house in Wilton Crescent, though handling her corner of it very effectively on that assumption, and being quite enlightened and liberal as to the books in the library, the pictures on the walls, the music in the portfolios, and the articles in the papers.

Her son, Stephen, comes in. He is a gravely correct young man under 25, taking himself very seriously, but still in some awe of his mother, from childish habit and bachelor shyness rather than from any weakness of character.

STEPHEN. Whats the matter?

LADY BRITOMART. Presently, Stephen.

Stephen submissively walks to the settee and sits down. He takes up a Liberal weekly called The Speaker.

10

LADY BRITOMART. Dont begin to read, Stephen. I shall require all your attention.

STEPHEN. It was only while I was waiting—

LADY BRITOMART. Dont make excuses, Stephen. (*He puts down The Speaker*). Now! (*She finishes her writing; rises; and comes to the settee*). I have not kept you waiting very long, I think.

STEPHEN. Not at all, mother.

LADY BRITOMART. Bring me my cushion. (*He takes the cushion from the chair at the desk and arranges it for her as she sits down on the settee*). Sit down. (*He sits down and fingers his tie nervously*). Dont fiddle with your tie, Stephen: there is nothing the matter with it.

20

STEPHEN. I beg your pardon. (*He fiddles with his watch chain instead*).

LADY BRITOMART. Now are you attending to me, Stephen?

STEPHEN. Of course, mother.

LADY BRITOMART. No: it's not of course. I

30

want something much more than your everyday matter-of-course attention. I am going to speak to you very seriously, Stephen. I wish you would let that chain alone.

STEPHEN (*hastily relinquishing the chain*). Have I done anything to annoy you, mother? If so, it was quite unintentional.

LADY BRITOMART (*astonished*). Nonsense! 40 (*With some remorse*) My poor boy, did you think I was angry with you?

STEPHEN. What is it, then, mother? You are making me very uneasy.

LADY BRITOMART (*squaring herself at him rather aggressively*). Stephen: may I ask how soon you intend to realize that you are a grown-up man, and that I am only a woman?

STEPHEN (*amazed*). Only a—

LADY BRITOMART. Dont repeat my words, 50 please: it is a most aggravating habit. You must learn to face life seriously, Stephen. I really cannot bear the whole burden of our family affairs any longer. You must advise me: you must assume the responsibility.

STEPHEN. I!

LADY BRITOMART. Yes, you, of course. You were 24 last June. Youve been at Harrow and Cambridge. Youve been to India and Japan. You must know a lot of things, now; unless 60 you have wasted your time most scandalously. Well, a d v i s e me.

STEPHEN (*much perplexed*). You know I have never interfered in the household—

LADY BRITOMART. No: I should think not. I dont want you to order the dinner.

STEPHEN. I mean in our family affairs.

LADY BRITOMART. Well, you must interfere now; for they are getting quite beyond me.

STEPHEN (*troubled*). I have thought some- 70 times that perhaps I ought; but really, mother, I know so little about them; and what I do know is so painful! it is so impossible to mention some things to you—(*he stops, ashamed*).

LADY BRITOMART. I suppose you mean your father.

STEPHEN (*almost inaudibly*). Yes.

LADY BRITOMART. My dear: we cant go on all our lives not mentioning him. Of course you were quite right not to open the subject until 80 I asked you to; but you are old enough now to be taken into my confidence, and to help me to deal with him about the girls.

STEPHEN. But the girls are all right. They are engaged.

LADY BRITOMART (*complacently*). Yes: I have made a very good match for Sarah. Charles Lomax will be a millionaire at 35. But that is ten years ahead; and in the meantime his trustees cannot under the terms of his father's will allow him more than £800 a year. 90

STEPHEN. But the will says also that if he increases his income by his own exertions, they may double the increase.

LADY BRITOMART. Charles Lomax's exertions are much more likely to decrease his income than to increase it. Sarah will have to find at least another £800 a year for the next ten years; and even then they will be as poor as church mice. And what about Barbara? I thought Barbara was going to make the most brilliant career 100 of all of you. And what does she do? Joins the Salvation Army; discharges her maid; lives on a pound a week; and walks in one evening with a professor of Greek whom she has picked up in the street, and who pretends to be a Salvationist, and actually plays the big drum for her in public because he has fallen head over ears in love with her.

STEPHEN. I was certainly rather taken aback when I heard they were engaged. Cusins is a 110 very nice fellow, certainly: nobody would ever guess that he was born in Australia; but—

LADY BRITOMART. Oh, Adolphus Cusins will make a very good husband. After all, nobody can say a word against Greek: it stamps a man at once as an educated gentleman. And my family, thank Heaven, is not a pig-headed Tory one. We are Whigs, and believe in liberty. Let snobbish people say what they please: Barbara shall marry, not the man they like, but the man 120 *I* like.

STEPHEN. Of course I was thinking only of his income. However, he is not likely to be extravagant.

LADY BRITOMART. Dont be too sure of that, Stephen. I know your quiet, simple, refined, poetic people like Adolphus: quite content with the best of everything! They cost more than your extravagant people, who are always as mean as they are second rate. No: Barbara will 130 need at least £2000 a year. You see it means two additional households. Besides, my dear, y o u must marry soon. I dont approve of the present fashion of philandering bachelors and late marriages; and I am trying to arrange something for you.

STEPHEN. It's very good of you, mother; but perhaps I had better arrange that for myself.

LADY BRITOMART. Nonsense! you are much too young to begin matchmaking: you would be taken in by some pretty little nobody. Of course I dont mean that you are not to be consulted: you know that as well as I do. (*Stephen closes his lips and is silent*). Now dont sulk, Stephen.

STEPHEN. I am not sulking, mother. What has all this got to do with—with—with my father?

LADY BRITOMART. My dear Stephen: where is the money to come from? It is easy enough for you and the other children to live on my income as long as we are in the same house; but I cant keep four families in four separate houses. You know how poor my father is: he has barely seven thousand a year now; and really, if he were not the Earl of Stevenage, he would have to give up society. He can do nothing for us. He says, naturally enough, that it is absurd that he should be asked to provide for the children of a man who is rolling in money. You see, Stephen, your father must be fabulously wealthy, because there is always a war going on somewhere.

STEPHEN. You need not remind me of that, mother. I have hardly ever opened a newspaper in my life without seeing our name in it. The Undershaft torpedo! The Undershaft quick firers! The Undershaft ten inch! the Undershaft disappearing rampart gun! the Undershaft submarine! and now the Undershaft aerial battleship! At Harrow they called me the Woolwich Infant. At Cambridge it was the same. A little brute at King's who was always trying to get up revivals, spoilt my Bible—your first birthday present to me—by writing under my name, 'Son and heir to Undershaft and Lazarus, Death and Destruction Dealers: address Christendom and Judea.' But that was not so bad as the way I was kowtowed to everywhere because my father was making millions by selling cannons.

LADY BRITOMART. It is not only the cannons, but the war loans that Lazarus arranges under cover of giving credit for the cannons. You know, Stephen, it's perfectly scandalous. Those two men, Andrew Undershaft and Lazarus, positively have Europe under their thumbs. That is why your father is able to behave as he does. He is above the law. Do you think Bismarck or Gladstone or Disraeli could have openly defied every social and moral obligation all their lives as your father has? They simply wouldnt have dared. I asked Gladstone to take it up. I asked The Times to take it up. I asked the Lord Chamberlain to take it up. But it was just like asking them to declare war on the Sultan. They w o u l d n t. They said they couldnt touch him. I believe they were afraid.

STEPHEN. What could they do? He does not actually break the law.

LADY BRITOMART. Not break the law! He is always breaking the law. He broke the law when he was born: his parents were not married.

STEPHEN. Mother! Is that true?

LADY BRITOMART. Of course it's true: that was why we separated.

STEPHEN. He married without letting you know this!

LADY BRITOMART (*rather taken aback by this inference*). Oh no. To do Andrew justice, that was not the sort of thing he did. Besides, you know the Undershaft motto: Unashamed. Everybody knew.

STEPHEN. But you said that was why you separated.

LADY BRITOMART. Yes, because he was not content with being a foundling himself: he wanted to disinherit you for another foundling. That was what I couldnt stand.

STEPHEN (*ashamed*). Do you mean for—for—for—

LADY BRITOMART. Dont stammer, Stephen. Speak distinctly.

STEPHEN. But this is so frightful to me, mother. To have to speak to you about such things!

LADY BRITOMART. It's not pleasant for me, either, especially if you are still so childish that you must make it worse by a display of embarrassment. It is only in the middle classes, Stephen, that people get into a state of dumb helpless horror when they find that there are wicked people in the world. In our class, we have to decide what is to be done with wicked people; and nothing should disturb our self-possession. Now ask your question properly.

STEPHEN. Mother: have you no consideration for me? For Heaven's sake either treat me as a child, as you always do, and tell me nothing at all; or tell me everything and let me take it as best I can.

LADY BRITOMART. Treat you as a child! What do you mean? It is most unkind and ungrateful of you to say such a thing. You know I have never treated any of you as children. I have always made you my companions and friends, and allowed you perfect freedom to do and say whatever you liked, so long as you liked what I could approve of.

STEPHEN (*desperately*). I daresay we have been the very imperfect children of a very perfect mother; but I do beg you to let me alone for once, and tell me about this horrible business of my father wanting to set me aside for another son.

LADY BRITOMART (*amazed*). Another son! I never said anything of the kind. I never dreamt of such a thing. This is what comes of interrupting me.

STEPHEN. But you said—

LADY BRITOMART (*cutting him short*). Now be a good boy, Stephen, and listen to me patiently. The Undershafts are descended from a foundling in the parish of St Andrew Undershaft in the city. That was long ago, in the reign of James the First. Well, this foundling was adopted by an armorer and gun-maker. In the course of time the foundling succeeded to the business; and from some notion of gratitude, or some vow or something, he adopted another foundling, and left the business to him. And that foundling did the same. Ever since that, the cannon business has always been left to an adopted foundling named Andrew Undershaft.

STEPHEN. But did they never marry? Were there no legitimate sons?

LADY BRITOMART. Oh yes: they married just as your father did; and they were rich enough to buy land for their own children and leave them well provided for. But they always adopted and trained some foundling to succeed them in the business; and of course they always quarrelled with their wives furiously over it. Your father was adopted in that way; and he pretends to consider himself bound to keep up the tradition and adopt somebody to leave the business to. Of course I was not going to stand that. There may have been some reason for it when the Undershafts could only marry women in their own class, whose sons were not fit to govern great estates. But there could be no excuse for passing over m y son.

STEPHEN (*dubiously*). I am afraid I should make a poor hand of managing a cannon foundry.

LADY BRITOMART. Nonsense! you could easily get a manager and pay him a salary.

STEPHEN. My father evidently had no great opinion of my capacity.

LADY BRITOMART. Stuff, child! you were only a baby: it had nothing to do with your capacity. Andrew did it on principle, just as he did every perverse and wicked thing on principle. When my father remonstrated, Andrew actually told him to his face that history tells us of only two successful institutions: one the Undershaft firm, and the other the Roman Empire under the Antonines. That was because the Antonine emperors all adopted their successors. Such rubbish! The Stevenages are as good as the Antonines, I hope; and you are a Stevenage. But that was Andrew all over. There you have the man! Always clever and unanswerable when he was defending nonsense and wickedness: always awkward and sullen when he had to behave sensibly and decently!

STEPHEN. Then it was on my account that your home life was broken up, mother. I am sorry.

LADY BRITOMART. Well, dear, there were other differences. I really cannot bear an immoral man. I am not a Pharisee, I hope; and I should not have minded his merely d o i n g wrong things: we are none of us perfect. But your father didnt exactly d o wrong things: he said them and thought them: that was what was so dreadful. He really had a sort of religion of wrongness. Just as one doesnt mind men practising immorality so long as they own that they are in the wrong by preaching morality; so I couldnt forgive Andrew for preaching immorality while he practised morality. You would all have grown up without principles, without any knowledge of right and wrong, if he had been in the house. You know, my dear, your father was a very attractive man in some ways. Chil-

dren did not dislike him; and he took advantage of it to put the wickedest ideas into their
340 heads, and make them quite unmanageable. I did not dislike him myself: very far from it; but nothing can bridge over moral disagreement.

STEPHEN. All this simply bewilders me, mother. People may differ about matters of opinion, or even about religion; but how can they differ about right and wrong? Right is right; and wrong is wrong; and if a man cannot distinguish them properly, he is either a
350 fool or a rascal: thats all.

LADY BRITOMART (*touched*). Thats my own boy (*she pats his cheek*)! Your father never could answer that: he used to laugh and get out of it under cover of some affectionate nonsense. And now that you understand the situation, what do you advise me to do?

STEPHEN. Well, what can you do?

LADY BRITOMART. I must get the money somehow.

360 STEPHEN. We cannot take money from him. I had rather go and live in some cheap place like Bedford Square or even Hampstead than take a farthing of his money.

LADY BRITOMART. But after all, Stephen, our present income comes from Andrew.

STEPHEN (*shocked*). I never knew that.

LADY BRITOMART. Well, you surely didnt suppose your grandfather had anything to give me. The Stevenages could not do everything for
370 you. We gave you social position. Andrew had to contribute something. He had a very good bargain, I think.

STEPHEN (*bitterly*). We are utterly dependent on him and his cannons, then?

LADY BRITOMART. Certainly not: the money is settled. But he provided it. So you see it is not a question of taking money from him or not: it is simply a question of how much. I dont want any more for myself.

380 STEPHEN. Nor do I.

LADY BRITOMART. But Sarah does; and Barbara does. That is, Charles Lomax and Adolphus Cusins will cost them more. So I must put my pride in my pocket and ask for it, I suppose. That is your advice, Stephen, is it not?

STEPHEN. No.

LADY BRITOMART (*sharply*). Stephen!

STEPHEN. Of course if you are determined—

LADY BRITOMART. I am not determined: I ask your advice; and I am waiting for it. I will not 390 have all the responsibility thrown on my shoulders.

STEPHEN (*obstinately*). I would die sooner than ask him for another penny.

LADY BRITOMART (*resignedly*). You mean that *I* must ask him. Very well, Stephen: it shall be as you wish. You will be glad to know that your grandfather concurs. But he thinks I ought to ask Andrew to come here and see the girls. After all, he must have some natural af- 400 fection for them.

STEPHEN. Ask him here!!!

LADY BRITOMART. Do not repeat my words, Stephen. Where else can I ask him?

STEPHEN. I never expected you to ask him at all.

LADY BRITOMART. Now dont tease, Stephen. Come! you see that it is necessary that he should pay us a visit, dont you?

STEPHEN (*reluctantly*). I suppose so, if the 410 girls cannot do without his money.

LADY BRITOMART. Thank you, Stephen: I knew you would give me the right advice when it was properly explained to you. I have asked your father to come this evening. (*Stephen bounds from his seat*). Dont jump, Stephen: it fidgets me.

STEPHEN (*in utter consternation*). Do you mean to say that my father is coming here tonight—that he may be here at any moment? 420

LADY BRITOMART (*looking at her watch*). I said nine. (*He gasps. She rises*). Ring the bell, please. (*Stephen goes to the smaller writing table! presses a button on it; and sits at it with his elbows on the table and his head in his hands, outwitted and overwhelmed*). It is ten minutes to nine yet; and I have to prepare the girls. I asked Charles Lomax and Adolphus to dinner on purpose that they might be here. Andrew had better see them in case he should 430 cherish any delusions as to their being capable of supporting their wives. (*The butler enters: Lady Britomart goes behind the settee to speak to him*). Morrison: go up to the drawing room and tell everybody to come down here at once. (*Morrison withdraws. Lady Britomart turns to Stephen*). Now remember, Stephen: I shall need all your countenance and authority. (*He rises and tries to recover some vestige of these attri-*

440 *butes*). Give me a chair, dear. (*He pushes a chair forward from the wall to where she stands, near the smaller writing table. She sits down; and he goes to the armchair, into which he throws himself*). I dont know how Barbara will take it. Ever since they made her a major in the Salvation Army she has developed a propensity to have her own way and order people about which quite cows me sometimes. It's not ladylike: I'm sure I dont know where she 450 picked it up. Anyhow, Barbara shant bully me; but still it's just as well that your father should be here before she has time to refuse to meet him or make a fuss. Dont look nervous, Stephen: it will only encourage Barbara to make difficulties. *I* am nervous enough, goodness knows; but I dont shew it.

Sarah and Barbara come in with their respective young men, Charles Lomax and Adolphus Cusins. Sarah is slender, bored, and mundane. 460 *Barbara is robuster, jollier, much more energetic. Sarah is fashionably dressed: Barbara is in Salvation Army uniform. Lomax, a young man about town, is like many other young men about town. He is afflicted with a frivolous sense of humor which plunges him at the most inopportune moments into paroxysms of imperfectly suppressed laughter. Cusins is a spectacled student, slight, thin haired, and sweet voiced, with a more complex form of Lomax's complaint.* 470 *His sense of humor is intellectual and subtle, and is complicated by an appalling temper. The lifelong struggle of a benevolent temperament and a high conscience against impluses of inhuman ridicule and fierce impatience has set up a chronic strain which has visibly wrecked his constitution. He is a most implacable, determined, tenacious, intolerant person who by mere force of character presents himself as—and indeed actually is—considerate,* 480 *gentle, explanatory, even mild and apologetic, capable possibly of murder, but not of cruelty or coarseness. By the operation of some instinct which is not merciful enough to blind him with the illusions of love, he is obstinately bent on marrying Barbara. Lomax likes Sarah and thinks it will be rather a lark to marry her. Consequently he has not attempted to resist Lady Britomart's arrangements to that end.*

All four look as if they had been having a good deal of fun in the drawing room. The girls enter first, leaving the swains outside. Sarah comes to the settee. Barbara comes in after her and stops at the door. 490

BARBARA. Are Cholly and Dolly to come in?

LADY BRITOMART (*forcibly*). Barbara: I will not have Charles called Cholly: the vulgarity of it positively makes me ill.

BARBARA. It's all right, mother: Cholly is quite correct nowadays. Are they to come in?

LADY BRITOMART. Yes, if they will behave 500 themselves.

BARBARA (*through the door*). Come in, Dolly; and behave yourself.

Barbara comes to her mother's writing table. Cusins enters smiling, and wanders towards Lady Britomart.

SARAH (*calling*). Come in, Cholly. (*Lomax enters, controlling his features very imperfectly, and places himself vaguely between Sarah and Barbara*). 510

LADY BRITOMART (*peremptorily*). Sit down, all of you. (*They sit. Cusins crosses to the window and seats himself there. Lomax takes a chair. Barbara sits at the writing table and Sarah on the settee*). I dont in the least know what you are laughing at, Adolphus. I am surprised at you, though I expected nothing better from Charles Lomax.

CUSINS (*in a remarkably gentle voice*). Barbara has been trying to teach me the West Ham 520 Salvation March.

LADY BRITOMART. I see nothing to laugh at in that; nor should you if you are really converted.

CUSINS (*sweetly*). You were not present. It was really funny, I believe.

LOMAX. Ripping.

LADY BRITOMART. Be quiet, Charles. Now listen to me, children. Your father is coming here this evening. 530

General stupefaction. Lomax, Sarah, and Barbara rise: Sarah scared, and Barbara amused and expectant.

LOMAX (*remonstrating*). Oh I say!

LADY BRITOMART. You are not called on to say anything, Charles.

SARAH. Are you serious, mother?

LADY BRITOMART. Of course I am serious. It is on your account, Sarah, and also on Charles's. (*Silence. Sarah sits, with a shrug. Charles looks painfully unworthy*). I hope you are not going to object, Barbara.

BARBARA. I! why should I? My father has a soul to be saved like anybody else. He's quite welcome as far as I am concerned. (*She sits on the table, and softly whistles 'Onward Christian Soldiers'*).

LOMAX (*still remonstrant*). But really, dont you know! Oh I say!

LADY BRITOMART (*frigidly*). What do you wish to convey, Charles?

LOMAX. Well, you must admit that this is a bit thick.

LADY BRITOMART (*turning with ominous suavity to Cusins*). Adolphus: you are a professor of Greek. Can you translate Charles Lomax's remarks into reputable English for us?

CUSINS (*cautiously*). If I may say so, Lady Brit, I think Charles has rather happily expressed what we all feel. Homer, speaking of Autolycus, uses the same phrase. πυκινὸν δόμον ἐλθεῖν means a bit thick.

LOMAX (*handsomely*). Not that I mind, you know, if Sarah dont. (*He sits*).

LADY BRITOMART (*crushingly*). Thank you. Have I y o u r permission, Adolphus, to invite my own husband to my own house?

CUSINS (*gallantly*). You have my unhesitating support in everything you do.

LADY BRITOMART. Tush! Sarah: have you nothing to say?

SARAH. Do you mean that he is coming regularly to live here?

LADY BRITOMART. Certainly not. The spare room is ready for him if he likes to stay for a day or two and see a little more of you; but there are limits.

SARAH. Well, he cant eat us, I suppose. *I* dont mind.

LOMAX (*chuckling*). I wonder how the old man will take it.

LADY BRITOMART. Much as the old woman will, no doubt, Charles.

LOMAX (*abashed*). I didnt mean—at least—

LADY BRITOMART. You didnt t h i n k, Charles. You never do; and the result is, you never mean anything. And now please attend to me, children. Your father will be quite a stranger to us.

LOMAX. I suppose he hasnt seen Sarah since she was a little kid.

LADY BRITOMART. Not since she was a little kid, Charles, as you express it with that elegance of diction and refinement of thought that seem never to desert you. Accordingly—er—(*impatiently*) Now I have forgotten what I was going to say. That comes of your provoking me to be sarcastic, Charles. Adolphus: will you kindly tell me where I was.

CUSINS (*sweetly*). You were saying that as Mr Undershaft has not seen his children since they were babies, he will form his opinion of the way you have brought them up from their behavior tonight, and that therefore you wish us all to be particularly careful to conduct ourselves well, especially Charles.

LADY BRITOMART (*with emphatic approval*). Precisely.

LOMAX. Look here, Dolly: Lady Brit didnt say that.

LADY BRITOMART (*vehemently*). I did, Charles. Adolphus's recollection is perfectly correct. It is most important that you should be good; and I do beg you for once not to pair off into opposite corners and giggle and whisper while I am speaking to your father.

BARBARA. All right, mother. We'll do you credit. (*She comes off the table, and sits in her chair with ladylike elegance*).

LADY BRITOMART. Remember, Charles, that Sarah will want to feel proud of you instead of ashamed of you.

LOMAX. Oh I say! theres nothing to be exactly proud of, dont you know.

LADY BRITOMART. Well, try and look as if there was.

Morrison, pale and dismayed, breaks into the room in unconcealed disorder.

MORRISON. Might I speak a word to you, my lady?

LADY BRITOMART. Nonsense! Shew him up.

MORRISON. Yes, my lady. (*He goes*).

LOMAX. Does Morrison know who it is?

LADY BRITOMART. Of course. Morrison has always been with us.

LOMAX. It must be a regular corker for him, dont you know.

LADY BRITOMART. Is this a moment to get on

my nerves, Charles, with your outrageous expressions?

LOMAX. But this is something out of the ordinary, really—

MORRISON (*at the door*). The—er—Mr Undershaft. (*He retreats in confusion*).

Andrew Undershaft comes in. All rise. Lady Britomart meets him in the middle of the room behind the settee.

Andrew is, on the surface, a stoutish, easygoing elderly man, with kindly patient manners, and an engaging simplicity of character. But he has a watchful, deliberate, waiting, listening face, and formidable reserves of power, both bodily and mental, in his capacious chest and long head. His gentleness is partly that of a strong man who has learnt by experience that his natural grip hurts ordinary people unless he handles them very carefully, and partly the mellowness of age and success. He is also a little shy in his present very delicate situation.

LADY BRITOMART. Good evening, Andrew.

UNDERSHAFT. How d'ye do, my dear.

LADY BRITOMART. You look a good deal older.

UNDERSHAFT (*apologetically*). I a m somewhat older. (*Taking her hand with a touch of courtship*) Time has stood still with you.

LADY BRITOMART (*throwing away his hand*). Rubbish! This is your family.

UNDERSHAFT (*surprised*). Is it so large? I am sorry to say my memory is failing very badly in some things. (*He offers his hand with paternal kindness to Lomax*).

LOMAX (*jerkily shaking his hand*). Ahdedoo.

UNDERSHAFT. I can see you are my eldest. I am very glad to meet you again, my boy.

LOMAX (*remonstrating*). No, but look here dont you know—(*Overcome*) Oh I say!

LADY BRITOMART (*recovering from momentary speechlessness*). Andrew: do you mean to say that you dont remember how many children you have?

UNDERSHAFT. Well, I am afraid I—. They have grown so much—er. Am I making any ridiculous mistake? I may as well confess: I recollect only one son. But so many things have happened since, of course—er—

LADY BRITOMART (*decisively*). Andrew: you are talking nonsense. Of course you have only one son.

UNDERSHAFT. Perhaps you will be good enough to introduce me, my dear.

LADY BRITOMART. That is Charles Lomax, who is engaged to Sarah.

UNDERSHAFT. My dear sir, I beg your pardon.

LOMAX. Notatall. Delighted, I assure you.

LADY BRITOMART. This is Stephen.

UNDERSHAFT (*bowing*). Happy to make your acquaintance, Mr Stephen. Then (*going to Cusins*) y o u must be my son. (*Taking Cusins' hands in his*) How are you, my young friend? (*To Lady Britomart*) He is very like you, my love.

CUSINS. You flatter me, Mr Undershaft. My name is Cusins: engaged to Barbara. (*Very explicitly*) That is Major Barbara Undershaft, of the Salvation Army. That is Sarah, your second daughter. This is Stephen Undershaft, your son.

UNDERSHAFT. My dear Stephen, I b e g your pardon.

STEPHEN. Not at all.

UNDERSHAFT. Mr Cusins: I am much indebted to you for explaining so precisely. (*Turning to Sarah*) Barbara, my dear—

SARAH (*prompting him*). Sarah.

UNDERSHAFT. Sarah, of course. (*They shake hands. He goes over to Barbara*) Barbara—I am right this time, I hope?

BARBARA. Quite right. (*They shake hands*).

LADY BRITOMART (*resuming command*). Sit down, all of you. Sit down, Andrew. (*She comes forward and sits on the settee. Cusins also brings his chair forward on her left. Barbara and Stephen resume their seats. Lomax gives his chair to Sarah and goes for another*).

UNDERSHAFT. Thank you, my love.

LOMAX (*conversationally, as he brings a chair forward between the writing table and the settee, and offers it to Undershaft*). Takes you some time to find out exactly where you are, dont it?

UNDERSHAFT (*accepting the chair, but remaining standing*). That is not what embarrasses me, Mr Lomax. My difficulty is that if I play the part of a father, I shall produce the effect of an intrusive stranger; and if I play the part of a discreet stranger, I may appear a callous father.

LADY BRITOMART. There is no need for you to play any part at all, Andrew. You had much better be sincere and natural.

UNDERSHAFT (*submissively*). Yes, my dear:

740 I daresay that will be best. (*He sits down comfortably*). Well, here I am. Now what can I do for you all?

LADY BRITOMART. You need not do anything, Andrew. You are one of the family. You can sit with us and enjoy yourself.

A painfully conscious pause. Barbara makes a face at Lomax, whose too long suppressed mirth immediately explodes in agonized neighings.

LADY BRITOMART (*outraged*). Charles Lomax: 750 if you can behave yourself, behave yourself. If not, leave the room.

LOMAX. I'm awfully sorry, Lady Brit; but really you know, upon my soul! (*He sits on the settee between Lady Britomart and Undershaft, quite overcome*).

BARBARA. Why dont you laugh if you want to, Cholly? It's good for your inside.

LADY BRITOMART. Barbara: you have had the education of a lady. Please let your father see 760 that; and dont talk like a street girl.

UNDERSHAFT. Never mind me, my dear. As you know, I am not a gentleman; and I was never educated.

LOMAX (*encouragingly*). Nobody'd know it, I assure you. You look all right, you know.

CUSINS. Let me advise you to study Greek, Mr Undershaft. Greek scholars are privileged men. Few of them know Greek; and none of them know anything else; but their position is 770 unchallengeable. Other languages are the qualifications of waiters and commercial travellers: Greek is to a man of position what the hallmark is to silver.

BARBARA. Dolly: dont be insincere. Cholly: fetch your concertina and play something for us.

LOMAX (*jumps up eagerly, but checks himself to remark doubtfully to Undershaft*). Perhaps that sort of thing isnt in your line, eh?

780 UNDERSHAFT. I am particularly fond of music.

LOMAX (*delighted*). Are you? Then I'll get it. (*He goes upstairs for the instrument*).

UNDERSHAFT. Do you play, Barbara?

BARBARA. Only the tambourine. But Cholly's teaching me the concertina.

UNDERSHAFT. Is Cholly also a member of the Salvation Army?

BARBARA. No: he says it's bad form to be a dissenter. But I dont despair of Cholly. I made 790 him come yesterday to a meeting at the dock gates, and take the collection in his hat.

UNDERSHAFT (*looks whimsically at his wife*)!!

LADY BRITOMART. It is not my doing, Andrew. Barbara is old enough to take her own way. She has no father to advise her.

BARBARA. Oh yes she has. There are no orphans in the Salvation Army.

UNDERSHAFT. Your father there has a great many children and plenty of experience, eh? 800

BARBARA (*looking at him with quick interest and nodding*). Just so. How did y o u come to understand that? (*Lomax is heard at the door trying the concertina*).

LADY BRITOMART. Come in, Charles. Play us something at once.

LOMAX. Righto! (*He sits down in his former place, and preludes*).

UNDERSHAFT. One moment, Mr. Lomax. I am rather interested in the Salvation Army. 810 Its motto might be my own: Blood and Fire.

LOMAX (*shocked*). But not your sort of blood and fire, you know.

UNDERSHAFT. My sort of blood cleanses: my sort of fire purifies.

BARBARA. So do ours. Come down tomorrow to my shelter—the West Ham shelter—and see what we're doing. We're going to march to a great meeting in the Assembly Hall at Mile End. Come and see the shelter and then march 820 with us: it will do you a lot of good. Can you play anything?

UNDERSHAFT. In my youth I earned pennies, and even shillings occasionally, in the streets and in public house parlors by my natural talent for stepdancing. Later on, I became a member of the Undershaft orchestral society, and performed passably on the tenor trombone.

LOMAX (*scandalized—putting down the concertina*). Oh I say! 830

BARBARA. Many a sinner has played himself into heaven on the trombone, thanks to the Army.

LOMAX (*to Barbara, still rather shocked*). Yes; but what about the cannon business, dont you know? (*To Undershaft*) Getting into heaven is not exactly in your line, is it?

LADY BRITOMART. Charles!!!

LOMAX. Well; but it stands to reason, dont it? The cannon business may be necessary and 840 all that: we cant get on without cannons; but it isnt right, you know. On the other hand, there may be a certain amount of tosh about the Salvation Army—I belong to the Established Church myself—but still you cant deny that it's religion; and you cant go against religion, can you? At least unless youre downright immoral, dont you know.

UNDERSHAFT. You hardly appreciate my position, Mr. Lomax—

LOMAX (*hastily*). I'm not saying anything against you personally—

UNDERSHAFT. Quite so, quite so. But consider for a moment. Here I am, a profiteer in mutilation and murder. I find myself in a specially amiable humor just now because, this morning, down at the foundry, we blew twenty-seven dummy soldiers into fragments with a gun which formerly destroyed only thirteen.

LOMAX (*leniently*). Well, the more destructive war becomes, the sooner it will be abolished, eh?

UNDERSHAFT. Not at all. The more destructive war becomes the more fascinating we find it. No, Mr Lomax: I am obliged to you for making the usual excuse for my trade; but I am not ashamed of it. I am not one of those men who keep their morals and their business in watertight compartments. All the spare money my trade rivals spend on hospitals, cathedrals, and other receptacles for conscience money, I devote to experiments and researches in improved methods of destroying life and property. I have always done so; and I always shall. Therefore your Christmas card moralities of peace on earth and goodwill among men are of no use to me. Your Christianity, which enjoins you to resist not evil, and to turn the other cheek, would make me a bankrupt. My morality—my religion—must have a place for cannons and torpedoes in it.

STEPHEN (*coldly—almost sullenly*). You speak as if there were half a dozen moralities and religions to choose from, instead of one true morality and one true religion.

UNDERSHAFT. For me there is only one true morality; but it might not fit you, as you do not manufacture aerial battleships. There is only one true morality for every man; but every man has not the same true morality.

LOMAX (*overtaxed*). Would you mind saying that again? I didnt quite follow it.

CUSINS. It's quite simple. As Euripides says, one man's meat is another man's poison morally as well as physically.

UNDERSHAFT. Precisely.

LOMAX. Oh, that! Yes, yes, yes. True. True.

STEPHEN. In other words, some men are honest and some are scoundrels.

BARBARA. Bosh! There are no scoundrels.

UNDERSHAFT. Indeed? Are there any good men?

BARBARA. No. Not one. There are neither good men nor scoundrels: there are just children of one Father; and the sooner they stop calling one another names the better. You neednt talk to me: I know them. Ive had scores of them through my hands: scoundrels, criminals, infidels, philanthropists, missionaries, county councillors, all sorts. Theyre all just the same sort of sinner; and theres the same salvation ready for them all.

UNDERSHAFT. May I ask have you ever saved a maker of cannons?

BARBARA. No. Will you let me try?

UNDERSHAFT. Well, I will make a bargain with you. If I go to see you tomorrow in your Salvation Shelter, will you come the day after to see me in my cannon works?

BARBARA. Take care. It may end in your giving up the cannons for the sake of the Salvation Army.

UNDERSHAFT. Are you sure it will not end in your giving up the Salvation Army for the sake of the cannons?

BARBARA. I will take my chance of that.

UNDERSHAFT. And I will take my chance of the other. (*They shake hands on it*). Where is your shelter?

BARBARA. In West Ham. At the sign of the cross. Ask anybody in Canning Town. Where are your works?

UNDERSHAFT. In Perivale St Andrews. At the sign of the sword. Ask anybody in Europe.

LOMAX. Hadnt I better play something?

BARBARA. Yes. Give us Onward, Christian Soldiers.

LOMAX. Well, thats rather a strong order to begin with, dont you know. Suppose I sing

Thourt passing hence, my brother. It's much the same tune.

BARBARA. It's too melancholy. You get saved, Cholly; and youll pass hence, my brother, without making such a fuss about it.

LADY BRITOMART. Really, Barbara, you go on as if religion were a pleasant subject. Do have some sense of propriety.

UNDERSHAFT. I do not find it an unpleasant subject, my dear. It is the only one that capable people really care for.

LADY BRITOMART (*looking at her watch*). Well, if you are determined to have it, I insist on having it in a proper and respectable way. Charles: ring for prayers.

General amazement. Stephen rises in dismay.

LOMAX (*rising*). Oh I say!

UNDERSHAFT (*rising*). I am afraid I must be going.

LADY BRITOMART. You cannot go now, Andrew: it would be most improper. Sit down. What will the servants think?

UNDERSHAFT. My dear: I have conscientious scruples. May I suggest a compromise? If Barbara will conduct a little service in the drawing room, with Mr Lomax as organist, I will attend it willingly. I will even take part, if a trombone can be procured.

LADY BRITOMART. Dont mock, Andrew.

UNDERSHAFT (*shocked—to Barbara*). You dont think I am mocking, my love, I hope.

BARBARA. No, of course not; and it wouldnt matter if you were: half the Army came to their first meeting for a lark. (*Rising*) Come along. (*She throws her arm round her father and sweeps him out, calling to the others from the threshold*) Come, Dolly. Come, Cholly.

Cusins rises.

LADY BRITOMART. I will not be disobeyed by everybody. Adolphus: sit down. (*He does not*). Charles: you may go. You are not fit for prayers: you cannot keep your countenance.

LOMAX. Oh I say! (*He goes out*).

LADY BRITOMART (*continuing*). But you, Adolphus, can behave yourself if you choose to. I insist on your staying.

CUSINS. My dear Lady Brit: there are things in the family prayer book that I couldnt bear to hear you say.

LADY BRITOMART. What things, pray?

CUSINS. Well, you would have to say before all the servants that we have done things we ought not to have done, and left undone things we ought to have done, and that there is no health in us. I cannot bear to hear you doing yourself such an injustice, and Barbara such an injustice. As for myself, I flatly deny it: I have done my best. I shouldnt dare to marry Barbara—I couldnt look you in the face—if it were true. So I must go to the drawing room.

LADY BRITOMART (*offended*). Well, go. (*He starts for the door*). And remember this, Adolphus (*he turns to listen*): I have a very strong suspicion that you went to the Salvation Army to worship Barbara and nothing else. And I quite appreciate the very clever way in which you systematically humbug me. I have found you out. Take care Barbara doesnt. Thats all.

CUSINS (*with unruffled sweetness*). Dont tell on me. (*He steals out*).

LADY BRITOMART. Sarah: if you want to go, go. Anything's better than to sit there as if you wished you were a thousand miles away.

SARAH (*languidly*). Very well, mamma. (*She goes*).

Lady Britomart, with a sudden flounce, gives way to a little gust of tears.

STEPHEN (*going to her*). Mother: whats the matter?

LADY BRITOMART (*swishing away her tears with her handkerchief*). Nothing. Foolishness. You can go with him, too, if you like, and leave me with the servants.

STEPHEN. Oh, you mustnt think that, mother. I—I dont like him.

LADY BRITOMART. The others do. That is the injustice of a woman's lot. A woman has to bring up her children; and that means to restrain them, to deny them things they want, to set them tasks, to punish them when they do wrong, to do all the unpleasant things. And then the father, who has nothing to do but pet them and spoil them, comes in when all her work is done and steals their affection from her.

STEPHEN. He has not stolen our affection from you. It is only curiosity.

LADY BRITOMART (*violently*). I wont be consoled, Stephen. There is nothing the matter with me. (*She rises and goes towards the door*). 1040

STEPHEN. Where are you going, mother?

LADY BRITOMART. To the drawing room, of course. (*She goes out. Onward, Christian Soldiers, on the concertina, with tambourine accompaniment, is heard when the door opens*). Are you coming, Stephen?

STEPHEN. No. Certainly not. (*She goes. He sits down on the settee, with compressed lips and an expression of strong dislike*).

ACT TWO

The yard of the West Ham shelter of the Salvation Army is a cold place on a January morning. The building itself, an old warehouse, is newly whitewashed. Its gabled end projects into the yard in the middle, with a door on the ground floor, and another in the loft above it without any balcony or ladder, but with a pulley rigged over it for hoisting sacks. Those who come from this central gable end into the yard have the gateway leading to the street on their left, with a stone horsetrough just beyond it, and, on the right, a penthouse shielding a table from the weather. There are forms at the table; and on them are seated a man and a woman, both much down on their luck, finishing a meal of bread (one thick slice each, with margarine and golden syrup) and diluted milk.

The man, a workman out of employment, is young, agile, a talker, a poser, sharp enough to be capable of anything in reason except honesty or altruistic considerations of any kind. The woman is a commonplace old bundle of poverty and hard-worn humanity. She looks sixty and probably is forty-five. If they were rich people, gloved and muffed and well wrapped up in furs and overcoats, they would be numbed and miserable; for it is a grindingly cold raw January day; and a glance at the background of grimy warehouses and leaden sky visible over the whitewashed walls of the yard would drive any idle rich person straight to the Mediterranean. But these two, being no more troubled with visions of the Mediterranean than of the moon, and being compelled to keep more of their clothes in the pawnshop, and less on their persons, in winter than in summer, are not depressed by the cold: rather are they stung into vivacity, to which their meal has just now given an almost jolly turn. The man takes a pull at his mug, and then gets up and moves about the yard with his hands deep in his pockets, occasionally breaking into a stepdance.

THE WOMAN. Feel better arter your meal, sir?

THE MAN. No. Call that a meal! Good enough for you, praps; but wot is it to me, an intelligent workin man.

THE WOMAN. Workin man! Wot are you?

THE MAN. Painter.

THE WOMAN (*sceptically*). Yus, I dessay.

THE MAN. Yus, you dessay! I know. Every loafer that cant do nothink calls isself a painter. 10 Well, I'm a real painter: grainer, finisher, thirty-eight bob a week when I can get it.

THE WOMAN. Then why dont you go and get it?

THE MAN. I'll tell you why. Fust: I'm intelligent—fffff! it's rotten cold here (*he dances a step or two*)—yes: intelligent beyond the station o life into which it has pleased the capitalists to call me; and they dont like a man that sees through em. Second, an intelligent bein 20 needs a doo share of appiness; so I drink somethink cruel when I get the chawnce. Third, I stand by my class and do as little as I can so's to leave arf the job for me fellow workers. Fourth, I'm fly enough to know wots inside the law and wots outside it; and inside it I do as the capitalists do: pinch wot I can lay me ands on. In a proper state of society I am sober, industrious and honest: in Rome, so to speak, I do as the Romans do. Wots the consequence? When trade is bad—and it's rotten bad just now—and the employers az to sack arf their men, they generally start on me.

THE WOMAN. Whats your name?

THE MAN. Price. Bronterre O'Brien Price. Usually called Snobby Price, for short.

THE WOMAN. Snobby's a carpenter, aint it? You said you was a painter.

PRICE. Not that kind of snob, but the genteel sort. I'm too uppish, owing to my intelligence, and my father being a Chartist and a reading, thinking man: a stationer, too. I'm none of your common hewers of wood and drawers of water; and dont you forget it. (*He returns to his seat at the table, and takes up his mug*). Wots y o u r name?

THE WOMAN. Rummy Mitchens, sir.

PRICE (*quaffing the remains of his milk to her*. Your elth, Miss Mitchens.

RUMMY (*correcting him*). Missis Mitchens.

PRICE. Wot! Oh Rummy, Rummy! Respectable married woman, Rummy, gittin rescued by the Salvation Army by pretendin to be a bad un. Same old game!

RUMMY. What am I to do? I cant starve. Them Salvation lasses is dear good girls; but the better you are, the worse they likes to think you were before they rescued you. Why shouldnt they av a bit o credit, poor loves? theyre worn to rags by their work. And where would they get the money to rescue us if we was to let on we're no worse than other people? You know what ladies and gentlemen are.

PRICE. Thievin swine! Wish I ad their job, Rummy, all the same. Wot does Rummy stand for? Pet name praps?

RUMMY. Short for Romola.

PRICE. For wot!?

RUMMY. Romola. It was out of a new book. Somebody me mother wanted me to grow up like.

PRICE. We're companions in misfortune, Rummy. Both on us got names that nobody cawnt pronounce. Consequently I'm Snobby and youre Rummy because Bill and Sally wasnt good enough for our parents. Such is life!

RUMMY. Who saved you, Mr Price? Was it Major Barbara?

PRICE. No: I come here on my own. I'm going to be Bronterre O'Brien Price, the converted painter. I know wot they like. I'll tell em how I blasphemed and gambled and wopped my poor old mother—

RUMMY (*shocked*). Used you to beat your mother?

PRICE. Not likely. She used to beat me. No matter: you come and listen to the converted painter, and youll hear how she was a pious woman that taught me prayers at er knee, an how I used to come home drunk and drag her out o bed be er snow white airs, an lam into er with the poker.

RUMMY. Thats whats so unfair to us women. Your confessions is just as big lies as ours: you dont tell what you really done no more than us; but you men can tell your lies right out at the meetins and be made much of for it; while the sort o confessions we az to make az to be wispered to one lady at a time. It aint right, spite of all their piety.

PRICE. Right! Do you spose the Army'd be allowed if it went and did right? Not much. It combs our air and makes us good little blokes to be robbed and put upon. But I'll play the game as good as any of em. I'll see somebody struck by lightnin, or hear a voice sayin 'Snobby Price: where will you spend eternity?' I'll av a time of it, I tell you.

RUMMY. You wont be let drink, though.

PRICE. I'll take it out in gorspellin, then. I dont want to drink if I can get fun enough any other way.

Jenny Hill, a pale, overwrought, pretty Salvation lass of 18, comes in through the yard gate, leading Peter Shirley, a half hardened, half worn-out elderly man, weak with hunger.

JENNY (*supporting him*). Come! pluck up. I'll get you something to eat. Youll be all right then.

PRICE (*rising and hurrying officiously to take the old man off Jenny's hands*). Poor old man!

Cheer up, brother: youll find rest and peace and appiness ere. Hurry up with the food, miss: e's fair done. (*Jenny hurries into the shelter*). Ere, buck up, daddy! she's fetchin y'a thick slice o breadn treacle, an a mug o skyblue. (*He seats him at the corner of the table*).

RUMMY (*gaily*). Keep up your old art! Never say die!

130 SHIRLEY. I'm not an old man. I'm ony 46. I'm as good as ever I was. The grey patch come in my hair before I was thirty. All it wants is three pennorth o hair dye: am I to be turned on the streets to starve for it? Holy God! Ive worked ten to twelve hours a day since I was thirteen, and paid my way all through; and now am I to be thrown into the gutter and my job given to a young man that can do it no better than me because Ive black hair that goes
140 white at the first change?

PRICE (*cheerfully*). No good jawrin about it. Your ony a jumped-up, jerked-off, orspittle-turned-out incurable of an ole workin man: who cares about you? Eh? Make the thievin swine give you a meal: theyve stole many a one from you. Get a bit o your own back. [*Jenny returns with the usual meal*]. There you are, brother. Awsk a blessin an tuck that into you.

150 SHIRLEY (*looking at it ravenously but not touching it, and crying like a child*). I never took anything before.

JENNY (*petting him*). Come, come! the Lord sends it to you: he wasnt above taking bread from his friends; and why should you be? Besides, when we find you a job you can pay us for it if you like.

SHIRLEY (*eagerly*). Yes, yes: thats true. I can pay you back: it's only a loan. (*Shivering*) Oh
160 Lord! oh Lord! (*He turns to the table and attacks the meal ravenously*).

JENNY. Well, Rummy, are you more comfortable now?

RUMMY. God bless you, lovey! youve fed my body and saved my soul, havnt you? (*Jenny, touched, kisses her*). Sit down and rest a bit: you must be ready to drop.

JENNY. Ive been going hard since morning. But theres more work than we can do. I
170 mustnt stop.

RUMMY. Try a prayer for just two minutes. Youll work all the better after.

JENNY (*her eyes lighting up*). Oh isnt it wonderful how a few minutes prayer revives you! I was quite lightheaded at twelve o'clock, I was so tired; but Major Barbara just sent me to pray for five minutes; and I was able to go on as if I had only just begun. (*To Price*) Did you have a piece of bread?

PRICE (*with unction*). Yes, miss; but Ive got 180 the piece that I value more; and thats the peace that passeth hall hannerstennin.

RUMMY (*fervently*). Glory Hallelujah!

Bill Walker, a rough customer of about 25, appears at the yard gate and looks malevolently at Jenny.

JENNY. That makes me so happy. When you say that, I feel wicked for loitering here. I must get to work again.

She is hurrying to the shelter, when the new- 190 *comer moves quickly up to the door and intercepts her. His manner is so threatening that she retreats as he comes at her truculently, driving her down the yard.*

BILL. Aw knaow. Youre the one that took awy maw girl. Youre the one that set er agen me. Well, I'm gowin to ev er aht. Not that Aw care a carse for er or you: see? Bat Aw'll let er knaow; and Aw'll let you knaow. Aw'm gowing to give her a doin thatll teach er to 200 cat awy from me. Nah in wiv you and tell er to cam aht afore Aw cam in and kick er aht. Tell er Bill Walker wants er. She'll knaow wot thet means; and if she keeps me witin itll be worse. You stop to jawr beck at me; and Aw'll stawt on you: d'ye eah? Theres your wy. In you gow. (*He takes her by the arm and slings her towards the door of the shelter. She falls on her hand and knee. Rummy helps her up again*).

PRICE (*rising, and venturing irresolutely to-* 210 *wards Bill*). Easy there, mate. She aint doin you no arm.

BILL. Oo are you callin mite? (*Standing over him threateningly*) Youre gowin to stend ap for er, aw yer? Put ap your ends.

RUMMY (*running indignantly to him to scold him*). Oh, you great brute— (*He instantly swings his left hand back against her face. She screams and reels back to the trough, where she sits down, covering her bruised face with* 220 *her hands and rocking herself and moaning with pain*).

JENNY (*going to her*). Oh, God forgive you! How could you strike an old woman like that?

BILL (*seizing her by the hair so violently that she also screams, and tearing her away from the old woman*). You Gawd forgimme again an Aw'll Gawk forgive you one on the jawr thetll stop you pryin for a week. (*Holding her and turning fiercely on Price*) Ev you ennything to sy agen it?

PRICE (*intimidated*). No, matey: she aint anything to do with me.

BILL. Good job for you! Aw'd pat two meals into you and fawt you with one finger arter, you stawved cur. [*To Jenny*] Nah are you gowin to fetch aht Mog Ebbijem; or em Aw to knock your fice off you and fetch her meself?

JENNY (*writhing in his grasp*). Oh please someone go in and tell Major Barbara—(*she screams again as he wrenches her head down; and Price and Rummy flee into the shelter*).

BILL. You want to gow in and tell your Mijor of me, do you?

JENNY. Oh please dont drag my hair. Let me go.

BILL. Do you or downt you? (*She stifles a scream*). Yus or nao?

JENNY. God give me strength—

BILL (*striking her with his fist in the face*). Gow an shaow her thet, and tell her if she wants one lawk it to cam and interfere with me. (*Jenny, crying with pain, goes into the shed. He goes to the form and addresses the old man*). Eah: finish your mess; an git aht o maw wy.

SHIRLEY (*springing up and facing him fiercely, with the mug in his hand*). You take a liberty with me, and I'll smash you over the face with the mug and cut your eye out. Aint you satisfied—young whelps like you—with takin the bread out o the mouths of your elders that have brought you up and slaved for you, but you must come shovin and cheekin and bullyin in here, where the bread o charity is sickenin in our stummicks?

BILL (*contemptuously, but backing a little*). Wot good are you, you aold palsy mag? Wot good are you?

SHIRLEY. As good as you and better. I'll do a day's work agen you or any fat young soaker of your age. Go and take my job at Horrockses, where I worked for ten year. They want young men there: they cant afford to keep men over forty-five. Theyre very sorry—give you a character and happy to help you to get anything suited to your years—sure a steady man wont be long out of a job. Well, let em try you. Theyll find the differ. What do *you* know? Not as much as how to beeyave yourself—layin your dirty fist across the mouth of a respectable woman!

BILL. Downt provowk me to ly it acrost yours: d'ye eah?

SHIRLEY (*with blighting contempt*). Yes: you like an old man to hit, dont you, when youve finished with the women. I aint seen you hit a young one yet.

BILL (*stung*). You loy, you aold soupkitchener, you. There was a yang menn eah. Did Aw offer to itt him or did Aw not?

SHIRLEY. Was he starvin or was he not? Was he a man or only a crosseyed thief an a loafer? Would you hit my son-in-law's brother?

BILL. Oo's ee?

SHIRLEY. Todger Fairmile o Balls Pond. Him that won £20 off the Japanese wrastler at the music hall by standin out 17 minutes 4 seconds agen him.

BILL (*sullenly*). Aw'm nao music awl wrastler. Ken he box?

SHIRLEY. Yes: an you cant.

BILL. Wot! Aw cawnt, cawnt Aw? Wots thet you sy (*threatening him*)?

SHIRLEY (*not budging an inch*). Will you box Todger Fairmile if I put him on to you? Say the word.

BILL (*subsiding with a slouch*). Aw'll stend ap to enny menn alawv, if he was ten Todger Fairmawls. But Aw dont set ap to be a perfeshnal.

SHIRLEY (*looking down on him with unfathomable disdain*). *You* box! Slap an old woman with the back o your hand! You hadnt even the sense to hit her where a magistrate couldnt see the mark of it, you silly young lump of conceit and ignorance. Hit a girl in the jaw and ony make her cry! If Todger Fairmile'd done it, she wouldnt a got up inside o ten minutes, no more than you would if he got on to you. Yah! I'd set about you myself if I had a week's feedin in me instead o two months' starvation. (*He turns his back on him and sits down moodily at the table*).

BILL (*following him and stooping over him to drive the taunt in*). You loy! youve the bread and treacle in you that you cam eah to beg.

330 SHIRLEY (*bursting into tears*). Oh God! it's true: I'm only an old pauper on the scrap heap. (*Furiously*) But youll come to it yourself; and then youll know. Youll come to it sooner than a teetotaller like me, fillin yourself with gin at this hour o the mornin!

BILL. Aw'm nao gin drinker, you oald lawr; bat wen Aw want to give my girl a bloomin good awdin Aw lawk to ev a bit o devil in me: see? An eah emm, talkin to a rotten aold

340 blawter like you sted o givin her wot for. (*Working himself into a rage*) Aw'm gowin in there to fetch her aht. (*He makes vengefully for the shelter door*).

SHIRLEY. Youre going to the station on a stretcher, more likely; and theyll take the gin and the devil out of you there when they get you inside. You mind what youre about: the major here is the Earl o Stevenage's granddaughter.

350 BILL (*checked*). Garn!

SHIRLEY. Youll see.

BILL (*his resolution oozing*). Well, Aw aint dan nathin to er.

SHIRLEY. Spose she said you did! who'd believe you?

BILL (*very uneasy, skulking back to the corner of the penthouse*). Gawd! theres no jastice in this cantry. To think wot them people can do! Aw'm as good as er.

360 SHIRLEY. Tell her so. It's just what a fool like you would do.

Barbara, brisk and businesslike, comes from the shelter with a note book, and addresses herself to Shirley. Bill, cowed, sits down in the corner on a form, and turns his back on them.

BARBARA. Good morning.

SHIRLEY (*standing up and taking off his hat*). Good morning, miss.

BARBARA. Sit down: make yourself at home.

370 (*He hesitates; but she puts a friendly hand on his shoulder and makes him obey*). Now then! since youve made friends with us, we want to know all about you. Names and addresses and trades.

SHIRLEY. Peter Shirley. Fitter. Chucked out two months ago because I was too old.

BARBARA (*not at all surprised*). Youd pass still. Why didnt you dye your hair?

SHIRLEY. I did. Me age come out at a coroner's inquest on me daughter. 380

BARBARA. Steady?

SHIRLEY. Teetotaller. Never out of a job before. Good worker. And sent to the knackers like an old horse!

BARBARA. No matter: if you did your part God will do his.

SHIRLEY (*suddenly stubborn*). My religion's no concern of anybody but myself.

BARBARA (*guessing*). *I* know. Secularist?

SHIRLEY (*hotly*). Did I offer to deny it? 390

BARBARA. Why should you? My own father's a Secularist, I think. Our Father—yours and mine—fulfils himself in many ways; and I daresay he knew what he was about when he made a Secularist of you. So buck up, Peter! we can always find a job for a steady man like you. (*Shirley, disarmed and a little bewildered, touches his hat. She turns from him to Bill*). Whats y o u r name?

BILL (*insolently*). Wots thet to you? 400

BARBARA (*calmly making a note*). Afraid to give his name. Any trade?

BILL. Oo's afride to give is nime? (*Doggedly, with a sense of heroically defying the House of Lords in the person of Lord Stevenage*) If you want to bring a chawge agen me, bring it. (*She waits, unruffled*). Moy nime's Bill Walker.

BARBARA (*as if the name were familiar: trying to remember how*). Bill Walker? (*Recollecting*) 410 Oh, I know: youre the man that Jenny Hill was praying for inside just now. (*She enters his name in her note book*).

BILL. Oo's Jenny Ill? And wot call as she to pry for me?

BARBARA. I dont know. Perhaps it was you that cut her lip.

BILL (*defiantly*). Yus, it w a s me that cat her lip. Aw aint afride o y o u.

BARBARA. How could you be, since youre not 420 afraid of God? Youre a brave man, Mr Walker. It takes some pluck to do o u r work here; but none of us dare lift our hand against a girl like that, for fear of her father in heaven.

BILL (*sullenly*). I want nan o your kentin jawr. I spowse you think Aw cam eah to beg from you, like this demmiged lot eah. Not me. Aw downt want your bread and scripe and ketlep. Aw dont blieve in your Gawd, no more than you do yourself.

BARBARA (*sunnily apologetic and ladylike, as on a new footing with him*). Oh, I beg your pardon for putting your name down, Mr Walker. I didnt understand. I'll strike it out.

BILL (*taking this as a slight, and deeply wounded by it*). Eah! you let maw nime alown. Aint it good enaff to be in your book?

BARBARA (*considering*). Well, you see, theres no use putting down your name unless I can do something for you, is there? Whats your trade?

BILL (*still smarting*). Thets nao concern o yours.

BARBARA. Just so. (*Very businesslike*) I'll put you down as (*writing*) the man who—struck—poor little Jenny Hill—in the mouth.

BILL (*rising threateningly*). See eah. Awve ed enaff o this.

BARBARA (*quite sunny and fearless*). What did you come to us for?

BILL. Aw cam for maw gel, see? Aw cam to tike her aht o this and to brike er jawr for er.

BARBARA (*complacently*). You see I was right about your trade. (*Bill, on the point of retorting furiously, finds himself, to his great shame and terror, in danger of crying instead. He sits down again suddenly*). Whats her name?

BILL (*dogged*). Er nime's Mog Ebbijem: thets wot her nime is.

BARBARA. Mog Habbijam! Oh, she's gone to Canning Town, to our barracks there.

BILL (*fortified by his resentment of Mog's perfidy*). Is she? (*Vindictively*) Then Aw'm gowin to Kennintahn arter her. (*He crosses to the gate; hesitates; finally comes back at Barbara*). Are you loyin to me to git shat o me?

BARBARA. I dont want to get shut of you. I want to keep you here and save your soul. Youd better stay: youre going to have a bad time today, Bill.

BILL. Oo's gowin to give it to me? You, preps?

BARBARA. Someone you dont believe in. But youll be glad afterwards.

BILL (*slinking off*). Aw'll gow to Kennintahn to be aht o reach o your tangue. (*Suddenly turning on her with intense malice*) And if Aw downt fawnd Mog there, Aw'll cam beck and do two years for you, selp me Gawd if Aw downt!

BARBARA (*a shade kindlier, if possible*). It's no use, Bill. She's got another bloke.

BILL. Wot!

BARBARA. One of her own converts. He fell in love with her when he saw her with her soul saved, and her face clean, and her hair washed.

BILL (*surprised*). Wottud she wash it for, the carroty slat? It's red.

BARBARA. It's quite lovely now, because she wears a new look in her eyes with it. It's a pity youre too late. The new bloke has put your nose out of joint, Bill.

BILL. Aw'll put his nowse aht o joint for him. Not that Aw care a carse for er, mawnd thet. But Aw'll teach her to drop me as if Aw was dirt. And Aw'll teach him to meddle with maw judy. Wots iz bleedin nime?

BARBARA. Sergeant Todger Fairmile.

SHIRLEY (*rising with grim joy*). I'll go with him, miss. I want to see them two meet. I'll take him to the infirmary when it's over.

BILL (*to Shirley, with undissembled misgiving*). Is thet im you was speakin on?

SHIRLEY. Thats him.

BILL. Im that wrastled in the music awl?

SHIRLEY. The competitions at the National Sportin Club was worth nigh a hundred a year to him. He's gev em up now for religion; so he's a bit fresh for want of the exercise he was accustomed to. He'll be glad to see you. Come along.

BILL. Wots is wight?

SHIRLEY. Thirteen four. (*Bill's last hope expires*).

BARBARA. Go and talk to him, Bill. He'll convert you.

SHIRLEY. He'll convert your head into a mashed potato.

BILL (*sullenly*). Aw aint afride of im. Aw aint afride of ennybody. Bat e can lick me. She's dan me. (*He sits down moodily on the edge of the horse trough*).

SHIRLEY. You aint going. I thought not. (*He resumes his seat*).

BARBARA (*calling*). Jenny!

JENNY (*appearing at the shelter door with a plaster on the corner of her mouth*). Yes, Major.

BARBARA. Send Rummy Mitchens out to clear away here.

JENNY. I think she's afraid.

BARBARA (*her resemblance to her mother flashing out for a moment*). Nonsense! she must do as she's told.

JENNY (*calling into the shelter*). Rummy: the Major says you must come.

Jenny comes to Barbara, purposely keeping on the side next Bill, lest he should suppose that she shrank from him or bore malice.

BARBARA. Poor little Jenny! Are you tired? (*Looking at the wounded cheek*) Does it hurt?

JENNY. No: it's all right now. It was nothing.

BARBARA (*critically*). It was as hard as he could hit, I expect. Poor Bill! You dont feel angry with him, do you?

JENNY. Oh no, no, no: indeed I dont, Major, bless his poor heart! (*Barbara kisses her; and she runs away merrily into the shelter. Bill writhes with an agonizing return of his new and alarming symptoms, but says nothing. Rummy Mitchens comes from the shelter*).

BARBARA (*going to meet Rummy*). Now Rummy, bustle. Take in those mugs and plates to be washed; and throw the crumbs about for the birds.

Rummy takes the three plates and mugs; but Shirley takes back his mug from her, as there is still some milk left in it.

RUMMY. There aint any crumbs. This aint a time to waste good bread on birds.

PRICE (*appearing at the shelter door*). Gentleman come to see the shelter, Major. Says he's your father.

BARBARA. All right. Coming. (*Snobby goes back into the shelter, followed by Barbara*).

RUMMY (*stealing across to Bill and addressing him in a subdued voice, but with intense conviction*). I'd av the lor of you, you flat eared pignosed potwalloper, if she'd let me. Youre no gentleman, to hit a lady in the face. (*Bill, with greater things moving in him, takes no notice*).

SHIRLEY (*following her*). Here! in with you and dont get yourself into more trouble by talking.

RUMMY (*with hauteur*). I aint ad the pleasure o being hintroduced to you, as I can remember. (*She goes into the shelter with the plates*).

SHIRLEY. Thats the—

BILL (*savagely*). Downt you talk to me, d'ye eah? You lea me alown, or Aw'll do you a mischief. Aw'm not dirt under your feet, ennywy.

SHIRLEY (*calmly*). Dont you be afeerd. You aint such prime company that you need expect to be sought after. (*He is about to go into the shelter when Barbara comes out, with Undershaft on her right*).

BARBARA. Oh, there you are, Mr Shirley! (*Between them*) This is my father: I told you he was a Secularist, didnt I? Perhaps youll be able to comfort one another.

UNDERSHAFT (*startled*). A Secularist! Not the least in the world: on the contrary, a confirmed mystic.

BARBARA. Sorry, I'm sure. By the way, papa, what is your religion? in case I have to introduce you again.

UNDERSHAFT. My religion? Well, my dear, I am a Millionaire. That is my religion.

BARBARA. Then I'm afraid you and Mr Shirley wont be able to comfort one another after all. Youre not a Millionaire, are you, Peter?

SHIRLEY. No; and proud of it.

UNDERSHAFT (*gravely*). Poverty, my friend, is not a thing to be proud of.

SHIRLEY (*angrily*). Who made your millions for you? Me and my like. Whats kep us poor? Keepin you rich. I wouldnt have your conscience, not for all your income.

UNDERSHAFT. I wouldnt have your income, not for all your conscience, Mr Shirley. (*He goes to the penthouse and sits down on a form*).

BARBARA (*stopping Shirley adroitly as he is about to retort*). You wouldnt think he was my father, would you, Peter? Will you go into the shelter and lend the lasses a hand for a while: we're worked off our feet.

SHIRLEY (*bitterly*). Yes: I'm in their debt for a meal, aint I?

BARBARA. Oh, not because youre in their debt, but for love of them, Peter, for love of them. (*He cannot understand, and is rather scandalized*) There! dont stare at me. In with you; and give that conscience of yours a holiday (*bustling him into the shelter*).

SHIRLEY (*as he goes in*). Ah! it's a pity you never was trained to use your reason, miss. Youd have been a very taking lecturer on Secularism.

Barbara turns to her father.

UNDERSHAFT. Never mind me, my dear. Go about your work; and let me watch it for a while.

BARBARA. All right.

UNDERSHAFT. For instance, whats the matter with that outpatient over there?

BARBARA (*looking at Bill, whose attitude has never changed, and whose expression of brooding wrath has deepened*). Oh, we shall cure him in no time. Just watch. (*She goes over to Bill and waits. He glances up at her and casts his eyes down again, uneasy, but grimmer than ever*). It w o u l d be nice to just stamp on Mog Habbijam's face, wouldnt it, Bill?

BILL (*starting up from the trough in consternation*). It's a loy: Aw never said so. (*she shakes her head*). Oo taold you wot was in moy mawnd?

BARBARA. Only your new friend.

BILL. Wot new friend?

BARBARA. The devil, Bill. When he gets round people they get miserable, just like you.

BILL (*with a heartbreaking attempt at devil-may-care cheerfulness*). Aw aint miserable. (*He sits down again, and stretches his legs in an attempt to seem indifferent*).

BARBARA. Well, if youre happy, why dont you look happy, as we do?

BILL (*his legs curling back in spite of him*). Aw'm eppy enaff, Aw tell you. Woy cawnt you lea me alown? Wot ev I dan to y o u? Aw aint smashed y o u r fice, ev Aw?

BARBARA (*softly: wooing his soul*). It's not me thats getting at you, Bill.

BILL. Oo else is it?

BARBARA. Somebody that doesnt intend you to smash women's faces, I suppose. Somebody or something that wants to make a man of you.

BILL (*blustering*). Mike a menn o m e! Aint Aw a menn? eh? Oo sez Aw'm not a menn?

BARBARA. Theres a man in you somewhere, I suppose. But why did he let you hit poor little Jenny Hill? That wasnt very manly of him, was it?

BILL (*tormented*). Ev dan wiv it, Aw tell you. Chack it. Aw'm sick o your Jenny Ill and er silly little fice.

BARBARA. Then why do you keep thinking about it? Why does it keep coming up against you in your mind? Youre not getting converted, are you?

BILL (*with conviction*). Not M E. Not lawkly.

BARBARA. Thats right, Bill. Hold out against it. Put out your strength. Dont lets get you cheap. Todger Fairmile said he wrestled for three nights against his salvation harder than he ever wrestled with the Jap at the music hall. He gave in to the Jap when his arm was going to break. But he didnt give in to his salvation until his heart was going to break. Perhaps youll escape that. You havnt any heart, have you?

BILL. Wot d'ye mean? Woy aint Aw got a awt the sime as ennybody else?

BARBARA. A man with a heart wouldnt have bashed poor little Jenny's face, would he?

BILL (*almost crying*). Ow, w i l l you lea me alown? Ev Aw ever offered to meddle with y o u, that you cam neggin and provowkin me lawk this? (*He writhes convulsively from his eyes to his toes*).

BARBARA (*with a steady soothing hand on his arm and a gentle voice that never lets him go*). It's your soul thats hurting you, Bill, and not me. Weve been through it all ourselves. Come with us, Bill. (*He looks wildly round*). To brave manhood on earth and eternal glory in heaven. (*He is on the point of breaking down*). Come. (*A drum is heard in the shelter; and Bill, with a gasp, escapes from the spell as Barbara turns quickly. Adolphus enters from the shelter with a big drum*). Oh! there you are, Dolly. Let me introduce a new friend of mine, Mr Bill Walker. This is my bloke, Bill: Mr Cusins. (*Cusins salutes with his drumstick*).

BILL. Gowin to merry im?

BARBARA. Yes.

BILL (*fervently*). Gawd elp im! Gaw-aw-aw-awd elp im!

BARBARA. Why? Do you think he wont be happy with me?

BILL. Awve aony ed to stend it for a mawnin: e'll ev to stend it for a lawftawm.

CUSINS. That is a frightful reflection, Mr Walker. But I cant tear myself away from her. 730

BILL. Well, Aw ken. (*To Barbara*) Eah! do you knaow where Aw'm gowin to, and wot Aw'm gowin to do?

BARBARA. Yes: youre going to heaven; and youre coming back here before the week's out to tell me so.

BILL. You loy. Aw'm gowin to Kennintahn, to spit in Todger Fairmawl's eye. Aw beshed Jenny Ill's fice; an nar Aw'll git me aown fice beshed and cam beck and shaow it to er. Ee'll 740 itt me ardern Aw itt her. Thatll mike us square. (*To Adolphus*) Is thet fair or is it not? Youre a genlmn: you oughter knaow.

BARBARA. Two black eyes wont make one white one, Bill.

BILL. Aw didnt awst y o u. Cawnt you never keep your mahth shat? Oy awst the genlmn.

CUSINS (*reflectively*). Yes: I think youre right, Mr Walker. Yes: I should do it. It's curious: it's exactly what an ancient Greek would 750 have done.

BARBARA. But what good will it do?

CUSINS. Well, it will give Mr Fairmile some exercise; and it will satisfy Mr Walker's soul.

BILL. Rot! there aint nao sach a thing as a saoul. Ah kin you tell wevver Awve a saoul or not? You never seen it.

BARBARA. Ive seen it hurting you when you went against it.

760 BILL (*with compressed aggravation*). If you was maw gel and took the word aht o me mahth lawk thet, Aw'd give you sathink youd feel urtin, Aw would. (*To Adolphus*) You tike maw tip, mite. Stop er jawr; or youll doy afoah your tawm (*With intense expression*) Wore aht: thets wot youll be: wore aht. (*He goes away through the gate*).

CUSINS (*looking after him*). I wonder!

BARBARA. Dolly! (*indignant, in her mother's* 770 *manner*).

CUSINS. Yes, my dear, it's very wearing to be in love with you. If it lasts, I quite think I shall die young.

BARBARA. Should you mind?

CUSINS. Not at all. (*He is suddenly softened, and kisses her over the drum, evidently not for the first time, as people cannot kiss over a big drum without practice. Undershaft coughs*).

BARBARA. It's all right, papa, weve not forgotten you. Dolly: explain the place to papa: I 780 havnt time. (*She goes busily into the shelter*).

Undershaft and Adolphus now have the yard to themselves. Undershaft, seated on a form, and still keenly attentive, looks hard at Adolphus. Adolphus looks hard at him.

UNDERSHAFT. I fancy you guess something of what is in my mind, Mr Cusins. (*Cusins flourishes his drumsticks as if in the act of beating a lively rataplan, but makes no sound*). Exactly so. But suppose Barbara finds you out! 790

CUSINS. You know, I do not admit that I am imposing on Barbara. I am quite genuinely interested in the views of the Salvation Army. The fact is, I am a sort of collector of religions; and the curious thing is that I find I can believe them all. By the way, have you any religion?

UNDERSHAFT. Yes.

CUSINS. Anything out of the common?

UNDERSHAFT. Only that there are two things necessary to Salvation. 800

CUSINS (*disappointed, but polite*). Ah, the Church Catechism. Charles Lomax also belongs to the Established Church.

UNDERSHAFT. The two things are—

CUSINS. Baptism and—

UNDERSHAFT. No. Money and gunpowder.

CUSINS (*surprised, but interested*). That is the general opinion of our governing classes. The novelty is in hearing any man confess it.

UNDERSHAFT. Just so. 810

CUSINS. Excuse me: is there any place in your religion for honor, justice, truth, love, mercy and so forth?

UNDERSHAFT. Yes: they are the graces and luxuries of a rich, strong, and safe life.

CUSINS. Suppose one is forced to choose between them and money or gunpowder?

UNDERSHAFT. Choose money a n d gunpowder; for without enough of both you cannot afford the others. 820

CUSINS. That is your religion?

UNDERSHAFT. Yes.

The cadence of this reply makes a full close in the conversation, Cusins twists his face dubiously and contemplates Undershaft. Undershaft contemplates him.

CUSINS. Barbara wont stand that. You will have to choose between your religion and Barbara.

830 UNDERSHAFT. So will you, my friend. She will find out that that drum of yours is hollow.

CUSINS. Father Undershaft: you are mistaken: I am a sincere Salvationist. You do not understand the Salvation Army. It is the army of joy, of love, of courage: it has banished the fear and remorse and despair of the old hell-ridden evangelical sects: it marches to fight the devil with trumpet and drum, with music and dancing, with banner and palm, as becomes a 840 sally from heaven by its happy garrison. It picks the waster out of the public house and makes a man of him: it finds a worm wriggling in a back kitchen, and lo! a woman! Men and women of rank too, sons and daughters of the Highest. It takes the poor professor of Greek, the most artificial and self-suppressed of human creatures, from his meal of roots, and lets loose the rhapsodist in him; reveals the true worship of Dionysos to him; sends him down the public 850 street drumming dithyrambs (*he plays a thundering flourish on the drum*).

UNDERSHAFT. You will alarm the shelter.

CUSINS. Oh, they are accustomed to these sudden ecstasies. However, if the drum worries you—(*he pockets the drumsticks; unhooks the drum; and stands it on the ground opposite the gateway*).

UNDERSHAFT. Thank you.

CUSINS. You remember what Euripides says 860 about your money and gunpowder?

UNDERSHAFT. No.

CUSINS (*declaiming*).

One and another
In money and guns may outpass his brother;
And men in their millions float and flow
And seethe with a million hopes as leaven;
And they win their will; or they miss their will;
And their hopes are dead or are pined for still;
But who'er can know
As the long days go 870
That to live is happy, has found h i s heaven.

My translation: what do you think of it?

UNDERSHAFT. I think, my friend, that if you wish to know, as the long days go, that to live is happy, you must first acquire money enough for a decent life, and power enough to be your own master.

CUSINS. You are damnably discouraging. (*He resumes his declamation*).

Is it so hard a thing to see 880
That the spirit of God—whate'er it be—
The law that abides and changes not, ages long,
The Eternal and Nature-born: t h e s e things be strong?
What else is Wisdom? What of Man's endeavor,
Or God's high grace so lovely and so great?
To stand from fear set free? to breathe and wait?
To hold a hand uplifted over Fate?
And shall not Barbara be loved for ever?

UNDERSHAFT. Euripides mentions Barbara, does he? 890

CUSINS. It is a fair translation. The word means Loveliness.

UNDERSHAFT. May I ask—as Barbara's father—how much a year she is to be loved for ever on?

CUSINS. As for Barbara's father, that is more your affair than mine. I can feed her by teaching Greek: that is about all.

UNDERSHAFT. Do you consider it a good match for her? 900

CUSINS (*with polite obstinacy*). Mr Undershaft: I am in many ways a weak, timid, ineffectual person; and my health is far from satisfactory. But whenever I feel that I must have anything, I get it, sooner or later. I feel that way about Barbara. I dont like marriage: I feel intensely afraid of it; and I dont know what I shall do with Barbara or what she will do with me. But I feel that I and nobody else must marry her. Please regard that as settled. 910 —Not that I wish to be arbitrary; but why should I waste your time in discussing what is inevitable?

UNDERSHAFT. You mean that you will stick at nothing: not even the conversion of the Salvation Army to the worship of Dionysos.

CUSINS. The business of the Salvation Army is to save, not to wrangle about the name of the pathfinder. Dionysos or another: what does it matter?

UNDERSHAFT (*rising and approaching him*). Professor Cusins: you are a young man after my own heart.

CUSINS. Mr Undershaft: you are, as far as I am able to gather, a most infernal old rascal; but you appeal very strongly to my sense of ironic humor.

Undershaft mutely offers his hand. They shake.

UNDERSHAFT (*suddenly concentrating himself*). And now to business.

CUSINS. Pardon me. We are discussing religion. Why go back to such an uninteresting and unimportant subject as business?

UNDERSHAFT. Religion is our business at present, because it is through religion alone that we can win Barbara.

CUSINS. Have you, too, fallen in love with Barbara?

UNDERSHAFT. Yes, with a father's love.

CUSINS. A father's love for a grown-up daughter is the most dangerous of all infatuations. I apologize for mentioning my own pale, coy, mistrustful fancy in the same breath with it.

UNDERSHAFT. Keep to the point. We have to win her; and we are neither of us Methodists.

CUSINS. That doesnt matter. The power Barbara wields here—the power that wields Barbara herself—is not Calvinism, not Presybterianism, not Methodism—

UNDERSHAFT. Not Greek Paganism either, eh?

CUSINS. I admit that. Barbara is quite original in her religion.

UNDERSHAFT (*triumphantly*). Aha! Barbara Undershaft would be. Her inspiration comes from within herself.

CUSINS. How do you suppose it got there?

UNDERSHAFT (*in towering excitement*). It is the Undershaft inheritance. I shall hand on my torch to my daughter. She shall make my converts and preach my gospel—

CUSINS. What! Money and gunpowder!

UNDERSHAFT. Yes, money and gunpowder. Freedom and power. Command of life and command of death.

CUSINS (*urbanely: trying to bring him down to earth*). This is extremely interesting, Mr Undershaft. Of course you know that you are mad.

UNDERSHAFT (*with redoubled force*). And you?

CUSINS. Oh, mad as a hatter. You are welcome to my secret since I have discovered yours. But I am astonished. Can a madman make cannons?

UNDERSHAFT. Would anyone else than a madman make them? And now (*with surging energy*) question for question. Can a sane man translate Euripides?

CUSINS. No.

UNDERSHAFT (*seizing him by the shoulder*). Can a sane woman make a man of a waster or a woman of a worm?

CUSINS (*reeling before the storm*). Father Colossus—Mammoth Millionaire—

UNDERSHAFT (*pressing him*). Are there two mad people or three in this Salvation shelter today?

CUSINS. You mean Barbara is as mad as we are?

UNDERSHAFT (*pushing him lightly off and resuming his equanimity suddenly and completely*). Pooh, Professor! let us call things by their proper names. I am a millionaire; you are a poet: Barbara is a savior of souls. What have we three to do with the common mob of slaves and idolators? (*He sits down again with a shrug of contempt for the mob*).

CUSINS. Take care! Barbara is in love with the common people. So am I. Have you never felt the romance of that love?

UNDERSHAFT (*cold and sardonic*). Have you ever been in love with Poverty, like St Francis? Have you ever been in love with Dirt, like St Simeon! Have you ever been in love with disease and suffering, like our nurses and philanthropists? Such passions are not virtues, but the most unnatural of all the vices. This love of the common people may please an earl's granddaughter and a university professor; but I have been a common man and a poor man; and it has no romance for me. Leave it to the poor to pretend that poverty is a blessing: leave it to the coward to make a religion of his cowardice by preaching humility: we know better than that. We three must stand together above the common people: how else can we help their children to climb up beside us? Barbara must belong to us, not to the Salvation Army.

CUSINS. Well, I can only say that if you think you will get her away from the Salvation Army by talking to her as you have been talking to me, you dont know Barbara.

UNDERSHAFT. My friend: I never ask for what I can buy.

CUSINS (*in a white fury*). Do I understand you to imply that you can buy Barbara?

UNDERSHAFT. No; but I can buy the Salvation Army.

CUSINS. Quite impossible.

UNDERSHAFT. You shall see. All religious organizations exist by selling themselves to the rich.

CUSINS. Not the Army. That is the Church of the poor.

UNDERSHAFT. All the more reason for buying it.

CUSINS. I dont think you quite know what the Army does for the poor.

UNDERSHAFT. Oh yes I do. It draws their teeth: that is enough for me as a man of business.

CUSINS. Nonsense! It makes them sober—

UNDERSHAFT. I prefer sober workmen. The profits are larger.

CUSINS. —honest—

UNDERSHAFT. Honest workmen are the most economical.

CUSINS. —attached to their homes—

UNDERSHAFT. So much the better: they will put up with anything sooner than change their shop.

CUSINS. —happy—

UNDERSHAFT. An invaluable safeguard against revolution.

CUSINS. —unselfish—

UNDERSHAFT. Indifferent to their own interests, which suits me exactly.

CUSINS. —with their thoughts on heavenly things—

UNDERSHAFT (*rising*). And not on Trade Unionism nor Socialism. Excellent.

CUSINS (*revolted*). You really are an infernal old rascal.

UNDERSHAFT (*indicating Peter Shirley, who has just come from the shelter and strolled dejectedly down the yard between them*). And this is an honest man!

SHIRLEY. Yes; and what av I got by it? (*he passes on bitterly and sits on the form, in the corner of the penthouse*).

Snobby Price, beaming sanctimoniously, and Jenny Hill, with a tambourine full of coppers, come from the shelter and go to the drum, on which Jenny begins to count the money.

UNDERSHAFT (*replying to Shirley*). Oh, your employers must have got a good deal by it from first to last. (*He sits on the table, with one foot on the side form, Cusins, overwhelmed, sits down on the same form nearer the shelter. Barbara comes from the shelter to the middle of the yard. She is excited and a little overwrought*).

BARBARA. Weve just had a splendid experience meeting at the other gate in Cripps's lane. Ive hardly ever seen them so much moved as they were by your confession, Mr Price.

PRICE. I could almost be glad of my past wickedness if I could believe that it would elp to keep hathers stright.

BARBARA. So it will, Snobby. How much, Jenny?

JENNY. Four and tenpence, Major.

BARBARA. Oh Snobby, if you had given your poor mother just one more kick, we should have got the whole five shillings!

PRICE. If she heard you say that, miss, she'd be sorry I didnt. But I'm glad. Oh what a joy it will be to her when she hears I'm saved!

UNDERSHAFT. Shall I contribute the odd twopence, Barbara? The millionaire's mite, eh? (*He takes a couple of pennies from his pocket*).

BARBARA. How did you make that twopence?

UNDERSHAFT. As usual. By selling cannons, torpedoes, submarines, and my new patent Grand Duke hand grenade.

BARBARA. Put it back in your pocket. You cant buy your salvation here for twopence: you must work it out.

UNDERSHAFT. Is twopence not enough? I can afford a little more, if your press me.

BARBARA. Two million millions would not be enough. There is bad blood on your hands; and nothing but good blood can cleanse them. Money is no use. Take it away. (*She turns to Cusins*). Dolly: you must write another letter for me to the papers. (*He makes a wry face*). Yes: I know you dont like it; but it must be done. The starvation this winter is beating us: everybody is unemployed. The General says we must close this shelter if we cant get more money. I force the collections at the meetings until I am ashamed: dont I, Snobby?

PRICE. It's a fair treat to see you work it, miss. The way you got them up from three-and-six to four-and-ten with that hymn, penny by penny and verse by verse, was a caution. Not a Cheap Jack on Mile End Waste could touch you at it.

BARBARA. Yes; but I wish we could do without it. I am getting at last to think more of the collection than of the people's souls. And what are those hatfuls of pence and halfpence? We want thousands! tens of thousands! hundreds of thousands! I want to convert people, not to be always begging for the Army in a way I'd die sooner than beg for myself.

UNDERSHAFT (*in profound irony*). Genuine unselfishness is capable of anything, my dear.

BARBARA (*unsuspectingly, as she turns away to take the money from the drum and put it in a cash bag she carries*). Yes, isnt it? (*Undershaft looks sardonically at Cusins*).

CUSINS (*aside to Undershaft*). Mephistopheles! Machiavelli!

BARBARA (*tears coming into her eyes as she ties the bag and pockets it*). How are we to feed them? I cant talk religion to a man with bodily hunger in his eyes. (*Almost breaking down*) It's frightful.

JENNY (*running to her*). Major, dear—

BARBARA (*rebounding*). No: dont comfort me. It will be all right. We shall get the money.

UNDERSHAFT. How?

JENNY. By praying for it, of course. Mrs Baines says she prayed for it last night; and she has never prayed for it in vain: never once. (*She goes to the gate and looks out into the street*).

BARBARA (*who has dried her eyes and regained her composure*). By the way, dad, Mrs Baines has come to march with us to our big meeting this afternoon; and she is very anxious to meet you, for some reason or other. Perhaps she'll convert you.

UNDERSHAFT. I shall be delighted, my dear.

JENNY (*at the gate: excitedly*). Major! Major! heres that man back again.

BARBARA. What man?

JENNY. The man that hit me. Oh, I hope he's coming back to join us.

Bill Walker, with frost on his jacket, comes through the gate, his hands deep in his pockets and his chin sunk between his shoulders, like a cleaned-out gambler. He halts between Barbara and the drum.

BARBARA. Hullo, Bill! Back already!

BILL (*nagging at her*). Bin talkin ever sence, ev you?

BARBARA. Pretty nearly. Well, has Todger paid you out for poor Jenny's jaw?

BILL. Nao e aint.

BARBARA. I thought your jacket looked a bit snowy.

BILL. Sao it is snaowy. You want to knaow where the snaow cam from, downt you?

BARBARA. Yes.

BILL. Well, it cam from orf the grahnd in Pawkinses Corner in Kennintahn. It got rabbed orf be maw shaoulders: see?

BARBARA. Pity you didnt rub some off with your knees, Bill! That would have done you a lot of good.

BILL (*with sour mirthless humor*). Aw was sivin anather menn's knees at the tawn. E was kneelin on moy ed, e was.

JENNY. Who was kneeling on your head?

BILL. Todger was. E was pryin for me: pryin camfortable wiv me as a cawpet. Sow was Mog. Sao was the aol bloomin meetin. Mog she sez 'Ow Lawd brike is stabborn sperrit; bat downt urt is dear art.' Thet was wot she said. 'Downt urt is dear art'! An er blowk—thirteen stun four!—kneelin wiv all is wight on me. Fanny, aint it?

JENNY. Oh no. We're so sorry, Mr Walker.

BARBARA (*enjoying it frankly*). Nonsense! of course it's funny. Served you right, Bill! You must have done something to him first.

BILL (*doggedly*). Aw did wot Aw said Aw'd do. Aw spit in is eye. E looks ap at the skoy and sez, 'Ow that Aw should be fahnd worthy to be spit upon for the gospel's sike!' e sez; an Mog sez 'Glaory Allelloolier!'; and then e called me Braddher, an dahned me as if Aw was a kid and e was me mather worshin me a Setterda nawt. Aw ednt jast nao shaow wiv im at all. Arf the street pryed; an the tather arf

1220 larfed fit to split theirselves. (*To Barbara*) There! are you settisfawd nah?

BARBARA (*her eyes dancing*). Wish I'd been there, Bill.

BILL. Yus: youd a got in a hextra bit o talk on me, wouldnt you?

JENNY. I'm so sorry, Mr Walker.

BILL (*fiercely*). Downt you gow being sorry for me: youve no call. Listen eah. Aw browk your jawr.

1230 JENNY. No, it didnt hurt me: indeed it didnt, except for a moment. It was only that I was frightened.

BILL. Aw downt want to be forgive be you, or be ennybody. Wot Aw did Aw'll py for. Aw trawd to gat me aown jawr browk to settisfaw you—

JENNY (*distressed*). Oh no—

BILL (*impatiently*). Tell y' Aw did: cawnt you listen to wots bein taold you? All Aw got 1240 be it was bein mide a sawt of in the pablic street for me pines. Well, if Aw cawnt settisfaw you one wy, Aw ken anather. Listen eah! Aw ed two quid sived agen the frost; and Awve a pahnd of it left. A mite o mawn last week ed words with the judy e's gowing to merry. E give er wot-for; an e's bin fawnd fifteen bob. E ed a rawt to itt er cause they was gowin to be merrid; but Aw ednt nao rawt to itt you; sao put anather fawv bob on an call it a pahnd's 1250 worth. (*He produces a sovereign*). Eahs the manney. Tike it; and lets ev no more o your forgivin an pryin and your Mijor jawrin me. Let wot Aw dan be dan an pide for; and let there be a end of it.

JENNY. Oh, I couldnt take it, Mr Walker. But if you would give a shilling or two to poor Rummy Mitchens! you really did hurt her; and she's old.

BILL (*contemptuously*). Not lawkly. Aw'd 1260 give her anather as soon as look at er. Let her ev the lawr o me as she threatened! She aint forgiven me: not mach. Wot Aw dan to er is not on me mawnd—wot she (*indicating Barbara*) mawt call on me conscience—no more than stickin a pig. It's this Christian gime o yours that Aw wownt ev plyed agen me: this bloomin forgivin an neggin an jawrin that mikes a menn thet sore that iz lawf's a burdn to im. Aw wownt ev it, Aw tell you; sao tike 1270 your manney and stop thraowin your silly beshed fice hap agen me.

JENNY. Major: may I take a little of it for the Army?

BARBARA. No: the Army is not to be bought. We want your soul, Bill; and we'll take nothing less.

BILL (*bitterly*). Aw knaow. Me an maw few shillins is not good enaff for you. Youre a earl's grendorter, you are. Nathink less than a andered pahnd for you. 1280

UNDERSHAFT. Come, Barbara! you could do a great deal of good with a hundred pounds. If you will set this gentleman's mind at ease by taking his pound, I will give the other ninety-nine.

Bill, dazed by such opulence, instinctively touches his cap.

BARBARA. Oh, youre too extravagant, papa. Bill offers twenty pieces of silver. All you need offer is the other ten. That will make the 1290 standard price to buy anybody who's for sale. I'm not; and the Army's not. (*To Bill*) Youll never have another quiet moment, Bill, until you come round to us. You cant stand out against your salvation.

BILL (*sullenly*). Aw cawnt stend aht agen music awl wrastlers and awtful tangued women. Awve offered to py. Aw can do no more. Tike it or leave it. There it is. (*He throws the sovereign on the drum, and sits down on the horse-* 1300 *trough. The coin fascinates Snobby Price, who takes an early opportunity of dropping his cap on it*).

Mrs Baines comes from the shelter. She is dressed as a Salvation Army Commissioner. She is an earnest looking woman of about 40, with a carressing, urgent voice, and an appealing manner.

BARBARA. This is my father, Mrs Baines. (*Undershaft comes from the table, taking his* 1310 *hat off with marked civility*). Try what you can do with him. He wont listen to me, because he remembers what a fool I was when I was a baby. (*She leaves them together and chats with Jenny*).

MRS BAINES. Have you been shewn over the shelter, Mr Undershaft? You know the work we're doing, of course.

UNDERSHAFT (*very civilly*). The whole nation knows it, Mrs Baines. 1320

MRS BAINES. No, sir: the whole nation does not know it, or we should not be crippled as we are for want of money to carry our work through the length and breadth of the land. Let me tell you that there would have been rioting this winter in London but for us.

UNDERSHAFT. You really think so?

MRS BAINES. I know it. I remember 1886, when you rich gentlemen hardened your hearts against the cry of the poor. They broke the windows of your clubs in Pall Mall.

UNDERSHAFT (*gleaming with approval of their method*). And the Mansion House Fund went up next day from thirty thousand pounds to seventy-nine thousand! I remember quite well.

MRS BAINES. Well, wont you help me to get at the people? They wont break windows then. Come here, Price. Let me shew you to this gentleman (*Price comes to be inspected*). Do you remember the window breaking?

PRICE. My ole father thought it was the revolution, maam.

MRS BAINES. Would you break windows now?

PRICE. Oh no, maam. The windows of eaven ave bin opened to me. I know now that the rich man is a sinner like myself.

RUMMY (*appearing above at the loft door*). Snobby Price!

SNOBBY. Wot is it?

RUMMY. Your mother's askin for you at the other gate in Cripps's Lane. She's heard about your confession (*Price turns pale*).

MRS BAINES. Go, Mr Price; and pray with her.

JENNY. You can go through the shelter, Snobby.

PRICE (*to Mrs Baines*). I couldnt face her now, maam, with all the weight of my sins fresh on me. Tell her she'll find her son at ome, waitin for her in prayer. (*He skulks off through the gate, incidentally stealing the sovereign on his way out by picking up his cap from the drum*).

MRS BAINES (*with swimming eyes*). You see how we take the anger and the bitterness against you out of their hearts, Mr Undershaft.

UNDERSHAFT. It is certainly most convenient and gratifying to all large employers of labor, Mrs Baines.

MRS BAINES. Barbara: Jenny: I have good news: most wonderful news. (*Jenny runs to her*). My prayers have been answered. I told you they would, Jenny, didnt I?

JENNY. Yes, yes.

BARBARA (*moving nearer to the drum*). Have we got money enough to keep the shelter open?

MRS BAINES. I hope we shall have enough to keep all the shelters open. Lord Saxmundham has promised us five thousand pounds—

BARBARA. Hooray!

JENNY. Glory!

MRS BAINES. —if—

BARBARA. 'If!' If what?

MRS BAINES. —if five other gentlemen will give a thousand each to make it up to ten thousand.

BARBARA. Who is Lord Saxmundham? I never heard of him.

UNDERSHAFT (*who has pricked up his ears at the peer's name, and is now watching Barbara curiously*). A new creation, my dear. You have heard of Sir Horace Bodger?

BARBARA. Bodger! Do you mean the distiller? Bodger's whisky!

UNDERSHAFT. That is the man. He is one of the greatest of our public benefactors. He restored the cathedral at Hakington. They made him a baronet for that. He gave half a million to the funds of his party: they made him a baron for that.

SHIRLEY. What will they give him for the five thousand?

UNDERSHAFT. There is nothing left to give him. So the five thousand, I should think, is to save his soul.

MRS BAINES. Heaven grant it may! Oh Mr Undershaft, you have some very rich friends. Cant you help us towards the other five thousand? We are going to hold a great meeting this afternoon at the Assembly Hall in the Mile End Road. If I could only announce that one gentleman had come forward to support Lord Saxmundham, others would follow. Dont you know somebody? couldnt you? wouldnt you? (*her eyes fill with tears*) oh, think of those poor people, Mr Undershaft: think of how much it means to them, and how little to a great man like you.

UNDERSHAFT (*sardonically gallant*). Mrs Baines: you are irresistible. I cant disappoint you; and I cant deny myself the satisfaction of making Bodger pay up. You shall have your five thousand pounds.

MRS BAINES. Thank God!

UNDERSHAFT. You dont thank me?

MRS BAINES. Oh sir, dont try to be cynical: dont be ashamed of being a good man. The Lord will bless you abundantly; and our pray- 1430 ers will be like a strong fortification round you all the days of your life. (*With a touch of caution*) You will let me have the cheque to shew at the meeting, wont you? Jenny: go in and fetch a pen and ink. (*Jenny runs to the shelter door*).

UNDERSHAFT. Do not disturb Miss Hill: I have a fountain pen (*Jenny halts. He sits at the table writes the cheque. Cusins rises to make room for him. They all watch him silently*).

1440 BILL (*cynically, aside to Barbara, his voice and accent horribly debased*). Wot prawce selvytion nah?

BARBARA. Stop. (*Undershaft stops writing: they all turn to her in surprise*). Mrs Baines: are you really going to take this money?

MRS BAINES (*astonished*). Why not, dear?

BARBARA. Why not! Do you know what my father is? Have you forgotten that Lord Saxmundham is Bodger the whisky man? Do you 1450 remembered how we implored the County Council to stop him from writing Bodger's Whisky in letters of fire against the sky; so that the poor drink-ruined creatures on the Embankment could not wake up from their snatches of sleep without being reminded of their deadly thirst by that wicked sky sign? Do you know that the worst thing I have had to fight here is not the devil, but Bodger, Bodger, Bodger, with his whisky, his distilleries, and his tied houses? Are 1460 you going to make our shelter another tied house for him, and ask me to keep it?

BILL. Rotten dranken whisky it is too.

MRS BAINES. Dear Barbara: Lord Saxmundham has a soul to be saved like any of us. If heaven has found the way to make a good use of his money, are we to set ourselves up against the answer to our prayers?

BARBARA. I know he has a soul to be saved. Let him come down here; and I'll do my best 1470 to help him to his salvation. But he wants to send his cheque down to buy us, and go on being as wicked as ever.

UNDERSHAFT (*with a reasonableness which Cusins alone perceives to be ironical*). My dear Barbara: alcohol is a very necessary article. It heals the sick—

BARBARA. It does nothing of the sort.

UNDERSHAFT. Well, it assists the doctor: that is perhaps a less questionable way of putting it. It makes life bearable to millions of people who 1480 could not endure their existence if they were quite sober. It enables Parliament to do things at eleven at night that no sane person would do eleven in the morning. Is it Bodger's fault that this inestimable gift is deplorably abused by less than one per cent of the poor? (*He turns again to the table; signs the cheque; and crosses it*).

MRS BAINES. Barbara: will there be less drinking or more if all those poor souls we are saving come tomorrow and find the doors of our 1490 shelters shut in their faces? Lord Saxmundham gives us the money to stop drinking—to take his own business from him.

CUSINS (*impishly*). Pure self-sacrifice on Bodger's part, clearly! Bless dear Bodger! (*Barbara almost breaks down as Adolphus, too, fails her*).

UNDERSHAFT (*tearing out the cheque and pocketing the book as he rises and goes past Cusins to Mrs Baines*). I also, Mrs Baines, may 1500 claim a little disinterestedness. Think of my business! think of the widows and orphans! the men and lads torn to pieces with shrapnel and poisoned with lyddite! (*Mrs Baines shrinks; but he goes on remorselessly*) the oceans of blood, not one drop of which is shed in a really just cause! the ravaged crops! the peaceful peasants forced, women and men, to till their fields under the fire of opposing armies on pain of starvation! the bad blood of the fierce little cowards 1510 at home who egg on others to fight for the gratification of their national vanity! All this makes money for me: I am never richer, never busier than when the papers are full of it. Well, it is your work to preach peace on earth and good will to men. (*Mrs Baines's face lights up again*). Every convert you make is a vote against war. (*Her lips move in prayer*). Yet I give you this money to help you to hasten my own commercial ruin. (*He gives her the cheque*). 1520

CUSINS (*mounting the form in an ecstasy of mischief*). The millennium will be inaugurated by the unselfishness of Undershaft and Bodger. Oh be joyful! (*He takes the drum-sticks from his pocket and flourishes them*).

MRS BAINES (*taking the cheque*). The longer I live the more proof I see that there is an Infinite Goodness that turns everything to the work of salvation sooner or later. Who would have thought that any good could have come out of war and drink? And yet their profits are brought today to the feet of salvation to do its blessed work. (*She is affected to tears*).

JENNY (*running to Mrs Baines and throwing her arms round her*). Oh dear! how blessed, how glorious it all is!

CUSINS (*in a convulsion of irony*). Let us seize this unspeakable moment. Let us march to the great meeting at once. Excuse me just an instant. (*He rushes into the shelter. Jenny takes her tambourine from the drum head*).

MRS BAINES. Mr Undershaft: have you ever seen a thousand people fall on their knees with one impulse and pray? Come with us to the meeting. Barbara shall tell them that the Army is saved, and saved through you.

CUSINS (*returning impetuously from the shelter with a flag and a trombone, and coming between Mrs Baines and Undershaft*). You shall carry the flag down the first street. Mrs Baines (*he gives her the flag*). Mr Undershaft is a gifted trombonist: he shall intone an Olympian diapason to the West Ham Salvation March. (*Aside to Undershaft, as he forces the trombone on him*) Blow, Machiavelli, blow.

UNDERSHAFT (*aside to him, as he takes the trombone*). The trumpet in Zion! (*Cusins rushes to the drum, which he takes up and puts on. Undershaft continues, aloud*) I will do my best. I could vamp a bass if I knew the tune.

CUSINS. It is a wedding chorus from one of Donizetti's operas; but we have converted it. We convert everything to good here, including Bodger. You remember the chorus. 'For thee immense rejoicing—immenso giubilo—immenso giubilo.' (*With drum obbligato*) Rum tum ti tum tum, tum tum ti ta—

BARBARA. Dolly: you are breaking my heart.

CUSINS. What is a broken heart more or less here? Dionysos Undershaft has descended. I am possessed.

MRS BAINES. Come, Barbara: I must have my dear Major to carry the flag with me.

JENNY. Yes, yes, Major darling.

CUSINS (*snatches the tambourine out of Jenny's hand and mutely offers it to Barbara*).

BARBARA (*coming forward a little as she puts the offer behind her with a shudder, whilst Cusins recklessly tosses the tambourine back to Jenny and goes to the gate*). I cant come.

JENNY. Not come!

MRS BAINES (*with tears in her eyes*). Barbara: do you think I am wrong to take the money?

BARBARA (*impulsively going to her and kissing her*). No, no: God help you, dear, you must: you are saving the Army. Go; and may you have a great meeting!

JENNY. But arnt you coming?

BARBARA. No. (*She begins taking off the silver S brooch from her collar*).

MRS BAINES. Barbara: what are you doing?

JENNY. Why are you taking your badge off? You cant be going to leave us, Major.

BARBARA (*quietly*). Father: come here.

UNDERSHAFT (*coming to her*). My dear! (*Seeing that she is going to pin the badge on his collar, he retreats to the penthouse in some alarm*).

BARBARA (*following him*). Dont be frightened. (*She pins the badge on and steps back towards the table, shewing him to the others*) There! It's not much for £5000, is it?

MRS BAINES. Barbara: if you wont come and pray with us, promise me you will pray for us.

BARBARA. I cant pray now. Perhaps I shall never pray again.

MRS BAINES. Barbara!

JENNY. Major!

BARBARA (*almost delirious*). I cant bear any more. Quick march!

CUSINS (*calling to the procession in the street outside*). Off we go. Play up, there! Immenso giubilo. (*He gives the time with his drum; and the band strikes up the march, which rapidly becomes more distant as the procession moves briskly away*).

MRS BAINES. I must go, dear. Youre overworked: you will be all right tomorrow. We'll never lose you. Now Jenny: step out with the old flag. Blood and Fire! (*She marches out through the gate with her flag*).

JENNY. Glory Hallelujah! (*flourishing her tambourine and marching*).

UNDERSHAFT (*to Cusins, as he marches out past him easing the slide of his trombone*). 'My ducats and my daughter'!

CUSINS (*following him out*). Money and gunpowder!

BARBARA. Drunkenness and Murder! My God: why hast thou forsaken me?

She sinks on the form with her face buried in her hands. The march passes away into silence. Bill Walker steals across to her.

BILL (*taunting*). Wot prawce selvytion nah?

SHIRLEY. Dont you hit her when she's down.

BILL. She itt me wen aw wiz dahn. Waw shouldnt Aw git a bit o me aown beck?

BARBARA (*raising her head*). I didnt take y o u r money, Bill. (*She crosses the yard to the gate and turns her back on the two men to hide her face from them*).

BILL (*sneering after her*). Naow, it warnt enaff for you. (*Turning to the drum, he misses the money*) Ellow! If you aint took it sammun else ez. Weres it gorn? Bly me if Jenny Ill didnt tike it arter all!

RUMMY (*screaming at him from the loft*). You lie, you dirty blackguard! Snobby Price pinched it off the drum when he took up his cap. I was up here all the time an see im do it.

BILL. Wot! Stowl maw manney! Waw didnt you call thief on him, you silly aold macker you?

RUMMY. To serve you aht for ittin me acrost the fice. It's cost y'pahnd, that az. (*Raising a pæan of squalid triumph*) I done you. I'm even with you. Uve ad it aht o y—(*Bill snatches up Shirley's mug and hurls it at her. She slams the loft door and vanishes. The mug smashes against the door and falls in fragments*).

BILL (*beginning to chuckle*). Tell us, aol menn, wot o'clock this mawnin was it wen im as they call Snobby Prawce was sived?

BARBARA (*turning to him more composedly, and with unspoiled sweetness*). About half past twelve, Bill. And he pinched your pound at a quarter to two. *I* know. Well, you cant afford to lose it. I'll send it to you.

BILL (*his voice and accent suddenly improving*). Not if Aw wiz to stawve for it. Aw aint to be bought.

SHIRLEY. Aint you? Youd sell yourself to the devil for a pint o beer; only there aint no devil to make the offer.

BILL (*unashamed*). Sao Aw would, mite, and often ev, cheerful. But she cawnt baw me. (*Approaching Barbara*) You wanted maw saoul, did you? Well, you aint got it.

BARBARA. I nearly got it, Bill. But weve sold it back to you for ten thousand pounds.

SHIRLEY. And dear at the money!

BARBARA. No, Peter: it was worth more than money.

BILL (*salvationproof*). It's nao good: you cawnt get rahnd me nah. Aw downt blieve in it; and Awve seen tody that Aw was rawt. (*Going*) Sao long, aol soupkitchener! Ta, ta, Mijor Earl's Grendorter! (*Turning at the gate*) Wot prawce selvytion nah? Snobby Prawce! Ha! ha!

BARBARA (*offering her hand*). Goodbye, Bill.

BILL (*taken aback, half plucks his cap off; then shoves it on again defiantly*). Git aht. (*Barbara drops her hand, discouraged. He has a twinge of remorse*). But thets aw rawt, you knaow. Nathink pasnl. Naow mellice. Sao long, Judy. (*He goes*).

BARBARA. No malice. So long, Bill.

SHIRLEY (*shaking his head*). You make too much of him, miss, in your innocence.

BARBARA (*going to him*). Peter: I'm like you now. Cleaned out, and lost my job.

SHIRLEY. Youve youth an hope. Thats two better than me.

BARBARA. I'll get you a job, Peter. Thats hope for you: the youth will have to be enough for me. (*She counts her money*). I have just enough left for two teas at Lockharts, a Rowton doss for you, and my tram and bus home. (*He frowns and rises with offended pride. She takes his arm*). Dont be proud, Peter: it's sharing between friends. And promise me youll talk to me and not let me cry. (*She draws him towards the gate*).

SHIRLEY. Well, I'm not accustomed to talk to the like of you—

BARBARA (*urgently*). Yes, yes: you must talk to me. Tell me about Tom Paine's books and Bradlaugh's lectures. Come along.

SHIRLEY. Ah, if you would only read Tom Paine in the proper spirit, miss! (*They go out through the gate together*).

ACT THREE

Next day after lunch Lady Britomart is writing in the library in Wilton Crescent. Sarah is reading in the armchair near the window. Barbara, in ordinary fashionable dress, pale and brooding, is on the settee. Charles Lomax enters. He starts on seeing Barbara fashionably attired and in low spirits.

LOMAX. Youve left off your uniform!

Barbara says nothing; but an expression of pain passes over her face.

LADY BRITOMART (*warning him in low tones to be careful*). Charles!

LOMAX (*much concerned, coming behind the settee and bending sympathetically over Barbara*). I'm awfully sorry, Barbara. You know I helped you all I could with the concertina and so forth. (*Momentously*) Still, I have never shut my eyes to the fact that there is a certain amount of tosh about the Salvation Army. Now the claims of the Church of England—

LADY BRITOMART. Thats enough, Charles. Speak of something suited to your mental capacity.

LOMAX. But surely the Church of England is suited to all our capacities.

BARBARA (*pressing his hand*). Thank you for your sympathy, Cholly. Now go and spoon with Sarah.

LOMAX (*dragging a chair from the writing table and seating himself affectionately by Sarah's side*). How is my ownest today?

SARAH. I wish you wouldnt tell Cholly to do things, Barbara. He always comes straight and does them. Cholly: we're going to the works this afternoon.

LOMAX. What works?

SARAH. The cannon works.

LOMAX. What? your governor's shop!

SARAH. Yes.

LOMAX. Oh I say!

Cusins enters in poor condition. He also starts visibly when he sees Barbara without her uniform.

BARBARA. I expected you this morning, Dolly. Didnt you guess that?

CUSINS (*sitting down beside her*). I'm sorry. I have only just breakfasted.

SARAH. But weve just finished lunch.

BARBARA. Have you had one of your bad nights?

CUSINS. No: I had rather a good night: in fact, one of the most remarkable nights I have ever passed.

BARBARA. The meeting?

CUSINS. No: after the meeting.

LADY BRITOMART. You should have gone to bed after the meeting. What were you doing?

CUSINS. Drinking.

LADY BRITOMART. Adolphus!
SARAH. Dolly!
BARBARA. Dolly!
LOMAX. Oh I say!

LADY BRITOMART. What were you drinking, may I ask?

CUSINS. A most devilish kind of Spanish burgundy, warranted free from added alcohol: a Temperance burgundy in fact. Its richness in natural alcohol made any addition superfluous.

BARBARA. Are you joking, Dolly?

CUSINS (*patiently*). No. I have been making a night of it with the nominal head of this household: that is all.

LADY BRITOMART. Andrew made you drunk!

CUSINS. No: he only provided the wine. I

think it was Dionysos who made me drunk. (*To Barbara*) I told you I was possessed.

70 LADY BRITOMART. Youre not sober yet. Go home to bed at once.

CUSINS. I have never before ventured to reproach you, Lady Brit; but how could you marry the Prince of Darkness?

LADY BRITOMART. It was much more excusable to marry him than to get drunk with him. That is a new accomplishment of Andrew's, by the way. He usent to drink.

CUSINS. He doesnt now. He only sat there 80 and completed the wreck of my moral basis, the rout of my convictions, the purchase of my soul. He cares for you, Barbara. That is what makes him so dangerous to me.

BARBARA. That has nothing to do with it, Dolly. There are larger loves and diviner dreams than the fireside onces. You know that, dont you?

CUSINS. Yes: that is our understanding. I know it. I hold to it. Unless he can win me on 90 that holier ground he may amuse me for a while; but he can get no deeper hold, strong as he is.

BARBARA. Keep to that; and the end will be right. Now tell me what happened at the meeting?

CUSINS. It was an amazing meeting. Mrs Baines almost died of emotion. Jenny Hill simply gibbered with hysteria. The Prince of Darkness played his trombone like a madman: its 100 brazen roarings were like the laughter of the damned. 117 conversions took place then and there. They prayed with the most touching sincerity and gratitude for Bodger, and for the anonymous donor of the £5000. Your father would not let his name be given.

LOMAX. That was rather fine of the old man, you know. Most chaps would have wanted the advertisement.

CUSINS. He said all the charitable institutions 110 would be down on him like kites on a battlefield if he gave his name.

LADY BRITOMART. Thats Andrew all over. He never does a proper thing without giving an improper reason for it.

CUSINS. He convinced me that I have all my life been doing improper things for proper reasons.

LADY BRITOMART. Adolphus: now that Barbara has left the Salvation Army, you had better leave it too. I will not have you playing 120 that drum in the streets.

CUSINS. Your orders are already obeyed, Lady Brit.

BARBARA. Dolly: were you ever really in earnest about it? Would you have joined if you had never seen me?

CUSINS (*disingenuously*). Well—er—well, possibly, as a collector of religions—

LOMAX (*cunningly*). Not as a drummer, though, you know. You are a very clearheaded 130 brainy chap, Dolly; and it must have been apparent to you that there is a certain amount of tosh about—

LADY BRITOMART. Charles: if you must drivel, drivel like a grown-up man and not like a schoolboy.

LOMAX (*out of countenance*). Well, drivel is drivel, dont you know, whatever a man's age.

LADY BRITOMART. In good society in England, Charles, men drivel at all ages by repeating silly 140 formulas with an air of wisdom. Schoolboys make their own formulas out of slang, like you. When they reach your age, and get political private secretaryships and things of that sort, they drop slang and get their formulas out of the Spectator or The Times. You had better confine yourself to The Times. You will find that there is a certain amount of tosh about The Times; but at least its language is reputable.

LOMAX (*overwhelmed*). You are so awfully 150 strong-minded, Lady Brit—

LADY BRITOMART. Rubbish! (*Morrison comes in*). What is it?

MORRISON. If you please, my lady, Mr Undershaft has just drove up to the door.

LADY BRITOMART. Well, let him in. (*Morrison hesitates*). Whats the matter with you?

MORRISON. Shall I announce him, my lady; or is he at home here, so to speak, my lady?

LADY BRITOMART. Announce him. 160

MORRISON. Thank you, my lady. You wont mind my asking, I hope. The occasion is in a manner of speaking new to me.

LADY BRITOMART. Quite right. Go and let him in.

MORRISON. Thank you, my lady. (*He withdraws*).

LADY BRITOMART. Children: go and get ready. (*Sarah and Barbara go upstairs for their out-of-*

door wraps). Charles: go and tell Stephen to come down here in five minutes: you will find him in the drawing room. (*Charles goes*). Adolphus: tell them to send round the carriage in about fifteen minutes. (*Adolphus goes*).

MORRISON (*at the door*). Mr Undershaft.

Undershaft comes in. Morrison goes out.

UNDERSHAFT. Alone! How fortunate!

LADY BRITOMART (*rising*). Dont be sentimental, Andrew. Sit down. (*She sits on the settee: he sits beside her, on her left. She comes to the point before he has time to breathe*). Sarah must have £800 a year until Charles Lomax comes into his property. Barbara will need more, and need it permanently, because Adolphus hasnt any property.

UNDERSHAFT (*resignedly*). Yes, my dear: I will see to it. Anything else? for yourself, for instance?

LADY BRITOMART. I want to talk to you about Stephen.

UNDERSHAFT (*rather wearily*). Dont, my dear. Stephen doesnt interest me.

LADY BRITOMART. He does interest me. He is our son.

UNDERSHAFT. Do you really think so? He has induced us to bring him into the world; but he chose his parents very incongruously, I think. I see nothing of myself in him, and less of you.

LADY BRITOMART. Andrew: Stephen is an excellent son, and a most steady, capable, high-minded young man. You are simply trying to find an excuse for disinheriting him.

UNDERSHAFT. My dear Biddy: the Undershaft tradition disinherits him. It would be dishonest of me to leave the cannon foundry to my son.

LADY BRITOMART. It would be most unnatural and improper of you to leave it to anyone else, Andrew. Do you suppose this wicked and immoral tradition can be kept up for ever? Do you pretend that Stephen could not carry on the foundry just as well as all the other sons of the big business houses?

UNDERSHAFT. Yes: he could learn the office routine without understanding the business, like all the other sons; and the firm would go on by its own momentum until the real Undershaft—probably an Italian or a German—would invent a new method and cut him out.

LADY BRITOMART. There is nothing that any Italian or German could do that Stephen could not do. And Stephen at least has breeding.

UNDERSHAFT. The son of a foundling! Nonsense!

LADY BRITOMART. My son, Andrew! And even you may have good blood in your veins for all you know.

UNDERSHAFT. True. Probably I have. That is another argument in favour of a foundling.

LADY BRITOMART. Andrew: dont be aggravating. And dont be wicked. At present you are both.

UNDERSHAFT. This conversation is part of the Undershaft tradition, Biddy. Every Undershaft's wife has treated him to it ever since the house was founded. It is mere waste of breath. If the tradition be ever broken it will be for an abler man than Stephen.

LADY BRITOMART (*pouting*). Then go away.

UNDERSHAFT (*deprecatory*). Go away!

LADY BRITOMART. Yes: go away. If you will do nothing for Stephen, you are not wanted here. Go to your foundling, whoever he is; and look after h i m.

UNDERSHAFT. The fact is, Biddy—

LADY BRITOMART. Dont call me Biddy. I dont call you Andy.

UNDERSHAFT. I will not call my wife Britomart: it is not good sense. Seriously, my love, the Undershaft tradition has landed me in a difficulty. I am getting on in years; and my partner Lazarus has at last made a stand and insisted that the succession must be settled one way or the other; and of course he is quite right. You see, I havent found a fit successor yet.

LADY BRITOMART (*obstinately*). There is Stephen.

UNDERSHAFT. Thats just it: all the foundlings I can find are exactly like Stephen.

LADY BRITOMART. Andrew!!

UNDERSHAFT. I want a man with no relations and no schooling: that is, a man who would be out of the running altogether if he were not a strong man. And I cant find him. Every blessed foundling nowadays is snapped up in his infancy by Barnardo homes, or School Board officers, or Boards of Guardians; and if he shews the least ability he is fastened on by schoolmasters; trained to win scholarships like a racehorse; crammed with secondhand ideas; drilled and disciplined in docility and what they call good taste; and lamed for life so that he is fit for nothing but teaching. If you want to keep the foundry in the family, you had better find an eligible foundling and marry him to Barbara.

LADY BRITOMART. Ah! Barbara! Your pet! You would sacrifice Stephen to Barbara.

280 UNDERSHAFT. Cheerfully. And you, my dear, would boil Barbara to make soup for Stephen.

LADY BRITOMART. Andrew: this is not a question of our likings and dislikings: it is a question of duty. It is your duty to make Stephen your successor.

UNDERSHAFT. Just as much as it is your duty to submit to your husband. Come, Biddy! these tricks of the governing class are of no use with me. I am one of the governing class myself; and

290 it is waste of time giving tracts to a missionary. I have the power in this matter; and I am not to be humbugged into using it for your purposes.

LADY BRITOMART. Andrew: you can talk my head off; but you cant change wrong into right. And your tie is all on one side. Put it straight.

UNDERSHAFT (*disconcerted*). It wont stay unless it's pinned (*he fumbles at it with childish grimaces*)—

300 *Stephen comes in.*

STEPHEN (*at the door*). I beg your pardon (*about to retire*).

LADY BRITOMART. No: come in, Stephen. (*Stephen comes forward to his mother's writing table*).

UNDERSHAFT (*not very cordially*). Good afternoon.

STEPHEN (*coldly*). Good afternoon.

UNDERSHAFT (*to Lady Britomart*). He knows

310 all about the tradition, I suppose?

LADY BRITOMART. Yes. (*To Stephen*) It is what I told you last night, Stephen.

UNDERSHAFT (*sulkily*). I understand you want to come into the cannon business.

STEPHEN. *I* go into trade! Certainly not.

UNDERSHAFT (*opening his eyes, greatly eased in mind and manner*). Oh! in that case—

LADY BRITOMART. Cannons are not trade, Stephen. They are enterprise.

320 STEPHEN. I have no intention of becoming a man of business in any sense. I have no capacity for business and no taste for it. I intend to devote myself to politics.

UNDERSHAFT (*rising*). My dear boy: this is an immense relief to me. And I trust it may prove an equally good thing for the country. I was afraid you would consider yourself disparaged and slighted. (*He moves towards Stephen as if to shake hands with him*).

LADY BRITOMART (*rising and interposing*). 330 Stephen: I cannot allow you to throw away an enormous property like this.

STEPHEN (*stiffly*). Mother: there must be an end of treating me as a child, if you please. (*Lady Britomart recoils, deeply wounded by his tone*). Until last night I did not take your attitude seriously, because I did not think you meant it seriously. But I find now that you left me in the dark as to matters which you should have explained to me years ago. I am extremely 340 hurt and offended. Any further discussion of my intentions had better take place with my father, as between one man and another.

LADY BRITOMART. Stephen! (*She sits down again, her eyes filling with tears*).

UNDERSHAFT (*with grave compassion*). You see, my dear, it is only the big men who can be treated as children.

STEPHEN. I am sorry, mother, that you have forced me— 350

UNDERSHAFT (*stopping him*). Yes, yes, yes, yes: thats all right, Stephen. She wont interfere with you any more: your independence is achieved: you have won your latchkey. Dont rub it in; and above all, dont apologize. (*He resumes his seat*). Now what about your future, as between one man and another—I beg your pardon, Biddy: as between two men and a woman.

LADY BRITOMART (*who has pulled herself together strongly*). I quite understand, Stephen. 360 By all means go your own way if you feel strong enough. (*Stephen sits down magisterially in the chair at the writing table with an air of affirming his majority*).

UNDERSHAFT. It is settled that you do not ask for the succession to the cannon business.

STEPHEN. I hope it is settled that I repudiate the cannon business.

UNDERSHAFT. Come, come! dont be so devilishly sulky: it's boyish. Freedom should be gen- 370 erous. Besides, I owe you a fair start in life in exchange for disinheriting you. You cant become prime minister all at once. Havnt you a turn for something? What about literature, art, and so forth?

STEPHEN. I have nothing of the artist about me, either in faculty or character, thank Heaven!

UNDERSHAFT. A philosopher, perhaps? Eh?

380 STEPHEN. I make no such ridiculous pretension.

UNDERSHAFT. Just so. Well, there is the army, the navy, the Church, the Bar. The Bar requires some ability. What about the Bar?

STEPHEN. I have not studied law. And I am afraid I have not the necessary push—I believe that is the name barristers give to their vulgarity—for success in pleading.

UNDERSHAFT. Rather a difficult case, Stephen.

390 Hardly anything left but the stage, is there? (*Stephen makes an impatient movement*). Well, come! is there a n y t h i n g you know or care for?

STEPHEN (*rising and looking at him steadily*). I know the difference between right and wrong.

UNDERSHAFT (*hugely tickled*). You dont say so! What! no capacity for business, no knowledge of law, no sympathy with art, no pretension to philosophy; only a simple knowledge of

400 the secret that has puzzled all the philosophers, baffled all the lawyers, muddled all the men of business, and ruined most of the artists: the secret of right and wrong. Why, man, youre a genius, a master of masters, a god! At twenty-four, too!

STEPHEN (*keeping his temper with difficulty*). You are pleased to be facetious. I pretend to be nothing more than any honorable English gentleman claims as his birthright (*he sits down*

410 *angrily*).

UNDERSHAFT. Oh, thats everybody's birthright. Look at poor little Jenny Hill, the Salvation lassie! she would think you were laughing at her if you asked her to stand up in the street and teach grammar or geography or mathematics or even drawing room dancing; but it never occurs to her to doubt that she can teach morals and religion. You are all alike, you respectable people. You cant tell me the bursting strain of

420 a ten-inch gun, which is a very simple matter; but you all think you can tell me the bursting strain of a man under temptation. You darent handle high explosives; but youre all ready to handle honesty and truth and justice and the whole duty of man, and kill one another at that game. What a country! What a world!

LADY BRITOMART (*uneasily*). What do you think he had better do, Andrew?

UNDERSHAFT. Oh, just what he wants to do. He knows nothing and he thinks he knows 430 everything. That points clearly to a political career. Get him a private secretaryship to someone who can get him an Under Secretaryship; and then leave him alone. He will find his natural and proper place in the end on the Treasury Bench.

STEPHEN (*springing up again*). I am sorry, sir, that you force me to forget the respect due to you as my father. I am an Englishman and I will not hear the Government of my country 440 insulted. (*He thrusts his hands in his pockets, and walks angrily across to the window*).

UNDERSHAFT (*with a touch of brutality*). The government of your country! *I* am the government of your country: I, and Lazarus. Do you suppose that you and half a dozen amateurs like you, sitting in a row in that foolish gabble shop, can govern Undershaft and Lazarus? No, my friend: you will do what pays u s. You will make war when it suits us, and keep peace 450 when it doesnt. You will find out that trade requires certain measures when we have decided on those measures. When I want anything to keep my dividends up, you will discover that my want is a national need. When other people want something to keep my dividends down, you will call out the police and military. And in return you shall have the support and applause of my newspapers, and the delight of imagining that you are a great statesman. Gov- 460 ernment of your country! Be off with you, my boy, and play with your caucuses and leading articles and historic parties and great leaders and burning questions and the rest of your toys. *I* am going back to my counting-house to pay the piper and call the tune.

STEPHEN (*actually smiling, and putting his hand on his father's shoulder with indulgent patronage*). Really, my dear father, it is impossible to be angry with you. You dont know 470 how absurd all this sounds to m e. You are very properly proud of having been industrious enough to make money; and it is greatly to your credit that you have made so much of it. But it has kept you in circles where you are valued for your money and deferred to for it, instead of in the doubtless very old-fashioned and behind-the-times public school and university where I formed my habits of mind. It is natural for you to think that money governs England; but you must allow me to think I know better.

UNDERSHAFT. And what d o e s govern England, pray?

STEPHEN. Character, father, character.

UNDERSHAFT. Whose character? Yours or mine?

STEPHEN. Neither yours nor mine, father, but the best elements in the English national character.

UNDERSHAFT. Stephen: Ive found your profession for you. Youre a born journalist. I'll start you with a high-toned weekly review. There!

Before Stephen can reply Sarah, Barbara, Lomax, and Cusins come in ready for walking. Barbara crosses the room to the window and looks out. Cusins drifts amiably to the armchair. Lomax remains near the door, whilst Sarah comes to her mother.
Stephen goes to the smaller writing table and busies himself with his letters.

SARAH. Go and get ready, mamma: the carriage is waiting. (*Lady Britomart leaves the room*).

UNDERSHAFT (*to Sarah*). Good day, my dear. Good afternoon, Mr Lomax.

LOMAX (*vaguely*). Ahdedoo.

UNDERSHAFT (*to Cusins*). Quite well after last night, Euripides, eh?

CUSINS. As well as can be expected.

UNDERSHAFT. Thats right. (*To Barbara*) So you are coming to see my death and devastation factory, Barbara?

BARBARA (*at the window*). You came yesterday to see my salvation factory. I promised you a return visit.

LOMAX (*coming forward between Sarah and Undershaft*). Youll find it awfully interesting. Ive been through the Woolwich Arsenal; and it gives you a ripping feeling of security, you know, to think of the lot of beggars we could kill if it came to fighting. (*To Undershaft, with sudden solemnity*) Still, it must be rather an awful reflection for you, from the religious point of view as it were. Youre getting on, you know, and all that.

SARAH. You dont mind Cholly's imbecility, papa, do you?

LOMAX (*much taken aback*). Oh I say!

UNDERSHAFT. Mr Lomax looks at the matter in a very proper spirit, my dear.

LOMAX. Just so. Thats all I meant, I assure you.

SARAH. Are you coming, Stephen?

STEPHEN. Well, I am rather busy—er—(*Magnanimously*) Oh well, yes: I'll come. That is, if there is room for me.

UNDERSHAFT. I can take two with me in a little motor I am experimenting with for field use. You wont mind its being rather unfashionable. It's not painted yet; but it's bullet proof.

LOMAX (*appalled at the prospect of confronting Wilton Crescent in an unpainted motor*). Oh I s a y!

SARAH. The carriage for me, thank you. Barbara doesnt mind what she's seen in.

LOMAX. I say, Dolly, old chap: do you really mind the car being a guy? Because of course if you do I'll go in it. Still—

CUSINS. I prefer it.

LOMAX. Thanks awfully, old man. Come, my ownest. (*He hurries out to secure his seat in the carriage. Sarah follows him*).

CUSINS (*moodily walking across to Lady Britomart's writing table*). Why are we two coming to this Works Department of Hell? that is what I ask myself.

BARBARA. I have always thought of it as a sort of pit where lost creatures with blackened faces stirred up smoky fires and were driven and tormented by my father? Is it like that, dad?

UNDERSHAFT (*scandalized*). My dear! It is a spotlessly clean and beautiful hillside town.

CUSINS. With a Methodist chapel? Oh d o say theres a Methodist chapel.

UNDERSHAFT. There are two: a Primitive one and a sophisticated one. There is even an Ethical Society; but it is not much patronized, as my men are all strongly religious. In the High Explosives Sheds they object to the presence of Agnostics as unsafe.

CUSINS. And yet they dont object to you!

BARBARA. Do they obey all your orders?

UNDERSHAFT. I never give them any orders. When I speak to one of them it is 'Well, Jones, is the baby doing well? and has Mrs Jones made a good recovery?' 'Nicely, thank you, sir.' And thats all.

CUSINS. But Jones has to be kept in order. How do you maintain discipline among your men?

UNDERSHAFT. I dont. They do. You see, the one thing Jones wont stand is any rebellion from the man under him, or any assertion of social equality between the wife of the man with 4 shillings a week less than himself, and Mrs Jones! Of course they all rebel against me, theoretically. Practically, every man of them keeps the man just below him in his place. I never meddle with them. I never bully them. I dont even bully Lazarus. I say that certain things are to be done; but I dont order anybody to do them. I dont say, mind you, that there is no ordering about and snubbing and even bullying. The men snub the boys and order them about; the carmen snub the sweepers; the artisans snub the unskilled laborers; the foremen drive and bully both the laborers and artisans; the assistant engineers find fault with the foremen; the chief engineers drop on the assistants; the departmental managers worry the chiefs; and the clerks have tall hats and hymnbooks and keep up the social tone by refusing to associate on equal terms with anybody. The result is a colossal profit, which comes to me.

CUSINS (*revolted*). You really are a—well, what I was saying yesterday.

BARBARA. What was he saying yesterday?

UNDERSHAFT. Never mind, my dear. He thinks I have made you unhappy. Have I?

BARBARA. Do you think I can be happy in this vulgar silly dress? I! who have worn the uniform. Do you understand what you have done to me? Yesterday I had a man's soul in my hand. I set him in the way of life with his face to salvation. But when we took your money he turned back to drunkenness and derision. (*With intense conviction*) I will never forgive you that. If I had a child, and you destroyed its body with your explosives—if you murdered Dolly with your horrible guns—I could forgive you if my forgiveness would open the gates of heaven to you. But to take a human soul from me, and turn it into the soul of a wolf! that is worse than any murder.

UNDERSHAFT. Does my daughter despair so easily? Can you strike a man to the heart and leave no mark on him?

BARBARA (*her face lighting up*). Oh, you are right: he can never be lost now: where was my faith?

CUSINS. Oh, clever clever devil!

BARBARA. You may be a devil; but God speaks through you sometimes. (*She takes her father's hands and kisses them*). You have given me back my happiness: I feel it deep down now, though my spirit is troubled.

UNDERSHAFT. You have learnt something. That always feels at first as if you had lost something.

BARBARA. Well, take me to the factory of death; and let me learn something more. There must be some truth or other behind all this frightful irony. Come, Dolly. (*She goes out*).

CUSINS. My guardian angel! (*To Undershaft*) Avaunt! (*He follows Barbara*).

STEPHEN (*quietly, at the writing table*). You must not mind Cusins, father. He is a very amiable good fellow; but he is a Greek scholar and naturally a little eccentric.

UNDERSHAFT. Ah, quite so, Thank you, Stephen. Thank you. (*He goes out*).

Stephen smiles patronizingly; buttons his coat responsibly; and crosses the room to the door. Lady Britomart, dressed for out-of-doors, opens it before he reaches it. She looks round for others; looks at Stephen; and turns to go without a word.

STEPHEN (*embarrassed*). Mother—

LADY BRITOMART. Dont be apologetic, Stephen. And dont forget that you have outgrown your mother. (*She goes out*).

Perivale St Andrews lies between two Middlesex hills, half climbing the northern one. It is an almost smokeless town of white walls, roofs of narrow green slates or red tiles, tall trees, domes, campaniles, and slender chimney shafts, beautifully situated and beautiful in itself. The best view of it is obtained from the crest of a slope about half a mile to the east, where the high explosives are dealt with. The foundry lies hidden in the depths between, the tops of its chimneys sprouting like huge skittles into the middle distance. Across the crest runs an emplacement of concrete, with a firestep, and a parapet which suggests a fortification, because there is a huge cannon of the obsolete Woolwich Infant pattern peering across it at the town. The cannon is mounted on an experimental gun carriage: possibly the original model of the Undershaft disappearing rampart gun alluded to by Stephen. The firestep, being a convenient place to sit, is furnished here and there with straw disc cushions; and at one place there is the additional luxury of a fur rug.

Barbara is standing on the firestep, looking over the parapet towards the town. On her right is the cannon; on her left the end of a shed raised on piles, with a ladder of three or four steps up to the door, which opens outwards and has a little wooden landing at the threshold, with a fire bucket in the corner of the landing. Several dummy soldiers more or less mutilated, with straw protruding from their gashes, have been shoved out of the way under the landing. A few others are nearly upright against the shed; and one has fallen forward and lies, like a grotesque corpse, on the emplacement. The parapet stops short of the shed, leaving a gap which is the beginning of the path down the hill through the foundry to the town. The rug is on the firestep near this gap. Down on the emplacement behind the cannon is a trolley carrying a huge conical bombshell with a red band painted on it. Further to the right is the door of an office, which, like the sheds, is of the lightest possible construction.

Cusins arrives by the path from the town.

BARBARA. Well?

CUSINS. Not a ray of hope. Everything perfect! wonderful! real! It only needs a cathedral to be a heavenly city instead of a hellish one.

670

BARBARA. Have you found out whether they have done anything for old Peter Shirley?

CUSINS. They have found him a job as gatekeeper and timekeeper. He's frightfully miserable. He calls the time-keeping brainwork, and says he isnt used to it; and his gate lodge is so splendid that he's ashamed to use the rooms, and skulks in the scullery.

BARBARA. Poor Peter!

Stephen arrives from town. He carries a fieldglass.

680

STEPHEN (*enthusiastically*). Have you two seen the place? Why did you leave us?

CUSINS. I wanted to see everything I was not intended to see; and Barbara wanted to make the men talk.

STEPHEN. Have you found anything discreditable?

CUSINS. No. They call him Dandy Andy and are proud of his being a cunning old rascal; but it's all horribly, frightfully, immorally, unanswerably perfect.

690

Sarah arrives.

SARAH. Heavens! what a place! (*She crosses to the trolley*). Did you see the nursing home!? (*She sits down on the shell*).

STEPHEN. Did you see the libraries and schools!?

SARAH. Did you see the ball room and the banqueting chamber in the Town Hall!?

STEPHEN. Have you gone into the insurance fund, the pension fund, the building society, the various applications of cooperation!?

700

Undershaft comes from the office, with a sheaf of telegrams in his hand.

UNDERSHAFT. Well, have you seen everything? I'm sorry I was called away. (*Indicating the telegrams*) Good news from Manchuria.

STEPHEN. Another Japanese victory?

UNDERSHAFT. Oh, I dont know. Which side wins does not concern us here. No: the good news is that the aerial battleship is a tremendous success. At the first trial it has wiped out a fort with three hundred soldiers in it.

710

CUSINS (*from the platform*). Dummy soldiers?

UNDERSHAFT (*striding across to Stephen and kicking the prostrate dummy brutally out of his way*). No: the real thing.

Cusins and Barbara exchange glances. Then Cusins sits on the step and buries his face in his

720 *hands. Barbara gravely lays her hand on his shoulder. He looks up at her in whimsical desperation.*

UNDERSHAFT. Well, Stephen, what do you think of the place?

STEHEN. Oh, magnificent. A perfect triumph of modern industry. Frankly, my dear father, I have been a fool: I had no idea of what it all meant: of the wonderful forethought, the power of organization, the administrative 730 capacity, the financial genius, the colossal capital it represents. I have been repeating to myself as I came through your streets 'Peace hath her victories no less renowned than War.' I have only one misgiving about it all.

UNDERSHAFT. Out with it.

STEPHEN. Well, I cannot help thinking that all this provision for every want of your workmen may sap their independence and weaken their sense of responsibility. And greatly as we 740 enjoyed our tea at that splendid restaurant—how they gave us all that luxury and cake and jam and cream for threepence I really cannot imagine!—still you must remember that restaurants break up home life. Look at the continent, for instance! Are you sure so much pampering is really good for the men's characters?

UNDERSHAFT. Well you see, my dear boy, when you are organizing civilization you have to make up your mind whether trouble and 750 anxiety are good things or not. If you decide that they are, then, I take it, you simply dont organize civilization; and there you are, with trouble and anxiety enough to make us all angels! But if you decide the other way, you may as well go through with it. However, Stephen, our characters are safe here. A sufficient dose of anxiety is always provided by the fact that we may be blown to smithereens at any moment.

760 SARAH. By the way, papa, where do you make the explosives?

UNDERSHAFT. In separate little sheds, like that one. When one of them blows up, it costs very little; and only the people quite close to it are killed.

Stephen, who is quite close to it, looks at it rather scaredly, and moves away quickly to the cannon. At the same moment the door of the shed is thrown abruptly open; and a foreman in overalls and list slippers comes out on the 770 *little landing and holds the door for Lomax, who appears in the doorway.*

LOMAX (*with studied coolness*). My good fellow: you neednt get into a state of nerves. Nothing's going to happen to you; and I suppose it wouldnt be the end of the world if anything did. A little bit of British pluck is what you want, old chap. (*He descends and strolls across to Sarah*).

UNDERSHAFT (*to the foreman*). Anything 780 wrong, Bilton?

BILTON (*with ironic calm*). Gentleman walked into the high explosives shed and lit a cigaret, sir: thats all.

UNDERSHAFT. Ah, quite so. (*Going over to Lomax*) Do you happen to remember what you did with the match?

LOMAX. Oh come! I'm not a fool. I took jolly good care to blow it out before I chucked it away. 790

BILTON. The top of it was red hot inside, sir.

LOMAX. Well, suppose it was! I didn't chuck it into any of your messes.

UNDERSHAFT. Think no more of it, Mr Lomax. By the way, would you mind lending me your matches.

LOMAX (*offering his box*). Certainly.

UNDERSHAFT. Thanks. (*He pockets the matches*).

LOMAX (*lecturing to the company generally*). 800 You know, these high explosives dont go off like gunpowder, except when theyre in a gun. When theyre spread loose, you can put a match to them without the least risk: they just burn quietly like a bit of paper. (*Warming to the scientific interest of the subject*) Did you know that, Undershaft? Have you ever tried?

UNDERSHAFT. Not on a large scale, Mr Lomax. Bilton will give you a sample of gun cotton when you are leaving if you ask him. 810 You can experiment with it at home. (*Bilton looks puzzled*).

SARAH. Bilton will do nothing of the sort, papa. I suppose it's your business to blow up the Russians and Japs; but you might really stop short of blowing up poor Cholly. (*Bilton gives it up and retires into the shed*).

LOMAX. My ownest, there is no danger. (*He sits beside her on the shell*).

820 *Lady Britomart arrives from the town with a bouquet.*

LADY BRITOMART (*impetuously*). Andrew: you shouldnt have let me see this place.

UNDERSHAFT. Why, my dear?

LADY BRITOMART. Never mind why: you shouldnt have: thats all. To think of all that (*indicating the town*) being yours! and that you have kept it to yourself all these years!

UNDERSHAFT. It does not belong to me. I be- 830 long to it. It is the Undershaft inheritance.

LADY BRITOMART. It is not. Your ridiculous cannons and that noisy banging foundry may be the Undershaft inheritance; but all that plate and linen, all that furniture and those houses and orchards and gardens belong to us. They belong to m e: they are not a man's business. I wont give them up. You must be out of your senses to throw them all away; and if you persist in such folly, I will call in a doctor.

840 UNDERSHAFT (*stooping to smell the bouquet*). Where did you get the flowers, my dear?

LADY BRITOMART. Your men presented them to me in your William Morris Labor Church.

CUSINS. Oh! It needed only that. A Labor Church! (*he mounts the firestep distractedly, and leans with his elbows on the parapet, turning his back to them*).

LADY BRITOMART. Yes, with Morris's words in mosaic letters ten feet high round the dome. 850 NO MAN IS GOOD ENOUGH TO BE ANOTHER MAN'S MASTER. The cynicism of it!

UNDERSHAFT. It shocked the men at first, I am afraid. But now they take no more notice of it than of the ten commandments in church.

LADY BRITOMART. Andrew: you are trying to put me off the subject of the inheritance by profane jokes. Well, you shant. I dont ask it any longer for Stephen: he has inherited far too much of your perversity to be fit for it. But 860 Barbara has rights as well as Stephen. Why should not Adolphus succeed to the inheritance? I could manage the town for him; and he can look after the cannons, if they are really necessary.

UNDERSHAFT. I should ask nothing better if Adolphus were a foundling. He is exactly the sort of new blood that is wanted in English business. But he's not a foundling; and theres an end of it. (*He makes for the office door*).

870 CUSINS (*turning to them*). Not quite. (*They all turn and stare at him*). I think—Mind! I am not committing myself in any way as to my future course—but I t h i n k the foundling difficulty can be got over. (*He jumps down to the emplacement*).

UNDERSHAFT (*coming back to him*). What do you mean?

CUSINS. Well, I have something to say which is in the nature of a confession.

SARAH.
LADY BRITOMART.
BARBARA.
STEPHEN. } Confession! 880

LOMAX. Oh I say!

CUSINS. Yes, a confession. Listen, all. Until I met Barbara I thought myself in the main an honorable, truthful man, because I wanted the approval of my conscience more than I wanted anything else. But the moment I saw Barbara, I wanted her far more than the approval of my conscience.

LADY BRITOMART. Adolphus!

890 CUSINS. It is true. You accused me yourself, Lady Brit, of joining the Army to worship Barbara; and so I did. She bought my soul like a flower at a street corner; but she bought it for herself.

UNDERSHAFT. What! Not for Dionysos or another?

CUSINS. Dionysos and all the others are in herself. I adored what was divine in her, and was therefore a true worshipper. But I was ro- 900 mantic about her too. I thought she was a woman of the people, and that a marriage with a professor of Greek would be far beyond the wildest social ambitions of her rank.

LADY BRITOMART. Adolphus!!

LOMAX. Oh I s a y!!!

CUSINS. When I learnt the horrible truth—

LADY BRITOMART. What do you mean by the horrible truth, pray?

CUSINS. That she was enormously rich; that 910 her grandfather was an earl; that her father was the Prince of Darkness—

UNDERSHAFT. Chut!

CUSINS. —and that I was only an adventurer trying to catch a rich wife, then I stooped to deceive her about my birth.

BARBARA (*rising*). Dolly!

LADY BRITOMART. Your birth! Now Adolphus,

dont dare to make up a wicked story for the sake of these wretched cannons. Remember: I have seen photographs of your parents; and the Agent General for South Western Australia knows them personally and has assured me that they are most respectable married people.

CUSINS. So they are in Australia; but here they are outcasts. Their marriage is legal in Australia, but not in England. My mother is my father's deceased wife's sister; and in this island I am consequently a foundling. (*Sensation*).

BARBARA. Silly! (*She climbs to the cannon, and leans, listening, in the angle it makes with the parapet*).

CUSINS. Is the subterfuge good enough, Machiavelli?

UNDERSHAFT (*thoughtfully*). Biddy: this may be a way out of the difficulty.

LADY BRITOMART. Stuff! A man cant make cannons any the better for being his own cousin instead of his proper self (*she sits down on the rug with a bounce that expresses her downright contempt for their casuistry*).

UNDERSHAFT (*to Cusins*). You are an educated man. That is against the tradition.

CUSINS. Once in ten thousand times it happens that the schoolboy is a born master of what they try to teach him. Greek has not destroyed my mind: it has nourished it. Besides, I did not learn it at an English public school.

UNDERSHAFT. Hm! Well, I cannot afford to be too particular: you have cornered the foundling market. Let it pass. You are eligible, Euripides: you are eligible.

BARBARA. Dolly: yesterday morning, when Stephen told us all about the tradition, you became very silent; and you have been strange and excited ever since. Were you thinking of your birth then?

CUSINS. When the finger of Destiny suddenly points at a man in the middle of his breakfast, it makes him thoughtful.

UNDERSHAFT. Aha! You have had your eye on the business, my young friend, have you?

CUSINS. Take care! There is an abyss of moral horror between me and your accursed aerial battleships.

UNDERSHAFT. Never mind the abyss for the present. Let us settle the practical details and leave your final decision open. You know that you will have to change your name. Do you object to that?

CUSINS. Would any man named Adolphus—any man called Dolly!—object to be called something else?

UNDERSHAFT. Good. Now, as to money! I propose to treat you handsomely from the beginning. You shall start at a thousand a year.

CUSINS (*with sudden heat, his spectacles twinkling with mischief*). A thousand! You dare offer a miserable thousand to the son-in-law of a millionaire! No, by Heavens, Machiavelli! you shall not cheat m e. You cannot do without me; and I can do without you. I must have two thousand five hundred a year for two years. At the end of that time, if I am a failure, I go. But if I am a success, and stay on, you must give me the other five thousand.

UNDERSHAFT. What other five thousand?

CUSINS. To make the two years up to five thousand a year. The two thousand five hundred is only half pay in case I should turn out a failure. The third year I must have ten per cent on the profits.

UNDERSHAFT (*taken aback*). Ten per cent! Why, man, do you know what my profits are?

CUSINS. Enormous, I hope: otherwise I shall require twenty-five per cent.

UNDERSHAFT. But, Mr Cusins, this is a serious matter of business. You are not bringing any capital into the concern.

CUSINS. What! no capital! Is my mastery of Greek no capital? Is my access to the subtlest thought, the loftiest poetry yet attained by humanity, no capital? My character! my intellect! my life! my career! what Barbara calls my soul! are these no capital? Say another word; and I double my salary.

UNDERSHAFT. Be reasonable—

CUSINS (*peremptorily*). Mr Undershaft: you have my terms. Take them or leave them.

UNDERSHAFT (*recovering himself*). Very well. I note your terms; and I offer you half.

CUSINS (*disgusted*). Half!

UNDERSHAFT (*firmly*). Half.

CUSINS. You call yourself a gentleman; and you offer me half!!

UNDERSHAFT. I do not call myself a gentleman; but I offer you half.

CUSINS. This to your future partner! your successor! your son-in-law!

BARBARA. You are selling your own soul, Dolly, not mine. Leave me out of the bargain, please.

UNDERSHAFT. Come! I will go a step further for Barbara's sake. I will give you three fifths; but that is my last word.

CUSINS. Done!

LOMAX. Done in the eye! Why, *I* get only eight hundred, you know.

CUSINS. By the way, Mac, I am a classical scholar, not an arithmetical one. Is three fifths more than half or less?

UNDERSHAFT. More, of course.

CUSINS. I would have taken two hundred and fifty. How you can succeed in business when you are willing to pay all that money to a University don who is obviously not worth a junior clerk's wages!—well! What will Lazarus say?

UNDERSHAFT. Lazarus is a gentle romantic Jew who cares for nothing but string quartets and stalls at fashionable theatres. He will be blamed for your rapacity in money matters, poor fellow! as he has hitherto been blamed for mine. You are a shark of the first order, Euripides. So much the better for the firm!

BARBARA. Is the bargain closed, Dolly? Does your soul belong to him now?

CUSINS. No: the price is settled: that is all. The real tug of war is still to come. What about the moral question?

LADY BRITOMART. There is no moral question in the matter at all, Adolphus. You must simply sell cannons and weapons to people whose cause is right and just, and refuse them to foreigners and criminals.

UNDERSHAFT (*determinedly*). No: none of that. You must keep the true faith of an Armorer, or you dont come in here.

CUSINS. What on earth is the true faith of an Armorer?

UNDERSHAFT. To give arms to all men who offer an honest price for them, without respect of persons or principles: to aristocrat and republican, to Nihilist and Tsar, to Capitalist and Socialist, to Protestant and Catholic, to burglar and policeman, to black man, white man and yellow man, to all sorts and conditions, all nationalities, all faiths, all follies, all causes and all crimes. The first Undershaft wrote up in his shop IF GOD GAVE THE HAND, LET NOT MAN WITHHOLD THE SWORD. The second wrote up ALL HAVE THE RIGHT TO FIGHT: NONE HAVE THE RIGHT TO JUDGE. The third wrote up TO MAN THE WEAPON: TO HEAVEN THE VICTORY. The fourth had no literary turn; so he did not write up anything; but he sold cannons to Napoleon under the nose of George the Third. The fifth wrote up PEACE SHALL NOT PREVAIL SAVE WITH A SWORD IN HER HAND. The sixth, my master, was the best of all. He wrote up NOTHING IS EVER DONE IN THIS WORLD UNTIL MEN ARE PREPARED TO KILL ONE ANOTHER IF IT IS NOT DONE. After that, there was nothing left for the seventh to say. So he wrote up, simply, UNASHAMED.

CUSINS. My good Machiavelli, I shall certainly write something up on the wall; only, as I shall write it in Greek, you wont be able to read it. But as to your Armorer's faith, if I take my neck out of the noose of my own morality I am not going to put it into the noose of yours. I shall sell cannons to whom I please and refuse them to whom I please. So there!

UNDERSHAFT. From the moment when you become Andrew Undershaft, you will never do as you please again. Dont come here lusting for power, young man.

CUSINS. If power were my aim I should not come here for it. You have no power.

UNDERSHAFT. None of my own, certainly.

CUSINS. I have more power than you, more will. You do not drive this place: it drives you. And what drives the place?

UNDERSHAFT (*enigmatically*). A will of which I am a part.

BARBARA (*startled*). Father! Do you know what you are saying; or are you laying a snare for my soul?

CUSINS. Dont listen to his metaphysics, Barbara. The place is driven by the most rascally part of society, the money hunters, the pleasure hunters, the military promotion hunters; and he is their slave.

UNDERSHAFT. Not necessarily. Remember the Armorer's Faith. I will take an order from a good man as cheerfully as from a bad one. If you good people prefer preaching and shirking to buying my weapons and fighting the rascals, dont blame me. I can make cannons: I cannot make courage and conviction. Bah! you tire me, Euripides, with your morality mongering. Ask Barbara: she understands. (*He suddenly reaches up and takes Barbara's hands, looking powerfully into her eyes*) Tell him, my love, what power really means.

BARBARA (*hypnotized*). Before I joined the Salvation Army, I was in my own power; and the consequence was that I never knew what to do with myself. When I joined it, I had not time enough for all the things I had to do.

1130 UNDERSHAFT (*approvingly*). Just so. And why was that, do you suppose?

BARBARA. Yesterday I should have said, because I was in the power of God. (*She resumes her self-possession, withdrawing her hands from his with a power equal to his own*). But you came and shewed me that I was in the power of Bodger and Undershaft. Today I feel—oh! how can I put it into words? Sarah: do you remember the earthquake at Cannes, when we

1140 were little children?—how little the surprise of the first shock mattered compared to the dread and horror of waiting for the second? That is how I feel in this place today. I stood on the rock I thought eternal; and without a word of warning it reeled and crumbled under me. I was safe with an infinite wisdom watching me, an army marching to Salvation with me; and in a moment, at a stroke of your pen in a cheque book, I stood alone; and the heavens were emp-

1150 ty. That was the first shock of the earthquake: I am waiting for the second.

UNDERSHAFT. Come, come, my daughter! dont make too much of your little tinpot tragedy. What do we do here when we spend years of work and thought and thousands of pounds of solid cash on a new gun or an aerial battleship that turns out just a hairsbreadth wrong after all? Scrap it. Scrap it without wasting another hour or another pound on it. Well, you

1160 have made for yourself something that you call a morality or a religion or what not. It doesnt fit the facts. Well, scrap it. Scrap it and get one that does fit. That is what is wrong with the world at present. It scraps its obsolete steam engines and dynamos; but it wont scrap its old prejudices and its old moralities and its old religions and its old political constitutions. Whats the result? In machinery it does very well; but in morals and religion and politics it is work-

1170 ing at a loss that brings it nearer bankruptcy every year. Dont persist in that folly. If your old religion broke down yesterday, get a newer and a better one for tomorrow.

BARBARA. Oh how gladly I would take a better one to my soul! But you offer me a worse one. (*Turning on him with sudden vehemence*). Justify yourself: shew me some light through the darkness of this dreadful place, with its beautifully clean workshops, and respectable workmen, and model homes. 1180

UNDERSHAFT. Cleanliness and respectability do not need justification, Barbara: they justify themselves. I see no darkness here, no dreadfulness. In your Salvation shelter I saw poverty, misery, cold and hunger. You gave them bread and treacle and dreams of heaven. I give from thirty shillings a week to twelve thousand a year. They find their own dreams; but I look after the drainage.

BARBARA. And their souls? 1190

UNDERSHAFT. I save their souls just as I saved yours.

BARBARA (*revolted*). You saved my soul! What do you mean?

UNDERSHAFT. I fed you and clothed you and housed you. I took care that you should have money enough to live handsomely—more than enough; so that you could be wasteful, careless, generous. That saved your soul from the seven deadly sins. 1200

BARBARA (*bewildered*). The seven deadly sins!

UNDERSHAFT. Yes, the deadly seven. (*Counting on his fingers*) Food, clothing, firing, rent, taxes, respectability and children. Nothing can lift those seven millstones from Man's neck but money; and the spirit cannot soar until the mill stones are lifted. I lifted them from your spirit. I enabled Barbara to become Major Barbara; and I saved her from the crime of poverty. 1210

CUSINS. Do you call poverty a crime?

UNDERSHAFT. The worst of crimes. All the other crimes are virtues beside it: all the other dishonors are chivalry itself by comparison. Poverty blights whole cities; spreads horrible pestilences; strikes dead the very souls of all who come within sight, sound, or smell of it. What you call crime is nothing: a murder here and a theft there, a blow now and a curse then: what do they matter? they are only the acci- 1220 dents and illnesses of life: there are not fifty genuine professional criminals in London. But there are millions of poor people, abject people, dirty people, ill fed, ill clothed people. They poison us morally and physically: they kill the happiness of society: they force us to do away with our own liberties and to organize unnatural cruelties for fear they should rise against us and drag us down into their abyss. Only fools fear crime: we all fear poverty. Pah! (*turning on Barbara*) you talk of your half-saved ruffian in West Ham: you accuse me of dragging his soul back to perdition. Well, bring him to me here; and I will drag his soul back again to salvation for you. Not by words and dreams; but by thirtyeight shillings a week, a sound house in a handsome street, and a permanent job. In three weeks he will have a fancy waistcoat; in three months a tall hat and a chapel sitting; before the end of the year he will shake hands with a duchess at a Primrose League meeting, and join the Conservative Party.

BARBARA. And will he be the better for that?

UNDERSHAFT. You know he will. Dont be a hypocrite, Barbara. He will be better fed, better housed, better clothed, better behaved; and his children will be pounds heavier and bigger. That will be better than an American cloth mattress in a shelter, chopping firewood, eating bread and treacle, and being forced to kneel down from time to time to thank heaven for it: knee drill, I think you call it. It is cheap work converting starving men with a Bible in one hand and a slice of bread in the other. I will undertake to convert West Ham to Mahometanism on the same terms. Try your hand on my men: their souls are hungry because their bodies are full.

BARBARA. And leave the east end to starve?

UNDERSHAFT (*his energetic tone dropping into one of bitter and brooding remembrance*). I was an east ender. I moralized and starved until one day I swore that I would be a full-fed free man at all costs; that nothing should stop me except a bullet, neither reason nor morals nor the lives of other men. I said 'Thou shalt starve ere I starve'; and with that word I became free and great. I was a dangerous man until I had my will: now I am a useful, beneficent, kindly person. That is the history of most self-made millionaires, I fancy. When it is the history of every Englishman we shall have an England worth living in.

LADY BRITOMART. Stop making speeches, Andrew. This is not the place for them.

UNDERSHAFT (*punctured*). My dear: I have no other means of conveying my ideas.

LADY BRITOMART. Your ideas are nonsense. You got on because you were selfish and unscrupulous.

UNDERSHAFT. Not at all. I had the strongest scruples about poverty and starvation. Your moralists are quite unscrupulous about both: they make virtues of them. I had rather be a thief than a pauper. I had rather be a murderer than a slave. I dont want to be either; but if you force the alternative on me, then, by Heaven, I'll chose the braver and more moral one. I hate poverty and slavery worse than any other crimes whatsoever. And let me tell you this. Poverty and slavery have stood up for centuries to your sermons and leading articles: they will not stand up to my machine guns. Dont preach at them: dont reason with them. Kill them.

BARBARA. Killing. Is that your remedy for everything?

UNDERSHAFT. It is the final test of conviction, the only lever strong enough to overturn a social system, the only way of saying Must. Let six hundred and seventy fools loose in the streets; and three policemen can scatter them. But huddle them together in a certain house in Westminster; and let them go through certain ceremonies and call themselves certain names until at last they get the courage to kill; and your six hundred and seventy fools become a government. Your pious mob fills up ballot papers and imagines it is governing its masters; but the ballot paper that really governs is the paper that has a bullet wrapped up in it.

CUSINS. That is perhaps why, like most intelligent people, I never vote.

UNDERSHAFT. Vote! Bah! When you vote, you only change the names of the cabinet. When you shoot, you pull down governments, inaugurate new epochs, abolish old orders and set up new. Is that historically true, Mr Learned Man, or is it not?

CUSINS. It is historically true. I loathe having to admit it. I repudiate your sentiments. I abhor your nature. I defy you in every possible way. Still, it is true. But it ought not to be true.

UNDERSHAFT. Ought! ought! ought! ought! ought! Are you going to spend your life saying ought, like the rest of our moralists? Turn your oughts into shalls, man. Come and make explosives with me. Whatever can blow men up can blow society up. The history of the world is the history of those who had courage enough to embrace this truth. Have you the courage to embrace it, Barbara?

LADY BRITOMART. Barbara: I positively forbid you to listen to your father's abominable wickedness. And you, Adolphus, ought to know better than to go about saying that wrong things are true. What does it matter whether they are true if they are wrong?

UNDERSHAFT. What does it matter whether they are wrong if they are true?

LADY BRITOMART (*rising*). Children: come home instantly. Andrew: I am exceedingly sorry I allowed you to call on us. You are wickeder than ever. Come at once.

BARBARA (*shaking her head*). It's no use running away from wicked people, mamma.

LADY BRITOMART. It is every use. It shews your disapprobation of them.

BARBARA. It does not save them.

LADY BRITOMART. I can see that you are going to disobey me. Sarah: are you coming home or are you not?

SARAH. I daresay it's very wicked of papa to make cannons; but I dont think I shall cut him on that account.

LOMAX (*pouring oil on the troubled waters*). The fact is, you know, there is a certain amount of tosh about this notion of wickedness. It doesnt work. You must look at facts. Not that I would say a word in favor of anything wrong; but then, you see, all sorts of chaps are always doing all sorts of things; and we have to fit them in somehow, dont you know. What I mean is that you cant go cutting everybody; and thats about what it comes to. (*Their rapt attention to his eloquence makes him nervous*). Perhaps I dont make myself clear.

LADY BRITOMART. You are lucidity itself, Charles. Because Andrew is successful and has plenty of money to give to Sarah, you will flatter him and encourage him in his wickedness.

LOMAX (*unruffled*). Well, where the carcase is, there will the eagles be gathered, dont you know. (*To Undershaft*) Eh? What?

UNDERSHAFT. Precisely. By the way, *may* I call you Charles?

LOMAX. Delighted. Cholly is the usual ticket.

UNDERSHAFT (*to Lady Britomart*). Biddy—

LADY BRITOMART (*violently*). Dont dare call me Biddy. Charles Lomax: you are a fool. Adolphus Cusins: you are a Jesuit. Stephen: you are a prig. Barbara: you are a lunatic. Andrew: you are a vulgar tradesman. Now you all know my opinion; and *my* conscience is clear, at all events (*she sits down with a vehemence that the rug fortunately softens*).

UNDERSHAFT. My dear: you are the incarnation of morality. (*She snorts*). Your conscience is clear and your duty done when you have called everybody names. Come, Euripides! it is getting late; and we all want to go home. Make up your mind.

CUSINS. Understand this, you old demon—

LADY BRITOMART. Adolphus!

UNDERSHAFT. Let him alone, Biddy. Proceed, Euripides.

CUSINS. You have me in a horrible dilemma. I want Barbara.

UNDERSHAFT. Like all young men, you greatly exaggerate the difference between one young woman and another.

BARBARA. Quite true, Dolly.

CUSINS. I also want to avoid being a rascal.

UNDERSHAFT (*with biting contempt*). You lust for personal righteousness, for self-approval, for what you call a good conscience, for what Barbara calls salvation, for what I call patronizing people who are not so lucky as yourself.

CUSINS. I do not: all the poet in me recoils from being a good man. But there are things in me that I must reckon with. Pity—

UNDERSHAFT. Pity! The scavenger of misery.

CUSINS. Well, love.

UNDERSHAFT. I know. You love the needy and the outcast: you love the oppressed races, the negro, the Indian ryot, the underdog everywhere. Do you love the Japanese? Do you love the French? Do you love the English?

CUSINS. No. Every true Englishman detests the English. We are the wickedest nation on earth; and our success is a moral horror.

UNDERSHAFT. That is what comes of your gospel of love, is it?

CUSINS. May I not love even my father-in-law?

UNDERSHAFT. Who wants your love, man? By what right do you take the liberty of offering it to me? I will have your due heed and respect, or I will kill you. But your love! Damn your impertinence!

CUSINS (*grinning*). I may not be able to control my affections, Mac.

UNDERSHAFT. You are fencing, Euripides.

You are weakening: your grip is slipping. Come! try your last weapon. Pity and love have broken in your hand: forgiveness is still left.

CUSINS. No: forgiveness is a beggar's refuge. I am with you there: we must pay our debts.

1440 UNDERSHAFT. Well said. Come! you will suit me. Remember the words of Plato.

CUSINS (*starting*). Plato! You dare quote Plato to me!

UNDERSHAFT. Plato says, my friend, that society cannot be saved until either the Professors of Greek take to making gunpowder, or else the makers of gunpowder become Professors of Greek.

CUSINS. Oh, tempter, cunning tempter!

1450 UNDERSHAFT. Come! choose, man, choose.

CUSINS. But perhaps Barbara will not marry me if I make the wrong choice.

BARBARA. Perhaps not.

CUSINS (*desperately perplexed*). You hear!

BARBARA. Father: do you love nobody?

UNDERSHAFT. I love my best friend.

LADY BRITOMART. And who is that, pray?

UNDERSHAFT. My bravest enemy. That is the man who keeps me up to the mark.

1460 CUSINS. You know, the creature is really a sort of poet in his way. Suppose he is a great man, after all!

UNDERSHAFT. Suppose you stop talking and make up your mind, my young friend.

CUSINS. But you are driving me against my nature. I hate war.

UNDERSHAFT. Hatred is the coward's revenge for being intimidated. Dare you make war on war? Here are the means: my friend Mr Lomax

1470 is sitting on them.

LOMAX (*springing up*). Oh I say! You dont mean that this thing is loaded, do you? My ownest: come off it.

SARAH (*sitting placidly on the shell*). If I am to be blown up, the more thoroughly it is done the better. Dont fuss, Cholly.

LOMAX (*to Undershaft, strongly remonstrant*). Your own daughter, you know!

UNDERSHAFT. So I see. (*To Cusins*). Well,

1480 my friend, may we expect you here at six tomorrow morning?

CUSINS (*firmly*). Not on any account. I will see the whole establishment blown up with its own dynamite before I will get up at five. My hours are healthy, rational hours: eleven to five.

UNDERSHAFT. Come when you please: before a week you will come at six and stay until I turn you out for the sake of your health. (*Calling*) Bilton! (*He turns to Lady Britomart, who*

1490 *rises*). My dear: let us leave these two young people to themselves for a moment. (*Bilton comes from the shed*). I am going to take you through the gun cotton shed.

BILTON (*barring the way*). You cant take anything explosive in here, sir.

LADY BRITOMART. What do you mean? Are you alluding to me?

BILTON (*unmoved*). No, maam. Mr Undershaft has the other gentleman's matches in his

1500 pocket.

LADY BRITOMART (*abruptly*). Oh! I beg your pardon. (*She goes into the shed*).

UNDERSHAFT. Quite right, Bilton, quite right: here you are. (*He gives Bilton the box of matches*). Come Stephen. Come, Charles. Bring Sarah. (*He passes into the shed*).

Bilton opens the box and deliberately drops the matches into the fire-bucket.

LOMAX. Oh! I say (*Bilton stolidly hands him*

1510 *the empty box*). Infernal nonsense! Pure scientific ignorance! (*He goes in*).

SARAH. Am I all right, Bilton?

BILTON. Youll have to put on list slippers, miss: that's all. Weve got em inside. (*She goes in*).

STEPHEN (*very seriously to Cusins*). Dolly, old fellow, think. Think before you decide. Do you feel that you are a sufficiently practical man? It is a huge undertaking, an enormous

1520 responsibility. All this mass of business will be Greek to you.

CUSINS. Oh, I think it will be much less difficult than Greek.

STEPHEN. Well, I just want to say this before I leave you to yourselves. Dont let anything I have said about right and wrong prejudice you against this great chance in life. I have satisfied myself that the business is one of the highest character and a credit to our country. (*Emo-*

1530 *tionally*) I am very proud of my father. I—(*Unable to proceed, he presses Cusins' hand and goes hastily into the shed, followed by Bilton*). *Barbara and Cusins, left alone together, look at one another silently.*

CUSINS. Barbara: I am going to accept this offer.

BARBARA. I thought you would.

CUSINS. You understand, dont you, that I had to decide without consulting you. If I had thrown the burden of the choice on you, you would sooner or later have despised me for it.

BARBARA. Yes: I did not want you to sell your soul for me any more than for this inheritance.

CUSINS. It is not the sale of my soul that troubles me: I have sold it too often to care about that. I have sold it for a professorship. I have sold it for an income. I have sold it to escape being imprisoned for refusing to pay taxes for hangmen's ropes and unjust wars and things that I abhor. What is all human conduct but the daily and hourly sale of our souls for trifles? What I am now selling it for is neither money nor position nor comfort, but for reality and for power.

BARBARA. You know that you will have no power, and that he has none.

CUSINS. I know. It is not for myself alone. I want to make power for the world.

BARBARA. I want to make power for the world too; but it must be spiritual power.

CUSINS. I think all power is spiritual: these cannons will not go off by themselves. I have tried to make spiritual power by teaching Greek. But the world can never be really touched by a dead language and a dead civilization. The people must have power; and the people cannot have Greek. Now the power that is made here can be wielded by all men.

BARBARA. Power to burn women's houses down and kill their sons and tear their husbands to pieces.

CUSINS. You cannot have power for good without having power for evil too. Even mother's milk nourishes murderers as well as heroes. This power which only tears men's bodies to pieces has never been so horribly abused as the intellectual power, the imaginative power, the poetic, religious power that can enslave men's souls. As a teacher of Greek I gave the intellectual man weapons against the common man. I now want to give the common man weapons against the intellectual man. I love the common people. I want to arm them against the lawyers, the doctors, the priests, the literary men, the professors, the artists, and the politicians, who, once in authority, are more disastrous and tyrannical than all the fools, rascals, and impostors. I want a power simple enough for common men to use, yet strong enough to force the intellectual oligarchy to use its genius for the general good.

BARBARA. Is there no higher power than that (*pointing to the shell*)?

CUSINS. Yes; but that power can destroy the higher powers just as a tiger can destroy a man: therefore Man must master that power first. I admitted this when the Turks and Greeks were last at war. My best pupil went out to fight for Hellas. My parting gift to him was not a copy of Plato's Republic, but a revolver and a hundred Undershaft cartridges. The blood of every Turk he shot—if he shot any—is on my head as well as on Undershaft's. That act committed me to this place for ever. Your father's challenge has beaten me. Dare I make war on war? I must. I will. And now, is it all over between us?

BARBARA (*touched by his evident dread of her answer*). Silly baby Dolly! How could it be!

CUSINS (*overjoyed*). Then you—you—you—Oh for my drum! (*He flourishes imaginary drumsticks*).

BARBARA (*angered by his levity*). Take care, Dolly, take care. Oh, if only I could get away from you and from father and from it all! if I could have the wings of a dove and fly away to heaven!

CUSINS. And leave m e!

BARBARA. Yes, you, and all the other naughty mischievous children of men. But I cant. I was happy in the Salvation Army for a moment. I escaped from the world into a paradise of enthusiasm and prayer and soul saving; but the moment our money ran short, it all came back to Bodger: it was he who saved our people: he, and the Prince of Darkness, my papa. Undershaft and Bodger: their hands stretch everywhere: when we feed a starving fellow creature, it is with their bread, because there is no other bread; when we tend the sick, it is in the hospitals they endow; if we turn from the churches they build, we must kneel on the stones of the streets they pave. As long as that lasts, there is no getting away from them. Turning our backs on Bodger and Undershaft is turning our backs on life.

CUSINS. I thought you were determined to turn your back on the wicked side of life.

1640 BARBARA. There is no wicked side: life is all one. And I never wanted to shirk my share in whatever evil must be endured, whether it be sin or suffering. I wish I could cure you of middle-class ideas, Dolly.

CUSINS (*gasping*). Middle cl—! A snub! A social snub to m e! from the daughter of a foundling!

BARBARA. That is why I have no class, Dolly: I come straight out of the heart of the whole 1650 people. If I were middle-class I should turn my back on my father's business; and we should both live in an artistic drawing room, with you reading the reviews in one corner, and I in the other at the piano, playing Schumann: both very superior persons, and neither of us a bit of use. Sooner than that, I would sweep out the guncotton shed, or be one of Bodger's barmaids. Do you know what would have happened if you had refused papa's offer?

1660 CUSINS. I wonder!

BARBARA. I should have given you up and married the man who accepted it. After all, my dear old mother has more sense than any of you. I felt like her when I saw this place—felt that I must have it—that never, never, never could I let it go; only she thought it was the houses and the kitchen ranges and the linen and china, when it was really all the human souls to be saved: not weak souls in starved 1670 bodies, sobbing with gratitude for a scrap of bread and treacle, but fullfed, quarrelsome, snobbish, uppish creatures, all standing on their little rights and dignities, and thinking that my father ought to be greatly obliged to them for making so much money for him—and so he ought. That is where salvation is really wanted. My father shall never throw it in my teeth again that my converts were bribed with bread. (*She is transfigured*). I have got rid of the bribe 1680 of bread. I have got rid of the bribe of heaven. Let God's work be done for its own sake: the work he had to create us to do because it cannot be done except by living men and women. When I die, let him be in my debt, not I in his; and let me forgive him as becomes a woman of my rank.

CUSINS. Then the way of life lies through the factory of death?

BARBARA. Yes, through the raising of hell to heaven and of man to God, through the un- 1690 veiling of an eternal light in the Valley of The Shadow. (*Seizing him with both hands*) Oh, did you think my courage would never come back? did you believe that I was a deserter? that I, who have stood in the streets, and taken my people to my heart, and talked of the holiest and greatest things with them, could ever turn back and chatter foolishly to fashionable people about nothing in a drawing room? Never, never, never, never: Major Barbara will die with the 1700 colors. Oh! and I have my dear little Dolly boy still; and he has found me my place and my work. Glory Hallelujah! (*She kisses him*).

CUSINS. My dearest: consider my delicate health. I cannot stand as much happiness as you can.

BARBARA. Yes: it is not easy work being in love with me, is it? But its good for you. (*She runs to the shed, and calls, childlike*) Mamma! Mamma! (*Bilton comes out of the shed, fol-* 1710 *lowed by Undershaft*). I want Mamma.

UNDERSHAFT. She is taking off her list slippers, dear. (*He passes on to Cusins*). Well? What does she say?

CUSINS. She has gone right up into the skies.

LADY BRITOMART (*coming from the shed and stopping on the steps, obstructing Sarah, who follows with Lomax. Barbara clutches like a baby at her mother's skirt*). Barbara: when will you learn to be independent and to act and 1720 think for yourself? I know as well as possible what that cry of 'Mamma, Mamma,' means. Always running to me!

SARAH (*touching Lady Britomart's ribs with her finger tips and imitating a bicycle horn*). Pip! pip!

LADY BRITOMART (*highly indignant*). How dare you say Pip! pip! to me, Sarah? You are both very naughty children. What do you want, Barbara? 1730

BARBARA. I want a house in the village to live in with Dolly. (*Dragging at the skirt*) Come and tell me which one to take.

UNDERSHAFT (*to Cusins*). Six o'clock tomorrow morning, Euripides.

THE END

Review Questions

1. Is Shaw primarily concerned with plot, character or ideas?
2. How real are the characters?
3. What farcical elements do you find?
4. What aspect of society does Undershaft symbolize?
5. What are the sources of comedy?
6. Is the play dated or are the ideas and problems still relevant?
7. Is the playwright didactic?
8. Who speaks for Shaw?
9. What is Shaw's purpose?
10. Is the opening situation believable in the light of Barbara's family background?
11. How does the comedy differ from *School for Scandal?*
12. Is Shaw more interested in the individual than in society?
13. Summarize the gospel of Undershaft.
14. Is the play an attack on the Salvation Army?
15. Should the Salvation Army take money from a distiller and cannon maker?
16. Comment on Undershaft's statement that "Money is the most important thing in the world. It represents health, strength, honor, generosity and beauty . . ."
17. Is the ending optimistic?
18. Contrast the difference in methods by which Shaw and Ibsen attack the ills of society.
19. What specific scenes or action stand out most vividly?

DESIRE UNDER THE ELMS

Eugene O'Neill (1888-1953)

Eugene O'Neill was born in New York the son of a famous romantic actor, James O'Neill. Eugene's early years were painful ones, as is evident in his autobiographical play, *Long Day's Journey Into Night.* His first one-act plays, based on his experiences as a seaman and prospector, were produced by the Provincetown Players in Massachusetts and later in New York. Critical recognition came to him with the New York production of his first full-length play, *Beyond the Horizon,* which won for O'Neill the first of his three Pulitzer Prizes.

He experimented freely with dramatic forms and theater techniques and became the first American playwright to achieve international stature, winning the *Nobel Prize* for literature in 1936. Outstanding O'Neill plays are *The Hairy Ape, The Great God Brown, Mourning Becomes Electra, Strange Interlude, Anna Christie, The Emperor Jones, The Iceman Cometh* and *Desire Under the Elms.*

An indication of O'Neill's objectives is suggested in his statement:

> To me the tragic alone has that significant beauty which is truth. It is the meaning of life —and the hope. The noblest is eternally the most tragic. The people who succeed and do not push on to a greater failure are the spiritual middle classes. Their stopping at success is the proof of their compromising insignificance. How petty their dreams must have been! . . . . Only through the unattainable does man achieve a hope worth living and dying for—and so attain himself. He with the spiritual guerdon of a hope in a hopelessness is nearest to the stars and the rainbow's foot.

From the Provincetown Playbill

ABOVE. Eugene O'Neill's sketches for the set of his play.

Friedman-Abeles

LEFT. George C. Scott plays Ephraim Cabot on an arena stage in the 1963 production at The Circle in the Square, New York.

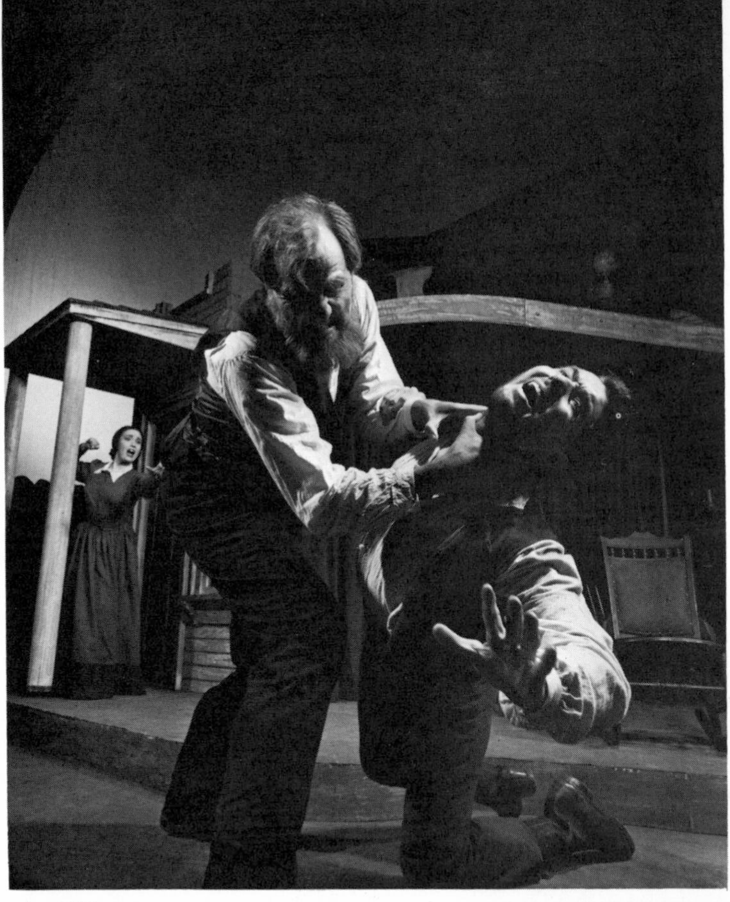

Arnold Newman

Arnold Newman

Karl Malden plays Cabot on a cut-away set.

Characters

EPHRAIM CABOT.
SIMEON, PETER, EBEN — *his sons.*
ABBIE PUTNAM.
YOUNG GIRL, TWO FARMERS, THE FIDDLER, A SHERIFF, *and other folk from the neighboring farms.*

The action of the entire play takes place in, and immediately outside of, the Cabot farmhouse in New England, in the year 1850. The south end of the house faces front to a stone wall with a wooden gate at center opening on a country road. The house is in good condition but in need of paint. Its walls are a sickly grayish, the green of the shutters faded. Two enormous elms are on each side of the house. They bend their trailing branches down over the roof. They appear to protect and at the same time subdue. There is a sinister maternity in their aspect, a crushing, jealous absorption. They have developed from their intimate contact with the life of man in the house an appalling humaneness. They brood oppressively over the house. They are like exhausted women resting their sagging breasts and hands and hair on its roof, and when it rains their tears trickle down monotonously and rot on the shingles.

There is a path running from the gate around the right corner of the house to the front door. A narrow porch is on this side. The end wall facing us has two windows in its upper story, two larger ones on the floor below. The two upper are those of the father's bedroom and that of the brothers. On the left, ground floor, is the kitchen—on the right, the parlor, the shades of which are always drawn down.

DESIRE UNDER THE ELMS

PART ONE *Scene One*

(Exterior of the Farmhouse. It is sunset of a day at the beginning of summer in the year 1850. There is no wind and everything is still. The sky above the roof is suffused with deep colors, the green of the elms glows, but the house is in shadow, seeming pale and washed out by contrast.

A door opens and EBEN CABOT *comes to the end of the porch and stands looking down the road to the right. He has a large bell in his hand and this he swings mechanically, awakening a deafening clangor. Then he puts his hands on his hips and stares up at the sky. He sighs with a puzzled awe and blurts out with halting appreciation.)*

EBEN. God! Purty! *(His eyes fall and he stares about him frowningly. He is twenty-five, tall and sinewy. His face is well-formed, good-looking, but its expression is resentful and defensive. His defiant, dark eyes remind one of a wild animal's in capitivity. Each day is a cage in which he finds himself trapped but inwardly unsubdued. There is a fierce repressed vitality about him. He has black hair, mustache, a thin curly trace of beard. He is dressed in rough farm clothes.)*

(He spits on the ground with intense disgust, turns and goes back into the house.)

*(*SIMEON *and* PETER *come in from their work in the fields. They are tall men, much older than their half-brother—*SIMEON *is thirty-nine and* PETER *thirty-seven—, built on a squarer, simpler model, fleshier in body, more bovine and homelier in face, shrewder and more practical. Their shoulders stoop a bit from years of farm work. They clump heavily along in their clumsy thick-soled boots caked with earth. Their clothes, their faces, hands, bare arms and throats are earth-stained. They smell of earth. They stand together for a moment in front of the house and, as if with the one impulse, stare dumbly up at the sky, leaning on their hoes. Their faces have a compressed, unresigned expression. As they look upward, this softens.)*

SIMEON *(grudgingly)*. Purty.

PETER. Ay-eh.

SIMEON *(suddenly)*. Eighteen year ago.

PETER. What?

SIMEON. Jenn. My woman. She died.

PETER. I'd fergot.

SIMEON. I rec'lect—now an' agin. Makes it lonesome. She'd hair long's a hoss' tail—an' yaller like gold!

PETER. Waal—she's gone. *(This with indifferent finality—then after a pause.)* They's gold in the West, Sim.

SIMEON *(still under the influence of sunset—vaguely)*. In the sky?

PETER. Waal—in a manner o' speakin'—thar's the promise. *(Growing excited.)* Gold in the sky—in the West—Golden Gate—Californi-a!—Goldest West!—fields o' gold!

SIMEON *(excited in his turn)*. Fortunes layin'

just atop o' the ground waitin' t' be picked! Solomon's mines, they says! (*For a moment they continue looking up at the sky—then their eyes drop.*)

PETER (*with sardonic bitterness*). Here—it's stones atop o' the ground—stones atop o' stones —makin' stone walls—year atop o' year—him 'n' yew 'n' me 'n' then Eben—makin' stone walls fur him to fence us in!

SIMEON. We've wuked. Give our strength. Give our years. Plowed 'em under in the ground —(*he stamps rebelliously*)—rottin'—makin' soil for his crops! (*A pause.*) Waal—the farm pays good for hereabouts.

PETER. If we plowed in Californi-a, they'd be lumps o' gold in the furrow!

SIMEON. Californi-a's t'other side o' earth, a'most. We got t' calc'late—

PETER (*after a pause*). 'Twould be hard fur me, too, to give up what we've 'arned here by our sweat. (*A pause.* EBEN *sticks his head out of the dining-room window, listening.*)

SIMEON. Ah-eh. (*A pause.*) Mebbe—he'll die soon.

PETER (*doubtfully*). Mebbe.

SIMEON. Mebbe—fur all we knows—he's dead now.

PETER. Ye'd need proof.

SIMEON. He's been gone two months—with no word.

PETER. Left us in the fields an evenin' like this. Hitched up an' druv off into the West. That's plumb onnateral. He hain't never been off this farm 'ceptin' t' the village in thirty year or more, not since he married Eben's maw. (*A pause. Shrewdly.*) I calc'late we might git him declared crazy by the court.

SIMEON. He skinned 'em too slick. He got the best o' all on 'em. They'd never b'lieve him crazy. (*A pause.*) We got t' wait—till he's under ground.

EBEN (*with a sardonic chuckle*). Honor thy father! (*They turn, startled, and stare at him. He grins, then scowls.*) I pray he's died. (*They stare at him. He continues matter-of-factly.*) Supper's ready.

SIMEON *and* PETER (*together*). Ay-eh.

EBEN (*gazing up at the sky*). Sun's downin' purty.

SIMEON *and* PETER (*together*). Ay-eh. They's gold in the West.

EBEN. Ay-eh. (*Pointing.*) Yonder atop o' the hill pasture, ye mean?

SIMEON *and* PETER (*together*). In Californi-a!

EBEN. Hunh? (*Stares at them indifferently for a second, then drawls.*) Waal—supper's gittin' cold. (*He turns back into kitchen.*)

SIMEON (*startled—smacks his lips*). I air hungry!

PETER (*sniffing*). I smells bacon!

SIMEON (*with hungry appreciation*). Bacon's good!

PETER (*in same tone*). Bacon's bacon! (*They turn, shouldering each other, their bodies bumping and rubbing together as they hurry clumsily to their food, like two friendly oxen toward their evening meal. They disappear around the right corner of house and can be heard entering the door.*)

(*The curtain falls.*)

Scene Two

(*The color fades from the sky. Twilight begins. The interior of the kitchen is now visible. A pine table is at center, a cook-stove in the right rear corner, four rough wooden chairs, a tallow candle on the table. In the middle of the rear wall is fastened a big advertizing poster with a ship in full sail and the word "Califorina" in big letters. Kitchen utensils hang from nails. Everything is neat and in order but the atmosphere is of a men's camp kitchen rather than that of a home.*)

(*Places for three are laid.* EBEN *takes boiled potatoes and bacon from the stove and puts them on the table, also a loaf of bread and a crock of water.* SIMEON *and* PETER *shoulder in, slump down in their chairs without a word.* EBEN *joins them. The three eat in silence for a moment, the two elder as naturally unrestrained as beasts of the field,* EBEN *picking at his food without appetite, glancing at them with a tolerant dislike.*)

SIMEON (*suddenly turns to* EBEN). Looky here! Ye'd oughtn't t' said that, Eben.

PETER. 'Twa'n't righteous.

EBEN. What?

SIMEON. Ye prayed he'd died.

EBEN. Waal—don't yew pray it? (*A pause.*)

PETER. He's our Paw.

EBEN (*violently*). Not mine!

SIMEON (*dryly*). Ye'd not let no one else say that about yer Maw! Ha! (*He gives one abrupt sardonic guffaw.* PETER *grins.*)

EBEN (*very pale*). I meant—I hain't his'n—I hain't like him—he hain't me!

PETER (*dryly*). Wait till ye've growed his age!

EBEN (*intensely*). I'm Maw—every drop o' blood! (*A pause. They stare at him with indifferent curiosity.*)

PETER (*reminiscently*). She was good t' Sim 'n' me. A good Step-maw's scurse.

SIMEON. She was good t' everyone.

EBEN (*greatly moved, gets to his feet and makes an awkward bow to each of them—stammering*). I be thankful t' ye. I'm her—her heir. (*He sits down in confusion.*)

PETER (*after a pause—judicially*). She was good even t' him.

EBEN (*fiercely*). An' fur thanks he killed her!

SIMEON (*after a pause*). No one never kills nobody. It's allus somethin'. That's the murderer.

EBEN. Didn't he slave Maw t' death?

PETER. He's slaved himself t' death. He's slaved Sim 'n' me 'n' yew t' death—on'y none o' us haint died—yit.

SIMEON. It's somethin'—drivin' him—t' drive us!

EBEN (*vengefully*). Waal—I hold him t' jedgment! (*Then scornfully.*) Somethin'! What's somethin'?

SIMEON. Dunno.

EBEN (*sardonically*). What's drivin' yew to Californi-a, mebbe? (*They look at him in surprise.*) Oh, I've heerd ye! (*Then, after a pause.*) But ye'll never go t' the gold fields!

PETER (*assertively*). Mebbe!

EBEN. Whar'll ye git the money?

PETER. We kin walk. It's an a'mighty ways —Californi-a—but if yew was t' put all the steps we've walked on this farm end t' end we'd be in the moon!

EBEN. The Injuns'll skulp ye on the plains.

SIMEON (*with grim humor*). We'll mebbe make 'em pay a hair fur a hair!

EBEN (*decisively*). But t'ain't that. Ye won't never go because ye'll wait here for yer share o' the farm, thinkin allus he'll die soon.

SIMEON (*after a pause*). We've a right.

PETER. Two-thirds belongs t'us.

EBEN (*jumping to his feet*). Ye've no right! She wa'n't yewr Maw! It was her farm! Didn't he steal it from her? She's dead. It's my farm.

SIMEON (*sardonically*). Tell that t' Paw—when he comes! I'll bet ye a dollar he'll laugh—fur once in his life. Ha! (*He laughs himself in one single mirthless bark.*)

PETER (*amused in turn, echoes his brother*). Ha!

SIMEON (*after a pause*). What've ye got held agin us, Eben? Year arter year it's skulked in yer eye—somethin'.

PETER. Ay-eh.

EBEN. Ay-eh. They's somethin'. (*Suddenly exploding.*) Why didn't ye never stand between him 'n' my Maw when he was slavin' her to her grave—t' pay her back fur the kindness she done t' yew? (*There is a long pause. They stare at him in surprise.*)

SIMEON. Waal—the stock'd got t' be watered.

PETER. 'R they was woodin' t' do.

SIMEON. 'R plowin'.

PETER. 'R hayin'.

SIMEON. 'R spreadin' manure.

PETER. 'R weedin'.

SIMEON. 'R prunin'.

PETER. 'R milkin'.

EBEN (*breaking in harshly*). An' makin' walls—stone atop o' stone—makin' walls till yer heart's a stone ye heft up out o' the way o' growth onto a stone wall t' wall in yer heart!

SIMEON (*matter-of-factly*). We never had no time t' meddle.

PETER (*to* EBEN). Yew was fifteen afore yer Maw died—an' big fur yer age. Why didn't ye never do nothin'?

EBEN (*harshly*). They was chores t' do, wa'n't they? (*A pause—then slowly.*) It was on'y arter she died I come to think o' it. Me cookin'—doin' her work—that made me know her, suffer her sufferin'—she'd come back t' help—come back t' bile potatoes—come back t' fry bacon—come back t' bake biscuits—come back all cramped up t' shake the fire, an' carry ashes, her eyes weepin' an' bloody with smoke an' cinders same's they used t' be. She still comes back—stands by the stove thar in the evenin'—she can't find it nateral sleepin' an' restin' in peace. She can't git used t' bein' free—even in her grave.

SIMEON. She never complained none.

EBEN. She'd got too tired. She'd got too used t' bein' too tired. That was what he done. (*With vengeful passion.*) An' sooner'r later, I'll meddle. I'll say the thin's I didn't say then t' him! I'll yell 'em at the top o' my lungs. I'll see t' it my Maw gits some rest an' sleep in her grave! (*He sits down again, relapsing into a brooding silence. They look at him with a queer indifferent curiosity.*)

PETER (*after a pause*). Whar in tarnation d'ye s'pose he went, Sim?

SIMEON. Dunno. He druv off in the buggy, all spick an' span, with the mare all breshed an' shiny, druv off clackin' his tongue an' wavin' his whip. I remember it right well. I was finishin' plowin', it was spring an' May an' sunset, an' gold in the West, an' he druv off into it. I yells "Whar ye goin', Paw?" an' he hauls up by the stone wall a jiffy. His old snake's eyes was glitterin' in the sun like he'd been drinkin' a jugful an' he says with a mule's grin: "Don't ye run away till I come back!"

PETER. Wonder if he knowed we was wantin' fur Californi-a?

SIMEON. Mebbe. I didn't say nothin' and he says, lookin' kinder queer an' sick: "I been hearin' the hens cluckin' an' the roosters crowin' all the durn day. I been listenin' t' the cows lowin' an' everythin' else kickin' up till I can't stand it no more. It's spring an' I'm feelin' damned," he says. "Damned like an old bare hickory tree fit on'y fur burnin'," he says. An' then I calc'late I must've looked a mite hopeful, fur he adds real spry and vicious: "But don't git no fool idee I'm dead. I've sworn t' live a hundred an' I'll do it, if on'y t' spite yer sinful greed! An' now I'm ridin' out t' learn God's message t' me in the spring, like the prophets done. An' yew git back t' yer plowin'," he says. An' he druv off singin' a hymn. I thought he was drunk—'r I'd stopped him goin'.

EBEN (*scornfully*). No, ye wouldn't! Ye're scared o' him. He's stronger—inside—than both o' ye put together!

PETER (*sardonically*). An' yew—be yew Samson?

EBEN. I'm gittin' stronger. I kin feel it growin' in me—growin' an' growin'—till it'll bust out—! (*He gets up and puts on his coat and a hat. They watch him, gradually breaking into grins.* EBEN *avoids their eyes sheepishly.*) I'm goin' out fur a spell—up the road.

PETER. T' the village?

SIMEON. T' see Minnie?

EBEN (*defiantly*). Ay-eh!

PETER (*jeeringly*). The Scarlet Woman!

SIMEON. Lust—that's what's growin' in ye!

EBEN. Waal—she's purty!

PETER. She's been purty fur twenty year!

SIMEON. A new coat o' paint'll make a heifer out of forty.

EBEN. She hain't forty!

PETER. If she hain't, she's teeterin' on the edge.

EBEN (*desperately*). What d'yew know—

PETER. All they is . . . Sim knew her—an' then me arter—

SIMEON. An' Paw kin tell yew somethin' too! He was fust!

EBEN. D'ye mean t'say he . . . ?

SIMEON (*with a grin*). Ay-eh! We air his heirs in everythin'!

EBEN (*intensely*). That's more to it! That grows on it! It'll bust soon! (*Then violently.*) I'll go smash my fist in her face! (*He pulls open the door in rear violently.*)

SIMEON (*with a wink at* PETER*—drawlingly*). Mebbe—but the night's wa'm—purty—by the time ye git thar mebbe ye'll kiss her instead!

PETER. Sart'n he will! (*They both roar with coarse laughter.* EBEN *rushes out and slams the door—then the outside front door—comes around the corner of the house and stands still by the gate, staring up at the sky.)*

SIMEON *(looking after him).* Like his Paw.

PETER. Dead spit an' image!

SIMEON. Dog'll eat dog!

PETER. Ay-eh. *(Pause. With yearning.)* Mebbe a year from now we'll be in Californi-a.

SIMEON. Ay-eh. *(A pause. Both yawn).* Let's git t'bed. *(He blows out the candle. They go out door in rear.* EBEN *stretches his arms up to the sky—rebelliously.)*

EBEN. Waal—thar's a star, an' somewhar's they's him, an' here's me, an' thar's Min up the road—in the same night. What if I does kiss her? She's like t'night. She's soft 'n' wa'm, her eyes kin wink like a star, her mouth's wa'm, her arms're wa'm, she smells like a wa'm plowed field, she's purty . . . Ay-eh! By God A'mighty she's purty, an' I don't give a damn how many sins she's sinned afore mine or who she's sinned 'em with, my sin's as purty as any one on 'em! *(He strides off down the road to the left.)*

Scene Three

(It is the pitch darkness just before dawn. EBEN *comes in from the left and goes around to the porch, feeling his way, chuckling bitterly and cursing half-aloud to himself.)*

EBEN. The cussed old miser! *(He can be heard going in the front door. There is a pause as he goes upstairs, then a loud knock on the bedroom door of the brothers.)* Wake up!

SIMEON *(startedly).* Who's thar?

EBEN *(pushing open the door and coming in, a lighted candle in his hand. The bedroom of the brothers is revealed. Its ceiling is the sloping roof. They can stand upright only close to the center dividing wall of the upstairs.* SIMEON *and* PETER *are in a double bed, front.* EBEN'S *cot is to the rear.* EBEN *has a mixture of silly grin and vicious scowl on his face).* I be.

PETER *(angrily).* What in hell's-fire . . . ?

EBEN. I got news fur ye! Ha! *(He gives one abrupt sardonic guffaw.)*

SIMEON *(angrily).* Couldn't ye hold it 'til we'd got our sleep?

EBEN. It's nigh sunup. *(Then explosively.)* He's gone an' married agen!

SIMEON *and* PETER *(explosively).* Paw?

EBEN. Got himself hitched to a female 'bout thirty-five—an' purty, they says . . .

SIMEON *(aghast).* It's a durn lie!

PETER. Who says?

SIMEON. They been stringin' ye!

EBEN. Think I'm a dunce, do ye? The hull village says. The preacher from New Dover, he brung the news—told it t'our preacher—New Dover, that's whar the old loon got himself hitched—that's whar the woman lived—

PETER *(no longer doubting—stunned).* Waal . . . !

SIMEON *(the same).* Waal . . . !

EBEN *(sitting down on a bed—with vicious hatred).* Ain't he a devil out o' hell? It's jest t' spite us—the damned old mule!

PETER *(after a pause).* Everythin'll go t' her now.

SIMEON. Ay-eh. *(A pause—dully.)* Waal—if it's done—

PETER. It's done us. *(Pause—then persuasively.)* They's gold in the fields o' Californi-a, Sim. No good a-stayin' here now.

SIMEON. Jest what I was a-thinkin'. *(Then with decision.)* S'well fust's last! Let's light out and git this mornin'.

PETER. Suits me.

EBEN. Ye must like walkin'.

SIMEON *(sardonically).* If ye'd grow wings on us we'd fly thar!

EBEN. Ye'd like ridin' better—on a boat.

wouldn't ye? (*Fumbles in his pocket and takes out a crumpled sheet of foolscap.*) Waal, if ye sign this ye kin ride on a boat. I've had it writ out an' ready in case ye'd ever go. It says fur three hundred dollars t' each ye agree yewr shares o' the farm is sold t' me. (*They look suspiciously at the paper. A pause.*)

60 SIMEON (*wonderingly*). But if he's hitched agen—

PETER. An' whar'd yew git that sum o' money, anyways?

EBEN (*cunningly*). I know whar it's hid. I been waitin'—Maw told me. She knew whar it lay fur years, but she was waitin' . . . It's her'n —the money he hoarded from her farm an' hid from Maw. It's my money by rights now.

PETER. Whar's it hid?

70 EBEN (*cunningly*). Whar yew won't never find it without me. Maw spied on him—'r she'd never knowed. (*A pause. They look at him suspiciously, and he at them.*) Waal, is it fa'r trade?

SIMEON. Dunno.

PETER. Dunno.

SIMEON (*looking at window*). Sky's grayin'.

PETER. Ye better start the fire, Eben.

SIMEON. An' fix some vittles.

80 EBEN. Ay-eh. (*Then with a forced jocular heartiness.*) I'll git ye a good one. If ye're startin' t' hoof it t' Californi-a ye'll need somethin' that'll stick t' yer ribs. (*He turns to the door, adding meaningly.*) But ye kin ride on a boat if ye'll swap. (*He stops at the door and pauses. They stare at him.*)

SIMEON (*suspiciously*). Whar was ye all night?

EBEN (*defiantly*). Up t' Min's. (*Then slowly.*) Walkin' thar, fust I felt 's if I'd kiss her; 90 then I got a-thinkin' o' what ye'd said o' him an' her an' I says, I'll bust her nose fur that! Then I got t' the village an' heerd the news an' I got madder'n hell an' run all the way t' Min's not knowin' what I'd do—(*He pauses—then sheepishly but more defiantly.*) Waal—when I seen her, I didn't hit her—nor I didn't kiss her nuther—I begun t' beller like a calf an' cuss at the same time, I was so durn mad—an' she got 100 scared—an' I jest grabbed holt an' tuk her! (*Proudly.*) Yes, sirree! I tuk her. She may've been his'n—an' your'n, too—but she's mine now!

SIMEON (*dryly*). In love, air yew?

EBEN (*with lofty scorn*). Love! I don't take no stock in sech slop!

PETER (*winking at* SIMEON). Mebbe Eben's aimin' t' marry, too.

SIMEON. Min'd make a true faithful he'p-meet! (*They snicker.*)

EBEN. What do I care fur her—'ceptin' she's 110 round an' wa'm? The p'int is she was his'n—an' now she b'longs t' me! (*He goes to the door —then turns—rebelliously.*) An' Min hain't sech a bad un. They's worse'n Min in the world, I'll bet ye! Wait'll we see this cow the Old Man's hitched t'! She'll beat Min, I got a notion! (*He starts to go out.*)

SIMEON (*suddenly*). Mebbe ye'll try t' make her your'n, too?

PETER. Ha! (*He gives a sardonic laugh of* 120 *relish at this idea.*)

EBEN (*spitting with disgust*). Her—here—sleepin' with him—stealin' my Maw's farm! I'd as soon pet a skunk 'r kiss a snake! (*He goes out. The two stare after him suspiciously. A pause. They listen to his steps receding.*)

PETER. He's startin' the fire.

SIMEON. I'd like t' ride t' Californi-a—but—

PETER. Min might o' put some scheme in his head. 130

SIMEON. Mebbe it's all a lie 'bout Paw maryin'. We'd best wait an' see the bride.

PETER. An' don't sign nothin' till we does!

SIMEON. Nor till we've tested it's good money! (*Then with a grin.*) But if Paw's hitched we'd be sellin' Eben somethin' we'd never git nohow!

PETER. We'll wait an' see. (*Then with sudden vindictive anger.*) An' till he comes, let's yew 'n' me not wuk a lick, let Eben tend to 140 thin's if he's a mind t', let's us jest sleep an' eat an' drink likker, an' let the hull damned farm go t' blazes!

SIMEON (*excitedly*). By God, we've 'arned a rest! We'll play rich fur a change. I hain't a-going to stir outa bed till breakfast's ready.

PETER. An' on the table!

SIMEON (*after a pause—thoughtfully*). What d'ye calc'late she'll be like—our new Maw? Like Eben thinks? 150

PETER. More'n' likely.

SIMEON (*vindictively*). Waal—I hope she's a she-devil that'll make him wish he was dead an' livin' in the pit o' hell fur comfort!

PETER (*fervently*). Amen!

SIMEON (*imitating his father's voice*). "I'm ridin' out t' learn God's message t' me in the spring like the prophets done," he says. I'll bet right then an' thar he knew plumb well he was goin' whorin', the stinkin' old hypocrite! 160

Scene Four

(*Same as Scene 2—shows the interior of the kitchen with a lighted candle on table. It is gray dawn outside.* SIMEON *and* PETER *are just finishing their breakfast.* EBEN *sits before his plate of untouched food, brooding frowningly.*)

PETER (*glancing at him rather irritably*). Lookin' glum don't help none.

SIMEON (*sarcastically*). Sorrowin' over his lust o' the flesh!

PETER (*with a grin*). Was she yer fust?

EBEN (*angrily*). None o' yer business. (*A pause.*) I was thinkin' o' him. I got a notion he's gittin' near—I kin feel him comin' on like yew kin feel malaria chill afore it takes ye.

10 PETER. It's too early yet.

SIMEON. Dunno. He'd like t' catch us nappin'—jest t' have somethin' t' hoss us 'round over.

PETER (*mechanically gets to his feet.* SIMEON *does the same*). Waal—let's git t' wuk. (*They both plod mechanically toward the door before they realize. Then they stop short.*)

SIMEON (*grinning*). Ye're a cussed fool, Pete —and I be wuss! Let him see we hain't wukin'!

20 We don't give a durn!

PETER (*as they go back to the table*). Not a damned durn! It'll serve t' show him we're done with him. (*They sit down again.* EBEN *stares from one to the other with surprise.*)

SIMEON (*grins at him*). We're aimin' t' start bein' lilies o' the field.

PETER. Nary a toil 'r spin 'r lick o' wuk do we put in!

SIMEON. Ye're sole owner—till he comes—

30 that's what ye wanted. Waal, ye got t' be sole hand, too.

PETER. The cows air bellerin'. Ye better hustle at the milkin'.

EBEN (*with excited joy*). Ye mean ye'll sign the paper?

SIMEON (*dryly*). Mebbe.

PETER. Mebbe.

SIMEON. We're considerin'. (*Peremptorily.*) Ye better git t' wuk.

EBEN (*with queer excitement*). It's Maw's farm agen! It's my farm! Them's my cows! I'll milk my durn fingers off fur cows o' mine! (*He goes out door in rear, they stare after him indifferently.*) 40

SIMEON. Like his Paw.

PETER. Dead spit 'n' image!

SIMEON. Waal—let dog eat dog! (EBEN *comes out of front door and around the corner of the house. The sky is beginning to grow flushed with sunrise.* EBEN *stops by the gate and stares around him with glowing, possessive eyes. He takes in the whole farm with his embracing glance of desire.*) 50

EBEN. It's purty! It's damned purty! It's mine! (*He suddenly throws his head back boldly and glares with hard, defiant eyes at the sky.*) Mine, d'ye hear? Mine! (*He turns and walks quickly off left, rear, toward the barn. The two brothers light their pipes.*)

SIMEON (*putting his muddy boots up on the table, tilting back his chair, and puffing defiantly*). Waal—this air solid comfort—fur once. 60

PETER. Ay-eh. (*He follows suit. A pause. Unconsciously they both sigh.*)

SIMEON (*suddenly*). He never was much o' a hand at milkin', Eben wa'n't.

PETER (*with a snort*). His hands air like hoofs! (*A pause.*)

SIMEON. Reach down the jug thar! Let's take a swaller. I'm feelin' kind o' low. 70

PETER. Good idee! (*He does so—gets two glasses—they pour out drinks of whisky.*) Here's t' the gold in Californi-a!

SIMEON. An' luck t' find it! (*They drink—puff resolutely—sigh—take their feet down from the table.*)

PETER. Likker don't pear t' sot right.

SIMEON. We hain't used t' it this early. (*A pause. They become very restless.*)

80 PETER. Gittin' close in this kitchen.

SIMEON (*with immense relief*). Let's git a breath o' air. (*They arise briskly and go out rear—appear around house and stop by the gate. They stare up at the sky with a numbed appreciation.*)

PETER. Purty!

SIMEON. Ay-eh. Gold's t' the East now.

PETER. Sun's startin' with us fur the Golden West.

90 SIMEON (*staring around the farm, his compressed face tightened, unable to conceal his emotion*). Waal—it's our last mornin'—mebbe.

PETER (*the same*). Ay-eh.

SIMEON (*stamps his foot on the earth and addresses it desperately*). Waal—ye've thirty year o' me buried in ye—spread out over ye—blood an' bone an' sweat—rotted away—fertilizin' ye—richin' yer soul—prime manure, by God, that's what I been t' ye!

100 PETER. Ay-eh! An' me!

SIMEON. An' yew, Peter. (*He sighs—then spits.*) Waal—no use'n cryin' over spilt milk.

PETER. They's gold in the West—an' freedom, mebbe. We been slaves t' stone walls here.

SIMEON (*defiantly*). We hain't nobody's slaves from this out—nor no thin's slaves nuther. (*A pause—restlessly.*) Speakin' o' milk, wonder how Eben's managin'?

PETER. I s'pose he's managin'.

110 SIMEON. Mebbe we'd ought t' help—this once.

PETER. Mebbe. The cows knows us.

SIMEON. An' likes us. They don't know him much.

PETER. An' the hosses, an' pigs, an' chickens. They don't know him much.

SIMEON. They knows us like brothers—an' likes us! (*Proudly.*) Hain't we raised 'em t' be fust-rate, number one prize stock?

120 PETER. We hain't—not no more.

SIMEON (*dully*). I was fergittin'. (*Then resignedly.*) Waal, let's go help Eben a spell an' git waked up.

PETER. Suits me. (*They are starting off down left, rear, for the barn when* EBEN *appears from there hurrying toward them, his face excited.*)

EBEN (*breathlessly*). Waal—har they be! The old mule an' the bride! I seen 'em from the barn down below at the turnin'. 130

PETER. How could ye tell that far?

EBEN. Hain't I as far-sight as he's near-sight? Don't I know the mare 'n' buggy, an' two people settin' in it? Who else . . . ? An' I tell ye I kin feel 'em a-comin', too! (*He squirms as if he had the itch.*)

PETER (*beginning to be angry*). Waal—let him do his own unhitchin'!

SIMEON (*angry in his turn*). Let's hustle in an' git our bundles an' be a-goin' as he's a-comin'. 140 I don't want never t' step inside the door agen arter he's back. (*They both start back around the corner of the house.* EBEN *follows them.*)

EBEN (*anxiously*). Will ye sign it afore ye go?

PETER. Let's see the color o' the old skinflint's money an' we'll sign. (*They disappear left. The two brothers clump upstairs to get their bundles.* EBEN *appears in the kitchen, runs to window, peers out, comes back and pulls up* 150 *a strip of flooring in under stove, takes out a canvas bag and puts it on table, then sets the floorboard back in place. The two brothers appear a moment after. They carry old carpet bags.*)

EBEN (*puts his hand on bag guardingly*). Have ye signed?

SIMEON (*shows paper in his hand*). Ay-eh. (*Greedily.*) Be that the money?

EBEN (*opens bag and pours out pile of twenty-* 160 *dollar gold pieces*). Twenty-dollar pieces—thirty on 'em. Count 'em. (PETER *does so, arranging them in stacks of five, biting one or two to test them.*)

PETER. Six hundred. (*He puts them in bag and puts it inside his shirt carefully.*)

SIMEON (*handing paper to* EBEN). Har ye be.

EBEN (*after a glance, folds it carefully and hides it under his shirt—gratefully*). Thank yew. 170

PETER. Thank yew fur the ride.

SIMEON. We'll send ye a lump o' gold fur

Christmas. (*A pause.* EBEN *stares at them and they at him.*)

PETER (*awkwardly*). Waal—we're a-goin'.

SIMEON. Comin' out t' the yard?

EBEN. No. I'm waitin' in here a spell. (*Another silence. The brothers edge awkwardly to door in rear—then turn and stand.*)

180 SIMEON. Waal—good-by.

PETER. Good-by.

EBEN. Good-by. (*They go out. He sits down at the table, faces the stove and pulls out the paper. He looks from it to the stove. His face, lighted up by the shaft of sunlight from the window, has an expression of trance. His lips move. The two brothers come out to the gate.*)

PETER (*looking off toward barn*). Thar he be—unhitchin'.

190 SIMEON (*with a chuckle*). I'll bet ye he's riled!

PETER. An' thar she be.

SIMEON. Let's wait 'n' see what our new Maw looks like.

PETER (*with a grin*). An' give him our partin' cuss!

SIMEON (*grinning*). I feel like raisin' fun. I feel light in my head an' feet.

PETER. Me, too. I feel like laffin' till I'd split 200 up the middle.

SIMEON. Reckon it's the likker?

PETER. No. My feet feel itchin' t' walk an' walk—an' jump high over thin's—an'. . . .

SIMEON. Dance? (*A pause.*)

PETER (*puzzled*). It's plumb onnateral.

SIMEON (*a light coming over his face*). I calc'late it's 'cause school's out. It's holiday. Fur once we're free!

PETER (*dazedly*). Free?

210 SIMEON. The halter's broke—the harness is busted—the fence bars is down—the stone walls air crumblin' an' tumblin'! We'll be kickin' up an' tearin' away down the road!

PETER (*drawing a deep breath—oratorically*). Anybody that wants this stinkin' old rock-pile of a farm kin hev it. T'ain't our'n, no sirree!

SIMEON (*takes the gate off its hinges and puts it under his arm*). We harby 'bolishes shet gates, an' open gates, an' all gates, by thunder!

220 PETER. We'll take it with us fur luck an' let 'er sail free down some river.

SIMEON (*as a sound of voices comes from left, rear*). Har they comes! (*The two brothers congeal into two stiff, grim-visaged statues.* EPHRAIM CABOT *and* ABBIE PUTNAM *come in.* CABOT *is seventy-five, tall and gaunt, with great, wiry, concentrated power, but stoop-shouldered from toil. His face is as hard as if it were hewn out of a boulder, yet there is a weakness in it, a petty pride in its own narrow strength. His* 230 *eyes are small, close together, and extremely near-sighted, blinking continually in the effort to focus on objects, their stare having a straining, ingrowing quality. He is dressed in his dismal black Sunday suit.* ABBIE *is thirty-five, buxom, full of vitality. Her round face is pretty but marred by its rather gross sensuality. There is strength and obstinacy in her jaw, a hard determination in her eyes, and about her whole personality the same unsettled, untamed, desperate* 240 *quality which is so apparent in* EBEN.)

CABOT (*as they enter—a queer strangled emotion in his dry cracking voice*). Har we be t' hum, Abbie.

ABBIE (*with lust for the word*). Hum! (*Her eyes gloating on the house without seeming to see the two stiff figures at the gate.*) It's purty —purty! I can't b'lieve it's r'ally mine.

CABOT (*sharply*). Yewr'n? Mine! (*He stares at her penetratingly. She stares back. He adds* 250 *relentingly.*) Our'n—mebbe! It was lonesome too long. I was growin' old in the spring. A hum's got t' hev a woman.

ABBIE (*her voice taking possession*). A woman's got t' hev a hum!

CABOT (*nodding uncertainly*). Ay-eh. (*Then irritably.*) Whar be they? Ain't thar nobody about—'r wukin'—'r nothin'?

ABBIE (*sees the brothers. She returns their stare of cold appraising contempt with interest* 260 *—slowly*). Thar's two men loafin' at the gate an' starin' at me like a couple o' strayed hogs.

CABOT (*straining his eyes*). I kin see 'em—but I can't make out. . . .

SIMEON. It's Simeon.

PETER. It's Peter.

CABOT (*exploding*). Why hain't ye wukin'?

SIMEON (*dryly*). We're waitin' t' welcome ye hum—yew an' the bride!

CABOT (*confusedly*). Huh? Waal—this be 270 yer new Maw, boys. (*She stares at them and they at her.*)

SIMEON (*turns away and spits contemptuously*). I see her!

PETER (*spits also*). An' I see her!

ABBIE (*with the conqueror's conscious superiority*). I'll go in an' look at *my* house. (*She goes slowly around to porch.*)

SIMEON (*with a snort*). *Her* house!

280 PETER (*calls after her*). Ye'll find Eben inside. Ye better not tell him it's *yewr* house.

ABBIE (*mouthing the name*). Eben. (*Then quietly.*) I'll tell Eben.

CABOT (*with a contemptuous sneer*). Ye needn't heed Eben. Eben's a dumb fool—like his Maw—soft an' simple!

SIMEON (*with his sardonic burst of laughter*). Ha! Eben's a chip o' yew—spit 'n' image—hard 'n' bitter's a hickory tree! Dog'll eat dog. He'll

290 eat ye yet, old man!

CABOT (*commandingly*). Ye git t' wuk!

SIMEON (*as* ABBIE *disappears in house—winks at* PETER *and says tauntingly*). So that thar's our new Maw, be it? Whar in hell did ye dig her up? (*He and* PETER *laugh.*)

PETER. Ha! Ye'd better turn her in the pen with the other sows. (*They laugh uproariously, slapping their thighs.*)

CABOT (*so amazed at their effrontery that he*

300 *stutters in confusion*). Simeon! Peter! What's come over ye? Air ye drunk?

SIMEON. We're free, old man—free o' yew an' the hull damned farm! (*They grow more and more hilarious and excited.*)

PETER. An' we're startin' out fur the gold fields o' Californi-a!

SIMEON. Ye kin take this place an' burn it!

PETER. An' bury it—fur all we cares!

SIMEON. We're free, old man! (*He cuts a*

310 *caper.*)

PETER. Free! (*He gives a kick in the air.*)

SIMEON (*in a frenzy*). Whoop!

PETER. Whoop! (*They do an absurd Indian war dance about the old man who is petrified between rage and the fear that they are insane.*)

SIMEON. We're free as Injuns! Lucky we don't skulp ye!

PETER. An' burn yer barn an' kill the stock!

SIMEON. An' rape yer new woman! Whoop!

320 (*He and* PETER *stop their dance, holding their sides, rocking with wild laughter.*)

CABOT (*edging away*). Lust fur gold—fur the sinful, easy gold o' Californi-a! It's made ye mad!

SIMEON (*tauntingly*). Wouldn't ye like us to send ye back some sinful gold, ye old sinner?

PETER. They's gold besides what's in Californi-a! (*He retreats back beyond the vision of the old man and takes the bag of money and flaunts it in the air above his head, laughing.*) 330

SIMEON. And sinfuller, too!

PETER. We'll be voyagin' on the sea! Whoop! (*He leaps up and down*).

SIMEON. Livin' free! Whoop! (*He leaps in turn.*)

CABOT (*suddenly roaring with rage*). My cuss on ye!

SIMEON. Take our'n in trade fur it! Whoop!

CABOT. I'll hev ye both chained up in the asylum! 340

PETER. Ye old skinflint! Good-by!

SIMEON. Ye old blood sucker! Good-by!

CABOT. Go afore I . . . !

PETER. Whoop! (*He picks a stone from the road.* SIMEON *does the same.*)

SIMEON. Maw'll be in the parlor.

PETER. Ay-eh! One! Two!

CABOT (*frightened*). What air ye. . . . ?

PETER. Three! (*They both throw, the stones hitting the parlor window with a crash of glass,* 350 *tearing the shade.*)

SIMEON. Whoop!

PETER. Whoop!

CABOT (*in a fury now, rushing toward them*). If I kin lay hands on ye—I'll break yer bones fur ye! (*But they beat a capering retreat before him,* SIMEON *with the gate still under his arm.* CABOT *comes back, panting with impotent rage. Their voices as they go off take up the song of the gold-seekers to the old tune of "Oh, Susan-* 360 *nah!"*)

I jumped aboard the Liza ship,
And traveled on the sea,
And every time I thought of home
I wished it wasn't me!
Oh! Californi-a,
That's the land fur me!
I'm off to Californi-a!
With my wash bowl on my knee.

(*In the meantime, the window of the upper* 370 *bedroom on right is raised and* ABBIE *sticks her head out. She looks down at* CABOT*—with a sigh of relief.*)

ABBIE. Waal—that's the last o' them two, hain't it? (*He doesn't answer. Then in posses-*

sive tones.) This here's a nice bedroom, Ephraim. It's a r'al nice bed. Is it my room, Ephraim?

CABOT (*grimly—without looking up*). Our'n! (*She cannot control a grimace of aversion and pulls back her head slowly and shuts the window. A sudden horrible thought seems to enter* CABOT's *head.*) They been up to somethin'! Mebbe—mebbe they've pizened the stock—'r somethin'! (*He almost runs off down toward the barn. A moment later the kitchen door is slowly pushed open and* ABBIE *enters. For a moment she stands looking at* EBEN. *He does not notice her at first. Her eyes take him in penetratingly with a calculating appraisal of his strength as against hers. But under this her desire is dimly awakened by his youth and good looks. Suddenly he becomes conscious of her presence and looks up. Their eyes meet. He leaps to his feet, glowering at her speechlessly.*)

ABBIE (*in her most seductive tones which she uses all through this scene*). Be you—Eben? I'm Abbie— (*She laughs.*) I mean, I'm yer new Maw.

EBEN (*viciously*). No, damn ye!

ABBIE (*as if she hadn't heard—with a queer smile*). Yer Paw's spoke a lot o' yew. . . .

EBEN. Ha!

ABBIE. Ye mustn't mind him. He's an old man. (*A long pause. They stare at each other.*) I don't want t' pretend playin' Maw t' ye, Eben. (*Admiringly.*) Ye're too big an' too strong fur that. I want t' be frens with ye. Mebbe with me fur a fren ye'd find ye'd like livin' here better. I kin make it easy fur ye with him, mebbe. (*With a scornful sense of power.*) I calc'late I kin git him t' do most anythin' fur me.

EBEN (*with bitter scorn*). Ha! (*They stare again,* EBEN *obscurely moved, physically attracted to her—in forced stilted tones.*) Yew kin go t' the devil!

ABBIE (*calmly*). If cussin' me does ye good, cuss all ye've a mind t'. I'm all prepared t' have ye agin me—at fust. I don't blame ye nuther. I'd feel the same at any stranger comin' t' take my Maw's place. (*He shudders. She is watching him carefully.*) Yew must've cared a lot fur yewr Maw, didn't ye? My Maw died afore I'd growed. I don't remember her none. (*A pause.*) But yew won't hate me long, Eben. I'm not the wust in the world—an' yew an' me've got a lot in common. I kin tell that by lookin' at ye. Waal—I've had a hard life, too—oceans o' trouble an' nuthin' but wuk fur reward. I was a orphan early an' had t' wuk fur others in other folks' hums. Then I married an' he turned out a drunken spreer an' so he had to wuk fur others an' me too agen in other folks' hums, an' the baby died, an' my husband got sick an' died too, an' I was glad sayin' now I'm free fur once, on'y diskivered right away all I was free fur was t' wuk agen in other folks' hums, doin' other folks' wuk till I'd most give up hope o' ever doin' my own wuk in my own hum, an' then your Paw come. . . . (CABOT *appears returning from the barn. He comes to the gate and looks down the road the brothers have gone. A faint strain of their retreating voices is heard: "Oh, Californi-a! That's the place for me." He stands glowering, his fist clenched, his face grim with rage.*)

EBEN (*fighting against his growing attraction and sympathy—harshly*). An' bought yew—like a harlot! (*She is stung and flushes angrily. She has been sincerely moved by the recital of her troubles. He adds furiously.*) An' the price he's payin' ye—this farm—was my Maw's, damn ye!—an' mine now!

ABBIE (*with a cool laugh of confidence*). Yewr'n? We'll see 'bout that! (*Then strongly.*) Waal—what if I did need a hum? What else'd I marry an old man like him fur?

EBEN (*maliciously*). I'll tell him ye said that!

ABBIE (*smiling*). I'll say ye're lyin' a-purpose —an' he'll drive ye off the place!

EBEN. Ye devil!

ABBIE (*defying him*). This be my farm—this be my hum—this be my kitchen—!

EBEN (*furiously, as if he were going to attack her*). Shut up, damn ye!

ABBIE (*walks up to him—a queer coarse expression of desire in her face and body—slowly*). An' upstairs—that be my bedroom—an' my bed! (*He stares into her eyes, terribly confused and torn. She adds softly.*) I hain't bad nor mean —'ceptin' fur an enemy—but I got t' fight fur what's due me out o' life, if I ever 'spect t' git it. (*Then putting her hand on his arm—seductively.*) Let's yew 'n' me be frens, Eben.

EBEN (*stupidly—as if hypnotized*). Ay-eh. (*Then furiously flinging off her arm.*) No, ye durned old witch! I hate ye! (*He rushes out the door.*)

ABBIE (*looks after him smiling satisfiedly—then half to herself, mouthing the word*). Eben's nice. (*She looks at the table, proudly.*) I'll wash up *my* dishes now. (EBEN *appears outside, slamming the door behind him. He comes around corner, stops on seeing his father, and stands staring at him with hate.*)

CABOT (*raising his arms to heaven in the fury he can no longer control*). Lord God o' Hosts, smite the undutiful sons with Thy wust cuss!

EBEN (*breaking in violently*). Yew 'n' yewr God! Allus cussin' folks—allus naggin' em!

CABOT (*oblivious to him—summoningly*). God o' the old! God o' the lonesome!

EBEN (*mockingly*). Naggin' His sheep t' sin! T' hell with yewr God! (CABOT *turns. He and* EBEN *glower at each other.*)

CABOT (*harshly*). So it's yew. I might've knowed it. (*Shaking his finger threateningly at him.*) Blasphemin' fool! (*Then quickly.*) Why hain't ye t' wuk?

EBEN. Why hain't yew? They've went. I can't wuk it all alone.

CABOT (*contemptuously*). Nor noways! I'm wuth ten o' ye yit, old's I be! Ye'll never be more'n half a man! (*Then, matter-of-factly.*) Waal—let's git t' the barn. (*They go. A last faint note of the "Californi-a" song is heard from the distance.* ABBIE *is washing her dishes.*)

(*The curtain falls.*)

PART TWO *Scene One*

(*The exterior of the farmhouse, as in Part I—a hot Sunday afternoon two months later.* ABBIE, *dressed in her best, is discovered sitting in a rocker at the end of the porch. She rocks listlessly, enervated by the heat, staring in front of her with bored, half-closed eyes.*)

(EBEN *sticks his head out of his bedroom window. He looks around furtively and tries to see—or hear—if anyone is on the porch, but although he has been careful to make no noise,* ABBIE *has sensed his movement. She stops rocking, her face grows animated and eager, she waits attentively.* EBEN *seems to feel her presence, he scowls back his thoughts of her and spits with exaggerated disdain—then withdraws back into the room.* ABBIE *waits, holding her breath as she listens with passionate eagerness for every sound within the house.*)

(EBEN *comes out. Their eyes meet. His falter, he is confused, he turns away and slams the door resentfully. At this gesture,* ABBIE *laughs tantalizingly, amused but at the same time piqued and irritated. He scowls, strides off the porch to the path and starts to walk past her to the road with a grand swagger of ignoring her existence. He is dressed in his store suit, spruced up, his face shines from soap and water.* ABBIE *leans forward on her chair, her eyes hard and angry now, and, as he passes her, gives a sneering, taunting chuckle.*)

EBEN (*stung—turns on her furiously*). What air yew cacklin' 'bout?

ABBIE (*triumphant*). Yew!

EBEN. What about me?

ABBIE. Ye look all slicked up like a prize bull.

EBEN (*with a sneer*). Waal—ye hain't so durned purty yerself, be ye? (*They stare into each other's eyes, his held by hers in spite of himself, hers glowingly possessive. Their physical attraction becomes a palpable force quivering in the hot air.*)

ABBIE (*softly*). Ye don't mean that, Eben. Ye may think ye mean it, mebbe, but ye don't. Ye can't. It's agin nature, Eben. Ye been fightin' yer nature ever since the day I come—tryin' t' tell yerself I hain't purty t'ye. (*She laughs a low humid laugh without taking her eyes from *his. A pause—her body squirms desirously—she* 20 *murmurs languorously.*) Hain't the sun strong an' hot? Ye kin feel it burnin' into the earth—Nature—makin' thin's grow—bigger 'n' bigger—burnin' inside ye—makin' ye want t' grow—into somethin' else—till ye're jined with it—an' it's your'n—but it owns ye, too—an' makes ye grow bigger—like a tree—like them elums—(*She laughs again softly, holding his eyes. He takes a step toward her, compelled against his will.*) Nature'll beat ye, Eben. Ye might's well 30 own up t' it fust 's last.

EBEN (*trying to break from her spell—confusedly*). If Paw'd hear ye goin' on. . . . (*Resentfully.*) But ye've made such a damned idjit out o' the old devil . . . ! (ABBIE *laughs.*)

ABBIE. Waal—hain't it easier fur yew with him changed softer?

EBEN (*defiantly*). No. I'm fightin' him—fightin' yew—fightin' fur Maw's rights t' her hum! (*This breaks her spell for him. He glowers at her.*) 40 An' I'm onto ye. Ye hain't foolin' me a mite. Ye're aimin' t' swaller up everythin' an' make it your'n. Waal, you'll find I'm a heap sight bigger hunk nor yew kin chew! (*He turns from her with a sneer.*)

ABBIE (*trying to regain her ascendancy—seductively*). Eben!

EBEN. Leave me be! (*He starts to walk away.*)

ABBIE (*more commandingly*). Eben!

50 EBEN (*stops—resentfully*). What d'ye want?

ABBIE (*trying to conceal a growing excitement*). Whar air ye goin'?

EBEN (*with malicious nonchalance*). Oh—up the road a spell.

ABBIE. T' the village?

EBEN (*airily*). Mebbe.

ABBIE (*excitedly*). T' see that Min, I s'pose?

EBEN. Mebbe.

ABBIE (*weakly*). What d'ye want t' waste 60 time on her fur?

EBEN (*revenging himself now—grinning at her*). Ye can't beat Nature, didn't ye say? (*He laughs and again starts to walk away.*)

ABBIE (*bursting out*). An ugly old hake!

EBEN (*with a tantalizing sneer*). She's purtier'n yew be!

ABBIE. That every wuthless drunk in the country has. . . .

EBEN (*tauntingly*). Mebbe—but she's better'n yew. She owns up fa'r 'n squar' t' her doin's. 70

ABBIE (*furiously*). Don't ye dare compare. . . .

EBEN. She don't go sneakin' an stealin'—what's mine.

ABBIE (*savagely seizing on his weak point*). Your'n? You mean—my farm!

EBEN. I mean the farm yew sold yerself fur like any other old whore—my farm!

ABBIE (*stung—fiercely*). Ye'll never live t' see the day when even a stinkin' weed on it 'll 80 belong t' ye! (*Then in a scream.*) Git out o' my sight! Go on t' yer slut—disgracin' yer Paw 'n' me! I'll git yer Paw t' horsewhip ye off the place if I want t'! Ye're only livin' here 'cause I tolerate ye! Git along! I hate the sight o' ye! (*She stops, panting and glaring at him.*)

EBEN (*returning her glance in kind*). An' I hate the sight o' yew! (*He turns and strides off up the road. She follows his retreating figure with concentrated hate. Old* CABOT *appears com-* 90 *ing up from the barn. The hard, grim expression of his face has changed. He seems in some queer way softened, mellowed. His eyes have taken on a strange, incongruous dreamy quality. Yet there is no hint of physical weakness about him—rather he looks more robust and younger.* ABBIE *sees him and turns away quickly with unconcealed aversion. He comes slowly up to her.*)

CABOT (*mildly*). War yew an' Eben quar- 100 relin' agen?

ABBIE (*shortly*). No.

CABOT. Ye was talkin' a'mighty loud. (*He sits down on the edge of porch*).

ABBIE (*snappishly*). If ye heerd us they hain't no need askin' questions.

CABOT. I didn't hear what ye said.

ABBIE (*relieved*). Waal—it wa'n't nothin' t' speak on.

CABOT (*after a pause*). Eben's queer. 110

ABBIE (*bitterly*). He's the dead spit 'n' image o' yew!

CABOT (*queerly interested*). D'ye think so, Abbie? (*After a pause, ruminatingly.*) Me 'n' Eben's allus fit 'n' fit. I never could b'ar him noways. He's so thunderin' soft—like his Maw.

ABBIE (*scornfully*). Ay-eh! 'Bout as soft as yew be!

CABOT (*as if he hadn't heard*). Mebbe I been too hard on him. 120

ABBIE (*jeeringly*). Waal—ye're gittin' soft now—soft as slop! That's what Eben was sayin'.

CABOT (*his face instantly grim and ominous*). Eben was sayin'? Waal, he'd best not do nothin' t' try me 'r he'll soon diskiver. . . . (*A pause. She keeps her face turned away. His gradually softens. He stares up at the sky.*) Purty, hain't it?

ABBIE (*crossly*). I don't see nothin' purty.

130 CABOT. The sky. Feels like a wa'm field up thar.

ABBIE (*sarcastically*). Air yew aimin' t' buy up over the farm too? (*She snickers contemptuously.*)

CABOT (*strangely*). I'd like t' own my place up thar. (*A pause.*) I'm gittin' old, Abbie. I'm gittin' ripe on the bough. (*A pause. She stares at him mystified. He goes on.*) It's allus lonesome cold in the house—even when it's bilin'

140 hot outside. Hain't yew noticed?

ABBIE. No.

CABOT. It's wa'm down t' the barn—nice smellin' an warm—with the cows. (*A pause.*) Cows is queer.

ABBIE. Like yew?

CABOT. Like Eben. (*A pause.*) I'm gittin' t' feel resigned t' Eben—jest as I got t' feel 'bout his Maw. I'm gittin' t' learn to b'ar his softness —jest like her'n. I calc'late I c'd a'most take t'

150 him—if he wa'n't sech a dumb fool! (*A pause.*) I s'pose it's old age a-creepin' in my bones.

ABBIE (*indifferently*). Waal—ye hain't dead yet.

CABOT (*roused*). No, I hain't, yew bet—not by a hell of a sight—I'm sound 'n' tough as hickory! (*Then moodily.*) But arter three score and ten the Lord warns ye t' prepare. (*A pause.*) That's why Eben's come in my head. Now that his cussed sinful brothers is gone their path t'

160 hell, they's no one left but Eben.

ABBIE (*resentfully*). They's me, hain't they? (*Agitatedly.*) What's all this sudden likin' ye've tuk to Eben? Why don't ye saying nothin' 'bout me? Hain't I yer lawful wife?

CABOT (*simply*). Ay-eh. Ye be. (*A pause—he stares at her desirously—his eyes grow avid —then with a sudden movement he seizes her hands and squeezes them, declaiming in a queer camp meeting preacher's tempo.*) Yew air my

170 Rose o' Sharon! Behold, yew air fair; yer eyes air doves; yer lips air like scarlet; yer two breasts air like two fawns; yer navel be like a round goblet; yer belly be like a heap o' wheat. . . . (*He covers her hands with kisses. She does not seem to notice. She stares before her with hard angry eyes.*)

ABBIE (*jerking her hands away—harshly*). So ye're plannin' t' leave the farm t' Eben, air ye?

CABOT (*dazedly*). Leave . . . ? (*Then with resentful obstinacy.*) I hain't a-givin' it t' no 180 one!

ABBIE (*remorselessly*). Ye can't take it with ye.

CABOT (*thinks a moment—then reluctantly*). No, I calc'late not. (*After a pause—with a strange passion.*) But if I could, I would, by the Etarnal! 'R if I could, in my dyin' hour, I'd set it afire an' watch it burn—this house an' every ear o' corn an' every tree down t' the last blade o' hay! I'd sit an' know it was all a-dying with 190 me an' no one else'd ever own what was mine, what I'd made out o' nothin' with my own sweat 'n' blood! (*A pause—then he adds with a queer affection.*) 'Ceptin' the cows. Them I'd turn free.

ABBIE (*harshly*). An' me?

CABOT (*with a queer smile*). Ye'd be turned free, too.

ABBIE (*furiously*). So that's the thanks I git fur marryin' ye—t' have ye change kind to 200 Eben who hates ye, an' talk o' turnin' me out in the road.

CABOT (*hastily*). Abbie! Ye know I wa'n't. . . .

ABBIE (*vengefully*). Just let me tell ye a thing or two 'bout Eben! Whar's he gone? T' see that harlot, Min! I tried fur t' stop him. Disgracin' yew an' me—on the Sabbath, too!

CABOT (*rather guiltily*). He's a sinner—nateral-born. It's lust eatin' his heart. 210

ABBIE (*enraged beyond endurance—wildly vindictive*). An' his lust fur me! Kin ye find excuses fur that?

CABOT (*stares at her—after a dead pause*). Lust—fur yew?

ABBIE (*defiantly*). He was tryin' t' make love t' me—when ye heerd us quarrelin'.

CABOT (*stares at her—then a terrible expression of rage comes over his face—he springs to his feet shaking all over*). By the A'mighty 220 God—I'll end him!

ABBIE (*frightened now for* EBEN). No! Don't ye!

CABOT (*violently*). I'll git the shotgun an'

blow his soft brains t' the top o' them elums!

ABBIE (*throwing her arms around him*). No, Ephraim!

CABOT (*pushing her away violently*). I will, by God!

230 ABBIE (*in a quieting tone*). Listen, Ephraim. 'Twa'n't nothin' bad—on'y a boy's foolin'—'twa'n't meant serious—jest jokin' an' teasin'. . . .

CABOT. Then why did ye say—lust?

ABBIE. It must hev sounded wusser'n I meant. An' I was mad at thinkin'—ye'd leave him the farm.

CABOT (*quieter but still grim and cruel*). Waal then, I'll horsewhip him off the place if

240 that much'll content ye.

ABBIE (*reaching out and taking his hand*). No. Don't think o' me! Ye mustn't drive him off. 'Tain't sensible. Who'll ye get to help ye on the farm? They's no one hereabouts.

CABOT (*considers this—then nodding his appreciation*). Ye got a head on ye. (*Then irritably.*) Waal, let him stay. (*He sits down on the edge of the porch. She sits beside him. He murmurs contemptuously.*) I oughtn't t' git

250 riled so—at that 'ere fool calf. (*pause.*) But har's the p'int. What son o' mine'll keep on here t' the farm—when the Lord does call me? Simeon an' Peter air gone to hell—an Eben's follerin' 'em.

ABBIE. They's me.

CABOT. Ye're on'y a woman.

ABBIE. I'm yewr wife.

CABOT. That hain't me. A son is me—my blood—mine. Mine ought t' git mine. An' then

260 it's still mine—even though I be six foot under. D'ye see?

ABBIE (*giving him a look of hatred*). Ay-eh. I see. (*She becomes very thoughtful, her face growing shrewd, her eyes studying* CABOT *craftily.*)

CABOT. I'm gittin' old—ripe on the bough. (*Then with a sudden forced reassurance.*) Not but what I hain't a hard nut t' crack even yet—an' fur many a year t' come! By the Etarnal, I kin break most o' the young fellers' backs at 270 any kind o' work any day o' the year!

ABBIE (*suddenly*). Mebbe the Lord'll give *us* a son.

CABOT (*turns and stares at her eagerly*). Ye mean—a son—t' me 'n' yew?

ABBIE (*with a cajoling smile*). Ye're a strong man yet, hain't ye? 'Taint noways impossible, be it? We know that. Why d'ye stare so? Hain't ye never thought o' that afore? I been thinkin' o' it all along. Ay-eh—an' I been prayin' 280 it'd happen, too.

CABOT (*his face growing full of joyous pride and a sort of religious ecstasy*). Ye been prayin', Abbie?—fur a son?—t' us?

ABBIE. Ay-eh. (*With a grim resolution.*) I want a son now.

CABOT (*excitedly clutching both of her hands in his*). It'd be the blessin' o' God, Abbie—the blessin' o' God A'mighty on me—in my old age—in my lonesomeness! They hain't 290 nothin' I wouldn't do fur ye then, Abbie. Ye'd hev on'y t' ask it—anythin' ye'd a mind t'!

ABBIE (*interrupting*). Would ye will the farm t' me then—t' me an' it . . . ?

CABOT (*vehemently*). I'd do anythin' ye axed, I tell ye! I swar it! May I be everlastin' damned t' hell if I wouldn't! (*He sinks to his knees pulling her down with him. He trembles all over with the fervor of his hopes.*) Pray t' the Lord agen, Abbie. It's the Sabbath! I'll jine 300 ye! Two prayers air better nor one. "An' God hearkened unto Rachel"! An' God hearkened unto Abbie! Pray, Abbie! Pray fur him to hearken! (*He bows his head, mumbling. She pretends to do likewise but gives him a side glance of scorn and triumph.*)

Scene Two

(*About eight in the evening. The interior of the two bedrooms on the top floor is shown.* EBEN *is sitting on the side of his bed in the room on the left. On account of the heat he has taken off everything but his undershirt and pants. His feet are bare. He faces front, brooding moodily, his chin propped on his hands, a desperate expression on his face.)*

(In the other room CABOT *and* ABBIE *are sitting side by side on the edge of their bed, an old four-poster with feather mattress. He is in his night shirt, she in her nightdress. He is still in the queer, excited mood into which the notion of a son has thrown him. Both rooms are lighted dimly and flickeringly by tallow candles.)*

CABOT. The farm needs a son.

ABBIE. I need a son.

CABOT. Ay-eh. Sometimes ye air the farm an' sometimes the farm be yew. That's why I clove t' ye in my lonesomeness. *(A pause. He pounds his knee with his fist.)* Me an' the farm has got t' beget a son!

ABBIE. Ye'd best go t' sleep. Ye're gittin' thin's all mixed.

CABOT *(with an impatient gesture)*. No, I hain't. My mind's clear's a well. Ye don't know me, that's it. *(He stares hopelessly at the floor.)*

ABBIE *(indifferently)*. Mebbe. *(In the next room* EBEN *gets up and paces up and down distractedly.* ABBIE *hears him. Her eyes fasten on the intervening wall with concentrated attention.* EBEN *stops and stares. Their hot glances seem to meet through the wall. Unconsciously he stretches out his arms for her and she half rises. Then aware, he mutters a curse at himself and flings himself face downward on the bed, his clenched fists above his head, his face buried in the pillow.* ABBIE *relaxes with a faint sigh but her eyes remain fixed on the wall; she listens with all her attention for some movement from* EBEN.)

CABOT *(suddenly raises his head and looks at her—scornfully)*. Will ye ever know me—'r will any man 'r woman? *(Shaking his head.)* No. I calc'late 't wa'n't t' be. *(He turns away.* ABBIE *looks at the wall. Then, evidently unable to keep silent about his thoughts, without looking at his wife, he puts out his hand and clutches her knee. She starts violently, looks at him, sees he is not watching her, concentrates again on the wall and pays no attention to what he says.)* Listen, Abbie. When I come here fifty odd year ago—I was jest twenty an' the strongest an' hardest ye ever seen—ten times as strong an' fifty times as hard as Eben. Waal—this place was nothin' but fields o' stones. Folks laughed when I tuk it. They couldn't know what I knowed. When ye kin make corn sprout out o' stones, God's livin' in yew! They wa'n't strong enuf fur that! They reckoned God was easy. They laughed. They don't laugh no more. Some died hereabouts. Some went West an' died. They're all under ground—fur follerin' arter an easy God. God hain't easy. *(He shakes his head slowly.)* An' I growed hard. Folks kept allus sayin' he's a hard man like 'twas sinful t' be hard, so's at last I said back at 'em: Waal then, by thunder, ye'll git me hard an' see how ye like it! *(Then suddenly.)* But I give in t' weakness once. 'Twas arter I'd been here two year. I got weak—despairful—they was so many stones. They was a party leavin', givin' up, goin' West. I jined 'em. We tracked on 'n' on. We come t' broad medders, plains, whar the soil was black an' rich as gold. Nary a stone. Easy. Ye'd on'y to plow an' sow an' then set an' smoke yer pipe an' watch thin's grow. I could o' been a rich man—but somethin' in me fit me an' fit me—the voice o' God sayin': "This hain't wuth nothin' t' Me. Git ye back t' hum!" I got afeerd o' that voice an' I lit out back t' hum here, leavin' my claim an' crops t' whoever'd a mind t' take 'em. Ay-eh. I actoolly give up what was rightful mine! God's hard, not easy! God's in the stones! Build my church on a rock—out o' stones an' I'll be in them! That's what He meant t' Peter! *(He sighs heavily—a pause.)* Stones. I picked 'em up an' piled 'em into walls. Ye kin read the years o' my life in them walls, every day a hefted stone, climbin' over the hills up and down, fencin' in the fields that was mine, whar I'd made thin's grow out o' nothin'—like the will o' God, like the servant o' His hand. It wa'n't easy. It was hard an' He made me hard fur it. *(He pauses.)* All the time I kept gittin' lonesomer. I tuk a wife. She bore Simeon an' Peter. She was a good woman. She wuked hard. We was married twenty year. She never knowed me. She helped but she never knowed what she was helpin'. I was allus lonesome. She died. After that it wa'n't so lonesome fur a spell. *(A pause.)* I lost count o' the years. I had no time t' fool away countin' 'em. Sim an' Peter helped. The farm growed. It was all mine! When I thought o' that I didn't feel lonesome. (*A pause.*) But ye can't hitch yer mind t' one thin' day an' night. I tuk another wife—Eben's Maw. Her folks contestin' me at law over my deeds t' the farm—my farm! That's why Eben keeps a-talkin' his fool talk o' this bein' his Maw's farm. She bore Eben. She was purty—but soft. She tried t' be hard. She couldn't. She never knowed me nor nothin'. It was lonesomer 'n hell with her. After a matter o' 100 sixteen odd years, she died. (*A pause.*) I lived with the boys. They hated me 'cause I was hard. I hated them 'cause they was soft. They coveted the farm without knowin' what it meant. It made me bitter 'n wormwood. It aged me—them coveting what I'd made fur mine. Then this spring the call come—the voice o' God cryin' in my wilderness, in my lonesomeness—t' go out an' seek an' find! (*Turning to her with strange passion.*) I sought ye an' I found ye! 110 Yew air my Rose o' Sharon! Yer eyes air like. . . . (*She has turned a blank face, resentful eyes to his. He stares at her for a moment—then harshly.*) Air ye any the wiser fur all I've told ye?

ABBIE (*confusedly*). Mebbe.

CABOT (*pushing her away from him—angrily*). Ye don't know nothin'—nor never will. If ye don't hev a son t' redeem ye. . . . (*This in a tone of cold threat.*)

120 ABBIE (*resentfully*). I've prayed, hain't I?

CABOT (*bitterly*). Pray agen—fur understandin'!

ABBIE (*a veiled threat in her tone*). Ye'll have a son out o' me, I promise ye.

CABOT. How kin ye promise?

ABBIE. I got second-sight, mebbe. I kin foretell. (*She gives a queer smile.*)

CABOT. I believe ye have. Ye give me the chills sometimes. (*He shivers.*) It's cold in this 130 house. It's oneasy. They's thin's pokin' about in the dark—in the corners. (*He pulls on his trousers, tucking in his night shirt, and pulls on his boots.*)

ABBIE (*surprised*). Whar air ye goin'?

CABOT (*queerly*). Down whar it's restful—whar it's warm—down t' the barn. (*Bitterly.*) I kin talk t' the cows. They know. They know the farm an' me. They'll give me peace. (*He turns to go out the door.*)

140 ABBIE (*a bit frightenedly*). Air ye ailin' tonight, Ephraim?

CABOT. Growin'. Growin' ripe on the bough. (*He turns and goes, his boots clumping down the stairs.* EBEN *sits up with a start, listening.* ABBIE *is conscious of his movement and stares at the wall.* CABOT *comes out of the house around the corner and stands by the gate, blinking at the sky. He stretches up his hands in a tortured gesture.*) God A'mighty, call from the dark!

(*He listens as if expecting an answer. Then his* 150 *arms drop, he shakes his head and plods off toward the barn.* EBEN *and* ABBIE *stare at each other through the wall.* EBEN *sighs heavily and* ABBIE *echoes it. Both become terribly nervous, uneasy. Finally* ABBIE *gets up and listens, her ear to the wall. He acts as if he saw every move she was making, he becomes resolutely still. She seems driven into a decision—goes out the door in rear determinedly. His eyes follow her. Then as the door of his room is opened softly, he* 160 *turns away, waits in an attitude of strained fixity.* ABBIE *stands for a second staring at him, her eyes burning with desire. Then with a little cry she runs over and throws her arms about his neck, she pulls his head back and covers his mouth with kisses. At first, he submits dumbly; then he puts his arms about her neck and returns her kisses, but finally, suddenly aware of his hatred, he hurls her away from him, springing to his feet. They stand speechless and breath-* 170 *less, panting like two animals.*)

ABBIE (*at last—painfully*). Ye shouldn't, Eben—ye shouldn't—I'd make ye happy!

EBEN (*harshly*). I don't want t' be happy—from yew!

ABBIE (*helplessly*). Ye do, Eben! Ye do! Why d'ye lie?

EBEN (*viciously*). I don't take t'ye, I tell ye! I hate the sight o'ye!

ABBIE (*with an uncertain troubled laugh*). 180 Waal, I kissed ye anyways—an' ye kissed back —yer lips was burnin'—ye can't lie 'bout that! (*Intensely.*) If ye don't care, why did ye kiss me back—why was yer lips burnin'?

EBEN (*wiping his mouth*). It was like pizen on 'em. (*Then tauntingly.*) When I kissed ye back, mebbe I thought 'twas someone else.

ABBIE (*wildly*). Min?

EBEN. Mebbe.

ABBIE (*torturedly*). Did ye go t' see her? 190

Did ye r'ally go? I thought ye mightn't. Is that why ye throwed me off jest now?

EBEN (*sneeringly*). What if it be?

ABBIE (*raging*). Then ye're a dog, Eben Cabot!

EBEN (*threateningly*). Ye can't talk that way t' me!

ABBIE (*with a shrill laugh*). Can't I? Did ye think I was in love with ye—a weak thin' like yew! Not much! I on'y wanted ye fur a pur- 200 pose o' my own—an' I'll hev ye fur it yet 'cause I'm stronger'n yew be!

EBEN (*resentfully*). I knowed well it was on'y part o' yer plan t' swaller everythin'!

ABBIE (*tauntingly*). Mebbe!

EBEN (*furious*). Git out o' my room!

ABBIE. This air my room an' ye're on'y hired help!

EBEN (*threateningly*). Git out afore I murder ye! 210

ABBIE (*quite confident now*). I hain't a mite afeered. Ye want me, don't ye? Yes, ye do! An yer Paw's son'll never kill what he wants! Look at yer eyes! They's lust fur me in 'em, burnin' 'em up! Look at yer lips now! They're tremblin' an' longin' t' kiss me, an' yer teeth t' bite! (*He is watching her now with a horrible fascination. She laughs a crazy triumphant laugh.*) I'm a-goin' t' make all o' this hum my hum! They's one room hain't mine yet, but it's a-goin' t' be 220 tonight. I'm a-goin' down now an' light up! (*She makes him a mocking bow.*) Won't ye come courtin' me in the best parlor, Mister Cabot?

EBEN (*staring at her—horribly confused—dully*). Don't ye dare! It hain't been opened since Maw died an' was laid out thar! Don't ye . . . ! (*But her eyes are fixed on his so burningly that his will seems to wither before hers. He stands swaying toward her helplessly.*)

ABBIE (*holding his eyes and putting all her* 230 *will into her words as she backs out the door*). I'll expect ye afore long, Eben.

EBEN (*stares after her for a while, walking toward the door. A light appears in the parlor window. He murmurs*). In the parlor? (*This seems to arouse connotations for he comes back and puts on his white shirt, collar, half ties the tie mechanically, puts on coat, takes his hat, stands barefooted looking about him in bewilderment, mutters wonderingly.*) Maw! Whar 240 air yew? (*Then goes slowly toward the door in rear.*)

Scene Three

(*A few minutes later. The interior of the parlor is shown. A grim, repressed room like a tomb in which the family has been interred alive.* ABBIE *sits on the edge of the horsehair sofa. She has lighted all the candles and the room is revealed in all its preserved ugliness. A change has come over the woman. She looks awed and frightened now, ready to run away.*)

(*The door is opened and* EBEN *appears. His face wears an expression of obsessed confusion. He stands staring at her, his arms hanging disjointedly from his shoulders, his feet bare, his hat in his hand.*)

ABBIE (*after a pause—with a nervous, formal politeness*). Won't ye set?

EBEN (*dully*). Ay-eh. (*Mechanically he places his hat carefully on the floor near the door and sits stiffly beside her on the edge of the sofa. A pause. They both remain rigid, looking straight ahead with eyes full of fear.*)

ABBIE. When I fust come in—in the dark—they seemed somethin' here.

EBEN (*simply*). Maw. 10

ABBIE. I kin still feel—somethin'. . . .

EBEN. It's Maw.

ABBIE. At first I was feered o' it. I wanted t' yell an' run. Now—since yew come—seems like it's growin' soft an' kind t' me. (*Addressing the air—queerly.*) Thank yew.

EBEN. Maw allus loved me.

ABBIE. Mebbe it knows I love yew, too. Mebbe that makes it kind t' me.

20 EBEN (*dully*). I dunno. I should think she'd hate ye.

ABBIE (*with certainty*). No. I kin feel it don't—not no more.

EBEN. Hate ye fur stealin' her place—here in her hum—settin' in her parlor whar she was laid— (*He suddenly stops, staring stupidly before him.*)

ABBIE. What is it, Eben?

EBEN (*in a whisper*). Seems like Maw didn't

30 want me t' remind ye.

ABBIE (*excitedly*). I knowed, Eben! It's kind t' me! It don't b'ar me no grudges fur what I never knowed an' couldn't help!

EBEN. Maw b'ars him a grudge.

ABBIE. Waal, so does all o' us.

EBEN. Ay-eh. (*With passion.*) I does, by God!

ABBIE (*taking one of his hands in hers and patting it*). Thar! Don't git riled thinkin' o'

40 him. Think o' yer Maw who's kind t' us. Tell me about yer Maw, Eben.

EBEN. They hain't nothin' much. She was kind. She was good.

ABBIE (*putting one arm over his shoulder. He does not seem to notice—passionately*). I'll be kind an' good t' ye!

EBEN. Sometimes she used t' sing fur me.

ABBIE. I'll sing fur ye!

EBEN. This was her hum. This was her farm.

50 ABBIE. This is my hum! This is my farm!

EBEN. He married her t' steal 'em. She was soft an' easy. He couldn't 'preciate her.

ABBIE. He can't 'preciate me!

EBEN. He murdered her with his hardness.

ABBIE. He's murderin' me!

EBEN. She died. (*A pause.*) Sometimes she used to sing fur me. (*He bursts into a fit of sobbing.*)

ABBIE (*both her arms around him—with wild*

60 *passion*). I'll sing fur ye! I'll die fur ye! (*In spite of her overwhelming desire for him, there is a sincere maternal love in her manner and voice—a horribly frank mixture of lust and mother love.*) Don't cry, Eben! I'll take yer Maw's place! I'll be everythin' she was t' ye! Let me kiss ye, Eben! (*She pulls his head around. He makes a bewildered pretense of resistance. She is tender.*) Don't be afeered! I'll kiss ye pure, Eben—same 's if I was a Maw t' ye—an' ye kin kiss me back 's if yew was my son—my 70 boy—sayin' good-night t' me! Kiss me, Eben. (*They kiss in restrained fashion. Then suddenly wild passion overcomes her. She kisses him lustfully again and again and he flings his arms about her and returns her kisses. Suddenly, as in the bedroom, he frees himself from her violently and springs to his feet. He is trembling all over, in a strange state of terror.* ABBIE *strains her arms toward him with fierce pleading.*) Don't ye leave me, Eben! Can't ye see it 80 hain't enuf—lovin' ye like a Maw—can't ye see it's got t' be that an' more—much more—a hundred times more—fur me t' be happy—fur yew t' be happy?

EBEN (*to the presence he feels in the room*). Maw! Maw! What d'ye want? What air ye tellin' me?

ABBIE. She's tellin' ye t' love me. She knows I love ye an' I'll be good t' ye. Can't ye feel it? Don't ye know? She's tellin' ye t' love me, 90 Eben!

EBEN. Ay-eh. I feel—mebbe she—but—I can't figger out—why—when ye've stole her place—here in her hum—in the parlor whar she was—

ABBIE (*fiercely*). She knows I love ye!

EBEN (*his face suddenly lighting up with a fierce, triumphant grin*). I see it! I sees why. It's her vengeance on him—so's she kin rest quiet in her grave! 100

ABBIE (*wildly*). Vengeance o' God on the hull o' us! What d'we give a durn? I love ye, Eben! God knows I love ye! (*She stretches out her arms for him.*)

EBEN (*throws himself on his knees beside the sofa and grabs her in his arms—releasing all his pent-up passion*). An' I love yew, Abbie! —now I kin say it! I been dyin' fur want o' ye —every hour since ye come! I love ye! (*Their lips meet in a fierce, bruising kiss.*) 110

Scene Four

(Exterior of the farmhouse. It is just dawn. The front door at right is opened and EBEN *comes out and walks around to the gate. He is dressed in his working clothes. He seems changed. His face wears a bold and confident expression, he is grinning to himself with evident satisfaction. As he gets near the gate, the window of the parlor is heard opening and the shutters are flung back and* ABBIE *sticks her head out. Her hair tumbles over her shoulders in disarray, her face is flushed, she looks at* EBEN *with tender, languorous eyes and calls softly.)*

ABBIE. Eben. *(As he turns—playfully.)* Jest one more kiss afore ye go. I'm goin' t' miss ye fearful all day.

EBEN. An me yew, ye kin bet! *(He goes to her. They kiss several times. He draws away, laughingly.)* Thar. That's enuf, hain't it? Ye won't hev none left fur next time.

ABBIE. I got a million o' 'em left fur yew! *(Then a bit anxiously.)* D'ye r'ally love me, Eben? 10

EBEN *(emphatically)*. I like ye better'n any gal I ever knowed! That's gospel!

ABBIE. Likin' hain't lovin'.

EBEN. Waal then—I love ye. Now air yew satisfied?

ABBIE. Ay-eh, I be. *(She smiles at him adoringly.)*

EBEN. I better git t' the barn. The old critter's liable t' suspicion an' come sneakin' up.

ABBIE *(with a confident laugh)*. Let him! I kin allus pull the wool over his eyes. I'm goin' t' leave the shutters open and let in the sun 'n' air. This room's been dead long enuf. Now it's goin' t' be my room! 20

EBEN *(frowning)*. Ay-eh.

ABBIE *(hastily)*. I meant—our room.

EBEN. Ay-eh.

ABBIE. We made it our'n last night, didn't we? We give it life—our lovin' did. *(A pause.)*

EBEN *(with a strange look)*. Maw's gone back t' her grave. She kin sleep now. 30

ABBIE. May she rest in peace! *(Then tenderly rebuking.)* Ye oughtn't t' talk o' sad thin's—this mornin'.

EBEN. It jest come up in my mind o' itself.

ABBIE. Don't let it. *(He doesn't answer. She yawns.)* Waal, I'm a-goin' t' steal a wink o' sleep. I'll tell the Old Man I hain't feelin' pert. Let him git his own vittles.

EBEN. I see him comin' from the barn. Ye better look smart an' git upstairs. 40

ABBIE. Ay-eh. Good-by. Don't ferget me. *(She throws him a kiss. He grins—then squares his shoulders and awaits his father confidently.* CABOT *walks slowly up from the left, staring up at the sky with a vague face.)*

EBEN *(jovially)*. Mornin', Paw. Stargazing' in daylight?

CABOT. Purty, hain't it?

EBEN *(looking around him possessively)*. It's a durned purty farm. 50

CABOT. I mean the sky.

EBEN *(grinning)*. How d'ye know? Them eyes o' your'n can't see that fur. *(This tickles his humor and he slaps his thigh and laughs.)* Ho-ho! That's a good un!

CABOT *(grimly sarcastic)*. Ye're feelin' right chipper, hain't ye? Whar'd ye steal the likker?

EBEN *(good-naturedly)*. 'Tain't likker. Jest life. *(Suddenly holding out his hand—soberly.)* Yew 'n' me is quits. Let's shake hands. 60

CABOT *(suspiciously)*. What's come over ye?

EBEN. Then don't. Mebbe it's jest as well. *(A moment's pause.)* What's come over me? *(Queerly.)* Didn't ye feel her passin'—goin' back t' her grave?

CABOT *(dully)*. Who?

EBEN. Maw. She kin rest now an' sleep content. She's quits with ye.

CABOT *(confusedly)*. I rested. I slept good—down with the cows. They know how t' sleep. They're teachin' me. 70

EBEN *(suddenly jovial again)*. Good fur the cows! Waal—ye better git t' work.

CABOT (*grimly amused*). Air yew bossin' me, ye calf?

EBEN (*beginning to laugh*). Ay-eh! I'm bossin' yew! Ha-ha-ha! See how ye like it! Ha-ha-ha! I'm the prize rooster o' this roost. Ha-ha-ha! (*He goes off toward the barn laughing.*)

80

CABOT (*looks after him with scornful pity*). Soft-headed. Like his Maw. Dead spit 'n' image. No hope in him! (*He spits with contemptuous disgust.*) A born fool! (*Then matter-of-factly.*) Waal—I'm gittin' peckish. (*He goes toward door.*)

(*The curtain falls.*)

PART THREE *Scene One*

(*A night in late spring the following year. The kitchen and the two bedrooms upstairs are shown. The two bedrooms are dimly lighted by a tallow candle in each.* EBEN *is sitting on the side of the bed in his room, his chin propped on his fists, his face a study of the struggle he is making to understand his conflicting emotions. The noisy laughter and music from below where a kitchen dance is in progress annoy and distract him. He scowls at the floor.*)

(*In the next room a cradle stands beside the double bed.*)

(*In the kitchen all is festivity. The stove has been taken down to give more room to the dancers. The chairs, with wooden benches added, have been pushed back against the walls. On these are seated, squeezed in tight against one another, farmers and their wives and their young folks of both sexes from the neighboring farms. They are all chattering and laughing loudly. They evidently have some secret joke in common. There is no end of winking, of nudging, of meaning nods of the head toward* CABOT *who, in a state of extreme hilarious excitement increased by the amount he has drunk, is standing near the rear door where there is a small keg of whisky and serving drinks to all the men. In the left corner, front, dividing the attention with her husband,* ABBIE *is sitting in a rocking chair, a shawl wrapped about her shoulders. She is very pale, her face is thin and drawn, her eyes are fixed anxiously on the open door in rear as if waiting for someone.*)

(*The* MUSICIAN *is tuning up his fiddle, seated in the far right corner. He is a lanky young fellow with a long, weak face. His pale eyes blink incessantly and he grins about him slyly with a greedy malice.*)

ABBIE (*suddenly turning to a* YOUNG GIRL *on her right*). Whar's Eben?

YOUNG GIRL (*eyeing her scornfully*). I dunno, Mrs. Cabot. I hain't seen Eben in ages. (*Meaningly.*) Seems like he's spent most o' his time t' hum since yew come.

ABBIE (*vaguely*). I tuk his Maw's place.

YOUNG GIRL. Ay-eh. So I've heerd. (*She turns away to retail this bit of gossip to her mother sitting next to her.* ABBIE *turns to her left to a big stoutish middle-aged* MAN *whose flushed face and starting eyes show the amount of "likker" he has consumed.*)

10

ABBIE. Ye hain't seen Eben, hev ye?

MAN. No, I hain't. (*Then he adds with a wink.*) If yew hain't, who would?

ABBIE. He's the best dancer in the county. He'd ought t' come an' dance.

MAN (*with a wink*). Mebbe he's doin' the dutiful an' walkin' the kid t' sleep. It's a boy, hain't it?

20

ABBIE (*nodding vaguely*). Ay-eh—born two weeks back—purty's a picter.

MAN. They all is—t' their Maws. (*Then in a whisper, with a nudge and a leer.*) Listen, Abbie—if ye ever git tired o' Eben, remember me! Don't fergit now! (*He looks at her uncomprehending face for a second—then grunts disgustedly.*) Waal—guess I'll likker agin. (*He goes over and joins* CABOT *who is arguing noisily with an old farmer over cows. They all drink.*)

ABBIE (*this time appealing to nobody in particular*). Wonder what Eben's a-doin'? (*Her remark is repeated down the line wtih many a guffaw and titter until it reaches the* FIDDLER. *He fastens his blinking eyes on* ABBIE.)

FIDDLER (*raising his voice*). Bet I kin tell ye, Abbie, what Eben's doin'! He's down t' the church offerin' up prayers o' thanksgivin'. (*They all titter expectantly.*)

A MAN. What fur? (*Another titter.*)

FIDDLER. 'Cause unto him a—(*he hesitates just long enough*) brother is born! (*A roar of laughter. They all look from* ABBIE *to* CABOT. *She is oblivious, staring at the door.* CABOT, *although he hasn't heard the words, is irritated by the laughter and steps forward, glaring about him. There is an immediate silence.*)

CABOT. What're ye all bleatin' about—like a flock o' goats? Why don't ye dance, damn ye? I axed ye here t' dance—t' eat, drink an' be merry—an' thar ye set cacklin' like a lot o' wet hens with the pip! Ye've swilled my likker an' guzzled my vittles like hogs, hain't ye? Then dance fur me, can't ye? That's fa'r an' squar', hain't it? (*A grumble of resentment goes around but they are all evidently in too much awe of him to express it openly.*)

FIDDLER (*slyly*). We're waitin' fur Eben. (*A suppressed laugh.*)

CABOT (*with a fierce exultation*). T'hell with Eben! Eben's done fur now! I got a new son! (*His mood switching with drunken suddenness.*) But ye needn't t' laugh at Eben, none o' ye! He's my blood, if he be a dumb fool. He's better nor any o' yew! He kin do a day's work a'most up t' what I kin—an' that'd put any o' yew pore critters t' shame!

FIDDLER. An' he kin do a good night's work, too! (*A roar of laughter.*)

CABOT. Laugh, ye damn fools! Ye're right jist the same, Fiddler. He kin work day an' night too, like I kin, if need be!

OLD FARMER (*from behind the keg where he is weaving drunkenly back and forth—with great simplicity*). They hain't many t' touch ye, Ephraim—a son at seventy-six. That's a hard man fur ye! I be on'y sixty-eight an' I couldn't do it. (*A roar of laughter in which* CABOT *joins uproariously.*)

CABOT (*slapping him on the back*). I'm sorry fur ye, Hi. I'd never suspicion sech weakness from a boy like yew!

OLD FARMER. An' I never reckoned yew had it in ye nuther, Ephraim. (*There in another laugh.*)

CABOT (*suddenly grim*). I got a lot in me—a hell of a lot—folks don't know on. (*Turning to the* FIDDLER.) Fiddle 'er up, durn ye! Give 'em somethin' t' dance t'! What air ye, an ornament? Hain't this a celebration? Then grease yer elbow an' go it!

FIDDLER (*seizes a drink which the* OLD FARMER *holds out to him and downs it*). Here goes! (*He starts to fiddle "Lady of the Lake." Four young fellows and four girls form in two lines and dance a square dance. The* FIDDLER *shouts directions for the different movements, keeping his words in the rhythm of the music and interspersing them with jocular personal remarks to the dancers themselves. The people seated along the walls stamp their feet and clap their hands in unison.* CABOT *is especially active in this respect. Only* ABBIE *remains apathetic, staring at the door as if she were alone in a silent room.*)

FIDDLER. Swing your partner t' the right! That's it, Jim! Give her a b'ar hug! Her Maw hain't lookin'. (*Laughter.*) Change partners! That suits ye, don't it, Essie, now ye got Reub afore ye? Look at her redden up, will ye? Waal, life is short an' so's love, as the feller says. (*Laughter.*)

CABOT (*excitedly, stamping his foot*). Go it, boys! Go it, gals!

FIDDLER (*with a wink at the others*). Ye're the spryest seventy-six ever I sees, Ephraim! Now if ye'd on'y good eyesight . . ! (*Suppressed laughter. He gives* CABOT *no chance to retort but roars.*) Promenade! Ye're walkin' like a bride down the aisle, Sarah! Waal, while they's life they's allus hope, I've heerd tell. Swing your partner to the left! Gosh A'mighty, look at Johnny Cook high-steppin'! They hain't goin' t'be much strength left fur howin' in the corn lot t'morrow. (*Laughter.*)

CABOT. Go it! Go it! (*Then suddenly, unable to restrain himself any longer, he prances into the midst of the dancers, scattering them, waving his arms about wildly.*) Ye're all hoofs! Git out o' my road! Give me room! I'll show ye dancin'. Ye're all too soft! (*He pushes them roughly away. They crowd back toward the walls, muttering, looking at him resentfully.*)

FIDDLER (*jeeringly*). Go it, Ephraim! Go it! (*He starts "Pop, Goes the Weasel," increasing the tempo with every verse until at the end he is fiddling crazily as fast as he can go.*)

CABOT (*starts to dance, which he does very well and wtih tremendous vigor. Then he begins to improvise, cuts incredibly grotesque capers, leaping up and cracking his heels together, prancing around in a circle with body bent in an Indian war dance, then suddenly straightening up and kicking as high as he can with both legs. He is like a monkey on a string. And all the while he intersperses his antics with shouts and derisive comments*). Whoop! Here's dancin' fur ye! Whoop! See that! Seventy-six, if I'm a day! Hard as iron yet! Beatin' the young 'uns like I allus done! Look at me! I'd invite ye t' dance on my hundredth birthday on'y ye'll all be dead by then. Ye're a sickly generation! Yer hearts air pink, not red! Yer veins is full o' mud an' water! I be the on'y man in the county! Whoop! See that! I'm a Injun! I've killed Injuns in the West afore ye was born—an' skulped 'em too! They's a arrer wound on my backside I c'd show ye! The hull tribe chased me. I outrun 'em all—with the arrer stuck in me! An' I tuk vengeance on 'em. Ten eyes fur an eye, that was my motter! Whoop! Look at me! I kin kick the ceilin' off the room! Whoop!

FIDDLER (*stops playing—exhaustedly*). God A'mighty, I got enuf. Ye got the devil's strength in ye.

CABOT (*delightedly*). Did I beat yew, too? Waal, ye played smart. Hev a swig. (*He pours whisky for himself and* FIDDLER. *They drink. The others watch* CABOT *silently with cold, hostile eyes. There is a dead pause. The* FIDDLER *rests.* CABOT *leans against the keg, panting, glaring around him confusedly. In the room above,* EBEN *gets to his feet and tiptoes out the door in rear, appearing a moment later in the other bedroom. He moves silently, even frightenedly, toward the cradle and stands there looking down at the baby. His face is as vague as his reactions are confused, but there is a trace of tenderness, of interested discovery. At the same moment that he reaches the cradle,* ABBIE *seems to sense something. She gets up weakly and goes to* CABOT.)

ABBIE. I'm goin' up t' the baby.

CABOT (*with real solicitation*). Air ye able fur the stairs? D'ye want me t' help ye, Abbie?

ABBIE. No. I'm able. I'll be down agen soon.

CABOT. Don't ye git wore out! He needs ye, remember—our son does! (*He grins affectionately, patting her on the back. She shrinks from his touch.*)

ABBIE (*dully*). Don't tech me. I'm goin'—up. (*She goes.* CABOT *looks after her. A whisper goes around the room.* CABOT *turns. It ceases. He wipes his forehead streaming with sweat. He is breathing pantingly.*)

CABOT. I'm a-goin' out t' git fresh air. I'm feelin' a mite dizzy. Fiddle up thar! Dance, all o' ye! Here's likker fur them as wants it. Enjoy yerselves. I'll be back. (*He goes, closing the door behind him.*)

FIDDLER (*sarcastically*). Don't hurry none on our account! (*A suppressed laugh. He imitates* ABBIE.) Whar's Eben? (*More laughter.*)

A WOMAN (*loudly*). What's happened in this house is plain as the nose on yer face! (ABBIE *appears in the doorway upstairs and stands looking in surprise and adoration at* EBEN *who does not see her.*)

A MAN. Ssshh! He's li'ble t' be listenin' at the door. That'd be like him. (*Their voices die to an intensive whispering. Their faces are concentrated on this gossip. A noise as of dead leaves in the wind comes from the room.* CABOT *has come out from the porch and stands by the gate, leaning on it, staring at the sky blinkingly.* ABBIE *comes across the room silently.* EBEN *does not notice her until quite near.*)

EBEN (*starting*). Abbie!

ABBIE. Ssshh! (*She throws her arms around him. They kiss—then bend over the cradle together.*) Ain't he purty?—dead spit'n' image o' yew!

EBEN (*pleased*). Air he? I can't tell none.

ABBIE. E-zactly like!

EBEN (*frowningly*). I don't like this. I don't like lettin' on what's mine's his'n. I been doin' that all my life. I'm gittin' t' the end o' b'arin' it!

ABBIE (*putting her finger on his lips*). We're

doin' the best we kin. We got t' wait. Somethin's bound t' happen. (*She puts her arms around him.*) I got t' go back.

EBEN. I'm goin' out. I can't b'ar it with the fiddle playin' an' the laughin'.

ABBIE. Don't git feelin' low. I love ye, EBEN. Kiss me. (*He kisses her. They remain in each other's arms.*)

CABOT (*at the gate, confusedly*). Even the music can't drive it out—somethin'. Ye kin feel it droppin' off the elums, climbin' up the roof, sneakin' down the chimney, pokin' in the corners! They's no peace in houses, they's no rest livin' with folks. Somethin's always livin' with ye. (*With a deep sigh.*) I'll go t' the barn an' rest a spell. (*He goes wearily toward the barn.*)

FIDDLER (*tuning up*). Let's celebrate the old skunk gittin' fooled! We kin have some fun now he's went. (*He starts to fiddle "Turkey in the Straw." There is real merriment now. The young folks get up to dance.*)

Scene Two

(*A half hour later—Exterior—*EBEN *is standing by the gate looking up at the sky, an expression of dumb pain bewildered by itself on his face.* CABOT *appears, returning from the barn, walking wearily, his eyes on the ground. He sees* EBEN *and his whole mood immediately changes. He becomes excited, a cruel, triumphant grin comes to his lips, he strides up and slaps* EBEN *on the back. From within comes the whining of the fiddle and the noise of stamping feet and laughing voices.*)

CABOT. So har ye be!

EBEN (*startled, stares at him with hatred for a moment—then dully*). Ay-eh.

CABOT (*surveying him jeeringly*). Why hain't ye been in t' dance? They was all axin' fur ye.

EBEN. Let 'em ax!

CABOT. They's a hull passel o' purty gals.

EBEN. T' hell with 'em!

CABOT. Ye'd ought t' be marryin' one o' 'em soon.

EBEN. I hain't marryin' no one.

CABOT. Ye might 'arn a share o' a farm that way.

EBEN (*with a sneer*). Like yew did, ye mean? I hain't that kind.

CABOT (*stung*). Ye lie! 'Twas yer Maw's folks aimed t' steal my farm from me.

EBEN. Other folks don't say so. (*After a pause—defiantly.*) An' I got a farm, anyways!

CABOT (*derisively*). Whar?

EBEN (*stamps a foot on the ground*). Har!

CABOT (*throws his head back and laughs coarsely*). Ho-ho! Ye hev, hev ye? Waal, that's a good un!

EBEN (*controlling himself—grimly*). Ye'll see!

CABOT (*stares at him suspiciously, trying to make him out—a pause—then with scornful confidence*). Ay-eh. I'll see. So'll ye. It's ye that's blind—blind as a mole underground. (EBEN *suddenly laughs, one short sardonic bark: "Ha." A pause.* CABOT *peers at him with renewed suspicion.*) What air ye hawin' 'bout? (EBEN *turns away without answering.* CABOT *grows angry.*) God A'mighty, yew air a dumb dunce! They's nothin' in that thick skull o' your'n but noise—like a empty keg it be! (EBEN *doesn't seem to hear.* CABOT's *rage grows.*) Yewr farm! God A'mighty! If ye wa'n't a born donkey ye'd know ye'll never own stick nor stone on it, specially now arter him bein' born. It's his'n, I tell ye—his'n arter I die—but I'll live a hundred jest t' fool ye all—an' he'll be growed then—yewr age a'most! (EBEN *laughs again his sardonic "Ha." This drives* CABOT *into a fury.*) Ha? Ye think ye kin git 'round that someways, do ye? Waal, it'll be her'n, too—Abbie's—ye won't git 'round her—she knows yer tricks—she'll be too much fur ye—she wants the farm her'n—she was afeerd o' ye—she told me ye was sneakin' 'round tryin' t' make love t' her t' git her on yer side . . . ye . . . ye mad fool, ye! (*He raises his clenched fists threateningly.*)

EBEN (*is confronting him, choking with rage*). Ye lie, ye old skunk! Abbie never said no sech thing!

CABOT (*suddenly triumphant when he sees how shaken* EBEN *is*). She did. An' I says, I'll blow his brains t' the top o' them elums—an' she says no, that hain't sense, who'll ye git t'help ye on the farm in his place—an' then she says yew'n me ought t' have a son—I know we kin, she says—an' I says, if we do, ye kin have anythin' I've got ye've a mind t'. An' she says, I wants Eben cut off so's this farm'll be mine when ye die! (*With terrible gloating.*) An' that's what's happened, hain't it? An' the farm's her'n! An' the dust o' the road—that's you'rn! Ha! Now who's hawin'?

EBEN (*has been listening, petrified with grief and rage—suddenly laughs wildly and brokenly*). Ha-ha-ha! So that's her sneakin' game—all along!—like I suspicioned at fust—t' swaller it all—an' me, too . . . ! (*Madly.*) I'll murder her! (*He springs toward the porch but* CABOT *is quicker and gets in between.*)

CABOT. No, ye don't!

EBEN. Git out o' my road! (*He tries to throw* CABOT *aside. They grapple in what becomes immediately a murderous struggle. The old man's concentrated strength is too much for* EBEN. CABOT *gets one hand on his throat and presses him back across the stone wall. At the same moment.* ABBIE *comes out on the porch. With a stifled cry she runs toward them.*)

ABBIE. Eben! Ephraim! (*She tugs at the hand on* EBEN's *throat.*) Let go, Ephraim! Ye're chokin' him!

CABOT (*removes his hand and flings* EBEN *sideways full length on the grass, gasping and choking. With a cry,* ABBIE *kneels beside him, trying to take his head on her lap, but he pushes her away.* CABOT *stands looking down with fierce triumph*). Ye needn't t've fret, Abbie, I wa'n't aimin' t' kill him. He hain't wuth hangin' fur—not by a hell of a sight! (*More and more triumphantly.*) Seventy-six an' him not thirty yit—an' look whar he be fur thinkin' his Paw was easy! No, by God, I hain't easy! An' him upstairs, I'll raise him t' be like me! (*He turns to leave them.*) I'm goin' in an' dance!—sing an' celebrate (*He walks to the porch—then turns with a great grin.*) I don't calc'late it's left in him, but if he gits pesky, Abbie, ye jest sing out. I'll come a-runnin' an' by the Etarnal, I'll put him across my knee an' birch him! Ha-ha-ha! (*He goes into the house laughing. A moment later his loud "whoop" is heard.*)

ABBIE (*tenderly*). Eben. Air ye hurt? (*She tries to kiss him but he pushes her violently away and struggles to a sitting position.*)

EBEN (*gaspingly*). T'hell—with ye!

ABBIE (*not believing her ears*). It's me, Eben—Abbie—don't ye know me?

EBEN (*glowering at her with hatred*). Ay-eh—I know ye—now! (*He suddenly breaks down, sobbing weakly.*)

ABBIE (*fearfully*). Eben—what's happened t' ye—why did ye look at me 's if ye hated me?

EBEN (*violently, between sobs and gasps*). I do hate ye! Ye're a whore—a damn trickin' whore!

ABBIE (*shrinking back horrified*). Eben! Ye don't know what ye're sayin'!

EBEN (*scrambling to his feet and following her—accusingly*). Ye're nothin' but a stinkin' passel o' lies! Ye've been lyin' t' me every word ye spoke, day an' night, since we fust—done it. Ye've kept sayin' ye loved me. . . .

ABBIE (*frantically*). I do love ye! (*She takes his hand but he flings hers away.*)

EBEN (*unheeding*). Ye've made a fool o' me—a sick, dumb fool—a-purpose! Ye've been on'y playin' yer sneakin', stealin' game all along—gittin' me t' lie with ye so's ye'd hev a son he'd think was his'n, an' makin' him promise he'd give ye the farm and let me eat dust, if ye did git him a son! (*Staring at her with anguished, bewildered eyes.*) They must be a devil livin' in ye! T'ain't human t' be as bad as that be!

ABBIE (*stunned—dully*). He told yew . . . ?

EBEN. Hain't it true? It hain't no good in yew lyin'.

ABBIE (*pleadingly*). Eben, listen—ye must listen—it was long ago—afore we done nothin'—yew was scornin' me—goin' t' see Min—when I was lovin' ye—an' I said it t' him t' git vengeance on ye!

EBEN (*unheedingly. With tortured passion*). I wish ye was dead! I wish I was dead along with ye afore this come! (*Ragingly.*) But I'll git my vengeance too! I'll pray Maw t' come back t' help me—t' put her cuss on yew an' him!

ABBIE (*brokenly*). Don't ye, Eben! Don't ye! (*She throws herself on her knees before him, weeping.*) I didn't mean t' do bad t'ye! Fergive me, won't ye?

160 EBEN (*not seeming to hear her—fiercely*). I'll git squar' with the old skunk—an' yew! I'll tell him the truth 'bout the son he's so proud o'! Then I'll leave ye here t' pizen each other—with Maw comin' out o' her grave at nights—an' I'll go t' the gold fields o' Californi-a whar Sim an' Peter be!

ABBIE (*terrified*). Ye won't—leave me? Ye can't!

EBEN (*with fierce determination*). I'm a 170 goin', I tell ye! I'll git rich thar an' come back an fight him fur the farm he stole—an' I'll kick ye both out in the road—t' beg an' sleep in the woods—an' yer son along with ye—t' starve an' die! (*He is hysterical at the end.*)

ABBIE (*with a shudder—humbly*). He's yewr son, too, Eben.

EBEN (*torturedly*). I wish he never was born! I wish he'd die this minit! I wish I'd never sot eyes on him! It's him—yew havin' 180 him—a-purpose t' steal—that's changed everythin'!

ABBIE (*gently*). Did ye believe I loved ye—afore he come?

EBEN. Ay-eh—like a dumb ox!

ABBIE. An' ye don't believe no more?

EBEN. B'lieve a lyin' thief! Ha!

ABBIE (*shudders—then humbly*). An' did ye r'ally love me afore?

EBEN (*brokenly*). Ay-eh—an' ye was trickin' 190 me!

ABBIE. An' ye don't love me now!

EBEN (*violently*). I hate ye, I tell ye!

ABBIE. An' ye're truly goin' West—goin' t' leave me—all account o' him being born?

EBEN. I'm a-goin' in the mornin'—or may God strike me t' hell!

ABBIE (*after a pause—with a dreadful cold intensity—slowly*). If that's what his comin' done t' me—killin' yewr love—takin' yew away 200 —my on'y joy—the on'y joy I ever knowed—like heaven t' me—purtier'n heaven—then I hate him, too, even if I be his Maw!

EBEN (*bitterly*). Lies! Ye love him! He'll steal the farm fur ye! (*Brokenly.*) But t'ain't the farm so much—not no more—it's yew foolin' me—gettin' me t' love ye—lyin' yew loved me—jes t' git a son t' steal!

ABBIE (*distractedly*). He won't steal! I'd kill him fust! I do love ye! I'll prove t' ye . . . !

EBEN (*harshly*). T'ain't no use lyin' no more. 210 I'm deaf t' ye! (*He turns away.*) I hain't seein' ye agen. Good-by!

ABBIE (*pale with anguish*). Hain't ye even goin' t' kiss me—not once—arter all we loved?

EBEN (*in a hard voice*). I hain't wantin' t' kiss ye never agen! I'm wantin' t' forgit I ever sot eyes on ye!

ABBIE. Eben!—ye mustn't—wait a spell—I want t' tell ye. . . .

EBEN. I'm a-goin' in t' git drunk. I'm a-goin' 220 t' dance.

ABBIE (*clinging to his arm—with passionate earnestness*). If I could make it—'s if he'd never come up between us—if I could prove t' ye I wa'n't schemin' t' steal from ye—so's everythin' could be jest the same with us, lovin' each other jest the same, kissin' an' happy the same's we've been happy afore he come—if I could do it—ye'd love me agen, wouldn't ye? Ye'd kiss me agen? Ye wouldn't never leave me, would 230 ye?

EBEN (*moved*). I calc'late not. (*Then shaking her hand off his arm—with a bitter smile.*) But ye hain't God, be ye?

ABBIE (*exultantly*). Remember ye've promised! (*Then with strange intensity.*) Mebbe I kin take back one thin' God does!

EBEN (*peering at her*). Ye're gittin cracked, hain't ye? (*Then going towards door.*) I'm a-goin' t' dance. 240

ABBIE (*calls after him intensely*). I'll prove t' ye! I'll prove I love ye better'n. . . . (*He goes in the door, not seeming to hear. She remains standing where she is, looking after him—then she finishes desperately.*) Bettern' everythin' else in the world!

Scene Three

(Just before dawn in the morning—shows the kitchen and CABOT'S *bedroom. In the kitchen, by the light of a tallow candle on the table,* EBEN *is sitting, his chin propped on his hands, his drawn face blank and expressionless. His carpetbag is on the floor beside him. In the bedroom, dimly lighted by a small whale-oil lamp,* CABOT *lies asleep.* ABBIE *is bending over the cradle, listening, her face full of terror yet with an undercurrent of desperate triumph. Suddenly, she breaks down and sobs, appears about to throw herself on her knees beside the cradle; but the old man turns restlessly, groaning in his sleep, and she controls herself, and, shrinking away from the cradle with a gesture of horror, backs swiftly toward the door in rear and goes out. A moment later she comes into the kitchen and, running to* EBEN, *flings her arms about his neck and kisses him wildly. He hardens himself, he remains unmoved and cold, he keeps his eyes straight ahead.)*

ABBIE *(hysterically)*. I done it, Eben! I told ye I'd do it! I've proved I love ye—better'n everythin'—so's ye can't never doubt me no more!

EBEN *(dully)*. Whatever ye done, it hain't no good now.

ABBIE *(wildly)*. Don't ye say that! Kiss me, Eben, won't ye? I need ye t' kiss me arter what I done! I need ye t' say ye love me!

EBEN *(kisses her without emotion—dully)*. That's fur good-by. I'm a-goin' soon.

ABBIE. No! No! Ye won't go—not now!

EBEN *(going on with his own thoughts)*. I been a-thinkin'—an' I hain't goin' t' tell Paw nothin'. I'll leave Maw t' take vengeance on ye. If I told him, the old skunk'd jest be stinkin' mean enuf to take it out on that baby. *(His voice showing emotion in spite of him.)* An' I don't want nothin' bad t' happen t' him. He hain't t' blame fur yew. *(He adds with a certain queer pride.)* An' he looks like me! An' by God, he's mine! An' some day I'll be a-comin' back an' . . . !

ABBIE *(too absorbed in her own thoughts to listen to him—pleadingly)*. They's no cause fur ye t' go now—they's no sense—it's all the same's it was—they's nothin' come b'tween us now—arter what I done!

EBEN *(something in her voice arouses him. He stares at her a bit frightenedly)*. Ye look mad, Abbie. What did ye do?

ABBIE. I—I killed him, Eben.

EBEN *(amazed)*. Ye killed him?

ABBIE *(dully)*. Ay-eh.

EBEN *(recovering from his astonishment—savagely)*. An' serves him right! But we got t' do somethin' quick t' make it look s'if the old skunk'd killed himself when he was drunk. We kin prove by 'em all how drunk he got.

ABBIE *(wildly)*. No! No! Not him! *(Laughing distractedly.)* But that's what I ought t' done, hain't it? I oughter killed him instead! Why didn't ye tell me?

EBEN *(appalled)*. Instead? What d'ye mean?

ABBIE. Not him.

EBEN *(his face grown ghastly)*. Not—not that baby!

ABBIE *(dully)*. Ay-eh!

EBEN *(falls to his knees as if he'd been struck—his voice trembling with horror)*. Oh God A'mighty! A'mighty God! Maw, whar was ye, why didn't ye stop her?

ABBIE *(simply)*. She went back t' her grave that night we fust done it, remember? I hain't felt her about since. *(A pause.* EBEN *hides his head in his hands, trembling all over as if he had the ague. She goes on dully.)* I left the piller over his little face. Then he killed himself. He stopped breathin'. *(She begins to weep softly.)*

EBEN *(rage beginning to mingle with grief)*. He looked like me. He was mine, damn ye!

ABBIE *(slowly and brokenly)*. I didn't want t' do it. I hated myself fur doin' it. I loved him.

He was so purty—dead spit 'n' image o' yew. But I loved yew more—an' yew was goin' away —far off whar I'd never see ye agen, never kiss ye, never feel ye pressed agin me agen—an' ye said ye hated me fur havin' him—ye said ye hated him an' wished he was dead—ye said if it hadn't been fur him comin' it'd be the same's afore between us.

EBEN (*unable to endure this, springs to his feet in a fury, threatening her, his twitching fingers seeming to reach out for her throat*). Ye lie! I never said—I never dreamed ye'd—I'd cut off my head afore I'd hurt his finger!

ABBIE (*piteously, sinking on her knees*). Eben, don't ye look at me like that—hatin' me —not after what I done fur ye—fur us—so's we could be happy agen—

EBEN (*furiously now*). Shut up, or I'll kill ye! I see yer game now—the same old sneakin' trick—ye're aimin' t' blame me fur the murder ye done!

ABBIE (*moaning—putting her hands over her ears*). Don't ye, Eben! Don't ye! (*She grasps his legs.*)

EBEN (*his mood suddenly changing to horror, shrinks away from her*). Don't ye tech me! Ye're pizen! How could ye—t' murder a pore little critter— Ye must've swapped yer soul t' hell! (*Suddenly raging.*) Ha! I kin see why ye done it! Not the lies ye jest told—but 'cause ye wanted t' steal agen—steal the last thin' ye'd left me—my part o' him—no, the hull o' him—ye saw he looked like me—ye knowed he was all mine—an' ye couldn't b'ar it—I know ye! Ye killed him fur bein' mine! (*All this has driven him almost insane. He makes a rush past her for the door—then turns—shaking both fists at her, violently.*) But I'll take vengeance now! I'll git the Sheriff! I'll tell him everythin'! Then I'll sing "I'm off to Californi-a!" an' go—gold —Golden Gate—gold sun—fields o' gold in the West! (*This last he half shouts, half croons incoherently, suddenly breaking off passionately.*) I'm a-goin' fur the Sheriff t' come an' git ye! I want ye tuk away, locked up from me! I can't stand t' luk at ye! Murderer an' thief 'r not, ye still tempt me! I'll give ye up t' the Sheriff! (*He turns and runs out, around the corner of house, panting and sobbing, and breaks into a swerving sprint down the road.*)

ABBIE (*struggling to her feet, runs to the door, calling after him*). I love ye, Eben! I love ye! (*She stops at the door weakly, swaying, about to fall.*) I don't care what ye do—if ye'll on'y love me agen— (*She falls limply to the floor in a faint.*)

Scene Four

(*About an hour later. Same as scene 3. Shows the kitchen and* CABOT'S *bedroom. It is after dawn. The sky is brilliant with the sunrise. In the kitchen,* ABBIE *sits at the table, her body limp and exhausted, her head bowed down over her arms, her face hidden. Upstairs,* CABOT *is still asleep but awakens with a start. He looks toward the window and gives a snort of surprise and irritation—throws back the covers and begins hurriedly pulling on his clothes. Without looking behind him, he begins talking to* ABBIE *whom he supposes beside him.*)

CABOT. Thunder 'n' lightin', Abbie! I hain't slept this late in fifty year! Looks 's if the sun was full riz a'most. Must've been the dancin' an' likker. Must be gittin' old. I hope Eben's t' wuk. Ye might've tuk the trouble t' rouse me, Abbie. (*He turns—sees no one there—surprised.*) Waal—whar air she? Gittin' vittles, I calc'late. (*He tiptoes to the cradle and peers down—proudly.*) Mornin', sonny. Purty's a picter! Sleepin' sound. He don't beller all night like most o' 'em. (*He goes quietly out the door in rear—a few moments later enters kitchen —sees* ABBIE*—with satisfaction.*) So thar ye be. Ye got any vittles cooked?

ABBIE (*without moving*). No.

CABOT (*coming to her, almost sympathetically*). Ye feelin' sick?

ABBIE. No.

CABOT (*pats her on shoulder. She shudders*). Ye'd best lie down a spell. (*Half jocularly.*) Yer son'll be needin' ye soon. He'd ought t' wake up with a gnashin' appetite, the sound way he's sleepin'.

ABBIE (*shudders—then in a dead voice*). He hain't never goin' t' wake up.

CABOT (*jokingly*). Takes after me this mornin'. I hain't slept so late in. . . .

ABBIE. He's dead.

CABOT (*stares at her—bewilderedly*). What. . . .

ABBIE. I killed him.

CABOT (*stepping back from her—aghast*). Air ye drunk—'r crazy—'r . . . !

ABBIE (*suddenly lifts her head and turns on him—wildly*). I killed him, I tell ye! I smothered him. Go up an' see if ye don't b'lieve me! (CABOT *stares at her a second, then bolts out the rear door, can be heard bounding up the stairs, and rushes into the bedroom and over to the cradle.* ABBIE *has sunk back lifelessly into her former position.* CABOT *puts his hand down on the body in the crib. An expression of fear and horror comes over his face.*)

CABOT (*shrinking away—trembling*). God A'mighty! God A'mighty. (*He stumbles out the door—in a short while returns to the kitchen—comes to* ABBIE, *the stunned expression still on his face—hoarsely.*) Why did ye do it? Why? (*As she doesn't answer, he grabs her violently by the shoulder and shakes her.*) I ax ye why ye done it! Ye'd better tell me 'r . . . !

ABBIE (*gives him a furious push which sends him staggering back and springs to her feet—with wild rage and hatred*). Don't ye dare tech me! What right hev ye t' question me 'bout him? He wa'n't your son! Think I'd have a son by yew? I'd die fust! I hate the sight o' ye an' allus did! It's yew I should've murdered, if I'd had good sense! I hate ye! I love Eben. I did from the fust. An' he was Eben's son—mine an' Eben's—not your'n!

CABOT (*stands looking at her dazedly—a pause—finding his words with an effort—dully*). That was it—what I felt—pokin' round the corners—while ye lied—holdin' yerself from me—sayin' ye'd a'ready conceived—. (*He lapses into crushed silence—then with a strange emotion.*) He's dead, sart'n. I felt his heart. Pore little critter! (*He blinks back one tear, wiping his sleeve across his nose.*)

ABBIE (*hysterically*). Don't ye! Don't ye! (*She sobs unrestrainedly.*)

CABOT (*with a concentrated effort that stiffens his body into a rigid line and hardens his face into a stony mask—through his teeth to himself*). I got t' be—like a stone—a rock o' jedgment! (*A pause. He gets complete control over himself—harshly.*) If he was Eben's, I be glad he air gone! An' mebbe I suspicioned it all along. I felt they was somethin' onnateral—somewhars—the house got so lonesome—an' cold—drivin' me down t' the barn—t' the beasts o' the field. . . . Ay-eh. I must've suspicioned—somethin'. Ye didn't fool me—not altogether, leastways—I'm too old a bird—growin' ripe on the bough. . . . (*He becomes aware he is wandering, straightens again, looks at* ABBIE *with a cruel grin.*) So ye'd liked t' hev murdered me 'stead o' him, would ye? Waal, I'll live to a hundred! I'll live t' see ye hung! I'll deliver ye up t' the jedgment o' God an' the law! I'll git the Sheriff now. (*Starts for the door.*)

ABBIE (*dully*). Ye needn't. Eben's gone fur him.

CABOT (*amazed*). Eben—gone fur the Sheriff?

ABBIE. Ay-eh.

CABOT. T' inform agen ye?

ABBIE. Ay-eh.

CABOT (*considers this—a pause—then in a hard voice*). Waal, I'm thankful fur him savin' me the trouble. I'll git t' wuk. (*He goes to the door—then turns—in a voice full of strange emotion.*) He'd ought t' been my son, Abbie. Ye'd ought t' loved me. I'm a man. If ye'd loved me, I'd never told no Sheriff on ye no matter what ye did, if they was t' brile me alive!

ABBIE (*defensively*). They's more to it nor yew know, makes him tell.

CABOT (*dryly*). Fur yewr sake, I hope they be. (*He goes out—comes around to the gate—stares up at the sky. His control relaxes. For a moment he is old and weary. He murmurs despairingly.*) God A'mighty, I be lonesomer'n ever! (*He hears running footsteps from the left, immediately is himself again.* EBEN *runs in, panting exhaustedly, wild-eyed and mad looking. He lurches through the gate.* CABOT *grabs him by the shoulder.* EBEN *stares at him dumbly.*) Did ye tell the Sheriff?

EBEN (*nodding stupidly*). Ay-eh.

CABOT (*gives him a push away that sends him sprawling—laughing with withering contempt*). Good fur ye! A prime chip o' yer Maw ye be! (*He goes toward the barn, laughing harshly.* EBEN *scrambles to his feet. Suddenly* CABOT *turns—grimly threatening.*) Git off this farm when the Sheriff takes her—or, by God, he'll have t' come back an' git me fur murder, too! (*He stalks off.* EBEN *does not appear to have heard him. He runs to the door and comes into the kitchen.* ABBIE *looks up with a cry of anguished joy.* EBEN *stumbles over and throws himself on his knees beside her—sobbing brokenly.*)

EBEN. Fergive me!

ABBIE (*happily*). Eben! (*She kisses him and pulls his head over against her breast.*)

EBEN. I love ye! Fergive me!

ABBIE (*ecstatically*). I'd fergive ye all the sins in hell fur sayin' that! (*She kisses his head, pressing it to her with a fierce passion of possession.*)

EBEN (*brokenly*). But I told the Sheriff. He's comin' fur ye!

ABBIE. I kin b'ar what happens t' me—now!

EBEN. I woke him up. I told him. He says, wait 'till I git dressed. I was waiting. I got to thinkin' o' yew. I got to thinkin' how I'd loved ye. It hurt like somethin' was bustin' in my chest an' head. I got t' cryin'. I knowed sudden I loved ye yet, an' allus would love ye!

ABBIE (*caressing his hair—tenderly*). My boy, hain't ye?

EBEN. I begun t' run back. I cut across the fields an' through the woods. I thought ye might have time t' run away—with me—an'. . . .

ABBIE (*shaking her head*). I got t' take my punishment—t' pay fur my sin.

EBEN. Then I want t' share it with ye.

ABBIE. Ye didn't do nothin'.

EBEN. I put it in yer head. I wisht he was dead! I as much as urged ye t' do it!

ABBIE. No. It was me alone!

EBEN. I'm as guilty as yew be! He was the child o' our sin.

ABBIE (*lifting her head as if defying God*). I don't repent that sin! I hain't askin' God t' fergive that!

EBEN. Nor me—but it led up t' the other—an' the murder ye did, ye did 'count o' me—an' it's my murder, too, I'll tell the Sheriff—an' if ye deny it, I'll say we planned it t'gether—an' they'll all b'lieve me, fur they suspicion everythin' we've done, an' it'll seem likely an' true to 'em. An' it is true—way down. I did help ye—somehow.

ABBIE (*laying her head on his—sobbing*). No! I don't want yew t' suffer!

EBEN. I got t' pay fur my part o' the sin! An' I'd suffer wuss leavin' ye, goin' West, thinkin' o' ye day an' night, bein' out when yew was in— (*Lowering his voice.*) 'r bein' alive when yew was dead. (*A pause.*) I want t' share with ye, Abbie—prison 'r death 'r hell 'r anythin'! (*He looks into her eyes and forces a trembling smile.*) If I'm sharin' with ye, I won't feel lonesome, leastways.

ABBIE (*weakly*). Eben! I won't let ye! I can't let ye!

EBEN (*kissing her—tenderly*). Ye can't he'p yerself. I got ye beat fur once!

ABBIE (*forcing a smile—adoringly*). I hain't beat—s'long's I got ye!

EBEN (*hears the sound of feet outside*). Ssshh! Listen! They've come t' take us!

ABBIE. No, it's him. Don't give him no chance to fight ye, Eben. Don't say nothin'—no matter what he says. An' I won't, neither. (*It is* CABOT. *He comes up from the barn in a great state of excitement and strides into the house and then into the kitchen.* EBEN *is kneeling beside* ABBIE, *his arm around her, hers around him. They stare straight ahead.*)

CABOT (*stares at them, his face hard. A long pause—vindictively*). Ye make a slick pair o' murderin' turtle doves! Ye'd ought t' be both hung on the same limb an' left thar t' swing in the breeze an' rot—a warnin' t' old fools like me t' b'ar their lonesomeness alone—an fur young fools like ye t' hobble their lust. (*A pause. The excitement returns to his face, his eyes snap, he looks a bit crazy.*) I couldn't work today. I couldn't take no interest. T' hell with the farm! I'm leavin' it! I've turned the cows an' other stock loose! I've druv 'em into the woods whar they kin be free! By freein' 'em, I'm freein' myself! I'm quittin' here today! I'll set fire t' house an' barn an' watch 'em burn, an' I'll leave yer Maw t' haunt the ashes, an' I'll will the fields back t' God, so that nothin' human kin never touch 'em! I'll be a-goin' to Californi-a—t' jine Simeon an' Peter—true sons o' mine if they be dumb fools—an' the Cabots'll find Solomon's Mines t'gether! (*He suddenly cuts a mad caper.*) Whoop! What was the song they sung? "Oh, Californi-a! That's the land fur me." (*He sings this—then gets on his knees by the floorboard under which the money was hid.*) An' I'll sail thar on one o' the finest clippers I kin find! I've got the money! Pity ye didn't know whar this was hidden so's ye could steal. . . . (*He has pulled up the board. He stares—feels—stares again. A pause of dead silence. He slowly turns, slumping into a sitting position on the floor, his eyes like those of a dead fish, his face the sickly green of an attack of nausea. He swallows painfully several times —forces a weak smile at last.*) So—ye did steal it!

EBEN (*emotionlessly*). I swapped it t' Sim an' Peter fur their share o' the farm—t' pay their passage t' Californi-a.

CABOT (*with one sardonic* "Ha!" *He begins to recover. Gets slowly to his feet—strangely.*). I calc'late God give it to 'em—not yew! God's hard, not easy! Mebbe they's easy gold in the West but it hain't God's gold. It hain't fur me. I kin hear His voice warnin' me agen t' be hard an' stay on my farm. I kin see his hand usin' Eben t' steal t' keep me from weakness. I kin feel I be in the palm o' His hand, His fingers guidin' me. (*A pause—then he mutters sadly.*) It's a-goin' t' be lonesomer now than ever it war afore—an' I'm gittin' old, Lord—ripe on the bough. . . . (*Then stiffening.*) Waal—what d'ye want? God's lonesome, hain't He? God's hard an' lonesome! (*A pause.* THE SHERIFF *with two men comes up the road from the left. They move cautiously to the door.* THE SHERIFF *knocks on it with the butt of his pistol.*)

SHERIFF. Open in the name o' the law! (*They start.*)

CABOT. They've come fur ye. (*He goes to the rear door.*) Come in, Jim! (*The three men enter.* CABOT *meets them in doorway.*) Jest a minit, Jim. I got 'em safe here. (THE SHERIFF *nods. He and his companions remain in the doorway.*)

EBEN (*suddenly calls*). I lied this mornin', Jim. I helped her do it. Ye kin take me, too.

ABBIE (*brokenly*). No!

CABOT. Take 'em both. (*He comes forward —stares at* EBEN *with a trace of grudging admiration.*) Purty good—fur yew! Waal, I got t' round up the stock. Good-by.

EBEN. Good-by.

ABBIE. Good-by. (CABOT *turns and strides past the men—comes out and around the corner of the house, his shoulders squared, his face stony, and stalks grimly toward the barn. In the meantime* THE SHERIFF *and men have come into the room.*)

SHERIFF (*embarrassedly*). Waal—we'd best start.

ABBIE. Wait. (*Turns to* EBEN.) I love ye, Eben.

EBEN. I love ye, Abbie. (*They kiss. The three men grin and shuffle embarrassedly.* EBEN *takes* ABBIE'*s hand. They go out the door in rear, the men following, and come from the house, walking hand in hand to the gate.* EBEN *stops there and points to the sunrise sky.*) Sun's a-rizin'. Purty, hain't it?

ABBIE. Ay-eh. (*They both stand for a moment looking up raptly in attitudes strangely aloof and devout.*)

SHERIFF (*looking around at the farm enviously—to his companion*). It's a jim-dandy farm, no denyin'. Wished I owned it!

(*The curtain falls.*)

Review Questions

1. Evaluate the play in terms of Gassner's description of it as a "peasant tragedy."
2. What are the characters' objectives? Do they reach them?
3. What aspects of melodrama are found in the play?
4. Is the plot unified?
5. How does the setting function dramatically?
6. O'Neill often shows his characters trapped by their environment. Comment on this play in that regard.
7. What is the feeling of Peter and Simeon towards Cabot?
8. What is accomplished in the first scene?
9. Indicate how O'Neill establishes local color.
10. Describe Cabot's first appearance. How has his entrance been built?
11. Does O'Neill treat his characters with compassion?
12. What does the abundance of explicit stage directions tell you about O'Neill?
13. What is the effect of Abbie's first entrance?
14. Comment on the dialogue from the standpoint of its purpose. Is it successful?
15. What is the effect of the denouement? Sentimental? Tragic?
16. Is the play an example of naturalism?
17. Evaluate Cabot as a dramatic character.
18. To what extent is this a play of crime and punishment?
19. What aspects of Puritanism do you find in the play?
20. What does the farm mean to Abbie? To Eben? To Cabot?
21. What are the "desires" in the play?
22. Is the violence meaningful?
23. Do the characters have free will?
24. Compare the Eben-Abbie relationship with that of Jean and Julie in *Miss Julie*.

THE CAUCASIAN CHALK CIRCLE

Bertolt Brecht (*1898-1956*)

ADAPTED BY
ERIC BENTLEY

The attitudes and career of Brecht, a German, were shaped not only by the violent upheaval of Communism, Nazism and two world wars but also by his earlier study of medicine and service during World War I in the medical corps of the German army. He has emerged as one of the most remarkable and stimulating of twentieth-century playwrights.

His first period of writing was an expression of his disillusionment which characterized the intellectual life of post-war Germany. He anticipated the absurdists in his treatment of the disintegration of human values and the impossibility of communication with *The Wedding* and *In the Jungle of Cities*. The most successful of his early works was *The Three Penny Opera,* which was based on the 18th century English ballad opera of John Gay.

Brecht's middle period shows him politically committed to Marxism, which he frankly espouses in such plays as *Saint Joan of the Stockyards*. In his final period, Brecht's plays show a maturation of his concept of "epic theater", in which didactic purpose gives way to artistic considerations, as in *Mother Courage, The Good Woman of Setzuan* and *The Caucasian Chalk Circle*. After World War II, Brecht gave a vivid demonstration of his gifts in his productions at the Berliner Ensemble.

Two terms are important in considering the production of Brecht's plays—"epic" and "alienation." Brecht called his plays epic because of their narrative or cinematic form.

He does not narrowly confine the audience's attention to a few characters engaged in a tightly structured sequence of cumulative action. Rather, as one famous European director, Piscator, said, Brecht's interest is "No longer the individual with his private, personal destiny, but the age itself." As a consequence of his social commitment, the playwright wants to challenge his audience to "complex seeing." The resulting succession of episodes made new demands on the stage in the use of music, light, sound and such pictorial devices as slides, motion pictures, maps and charts—all used in a frankly theatrical way in which actor, spectator and stage are all a part of the same theater, devoid of illusion or separation by a fourth wall. As for the actor, Brecht's intention was to present him free from emotional attachment with his role in order that "alienation" might take place—the audience will not enter into the play empathically because a distance will be maintained. Character identification, the objective of the "method" actor, was rejected because the actor became too absorbed in "psychological truth" to be aware of "social truth." All aspects of epic theater—the play, the production and the acting—were intended to neutralize the audience's emotional attachment so as to awaken them to the playwright's ideas.

The story of the Noble Child begins. Georgi Abashwili, the governor, stands in the foreground holding his son in the cradle. The Fat Prince stands at his elbow. Natella Abashwili, the governor's wife, looks on from behind. In the far background is the Singer, surrounded by his audience and chorus. From the 1966 Lincoln Center Reperatory Company production.

Peter Daness

Peter Daness

LEFT. Grusha at the Rotten Bridge.

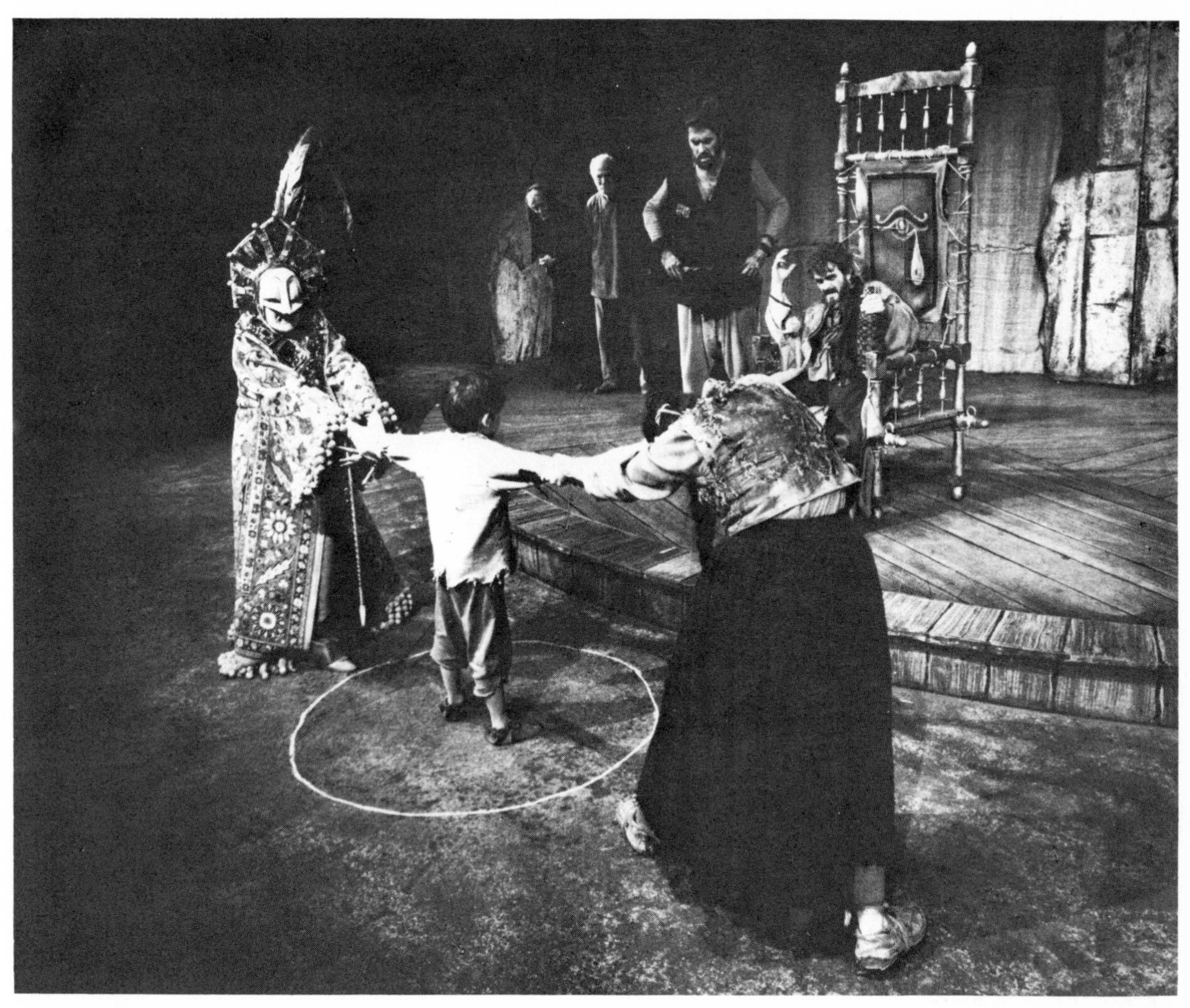

Peter Daness

ABOVE. Azdak's test of the Chalk Circle.

Characters

Old Man, *on the right*
Peasant Woman, *on the right*
Young Peasant
A Very Young Worker
Old Man, *on the left*
Peasant Woman, *on the left*
Agriculturist Kato
Girl Tractorist
Wounded Soldier
The Delegate *from the capital*
The Singer
Georgi Abashwili, *the Governor*
Natella, *the Governor's wife*
Michael, *their son*
Shalva, *an adjutant*
Arsen Kazbeki, *a fat prince*
Messenger, *from the capital*
Niko Mikadze *and* Mika Loladze, *doctors*
Simon Shashava, *a soldier*
Grusha Vashnadze, *a kitchen maid*
Old Peasant, *with the milk*
Corporal and Private
Peasant *and his wife*
Lavrenti Vashnadze, Grusha's *brother*
Aniko, *his wife*
Peasant Woman, *for a while* Grusha's *mother-in-law*
Jussup, *her son*
Monk
Azdak, *village recorder*
Shauwa, *a policeman*
Grand Duke
Doctor
Invalid
Limping Man
Blackmailer
Ludovica
Innkeeper, *her father-in-law*
Stableboy
Poor Old Peasant Woman
Irakli, *her brother-in-law, a bandit*
Three Wealthy Farmers
Illo Shuboladze *and* Sandro Oboladze, *lawyers*
Old Married Couple
Soldiers, Servants,
Peasants, Beggars,
Musicians, Merchants,
Nobles, Architects

THE CAUCASIAN CHALK CIRCLE

Prologue

*Among the ruins of a war-ravaged Caucasian village the members of two Kolkhoz * villages, mostly women and older men, are sitting in a circle, smoking and drinking wine. With them is a delegate of the state reconstruction commission from Nuka, the capital.*

PEASANT WOMAN (*Left*) (*Pointing*). In those hills over there we stopped three Nazi tanks, but the apple orchard was already destroyed.

OLD MAN (*Right*). Our beautiful dairy farm: a ruin.

GIRL TRACTORIST. I laid the fire, Comrade. (*Pause*)

THE DELEGATE. Now listen to the report. Delegates from the goat-breeding Kolkhoz "Rosa Luxemburg" have been to Nuka. When Hitler's armies approached, the Kolkhoz had moved its goat-herds further east on orders from the authorities. They are now thinking of returning. Their delegates have investigated the village and the land and found a lot of it destroyed.

(DELEGATES *on right nod*)

The neighboring fruit-culture Kolkhoz (*To the left*) "Galinsk" is proposing to use the former grazing land of Kolkhoz "Rosa Luxemburg," a valley with scanty growth of grass, for orchards and vineyards. As a delegate of the Reconstruction Commission, I request that the two Kolkhoz villages decide between themselves whether Kolkhoz "Rosa Luxemburg" shall return here or not.

OLD MAN (*Right*). First of all, I want to protest against the restriction of time for discussion. We of Kolkhoz "Rosa Luxemburg" have spent three days and three nights getting here. And now discussion is limited to half a day.

WOUNDED SOLDIER (*Left*). Comrade, we haven't as many villages as we used to have. We haven't as many hands. We haven't as much time.

GIRL TRACTORIST. All pleasures have to be rationed. Tobacco is rationed, and wine. Discussion should be rationed.

OLD MAN (*Right*) (*Sighing*). Death to the fascists! But I will come to the point and explain why we want our valley back. There are a great many reasons, but I'll begin with one of the simplest. Makina Abakidze, unpack the goat cheese. (*A* PEASANT WOMAN *from right takes from a basket an enormous cheese wrapped in a cloth. Applause and laughter*) Help yourselves, Comrades, start in!

OLD MAN (*Left*) (*Suspiciously*). Is this a way of influencing us?

OLD MAN (*Right*) (*Amid laughter*). How could it be a way of influencing you, Surab, you valley-thief? Everyone knows you will take

* **Kolkhoz** a collective farm in the Soviet Union

the cheese and the valley, too. (*Laughter*) All I expect from you is an honest answer. Do you like the cheese?

OLD MAN (*Left*). The answer is: yes.

OLD MAN (*Right*). Really. (*Bitterly*) I ought to have known you know nothing about cheese.

OLD MAN (*Left*). Why not? When I tell you I like it?

OLD MAN (*Right*). Because you can't like it. Because it's not what it was in the old days. And why not? Because our goats don't like the new grass as they did the old. Cheese is not cheese because grass is not grass, that's the thing. Please put that in your report.

OLD MAN (*Left*). But your cheese is excellent.

OLD MAN (*Right*). It isn't excellent. It's just passable. The new grazing land is no good, whatever the young people may say. One can't live there. It doesn't even smell of morning in the morning. (SEVERAL PEOPLE *laugh*)

THE DELEGATE. Don't mind their laughing: they understand you. Comrades, why does one love one's country? Because the bread tastes better there, the air smells better, voices sound stronger, the sky is higher, the ground is easier to walk on. Isn't that so?

OLD MAN (*Right*). The valley has belonged to us from all eternity.

SOLDIER (*Left*). What does *that* mean—from all eternity? Nothing belongs to anyone from all eternity. When you were young you didn't even belong to yourself. You belonged to the Kazbeki princes.

OLD MAN (*Right*). Doesn't it make a difference, though, what kind of trees stand next to the house you are born in? Or what kind of neighbors you have? Doesn't that make a difference? We want to go back just to have you as our neighbors, valley-thieves! Now you can all laugh again.

OLD MAN (*Left*) (*Laughing*). Then why don't you listen to what your neighbor, Kato Wachtang, our agriculturist, has to say about the valley?

PEASANT WOMAN (*Right*). We've not said all there is to be said about our valley. By no means. Not all the houses are destroyed. As for the dairy farm, at least the foundation wall is still standing.

DELEGATE. You can claim State support—here and there—you know that. I have suggestions here in my pocket.

PEASANT WOMAN (*Right*). Comrade Specialist, we haven't come here to bargain. I can't take your cap and hand you another, and say "This one's better." The other one might *be* better; but you *like* yours better.

GIRL TRACTORIST. A piece of land is not a cap—not in our country, Comrade.

DELEGATE. Don't get angry. It's true we have to consider a piece of land as a tool to produce something useful, but it's also true that we must recognize love for a particular piece of land. As far as I'm concerned, I'd like to find out more exactly what you (*To those on the left*) want to do with the valley.

OTHERS. Yes, let Kato speak.

DELEGATE. Comrade Agriculturist!

KATO (*Rising,* SHE'S *in military uniform*). Comrades, last winter, while we were fighting in these hills as Partisans, we discussed how, after the expulsion of the Germans, we could build up our fruit culture to ten times its original size. I've prepared a plan for an irrigation project. By means of a cofferdam on our mountain lake, 300 hectares of unfertile land can be irrigated. Our Kolkhoz could not only cultivate more fruit, but also have vineyards. The project, however, would pay only if the disputed valley of Kolkhoz "Galinsk" were also included. Here are the calculations. (SHE *hands the* DELEGATE *a briefcase*)

OLD MAN (*Right*). Write into a report that our Kolkhoz plans to start a new stud farm.

GIRL TRACTORIST. Comrades, the project was conceived during days and nights when we had to take cover in the mountains. We were often without ammunition for our half-dozen rifles. Even getting a pencil was difficult. (*Applause from both sides*)

OLD MAN (*Right*). Our thanks to the Comrades of Kolkhoz "Galinsk" and all who have defended our country! (THEY *shake hands and embrace*)

PEASANT WOMAN (*Left*). In doing this our thought was that our soldiers—both your men

87 **Kazbeki** a Caucasian district

and our men—should return to a still more productive homeland.

GIRL TRACTORIST. As the poet Mayakovsky said: "The home of the Soviet people shall also be the home of Reason"!

(*The* DELEGATES *including the* OLD MAN *have got up, and with the* DELEGATE *specified proceed to study the Agriculturist's drawings . . . exclamations such as: "Why is the altitude of all* 160 *22 meters?"—"This rock must be blown up"—"Actually, all they need is cement and dynamite"—"They force the water to come down here, that's clever!"*)

A VERY YOUNG WORKER (*Right*) (*To* OLD MAN, *right*). They're going to irrigate all the fields between the hills, look at that, Aleko!

OLD MAN (*Right*). I'm not going to look. I knew the project would be good. I won't have a revolver aimed at my chest.

170 DELEGATE. But they only want to aim a pencil at your chest. (*Laughter*)

OLD MAN (*Right*) (*Gets up gloomily, and walks over to look at the drawings*) These valley-thieves know only too well that we can't resist machines and projects in this country.

PEASANT WOMAN (*Right*). Aleko Bereshwili, you have a weakness for new projects. That's well known.

DELEGATE. What about my report? May I 180 write that you will all support the cession of your old valley in the interests of this project when you get back to your Kolkhoz?

PEASANT WOMAN (*Right*). I will. What about you, Aleko?

OLD MAN (*Right*) (*Bent over drawings*). I suggest that you give us copies of the drawings to take along.

PEASANT WOMAN (*Right*). Then we can sit down and eat. Once he has the drawings and 190 he's ready to discuss them, the matter is settled. I know him. And it will be the same with the rest of us. (DELEGATES *laughingly embrace again*)

OLD MAN (*Left*). Long live the Kolkhoz "Rosa Luxemburg" and much luck to your horsebreeding project!

PEASANT WOMAN (*Left*). In honor of the visit of the delegates from Kolkhoz "Rosa Luxemburg" and of the Specialist, the plan is that we all hear a presentation of the Singer Arkadi Tscheidse. (*Applause.* GIRL TRACTORIST *has gone* 200 *off to bring the* SINGER)

PEASANT WOMAN (*Right*). Comrades, your entertainment had better be good. We're going to pay for it with a valley.

PEASANT WOMAN (*Left*). Arkadi Tscheidse knows about our discussion. He's promised to perform something that has a bearing on the problem.

KATO. We wired to Tiflis three times. The whole thing nearly fell through at the last 210 minute because his driver had a cold.

PEASANT WOMAN (*Left*). Arkadi Tscheidse knows 21,000 lines of verse.

OLD MAN (*Left*). It's very difficult to get him. You and the Planning Commission should see to it that you get him to come North more often, Comrade.

DELEGATE. We are more interested in economics, I'm afraid.

OLD MAN (*Left*) (*Smiling*). You arrange the 220 redistribution of vines and tractors, why not of songs?

(*Enter the* SINGER ARKADI TSCHEIDSE, *led by* GIRL TRACTORIST. HE *is a well-built man of simple manners, accompanied by* FOUR MUSICIANS *with their instruments. The* ARTISTS *are greeted with applause*)

GIRL TRACTORIST. This is the Comrade Specialist, Arkadi. (*The* SINGER *greets them all*)

DELEGATE. I'm honored to make your ac- 230 quaintance. I heard about your songs when I was a boy at school. Will it be one of the old legends?

THE SINGER. A very old one. It's called The Chalk Circle and comes from the Chinese. But we'll do it, of course, in a changed version. Comrades, it's an honor for me to entertain you after a difficult debate. We hope you will find that the voice of the old poet also sounds well in the shadow of Soviet tractors. It may be a mistake to mix different wines, but old and 240 new wisdom mix admirably. Now I hope we'll get something to eat before the performance begins—it would certainly help.

153 Vladimir **Mayakovsky** (1894–1930) one of the greatest Russian poets of this century

209 **Tiflis** capital of the Georgian Republic of the U.S.S.R.

VOICES. Surely. Everyone into the Club House! (*While* EVERYONE *begins to move, the* DELEGATE *turns to the* GIRL TRACTORIST)

DELEGATE. I hope it won't take long. I've got to get back tonight.

GIRL TRACTORIST. How long will it last, Arkadi? The Comrade Specialist must get back to Tiflis tonight.

THE SINGER (*Casually*). It's actually two stories. An hour or two.

GIRL TRACTORIST (*Confidentially*). Couldn't you make it shorter?

THE SINGER. No.

VOICE. Arkadi Tscheidse's performance will take place here in the square after the meal. (*And* THEY ALL *go happily to eat*)

1. *The Noble Child*

As the lights go up, THE SINGER *is seen sitting on the floor, a black sheepskin cloak round his shoulders, and a little well-thumbed notebook in his hand. A small group of listeners—the* CHORUS—*sits with him. The manner of his recitation makes it clear that* HE *has told his story over and over again.* HE *mechanically fingers the pages, seldom looking at them. With appropriate gestures,* HE *gives the signal for each scene to begin.*

THE SINGER.
In olden times, in a bloody time,
There ruled in a Caucasian city—
Men called it City of the Damned—
A governor.
His name was Georgi Abashwili.
He was rich as Croesus
He had a beautiful wife
He had a healthy baby.
No other governor in Grusinia
Had so many horses in his stable
So many beggars on his doorstep
So many soldiers in his service
So many petitioners in his courtyard.
Georgi Abashwili—how shall I describe him to you?
He enjoyed his life.
On the morning of Easter Sunday
The governor and his family went to church.

(*At the left a large doorway, at the right an even larger gateway.* BEGGARS *and* PETITIONERS *pour from the gateway, holding up thin* CHILDREN, *crutches, and petitions.* THEY *are followed by* IRONSHIRTS, *and then, expensively dressed, the* GOVERNOR'S FAMILY)

BEGGARS AND PETITIONERS.
Mercy! Mercy, Your Grace! The taxes are too high.
—I lost my leg in the Persian War, where can I get . . .
—My brother is innocent, Your Grace, a misunderstanding . . .
—The child is starving in my arms!
—Our petition is for our son's discharge from the army, our last remaining son!
—Please, Your Grace, the water inspector takes bribes.

(ONE SERVANT *collects the petitions,* ANOTHER *distributes coins from a purse.* SOLDIERS *push the* CROWD *back, lashing at them with thick leather whips*)

THE SOLDIER. Get back! Clear the church door! (*Behind the* GOVERNOR, HIS WIFE, *and the* ADJUTANT, *the* GOVERNOR'S CHILD *is brought through the gateway in an ornate carriage*)

THE CROWD.
—The baby!
—I can't see it, don't shove so hard!
—God bless the child, Your Grace!

THE SINGER (*While the* CROWD *is driven back with whips*).
For the first time on that Easter Sunday, the people saw the Governor's heir.
Two doctors never moved from the noble child, apple of the Governor's eye.
Even the mighty Prince Kazbeki bows before

him at the church door. (A FAT PRINCE *steps forward and greets the family*)

THE FAT PRINCE. Happy Easter, Natella Abashwili! What a day! When it was raining last night, I thought to myself, gloomy holidays! But this morning the sky was gay. I love a gay sky, a simple heart, Natella Abashwili. And little Michael is a governor from head to foot! Tititi! (HE *tickles the* CHILD)

THE GOVERNOR'S WIFE. What do you think, Arsen, at last Georgi has decided to start building the wing on the east side. All those wretched slums are to be torn down to make room for the garden.

THE FAT PRINCE. Good news after so much bad! What's the latest on the war, Brother Georgi? (*The* GOVERNOR *indicates a lack of interest*)

THE FAT PRINCE. Strategical retreat, I hear. Well, minor reverses are to be expected. Sometimes things go well, sometimes not. Such is war. Doesn't mean a thing, does it?

THE GOVERNOR'S WIFE. He's coughing. Georgi, did you hear? (SHE *speaks sharply to the* DOCTORS, *two dignified men standing close to the little carriage*) He's coughing!

THE FIRST DOCTOR (*To the* SECOND). May I remind you, Niko Mikadze, that I was against the lukewarm bath? (*To the* GOVERNOR'S WIFE) There's been a little error over warming the bath water, Your Grace.

THE SECOND DOCTOR (*Equally polite*). Mika Loladze, I'm afraid I can't agree with you. The temperature of the bath water was exactly what our great, beloved Mishiko Oboladze prescribed. More likely a slight draft during the night, Your Grace.

THE GOVERNOR'S WIFE. But do pay more attention to him. He looks feverish, Georgi.

THE FIRST DOCTOR (*Bending over the* CHILD). No cause for alarm, Your Grace. The bath water will be warmer. It won't occur again.

THE SECOND DOCTOR (*With a venomous glance at the* FIRST). I won't forget that, my dear Mika Loladze. No cause for concern, Your Grace.

THE FAT PRINCE. Well, well, well! I always say: "A pain in my liver? Then the doctor gets fifty strokes on the soles of his feet." We live in a decadent age. In the old days one said: "Off with his head!"

THE GOVERNOR'S WIFE. Let's go into church. Very likely it's the draft here.

(*The procession of* FAMILY *and* SERVANTS *turns into the doorway. The* FAT PRINCE *follows, but the* GOVERNOR *is kept back by the* ADJUTANT, *a handsome young man. When the crowd of* PETITIONERS *has been driven off, a young dust-stained* RIDER, *his arm in a sling, remains behind*)

THE ADJUTANT (*Pointing at the* RIDER, *who steps forward*). Won't you hear the messenger from the capital, your Excellency? He arrived this morning. With confidential papers.

THE GOVERNOR. Not before Service, Shalva. But did you hear Brother Kazbeki wish me a happy Easter? Which is all very well, but I don't believe it did rain last night.

THE ADJUTANT (*Nodding*). We must investigate.

THE GOVERNOR. Yes, at once. Tomorrow.

(THEY *pass through the doorway. The* RIDER, *who has waited in vain for an audience, turns sharply round and, muttering a curse, goes off. Only one of the palace guards*—SIMON SHASHAVA—*remains at the door*)

THE SINGER.
The city is still.
Pigeons strut in the church square.
A soldier of the Palace Guard
Is joking with a kitchen maid
As she comes up from the river with a bundle.

(*A girl*—GRUSHA VASHADZE—*comes through the gateway with a bundle made of large green leaves under her arm*)

SIMON. What, the young lady is not in church? Shirking?

GRUSHA. I was dressed to go. But they needed another goose for the banquet. And they asked me to get it. I know about geese.

SIMON. A goose? (HE *feigns suspicion*) I'd like to see that goose. (GRUSHA *does not understand*) One has to be on one's guard with women. "I only went for a fish," they tell you, but it turns out to be something else.

GRUSHA (*Walking resolutely toward him and showing him the goose*). There! If it isn't a fifteen-pound goose stuffed full of corn, I'll eat the feathers.

SIMON. A queen of a goose! The Governor himself will eat it. So the young lady has been down to the river again?

GRUSHA. Yes, at the poultry farm.

SIMON. Really? At the poultry farm, down by the river . . . not higher up maybe? Near those willows?

GRUSHA. I only go to the willows to wash the linen.

SIMON (*Insinuatingly*). Exactly.

GRUSHA. Exactly what?

SIMON (*Winking*). Exactly that.

GRUSHA. Why shouldn't I wash the linen by the willows?

SIMON (*With exaggerated laughter*). "Why shouldn't I wash the linen by the willows!" That's good, really good!

GRUSHA. I don't understand the soldier. What's so good about it?

SIMON (*Slyly*). "If something I know someone learns, she'll grow hot and cold by turns!"

GRUSHA. I don't know what I could learn about those willows.

SIMON. Not even if there was a bush opposite? That one could see everything from? Everything that goes on there when a certain person is—"washing linen"?

GRUSHA. What does go on? Won't the soldier say what he means and have done?

SIMON. Something goes on. And something can be seen.

GRUSHA. Could the soldier mean I dip my toes in the water when it is hot? There is nothing else.

SIMON. More. Your toes. And more.

GRUSHA. More what? At most my foot?

SIMON. Your foot. And a little more. (HE *laughs heartily*)

GRUSHA (*Angrily*). Simon Shashava, you ought to be ashamed of yourself! To sit in a bush on a hot day and wait till someone comes and dips her leg in the river! And I bet you bring a friend along too! (SHE *runs off*)

SIMON (*Shouting after her*). I didn't bring any friend along! (*As the* SINGER *resumes his tale, the* SOLDIER *steps into the doorway as though to listen to the service*)

THE SINGER.

The city lies still
But why are there armed men?
The Governor's palace is at peace
But why is it a fortress?
And the Governor returned to his palace
And the fortress was a trap
And the goose was plucked and roasted
But the goose was not eaten this time
And noon was no longer the hour to eat:
Noon was the hour to die.

(*From the doorway at the left the* FAT PRINCE *quickly appears, stands still, looks around. Before the gateway at the right* TWO IRONSHIRTS *are squatting and playing dice. The* FAT PRINCE *sees them, walks slowly past, making a sign to them.* THEY *rise:* ONE *goes through the gateway, the* OTHER *goes off at the right. Muffled voices are heard from various directions in the rear: "To your posts!" The palace is surrounded. The* FAT PRINCE *quickly goes off. Church bells in the distance. Enter, through the doorway, the* GOVERNOR'S FAMILY *and* PROCESSION, *returning from church*)

THE GOVERNOR'S WIFE (*Passing the* ADJUTANT). It's impossible to live in such a slum. But Georgi, of course, will only build for his little Michael. Never for me! Michael is all! All for Michael!

(*The* PROCESSION *turns into the gateway. Again the* ADJUTANT *lingers behind.* HE *waits. Enter the* WOUNDED RIDER *from the doorway.* TWO IRONSHIRTS *of the palace guard have taken up positions by the gateway*)

THE ADJUTANT (*To the* RIDER). The Governor does not wish to receive military reports before dinner—especially if they're depressing, as I assume. In the afternoon His Excellency will confer with prominent architects. They're coming to dinner too. And here they are! (*Enter* THREE GENTLEMEN *through the doorway*) Go in the kitchen and get yourself something to eat, my friend. (*As the* RIDER *goes, the* ADJUTANT *greets the* ARCHITECTS) Gentlemen, His Excellency expects you at dinner. He will devote all his time to you and your great new plans. Come!

ONE OF THE ARCHITECTS. We marvel that His Excellency intends to build. There are disquieting rumors that the war in Persia has taken a turn for the worse.

THE ADJUTANT. All the more reason to build! There's nothing to those rumors anyway. Persia is a long way off, and the garrison here would let itself be hacked to bits for its Governor. (*Noise from the palace. The shrill scream of a woman. Someone is shouting orders. Dumbfounded, the* ADJUTANT *moves toward the gateway. An* IRONSHIRT *steps out, points his lance at him*) What's this? Put down that lance, you dog. 250

ONE OF THE ARCHITECTS. It's the Princes! Don't you know the Princes met last night in the capital? And they're against the Grand Duke and his Governors? Gentlemen, we'd better make ourselves scarce. (THEY *rush off. The* ADJUTANT *remains helplessly behind*)

THE ADJUTANT (*Furiously to the* PALACE GUARD). Down with those lances! Don't you see the Governor's life is threatened? 260

(*The* IRONSHIRTS *of the Palace Guard refuse to obey.* THEY *stare coldly and indifferently at the* ADJUTANT *and follow the next events without interest*)

THE SINGER.
O blindness of the great!
They go their way like gods,
Great over bent backs,
Sure of hired fists,
Trusting in the power
Which has lasted so long. 270
But long is not forever.
O change from age to age!
Thou hope of the people!

(*Enter the* GOVERNOR, *through the gateway, between* TWO SOLDIERS *armed to the teeth.* HE *is in chains. His face is gray*)

Up, great sir, deign to walk upright!
From your palace the eyes of many foes follow you!
And now you don't need an architect, a carpenter will do.
You won't be moving into a new palace 280
But into a little hole in the ground.
Look about you once more, blind man!

(*The arrested man looks round*)

Does all you had please you?
Between the Easter Mass and the Easter meal
You are walking to a place whence no one returns.

(*The* GOVERNOR *is led off. A horn sounds an alarm. Noise behind the gateway*)

When the house of a great one collapses
Many little ones are slain. 290
Those who had no share in the *good* fortunes of the mighty
Often have a share in their *mis*fortunes.
The plunging wagon
Drags the sweating oxen down with it
Into the abyss.

(*The* SERVANTS *come rushing through the gateway in panic*)

THE SERVANTS (*Among themselves*).
—The baskets! 300
—Take them all into the third courtyard! Food for five days!
—The mistress has fainted! Someone must carry her down.
—She must get away.
—What about us? We'll be slaughtered like chickens, as always.
—Goodness, what'll happen? There's bloodshed already in the city, they say.
—Nonsense, the Governor has just been asked to appear at a Princes' meeting. All very correct. Everything'll be ironed out. I heard this on the best authority . . . 310

(*The* TWO DOCTORS *rush into the courtyard*)

THE FIRST DOCTOR (*Trying to restrain the other*). Niko Mikadze, it is your duty as a doctor to attend Natella Abashwili.

THE SECOND DOCTOR. My duty! It's yours!

THE FIRST DOCTOR. Whose turn is it to look after the child today, Niko Mikadze, yours or mine? 320

THE SECOND DOCTOR. Do you really think, Mika Loladze, I'm going to stay a minute longer in this accursed house on that little brat's account?

(THEY *start fighting. All one hears is: "You neglect your duty!" and "Duty, my foot!" Then the* SECOND DOCTOR *knocks the* FIRST *down*)

Go to hell! (*Exit*)

(*Enter the* SOLDIER, SIMON SHASHAVA. HE *searches in the crowd for* GRUSHA) 330

SIMON. Grusha! There you are at last! What are you going to do?

GRUSHA. Nothing. If worst comes to worst, I've a brother in the mountains. How about you?

SIMON. Forget about me. (*Formally again*) Grusha Vashnadze, your wish to know my plans fills me with satisfaction. I've been ordered to accompany Madam Natella Abashwili as her guard.

GRUSHA. But hasn't the Palace Guard mutinied?

SIMON (*Seriously*). That's a fact.

GRUSHA. Isn't it dangerous to go with her?

SIMON. In Tiflis, they say: Isn't the stabbing dangerous for the knife?

GRUSHA. You're not a knife, you're a man, Simon Shashava, what has that woman to do with you?

SIMON. That woman has nothing to do with me. I have my orders, and I go.

GRUSHA. The soldier is pigheaded: he is getting himself into danger for nothing—nothing at all. I must get into the third courtyard, I'm in a hurry.

SIMON. Since we're both in a hurry we shouldn't quarrel. You need time for a good quarrel. May I ask if the young lady still has parents?

GRUSHA. No, just a brother.

SIMON. As time is short—my second question is this: Is the young lady as healthy as a fish in water?

GRUSHA. I may have a pain in the right shoulder once in a while. Otherwise I'm strong enough for my job. No one has complained. So far.

SIMON. That's well-known. When it's Easter Sunday, and the question arises who'll run for the goose all the same, she'll be the one. My third question is this: Is the young lady impatient? Does she want apples in winter?

GRUSHA. Impatient? No. But if a man goes to war without any reason and then no message comes—that's bad.

SIMON. A message will come. And now my final question . . .

GRUSHA. Simon Shashava, I must get to the third courtyard at once. My answer is yes.

SIMON (*Very embarrassed*). Haste, they say, is the wind that blows down the scaffolding. But they also say: The rich don't know what haste is. I'm from . . .

GRUSHA. Kutsk . . .

SIMON. So the young lady has been inquiring about me? I'm healthy, I have no dependants, I make ten piasters a month, as paymaster twenty piasters, and I'm asking—very sincerely—for your hand.

GRUSHA. Simon Shashava, it suits me well.

SIMON (*Taking from his neck a thin chain with a little cross on it*). My mother gave me this cross, Grusha Vashnadze. The chain is silver. Please wear it.

GRUSHA. Many thanks, Simon.

SIMON (*Hangs it round her neck*). It would be better for the young lady to go to the third courtyard now. Or there'll be difficulties. Anyway, I must harness the horses. The young lady will understand?

GRUSHA. Yes, Simon. (THEY *stand undecided*)

SIMON. I'll just take the mistress to the troops that have stayed loyal. When the war's over, I'll be back. In two weeks. Or three. I hope my intended won't get tired, awaiting my return.

GRUSHA.

Simon Shashava, I shall wait for you.
Go calmly into battle, soldier
The bloody battle, the bitter battle
From which not everyone returns:
When you return I shall be there.
I shall be waiting for you under the green elm
I shall be waiting for you under the bare elm
I shall wait until the last soldier has returned
And longer.
When you come back from the battle
No boots will stand at my door
The pillow beside mine will be empty
And my mouth will be unkissed.
When you return, when you return
You will be able to say: It is just as it was.

SIMON. I thank you, Grusha Vashnadze. And goodbye! (HE *bows low before her.* SHE *does the same before him. Then* SHE *runs quickly off without looking round. Enter the* ADJUTANT *from the gateway*)

THE ADJUTANT (*Harshly*). Harness the horses to the carriage! Don't stand there doing nothing, louse! (SIMON SHASHAVA *stands to attention and goes off*)

(TWO SERVANTS *crowd from the gateway, bent low under huge trunks. Behind them, supported by her* WOMEN, *stumbles* NATELLA ABASHWILI. SHE *is followed by a* WOMAN *carrying the* CHILD)

THE GOVERNOR'S WIFE. I hardly know if my head's still on. Where's Michael? Don't hold him so clumsily. Pile the trunks onto the carriage. Shalva, is there no news from the city? 440

THE ADJUTANT. None. All's quiet so far, but there's not a minute to lose. No room for all these trunks in the carriage. Pick out what you need. (*Exit quickly*)

THE GOVERNOR'S WIFE. Only essentials! Quick, open the trunks! I'll tell you what I need. (*The trunks are lowered and opened.* SHE *points at some brocade dresses*) The green one! And, of course, the one with the fur trimming. Where are Niko Mikadze and Mika Loladze? I've 450 suddenly got the most terrible migraine again. It always starts in the temples.

(*Enter* GRUSHA)

Taking your time, eh? Go at once and get the hot water bottles! (GRUSHA *runs off, returns later with hot water bottles; the* GOVERNOR'S WIFE *orders her about by signs*) Don't tear the sleeves.

A YOUNG WOMAN. Pardon, madam, no harm has come to the dress.

THE GOVERNOR'S WIFE. Because I stopped you. 460 I've been watching you for a long time. Nothing in your head but making eyes at Shalva Tzereteli. I'll kill you, you bitch! (SHE *beats the woman*)

THE ADJUTANT (*Appearing in the gateway*). Please make haste, Natella Abashwili. Firing has broken out in the city. (*Exit*)

THE GOVERNOR'S WIFE (*Letting go of the* YOUNG WOMAN). Oh dear, do you think they'll lay hands on us? Why should they? Why? (SHE 470 *herself begins to rummage in the trunks*) How's Michael? Asleep?

THE WOMAN WITH THE CHILD. Yes, madam.

THE GOVERNOR'S WIFE. Then put him down a moment and get my little saffron-colored boots from the bedroom. I need them for the green dress. (*The* WOMAN *puts down the* CHILD *and goes off*) Just look how these things have been packed! No love! No understanding! If you don't give them every order yourself . . . 480 At such moments you realize what kind of servants you have! They gorge themselves at your expense, and never a word of gratitude! I'll remember this.

THE ADJUTANT (*Entering, very excited*). Natella, you must leave at once!

THE GOVERNOR'S WIFE. Why? I've got to take this silver dress—it cost a thousand piasters. And that one there, and where's the wine-colored one? 490

THE ADJUTANT (*Trying to pull her away*). Riots have broken out! We must leave at once. Where's the baby?

THE GOVERNOR'S WIFE (*Calling to the* YOUNG WOMAN *who was holding the baby*). Maro, get the baby ready! Where on earth are you?

THE ADJUTANT (*Leaving*). We'll probably have to leave the carriage behind and go ahead on horseback.

(*The* GOVERNOR'S WIFE *rummages again among* 500 *her dresses, throws some onto the heap of chosen clothes, then takes them off again. Noises, drums are heard. The* YOUNG WOMAN *who was beaten creeps away. The sky begins to grow red*)

THE GOVERNOR'S WIFE (*Rummaging desperately*). I simply cannot find the wine-colored dress. Take the whole pile to the carriage. Where's Asja? And why hasn't Maro come back? Have you all gone crazy?

THE ADJUTANT (*Returning*). Quick! Quick! 510

THE GOVERNOR'S WIFE (*To the* FIRST WOMAN). Run! Just throw them into the carriage!

THE ADJUTANT. We're not taking the carriage. And if you don't come now, I'll ride off on my own.

THE GOVERNOR'S WIFE (*As the* FIRST WOMAN *can't carry everything*). Where's the bitch Asja? (*The* ADJUTANT *pulls her away*) Maro, bring the baby! (*To the* FIRST WOMAN) Go and look for Masha. No, first take the dresses to 520 the carriage. Such nonsense! I wouldn't dream of going on horseback!

(*Turning round,* SHE *sees the red sky, and starts back rigid. The fire burns.* SHE *is pulled out by the* ADJUTANT. *Shaking, the* FIRST WOMAN *follows with the dresses*)

MARO (*From the doorway with the boots*). Madam! (SHE *sees the trunks and dresses and runs toward the* BABY, *picks it up, and holds it*

530 *a moment*) They left it behind, the beasts. (SHE *hands it to* GRUSHA) Hold it a moment. (SHE *runs off, following the* GOVERNOR'S WIFE)

(*Enter* SERVANTS *from the gateway*)

THE COOK. Well, so they've actually gone. Without the food wagons, and not a minute too early. It's time for us to clear out.

A GROOM. This'll be an unhealthy neighborhood for quite a while. (*To one of the* WOMEN) Suliko, take a few blankets and wait for me in

540 the foal stables.

GRUSHA. What have they done with the governor?

THE GROOM (*Gesturing throat cutting*). Ffffft.

A FAT WOMAN (*Seeing the gesture and becoming hysterical*). Oh dear, oh dear, oh dear, oh dear! Our master Georgi Abashwili! A picture of health he was, at the Morning Mass—and now! Oh, take me away, we're all lost, we must

550 die in sin like our master, Georgi Abashwili!

THE OTHER WOMAN (*Soothing her*). Calm down, Nina! You'll be taken to safety. You've never hurt a fly.

THE FAT WOMAN (*Being led out*). Oh dear, oh dear, oh dear! Quick! Let's all get out before they come, before they come!

A YOUNG WOMAN. Nina takes it more to heart than the mistress, that's a fact. They even have to have their weeping done for them.

560 THE COOK. We'd better get out, all of us.

ANOTHER WOMAN (*Glancing back*). That must be the East Gate burning.

THE YOUNG WOMAN (*Seeing the* CHILD *in* GRUSHA'S *arms*). The baby! What are you doing with it?

GRUSHA. It got left behind.

THE YOUNG WOMAN. She simply left it there. Michael, who was kept out of all the drafts!

(*The* SERVANTS *gather round the* CHILD)

570 GRUSHA. He's waking up.

THE GROOM. Better put him down, I tell you. I'd rather not think what'd happen to anybody who was found with that baby.

THE COOK. That's right. Once they get started, they'll kill each other off, whole families at a time. Let's go.

(*Exeunt all but* GRUSHA, *with the* CHILD *on her arm, and* TWO WOMEN)

THE TWO WOMEN. Didn't you hear? Better put him down.

580

GRUSHA. The nurse asked me to hold him a moment.

THE OLDER WOMAN. She's not coming back, you simpleton.

THE YOUNGER WOMAN. Keep your hands off it.

THE OLDER WOMAN (*Amiably*). Grusha, you're a good soul, but you're not very bright, and you know it. I tell you, if he had the plague he couldn't be more dangerous.

590

GRUSHA (*Stubbornly*). He hasn't got the plague. He looks at me! He's human!

THE OLDER WOMAN. Don't look at *him*. You're a fool—the kind that always gets put upon. A person need only say, "Run for the salad, you have the longest legs," and you run. My husband has an ox cart—you can come with us if you hurry! Lord, by now the whole neighborhood must be in flames.

600

(BOTH WOMEN *leave, sighing. After some hesitation,* GRUSHA *puts the sleeping* CHILD *down, looks at it for a moment, then takes a brocade blanket from the heap of clothes and covers it. Then* BOTH WOMEN *return, dragging bundles.* GRUSHA *starts guiltily away from the* CHILD *and walks a few steps to one side*)

THE YOUNGER WOMAN. Haven't you packed anything yet? There isn't much time, you know. The Ironshirts will be here from the barracks.

610

GRUSHA. Coming. (SHE *runs through the doorway.* BOTH WOMEN *go to the gateway and wait. The sound of horses is heard.* THEY *flee, screaming*)

(*Enter the* FAT PRINCE *with drunken* IRONSHIRTS. *One of them carries the governor's head on a lance*)

THE FAT PRINCE. Here! In the middle! (ONE SOLDIER *climbs onto the other's back, takes the head, holds it tentatively over the door*) That's not the middle. Farther to the right. That's it.

620

What I do, my friends, I do well. (*While, with hammer and nail, the* SOLDIER *fastens the head to the wall by its hair*) This morning at the church door I said to Georgi Abashwili: "I love a clear sky." Actually, I prefer the lightning that comes out of a clear sky. Yes, indeed. It's a pity they took the brat along, though, I need him, urgently.

(*Exit with* IRONSHIRTS *through the gateway.* 630 *Trampling of horses again. Enter* GRUSHA *through the doorway looking cautiously about her. Clearly* SHE *has waited for the* IRONSHIRTS *to go. Carrying a bundle,* SHE *walks toward the gateway. At the last moment,* SHE *turns to see if the* CHILD *is still there. Catching sight of the head over the doorway,* SHE *screams. Horrified,* SHE *picks up her bundle again, and is about to leave when the* SINGER *starts to speak.* SHE *stands rooted to the spot*)

THE SINGER.

As she was standing between courtyard and
gate, 640
She heard or she thought she heard a low voice calling.
The child called to her,
Not whining, but calling quite sensibly,
Or so it seemed to her.
"Woman," it said, "help me."
And it went on, not whining, but saying quite sensibly:
"Know, woman, he who hears not a cry for help
But passes by with troubled ears will never hear
The gentle call of a lover nor the blackbird at dawn
Nor the happy sigh of the tired grape-picker as
the Angelus rings." 650

(SHE *walks a few steps toward the* CHILD *and bends over it*)

Hearing this she went back for one more look at the child:
Only to sit with him for a moment or two,
Only till someone should come,
His mother, or anyone.

(*Leaning on a trunk,* SHE *sits facing the* CHILD)

Only till she would have to leave, for the danger was too great,
The city was full of flame and crying.

(*The light grows dimmer, as though evening and night were coming on*) 660

Fearful is the seductive power of goodness!

(GRUSHA *now settles down to watch over the* CHILD *through the night. Once,* SHE *lights a small lamp to look at it. Once,* SHE *tucks it in with a coat. From time to time* SHE *listens and looks to see whether someone is coming*)

And she sat with the child a long time,
Till evening came, till night came, till dawn came.
She sat too long, too long she saw 670
The soft breathing, the small clenched fists,
Till toward morning the seduction was complete
And she rose, and bent down and, sighing, took the child
And carried it away.

(SHE *does what the* SINGER *says as* HE *describes it*)

As if it was stolen goods she picked it up.
As if she was a thief she crept away.

2. *The Flight into the Northern Mountains*

THE SINGER.

When Grusha Vashnadze left the city
On the Grusinian highway
On the way to the Northern Mountains
She sang a song, she bought some milk.

THE CHORUS.

How will this human child escape
The bloodhounds, the trap-setters?
Into the deserted mountains she journeyed
Along the Grusinian highway she journeyed
She sang a song, she bought some milk.

(GRUSHA VASHNADZE *walks on. On her back* SHE 10 *carries the* CHILD *in a sack, in one hand is a large stick, in the other a bundle.* SHE *sings*)

THE SONG OF THE FOUR GENERALS

Four generals
Set out for Iran.

With the first one, war did not agree.
The second never won a victory.
For the third the weather never was right.
For the fourth the men would never fight.
Four generals
And not a single man!

Sosso Robakidse
Went marching to Iran
With him the war did so agree
He soon had won a victory.
For him the weather was always right.
For him the men would always fight.
Sosso Robakidse,
He is our man!

(*A peasant's cottage appears*)

GRUSHA (*To the* CHILD). Noontime is meal time. Now we'll sit hopefully in the grass, while the good Grusha goes and buys a little pitcher of milk. (SHE *lays the* CHILD *down and knocks at the cottage door. An* OLD MAN *opens it*) Grandfather, could I have a little pitcher of milk? And a corn cake, maybe?

THE OLD MAN. Milk? We have no milk. The soldiers from the city have our goats. Go to the soldiers if you want milk.

GRUSHA. But grandfather, you must have a little pitcher of milk for a baby?

THE OLD MAN. And for a God-bless-you, eh?

GRUSHA. Who said anything about a God-bless-you? (SHE *shows her purse*) We'll pay like princes. "Head in the clouds, backside in the water." (*The* PEASANT *goes off, grumbling, for milk*) How much for the milk?

THE OLD MAN. Three piasters. Milk has gone up.

GRUSHA. Three piasters for this little drop? (*Without a word the* OLD MAN *shuts the door in her face*) Michael, did you hear that? Three piasters! We can't afford it! (SHE *goes back, sits down again, and gives the* CHILD *her breast*) Suck. Think of the three piasters. There's nothing there, but you *think* you're drinking, and that's something. (*Shaking her head,* SHE *sees that the* CHILD *isn't sucking any more.* SHE *gets up, walks back to the door, and knocks again*) Open grandfather, we'll pay. (*Softly*) May lightning strike you! (*When the* OLD MAN *appears*) I thought it would be half a piaster. But the baby must be fed. How about one piaster for that little drop?

THE OLD MAN. Two.

GRUSHA. Don't shut the door again. (SHE *fishes a long time in her bag*) Here are two piasters. The milk better be good. I still have two days' journey ahead of me. It's a murderous business you have here—and sinful, too!

THE OLD MAN. Kill the soldiers if you want milk.

GRUSHA (*Giving the* CHILD *some milk*). This is an expensive joke. Take a sip, Michael, it's a week's pay. Around here they think we earned our money just sitting around. Oh, Michael, Michael, you're a nice little load for a girl to take on! (*Uneasy,* SHE *gets up, puts the* CHILD *on her back, and walks on. The* OLD MAN, *grumbling, picks up the pitcher and looks after her unmoved*)

THE SINGER.
As Grusha Vashnadze went northward
The Princes' Ironshirts went after her.

THE CHORUS.
How will the barefoot girl escape the Ironshirts,
The bloodhounds, the trap-setters?
They hunt even by night.
Pursuers never tire.
Butchers sleep little.

(TWO IRONSHIRTS *are trudging along the highway*)

THE CORPORAL. You'll never amount to anything, blockhead, your heart's not in it. Your senior officer sees this in little things. Yesterday, when I made the fat gal, yes, you grabbed her husband as I commanded, and you did kick him in the stomach, at my request, but did you *enjoy* it, like a loyal Private, or were you just doing your duty? I've kept an eye on you blockhead, you're a hollow reed and a tinkling cymbal, you won't get promoted. (THEY *walk a while in silence*) Don't think I've forgotten how insubordinate you are, either. Stop limping! I forbid you to limp! You limp because I sold the horses, and I sold the horses because I'd never have got that price again. You limp to show me you don't like marching. I know you. It won't help. You wait. Sing!

THE TWO IRONSHIRTS (*Singing*).
Sadly to war I went my way
Leaving my loved one at her door.

My friends will keep her honor safe
Till from the war I'm back once more.

THE CORPORAL. Louder!

THE TWO IRONSHIRTS (*Singing*).

When 'neath a headstone I shall be
My love a little earth will bring:
"Here rest the feet that oft would run to me
And here the arms that oft to me would cling."

(THEY *begin to walk again in silence*)

120 THE CORPORAL. A good soldier has his heart and soul in it. When he receives an order, he gets a hard on, and when he drives his lance into the enemy's guts, he comes. (HE *shouts for joy*) He lets himself be torn to bits for his superior officer, and as he lies dying he takes note that his corporal is nodding approval, and that is reward enough, it's his dearest wish. *You* won't get any nod of approval, but you'll croak all right. Christ, how'm I to get my hands on 130 the Governor's bastard with the help of a fool like you! (THEY *stay on stage behind*)

THE SINGER.

When Grusha Vashnadze came to the River Sirra
Flight grew too much for her, the helpless child too heavy.
In the cornfields the rosy dawn
Is cold to the sleepless one, only cold.
The gay clatter of the milk cans in the farm-
140 yard where the smoke rises
Is only a threat to the fugitive.
She who carries the child feels its weight and little more.

(GRUSHA *stops in front of a farm. A* FAT PEASANT WOMAN *is carrying a milk can through the door.* GRUSHA *waits until* SHE *has gone in, then approaches the house cautiously*)

GRUSHA (*To the* CHILD). Now you've wet yourself again, and you know I've no linen. 150 Michael, this is where we part company. It's far enough from the city. They wouldn't want you *so* much that they'd follow you all *this* way, little good-for-nothing. The peasant woman is kind, and can't you just smell the milk? (SHE *bends down to lay the* CHILD *on the threshold*) So farewell, Michael, I'll forget how you kicked me in the back all night to make me walk faster. And you can forget the meager fare—it was meant well. I'd like to have kept you—your 160 nose is so tiny—but it can't be. I'd have shown you your first rabbit, I'd have trained you to keep dry, but now I must turn around. My sweetheart the soldier might be back soon, and suppose he didn't find me? You can't ask that, can you?

(SHE *creeps up to the door and lays the* CHILD *on the threshold. Then, hiding behind a tree,* SHE *waits until the* PEASANT WOMAN *opens the door and sees the bundle*)

THE PEASANT WOMAN. Good heavens, what's 170 this? Husband!

THE PEASANT. What is it? Let me finish my soup.

THE PEASANT WOMAN (*To the* CHILD). Where's your mother then? Haven't you got one? It's a boy. Fine linen. He's from a good family, you can see that. And they just leave him on our doorstep. Oh, these are times!

THE PEASANT. If they think we're going to feed it, they're wrong. You can take it to the 180 priest in the village. That's the best we can do.

THE PEASANT WOMAN. What'll the priest do with him? He needs a mother. There, he's waking up. Don't you think we could keep him, though?

THE PEASANT (*Shouting*). No!

THE PEASANT WOMAN. I could lay him in the corner by the armchair. All I need is a crib. I can take him into the fields with me. See him laughing? Husband, we have a roof 190 over our heads. We can do it. Not another word out of you!

(SHE *carries the* CHILD *into the house. The* PEASANT *follows protesting.* GRUSHA *steps out from behind the tree, laughs, and hurries off in the opposite direction*)

THE SINGER.

Why so cheerful, making for home?

THE CHORUS.

Because the child has won new parents with a 200 laugh,
Because I'm rid of the little one, I'm cheerful.

THE SINGER.

And why so sad?

THE SINGER.

Because I'm single and free, I'm sad
Like someone who's been robbed
Someone who's newly poor.

(SHE *walks for a short while, then meets the* TWO IRONSHIRTS, *who point their lances at her*)

210

THE CORPORAL. Lady, you are running straight into the arms of the Armed Forces. Where are you coming from? And when? Are you having illicit relations with the enemy? Where is he hiding? What movements is he making in your rear? How about the hills? How about the valleys? How are your stockings fastened? (GRUSHA *stands there frightened*) Don't be scared, we always stage a retreat, if necessary . . . what, blockhead? I always stage retreats. In that respect at least, I can be relied on. Why are you staring like that at my lance? In the field no soldier drops his lance, that's a rule. Learn it by heart, blockhead. Now, lady, where are you headed?

220

GRUSHA. To meet my intended, one Simon Shashava, of the Palace Guard in Nuka.

THE CORPORAL. Simon Shashava? Sure, I know him. He gave me a key so I could look you up once in a while. Blockhead, we are getting to be unpopular. We must make her realize we have honorable intentions. Lady, behind apparent frivolity I conceal a serious nature, so let me tell you officially: I want a child from you. (GRUSHA *utters a little scream*) Blockhead, she understood me. Uh-huh, isn't it a sweet shock? "Then first I must take the noodles out of the oven, Officer. Then first I must change my torn shirt, Colonel." But away with jokes, away with my lance! We are looking for a baby. A baby from a good family. Have you heard of such a baby, from the city, dressed in fine linen, and suddenly turning up here?

230

240

GRUSHA. No, I haven't heard a thing.

(*Suddenly* SHE *turns round and runs back, panic-stricken. The* IRONSHIRTS *glance at each other, then follow her, cursing*)

THE SINGER.

Run, kind girl! The killers are coming!
Help the helpless babe, helpless girl!
And so she runs!

250

THE CHORUS.

In the bloodiest times
There are kind people.

(*As* GRUSHA *rushes into the cottage, the* PEASANT WOMAN *is bending over the* CHILD's *crib*)

GRUSHA. Hide him. Quick! The Ironshirts are coming! I laid him on your doorstep. But he isn't mine. He's from a good family.

260

THE PEASANT WOMAN. Who's coming? What Ironshirts?

GRUSHA. Don't ask questions. The Ironshirts that are looking for it.

THE PEASANT WOMAN. They've no business in my house. But I must have a little talk with you, it seems.

GRUSHA. Take off the fine linen. It'll give us away.

THE PEASANT WOMAN. Linen, my foot! In this house I make the decisions! "*You* can't vomit in *my* room!" Why did you abandon it? It's a sin.

270

GRUSHA (*Looking out of the window*). Look, they're coming out from behind those trees! I shouldn't have run away, it made them angry. Oh, what shall I do?

THE PEASANT WOMAN (*Looking out of the window and suddenly starting with fear*). Gracious! Ironshirts!

280

GRUSHA. They're after the baby.

THE PEASANT WOMAN. Suppose they come in!

GRUSHA. You mustn't give him to them. Say he's yours.

THE PEASANT WOMAN. Yes.

GRUSHA. They'll run him through if you hand him over.

THE PEASANT WOMAN. But suppose they ask for it? The silver for the harvest is in the house.

290

GRUSHA. If you let them have him, they'll run him through, right here in this room! You've got to say he's yours!

THE PEASANT WOMAN. Yes. But what if they don't believe me?

GRUSHA. You must be firm.

THE PEASANT WOMAN. They'll burn the roof over our heads.

GRUSHA. That's why you must say he's yours. His name's Michael. But I shouldn't have told you. (*The* PEASANT WOMAN *nods*) Don't nod like that. And don't tremble—they'll notice.

300

THE PEASANT WOMAN. Yes.

GRUSHA. And stop saying yes, I can't stand it. (SHE *shakes the* WOMAN) Don't you have any children?

THE PEASANT WOMAN (*Muttering*). He's in the war.

GRUSHA. Then maybe *he's* an Ironshirt? Do you want *him* to run children through with a lance? You'd bawl him out. "No fooling with lances in *my* house!" you'd shout, "is that what I've reared you for? Wash your neck before you speak to your mother!"

THE PEASANT WOMAN. That's true, he couldn't get away with anything around here!

GRUSHA. So you'll say he's yours?

THE PEASANT WOMAN. Yes.

GRUSHA. Look! They're coming!

(*There is a knocking at the door. The* WOMEN *don't answer. Enter* IRONSHIRTS. *The* PEASANT WOMAN *bows low*)

THE CORPORAL. Well, here she is. What did I tell you? What a nose I have! I *smelt* her. Lady, I have a question for you. Why did you run away? What did you think I would do to you? I'll bet it was something dirty. Confess!

GRUSHA (*While the* PEASANT WOMAN *bows again and again*). I'd left some milk on the stove, and I suddenly remembered it.

THE CORPORAL. Or maybe you imagined I looked at you in a dirty way? Like there could be something between us? A lewd sort of look, know what I mean?

GRUSHA. I didn't see it.

THE CORPORAL. But it's possible, huh? You admit that much. After all, I might be a pig. I'll be frank with you: I could think of all sorts of things if we were alone. (*To the* PEASANT WOMAN) Shouldn't you be busy in the yard? Feeding the hens?

THE PEASANT WOMAN (*falling suddenly to her knees*). Soldier, I didn't know a thing about it. Please don't burn the roof over our heads.

THE CORPORAL. What are you talking about?

THE PEASANT WOMAN. I had nothing to do with it. She left it on my doorstep, I swear it!

THE CORPORAL (*Suddenly seeing the* CHILD *and whistling*). Ah, so there's a little something in the crib! Blockhead, I smell a thousand piasters. Take the old girl outside and hold on to her. It looks like I have a little cross-examining to do.

(*The* PEASANT WOMAN *lets herself be led out by the* PRIVATE, *without a word*)

So, you've got the child I wanted from you! (HE *walks toward the crib*)

GRUSHA. Officer, he's mine. He's not the one you're after.

THE CORPORAL. I'll just take a look. (HE *bends over the crib.* GRUSHA *looks round in despair*)

GRUSHA. He's mine! He's mine!

THE CORPORAL. Fine linen!

(GRUSHA *dashes at him to pull him away.* HE *throws her off and again bends over the crib. Again looking round in despair,* SHE *sees a log of wood, seizes it, and hits the* CORPORAL *over the head from behind. The* CORPORAL *collapses.* SHE *quickly picks up the* CHILD *and rushes off*)

THE SINGER.
And in her flight from the Ironshirts
After twenty-two days of journeying
At the foot of the Janga-Tu Glacier
Grusha Vashnadze decided to adopt the child.

THE CHORUS.
The helpless girl adopted the helpless child.

(GRUSHA *squats over a half-frozen stream to get the* CHILD *water in the hollow of her hand*)

GRUSHA.
Since no one else will take you, son,
I must take you.
Since no one else will take you, son,
You must take me.
O black day in a lean, lean year,
The trip was long, the milk was dear,
My legs are tired, my feet are sore:
But I wouldn't be without you any more.
I'll throw your silken shirt away
And dress you in rags and tatters.
I'll wash you, son, and christen you in glacier water.
We'll see it through together.

(SHE *has taken off the* CHILD's *fine linen and wrapped it in a rag*)

THE SINGER.
When Grusha Vashnadze
Pursued by the Ironshirts
Came to the bridge on the glacier
Leading to the villages of the Eastern Slope
She sang the Song of the Rotten Bridge
And risked two lives.

(*A wind has risen. The bridge on the glacier is visible in the dark. One rope is broken and half the bridge is hanging down the abyss.* MERCHANTS, TWO MEN *and a* WOMAN, *stand undecided before the bridge as* GRUSHA *and the* CHILD *arrive.* ONE MAN *is trying to catch the hanging rope with a stick*)

410 THE FIRST MAN. Take your time, young woman. You won't get across here anyway.

GRUSHA. But I *have* to get the baby to the east side. To my brother's place.

THE MERCHANT WOMAN. Have to? How d'you mean, "have to"? I have to get there, too—because I have to buy carpets in Atum—carpets a woman had to sell because her husband had to die. But can *I* do what I have to? Can she? Andrei's been fishing for that rope 420 for hours. And I ask you, how are we going to fasten it, even if he gets it up?

THE FIRST MAN (*Listening*). Hush, I think I hear something.

GRUSHA. The bridge isn't quite rotted through. I think I'll try it.

THE MERCHANT WOMAN. *I* wouldn't—if the devil himself were after me. It's suicide.

THE FIRST MAN (*Shouting*). Hi!

GRUSHA. Don't shout! (*To the* MERCHANT 430 WOMAN) Tell him not to shout.

THE FIRST MAN. But there's someone down there calling. Maybe they've lost their way.

THE MERCHANT WOMAN. Why shouldn't he shout? Is there something funny about you? Are they after you?

GRUSHA. All right, I'll tell. The Ironshirts are after me. I knocked one down.

THE SECOND MAN. Hide our merchandise!

(*The* WOMAN *hides a sack behind a rock*)

440 THE FIRST MAN. Why didn't you say so right away? (*To the* OTHERS) If they catch her they'll make mincemeat out of her!

GRUSHA. Get out of my way. I've got to cross that bridge.

THE SECOND MAN. You can't. The precipice is two thousand feet deep.

THE FIRST MAN. Even with the rope it'd be no use. We could hold it up with our hands. But then we'd have to do the same for the 450 Ironshirts.

GRUSHA. Go away.

(*There are calls from the distance: "Hi, up there!"*)

THE MERCHANT WOMAN. They're getting near. But you can't take the child on that bridge. It's sure to break. And look!

(GRUSHA *looks down into the abyss. The* IRONSHIRTS *are heard calling again from below*)

THE SECOND MAN. Two thousand feet!

GRUSHA. But those men are worse. 460

THE FIRST MAN. You can't do it. Think of the baby. Risk your life but not a child's.

THE SECOND MAN. With the child she's that much heavier!

THE MERCHANT WOMAN. Maybe she's *really* got to get across. Give *me* the baby. I'll hide it. Cross the bridge alone!

GRUSHA. I won't. We belong together. (*To the* CHILD) "Live together, die together."

(SHE *sings*) 470

THE SONG OF THE ROTTEN BRIDGE

Deep is the abyss, son,
I see the weak bridge sway
But it's not for us, son,
To choose the way.

The way I know
Is the one you must tread,
And all you will eat
Is my bit of bread.

Of every four pieces 480
You shall have three.
Would that I knew
How big they will be!

Get out of my way, I'll try it without the rope.

THE MERCHANT WOMAN. You are tempting God!

(*There are shouts from below*)

GRUSHA. Please, throw that stick away, or they'll get the rope and follow me.

(*Pressing the* CHILD *to her,* SHE *steps onto the swaying bridge. The* MERCHANT WOMAN *screams when it looks as though the bridge is about to collapse. But* GRUSHA *walks on and reaches the far side*) 490

THE FIRST MAN. She made it!

THE MERCHANT WOMAN (*Who has fallen on*

416 **Atum** a trading center

her knees and begun to pray, angrily). I still think it was a sin.

(*The* IRONSHIRTS *appear; the* CORPORAL'S *head is bandaged*)

500

THE CORPORAL. Seen a woman with a child?

THE FIRST MAN (*While the* SECOND MAN *throws the stick into the abyss*). Yes, there! But the bridge won't carry you!

THE CORPORAL. You'll pay for this, blockhead!

(GRUSHA, *from the far bank, laughs and shows the* CHILD *to the* IRONSHIRTS. SHE *walks on. The wind blows*)

510

GRUSHA (*Turning to the* CHILD). You mustn't be afraid of the wind. He's a poor thing too. He has to push the clouds along and he gets quite cold doing it. (*Snow starts falling*) And the snow isn't so bad, either, Michael. It covers the little fir trees so they won't die in winter. Let me sing you a little song. (SHE *sings*)

THE SONG OF THE CHILD

Your father is a bandit
A harlot the mother who bore you.
Yet honorable men
Shall kneel down before you.

520

Food to the baby horses
The tiger's son will take.
The mothers will get milk
From the son of the snake.

3. *In The Northern Mountains*

THE SINGER.
Seven days the sister, Grusha Vashnadze,
Journeyed across the glacier
And down the slopes she journeyed.
"When I enter my brother's house," she thought
"He will rise and embrace me."
"Is that you, sister?" he will say,
"I have long expected you.
This is my dear wife,
And this is my farm, come to me by marriage,
With eleven horses and thirty-one cows. Sit down.

10

Sit down with your child at our table and eat."
The brother's house was in a lovely valley.
When the sister came to the brother,
She was ill from walking.
The brother rose from the table.

(*A* FAT PEASANT COUPLE *rise from the table.* LAVRENTI VASHNADZE *still has a napkin round his neck, as* GRUSHA, *pale and supported by a* SERVANT, *enters with the* CHILD)

20

LAVRENTI. Where've *you* come from, Grusha?

GRUSHA (*Feebly*). Across the Janga-Tu Pass, Lavrenti.

THE SERVANT. I found her in front of the hay barn. She has a baby with her.

THE SISTER-IN-LAW. Go and groom the mare. (*Exit the* SERVANT)

LAVRENTI. This is my wife Aniko.

THE SISTER-IN-LAW. I thought you were in service in Nuka.

GRUSHA (*Barely able to stand*). Yes, I was.

30

THE SISTER-IN-LAW. Wasn't it a good job? We were told it was.

GRUSHA. The Governor got killed.

LAVRENTI. Yes, we heard there were riots. Your aunt told us. Remember, Aniko?

THE SISTER-IN-LAW. Here with us, it's very quiet. City people always want something going on. (SHE *walks toward the door, calling*) Sosso, Sosso, don't take the cake out of the oven yet, d'you hear? Where on earth are you?

40

(*Exit, calling*)

LAVRENTI (*Quietly, quickly*). Is there a father? (*As* SHE *shakes her head*) I thought not. We must think up something. She's religious.

THE SISTER-IN-LAW (*Returning*). Those servants! (*To* GRUSHA) You have a child.

GRUSHA. It's mine.

(SHE *collapses.* LAVRENTI *rushes to her assistance*)

THE SISTER-IN-LAW. Heavens, she's ill—what are we going to do?

LAVRENTI (*Escorting her to a bench near the stove*). Sit down, sit. I think it's just weakness, Aniko.

THE SISTER-IN-LAW. As long as it's not scarlet fever!

LAVRENTI. She'd have spots if it was. It's only weakness. Don't worry, Aniko. (*To* GRUSHA) Better, sitting down?

THE SISTER-IN-LAW. Is the child hers?

GRUSHA. Yes, mine.

LAVRENTI. She's on her way to her husband.

THE SISTER-IN-LAW. I see. Your meat's getting cold. (LAVRENTI *sits down and begins to eat*) Cold food's not good for you, the fat mustn't get cold, you know your stomach's your weak spot. (*To* GRUSHA) If your husband's not in the city, where is he?

LAVRENTI. She got married on the other side of the mountain, she says.

THE SISTER-IN-LAW. On the other side of the mountain. I see. (SHE *also sits down to eat*)

GRUSHA. I think I should lie down somewhere, Lavrenti.

THE SISTER-IN-LAW. If it's consumption we'll all get it. (SHE *goes on cross-examining her*) Has your husband got a farm?

GRUSHA. He's a soldier.

LAVRENTI. But he's coming into a farm—a small one—from his father.

THE SISTER-IN-LAW. Isn't he in the war? Why not?

GRUSHA (*With effort*). Yes, he's in the war.

THE SISTER-IN-LAW. Then why d'you want to go to the farm?

LAVRENTI. When he comes back from the war, he'll return to his farm.

THE SISTER-IN-LAW. But you're going there now?

LAVRENTI. Yes, to wait for him.

THE SISTER-IN-LAW (*Calling shrilly*). Sosso, the cake!

GRUSHA (*Murmuring feverishly*). A farm—a soldier—waiting—sit down, eat.

THE SISTER-IN-LAW. It's scarlet fever.

GRUSHA (*Starting up*). Yes, he's got a farm!

LAVRENTI. I think it's just weakness, Aniko. Would you look after the cake yourself, dear?

THE SISTER-IN-LAW. But when will he come back if war's broken out again as people say? (SHE *waddles off, shouting*) Sosso! Where on earth are you? Sosso!

LAVRENTI (*Getting up quickly and going to* GRUSHA). You'll get a bed in a minute. She has a good heart. But wait till after supper.

GRUSHA (*Holding out the* CHILD *to him*) Take him.

LAVRENTI (*Taking it and looking around*). But you can't stay here long with the child. She's religious, you see.

(GRUSHA *collapses.* LAVRENTI *catches her*)

THE SINGER.
The sister was so ill,
The cowardly brother had to give her shelter.
Summer departed, winter came.
The winter was long, the winter was short
People mustn't know anything,
Rats mustn't bite,
Spring mustn't come.

(GRUSHA *sits over the weaving loom in a workroom.* SHE *and the* CHILD, *who is squatting on the floor, are wrapped in blankets.*)
(SHE *sings*)

THE SONG OF THE CENTER

And the lover started to leave
And his betrothed ran pleading after him
Pleading and weeping, weeping and teaching:
"Dearest mine, dearest mine
When you go to war as now you do
When you fight the foe as soon you will
Don't lead with the front line
And don't push with the rear line
At the front is red fire
In the rear is red smoke
Stay in the war's center
Stay near the standard bearer
The first always die
The last are also hit
Those in the center come home."

Michael, we must be clever. If we make ourselves as small as cockroaches, the sister-in-law will forget we're in the house, and then we can stay till the snow melts.

(*Enter* LAVRENTI. HE *sits down beside his* SISTER)

LAVRENTI. Why are you sitting there muffled up like coachmen, you two? Is it too cold in the room?

GRUSHA (*Hastily removing one shawl*). It's not too cold, Lavrenti.

LAVRENTI. If it's too cold, you shouldn't be sitting here with the child. Aniko would never forgive herself! (*Pause*) I hope our priest didn't question you about the child? 150

GRUSHA. He did, but I didn't tell him anything.

LAVRENTI. That's good. I wanted to speak to you about Aniko. She has a good heart but she's very, very sensitive. People need only mention our farm and she's worried. She takes everything hard, you see. One time our milkmaid went to church with a hole in her stocking. Ever since, Aniko has worn two pairs of stockings in church. It's the old family in her. 160 (HE *listens*) Are you sure there are no rats around? If there are rats, you couldn't live here.

(*There are sounds as of dripping from the roof*)

What's that, dripping?

GRUSHA. It must be a barrel leaking.

LAVRENTI. Yes, it must be a barrel. You've been here six months, haven't you? Was I talking about Aniko? 170 (THEY *listen again to the snow melting*) You can't imagine how worried she gets about your soldier-husband. "Suppose he comes back and can't find her!" she says and lies awake. "He can't come before the spring," I tell her. The dear woman! (*The drops begin to fall faster*) When d'you think he'll come? What do *you* think? (GRUSHA *is silent*) Not before the spring, you agree? (GRUSHA *is silent*) You don't believe he'll come at all? 180 (GRUSHA *is silent*) But when the spring comes and the snow melts here and on the passes, you can't stay on. They may come and look for you. There's already talk of an illegitimate child. (*The "glockenspiel" of the falling drops has grown faster and steadier*) Grusha, the snow is melting on the roof. Spring is here.

GRUSHA. Yes.

LAVRENTI (*Eagerly*). I'll tell you what we'll do. You need a place to go, and, because of the child, 190 (HE *sighs*) you have to have a husband, so people won't talk. Now I've made cautious inquiries to see if we can find you a husband. Grusha, I *have* one. I talked to a peasant woman who has a son. Just the other side of the mountain. A small farm. And she's willing.

GRUSHA. But I *can't* marry! I must wait for Simon Shashava.

LAVRENTI. Of course. That's all been taken care of. You don't need a man in bed—you 200 need a man on paper. And I've found you one. The son of this peasant woman is going to die. Isn't that wonderful? He's at his last gasp. And all in line with our story—a husband from the other side of the mountain! And when you met him he was at the last gasp. So you're a widow. What do you say?

GRUSHA. It's true I could use a document with stamps on it for Michael.

LAVRENTI. Stamps make all the difference. 210 Without something in writing the Shah couldn't prove he's a Shah. And you'll have a place to live.

GRUSHA. How much does the peasant woman want?

LAVRENTI. Four hundred piasters.

GRUSHA. Where will you find it?

LAVRENTI (*Guiltily*). Aniko's milk money.

GRUSHA. No one would know us there. I'll do it. 220

LAVRENTI (*Getting up*). I'll let the peasant woman know. (*Quick exit*)

GRUSHA. Michael, you cause a lot of fuss. I came to you as the pear tree comes to the sparrows. And because a Christian bends down and picks up a crust of bread so nothing will go to waste. Michael, it would have been better had I walked quickly away on that Easter Sunday in Nuka in the second courtyard. Now I *am* a fool. 230

THE SINGER.

The bridegroom was lying on his deathbed
when the bride arrived.
The bridegroom's mother was waiting at the
door, telling her to hurry.
The bride brought a child along.
The witness hid it during the wedding.

(*On one side the bed. Under the mosquito net lies a very* SICK MAN. GRUSHA *is pulled in at a run by her future* MOTHER-IN-LAW. THEY *are* 240 *followed by* LAVRENTI *and the* CHILD)

THE MOTHER-IN-LAW. Quick! Quick! Or he'll die on us before the wedding. (*To* LAVRENTI) I was never told she had a child already.

LAVRENTI. What difference does it make? (*Pointing toward the* DYING MAN) It can't matter to him—in his condition.

THE MOTHER-IN-LAW. To him? But *I'll* never survive the shame! We are honest people. (SHE *begins to weep*) My Jussup doesn't have to marry a girl with a child!

LAVRENTI. All right, make it another two hundred piasters. You'll have it in writing that the farm will go to you: but she'll have the right to live here for two years.

THE MOTHER-IN-LAW (*Drying her tears*). It'll hardly cover the funeral expenses. I hope she'll really lend a hand with the work. And what's happened to the monk? He must have slipped out through the kitchen window. We'll have the whole village round our necks when they hear Jussup's end is come! Oh dear! I'll run and get the monk. But he mustn't see the child!

LAVRENTI. I'll take care he doesn't. But why only a monk? Why not a priest?

THE MOTHER-IN-LAW. Oh, he's just as good. I only made one mistake: I paid half his fee in advance. Enough to send him to the tavern. I only hope . . . (SHE *runs off*)

LAVRENTI. She saved on the priest, the wretch! Hired a cheap monk.

GRUSHA. You *will* send Simon Shashava over to see me if he turns up after all?

LAVRENTI. Yes. (*Pointing at the* SICK MAN) Won't you take a look at him?

(GRUSHA, *taking* MICHAEL *to her, shakes her head*)

He's not moving an eyelid. I hope we aren't too late.

(THEY *listen. On the opposite side enter* NEIGHBORS *who look around and take up positions against the walls, thus forming another wall near the bed, yet leaving an opening so that the bed can be seen.* THEY *start murmuring prayers. Enter the* MOTHER-IN-LAW *with a* MONK. *Showing some annoyance and surprise,* SHE *bows to the* GUESTS)

THE MOTHER-IN-LAW. I hope you won't mind waiting a few moments? My son's bride has just arrived from the city. An emergency wedding is about to be celebrated. (*To the* MONK *in the bedroom*) I might have known you couldn't keep your trap shut. (*To* GRUSHA) The wedding can take place at once. Here's the license. I myself and the bride's brother (LAVRENTI *tries to hide in the background, after having quietly taken* MICHAEL *back from* GRUSHA. *The* MOTHER-IN-LAW *waves him away*), who will be here in a moment, are the witnesses.

(GRUSHA *has bowed to the* MONK. THEY *go to the bed. The* MOTHER-IN-LAW *lifts the mosquito net. The* MONK *starts reeling off the marriage ceremony in Latin. Meanwhile, the* MOTHER-IN-LAW *beckons to* LAVRENTI *to get rid of the* CHILD, *but fearing that it will cry* HE *draws its attention to the ceremony.* GRUSHA *glances once at the* CHILD, *and* LAVRENTI *waves the* CHILD'S *hand in a greeting*)

THE MONK. Are you prepared to be a faithful, obedient, and good wife to this man, and to cleave to him until death you do part?

GRUSHA (*Looking at the* CHILD). I am.

THE MONK (*To the* SICK PEASANT). And are you prepared to be a good and loving husband to your wife until death you do part?

(*As the* SICK PEASANT *does not answer, the* MONK *looks inquiringly around*)

THE MOTHER-IN-LAW. Of course he is! Didn't you hear him say yes?

THE MONK. All right. We declare the marriage contracted! How about extreme unction?

THE MOTHER-IN-LAW. Nothing doing! The wedding cost quite enough. Now I must take care of the mourners. (*To* LAVRENTI) Did we say seven hundred?

LAVRENTI. Six hundred. (HE *pays*) Now I don't want to sit with the guests and get to know people. So farewell, Grusha, and if my widowed sister comes to visit me, she'll get a welcome from my wife, or I'll show my teeth. (*Nods, gives the* CHILD *to* GRUSHA, *and leaves*)

(*The* MOURNERS *glance after him without interest*)

THE MONK. May one ask where this child comes from?

THE MOTHER-IN-LAW. Is there a child? I don't see a child. And you don't see a child either—you understand? Or it may turn out I saw all sorts of things in the tavern! Now come on.

(*After* GRUSHA *has put the* CHILD *down and told him to be quiet,* THEY *move over left,* GRUSHA *is introduced to the* NEIGHBORS)

This is my daughter-in-law. She arrived just in time to find dear Jussup still alive.

ONE WOMAN. He's been ill now a whole year, hasn't he? When our Vassili was drafted he was there to say goodbye.

ANOTHER WOMAN. Such things are terrible for a farm. The corn all ripe and the farmer in bed! It'll really be a blessing if he doesn't suffer too long, I say.

THE FIRST WOMAN (*Confidentially*). You know why we thought he'd taken to his bed? Because of the draft! And now his end is come!

THE MOTHER-IN-LAW. Sit yourselves down, please! And have some cakes!

(SHE *beckons to* GRUSHA *and* BOTH WOMEN *go into the bedroom, where* THEY *pick up the cake pans off the floor. The* GUESTS, *among them the* MONK, *sit on the floor and begin conversing in subdued voices*)

ONE PEASANT (*To whom the* MONK *has handed the bottle which* HE *has taken from his soutane*). There's a child, you say! How can that have happened to Jussup?

A WOMAN. She was certainly lucky to get herself hitched, with him so sick!

THE MOTHER-IN-LAW. They're gossiping already. And gorging themselves on the funeral cakes at the same time! If he doesn't die today, I'll have to bake some more tomorrow!

GRUSHA. I'll bake them for you.

THE MOTHER-IN-LAW. Yesterday some horsemen rode by, and I went out to see who it was. When I came in again he was lying there like a corpse! So I sent for you. It can't take much longer. (SHE *listens*)

THE MONK. Dear wedding and funeral guests! Deeply touched, we stand before a bed of death and marriage. The bride gets a veil; the groom, a shroud: how varied, my children, are the fates of men! Alas! One man dies and has a roof over his head, and the other is married and the flesh turns to dust from which it was made. Amen.

THE MOTHER-IN-LAW. He's getting his own back. I shouldn't have hired such a cheap one. It's what you'd expect. A more expensive monk would behave himself. In Sura there's one with a real air of sanctity about him, but of course he charges a fortune. A fifty-piaster monk like that has no dignity, and as for piety, just fifty piasters' worth and no more! When I came to get him in the tavern he'd just made a speech, and he was shouting: "The war is over, beware of the peace!" We must go in.

GRUSHA (*Giving* MICHAEL *a cake*). Eat this cake, and keep nice and still, Michael.

(*The* TWO WOMEN *offer cakes to the* GUESTS. *The* DYING MAN *sits up in bed.* HE *puts his head out from under the mosquito net, stares at the* TWO WOMEN, *then sinks back again. The* MONK *takes two bottles from his soutane and offers them to the* PEASANT *beside him. Enter* THREE MUSICIANS *who are greeted with a sly wink by the* MONK)

THE MOTHER-IN-LAW (*To the* MUSICIANS). What are you doing here? With instruments?

ONE MUSICIAN. Brother Anastasius here (*Points at the* MONK) told us there was a wedding on.

THE MOTHER-IN-LAW. What? You brought them? Three more on my neck! Don't you know there's a dying man in the next room?

THE MONK. A very tempting assignment for a musician: something that could be either a subdued Wedding March or a spirited Funeral Dance.

THE MOTHER-IN-LAW. Well, you might as well play. Nobody can stop you eating in any case.

(*The* MUSICIANS *play a potpouri. The* WOMEN *serve cakes*)

THE MONK. The trumpet sounds like a whining baby. And you, little drum, what have you got to tell the world?

THE DRUNKEN PEASANT (*Beside the* MONK, *sings*).

Miss Roundass took the old old man
And said that marriage was the thing
To everyone who met 'er.
She later withdrew from the contract because
Candles are better.

(*The* MOTHER-IN-LAW *throws the* DRUNKEN PEASANT *out. The music stops. The* GUESTS *are embarrassed*)

THE GUESTS (*Loudly*).
—Have you heard? The Grand Duke is back! But the Princes are against him.
—They say the Shah of Persia has lent him a great army to restore order in Grusinia.
—But how is that possible? The Shah of Persia is the enemy . . .
—The enemy of Grusinia, you donkey, not the enemy of the Grand Duke!
—In any case, the war's over, so our soldiers are coming back.

(GRUSHA *drops a cake pan,* GUESTS *help her pick up the cake*)

AN OLD WOMAN (*To* GRUSHA). Are you feeling bad? It's just excitement about dear Jussup. Sit down and rest a while, my dear. (GRUSHA *staggers*)

THE GUESTS. Now everything'll be the way it was. Only the taxes'll go up because now we'll have to pay for the war.

GRUSHA (*Weakly*). Did someone say the soldiers are back?

A MAN. I did.

GRUSHA. It can't be true.

THE FIRST MAN (*To a* WOMAN). Show her the shawl. We bought it from a soldier. It's from Persia.

GRUSHA (*Looking at the shawl*). They are here. (SHE *gets up, takes a step, kneels down in prayer, takes the silver cross and chain out of her blouse, and kisses it*)

THE MOTHER-IN-LAW (*While the* GUESTS *silently watch* GRUSHA). What's the matter with you? Aren't you going to look after our guests? What's all this city nonsense got to do with us?

THE GUESTS (*Resuming conversation while* GRUSHA *remains in prayer*).
—You can buy Persian saddles from the soldiers too. Though many want crutches in exchange for them.
—The big shots on one side can win a war, the soldiers on both sides lose it.
—Anyway, the war's over. It's something they can't draft you any more.

(*The* DYING MAN *sits bolt upright in bed.* HE *listens*)

—What we need is two weeks of good weather.
—Our pear trees are hardly bearing a thing this year.

THE MOTHER-IN-LAW (*Offering cakes*). Have some more cakes and welcome! There are more!

(*The* MOTHER-IN-LAW *goes to the bedroom with the empty cake pans. Unaware of the* DYING MAN, SHE *is bending down to pick up another tray when* HE *begins to talk in a hoarse voice*)

THE PEASANT. How many more cakes are you going to stuff down their throats? Think I'm a fucking goldmine?

(*The* MOTHER-IN-LAW *starts, stares at him aghast, while* HE *climbs out from behind the mosquito net*)

THE FIRST WOMAN (*Talking kindly to* GRUSHA *in the next room*). Has the young wife got someone at the front?

A MAN. It's good news that they're on their way home, huh?

THE PEASANT. Don't stare at me like that! Where's this wife you've hung round my neck?

(*Receiving no answer,* HE *climbs out of bed and in his nightshirt staggers into the other room. Trembling,* SHE *follows him with the cake pan*)

THE GUESTS (*Seeing him and shrieking*). Good God! Jussup!

(EVERYONE *leaps up in alarm. The* WOMEN *rush to the door.* GRUSHA, *still on her knees, turns round and stares at the* MAN)

THE PEASANT. A funeral supper! You'd enjoy that, wouldn't you? Get out before I throw you out! (*As the* GUESTS *stampede from the house, gloomily to* GRUSHA) I've upset the apple cart, huh? (*Receiving no answer,* HE *turns round and takes a cake from the pan which his* MOTHER *is holding*)

THE SINGER.
O confusion! The wife discovers she has a husband.
By day there's the child, by night there's the husband.
The lover is on his way both day and night.
Husband and wife look at each other.
The bedroom is small.

530 (*Near the bed the* PEASANT *is sitting in a high wooden bathtub, naked, the* MOTHER-IN-LAW *is pouring water from a pitcher. Opposite* GRUSHA *cowers with* MICHAEL, *who is playing at mending straw mats*)

THE PEASANT (*To his* MOTHER). That's her work, not yours. Where's she hiding out now?

THE MOTHER-IN-LAW (*Calling*). Grusha! The peasant wants you!

GRUSHA (*To* MICHAEL). There are still two holes to mend.

540 THE PEASANT (*When* GRUSHA *approaches*). Scrub my back!

GRUSHA. Can't the peasant do it himself?

THE PEASANT. "Can't the peasant do it himself?" Get the brush! To hell with you! Are you the wife here? Or are you a visitor? (*To the* MOTHER-IN-LAW). It's too cold!

THE MOTHER-IN-LAW. I'll run for hot water.

GRUSHA. Let me go.

THE PEASANT. You stay here. (*The* MOTHER-
550 IN-LAW *exits*) Rub harder. And no shirking. You've seen a naked fellow before. That child didn't come out of thin air.

GRUSHA. The child was not conceived in joy, if that's what the peasant means.

THE PEASANT (*Turning and grinning*). You don't look the type. (GRUSHA *stops scrubbing him, starts back*)

(*Enter the* MOTHER-IN-LAW)

THE PEASANT. A nice thing you've hung
560 around my neck! A simpleton for a wife!

THE MOTHER-IN-LAW. She just isn't co-operative.

THE PEASANT. Pour—but go easy! Ow! Go easy, I said. (*To* GRUSHA) Maybe you did something wrong in the city . . . I wouldn't be surprised. Why else should you be here? But I won't talk about that. I've not said a word about the illegitimate object you brought into my house either. But my patience has limits!
570 It's against nature. (*To the* MOTHER-IN-LAW) More! (*To* GRUSHA) And even if your soldier does come back, you're married.

GRUSHA. Yes.

THE PEASANT. But your soldier won't come back. Don't you believe it.

GRUSHA. No.

THE PEASANT. You're cheating me. You're my wife and you're not my wife. Where you lie, nothing lies, and yet no other woman can lie
580 there. When I go to work in the morning I'm tired—when I lie down at night I'm awake as the devil. God has given you sex—and what d'you do? I don't have ten piasters to buy myself a woman in the city. Besides, it's a long way. Woman weeds the fields and opens up her legs, that's what our calendar says. D'you hear?

GRUSHA (*Quietly*). Yes. I didn't mean to cheat you out of it.

THE PEASANT. She didn't mean to cheat me
590 out of it! Pour some more water! (*The* MOTHER-IN-LAW *pours*) Ow!

THE SINGER.

As she sat by the stream to wash the linen
She saw his image in the water
And his face grew dimmer with the passing moons.
As she raised herself to wring the linen
She heard his voice from the murmuring maple
And his voice grew fainter with the passing
600 moons.
Evasions and sighs grew more numerous,
Tears and sweat flowed.
With the passing moons the child grew up.

(GRUSHA *sits by a stream, dipping linen into the water. In the rear, a few* CHILDREN *are standing*)

GRUSHA (*To* MICHAEL). You can play with them, Michael, but don't let them boss you around just because you're the littlest.

(MICHAEL *nods and joins the* CHILDREN. THEY
610 *start playing*)

THE BIGGEST BOY. Today it's the Heads-Off Game. (*To a* FAT BOY) You're the Prince and you laugh. (*To* MICHAEL) You're the Governor. (*To a* GIRL) You're the Governor's wife and you cry when his head's cut off. And I do the cutting. (HE *shows his wooden sword*) With this. First, they lead the Governor into the yard. The Prince walks in front. The Governor's wife comes last.

620 (THEY *form a procession. The* FAT BOY *is first and laughs. Then comes* MICHAEL, *then the* BIGGEST BOY, *and then the* GIRL, *who weeps*)

MICHAEL (*Standing still*). Me cut off head!

THE BIGGEST BOY. That's my job. You're the littlest. The Governor's the easy part. All you do is kneel down and get your head cut off—simple.

MICHAEL. Me want sword!

THE BIGGEST BOY. It's mine! (HE *gives him a* 630 *kick*)

THE GIRL (*Shouting to* GRUSHA). He won't play his part!

GRUSHA (*Laughing*). Even the little duck is a swimmer, they say.

THE BIGGEST BOY. You can be the Prince if you can laugh.

(MICHAEL *shakes his head*)

THE FAT BOY. I laugh best. Let him cut off the head just once. Then you do it, then me.

640 (*Reluctantly, the* BIGGEST BOY *hands* MICHAEL *the wooden sword and kneels down. The* FAT BOY *sits down slaps his thigh, and laughs with all his might. The* GIRL *weeps loudly.* MICHAEL *swings the big sword and "cuts off" the head. In doing so,* HE *topples over*)

THE BIGGEST BOY. Hey! I'll show you how to cut heads off!

(MICHAEL *runs away. The* CHILDREN *run after him.* GRUSHA *laughs, following them with her* 650 *eyes. On looking back,* SHE *sees* SIMON SHASHAVA *standing on the opposite bank.* HE *wears a shabby uniform*)

GRUSHA. Simon!

SIMON. Is that Grusha Vashnadze?

GRUSHA. Simon!

SIMON (*Formally*). A good morning to the young lady. I hope she is well.

GRUSHA (*Getting up gaily and bowing low*). A good morning to the soldier. God be thanked 660 he has returned in good health.

SIMON. They found better fish, so they didn't eat me, said the haddock.

GRUSHA. Courage, said the kitchen boy. Good luck, said the hero.

SIMON. How are things here? Was the winter bearable? The neighbor considerate?

GRUSHA. The winter was a trifle rough, the neighbor as usual, Simon.

SIMON. May one ask if a certain person still 670 dips her foot in the water when rinsing the linen?

GRUSHA. The answer is no. Because of the eyes in the bushes.

SIMON. The young lady is speaking of soldiers. Here stands a paymaster.

GRUSHA. A job worth twenty piasters?

SIMON. And lodgings.

GRUSHA (*With tears in her eyes*). Behind the barracks under the date trees.

SIMON. Yes, there. A certain person has kept 680 her eyes open.

GRUSHA. She has, Simon.

SIMON. And has not forgotten (GRUSHA *shakes her head*) So the door is still on its hinges as they say? (GRUSHA *looks at him in silence and shakes her head again*) What's this? Is something not as it should be?

GRUSHA. Simon Shashava, I can never return to Nuka. Something has happened.

SIMON. What can have happened? 690

GRUSHA. For one thing, I knocked an Ironshirt down.

SIMON. Grusha Vashnadze must have had her reasons for that.

GRUSHA. Simon Shashava, I am no longer called what I used to be called.

SIMON (*After a pause*). I do not understand.

GRUSHA. When do women change their names, Simon? Let me explain. Nothing stands between us. Everything is just as it was. You 700 must believe that.

SIMON. Nothing stands between us and yet there's something?

GRUSHA. How can I explain it so fast and with the stream between us? Couldn't you cross the bridge there?

SIMON. Maybe it's no longer necessary.

(GRUSHIA. It is very necessary. Come over on this side, Simon. Quick!

SIMON. Does the young lady wish to say 710 someone has come too late?

(GRUSHA *looks up at him in despair, her face streaming with tears.* SIMON *stares before him.* HE *picks up a piece of wood and starts cutting it*)

THE SINGER.

So many words are said, so many left unsaid.
The soldier has come.
Where he comes from, he does not say.
Hear what he thought and did not say:
"The battle began, gray at dawn, grew bloody 720
at noon.
The first man fell in front of me, the second
behind me, the third at my side.

I trod on the first, left the second behind, the third was run through by the captain.
One of my brothers died by steel, the other by smoke.
My neck caught fire, my hands froze in my gloves, my toes in my socks.
730 I fed on aspen buds, I drank maple juice, I slept on stone, in water."

SIMON. I see a cap in the grass. Is there a little one already?

GRUSHA. There is, Simon. There's no keeping that from you. But please don't worry, it is not mine.

SIMON. When the wind once starts to blow, they say, it blows through every cranny. The wife need say no more.

740 (GRUSHA *looks into her lap and is silent*)

THE SINGER.
There was yearning but there was no waiting.
The oath is broken. Neither could say why.
Hear what she thought but did not say:
"While you fought in the battle, soldier,
The bloody battle, the bitter battle
I found a helpless infant
I had not the heart to destroy him
I had to care for a creature that was lost
I had to stoop for breadcrumbs on the floor
I had to break myself for that which was not mine
750 That which was other people's.
Someone must help!
For the little tree needs water
The lamb loses its way when the shepherd is asleep
And its cry is unheard!"

SIMON. Give me back the cross I gave you. Better still, throw it in the stream. (HE *turns to go*)

GRUSHA (*Getting up*). Simon Shashava, don't go away! He isn't mine! He isn't mine! (SHE *hears the* CHILDREN *calling*) What's the matter, children? 760

VOICES. Soldiers! And they're taking Michael away!

(GRUSHA *stands aghast as* TWO IRONSHIRTS, *with* MICHAEL *between them, come toward her*)

ONE OF THE IRONSHIRTS. Are you Grusha? (SHE *nods*) Is this your child?

GRUSHA. Yes. (SIMON *goes*) Simon! 770

THE IRONSHIRT. We have orders, in the name of the law, to take this child, found in your custody, back to the city. It is suspected that the child is Michael Abashwili, son and heir of the late Governor Georgi Abashwili, and his wife, Natella Abashwili. Here is the document and the seal. (THEY *lead the* CHILD *away*)

GRUSHA (*Running after them, shouting*). Leave him here. Please! He's mine!

THE SINGER.
The Ironshirts took the child, the beloved child.
The unhappy girl followed them to the city, the dreaded city.
She who had borne him demanded the child. 780
She who had raised him faced trial.
Who will decide the case?
To whom will the child be assigned?
Who will the judge be? A good judge? A bad?
The city was in flames.
In the judge's seat sat Azdak.

4. *The Story of the Judge*

THE SINGER.
Hear the story of the judge
How he turned judge, how he passed judgment, what kind of judge he was.
On that Easter Sunday of the great revolt, when the Grand Duke was overthrown
And his Governor Abashwili, father of our child, lost his head
The Village Scrivener Azdak found a fugitive in the woods and hid him in his hut.

788 The name **Azdak** should be accented on the second syllable.

(AZDAK, *in rags and slightly drunk, is helping an* OLD BEGGAR *into his cottage*)

AZDAK. Stop snorting, you're not a horse. And it won't do you any good with the police, to run like a snotty nose in April. Stand still, I say. (HE *catches the* OLD MAN, *who has marched into the cottage as if* HE'D *like to go through the walls*) Sit down. Feed. Here's a hunk of cheese. (*From under some rags, in a chest,* HE *fishes out some cheese, and the* OLD MAN *greedily begins to eat*) Haven't eaten in a long time, huh? (*The* OLD MAN *growls*) Why were you running like that, asshole? The cop wouldn't even have seen you.

THE OLD MAN. Had to! Had to!

AZDAK. Blue Funk? (*The* OLD MAN *stares, uncomprehending*) Cold feet? Panic? Don't lick your chops like a Grand Duke. Or an old sow. I can't stand it. We have to accept respectable stinkers as God made them, but not you! I once heard of a senior judge who farted at a public dinner to show an independent spirit! Watching you eat like that gives me the most awful ideas. Why don't you say something? (*Sharply*) Show me your hand. Can't you hear? (*The* OLD MAN *slowly puts out his hand*) White! So you're not a beggar at all! A fraud, a walking swindle! And I'm hiding you from the cops as though you were an honest man! Why were you running like that if you're a landowner? For that's what you are. Don't deny it! I see it in your guilty face! (HE *gets up*) Get out! (*The* OLD MAN *looks at him uncertainly*) What are you waiting for, peasant-flogger?

THE OLD MAN. Pursued. Need undivided attention. Make proposition . . .

AZDAK. Make what? A proposition? Well, if that isn't the height of insolence. He's making me a proposition! The bitten man scratches his fingers bloody, and the leech that's biting him makes him a proposition! Get out, I tell you!

THE OLD MAN. Understand point of view! Persuasion! Pay hundred thousand piasters one night! Yes?

AZDAK. What, you think you can buy me? For a hundred thousand piasters? Let's say a hundred and fifty thousand. Where are they?

THE OLD MAN. Have not them here. Of course. Will be sent. Hope do not doubt.

AZDAK. Doubt very much. Get out!

(*The* OLD MAN *gets up, waddles to the door. A* VOICE *is heard off stage*)

A VOICE. Azdak!

(*The* OLD MAN *turns, waddles to the opposite corner, stands still*)

AZDAK (*Calling out*). I'm not in! (HE *walks to door*) So you're sniffing around here again, Shauwa?

POLICEMAN SHAUWA (*Reproachfully*). You've caught another rabbit, Azdak. And you promised me it wouldn't happen again!

AZDAK (*Severely*). Shauwa, don't talk about things you don't understand. The rabbit is a dangerous and destructive beast. It feeds on plants, especially on the species of plants known as weeds. It must therefore be exterminated.

SHAUWA. Azdak, don't be so hard on me. I'll lose my job if I don't arrest you. I know you have a good heart.

AZDAK. I do not have a good heart! How often must I tell you I'm a man of intellect?

SHAUWA (*Slyly*). I know, Azdak. You're a superior person. You say so yourself. I'm just a Christian and an ignoramus. So I ask you: When one of the Prince's rabbits is stolen, and I'm a policeman, what should I do with the offending party?

AZDAK. Shauwa, Shauwa, shame on you. You stand and ask me a question, than which nothing could be more seductive. It's like you were a woman—let's say that bad girl Nunowna, and you showed me your thigh—Nunowna's thigh, that would be—and asked me: "What shall I do with my thigh, it itches?" Is she as innocent as she pretends? Of course not. I catch a rabbit, but you catch a man. Man is made in God's image. Not so a rabbit, you know that. I'm a rabbit-eater, but you're a man-eater, Shauwa. And God will pass judgment on you. Shauwa, go home and repent. No, stop, there's something . . . (HE *looks at the* OLD MAN *who stands trembling in the corner*) No, it's nothing. Go home and repent. (HE *slams the door behind* SHAUWA) Now you're surprised, huh? Surprised I didn't hand you over? I couldn't hand over a bedbug to that animal. It goes against the grain. Now don't tremble because of a cop! So old and still so scared? Finish your cheese, but eat it like a poor man, or else they'll still catch you. Must I even explain how a poor man behaves? (HE *pushes him down, and then gives him back the cheese*) That box is the table. Lay your elbows on the table. Now, encircle the cheese on the plate like it might be snatched from you at any moment—what right have you to be safe, huh? —now, hold your knife like an undersized sickle, and give your cheese a troubled look because, like all beautiful things, it's already fading away. (AZDAK *watches him*) They're after you, which speaks in your favor, but how can we be sure they're not mistaken about you? In Tiflis one time they hanged a landowner, a Turk, who could prove he quartered his peasants instead of merely cutting them in half, as is the custom, and he squeezed twice the usual amount of taxes out of them, his zeal was above suspicion. And yet they hanged him like a common criminal—because he was a Turk—a thing he couldn't do much about. What injustice! He got onto the gallows by a sheer fluke. In short, I don't trust you.

THE SINGER.

Thus Azdak gave the old beggar a bed,
And learned that old beggar was the old butcher, the Grand Duke himself,
And was ashamed.
He denounced himself and ordered the policeman to take him to Nuka, to court, to be judged.

(*In the court of justice* THREE IRONSHIRTS *sit drinking. From a beam hangs a man in judge's robes. Enter* AZDAK, *in chains, dragging* SHAUWA *behind him*)

AZDAK (*Shouting*). I've helped the Grand Duke, the Grand Thief, the Grand Butcher, to escape! In the name of justice I ask to be severely judged in public trial!

THE FIRST IRONSHIRT. Who's this queer bird?

SHAUWA. That's our Village Scrivener, Azdak.

AZDAK. I am contemptible! I am a traitor! A branded criminal! Tell them, flat-foot, how I insisted on being chained up and brought to the capital. Because I sheltered the Grand Duke, the Grand Swindler, by mistake. And how I found out afterwards. See the marked man denounce himself! Tell them how I forced you to walk with me half the night to clear the whole thing up.

SHAUWA. And all by threats. That wasn't nice of you, Azdak.

AZDAK. Shut your mouth, Shauwa. You don't understand. A new age is upon us! It'll go thundering over you. You're finished. The police will be wiped out—poof! Everything will be gone into, everything will be brought into the open. The guilty will give themselves up. Why? They couldn't escape the people in any case. (*To* SHAUWA) Tell them how I shouted all along Shoemaker Street: (*With big gestures, looking at the* IRONSHIRTS) "In my ignorance I let the Grand Swindler escape! So tear me to pieces, brothers! I wanted to get it in first.

THE FIRST IRONSHIRT. And what did your brothers answer?

SHAUWA. They comforted him in Butcher Street, and they laughed themselves sick in Shoemaker Street. That's all.

AZDAK. But with you it's different. I can see you're men of iron. Brothers, where's the judge? I must be tried.

THE FIRST IRONSHIRT (*Points at the hanged man*). There's the judge. And please stop "bothering" us. It's rather a sore spot this evening.

AZDAK. "There's the judge." An answer never heard in Grusinia before. Townsman, where's His Excellency the Governor? (*Pointing to the floor*) There's His Excellency, stranger. Where's the Chief Tax Collector? Where's the official Recruiting Officer? The Patriarch? The Chief of Police? There, there, there—all there. Brothers, I expected no less of you.

THE SECOND IRONSHIRT. What? *What* was it you expected, funny man?

AZDAK. What happened in Persia, brother, what happened in Persia?

THE SECOND IRONSHIRT. What did happen in Persia?

AZDAK. Everybody was hanged. Viziers, tax collectors. Everybody. Forty years ago now. My grandfather, a remarkable man by the way, saw it all. For three whole days. Everywhere.

THE SECOND IRONSHIRT. And who ruled when the Vizier was hanged?

AZDAK. A peasant ruled when the Vizier was hanged.

THE SECOND IRONSHIRT. And who commanded the army?

AZDAK. A soldier, a soldier.

THE SECOND IRONSHIRT. And who paid the wages?

AZDAK. A dyer. A dyer paid the wages.

THE SECOND IRONSHIRT. Wasn't it a weaver, maybe?

THE FIRST IRONSHIRT. And why did all this happen, Persian?

AZDAK. Why did all this happen? Must there be a special reason? Why do you scratch yourself, brother? War! Too long a war! And no justice! My grandfather brought back a song that tells how it was. I will sing it for you. With my friend the policeman. (*To* SHAUWA) And hold the rope tight. It's very suitable.

(HE *sings, with* SHAUWA *holding the rope tight around him*)

THE SONG OF INJUSTICE IN PERSIA

Why don't our sons bleed any more? Why don't our daughters weep?
Why do only the slaughter-house cattle have blood in their veins?
Why do only the willows shed tears on Lake Urmi?

The king must have a new province, the peasant must give up his savings.
That the roof of the world might be conquered, the roof of the cottage is torn down.
Our men are carried to the ends of the earth, so that great ones can eat at home.
The soldiers kill each other, the marshals salute each other.
They bite the widow's tax money to see if it's good, their swords break.
The battle was lost, the helmets were paid for.
(*Refrain*)
Is it so? Is it so?
(*Refrain*) (*By* SHAUWA)
Yes, yes, yes, yes, yes it's so.

AZDAK. Do you want to hear the rest of it? (*The* FIRST IRONSHIRT *nods*)

THE SECOND IRONSHIRT (*To* SHAUWA). Did he teach you that song?

SHAUWA. Yes, only my voice isn't very good.

THE SECOND IRONSHIRT. No. (*To* AZDAK) Go on singing.

AZDAK. The second verse is about the peace. (HE *sings*)

The offices are packed, the streets overflow with officials.
The rivers jump their banks and ravage the fields.
Those who cannot let down their own trousers rule countries.
They can't count up to four, but they devour eight courses.
The corn farmers, looking round for buyers, see only the starving.
The weavers go home from their looms in rags.
(*Refrain*)
Is it so? Is it so?
(*Refrain*) (*By* SHAUWA)
Yes, yes, yes, yes, yes it's so.

AZDAK.
That's why our sons don't bleed any more, that's why our daughters don't weep.
That's why only the slaughter-house cattle have blood in their veins,
And only the willows shed tears by Lake Urmi toward morning.

THE FIRST IRONSHIRT. Are you going to sing that song here in town?

AZDAK. Sure. What's wrong with it?

THE FIRST IRONSHIRT. Have you noticed that the sky's getting red? (*Turning round,* AZDAK *sees the sky red with fire*) It's the people's quarters. On the outskirts of town. The carpet weavers have caught the "Persian Sickness," too. And they've been asking if Prince Kazbeki isn't eating too many courses. This morning they strung up the city judge. As for us we beat them to pulp. We were paid one hundred piasters per man, you understand?

AZDAK (*After a pause*). I understand.

(HE *glances shyly round and, creeping away, sits down in a corner, his head in his hands*)

THE IRONSHIRTS (*To each other*).
—If there ever was a trouble-maker it's him.
—He must've come to the capital to fish in the troubled waters.

SHAUWA. Oh, I don't think he's a really bad character, gentlemen. Steals a few chickens here and there. And maybe a rabbit.

THE SECOND IRONSHIRT (*Approaching* AZDAK). Came to fish in the troubled waters, huh?

AZDAK (*Looking up*). I don't know why I came.

280 THE SECOND IRONSHIRT. Are you in with the carpet weavers maybe? (AZDAK *shakes his head*) How about that song?

AZDAK. From my grandfather. A silly and ignorant man.

THE SECOND IRONSHIRT. Right. And how about the dyer who paid the wages?

AZDAK (*Muttering*). That was in Persia.

THE FIRST IRONSHIRT. And this denouncing of yourself? Because you didn't hang the Grand 290 Duke with your own hands?

AZDAK. Didn't I tell you I let him run? (HE *creeps farther away and sits on the floor*)

SHAUWA. I can swear to that: he let him run.

(*The* IRONSHIRTS *burst out laughing and slap* SHAUWA *on the back*. AZDAK *laughs loudest.* THEY *slap* AZDAK *too, and unchain him.* THEY ALL *start drinking as the* FAT PRINCE *enters with a* YOUNG MAN)

THE FIRST IRONSHIRT (*To* AZDAK, *pointing at* 300 *the* FAT PRINCE). There's your "new age" for you! (*More laughter*)

THE FAT PRINCE. Well, my friends, what is there to laugh about? Permit me a serious word. Yesterday morning the Princes of Grusinia overthrew the war-mongering government of the Grand Duke and did away with his Governors. Unfortunately the Grand Duke himself escaped. In this fateful hour our carpet weavers, those eternal trouble-makers, had the effrontery 310 to stir up a rebellion and hang the universally loved city judge, our dear Illo Orbeliani. Ts-ts-ts. My friends, we need peace, peace, peace in Grusinia! And Justice! So I've brought along my dear nephew Bizergan Kazbeki. He'll be the new judge, hm? A very gifted fellow. What do you say? I want your opinion. Let the people decide!

THE SECOND IRONSHIRT. Does this mean *we* elect the judge?

320 THE FAT PRINCE. Precisely. Let the people propose some very gifted fellow! Confer among yourselves, my friends. (*The* IRONSHIRTS *confer*) Don't worry, my little fox. The job's yours. And when we catch the Grand Duke we won't have to kiss this rabble's ass any longer.

THE IRONSHIRTS (*Between themselves*).

—Very funny: they're wetting their pants because they haven't caught the Grand Duke.

—When the outlook isn't so bright, they say: 330
"My friends!" and "Let the people decide!"

—Now he even wants justice for Grusinia! But fun is fun as long as it lasts!

(*Pointing at* AZDAK)

—*He* knows all about justice. Hey, rascal, would you like this nephew fellow to be the judge?

AZDAK. Are you asking me? You're not asking *me?!*

THE FIRST IRONSHIRT. Why not? Anything 340 for a laugh!

AZDAK. You'd like to test him to the marrow, correct? Have you a criminal on hand? An experienced one? So the candidate can show what he knows?

THE SECOND IRONSHIRT. Let's see. We do have a couple of doctors downstairs. Let's use them.

AZDAK. Oh, no, that's no good, we can't take real criminals till we're sure the judge 350 will be appointed. He may be dumb, but he must be appointed, or the Law is violated. And the Law is a sensitive organ. It's like the spleen, you mustn't hit it—that would be fatal. Of course you can hang those two without violating the Law, because there was no judge in the vicinity. But Judgment, when pronounced, must be pronounced with absolute gravity—it's all such nonsense. Suppose, for instance, a judge jails a woman—let's say she's stolen a 360 corncake to feed her child—and this judge isn't wearing his robes—or maybe he's scratching himself while passing sentence and half his body is uncovered—a man's thigh *will* itch once in a while—the sentence this judge passes is a disgrace and the Law is violated. In short it would be easier for a judge's robe and a judge's hat to pass judgment than for a man with no robe and no hat. If you don't treat it with respect, the Law just disappears on you. 370 Now you don't try out a bottle of wine by offering it to a dog; you'd only lose your wine.

THE FIRST IRONSHIRT. Then what do you suggest, hair-splitter?

AZDAK. I'll be the defendant.

THE FIRST IRONSHIRT. You? (HE *bursts out laughing*)

THE FAT PRINCE. What have you decided?

THE FIRST IRONSHIRT. We've decided to stage a rehearsal. Our friend here will be the defen- 380 dant. Let the candidate be the judge and sit there.

THE FAT PRINCE. It isn't customary, but why not? (*To the* NEPHEW) A mere formality, my little fox. What have I taught you? Who got there first—the slow runner or the fast?

THE NEPHEW. The silent runner, Uncle Arsen.

(*The* NEPHEW *takes the chair. The* IRONSHIRTS *and the* FAT PRINCE *sit on the steps. Enter* AZDAK, *mimicking the gait of the Grand Duke*)

AZDAK (*In the Grand Duke's accent*). Is any here knows me? Am Grand Duke.

THE IRONSHIRTS.
—*What* is he?
—The Grand Duke. He knows him, too.
—Fine. So get on with the trial.

AZDAK. Listen! Am accused instigating war? Ridiculous! Am saying ridiculous! That enough? If not, have brought lawyers. Believe five hundred. (HE *points behind him, pretending to be surrounded by lawyers*) Requisition all available seats for lawyers!

(*The* IRONSHIRTS *laugh, the* FAT PRINCE *joins in*)

THE NEPHEW (*To the* IRONSHIRTS). You really wish me to try this case? I find it rather unusual. From the taste angle, I mean.

THE FIRST IRONSHIRT. Let's go!

THE FAT PRINCE (*Smiling*). Let him have it, my little fox!

THE NEPHEW. All right. People of Grusinia versus Grand Duke. Defendant, what have you got to say for yourself?

AZDAK. Plenty. Naturally, have read war lost. Only started on the advice of patriots. Like Uncle Arsen Kazbeki. Call Uncle Arsen as witness.

THE FAT PRINCE (*To the* IRONSHIRTS, *delightedly*). What a screw-ball!

THE NEPHEW. Motion rejected. One cannot be arraigned for declaring a war, which every ruler has to do once in a while, but only for running a war badly.

AZDAK. Rubbish! Did not run it at all! Had it run! Had it run by Princes! Naturally, they messed it up.

THE NEPHEW. Do you by any chance deny having been commander-in-chief?

AZDAK. Not at all! Always *was* commander-in-chief. At birth shouted at wet nurse. Was trained drop turds in toilet, grew accustomed to command. Always commanded officials rob my cash box. Officers flog soldiers only on command. Landowners sleep with peasants' wives only on strictest command. Uncle Arsen here grew his belly at *my* command!

THE IRONSHIRTS (*Clapping*). He's good! Long live the Grand Duke!

THE FAT PRINCE. Answer him, my little fox. I'm with you.

THE NEPHEW. I shall answer him according to the dignity of the law. Defendant, preserve the dignity of the law!

AZDAK. Agreed. Command you to proceed with the trial!

THE NEPHEW. It is not your place to command me. You claim that the Princes forced you to declare war. How can you claim, then, that they—er—"messed it up"?

AZDAK. Did not send enough people. Embezzled funds. Sent sick horses. During attack, drinking in whorehouse. Call Uncle Arsen as witness.

THE NEPHEW. Are you making the outrageous suggestion that the Princes of this country did not fight?

AZDAK. No. Princes fought. Fought for war contracts.

THE FAT PRINCE (*Jumping up*). That's too much! This man talks like a carpet weaver!

AZDAK. Really? I told nothing but the truth.

THE FAT PRINCE. Hang him! Hang him!

THE FIRST IRONSHIRT (*Pulling the* PRINCE *down*). Keep quiet! Go on, Excellency!

THE NEPHEW. Quiet! I now render a verdict: You must be hanged! By the neck! Having lost war!

AZDAK. Young man, seriously advise not fall publicly into jerky clipped manner of speech. Cannot be employed as watchdog if howl like wolf. Got it? If people realize Princes speak same language as Grand Duke, may hang Grand Duke *and Princes,* huh? By the way, must overrule verdict. Reason? War lost, but not for Princes. Princes won their war. Got 3,863,000 piasters for horses not delivered, 8,240,000 piasters for food supplies not produced. Are therefore victors. War lost only for Grusinia, which as such is not present in this court.

480 THE FAT PRINCE. I think that will do, my friends. (*To* AZDAK) You can withdraw, funny man. (*To the* IRONSHIRTS) you may now ratify the new judge's appointment, my friends.

THE FIRST IRONSHIRT. Yes, we can. Take down the judge's gown.

(ONE IRONSHIRT *climbs on the back of the* OTHER, *pulls the gown off the hanged man*)

THE FIRST IRONSHIRT (*To the* NEPHEW). Now you run away so the right ass can get
490 on the right chair. (*To* AZDAK) Step forward! Go to the judge's seat! Now sit in it!

(AZDAK *steps up, bows, and sits down*)

The judge was always a rascal! Now the rascal shall be a judge!

(*The judge's gown is placed round his shoulders, the hat on his head*)

And what a judge!

THE SINGER.

And there was civil war in the land.
The mighty were not safe.
500 And Azdak was made a judge by the Ironshirts.
And Azdak remained a judge for two years.

THE SINGER AND CHORUS.

When the towns were set afire
And rivers of blood rose higher and higher,
Cockroaches crawled out of every crack.
And the court was full of schemers
And the church of foul blasphemers.
In the judge's cassock sat Azdak.

(AZDAK *sits in the judge's chair, peeling an apple.* SHAUWA *is sweeping out the hall. On*
510 *one side an* INVALID *in a wheelchair. Opposite, a* YOUNG MAN *accused of blackmail. An* IRONSHIRT *stands guard, holding the Ironshirt's banner*)

AZDAK. In consideration of the large number of cases, the Court today will hear two cases at a time. Before I open the proceedings, a short announcement—I accept.

(HE *stretches out his hand. The* BLACKMAILER *is the only one to produce any money.* HE *hands*
520 *it to* AZDAK)

I reserve the right to punish one of the parties for contempt of court. (HE *glances at* THE INVALID) You (*To the* DOCTOR) are a doctor, and you (*To the* INVALID) are bringing a complaint against him. Is the doctor responsible for your condition?

THE INVALID. Yes. I had a stroke on his account.

AZDAK. That would be professional negligence. 530

THE INVALID. Worse than negligence. I gave this man money for his studies. So far, he hasn't paid me back a cent. It was when I heard he was treating a patient free that I had my stroke.

AZDAK. Rightly. (*To a* LIMPING MAN) And what are *you* doing here?

THE LIMPING MAN. I'm the patient, your honor.

AZDAK. He treated your leg for nothing? 540

THE LIMPING MAN. The wrong leg! My rheumatism was in the left leg, and he operated on the right. That's why I limp now.

AZDAK. And you were treated free?

THE INVALID. A five-hundred-piaster operation free! For nothing! For a God-bless-you! And I paid for this man's studies! (*To the* DOCTOR) Did they teach you to operate free?

THE DOCTOR. Your Honor, it is actually the custom to demand the fee before the operation, 550 as the patient is more willing to pay before an operation than after. Which is only human. In the case in question I was convinced, when I started the operation, that my servant had already received the fee. In this I was mistaken.

THE INVALID. He was mistaken! A good doctor doesn't make mistakes! He examines before he operates!

AZDAK. That's right. (*To* SHAUWA) Public Prosecutor, what's the other case about? 560

SHAUWA (*Busily sweeping*). Blackmail.

THE BLACKMAILER. High Court of Justice, I'm innocent. I only wanted to find out from the landowner concerned if he really *had* raped his niece. He informed me very politely that this was not the case, and gave me the money only so I could pay for my uncle's studies.

AZDAK. Hm. (*To the* DOCTOR) You, on the other hand, can cite no extenuating circumstances for your offense, huh? 570

THE DOCTOR. Except that to err is human.

AZDAK. And you are aware that in money matters a good doctor is a highly responsible person? I once heard of a doctor who got a thousand piasters for a sprained finger by remarking that sprains have something to do with blood circulation, which after all a less good doctor might have overlooked, and who, on another occasion made a real gold mine out of a somewhat disordered gall bladder, he treated it with such loving care. You have no excuse, Doctor. The corn merchant, Uxu, had his son study medicine to get some knowledge of trade, our medical schools are so good. (*To the* BLACKMAILER) What's the landowner's name?

SHAUWA. He doesn't want it mentioned.

AZDAK. In that case I will pass judgment. The Court considers the blackmail proved. And you (*To the* INVALID) are sentenced to a fine of one thousand piasters. If you have a second stroke, the doctor will have to treat you free. Even if he has to amputate. (*To the* LIMPING MAN) As compensation, you will receive a bottle of rubbing alcohol. (*To the* BLACKMAILER) You are sentenced to hand over half the proceeds of your deal to the Public Prosecutor to keep the landowner's name secret. You are advised, moreover, to study medicine—you seem well suited to that calling. (*To the* DOCTOR) You have perpetrated an unpardonable error in the practice of your profession: you are acquitted. Next cases!

THE SINGER AND CHORUS.

Men won't do much for a shilling.
For a pound they may be willing.
For 20 pounds the verdict's in the sack.
As for the many, all too many,
Those who've only got a penny—
They've one single, sole recourse: Azdak.

(*Enter* AZDAK *from the caravansary on the highroad, followed by an old bearded* INNKEEPER. *The judge's chair is carried by a* STABLEMAN *and* SHAUWA. *An* IRONSHIRT, *with a banner, takes up his position*)

AZDAK. Put me down. Then we'll get some air, maybe even a good stiff breeze from the lemon grove there. It does justice good to be done in the open: the wind blows her skirts up and you can see what she's got. Shauwa, we've been eating too much. These official journeys are exhausting. (*To the* INNKEEPER) It's a question of your daughter-in-law?

THE INNKEEPER. Your Worship, it's a question of the family honor. I wish to bring an action on behalf of my son, who's on business on the other side of the mountain. This is the offending stableman, and here's my daughter-in-law.

(*Enter the* DAUGHTER-IN-LAW, *a voluptuous wench.* SHE *is veiled*)

AZDAK (*Sitting down*). I accept.

(*Sighing, the* INNKEEPER *hands him some money*)

Good. Now the formalities are disposed of. This is a case of rape?

THE INNKEEPER. Your Honor, I caught the fellow in the act. Ludovica was in the straw on the stable floor.

AZDAK. Quite right, the stable. Lovely horses! I specially liked the little roan.

THE INNKEEPER. The first thing I did, of course, was to question Ludovica. On my son's behalf.

AZDAK (*Seriously*). I said I specially liked the little roan.

THE INNKEEPER (*Coldly*). Really? Ludovica confessed the stableman took her against her will.

AZDAK. Take your veil off, Ludovica. (SHE *does so*) Ludovica, you please the Court. Tell us how it happened.

LUDOVICA (*Well-schooled*). When I entered the stable to see the new foal the stableman said to me on his own accord: "It's hot today!" and laid his hand on my left breast. I said to him: "Don't do that!" But he continued to handle me indecently, which provoked my anger. Before I realized his sinful intentions, he got much closer. It was all over when my father-in-law entered and accidentally trod on me.

THE INNKEEPER (*Explaining*). On my son's behalf.

AZDAK (*To the* STABLEMAN). You admit you started it?

THE STABLEMAN. Yes.

AZDAK. Ludovica, you like to eat sweet things?

LUDOVICA. Yes, sunflower seeds!

AZDAK. You like to lie a long time in the bathtub?

LUDOVICA. Half an hour or so.

AZDAK. Public Prosecutor, drop your knife—there—on the ground. (SHAUWA *does so*) Ludovica, pick up that knife. (LUDOVICA, *swaying her hips, does so*) See that? (HE *points at her*) The way it moves? The rape is now proven. By eating too much—sweet things, especially—by lying too long in warm water, by laziness and too soft a skin, you have raped that unfortunate man. Think you can run around with a behind like that and get away with it in court? This is a case of intentional assault with a dangerous weapon! You are sentenced to hand over to the Court the little roan which your father liked to ride "on his son's behalf." And now, come with me to the stables, so the Court may inspect the scene of the crime, Ludovica.

THE SINGER AND THE CHORUS.

When the sharks the sharks devour
Little fishes have their hour.
For a while the load is off their back.
On Grusinia's highways faring
Fixed-up scales of justice bearing
Strode the poor man's magistrate: Azdak.

And he gave to the forsaken
All that from the rich he'd taken.
And a bodyguard of roughnecks was Azdak's.
And our good and evil man, he
Smiled upon Grusinia's Granny.
His emblem was a tear in sealing wax.

All mankind should love each other
But when visiting your brother
Take an ax along and hold it fast.
Not in theory but in practice
Miracles are wrought with axes
And the age of miracles is not past.

(AZDAK'S *judge's chair is in a tavern.* THREE RICH FARMERS *stand before* AZDAK. SHAUWA *brings him wine. In a corner stands an* OLD PEASANT WOMAN. *In the open doorway, and outside, stand* VILLAGERS *looking on. An* IRONSHIRT *stands guard with a banner*)

AZDAK. The Public Prosecutor has the floor.

SHAUWA. It concerns a cow. For five weeks the defendant has had a cow in her stable, the property of the farmer Suru. She was also found to be in possession of a stolen ham, and a number of cows belonging to Shutoff were killed after he asked the defendant to pay the rent on a piece of land.

THE FARMERS.

—It's a matter of my ham, Your Honor.
—It's a matter of my cow, Your Honor.
—It's a matter of my land, Your Honor.

AZDAK. Well, Granny, what have *you* got to say to all this?

THE OLD WOMAN. Your Honor, one night toward morning, five weeks ago, there was a knock at my door, and outside stood a bearded man with a cow. "My dear woman," he said, "I am the miracle-working Saint Banditus and because your son has been killed in the war, I bring you this cow as a souvenir. Take good care of it."

THE FARMERS.

—The robber, Irakli, Your Honor!
—Her brother-in-law, Your Honor!
—The cow-thief!
—The incendiary!
—He must be beheaded!

(*Outside, a* WOMAN *screams. The* CROWD *grows restless, retreats. Enter the* BANDIT IRAKLI *with a huge ax*)

THE BANDIT. A very good evening, dear friends! A glass of vodka!

THE FARMERS (*Crossing themselves*). Irakli!

AZDAK. Public Prosecutor, a glass of vodka for our guest. And who are you?

THE BANDIT. I'm a wandering hermit, Your Honor. Thanks for the gracious gift.

(HE *empties the glass which* SHAUWA *has brought*)

Another!

AZDAK. I am Azdak. (HE *gets up and bows. The* BANDIT *also bows*) The Court welcomes the foreign hermit. Go on with your story, Granny.

THE OLD WOMAN. Your Honor, that first night I didn't yet know Saint Banditus could work miracles, it was only the cow. But one night, a few days later, the farmer's servants came to take the cow away again. Then they turned round in front of my door and went off without the cow. And bumps as big as a fist sprouted on their heads. So I knew that Saint Banditus had changed their hearts and turned them into friendly people. (*The* BANDIT *roars with laughter*)

THE FIRST FARMER. I know what changed them.

770 AZDAK. That's fine. You can tell us later. Continue.

THE OLD WOMAN. Your Honor, the next one to become a good man was the farmer Shutoff—a devil, as everyone knows. But Saint Banditus arranged it so he let me off the rent on the little piece of land.

THE SECOND FARMER. Because my cows were killed in the field. (*The* BANDIT *laughs*)

THE OLD WOMAN (*Answering* AZDAK'*s sign to*
780 *continue*). Then one morning the ham came flying in at my window. It hit me in the small of the back. I'm still lame, Your Honor, look. (SHE *limps a few steps*) (*The* BANDIT *laughs*) Your Honor, was there ever a time when a poor old woman could get a ham *without* a miracle?

(*The* BANDIT *starts sobbing*)

AZDAK (*Rising from his chair*). Granny, that's a question that strikes straight at the
790 Court's heart. Be so kind as to sit here.

(*The* OLD WOMAN, *hesitating, sits in the judge's chair*)

AZDAK (*Sits on the floor, glass in hand, reciting*).

Granny
We could almost call you Granny Grusinia
The Woebegone
The Bereaved Mother
Whose sons have gone to war
800 Receiving the present of a cow
She bursts out crying.
When she is beaten
She remains hopeful.
When she's not beaten
She's surprised.
On us
Who are already damned
May you render a merciful verdict
Granny Grusinia!
810 (*Bellowing at the* FARMERS)
Admit you don't believe in miracles, you atheists! Each of you is sentenced to pay five hundred piasters! For godlessness! Get out!

(*The* FARMERS *slink out*)

And you Granny, and you (*To the* BANDIT) pious man, empty a pitcher of wine with the Public Prosecutor and Azdak!

THE SINGER AND THE CHORUS.

And he broke the rules to save them.
Broken law like bread he gave them,
Brought them to shore upon his crooked back. 820
At long last the poor and lowly
Had someone who was not too holy
To be bribed by empty hands: Azdak.

For two years it was his pleasure
To give the beasts of prey short measure:
He became a wolf to fight the pack.
From All Hallows to All Hallows
On his chair beside the gallows
Dispensing justice in his fashion sat Azdak.

THE SINGER.

But the era of disorder came to an end. 830
The Grand Duke returned.
The Governor's wife returned.
A trial was held.
Many died.
The people's quarters burned anew.
And fear seized Azdak.

(AZDAK'*s judge's chair stands again in the court of justice.* AZDAK *sits on the floor, shaving and talking to* SHAUWA. *Noises outside. In the rear the* FAT PRINCE'*s head is carried by on a lance*) 840

AZDAK. Shauwa, the days of your slavery are numbered, maybe even the minutes. For a long time now I have held you in the iron curb of reason, and it has torn your mouth till it bleeds. I have lashed you with reasonable arguments, I have manhandled you with logic. You are by nature a weak man, and if one slyly throws an argument in your path, you *have* to snap it up, you can't resist. It is your nature to lick the hand of some superior being. 850 But superior beings can be of very different kinds. And now, with your liberation, you will soon be able to follow your natural inclinations, which are low. You will be able to follow your infallible instinct, which teaches you to plant your fat heel on the faces of men. Gone is the era of confusion and disorder, which I find described in the Song of Chaos. Let us now sing that song together in memory of those terrible days. Sit down and don't do violence 860 to the music. Don't be afraid. It sounds all right. And it has a fine refrain. (HE *sings*)

THE SONG OF THE CHAOS

Sister, hide your face! Brother, take your knife!
The times are out of joint!
Big men are full of complaint
And small men full of joy.
The city says:
"Let us drive the strong ones from our midst!"
Offices are raided. Lists of serfs are destroyed.
870 They have set Master's nose to the grindstone.
They who lived in the dark have seen the light.
The ebony poor box is broken.
Magnificent sesnem wood is sawed up for beds.
Who had no bread have barns full.
Who begged for alms of corn now mete it out.

SHAUWA (*Refrain*). Oh, oh, oh, oh.

AZDAK (*Refrain*).
Where are you, General, where are you?
Please, please, please, restore order!

The nobleman's son can no longer be recog-
880 nized;
The lady's child becomes the son of her slave.
The councilors meet in a shed.
Once, this man was barely allowed to sleep on the wall;
Now, he stretches his limbs in a bed.
Once, this man rowed a boat; now, he owns ships.
Their owner looks for them, but they're his no longer.
Five men are sent on a journey by their master.
"Go yourself," they say, "we have arrived."

SHAUWA (*Refrain*). Oh, oh, oh, oh.

890 AZDAK (*Refrain*).
Where are you, General, where are you?
Please, please, please, restore order!

Yes, So it might have been, had order been neglected much longer. But now the Grand Duke has returned to the capital, and the Persians have lent him an army to restore order with. The suburbs are already aflame. Go and get me the big book I always sit on. (SHAUWA *brings the big book from the judge's chair.* Azdak opens it) This is the Statue Book and I've always used it, as you can testify. Now I'd better look in this book and see what they can do to me. I've let the down-and-outs get away with murder, and I'll have to pay for it. I helped poverty onto its skinny legs, so they'll hang me for drunkedness. I peeped into the rich man's pocket, which is bad taste. And I can't hide anywhere—everybody knows me because I've helped everybody. 900 910

SHAUWA. Someone's coming!

AZDAK (*In panic,* HE *walks trembling to the chair*). It's the end. And now they'd enjoy seeing what a Great Man I am. I'll deprive them of that pleasure. I'll beg on my knees for mercy. Spittle will slobber down my chin. The fear of death is in me.

(*Enter* NATELLA ABASHWILI, *the* GOVERNOR'S WIFE, *followed by the* ADJUTANT *and an* IRONSHIRT)

THE GOVERNOR'S WIFE. What sort of a creature is that, Shalva? 920

AZDAK. A willing one, Your Highness, a man ready to oblige.

THE ADJUTANT. Natella Abashwili, wife of the late Governor, has just returned. She is looking for her two-year-old son, Michael. She has been informed that the child was carried off to the mountains by a former servant.

AZDAK. The child will be brought back, Your Highness, at your service. 930

THE ADJUTANT. They say that the person in question is passing it off as her own.

AZDAK. She will be beheaded, Your Highness, at your service.

THE ADJUTANT. That is all.

THE GOVERNOR'S WIFE (*Leaving*). I don't like the man.

AZDAK (*Following her to door, bowing*). At your service, Your Highness, it will all be arranged.

5. The Chalk Circle

THE SINGER.
Hear now the story of the trial
Concerning Governor Abashwili's child
And the establishing of the true mother
By the famous test of the Chalk Circle.

(*The court of justice in Nuka.* IRONSHIRTS *lead* MICHAEL *across stage and out at the back.* IRONSHIRTS *hold* GRUSHA *back with their lances under the gateway until the* CHILD *has been led through. Then* SHE *is admitted.* SHE *is accompanied by the former governor's* COOK. *Distant noises and a fire-red sky*)

GRUSHA (*Trying to hide*). He's brave, he can wash himself now.

THE COOK. You're lucky. It's not a real judge. It's Azdak, a drunk who doesn't know what he's doing. The biggest theives have got by through him. Because he gets everything mixed up and the rich never offer him big enough bribes, the likes of us sometimes do pretty well.

GRUSHA. I *need* luck right now.

THE COOK. Touch wood. (SHE *crosses herself*) I'd better offer up another prayer that the judge may be drunk.

(SHE *prays with motionless lips, while* GRUSHA *looks around, in vain, for the* CHILD)

Why must you hold on to it at any price if it isn't yours? In days like these?

GRUSHA. He's mine. I brought him up.

THE COOK. Have you never thought what'd happen when she came back?

GRUSHA. At first I thought I'd give him to her. Then I thought she wouldn't come back.

THE COOK. And even a borrowed coat keeps a man warm, hm? (GRUSHA *nods*) I'll swear to anything for you. You're a decent girl. (SHE *sees the soldier* SIMON SHASHAVA *approaching*) You've done wrong by Simon, though. I've been talking with him. He just can't understand.

GRUSHA (*Unaware of* SIMON'S *presence*). Right now I can't be bothered whether he understands or not!

THE COOK. He knows the child isn't yours, but you married and not free "til death you do part"—he can't understand *that.*

(GRUSHA *sees* SIMON *and greets him*)

SIMON (*Gloomily*). I wish the lady to know I will swear I am the father of the child.

GRUSHA (*Low*). Thank you, Simon.

SIMON. At the same time I wish the lady to know my hands are not tied—nor are hers.

THE COOK. You needn't have said that. You know she's married.

SIMON. And it needs no rubbing in.

(*Enter an* IRONSHIRT)

THE IRONSHIRT. Where's the judge? Has anyone seen the judge?

ANOTHER IRONSHIRT (*stepping forward*). The judge isn't here yet. Nothing but a bed and a pitcher in the whole house!

(*Exeunt* IRONSHIRTS)

THE COOK. I hope nothing has happened to him. With any other judge you'd have about as much chance as a chicken has teeth.

GRUSHA (*Who has turned away and covered her face*). Stand in front of me. I shouldn't have come to Nuka. If I run into the Ironshirt, the one I hit over the head . . .

(SHE *screams. An* IRONSHIRT *had stopped and, turning his back, had been listening to her.* HE *now wheels around. It is the* CORPORAL, *and* HE *has a huge scar across his face*)

THE IRONSHIRT (*In the gateway*). What's the matter, Shotta? Do you know her?

THE CORPORAL (*After staring for some time*). No.

THE IRONSHIRT. She's the one who stole the Abashwili child, or so they say. If you know anything about it you can make some money, Shotta. (*Exit the* CORPORAL, *cursing*)

80 THE COOK. Was it him? (GRUSHA *nods*) I think he'll keep his mouth shut, or he'd be admitting he was after the child.

GRUSHA. I'd almost forgotten him.

(*Enter* THE GOVERNOR'S WIFE, *followed by the* ADJUTANT *and* TWO LAWYERS)

THE GOVERNOR'S WIFE. At least there are no common people here, thank God. I can't stand their smell. It always gives me migraine.

THE FIRST LAWYER. Madam, I must ask you 90 to be careful what you say until we have another judge.

THE GOVERNOR'S WIFE. But I didn't say anything, Illo Shuboladze. I love the people with their simple straightforward minds. It's only that their smell brings on my migraine.

THE SECOND LAWYER. There won't be many spectators. The whole population is sitting at home behind locked doors because of the riots on the outskirts of town.

100 THE GOVERNOR'S WIFE (*Looking at* GRUSHA). Is that the creature?

THE FIRST LAWYER. Please, most gracious Natella Abashwili, abstain from invective until it is certain the Grand Duke has appointed a new judge and we're rid of the present one, who's about the lowest fellow ever seen in judge's gown. Things are all set to move, you see.

(*Enter* IRONSHIRTS *from the courtyard*)

110 THE COOK. Her Grace would pull your hair out on the spot if she didn't know Azdak is for the poor. He goes by the face.

(IRONSHIRTS *begin fastening a rope to a beam.* AZDAK, *in chains, is led in, followed by* SHAUWA, *also in chains. The* THREE FARMERS *bring up the rear*)

AN IRONSHIRT. Trying to run away, were you? (HE *strikes* AZDAK)

ONE FARMER. Off with his judge's gown be-120 fore we string him up!

(IRONSHIRTS *and* FARMERS *tear off* AZDAK'S *gown. His torn underwear is visible. Then someone kicks him*)

AN IRONSHIRT (*Pushing him into someone else*). If you want a heap of justice, here it is!

(*Accompanied by shouts of "You take it!" and "Let me have him, Brother!"* THEY *throw* AZDAK *back and forth until* HE *collapses. Then* HE *is lifted up and dragged under the noose*)

THE GOVERNOR'S WIFE (*Who, during this* 130 *"Ball-game," has clapped her hands hysterically*). I disliked that man from the moment I first saw him.

AZDAK (*Covered with blood, panting*). I can't see. Give me a rag.

AN IRONSHIRT. What is it you want to see?

AZDAK. You, you dogs! (HE *wipes the blood out of his eyes with his shirt*) Good morning, dogs! How goes it, dogs! How's the dog world! Does it smell good? Got another boot for me 140 to lick? Are you back at each other's throats, dogs?

(*Accompanied by a* CORPORAL, *a dust-covered* RIDER *enters.* HE *takes some documents from a leather case, looks at them, then interrupts*)

THE RIDER. Stop! I bring a dispatch from the Grand Duke, containing the latest appointments.

THE CORPORAL (*Bellowing*). Atten-shun!

THE RIDER. Of the new judge it says: "We appoint a man whom we have to thank for 150 saving a life indispensable to the country's welfare—a certain Azdak of Nuka." Which is he?

SHAUWA (*Pointing*). That's him, Your Excellency.

THE CORPORAL (*Bellowing*). What's going on here?

AN IRONSHIRT. I beg to report that His Honor Azdak was already His Honor Azdak, but on these farmers' denunciation was pronounced the 160 Grand Duke's enemy.

THE CORPORAL (*Pointing at the* FARMERS). March them off! (THEY *are marched off.* THEY *bow all the time*) See to it that His Honor Azdak is exposed to no more violence.

(*Exeunt* RIDER *and* CORPORAL)

THE COOK (*To* SHAUWA). She clapped her hands! I hope he saw it!

THE FIRST LAWYER. It's a catastrophe.

(AZDAK *has fainted. Coming to,* HE *is dressed* 170 *again in judge's robes.* HE *walks, swaying, toward the* IRONSHIRTS)

AN IRONSHIRT. What does Your Honor desire?

AZDAK. Nothing, fellow dogs, or just an occasional boot to lick. (*To* SHAUWA) I pardon you. (HE *is unchained*) Get me some red wine, the sweet kind.

(SHAUWA *stumbles off*)

Get out of here, I've got to judge a case.

(*Exeunt* IRONSHIRTS. SHAUWA *returns with a pitcher of wine.* AZDAK *gulps it down*)

AZDAK. Something for my backside. (SHAUWA *brings the Statute Book, puts it on the judge's chair.* AZDAK *sits on it*) I accept.

(*The* PROSECUTORS, *among whom a worried council has been held, smile with relief.* THEY *whisper*)

THE COOK. Oh dear!

SIMON. A well can't be filled with dew, they say.

THE LAWYERS (*Approaching* AZDAK, *who stands up, expectantly*). A quite ridiculous case, Your Honor. The accused has abducted a child and refuses to hand it over.

AZDAK (*Stretching out his hand, glancing at* GRUSHA). A most attractive person. (HE *fingers the money, then sits down, satisfied*) I declare the proceedings open and demand the whole truth. (*To* GRUSHA) Especially from you.

THE FIRST LAWYER. High Court of Justice! Blood, as the popular saying goes, is thicker than water. This old adage . . .

AZDAK (*Interrupting*). The Court wants to know the lawyers' fee.

THE FIRST LAWYER (*Surprised*). I beg your pardon? (AZDAK, *smiling, rubs his thumb and index finger*) Oh, I see. Five hundred piasters, Your Honor, to answer the Court's somewhat unusual question.

AZDAK. Did you hear? The question is unusual. I ask it because I listen in quite a different way when I know you're good.

THE FIRST LAWYER (*Bowing*). Thank you, Your Honor. High Court of Justice, of all ties the ties of blood are strongest. Mother and child—is there a more intimate relationship? Can one tear a child from its mother? High Court of Justice, she has conceived it in the holy ecstasies of love. She has carried it in her womb. She has fed it with her blood. She has borne it with pain. High Court of Justice, it has been observed that even the wild tigress, robbed of her young, roams restless through the mountains, shrunk to a shadow. Nature herself . . .

AZDAK (*Interrupting, to* GRUSHA). What's your answer to all this and anything else that lawyer might have to say?

GRUSHA. He's mine.

AZDAK. Is that all? I hope you can prove it. Why should I assign the child to you in any case?

GRUSHA. I brought him up like the priest says "according to my best knowledge and conscience." I always found him something to eat. Most of the time he had a roof over his head. And I went to such trouble for him. I had expenses too. I didn't look out for my own comfort. I brought the child up to be friendly with everyone, and from the beginning taught him to work. As well as he could, that is. He's still very little.

THE FIRST LAWYER. Your Honor, it is significant that the girl herself doesn't claim any tie of blood between her and the child.

AZDAK. The Court takes note of that.

THE FIRST LAWYER. Thank you, Your Honor. And now permit a woman bowed in sorrow—who has already lost her husband and now has also to fear the loss of her child—to address a few words to you. The gracious Natella Abashwili is . . .

THE GOVERNOR'S WIFE (*Quietly*). A most cruel fate, Sir, forces me to describe to you the tortures of a bereaved mother's soul, the anxiety, the sleepless nights, the . . .

THE SECOND LAWYER (*Bursting out*). It's outrageous the way this woman is being treated! Her husband's palace is closed to her! The revenue of her estates is blocked, and she is cold-bloodedly told that it's tied to the heir. She can't do a thing without that child. She can't even pay her lawyers!! (*To the* FIRST LAWYER, *who desperate about this outburst, makes frantic gestures to keep him from speaking*) Dear Illo Shuboladze, surely it can be divulged now that the Abashwili estates are at stake?

THE FIRST LAWYER. Please, Honored Sandro Oboladze! We agreed . . . (*To* AZDAK) Of course it is correct that the trial will also decide if our noble client can dispose of the Abashwili estates, which are rather extensive. I say "also" advisedly, for in the foreground stands the human tragedy of a mother, as Natella Abashwili very properly explained in the first words of her moving statement. Even if Michael Abashwili were not heir to the estates, he would still be the dearly beloved child of my client.

AZDAK. Stop! The Court is touched by the mention of estates. It's a proof of human feeling.

THE SECOND LAWYER. Thanks, Your Honor. Dear Illo Shuboladze, we can prove in any case that the woman who took the child is not the child's mother. Permit me to lay before the Court the bare facts. High Court of Justice, by an unfortunate chain of circumstances, Michael Abashwili was left behind on that Easter Sunday while his mother was making her escape. Grusha, a palace kitchen maid, was seen with the baby . . .

THE COOK. All her mistress was thinking of was what dresses she'd take along!

THE SECOND LAWYER (*Unmoved*). Nearly a year later Grusha turned up in a mountain village with a baby and there entered into the state of matrimony with . . .

AZDAK. How did you get to that mountain village?

GRUSHA. On foot, Your Honor. And it was mine.

SIMON. I am the father, Your Honor.

THE COOK. I used to look after it for them, Your Honor. For five piasters.

THE SECOND LAWYER. This man is engaged to Grusha, High Court of Justice: his testimony is not trustworthy.

AZDAK. Are you the man she married in the mountain village?

SIMON. No, Your Honor, she married a peasant.

AZDAK (*To* GRUSHA). Why? (*Pointing at* SIMON) Is he no good in bed? Tell the truth.

GRUSHA. We didn't get that far. I married because of the baby. So it'd have a roof over his head. (*Pointing at* SIMON) He was in the war, Your Honor.

AZDAK. And now he wants you back again, huh?

SIMON. I wish to state in evidence . . .

GRUSHA (*Angrily*). I am no longer free, Your Honor.

AZDAK. And the child, you claim, comes from whoring? (GRUSHA *doesn't answer*) I'm going to ask you a question: What kind of child is it? Is it a ragged little bastard or from a well-to-do family?

GRUSHA (*Angrily*). He's just an ordinary child.

AZDAK. I mean—did he have refined features from the beginning?

GRUSHA. He had a nose on his face.

AZDAK. A very significant comment! It has been said of me that I went out one time and sniffed at a rosebush before rendering a verdict—tricks like that are needed nowadays. Well, I'll make it short, and not listen to any more lies. (*To* GRUSHA) Especially not yours. (*To* ALL *the accused*) I can imagine what you've cooked up to cheat me! I know you people. You're swindlers.

GRUSHA (*Suddenly*). I can understand your wanting to cut it short, now I've seen what you accepted!

AZDAK. Shut up! Did I accept anything from you?

GRUSHA (*While the* COOK *tries to restrain her*). I haven't got anything.

AZDAK. True. Quite true. From starvelings I never get a thing. I might just as well starve, myself. You want justice, but do you want to pay for it, hm? When you go to a butcher you know you have to pay, but you people go to a judge as if you were going to a funeral supper.

SIMON (*Loudly*). When the horse was shod, the horse-fly held out its leg, as the saying is.

AZDAK (*Eagerly accepting the challenge*). Better a treasure in manure than a stone in a mountain stream.

SIMON. A fine day. Let's go fishing, said the angler to the worm.

AZDAK. I'm my own master, said the servant, and cut off his foot.

SIMON. I love you as a father, said the Czar to the peasants, and had the Czarevitch's head chopped off.

AZDAK. A fool's worst enemy is himself.

SIMON. However, a fart has no nose.

AZDAK. Fined ten piasters for indecent language in court! That'll teach you what justice is.

GRUSHA (*Furiously*). A fine kind of justice! You play fast and loose with us because we don't talk as refined as that crowd with their lawyers!

AZDAK. That's true. You people are too dumb. It's only right you should get it in the neck.

380 GRUSHA. You want to hand the child over to her, and she wouldn't even know how to keep it dry, she's so "refined"! You know about as much about justice as I do!

AZDAK. There's something in that. I'm an ignorant man. Haven't even a decent pair of pants on under this gown. Look! With me, everything goes for food and drink—I was educated at a convent. Incidentally, I'll fine you ten piasters for contempt of court. And you're a 390 very silly girl, to turn me against you, instead of making eyes at me and wiggling your backside a little to keep me in a good temper. Twenty piasters!

GRUSHA. Even if it was thirty, I'd tell you what I think of your justice, you drunken onion! (*Incoherently*) How dare you talk to me like the cracked Isaiah on the church window? As if you were somebody? For you weren't born to this. You weren't born to rap your own 400 mother on the knuckles if she swipes a little bowl of salt someplace. Aren't you ashamed of yourself when you see how I tremble before you? You've made yourself their servant so no one will take their houses from them—houses they had stolen! Since when have houses belonged to the bedbugs? But you're on the watch, or they couldn't drag our men into their wars! You bribe-taker! (AZDAK *half gets up, starts beaming. With his little hammer* HE 410 *half-heartedly knocks on the table as if to get silence. As* GRUSHA'S *scolding continues,* HE *only beats time with his hammer*). I've no respect for you. No more than for a thief or a bandit with a knife! You can do what you want. You can take the child away from me, a hundred against one, but I tell you one thing: only extortioners should be chosen for a profession like yours, and men who rape children! As punishment! Yes, let *them* sit in 420 judgment on their fellow creatures. It is worse than to hang from the gallows.

AZDAK (*Sitting down*). Now it'll be thirty! And I won't go on squabbling with you—we're not in a tavern. What'd happen to my dignity as a judge? Anyway, I've lost interest in your case. Where's the couple who wanted a divorce? (*To* SHAUWA) Bring 'em in. This case is adjourned for fifteen minutes.

THE FIRST LAWYER (*To the* GOVERNOR'S WIFE). Even without using the rest of the evidence, 430 Madam, we have the verdict in the bag.

THE COOK (*To* GRUSHA). You've gone and spoiled your chances with him. You won't get the child now.

THE GOVERNOR'S WIFE. Shalva, my smelling salts!

(*Enter a* VERY OLD COUPLE)

AZDAK. I accept. (*The* OLD COUPLE *don't understand*) I hear you want to be divorced. How long have you been together? 440

THE OLD WOMAN. Forty years, Your Honor.

AZDAK. And why do you want a divorce?

THE OLD MAN. We don't like each other, Your Honor.

AZDAK. Since when?

THE OLD WOMAN. Oh, from the very beginning, Your Honor.

AZDAK. I'll think about your request and render my verdict when I'm through with the other case. (SHAUWA *leads them back*) I need 450 the child. (HE *beckons* GRUSHA *to him and bends not unkindly toward her*) I've noticed you have a soft spot for justice. I don't believe he's your child, but if he *were* yours, woman, wouldn't you want him to be rich? You'd only have to say he wasn't yours, and he'd have a palace and many horses in his stable and many beggars on his doorstep and many soldiers in his service and many petitioners in his courtyard, wouldn't he? What do you say—don't you want him to 460 be rich? (GRUSHA *is silent*)

THE SINGER.

Hear now what the angry girl thought but did not say:

Had he golden shoes to wear
He'd be cruel as a bear.
Evil would his life disgrace.
He'd laugh in my face.
Carrying a heart of flint
Is too troublesome a stint.
Being powerful and bad 470
Is hard on a lad.

Then let hunger be his foe!
Hungry men and women, no.
Let him fear the darksome night
But not daylight!

AZDAK. I think I understand you, woman.

GRUSHA (*Suddenly and loudly*). I won't give him up. I've raised him, and he knows me.

(*Enter* SHAUWA *with the* CHILD)

480 THE GOVERNOR'S WIFE. It's in rags!

GRUSHA. That's not true. But I wasn't given time to put his good shirt on.

THE GOVERNOR'S WIFE. It must have been in a pigsty.

GRUSHA (*Furiously*). I'm not a pig, but there are some who are! Where did you leave your baby?

THE GOVERNOR'S WIFE. I'll show you, you vulgar creature! (SHE *is about to throw herself* 490 *on* GRUSHA, *but is restrained by her* LAWYERS) She's a criminal, she must be whipped. Immediately!

THE SECOND LAWYER (*Holding his hand over her mouth*). Natella Abashwili, your promised . . . Your Honor, the plaintiff's nerves . . .

AZDAK. Plaintiff and defendant! The Court has listened to your case, and has come to no decision as to who the real mother is, therefore, I, the judge, am obliged to *choose* a mother for 500 the child. I'll make a test. Shauwa, get a piece of chalk and draw a circle on the floor.

(SHAUWA *does so*)

AZDAK. Now place the child in the center. (SHAUWA *puts* MICHAEL, *who smiles at* GRUSHA, *in the center of the circle*) Stand near the circle, both of you. (THE GOVERNOR'S WIFE *and* GRUSHA *step up to the circle*) Now each of you take the child by one hand. (THEY *do so*) The true mother is she who can pull the child out of the 510 circle.

THE SECOND LAWYER (*Quickly*). High Court of Justice, I object! The fate of the great Abashwili estates, which are tied to the child, as the heir, should not be made dependent on such a doubtful duel. In addition, my client does not command the strength of this person, who is accustomed to physical work.

AZDAK. She looks pretty well fed to me. Pull! (GOVERNOR'S WIFE *pulls the* CHILD *out of the circle on her side;* GRUSHA *has let go and stands* 520 *aghast*) What's the matter with you? You didn't pull!

GRUSHA. I didn't hold on to him.

THE FIRST LAWYER (*Congratulating the* GOVERNOR'S WIFE). What did I say! The ties of blood!

GRUSHA (*Running to* AZDAK). Your Honor, I take back everything I said against you. I ask your forgiveness. But could I keep him till he can speak all the words? He knows a few. 530

AZDAK. Don't influence the Court. I bet you only know about twenty words yourself. All right, I'll make the test once more, just to be certain. (*The* TWO WOMEN *take up their positions again*) Pull! (*Again* GRUSHA *lets go of the* CHILD)

GRUSHA (*In despair*). I brought him up! Shall I also tear him to pieces? I can't!

AZDAK (*Rising*). And in this manner the Court has established the true mother. (*To* 540 GRUSHA) Take your child and be off. I advise you not to stay in the city with him. (*To the* GOVERNOR'S WIFE) And you disappear before I fine you for fraud. Your estates fall to the city. They'll be converted into a playground for the children. They need one, and I've decided it shall be called after me: Azdak's Garden. (THE GOVERNOR'S WIFE *has fainted and is carried out by the* LAWYERS *and the* ADJUTANT. GRUSHA *stands motionless.* SHAUWA *leads the* CHILD *to-* 550 *ward her*) Now I'll take off this judge's gown —it's grown too hot for me. I'm not cut out for a hero. In token of farewell I invite you all to a little dance outside on the meadow. Oh, I'd almost forgotten something in my excitement . . . to sign the divorce decree.

(*Using the judge's chair as a table,* HE *writes something on a piece of paper, and prepares to leave. Dance music has started*)

SHAUWA (*Having read what is on the paper*). 560 But that's not right. You've not divorced the old people. You've divorced Grusha!

AZDAK. Have I divorced the wrong couple? What a pity! And I never retract! If I did, how could we keep order in the land? (*To the* OLD COUPLE) I'll invite you to my party instead. You don't mind dancing with each other, do you?

(*To* GRUSHA *and* SIMON) I've got forty piasters coming from you.

570 SIMON (*Pulling out his purse*). Cheap at the price, Your Honor. And many thanks.

AZDAK (*Pocketing the cash*). I'll be needing this.

GRUSHA (*To* MICHAEL). So we'd better leave the city tonight, Michael. (*To* SIMON) You like him?

SIMON. With my respects, I like him.

GRUSHA. Now I can tell you: I took him because on that Easter Sunday I got engaged to

580 you. So he's a child of love. Michael, let's dance.

(SHE *dances with* MICHAEL, SIMON *dances with the* COOK, *the* OLD COUPLE *with each other.* AZDAK *stands lost in thought. The* DANCERS *soon hide him from view. Occasionally* HE *is seen, but less and less as* MORE COUPLES *join the dance*)

THE SINGER.

And after that evening Azdak vanished and was never seen again.
The people of Grusinia did not forget him but long remembered
The period of his judging as a brief golden age,
Almost an age of justice.

(ALL THE COUPLES *dance off.* ADZAK *has disappeared*) 590

THE SINGER.

But you, you who have listened to the Story of the Chalk Circle,
Take note what men of old concluded:
That what there is shall go to those who are good for it,
Children to the motherly, that they prosper,
Carts to good drivers, that they be driven well,
The valley to the waterers, that it yield fruit.

Review Questions

1. What are the advantages of Brecht's "epic" style?
2. What is the function of the Story Teller?
3. What problems does the "epic" style create?
4. What important actions happen off-stage? How are they made known to the audience?
5. What is Brecht's point of view? Cite specific evidence.
6. Does the play achieve any kind of unity?
7. Describe the proposal scene between Grusha and Simon.
8. What is the tone of the play? Is the denouement consistent with the tone?
9. Discuss the use of sound in establishing atmosphere.
10. What conflicts are raised?
11. Does Brecht create suspense?
12. What do the songs contribute to the total effect?
13. Describe the wedding ceremony. Why is it treated comically?
14. What is the effect of the opening scene?
15. Describe the reunion of Simon and Grusha.
16. What is the point of the children's games?
17. Describe the character of Azdak.
18. Describe the trial scenes.
19. What is the function of the dance at the end of the play?
20. What are the problems of producing such a play?
21. Does Brecht's political bias limit the play's appeal?
22. What are the most memorable scenes? Why?

THE GLASS MENAGERIE

Tennessee Williams (1914–   )

Thomas Lanier ("Tennessee") Williams' early life was associated with the South. He was born in Mississippi and attended high school in St. Louis, Missouri. He began his college education at the University of Missouri, but financial pressure forced him to find work in a shoe factory for two years before resuming his academic career at Washington University, in St. Louis, and then at the University of Iowa.

He was constantly striving to become a writer, turning out a steady stream of poetry, stories and plays. He wandered about the country working at a variety of jobs until he reached New York, determined to make a career of the theater.

A series of one-act plays attracted attention to Williams, and in 1940 the Theatre Guild sponsored his first professional full-length production of *Battle of Angels* in Boston. The play failed to reach New York but his next effort, *The Glass Menagerie,* after a long tryout in Chicago, came to New York in 1945 and was a popular and critical success, winning the Drama Critics Circle Award. Two years later he triumphed again with *A Streetcar Named Desire*. Other plays of Williams include *Orpheus Descending, Summer and Smoke, Sweet Bird of Youth, Cat on a Hot Tin Roof, The Rose Tatoo* and *The Night of the Iguana.*

Williams' production notes on the play are helpful in visualizing his intent.

> Being a "memory play," *The Glass Menagerie* can be presented with unusual freedom of convention. Because of its considerably delicate or tenuous material, atmospheric touches and subtleties of direction play a particularly important part . . . When a play employs unconventional techniques, it is not, or certainly shouldn't be, trying to escape its responsibility of dealing with reality, or interpreting experience, but is actually or should be attempting to find a closer approach, a more penetrating and vivid expression of things as they are. The straight realistic play with its genuine frigidaire and authentic icecubes, its characters that speak exactly as the audience speaks, corresponds to the academic landscape and has the same virtue of a photographic likeness. Everyone should know nowadays the unim-

portance of the photographic in art: that truth, life, or reality is an organic thing which the poetic imagination can represent or suggest, in essence, only through transformation, through changing into other forms than those which were merely present in appearance.

The lighting in the play is not realistic. In keeping with the atmosphere of memory, the stage is dim. Shafts of light are focused on selected areas or actors . . . The light upon Laura should be distinct from the others, have a peculiar pristine clarity such as light used in early religious portraits of female saints or madonnas.

Another extra-literary accent in this play is provided by the use of music. A single recurring tune, "The Glass Menagerie," is used to give emotional emphasis to suitable passages. This tune is like circus music when you are at some distance . . . It expresses the surface vivacity of life with the underlying strain of immutable and inexpressible sorrow. When you look at a piece of delicately spun glass you think of two things: how beautiful it is and how easily it can be broken. Both of these ideas should be woven into the recurring tune . . . It serves as a thread of connection and allusion between the narrator with his separate point in time and space and the subject of his story. Between each episode it returns as a reference to the emotion, nostalgia, which is the first condition of the play. It is primarily Laura's music and therefore comes out most clearly when the play focuses upon her and the lovely fragility which is her image.

Williams also intended to use a screen device in an attempt to emphasize the most important points in each episode and to provide appropriate emotional reinforcement, but the device was eliminated from the original production.

A schematic diagram of the *Glass Menagerie* set.

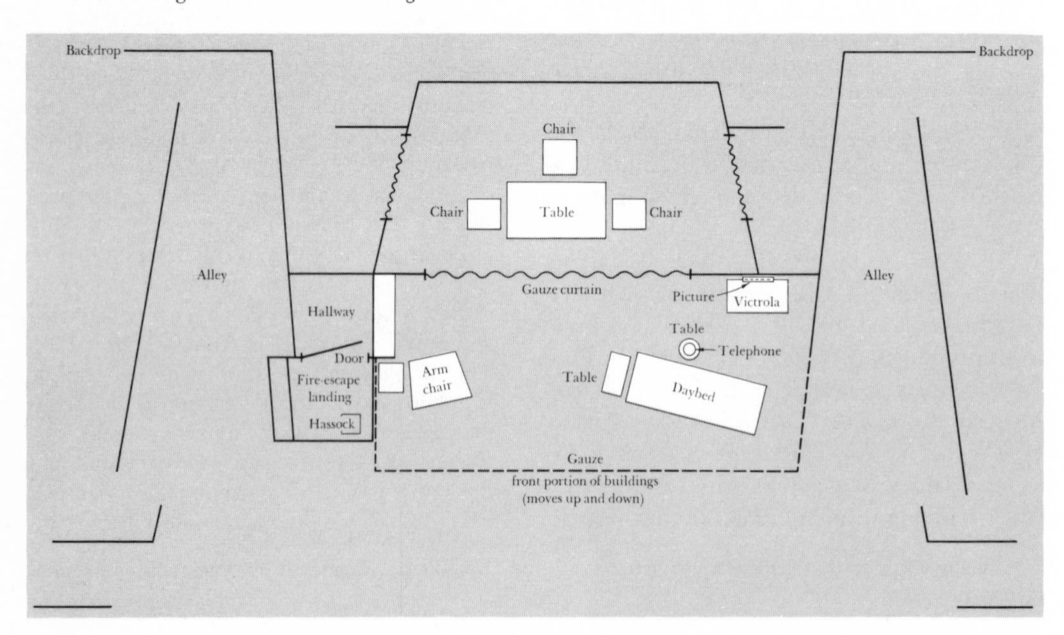

CBS Television Network

ABOVE. Shirley Booth, Hal Holbrook, and Barbara Loden in the 1966 CBS television play.

CBS Television Network

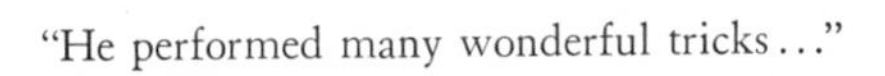

"He performed many wonderful tricks..."

George Karger—PIX

Amanda prepares Laura for the gentleman caller, from the beginning of Scene Six of the 1945 production, with Eddie Dowling as Tom, Julie Haydon as Laura, and Laurette Taylor as Amanda. Here can be seen the use of the transparent scrim.

George Karger—PIX

The gentleman caller comes to dinner. Anthony Ross plays Jim O'Conner.

"Gives you an idea of what the future will be like in America, even more wonderful than the present time is."

George Karger—PIX

Characters

AMANDA WINGFIELD, *the mother*
LAURA WINGFIELD, *her daughter*
TOM WINGFIELD, *her son*
JIM O'CONNOR, *the gentleman caller*

Scene: *An Alley in St. Louis*

Part I. Preparation for a Gentleman Caller
Part II. The Gentleman calls

Time: *Now and the Past*

THE GLASS MENAGERIE

Scene One

[The Wingfield apartment is in the rear of the building, one of those vast hive-like conglomerations of cellular living-units that flower as warty growths in overcrowded urban centers of lower middle-class population and are symptomatic of the impulse of this largest and fundamentally enslaved section of American society to avoid fluidity and differentiation and to exist and function as one interfused mass of automatism.

The apartment faces an alley and is entered by a fire-escape, a structure whose name is a touch of accidental poetic truth, for all of these huge buildings are always burning with the slow and implacable fires of human desperation. The fire-escape is included in the set—that is, the landing of it and steps descending from it.

The scene is memory and is therefore nonrealistic. Memory takes a lot of poetic license. It omits some details; others are exaggerated, according to the emotional value of the articles it touches, for memory is seated predominantly in the heart. The interior is therefore rather dim and poetic.

At the rise of the curtain, the audience is faced with the dark, grim rear wall of the Wingfield tenement. This building, which runs parallel to the footlights, is flanked on both sides by dark, narrow alleys which run into murky canyons of tangled clotheslines, garbage cans and the sinister lattice-work of neighboring fire-escapes. It is up and down these side alleys that exterior entrances and exits are made, during the play. At the end of TOM'S *opening commentary, the dark tenement wall slowly reveals (by means of a transparency) the interior of the ground floor Wingfield apartment.*

Downstage is the living room, which also serves as a sleeping room for LAURA, *the sofa unfolding to make her bed. Upstage, center, and divided by a wide arch or second proscenium with transparent faded portieres (or second curtain), is the dining room. In an old-fashioned what-not in the living room are seen scores of transparent glass animals. A blown-up photograph of the father hangs on the wall of the living room, facing the audience, to the left of the archway. It is the face of a very handsome young man in a doughboy's First World War cap. He is gallantly smiling, ineluctably smiling, as if to say, "I will be smiling forever."*

The audience hears and sees the opening scene in the dining room through both the transparent fourth wall of the building and the transparent gauze portieres of the dining-room arch. It is during this revealing scene that the fourth wall slowly ascends, out of sight. This transparent exterior wall is not brought down again until the very end of the play, during TOM'S *final speech.*

The narrator is an undisguised convention of the play. He takes whatever license with dramatic convention as is convenient to his purposes.

TOM *enters dressed as a merchant sailor from alley, stage left, and strolls across the front of the stage to the fire-escape. There he stops and lights a cigarette. He addresses the audience.*]

TOM. Yes, I have tricks in my pocket, I have things up my sleeve. But I am the opposite of a stage magician. He gives you illusion that has the appearance of truth. I give you truth in the pleasant disguise of illusion. To begin with, I turn back time. I reverse it to that quaint period, the thirties, when the huge middle class of America was matriculating in a school for the blind. Their eyes had failed them, or they had failed their eyes, and so they were having their fingers pressed forcibly down on the fiery Braille alphabet of a dissolving economy. In Spain there was revolution. Here there was only shouting and confusion. In Spain there was Guernica. Here there were disturbances of labor, sometimes pretty violent, in otherwise peaceful cities such as Chicago, Cleveland, Saint Louis . . . This is the social background of the play.

(MUSIC.)

The play is memory. Being a memory play, it is dimly lighted, it is sentimental, it is not realistic. In memory everything seems to happen to music. That explains the fiddle in the wings. I am the narrator of the play, and also a character in it. The other characters are my mother, Amanda, my sister, Laura, and a gentleman caller who appears in the final scenes. He is the most realistic character in the play, being an emissary from a world of reality that we were somehow set apart from. But since I have a poet's weakness for symbols, I am using this character also as a symbol; he is the long delayed but always expected something that we live for. There is a fifth character in the play who doesn't appear except in this larger-than-life photograph over the mantel. This is our father who left us a long time ago. He was a telephone man who fell in love with long distances; he gave up his job with the telephone company and skipped the light fantastic out of town . . . The last we heard of him was a picture post-card from Mazatlan, on the Pacific coast of Mexico, containing a message of two words— "Hello—Good-bye!" and no address. I think the rest of the play will explain itself. . . .

(AMANDA'S *voice becomes audible through the portieres.*)

(LEGEND ON SCREEN: "OÙ SONT LES NEIGES.")

(*He divides the portieres and enters the upstage area.*)

(AMANDA *and* LAURA *are seated at a drop-leaf table. Eating is indicated by gestures without food or utensils.* AMANDA *faces the audience.* TOM *and* LAURA *are seated in profile.*)

(*The interior has lit up softly and through the scrim we see* AMANDA *and* LAURA *seated at the table in the upstage area.*)

AMANDA (*calling*). Tom?

TOM. Yes, Mother.

AMANDA. We can't say grace until you come to the table!

TOM. Coming, Mother. (*He bows slightly and withdraws, reappearing a few moments later in his place at the table.*)

AMANDA (*to her son*). Honey, don't *push* with your *fingers.* If you have to push with something, the thing to push with is a crust of bread. And chew—chew! Animals have sections in their stomachs which enable them to digest food without mastication, but human beings are supposed to chew their food before they swallow it down. Eat food leisurely, son, and really enjoy it. A well-cooked meal has lots of delicate flavors that have to be held in the mouth for appreciation. So chew your food and give your salivary glands a chance to function!

(TOM *deliberately lays his imaginary fork down and pushes his chair back from the table.*)

TOM. I haven't enjoyed one bite of this dinner because of your constant directions on how to eat it. It's you that make me rush through meals with your hawk-like attention to every bite I take. Sickening—spoils my appetite—all this discussion of animals' secretion—salivary glands—mastication!

AMANDA (*lightly*). Temperament like a Metropolitan star! (*He rises and crosses downstage.*) You're not excused from the table.

TOM. I'm getting a cigarette.

AMANDA. You smoke too much.

(LAURA *rises.*)

LAURA. I'll bring in the blanc mange.

(*He remains standing with his cigarette by the portieres during the following.*)

AMANDA (*rising*). No, sister, no, sister—you be the lady this time and I'll be the darky.

LAURA. I'm already up.

100 AMANDA. Resume your seat, little sister—I want you to stay fresh and pretty—for gentlemen callers!

LAURA. I'm not expecting any gentlemen callers.

AMANDA (*crossing out to kitchenette. Airily*). Sometimes they come when they are least expected! Why, I remember one Sunday afternoon in Blue Mountain— (*Enters kitchenette.*)

TOM. I know what's coming!

110 LAURA. Yes. But let her tell it.

TOM. Again?

LAURA. She loves to tell it.

(AMANDA *returns with bowl of dessert.*)

AMANDA. One Sunday afternoon in Blue Mountain—your mother received—*seventeen!*—gentlemen callers! Why, sometimes there weren't chairs enough to accommodate them all. We had to send the nigger over to bring in folding chairs from the parish house.

120 TOM (*remaining at portieres*). How did you entertain those gentlemen callers?

AMANDA. I understood the art of conversation!

TOM. I bet you could talk.

AMANDA. Girls in those days *knew* how to talk, I can tell you.

TOM. Yes?

(IMAGE: AMANDA AS A GIRL ON A PORCH, GREETING CALLERS.)

130 AMANDA. They knew how to entertain their gentlemen callers. It wasn't enough for a girl to be possessed of a pretty face and a graceful figure—although I wasn't slighted in either respect. She also needed to have a nimble wit and a tongue to meet all occasions.

TOM. What did you talk about?

AMANDA. Things of importance going on in the world! Never anything coarse or common or vulgar. (*She addresses* TOM *as though he were seated in the vacant chair at the table* 140 *though he remains by portieres. He plays this scene as though he held the book.*) My callers were gentlemen—all! Among my callers were some of the most prominent young planters of the Mississippi Delta—planters and sons of planters!

(TOM *motions for music and a spot of light on* AMANDA.)

(*Her eyes lift, her face glows, her voice becomes rich and elegiac.*) 150

(SCREEN LEGEND: "OÙ SONT LES NEIGES.")

There was young Champ Laughlin who later became vice-president of the Delta Planters Bank. Hadley Stevenson who was drowned in Moon Lake and left his widow one hundred and fifty thousand in Government bonds. There were the Cutrere brothers, Wesley and Bates. Bates was one of my bright particular beaux! He got in a quarrel with that wild Wainwright boy. They shot it out on the floor of Moon Lake 160 Casino. Bates was shot through the stomach. Died in the ambulance on his way to Memphis. His widow was also well-provided for, came into eight or ten thousand acres, that's all. She married him on the rebound—never loved her—carried my picture on him the night he died! And there was that boy that every girl in the Delta had set her cap for! That beautiful, brilliant young Fitzhugh boy from Greene County!

TOM. What did he leave his widow? 170

AMANDA. He never married! Gracious, you talk as though all of my old admirers had turned up their toes to the daisies!

TOM. Isn't this the first you've mentioned that still survives?

AMANDA. That Fitzhugh boy went North and made a fortune—came to be known as the Wolf of Wall Street! He had the Midas touch, whatever he touched turned to gold! And I could have been Mrs. Duncan J. Fitzhugh, 180 mind you! But—I picked your *father!*

LAURA (*rising*). Mother, let me clear the table.

AMANDA. No, dear, you go in front and

study your typewriter chart. Or practice your shorthand a little. Stay fresh and pretty!—It's almost time for our gentlemen callers to start arriving. (*She flounces girlishly toward the kitchenette.*) How many do you suppose we're going to entertain this afternoon? 190

(TOM *throws down the paper and jumps up with a groan.*)

LAURA (*alone in the dining room*). I don't believe we're going to receive any, Mother.

AMANDA (*reappearing, airily*). What? No one—not one? You must be joking! (LAURA *nervously echoes her laugh. She slips in a fugitive manner through the half-open portieres and draws them gently behind her. A shaft of very clear light is thrown on her face against the faded tapestry of the curtains.* MUSIC: "THE GLASS MENAGERIE" UNDER FAINTLY. *Lightly:*) Not one gentleman caller? It can't be true! There must be a flood, there must have been a tornado! 200

LAURA. It isn't a flood, it's not a tornado, Mother. I'm just not popular like you were in Blue Mountain. . . . (TOM *utters another groan.* LAURA *glances at him with a faint, apologetic smile. Her voice catching a little.*) Mother's afraid I'm going to be an old maid. 210

THE SCENE DIMS OUT WITH "GLASS MENAGERIE" MUSIC.

Scene Two

[*"Laura, Haven't You Ever Liked Some Boy?"*

On the dark stage the screen is lighted with the image of blue roses.

Gradually LAURA's *figure becomes apparent and the screen goes out.*

The music subsides.

LAURA *is seated in the delicate ivory chair at the small claw-foot table.*

She wears a dress of soft violet material for a kimono—her hair tied back from her forehead with a ribbon.

She is washing and polishing her collection of glass.

AMANDA *appears on the fire-escape steps. At the sound of her ascent,* LAURA *catches her breath, thrusts the bowl of ornaments away and seats herself stiffly before the diagram of the typewriter keyboard as though it held her spellbound. Something has happened to* AMANDA. *It is written in her face as she climbs to the landing: a look that is grim and hopeless and a little absurd.*

She has on one of those cheap or imitation velvety-looking cloth coats with imitation fur collar. Her hat is five or six years old, one of those dreadful cloche hats that were worn in the late twenties and she is clasping an enormous black patent-leather pocketbook with nickel clasps and initials. This is her full-dress outfit, the one she usually wears to the D.A.R.

Before entering she looks through the door.

She purses her lips, opens her eyes wide, rolls them upward and shakes her head.

Then she slowly lets herself in the door. Seeing her mother's expression LAURA *touches her lips with a nervous gesture.*]

LAURA. Hello, Mother, I was— (*She makes a nervous gesture toward the chart on the wall.* AMANDA *leans against the shut door and stares at* LAURA *with a martyred look.*)

AMANDA. Deception? Deception? (*She slowly removes her hat and gloves, continuing the sweet suffering stare. She lets the hat and gloves fall on the floor—a bit of acting.*)

LAURA (*shakily*). How was the D.A.R. meeting? (AMANDA *slowly opens her purse and removes a dainty white handkerchief which she shakes out delicately and delicately touches* 10 *to her lips and nostrils.*) Didn't you go to the D.A.R. meeting, Mother?

AMANDA (*faintly, almost inaudibly*). —No. —No. (*Then more forcibly:*) I did not have the strength—to go to the D.A.R. In fact, I did not have the courage! I wanted to find a hole in the ground and hide myself in it forever! (*She crosses slowly to the wall and removes the diagram of the typewriter keyboard. She holds it in front of her for a second, staring at it sweetly and sorrowfully—then bites her lips and tears it in two pieces.*) 20

LAURA (*faintly*). Why did you do that, Mother? (AMANDA *repeats the same procedure with the chart of the Gregg Alphabet.*) Why are you—

AMANDA. Why? Why? How old are you, Laura? 30

LAURA. Mother, you know my age.

AMANDA. I thought that you were an adult; it seems that I was mistaken. (*She crosses slowly to the sofa and sinks down and stares at* LAURA.)

LAURA. Please don't stare at me, Mother.

(AMANDA *closes her eyes and lowers her head. Count ten.*)

AMANDA. What are we going to do, what is going to become of us, what is the future? 40

(*Count ten.*)

LAURA. Has something happened, Mother?

(AMANDA *draws a long breath and takes out the handkerchief again. Dabbing process.*)

Mother, has—something happened?

AMANDA. I'll be all right in a minute. I'm just bewildered—(*Count five*)—by life. . . .

LAURA. Mother, I wish that you would tell me what's happened!

AMANDA. As you know, I was supposed to be inducted into my office at the D.A.R. this afternoon. (IMAGE: A SWARM OF TYPEWRITERS.) But I stopped off at Rubicam's Business College to speak to your teachers about your having a cold and ask them what progress they thought you were making down there. 50

LAURA. Oh. . . .

AMANDA. I went to the typing instructor and introduced myself as your mother. She didn't know who you were. Wingfield, she said. We don't have any such student enrolled at the school! I assured her she did, that you had been going to classes since early in January. "I wonder," she said, "if you could be talking about that terribly shy little girl who dropped out of school after only a few days' attendance?" "No," I said, "Laura, my daughter has been going to school every day for the past six weeks!" "Excuse me," she said. She took the attendance book out and there was your name, unmistakably printed, and all the dates you were absent until they decided that you had dropped out of school. I still said, "No, there must have been some mistake! There must have been some mix-up in the records!" And she said, "No—I remember her perfectly now. Her hands shook so that she couldn't hit the right keys! The first time we gave a speed-test, she broke down completely—was sick at the stomach and almost had to be carried into the wash-room! After that morning she never showed up any more. We phoned the house but never got any answer—while I was working at Famous and Barr, I suppose, demonstrating those— Oh!" I felt so weak I could barely keep on my feet! I had to sit down while they got me a glass of water! Fifty dollars' tuition, all of our plans—my hopes and ambitions for you—just gone up the spout, just gone up the spout like that. (LAURA *draws a long breath and gets awkwardly to her feet. She crosses to the victrola and winds it up.*) What are you doing? 60 70 80 90

LAURA. Oh! (*She releases the handle and returns to her seat.*)

AMANDA. Laura, where have you been going when you've gone out pretending that you were going to business college?

LAURA. I've just been going out walking.

AMANDA. That's not true. 100

LAURA. It is. I just went walking.

AMANDA. Walking? Walking? In winter? Deliberately courting pneumonia in that light coat? Where did you walk to, Laura?

LAURA. All sorts of places—mostly in the park.

AMANDA. Even after you'd started catching that cold?

LAURA. It was the lesser of two evils, Mother. (IMAGE: WINTER SCENE IN PARK.) 110

I couldn't go back up. I—threw up—on the floor!

AMANDA. From half past seven till after five every day you mean to tell me you walked around in the park, because you wanted to make me think that you were still going to Rubicam's Business College?

LAURA. It wasn't as bad as it sounds. I went inside places to get warmed up.

120 AMANDA. Inside where?

LAURA. I went in the art museum and the bird-houses at the Zoo. I visited the penguins every day! Sometimes I did without lunch and went to the movies. Lately I've been spending most of my afternoons in the Jewel-box, that big glass house where they raise the tropical flowers.

AMANDA. You did all this to deceive me, just for deception? (LAURA *looks down.*) Why?

130 LAURA. Mother, when you're disappointed, you get that awful suffering look on your face, like the picture of Jesus' mother in the museum!

AMANDA. Hush!

LAURA. I couldn't face it.

(*Pause. A whisper of strings.*)

(LEGEND: "THE CRUST OF HUMILITY.")

AMANDA (*hopelessly fingering the huge pocketbook*). So what are we going to do the rest

140 of our lives? Stay home and watch the parades go by? Amuse ourselves with the glass menagerie, darling? Eternally play those worn-out phonograph records your father left as a painful reminder of him? We won't have a business career—we've given that up because it gave us nervous indigestion! (*Laughs wearily.*) What is there left but dependency all our lives? I know so well what becomes of unmarried women who aren't prepared to occupy a posi-

150 tion. I've seen such pitiful cases in the South —barely tolerated spinsters living upon the grudging patronage of sister's husband or brother's wife!—stuck away in some little mouse-trap of a room—encouraged by one in-law to visit another—little birdlike women without any nest—eating the crust of humility all their life! Is that the future that we've mapped out for ourselves? I swear it's the only alternative I can think of! It isn't a very pleas-

160 ant alternative, is it? Of course—some girls *do marry.* (LAURA *twists her hands nervously.*) Haven't you ever liked some boy?

LAURA. Yes. I liked one once. (*Rises.*) I came across his picture a while ago.

AMANDA (*with some interest*). He gave you his picture?

LAURA. No, it's in the year-book.

AMANDA (*disappointed*). Oh—a high-school boy.

170 (SCREEN IMAGE: JIM AS HIGH-SCHOOL HERO BEARING A SILVER CUP.)

LAURA. Yes. His name was Jim. (LAURA *lifts the heavy annual from the claw-foot table.*) Here he is in *The Pirates of Penzance.*

LAURA. The operetta the senior class put on. He had a wonderful voice and we sat across the aisle from each other Mondays, Wednesdays and Fridays in the Aud. Here he is with the silver cup for debating! See his grin?

180 AMANDA (*absently*). He must have had a jolly disposition.

LAURA. He used to call me—Blue Roses.

(IMAGE: BLUE ROSES.)

AMANDA. Why did he call you such a name as that?

LAURA. When I had that attack of pleurosis —he asked me what was the matter when I came back. I said pleurosis—he thought that I said Blue Roses! So that's what he always

190 called me after that. Whenever he saw me, he'd holler, "Hello, Blue Roses!" I didn't care for the girl that he went out with. Emily Meisenbach. Emily was the best-dressed girl at Soldan. She never struck me, though, as being sincere . . . It says in the Personal Section—they're engaged. That's—six years ago! They must be married by now.

AMANDA. Girls that aren't cut out for business careers usually wind up married to some

200 nice man. (*Gets up with a spark of revival.*) Sister, that's what you'll do!

(LAURA *utters a startled, doubtful laugh. She reaches quickly for a piece of glass.*)

LAURA. But, Mother—

AMANDA. Yes? (*Crossing to photograph.*)

LAURA (*in a tone off frightened apology*). I'm—crippled!

(IMAGE: SCREEN.)

AMANDA. Nonsense! Laura, I've told you never, never to use that word. Why, you're not crippled, you just have a little defect—hardly noticeable, even! When people have some slight disadvantage like that, they cultivate other things to make up for it—develop charm—and vivacity—and—*charm!* That's all you have to do! (*She turns again to the photograph.*) One thing your father had *plenty of*—was *charm!*

(TOM *motions to the fiddle in the wings.*)

THE SCENE FADES OUT WITH MUSIC

Scene Three

LEGEND ON SCREEN: "AFTER THE FIASCO—"

(TOM *speaks from the fire-escape landing.*)

TOM. After the fiasco at Rubicam's Business College, the idea of getting a gentleman caller for Laura began to play a more important part in Mother's calculations. It became an obsession. Like some archetype of the universal unconscious, the image of the gentleman caller haunted our small apartment. . . . (IMAGE: YOUNG MAN AT DOOR WITH FLOWERS.) An evening at home rarely passed without some allusion to this image, this spectre, this hope. . . . Even when he wasn't mentioned, his presence hung in Mother's preoccupied look and in my sister's frightened, apologetic manner—hung like a sentence passed upon the Wingfields! Mother was a woman of action as well as words. She began to take logical steps in the planned direction. Late that winter and in the early spring—realizing that extra money would be needed to properly feather the nest and plume the bird—she conducted a vigorous campaign on the telephone, roping in subscribers to one of those magazines for matrons called *The Home-maker's Companion,* the type of journal that features the serialized sublimations of ladies of letters who think in terms of delicate cup-like breasts, slim, tapering waists, rich, creamy thighs, eyes like wood-smoke in autumn, fingers that soothe and caress like strains of music, bodies as powerful as Etruscan sculpture.

(SCREEN IMAGES: GLAMOR MAGAZINE COVER.)

(AMANDA *enters with phone on long extension cord. She is spotted in the dim stage.*)

AMANDA. Ida Scott? This is Amanda Wingfield! We *missed* you at the D.A.R. last Monday! I said to myself: She's probably suffering with that sinus condition! How is that sinus condition? Horrors! Heaven have mercy!—You're a Christian martyr, yes, that's what you are, a Christian martyr! Well, I just now happened to notice that your subscription to the *Companion's* about to expire! Yes, it expires with the next issue, honey!—just when that wonderful new serial by Bessie Mae Hopper is getting off to such an exciting start. Oh, honey, it's something that you can't miss! You remember how *Gone With the Wind* took everybody by storm? You simply couldn't go out if you hadn't read it. All everybody *talked* was Scarlett O'Hara. Well, this is a book that critics already compare to *Gone With the Wind*. It's the *Gone With the Wind* of the post-World War generation!—What?—Burning?—Oh, honey, don't let them burn, go take a look in the oven and I'll hold the wire! Heavens—I think she's hung up!

DIM OUT

(LEGEND ON SCREEN: "YOU THINK I'M IN LOVE WITH CONTINENTAL SHOEMAKERS?")

(*Before the stage is lighted, the violent voices of* TOM *and* AMANDA *are heard.*)

(They are quarreling behind the portieres. In front of them stands LAURA *with clenched hands and panicky expression.)*

(A clear pool of light on her figure throughout this scene.)

TOM. What in Christ's name am I—

70 AMANDA *(shrilly)*. Don't you use that—

TOM. Supposed to do!

AMANDA. Expression! Not in my—

TOM. Ohhh!

AMANDA. Presence! Have you gone out of your senses?

TOM. I have, that's true, *driven* out!

AMANDA. What is the matter with you, you —big—big—IDIOT!

TOM. Look—I've got *no thing,* no single

80 thing—

AMANDA. Lower your voice!

TOM. In my life here that I can call my OWN! Everything is—

AMANDA. Stop that shouting!

TOM. Yesterday you confiscated my books! You had the nerve to—

AMANDA. I took that horrible novel back to the library—yes! That hideous book by that insane Mr. Lawrence. (TOM *laughs wildly.*) I

90 cannot control the output of diseased minds or people who cater to them—(TOM *laughs still more wildly.*) BUT I WON'T ALLOW SUCH FILTH BROUGHT INTO MY HOUSE! No, no, no, no, no!

TOM. House, house! Who pays rent on it, who makes a slave of himself to—

AMANDA *(fairly screeching)*. Don't you DARE to—

TOM. No, no, *I* mustn't say things! *I've* got

100 to just—

AMANDA. Let me tell you—

TOM. I don't want to hear any more! *(He tears the portieres open. The upstage area is lit with a turgid smoky red glow.)*

(AMANDA'*s hair is in metal curlers and she wears a very old bathrobe, much too large for her slight figure, a relic of the faithless Mr. Wingfield.)*

(An upright typewriter and a wild disarray

110 *of manuscripts is on the drop-leaf table. The quarrel was probably precipitated by* AMANDA'*s interruption of his creative labor. A chair lying overthrown on the floor.)*

(Their gesticulating shadows are cast on the ceiling by the fiery glow.)

AMANDA. You *will* hear more, you—

TOM. No, I won't hear more, I'm going out!

AMANDA. You come right back in—

TOM. Out, out out! Because I'm—

AMANDA. Come back here, Tom Wingfield! 120

I'm not through talking to you!

TOM. Oh, go—

LAURA *(desperately)*. —Tom!

AMANDA. You're going to listen, and no more insolence from you! I'm at the end of my patience! *(He comes back toward her.)*

TOM. What do you think I'm at? Aren't I suppose to have any patience to reach the end of, Mother? I know, I know. It seems unimportant to you, what I'm *doing*—what I 130 *want* to do—having a little *difference* between them! You don't think that—

AMANDA. I think you've been doing things that you're ashamed of. That's why you act like this. I don't believe that you go every night to the movies. Nobody goes to the movies night after night. Nobody in their right minds goes to the movies as often as you pretend to. People don't go to the movies at nearly midnight, and movies don't let out at two A.M. 140 Come in stumbling. Muttering to yourself like a maniac! You get three hours' sleep and then go to work. Oh, I can picture the way you're doing down there. Moping, doping, because you're in no condition.

TOM *(wildly)*. No, I'm in no condition!

AMANDA. What right have you got to jeopardize your job? Jeopardize the security of us all? How do you think we'd manage if you were— 150

TOM. Listen! You think I'm crazy *about* the *warehouse? (He bends fiercely toward her slight figure.)* You think I'm in love with the Continental Shoemakers? You think I want to spend fifty-five *years* down there in that—*celotex interior! with—fluorescent—tubes!* Look! I'd rather somebody picked up a crowbar and battered out my brains—than go back mornings! I *go!* Every time you come in yelling that God damn *"Rise and Shine!" "Rise and* 160 *Shine!"* I say to myself, "How *lucky dead* people are!" But I get up. I *go!* For sixty-five dollars a month I give up all that I dream of doing and being *ever!* And you say self—*self's* all I ever think of. Why, listen, if self is what I thought of, Mother, I'd be where he is—GONE! (*Pointing to father's picture.*) As far as the system of transportation reaches! (*He starts past her. She grabs his arm.*) Don't grab at me, Mother!

170

AMANDA. Where are you going?

TOM. I'm going to the *movies!*

AMANDA. I don't believe that lie!

TOM (*crouching toward her, overtowering her tiny figure. She backs away, gasping*). I'm going to opium dens! Yes, opium dens, dens of vice and criminals' hang-outs, Mother. I've joined the Hogan gang, I'm a hired assassin, I carry a tommy-gun in a violin case! I run a string of cat-houses in the Valley! They call me Killer, Killer Wingfield, I'm leading a double-life, a simple, honest warehouse worker by day, by night, a dynamic *czar* of the *underworld, Mother.* I go to gambling casinos, I spin away fortunes on the roulette table! I wear a patch over one eye and a false mustache, sometimes I put on green whiskers. On those occasions they call me—*El Diablo!* Oh, I could tell you things to make you sleepless! My enemies plan to dynamite this place. They're going to blow us all sky-high some night! I'll be glad, very happy, and so will you! You'll go up, up on a broomstick, over Blue Mountain with seventeen gentlemen callers! You ugly—babbling old—*witch. . . .* (*He goes through a series of violent, clumsy movements, seizing his overcoat, lunging to the door, pulling it fiercely open. The women watch him, aghast. His arm catches in the sleeve of the coat as he struggles to pull it on. For a moment he is pinioned by the bulky garment. With an outraged groan he tears the coat off again, splitting the shoulder of it, and hurls it across the room. It strikes against the shelf of* LAURA's *glass collection, there is a tinkle of shattering glass.* LAURA *cries out as if wounded.*)

180

190

200

(MUSIC LEGEND: "THE GLASS MENAGERIE.")

LAURA (*shrilly*). *My glass!—menagerie. . . .* (*She covers her face and turns away.*)

(*But* AMANDA *is still stunned and stupefied by the "ugly witch" so that she barely notices this occurrence. Now she recovers her speech.*)

210

AMANDA (*in an awful voice*). I won't speak to you—until you apologize! (*She crosses through portieres and draws them together behind her.* TOM *is left with* LAURA. LAURA *clings weakly to the mantel with her face averted.* TOM *stares at her stupidly for a moment. Then he crosses to shelf. Drops awkwardly on his knees to collect the fallen glass, glancing at* LAURA *as if he would speak but couldn't.*)

220

"The Glass Menagerie" steals in as
THE SCENE DIMS OUT

Scene Four

[*The interior is dark. Faint light in the alley.*

A deep-voice bell in a church is tolling the hour of five as the scene commences.

TOM *appears at the top of the alley. After each solemn boom of the bell in the tower, he shakes a little noise-maker or rattle as if to express the tiny spasm of man in contrast to the sustained power and dignity of the Almighty. This and the unsteadiness of his advance make it evident that he has been drinking.*

As he climbs the few steps to the fire-escape landing light steals up inside. LAURA *appears in night-dress, observing* TOM's *empty bed in the front room.*

TOM *fishes in his pockets for door-key, removing a motley assortment of articles in the search, including a perfect shower of movie-ticket stubs and an empty bottle. At last he finds the key, but just as he is about to insert it, it slips from his fingers. He strikes a match and crouches below the door.*]

TOM (*bitterly*). One crack—and it falls through!

(LAURA *opens the door.*)

LAURA. Tom! Tom, what are you doing?

TOM. Looking for a door-key.

LAURA. Where have you been all this time?

TOM. I have been to the movies.

LAURA. All this time at the movies?

TOM. There was a very long program. There was a Garbo picture and a Mickey Mouse and a travelogue and a newsreel and a preview of coming attractions. And there was an organ solo and a collection for the milk-fund—simultaneously—which ended up in a terrible fight between a fat lady and an usher!

LAURA (*innocently*). Did you have to stay through everything?

TOM. Of course! And, oh, I forgot! There was a big stage show! The headliner on this stage show was Malvolio the Magician. He performed wonderful tricks, many of them, such as pouring water back and forth between pitchers. First it turned to wine and then it turned to beer and then it turned to whiskey. I know it was whiskey it finally turned into because he needed somebody to come up out of the audience to help him, and I came up—both shows! It was Kentucky Straight Bourbon. A very generous fellow, he gave souvenirs. (*He pulls from his back pocket a shimmering rainbow-colored scarf.*) He gave me this. This is his magic scarf. You can have it, Laura. You wave it over a canary cage and you get a bowl of gold-fish. You wave it over the gold-fish bowl and they fly away canaries. . . . But the wonderfullest trick of all was the coffin trick. We nailed him into a coffin and he got out of the coffin without removing one nail. (*He has come inside.*) There is a trick that would come in handy for me—get me out of this 2 by 4 situation! (*Flops onto bed and starts removing shoes.*)

LAURA. Tom—Shhh!

TOM. What're you shushing me for?

LAURA. You'll wake up Mother.

TOM. Goody, goody! Pay 'er back for all those "Rise an' Shines." (*Lies down, groaning.*) You know it don't take much intelligence to get yourself into a nailed-up coffin, Laura. But who in hell ever got out himself out of one without removing one nail?

(*As if in answer, the father's grinning photograph lights up.*)

SCENE DIMS OUT

(*Immediately following: The church bell is heard striking six. At the sixth stroke the alarm clock goes off in* AMANDA'S *room, and after a few moments we hear her calling: "Rise and Shine! Rise and Shine! Laura, go tell your brother to rise and shine!"*)

TOM (*Sitting up slowly*). I'll rise—but I won't shine.

(*The light increases.*)

AMANDA. Laura, tell your brother his coffee is ready.

(LAURA *slips into front room.*)

LAURA. Tom it's nearly seven. Don't make Mother nervous. (*He stares at her stupidly. Beseechingly.*) Tom, speak to Mother this morning. Make up with her, apologize, speak to her!

TOM. She won't to me. It's her that started not speaking.

LAURA. If you just say you're sorry she'll start speaking.

TOM. Her not speaking—is that such a tragedy?

LAURA. Please—please!

AMANDA (*calling from kitchenette*). Laura, are you going to do what I asked you to do, or do I have to get dressed and go out myself?

LAURA. Going, going—soon as I get on my coat! (*She pulls on a shapeless felt hat with nervous, jerky movement, pleadingly glancing at* TOM. *Rushes awkwardly for coat. The coat is one of* AMANDA'S, *inaccurately made-over, the sleeves too short for* LAURA.) Butter and what else?

AMANDA (*entering upstage*). Just butter. Tell them to charge it.

LAURA. Mother, they make such faces when I do that.

AMANDA. Sticks and stones can break our bones, but the expression on Mr. Garfinkel's face won't harm us! Tell your brother his coffee is getting cold.

LAURA (*at door*). Do what I asked you, will you, will you, Tom?

(*He looks sullenly away.*)

AMANDA. Laura, go now or just don't go at all!

LAURA (*rushing out*). Going—going! (*A second later she cries out.* TOM *springs up and crosses to door.* AMANDA *rushes anxiously in.* TOM *opens the door.*)

TOM. Laura?

LAURA. I'm all right. I slipped, but I'm all right.

AMANDA (*peering anxiously after her*). If anyone breaks a leg on those fire-escape steps, the landlord ought to be sued for every cent he possesses! (*She shuts door. Remembers she isn't speaking and returns to other room.*)

(*As* TOM *enters listlessly for his coffee, she turns her back to him and stands rigidly facing the window on the gloomy gray vault of the areaway. Its light on her face with its aged but childish features is cruelly sharp, satirical as a Daumier print.*)

(MUSIC UNDER: "AVE MARIE.")

(TOM *glances sheepishly but sullenly at her averted figure and slumps at the table. The coffee is scalding hot; he sips it and gasps and spits it back in the cup. At his gasp,* AMANDA *catches her breath and half turns. Then catches herself and turns back to window.*)

(TOM *blows on his coffee, glancing sidewise at his mother. She clears her throat.* TOM *clears his. He starts to rise. Sinks back down again, scratches his head, clears his throat again.* AMANDA *coughs.* TOM *raises his cup in both hands to blow on it, his eyes staring over the rim of it at his mother for several moments. Then he slowly sets the cup down and awkwardly and hesitantly rises from the chair.*)

TOM (*hoarsely*). Mother. I—I apologize. Mother. (AMANDA *draws a quick, shuddering breath. Her face works grotesquely. She breaks into childlike tears.*) I'm sorry for what I said, for everything that I said, I didn't mean it.

AMANDA (*sobbingly*). My devotion has made me a witch and so I make myself hateful to my children!

TOM. *No,* you *don't.*

AMANDA. I worry so much, don't sleep, it makes me nervous!

TOM (*gently*). I understand that.

AMANDA. I've had to pull up a solitary battle all these years. But you're my right-hand bower! Don't fall down, don't fail!

TOM (*gently*). I try, Mother.

AMANDA (*with great enthusiasm*). Try and you will SUCCEED! (*The notion makes her breathless.*) Why, you—you're just *full* of natural endowments! Both of my children—they're *unusual* children! Don't you think I know it? I'm so—*proud!* Happy and—feel I've—so much to be thankful for but—Promise me one thing, son!

TOM. What, Mother?

AMANDA. Promise, son, you'll—never be a drunkard!

TOM (*turns to her grinning*). I will never be a drunkard, Mother.

AMANDA. That's what frightened me so, that you'd be drinking! Eat a bowl of Purina!

TOM. Just coffee, Mother.

AMANDA. Shredded wheat biscuit?

TOM. No. No, Mother, just coffee.

AMANDA. You can't put in a day's work on an empty stomach. You've got ten minutes—don't gulp! Drinking too-hot liquids makes cancer of the stomach. . . . Put cream in.

TOM. No, thank you.

AMANDA. To cool it.

TOM. No! No, thank you, I want it black.

AMANDA. I know, but it's not good for you. We have to do all that we can to build ourselves up. In these trying times we live in, all that we have to cling to is—each other. . . . That's why it's so important to—Tom, I—I sent out your sister so I could discuss something with you. If you hadn't spoken I would have spoken to you. (*Sits down.*)

TOM (*gently*). What is it, Mother, that you want to discuss?

AMANDA. *Laura!*

(TOM *puts his cup down slowly.*)

(LEGEND ON SCREEN: "LAURA.")

(MUSIC: "THE GLASS MENAGERIE.")

190 TOM. —Oh.—Laura . . .

AMANDA (*touching his sleeve*). You know how Laura is. So quiet but—still water runs deep! She notices things and I think she—broods about them. (TOM *looks up*). A few days ago I came in and she was crying.

TOM. What about?

AMANDA. You.

TOM. Me?

AMANDA. She has an idea that you're not 200 happy here.

TOM. What gave her that idea?

AMANDA. What gives her any idea? However, you do act strangely. I—I'm not criticizing, understand *that!* I know your ambitions do not lie in the warehouse, that like everybody in the whole wide world—you've had to—make sacrifices, but—Tom—Tom—life's not easy, it calls for—Spartan endurance! There's so many things in my heart that I cannot describe to 210 you! I've never told you but I—*loved* your father. . . .

TOM (*gently*). I know that, Mother.

AMANDA. And you—when I see you taking after his ways! Staying out late—and—well, you *had* been drinking the night you were in that —terrifying condition! Laura says that you hate the apartment and that you go out nights to get away from it! Is that true, Tom?

TOM. No. You say there's so much in your 220 heart that you can't describe to me. That's true of me, too. There's so much in my heart that I can't describe to *you!* So let's respect each other's—

AMANDA. But, why—*why,* Tom—are you always so *restless?* Where do you *go* to, nights?

TOM. I—go to the movies.

AMANDA. Why do you go to the movies so much, Tom?

TOM. I go to the movies because—I like ad-230 venture. Adventure is something I don't have much of at work, so I go to the movies.

AMANDA. But, Tom, you go to the movies *entirely* too *much!*

TOM. I like a lot of adventure.

(AMANDA *looks baffled, then hurt. As the familiar inquisition resumes he becomes hard and impatient again.* AMANDA *slips back into her querulous attitude toward him.*)

(IMAGE ON SCREEN: SAILING VESSEL WITH JOLLY ROGER.) 240

AMANDA. Most young men find adventure in their careers.

TOM. Then most young men are not employed in a warehouse.

AMANDA. The world is full of young men employed in warehouses and offices and factories.

TOM. Do all of them find adventure in their careers?

AMANDA. They do or they do without it! Not everybody has a craze for adventure. 250

TOM. Man is by instinct a lover, a hunter, a fighter, and none of those instincts are given much play at the warehouse!

AMANDA. Man is by instinct! Don't quote instinct to me! Instinct is something that people have got way from! It belongs to animals! Christian adults don't want it!

TOM. What do Christian adults want, then, Mother?

AMANDA. Superior things! Things of the 260 mind and the spirit! Only animals have to satisfy instincts! Surely your aims are somewhat higher than theirs! Than monkeys—pigs—

TOM. I reckon they're not.

AMANDA. You're joking. However, that isn't what I wanted to discuss.

TOM (*rising*). I haven't much time.

AMANDA (*pushing his shoulders*). Sit down.

TOM. You want me to punch in red at the warehouse, Mother? 270

AMANDA. You have five minutes. I want to talk about Laura.

(LEGEND: "PLANS AND PROVISIONS.")

TOM. All right! What about Laura?

AMANDA. We have to be making plans and provisions for her. She's older than you, two years, and nothing has happened. She just drifts along doing nothing. It frightens me terribly how she just drifts along.

TOM. I guess she's the type that people call 280 home girls.

AMANDA. There's no such type, and if there is, it's a pity! That is unless the home is hers, with a husband!

TOM. What?

AMANDA. Oh, I can see the handwriting on the wall as plain as I see the nose in front

of my face! It's terrifying! More and more you remind me of your father! He was out all hours
290 without explanation—Then *left! Good-bye!* And me with the bag to hold. I saw that letter you got from the Merchant Marine. I know what you're dreaming of. I'm not standing here blindfolded. Very well, then. Then *do* it! But not till there's somebody to take your place.

TOM. What do you mean?

AMANDA. I mean that as soon as Laura has got somebody to take care of her, married, a home of her own, independent—why, then
300 you'll be free to go wherever you please, on land, on sea, whichever way the wind blows you! But until that time you've got to look out for your sister. I don't say me because I'm old and don't matter! I say for your sister because she's young and dependent. I put her in business college—a dismal failure! Frightened her so it made her sick to her stomach. I took her over to the Young People's League at the church. Another fiasco. She spoke to nobody,
310 nobody spoke to her. Now all she does is fool with those pieces of glass and play those worn-out records. What kind of a life is that for a girl to lead?

TOM. What can I do about it?

AMANDA. Overcome selfishness! Self, self, self is all that you ever think of! (TOM *springs up and crosses to get his coat. It is ugly and bulky. He pulls on a cap with earmuffs.*) Where is your muffler? Put your wool muffler on! (*He*
320 *snatches it angrily from the closet and tosses it around his neck and pulls both ends tight.*) Tom! I haven't said what I had in mind to ask you.

TOM. I'm too late to—

AMANDA (*catching his arm—very importunately. Then shyly*). Down at the warehouse, aren't there some—nice young men?

TOM. No!

AMANDA. There *must* be—*some* . . .

TOM. Mother— 330

(*Gesture.*)

AMANDA. Find out one that's clean-living—doesn't drink and—ask him out for sister!

TOM. What?

AMANDA. For *sister!* To *meet!* Get *acquainted!*

TOM (*stamping to door*). Oh, my *go-osh!*

AMANDA. Will you? (*He opens door. Imploringly.*) Will you? (*He starts down.*) Will you? *Will* you, dear?

TOM (*calling back*). YES! 340

(AMANDA *closes the door hesitantly and with a troubled but faintly hopeful expression.*)

(SCREEN IMAGE: GLAMOR MAGAZINE COVER.)

(*Spot* AMANDA *at phone.*)

AMANDA. Ella Cartwright? This is Amanda Wingfield! How are you, honey? How is that kidney condition? (*Count five.*) *Horrors!* (*Count five.*) You're a Christian martyr, yes, honey, that's what you are, a Christian martyr! Well, I just happened to notice in my little red 350 book that your subscription to the *Companion* has just run out! I knew that you wouldn't want to miss out on the wonderful serial starting in this new issue. It's by Bessie Mae Hopper, the first thing she's written since *Honeymoon for Three.* Wasn't that a strange and interesting story? Well, this one is even lovelier, I believe. It has a sophisticated, society background. It's all about the horsey set on Long Island!

FADE OUT

Scene Five

LEGEND ON SCREEN: "ANNUNCIATION." *Fade with music.*

[*It is early dusk of a spring evening. Supper has just been finished in the Wingfield apartment.* AMANDA *and* LAURA *in light colored dresses are removing dishes from the table, in the upstage area, which is shadowy, their movements formalized almost as a dance or ritual, their moving forms as pale and silent as moths.*

TOM, *in white shirt and trousers, rises from the table and crosses toward the fire-escape.*]

AMANDA (*as he passes her*). Son, will you do me a favor?

TOM. What?

AMANDA. Comb your hair! You look so pretty when your hair is combed! (TOM *slouches on sofa with evening paper. Enormous caption "Franco Triumphs."*) There is only one respect in which I would like you to emulate your father.

10 TOM. What respect is that?

AMANDA. The care he always took of his appearance. He never allowed himself to look untidy. (*He throws down the paper and crosses to fire-escape.*) Where are you going?

TOM. I'm going out to smoke.

AMANDA. You smoke too much. A pack a day at fifteen cents a pack. How much would that amount to in a month? Thirty times fifteen is how much, Tom? Figure it out and you will 20 be astounded at what you could save. Enough to give you a night-school course in accounting at Washington U! Just think what a wonderful thing that would be for you, son!

(TOM *is unmoved by the thought.*)

TOM. I'd rather smoke. (*He steps out on landing, letting the screen door slam.*)

AMANDA (*sharply*). I know! That's the tragedy of it. . . . (*Alone, she turns to look at her husband's picture.*)

(DANCE MUSIC: "ALL THE WORLD IS WAITING FOR 30 THE SUNRISE!")

TOM (*to the audience*). Across the alley from us was the Paradise Dance Hall. On evenings in spring the windows and doors were open and the music came outdoors. Sometimes the lights were turned out except for a large glass sphere that hung from the ceiling. It would turn slowly about and filter the dusk with delicate rainbow colors. Then the orchestra played a waltz or a tango, something that had a slow and 40 sensuous rhythm. Couples would come outside, to the relative privacy of the alley. You could see them kissing behind ash-pits and telephone poles. This was the compensation for lives that passed like mine, without any change or adventure. Adventure and change were imminent in this year. They were waiting around the corner for all these kids. Suspended in the mist over Berchtesgaden, caught in the folds of Chamberlain's umbrella—In Spain there was 50 Guernica! But here there was only hot swing music and liquor, dance halls, bars, and movies, and sex that hung in the gloom like a chandelier and flooded the world with brief, deceptive rainbows. . . . All the world was waiting for bombardments!

(AMANDA *turns from the picture and comes outside.*)

AMANDA (*Sighing*). A fire-escape landing's a poor excuse for a porch. (*She spreads a news-* 60 *paper on a step and sits down, gracefully and demurely as if she were settling into a swing on a Mississippi veranda.*) What are you looking at?

TOM. The moon.

AMANDA. Is there a moon this evening?

TOM. It's rising over Garfinkel's Delicatessen.

AMANDA. So it is! A little silver slipper of a moon. Have you made a wish on it yet?

70 TOM. Um-hum.

AMANDA. What did you wish for?

TOM. That's a secret.

AMANDA. A secret, huh? Well, I won't tell tell mine either. I will be just as mysterious as you.

TOM. I bet I can guess what yours is.

AMANDA. Is my head so transparent?

TOM. You're not a sphinx.

AMANDA. No, I don't have secrets. I'll tell 80 you what I wished for on the moon. Success and happiness for my precious children! I wish for that whenever there's a moon, and when there isn't a moon, I wish for it, too.

TOM. I thought perhaps you wished for a gentleman caller.

AMANDA. Why do you say that?

TOM. Don't you remember asking me to fetch one?

AMANDA. I remember suggesting that it 90 would be nice for your sister if you brought home some nice young man from the warehouse. I think that I've made that suggestion more than once.

TOM. Yes, you have made it repeatedly.

AMANDA. Well?

TOM. We are going to have one.

AMANDA. *What?*

TOM. A gentleman caller!

(THE ANNUNCIATION IS CELEBRATED WITH MUSIC.)

100 (AMANDA *rises.*)

(IMAGE ON SCREEN: CALLER WITH BOUQUET.)

AMANDA. You mean you have asked some nice young man to come over?

TOM. Yep. I've asked him to dinner.

AMANDA. You really did?

TOM. I did!

AMANDA. You did, and did he—*accept?*

TOM. He did!

AMANDA. Well, well—well, well! That's— 110 lovely!

TOM. I thought that you would be pleased.

AMANDA. It's definite, then?

TOM. Very definite.

AMANDA. Soon?

TOM. Very soon.

AMANDA. For heaven's sake, stop putting on and tell me some things, will you?

TOM. What things do you want me to tell you?

AMANDA. *Naturally* I would like to know 120 when he's *coming!*

TOM. He's coming tomorrow.

AMANDA. *Tomorrow?*

TOM. Yep. Tomorrow.

AMANDA. But, Tom!

TOM. Yes, Mother?

AMANDA. Tomorrow gives me no time!

TOM. Time for what?

AMANDA. Preparations! Why didn't you phone me at once, as soon as you asked him, 130 the minute that he accepted? Then, don't you see, I could have been getting ready!

TOM. You don't have to make any fuss.

AMANDA. Oh, Tom, Tom, Tom, of course I have to make a fuss! I want things nice, not sloppy! Not thrown together. I'll certainly have to do some fast thinking, won't I?

TOM. I don't see why you have to think at all.

AMANDA. You just don't know. We can't 140 have a gentleman caller in a pig-sty! All my wedding silver has to be polished, the monogrammed table linen ought to be laundered! The windows have to be washed and fresh curtains put up. And how about clothes? We have to *wear* something, don't we?

TOM. Mother, this boy is no one to make a fuss over!

AMANDA. Do you realize he's the first young man we've introduced to your sister? It's terri- 150 ble, dreadful, disgraceful that poor little sister has never received a single gentleman caller! Tom, come inside! (*She opens the screen door.*)

TOM. What for?

AMANDA. I want to ask you some things.

TOM. If you're going to make such a fuss, I'll call it off, I'll tell him not to come!

AMANDA. You certainly won't do anything of the kind. Nothing offends people worse than broken engagements. It simply means I'll have 160 to work like a Turk! We won't be brilliant, but we will pass inspection. Come on inside. (TOM *follows, groaning.*) Sit down.

TOM. Any particular place you would like me to sit?

AMANDA. Thank heavens I've got that new

sofa! I'm also making payments on a floor lamp I'll have sent out! And put the chintz covers on, they'll brighten things up! Of course I'd hoped to have these walls re-papered. . . . What is the young man's name? 170

TOM. His name is O'Connor.

AMANDA. That, of course, means fish—tomorrow is Friday! I'll have that salmon loaf—with Durkee's dressing! What does he do? He works at the warehouse?

TOM. Of course! How else would I—

AMANDA. Tom, he—doesn't drink?

TOM. Why do you ask me that?

180 AMANDA. Your father *did!*

TOM. Don't get started on that!

AMANDA. He *does* drink, then?

TOM. Not that I know of!

AMANDA. Make sure, be certain! The last thing I want for my daughter's a boy who drinks!

TOM. Aren't you being a little bit premature? Mr. O'Connor has not yet appeared on the scene!

190 AMANDA. But will tomorrow. To meet your sister, and what do I know about his character? Nothing! Old maids are better off than wives of drunkards!

TOM. Oh, my God!

AMANDA. Be still!

TOM (*leaning forward to whisper*). Lots of fellows meet girls whom they don't marry!

AMANDA. Oh, talk sensibly, Tom—and don't be sarcastic! (*She has gotten a hairbrush.*)

200 TOM. What are you doing?

AMANDA. I'm brushing that cow-lick down! What is this young man's position at the warehouse?

TOM (*submitting grimly to the brush and the interrogation*). This young man's position is that of a shipping clerk, Mother.

AMANDA. Sounds to me like a fairly responsible job, the sort of a job *you* would be in if you just had more *get-up*. What is his salary? Have you any idea? 210

TOM. I would judge it to be approximately eighty-five dollars a month.

AMANDA. Well—not princely, but—

TOM. Twenty more than I make.

AMANDA. Yes, how well I know! But for a family man, eighty-five dollars a month is not much more than you can just get by on. . . .

TOM. Yes, but Mr. O'Connor is not a family man.

AMANDA. He might be, mightn't he? Some time in the future? 220

TOM. I see. Plans and provisions.

AMANDA. You are the only young man that I know of who ignores the fact that the future becomes the present, the present the past, and the past turns into everlasting regret if you don't plan for it!

TOM. I will think that over and see what I can make of it.

AMANDA. Don't be supercilious with your mother! Tell me some more about this—what do you call him? 230

TOM. James D. O'Connor. The D. is for Delaney.

AMANDA. Irish on *both* sides! *Gracious!* And doesn't drink?

TOM. Shall I call him up and ask him right this minute?

AMANDA. The only way to find out about those things is to make discreet inquiries at the proper moment. When I was a girl in Blue Mountain and it was suspected that a young man drank, the girl whose attentions he had been receiving, if any girl *was,* would sometimes speak to the minister of his church, or rather her father would if her father was living, and sort of feel him out on the young man's character. That is the way such things are discreetly handled to keep a young woman from making a tragic mistake! 240 250

TOM. Then how did you happen to make a tragic mistake?

AMANDA. That innocent look of your father's had everyone fooled! He *smiled*—the world was *enchanted!* No girl can do worse than put herself at the mercy of a handsome appearance! I hope that Mr. O'Connor is not too good-looking.

TOM. No, he's not too good-looking. He's covered with freckles and hasn't too much of a nose. 260

AMANDA. He's not right-down homely, though?

TOM. Not right-down homely. Just medium homely, I'd say.

AMANDA. Character's what to look for in a man.

TOM. That's what I've always said, Mother.

AMANDA. You've never said anything of the

kind and I suspect you would never give it a
270 thought.

TOM. Don't be so suspicious of me.

AMANDA. At least I hope he's the type that's up and coming.

TOM. I think he really goes in for self-improvement.

AMANDA. What reason have you to think so?

TOM. He goes to night school.

AMANDA (*beaming*). Splendid! What does he do, I mean study?

280 TOM. Radio engineering and public speaking!

AMANDA. Then he has visions of being advanced in the world! Any young man who studies public speaking is aiming to have an executive job some day! And radio engineering? A thing for the future! Both of these facts are very illuminating. Those are the sort of things that a mother should know concerning any young man who comes to call on her daughter. Seriously or—not.

290 TOM. One little warning. He doesn't know about Laura. I didn't let on that we had dark ulterior motives. I just said, why don't you come and have dinner with us? He said okay and that was the whole conversation.

AMANDA. I bet it was! You're eloquent as an oyster. However, he'll know about Laura when he gets here. When he sees how lovely and sweet and pretty she is, he'll thank his lucky stars he was asked to dinner.

300 TOM. Mother, you mustn't expect too much of Laura.

AMANDA. What do you mean?

TOM. Laura seems all those things to you and me because she's ours and we love her. We don't even notice she's crippled any more.

AMANDA. Don't say crippled! You know that I never allow that word to be used!

TOM. But face facts, Mother. She is and—that's not all—

310 AMANDA. What do you mean "not all"?

TOM. Laura is very different from other girls.

AMANDA. I think the difference is all to her advantage.

TOM. Not quite all—in the eyes of others—strangers—she's terribly shy and lives in a world of her own and those things make her seem a little peculiar to people outside the house.

AMANDA. Don't say peculiar.

TOM. Face the facts. She is. 320

(THE DANCE-HALL MUSIC CHANGES TO A TANGO THAT HAS A MINOR AND SOMEWHAT OMINOUS TONE.)

AMANDA. In what way is she peculiar—may I ask?

TOM (*gently*). She lives in a world of her own—a world of—little glass ornaments, Mother. . . . (*Gets up.* AMANDA *remains holding brush, looking at him, troubled.*) She plays old phonograph records and—that's about all— 330 (*He glances at himself in the mirror and crosses to door.*)

AMANDA (*sharply*). Where are you going?

TOM. I'm going to the movies. (*Out screen door.*)

AMANDA. Not to the movies, every night to the movies! (*Follows quickly to screen door.*) I don't believe you always go to the movies! (*He is gone.* AMANDA *looks worriedly after him for a moment. Then vitality and optimism return* 340 *and she turns from the door. Crossing to portieres.*) Laura! Laura! (LAURA *answers from kitchenette.*)

LAURA. Yes, Mother.

AMANDA. Let those dishes go and come in front! (LAURA *appears with dish towel. Gaily.*) Laura, come here and make a wish on the moon!

LAURA (*entering*). Moon—moon?

AMANDA. A little silver slipper of a moon. 350 Look over your left shoulder, Laura, and make a wish! (LAURA *looks faintly puzzled as if called out of sleep.* AMANDA *seizes her shoulders and turns her at an angle by the door.*) No! Now, darling, *wish!*

LAURA. What shall I wish for, Mother?

AMANDA (*her voice trembling and her eyes suddenly filling with tears*). Happiness! Good Fortune!

(*The violin rises and the stage dims out.*) 360

Scene Six

(IMAGE: HIGH SCHOOL HERO.)

TOM. And so the following evening I brought Jim home to dinner. I had known Jim slightly in high school. In high school Jim was a hero. He had tremendous Irish good nature and vitality with the scrubbed and polished look of white chinaware. He seemed to move in a continual spotlight. He was a star in basketball, captain of the debating club, president of the senior class and the glee club and he sang the male lead in the annual light operas. He was always running or bounding, never just walking. He seemed always at the point of defeating the law of gravity. He was shooting with such velocity through his adolescence that you would logically expect him to arrive at nothing short of the White House by the time he was thirty. But Jim apparently ran into more interference after his graduation from Soldan. His speed had definitely slowed. Six years after he left high school he was holding a job that wasn't much better than mine.

(IMAGE: CLERK.)

He was the only one at the warehouse with whom I was on friendly terms. I was valuable to him as someone who could remember his former glory, who had seen him win basketball games and the silver cup in debating. He knew of my secret practice of retiring to a cabinet of the washroom to work on poems when business was slack in the warehouse. He called me Shakespeare. And while the other boys in the warehouse regarded me with suspicious hostility, Jim took a humorous attitude toward me. Gradually his attitude affected the others, their hostility wore off and they also began to smile at me as people smile at an oddly fashioned dog who trots across their path at some distance.

I knew that Jim and Laura had known each other at Soldan, and I had heard Laura speak admiringly of his voice. I didn't know if Jim remembered her or not. In high school Laura had been as unobtrusive as Jim had been astonishing. If he did remember Laura, it was not as my sister, for when I asked him to dinner, he grinned and said, "You know, Shakespeare, I never thought of you as having folks!"

He was about to discover that I did. . . .

(LIGHT UP STAGE.)

(LEGEND ON SCREEN: "THE ACCENT OF A COMING FOOT.")

(*Friday evening. It is about five o'clock of a late spring evening which comes "scattering poems in the sky."*)

(*A delicate lemony light is in the Wingfield apartment.*)

(AMANDA *has worked like a Turk in preparation for the gentleman caller. The results are astonishing. The new floor lamp with its rose-silk shade is in place, a colored paper lantern conceals the broken light fixture in the ceiling, new billowing white curtains are at the windows, chintz covers are on chairs and sofa, a pair of new sofa pillows make their initial appearance.*)

(*Open boxes and tissue paper are scattered on the floor.*)

(LAURA *stands in the middle with lifted arms while* AMANDA *crouches before her, adjusting the hem of the new dress, devout and ritualistic. The dress is colored and designed by memory. The arrangement of* LAURA'*s hair is changed; it is softer and more becoming. A fragile, unearthly prettiness has come out in* LAURA: *she is like a piece of translucent glass touched by light, given a momentary radiance, not actual, not lasting.*)

AMANDA (*impatiently*). Why are you trembling?

LAURA. Mother, you've made me so nervous!

AMANDA. How have I made you nervous?

LAURA. By all this fuss! You make it seem so important!

AMANDA. I don't understand you, Laura. You couldn't be satisfied with just sitting home, and yet whenever I try to arrange something for you, you seem to resist it. (*She gets up.*) Now take a look at yourself. No, wait! Wait just a moment—I have an idea!

LAURA. What is it now?

(AMANDA *produces two powder puffs which she wraps in hankerchiefs and stuffs in* LAURA'S *bosom.*)

LAURA. Mother, what are you doing?

AMANDA. They call them "Gay Deceivers"!

LAURA. I won't wear them!

AMANDA. You will!

LAURA. Why should I?

AMANDA. Because, to be painfully honest, your chest is flat.

LAURA. You make it seem like we were setting a trap.

AMANDA. All pretty girls are a trap, a pretty trap, and men expect them to be. (LEGEND: "A PRETTY TRAP.") Now look at yourself, young lady. This is the prettiest you will ever be! I've got to fix myself now! You're going to be surprised by your mother's appearance! (*She crosses through portieres, humming gaily.*)

(LAURA *moves slowly to the long mirror and stares solemnly at herself.*)

(*A wind blows the white curtains inward in a slow, graceful motion and with a faint, sorrowful sighing.*)

AMANDA (*off stage*). It isn't dark enough yet. (*She turns slowly before the mirror with a troubled look.*)

(LEGEND ON SCREEN: "THIS IS MY SISTER: CELEBRATE HER WITH STRINGS!" MUSIC.)

AMANDA (*laughing, off*). I'm going to show you something. I'm going to make a spectacular appearance!

LAURA. What is it, Mother?

AMANDA. Possess your soul in patience—you will see! Something I've resurrected from that old trunk! Styles haven't changed so terribly much after all. . . . (*She parts the portieres.*) Now just look at your mother! (*She wears a girlish frock of yellowed voile with a blue silk sash. She carries a bunch of jonquils—the legend of her youth is nearly revived. Feverishly*) This is the dress in which I led the cotillion. Won the cakewalk twice at Sunset Hill, wore one spring to the Governor's ball in Jackson! See how I sashayed around the ballroom, Laura? (*She raises her skirt and does a mincing step around the room.*) I wore it on Sundays for my gentlemen callers! I had it on the day I met your father—I had malaria fever all that spring. The change of climate from East Tennessee to the Delta—weakened resistance—I had a little temperature all the time—not enough to be serious—just enough to make me restless and giddy! Invitations poured in—parties all over the Delta!—"Stay in bed," said Mother, "you have fever!"—but I just wouldn't.—I took quinine but kept on going, going!—Evenings, dances!—Afternoons, long, long rides! Picnics—lovely!—So lovely, that country in May.—All lacy with dogwood, literally flooded with jonquils!—That was the spring I had the craze for jonquils. Jonquils became an absolute obsession. Mother said, "Honey, there's no more room for jonquils." And still I kept on bringing in more jonquils. Whenever, wherever I saw them, I'd say, "Stop! Stop! I see jonquils!" I made the young men help me gather the jonquils! It was a joke, Amanda and her jonquils! Finally there were no more vases to hold them, every available space was filled with jonquils. No vases to hold them? All right, I'll hold them myself! And then I—(*She stops in front of the picture:* MUSIC.) met your father! Malaria fever and jonquils and then—this—boy. . . . (*She switches on the rose-colored lamp.*) I hope they get here before it starts to rain. (*She crosses upstage and places the jonquils in bowl on table.*) I gave your brother a little extra change so he and Mr. O'Connor could take the service car home.

LAURA (*with altered look*). What did you say his name was?

AMANDA. O'Connor.

LAURA. What is his first name?

AMANDA. I don't remember. Oh, yes. I do. It was—Jim!

(LAURA *sways slightly and catches hold of a chair.*)

(LEGEND ON SCREEN: "NOT JIM!")

180 LAURA (*faintly*). Not—Jim!

AMANDA. Yes, that was it, it was Jim! I've never known a Jim that wasn't nice!

(MUSIC: OMINOUS.)

LAURA. Are you sure his name is Jim O'Connor?

AMANDA. Yes. Why?

LAURA. Is he the one that Tom used to know in high school?

AMANDA. He didn't say so. I think he just
190 got to know him at the warehouse.

LAURA. There was a Jim O'Connor we both knew in high school—(*Then, with effort.*) If that is the one that Tom is bringing to dinner —you'll have to excuse me, I won't come to the table.

AMANDA. What sort of nonsense is this?

LAURA. You asked me once if I'd ever liked a boy. Don't you remember I showed you this boy's picture?

200 AMANDA. You mean the boy you showed me in the year book?

LAURA. Yes, that boy.

AMANDA. Laura, Laura, were you in love with that boy?

LAURA. I don't know, Mother. All I know is I couldn't sit at the table if it was him!

AMANDA. It won't be him! It isn't the least bit likely. But whether it is or not, you will come to the table. You will not be excused.

210 LAURA. I'll have to be, Mother.

AMANDA. I don't intend to humor your silliness, Laura. I've had too much from you and your brother, both! So just sit down and compose yourself till they come. Tom has forgotten his key so you'll have to let them in, when they arrive.

LAURA (*panicky*). Oh, Mother—*you* answer the door!

AMANDA (*lightly*). I'll be in the kitchen—
220 busy!

LAURA. Oh, Mother, please answer the door, don't make me do it!

AMANDA (*crossing into kitchenette*). I've got to fix the dressing for the salmon. Fuss, fuss —silliness!—over a gentleman caller!

(*Door swings shut.* LAURA *is left alone.*)

(LEGEND: "TERROR!")

(*She utters a low moan and turns off the lamp —sits stiffly on the edge of the sofa, knotting her fingers together.*) 230

(LEGEND ON SCREEN: "THE OPENING OF A DOOR!")

(TOM *and* JIM *appear on the fire-escape steps and climb to landing. Hearing their approach,* LAURA *rises with a panicky gesture. She retreats to the portieres.*)

(*The doorbell.* LAURA *catches her breath and touches her throat. Low drums.*)

AMANDA (*calling*). Laura, sweetheart! The door!

(LAURA *stares at it without moving.*) 240

JIM. I think we just beat the rain.

TOM. Uh-huh. (*He rings again, nervously,* JIM *whistles and fishes for a cigarette.*)

AMANDA (*very, very gaily*). Laura, that is your brother and Mr. O'Connor! Will you let them in, darling?

(LAURA *crosses toward kitchenette door.*)

LAURA (*breathlessly*). Mother—you go to the door!

(AMANDA *steps out of kitchenette and stares* 250 *furiously at* LAURA. *She points imperiously at the door.*)

LAURA. Please, please!

AMANDA (*in a fierce whisper*). What is the matter with you, you silly thing?

LAURA (*desperately*). Please, you answer it, *please!*

AMANDA. I told you I wasn't going to humor you, Laura. Why have you chosen this moment to lose your mind? 260

LAURA. Please, please, please, you go!

AMANDA. You'll have to go to the door because I can't!

LAURA (*despairingly*). I can't either!

AMANDA. *Why?*

LAURA. I'm *sick!*

AMANDA. I'm sick, too—of your nonsense! Why can't you and your brother be normal people? Fantastic whims and behavior! (TOM *gives a long ring.*) Preposterous goings on! 270 Can you give me one reason—(*Calls out lyrically:*) COMING! JUST ONE SECOND!—why you should be afraid to open a door? Now you answer it, Laura!

LAURA. Oh, oh, oh . . . (*She returns through the portieres. Darts to the victrola and winds it frantically and turns it on.*)

AMANDA. Laura Wingfield, you march right to that door!

280 LAURA. Yes—yes, Mother!

(*A faraway, scratchy rendition of "Dardanella" softens the air and gives her strength to move through it. She slips to the door and draws it cautiously open.*)

(TOM *enters with the caller,* JIM O'CONNOR.)

TOM. Laura, this is Jim. Jim, this is my sister, Laura.

JIM (*stepping inside*). I didn't know that Shakespeare had a sister!

290 LAURA (*retreating stiff and trembling from the door*). How—how do you do?

JIM (*heartily extending his hand*). Okay!

(LAURA *touches it hesitantly with hers.*)

JIM. Your hand's *cold,* Laura!

LAURA. Yes, well—I've been playing the victrola. . . .

JIM. Must have been playing classical music on it! You ought to play a little hot swing music to warm you up!

300 LAURA. Excuse me—I haven't finished playing the victrola. . . .

(*She turns awkwardly and hurries into the front room. She pauses a second by the victrola. Then catches her breath and darts through the portieres like a frightened deer.*)

JIM (*grinning*). What was the matter?

TOM. Oh—with Laura? Laura is—terribly shy.

JIM. Shy, huh? It's unusual to meet a shy

310 girl nowadays. I don't believe you ever mentioned you had a sister.

TOM. Well, now you know. I have one. Here is the *Post Dispatch.* You want a piece of it?

JIM. Uh-huh.

TOM. What piece? The comics?

JIM. Sports! (*Glances at it.*) Ole Dizzy Dean is on his bad behavior.

TOM (*disinterest*). Yeah? (*Lights cigarette and crosses back to fire-escape door.*) 320

JIM. Where are *you* going?

TOM. I'm going out on the terrace.

JIM (*goes after him*). You know, Shakespeare—I'm going to sell you a bill of goods!

TOM. What goods?

JIM. A course I'm taking.

TOM. Huh?

JIM. In public speaking! You and me, we're not the warehouse type.

TOM. Thanks—that's good news. But what 330 has public speaking got to do with it?

JIM. It fits you for—executive positions!

TOM. Awww.

JIM. I tell you it's done a helluva lot for me.

(IMAGE: EXECUTIVES AT DESK.)

TOM. In what respect?

JIM. In every! Ask yourself what is the difference between you an' me and men in the office down front? Brains?—No!—Ability?— 340 No! Then what? Just one little thing—

TOM. What is that one little thing?

JIM. Primarily it amounts to—social poise! Being able to square up to people and hold your own on any social level!

AMANDA (*off stage*). Tom?

TOM. Yes, Mother?

AMANDA. Is that you and Mr. O'Connor?

TOM. Yes, Mother.

AMANDA. Well, you just make yourselves 350 comfortable in there.

TOM. Yes, Mother.

AMANDA. Ask Mr. O'Connor if he would like to wash his hands.

JIM. Aw, no—no—thank you—I took care of that at the warehouse. Tom—

TOM. Yes?

JIM. Mr. Mendoza was speaking to me about you.

TOM. Favorably? 360

JIM. What do you think?

TOM. Well—

JIM. You're going to be out of a job if you don't wake up.

TOM. I am waking up—

JIM. You show no signs.

TOM. The signs are interior.

(IMAGE ON SCREEN: THE SAILING VESSEL WITH JOLLY ROGER AGAIN.)

370 TOM. I'm planning to change. (*He leans over the rail speaking with quiet exhilaration. The incandescent marquees and signs of the first-run movie houses light his face from across the alley. He looks like a voyager.*) I'm right at the point of committing myself to a future that doesn't include the warehouse and Mr. Mendoza or even a night-school course in public speaking.

JIM. What are you gassing about?

380 TOM. I'm tired of the movies.

JIM. Movies!

TOM. Yes, movies! Look at them—(*A wave toward the marvels of Grand Avenue.*) All of those glamorous people—having adventures—hogging it all, gobbling the whole thing up! You know what happens? People go to the *movies* instead of *moving!* Hollywood characters are supposed to have all the adventures for everybody in America, while everybody in
390 America sits in a dark room and watches them have them! Yes, until there's a war. That's when adventure becomes available to the masses! *Everyone's* dish, not only Gable's! Then the people in the dark room come out of the dark room to have some adventures themselves—Goody, goody!—It's our turn now, to go to the South Sea Islands—to make a safari—to be exotic, far-off!—But I'm not patient. I don't want to wait till then. I'm tired of the *movies* and I
400 am *about* to *move!*

JIM (*incredulously*). Move?

TOM. Yes.

JIM. When?

TOM. Soon!

JIM. Where? Where?

(THEME THREE MUSIC SEEMS TO ANSWER THE QUESTION, WHILE TOM THINKS IT OVER. HE SEARCHES AMONG HIS POCKETS.)

TOM. I'm starting to boil inside. I know I
410 seem dreamy, but inside—well, I'm boiling! Whenever I pick up a shoe, I shudder a little thinking how short life is and what I am doing!—Whatever that means, I know it doesn't mean shoes—except as something to wear on a traveler's feet! (*Finds paper.*) Look—

JIM. What?

TOM. I'm a member.

JIM (*reading*). The Union of Merchant Seamen.

420 TOM. I paid my dues this month, instead of the light bill.

JIM. You will regret it when they turn the lights off.

TOM. I won't be here.

JIM. How about your mother?

TOM. I'm like my father. The bastard son of a bastard! See how he grins? And he's been absent going on sixteen years!

JIM. You're just talking, you drip. How
430 does your mother feel about it?

TOM. Shhh!—Here comes Mother! Mother is not acquainted with my plans!

AMANDA (*enters portieres*). Where are you all?

TOM. On the terrace, Mother.

(*They start inside. She advances to them.* TOM *is distinctly shocked at her appearance. Even* JIM *blinks a little. He is making his first contact with girlish Southern vivacity and in spite*
440 *of the night-school course in public speaking is somewhat thrown off the beam by the unexpected outlay of social charm.*)

(*Certain responses are attempted by* JIM *but are swept aside by* AMANDA'*s gay laughter and chatter.* TOM *is embarrassed but after the first shock* JIM *reacts very warmly. Grins and chuckles, is altogether won over.*)

(IMAGE: AMANDA AS A GIRL.)

AMANDA (*coyly smiling, shaking her girlish*
450 *ringlets*). Well, well, well, so this is Mr. O'Connor. Introductions entirely unnecessary. I've heard so much about you from my boy. I finally said to him, Tom—good gracious!—why don't you bring this paragon to supper? I'd like to meet this nice young man at the warehouse!—Instead of just hearing him sing your praises so much! I don't know why my son is so standoffish—that's not Southern behavior! Let's sit down and—I think we could stand
460 a little more air in here! Tom, leave the door open. I felt a nice fresh breeze a moment ago. Where has it gone to? Mmm, so warm already! And not quite summer, even. We're going to burn up when summer really gets started. However, we're having—we're having a very

light supper. I think light things are better fo' this time of year. The same as light clothes are. Light clothes an' light food are what warm weather calls fo'. You know our blood gets so thick during th' winter—it takes a while fo' us to *adjust* ou'selves!—when the season changes . . . It's come so quick this year. I wasn't prepared. All of a sudden—heavens! Already summer!—I ran to the trunk an' pulled out this light dress—Terribly old! Historical almost! But feels so good—so good an' co-ol, y'know. . . .

TOM. Mother—

AMANDA. Yes, honey?

TOM. How about—supper?

AMANDA. Honey, you go ask Sister if supper is ready! You know that Sister is in full charge of supper! Tell her you hungry boys are waiting for it. (*To* JIM.) Have you met Laura?

JIM. She—

AMANDA. Let you in? Oh, good, you've met already! It's rare for a girl as sweet an' pretty as Laura to be domestic! But Laura is, thank heavens, not only pretty but also very domestic. I'm not at all. I never was a bit. I never could make a thing but angel-food cake. Well, in the South we had so many servants. Gone, gone, gone. All vestige of gracious living! Gone completely! I wasn't prepared for what the future brought me. All of my gentlemen callers were sons of planters and so of course I assumed that I would be married to one and raise my family on a large piece of land with plenty of servants. But man proposes—and woman accepts the proposal!—To vary that old, old saying a little bit—I married no planter! I married a man who worked for the telephone company! —That gallantly smiling gentleman over there! (*Points to the picture.*) A telephone man who —fell in love with long-distance!—Now he travels and I don't even know where!—But what am I going on for about my—tribulations? Tell me yours—I hope you don't have any! Tom?

TOM (*returning*). Yes, Mother?

AMANDA. Is supper nearly ready?

TOM. It looks to me like supper is on the table.

AMANDA. Let me look—(*She rises prettily and looks through portieres.*) Oh, lovely!—But where is Sister?

TOM. Laura is not feeling well and she says that she thinks she'd better not come to the table.

AMANDA. What?—Nonsense!—Laura? Oh, Laura!

LAURA (*off stage, faintly*). Yes, Mother.

AMANDA. You really must come to the table. We won't be seated until you come to the table! Come in, Mr. O'Connor. You sit over there, and I'll—Laura? Laura Wingfield! You're keeping us waiting, honey! We can't say grace until you come to the table!

(*The back door is pushed weakly open and* LAURA *comes in. She is obviously quite faint, her lips trembling, her eyes wide and staring. She moves unsteadily toward the table.*)

(LEGEND: "TERROR!")

(*Outside a summer storm is coming abruptly. The white curtains billow inward at the windows and there is a sorrowful murmur and deep blue dusk.*)

(LAURA *suddenly stumbles—she catches at a chair with a faint moan.*)

TOM. Laura!

AMANDA. Laura! (*There is a clap of thunder.*) (LEGEND: "AH") (*Despairingly*). Why, Laura, you *are* sick, darling! Tom, help your sister into the living room, dear! Sit in the living room, Laura—rest on the sofa. Well! (*To the gentleman caller.*) Standing over the hot stove made her ill!—I told her that it was just too warm this evening, but—(TOM *comes back in.* LAURA *is on the sofa.*) Is Laura all right now?

TOM. Yes.

AMANDA. What *is* that? Rain? A nice cool rain has come up! (*She gives the gentleman caller a frightened look.*) I think we may—have grace—now . . . (TOM *looks at her stupidly.*) Tom, honey—you say grace!

TOM. Oh . . . "For these and all thy mercies—" (*They bow their heads,* AMANDA *stealing a nervous glance at* JIM. *In the living room* LAURA, *stretched on the sofa, clenches her hand to her lips, to hold back a shuddering sob.*) God's Holy Name be praised—

THE SCENE DIMS OUT

Scene Seven

[A Souvenir.]

[*Half an hour later. Dinner is just being finished in the upstage area which is concealed by the drawn portieres.*

As the curtain rises LAURA *is still huddled upon the sofa, her feet drawn under her, her head resting on a pale blue pillow, her eyes wide and mysteriously watchful. The new floor lamp with its shade of rose-colored silk gives a soft, becoming light to her face, bringing out the fragile, unearthly prettiness which usually escapes attention. There is a steady murmur of rain, but it is slackening and stops soon after the scene begins; the air outside becomes pale and luminous as the moon breaks out.*

A moment after the curtain rises, the lights in both rooms flicker and go out.]

JIM. Hey, there, Mr. Light Bulb!

(AMANDA *laughs nervously.*)

(LEGEND: "SUSPENSION OF A PUBLIC SERVICE.")

AMANDA. Where was Moses when the lights went out? Ha-ha. Do you know the answer to that one, Mr. O'Connor?

JIM. No, Ma'am, what's the answer?

AMANDA. In the dark! (JIM *laughs appreciably.*) Everybody sit still. I'll light the candles. 10 Isn't it lucky we have them on the table? Where's a match? Which of you gentlemen can provide a match?

JIM. Here.

AMANDA. Thank you, sir.

JIM. Not at all, Ma'am!

AMANDA. I guess the fuse has burnt out. Mr. O'Connor, can you tell a burnt-out fuse? I know I can't and Tom is a total loss when it comes to mechanics. (SOUND: GETTING UP: VOICES 20 RECEDE A LITTLE TO KITCHENETTE.) Oh, be careful you don't bump into something. We don't want our gentleman caller to break his neck. Now wouldn't that be a fine howdy-do?

JIM. Ha-ha! Where is the fuse-box?

AMANDA. Right here next to the stove. Can you see anything?

JIM. Just a minute.

AMANDA. Isn't electricity a mysterious thing? Wasn't it Benjamin Franklin who tied a key to a kite? We live in such a mysterious uni- 30 verse, don't we? Some people say that science clears up all the mysteries for us. In my opinion it only creates more! Have you found it yet?

JIM. No, Ma'am. All these fuses look okay to me.

AMANDA. Tom!

TOM. Yes, Mother?

AMANDA. That light bill I gave you several days ago. The one I told you we got the notices about? 40

TOM. Oh—Yeah.

(LEGEND: "HA!")

AMANDA. You didn't neglect to pay it by any chance?

TOM. Why, I—

AMANDA. Didn't! I might have known it!

JIM. Shakespeare probably wrote a poem on that light bill, Mrs. Wingfield.

AMANDA. I might have known better than to trust him with it! There's such a high price for 50 negligence in this world!

JIM. Maybe the poem will win a ten-dollar prize.

AMANDA. We'll just have to spend the remainder of the evening in the nineteenth century, before Mr. Edison made the Mazda lamp!

JIM. Candlelight is my favorite kind of light.

AMANDA. That shows you're romantic! But

60 that's no excuse for Tom. Well, we got through dinner. Very considerate of them to let us get through dinner before they plunged us into everlasting darkness, wasn't it, Mr. O'Connor?

JIM. Ha-ha!

AMANDA. Tom, as a penalty for your carelessness you can help me with the dishes.

JIM. Let me give you a hand.

AMANDA. Indeed you will not!

JIM. I ought to be good for something.

70 AMANDA. Good for something? (*Her tone is rhapsodic.*) You? Why, Mr. O'Connor, nobody, *nobody's* given me this much entertainment in years—as you have!

JIM. Aw, now, Mrs. Wingfield!

AMANDA. I'm not exaggerating, not one bit! But Sister is all by her lonesome. You go keep her company in the parlor! I'll give you this lovely old candelabrum that used to be on the altar at the church of the Heavenly Rest. It was 80 melted a little out of shape when the church burnt down. Lightning struck it one spring. Gypsy Jones was holding a revival at the time and he intimated that the church was destroyed because the Episcopalians gave card parties.

JIM. Ha-ha.

AMANDA. And how about you coaxing Sister to drink a little wine? I think it would be good for her! Can you carry both at once?

JIM. Sure. I'm Superman!

90 AMANDA. Now, Thomas, get into this apron!

(*The door of kitchenette swings closed on* AMANDA's *gay laughter; the flickering light approaches the portieres.*)

(LAURA *sits up nervously as he enters. Her speech at first is low and breathless from the almost intolerable strain of being alone with a stranger.*)

(THE LEGEND: "I DON'T SUPPOSE YOU REMEMBER ME AT ALL!")

100 (*In her first speeches in this scene, before* JIM's *warmth overcomes her paralyzing shyness,* LAURA's *voice is thin and breathless as though she has just run up a steep flight of stairs.*)

(JIM's *attitude is gently humorous. In playing this scene it should be stressed that while the incident is apparently unimportant, it is to* LAURA *the climax of her secret life.*)

JIM. Hello, there, Laura.

LAURA (*faintly*). Hello. (*She clears her throat.*) 110

JIM. How are you feeling now? Better?

LAURA. Yes. Yes, thank you.

JIM. This is for you. A little dandelion wine. (*He extends it toward her with extravagant gallantry.*)

LAURA. Thank you.

JIM. Drink it—but don't get drunk! (*He laughs heartily.* LAURA *takes the glass uncertainly; laughs shyly.*) Where shall I set the candles?

LAURA. Oh—oh, anywhere . . . 120

JIM. How about here on the floor? Any objections?

LAURA. No.

JIM. I'll spread a newspaper under to catch the drippings. I like to sit on the floor. Mind if I do?

LAURA. Oh, no.

JIM. Give me a pillow?

LAURA. What?

JIM. A pillow! 130

LAURA. Oh . . . (*Hands him one quickly.*)

JIM. How about you? Don't you like to sit on the floor?

LAURA. Oh—yes.

JIM. Why don't you, then?

LAURA. I—will.

JIM. Take a pillow! (LAURA *does. Sits on the other side of the candelabrum.* JIM *crosses his legs and smiles engagingly at her.*) I can't hardly see you sitting way over there. 140

LAURA. I can—see you.

JIM. I know, but that's not fair, I'm in the limelight. (LAURA *moves her pillow closer.*) Good! Now I can see you! Comfortable?

LAURA. Yes.

JIM. So am I. Comfortable as a cow. Will you have some gum?

LAURA. No, thank you.

JIM. I think that I will indulge, with your permission. (*Musingly unwraps it and holds it up.*) 150 Think of the fortune made by the guy that invented the first piece of chewing gum. Amazing, huh? The Wrigley Building is one of the sights of Chicago.—I saw it summer before last when I went up to the Century of Progress. Did you take in the Century of Progress?

LAURA. No, I didn't.

JIM. Well, it was quite a wonderful exposition. What impressed me most was the Hall of Science. Gives you an idea of what the future will be in America, even more wonderful than the present time is! (*Pause. Smiling at her.*) Your brother tells me you're shy. Is that right, Laura?

LAURA. I—don't know.

JIM. I judge you to be an old-fashioned type of girl. Well, I think that's a pretty good type to be. Hope you don't think I'm being too personal—do you?

LAURA (*hastily, out of embarrassment*). I believe I *will* take a piece of gum, if you—don't mind. (*Clearing her throat.*) Mr. O'Connor, have you—kept up with your singing?

JIM. Singing? Me?

LAURA. Yes. I remember what a beautiful voice you had.

JIM. When did you hear me sing?

(VOICE OFF STAGE IN THE PAUSE.)

VOICE (*off stage*).

O blow, ye winds, heigh-ho,
A-roving I will go!
I'm off to my love
With a boxing glove—
Ten thousand miles away!

JIM. You say you've heard me sing?

LAURA. Oh! yes! Yes, very often . . . I—don't suppose you remember me—at all?

JIM (*smiling doubtfully*). You know I have an idea I've seen you before. I had that idea soon as you opened the door. It seemed almost like I was about to remember your name. But the name that I started to call you—wasn't a name! And so I stopped myself before I said it.

LAURA. Wasn't it—Blue Roses?

JIM (*springs up. Grinning*). Blue Roses! My gosh, yes—Blue Roses! That's what I had on my tongue when you opened the door! Isn't it funny what tricks your memory plays? I didn't connect you with high school somehow or other. But that's where it was; it was high school. I didn't even know you were Shakespeare's sister! Gosh, I'm sorry.

LAURA. I didn't expect you to. You—barely knew me!

JIM. But we did have a speaking acquaintance, huh?

LAURA. Yes, we—spoke to each other.

JIM. When did you recognize me?

LAURA. Oh, right away!

JIM. Soon as I came in the door?

LAURA. When I heard your name I thought it was probably you. I knew that Tom used to know you a little in high school. So when you came in the door—Well, then I was—sure.

JIM. Why didn't you *say* something, then?

LAURA (*breathlessly*). I didn't know what to say, I was—too surprised!

JIM. For goodness' sakes! You know, this sure is funny!

LAURA. Yes! Yes, isn't it, though . . .

JIM. Didn't we have a class in something together?

LAURA. Yes, we did.

JIM. What class was that?

LAURA. It was—singing—Chorus!

JIM. Aw!

LAURA. I sat across the aisle from you in the Aud.

JIM. Aw.

LAURA. Mondays, Wednesdays and Fridays.

JIM. Now I remember—you always came in late.

LAURA. Yes, it was so hard for me, getting upstairs. I had that brace on my leg—it clumped so loud!

JIM. I never heard any clumping.

LAURA (*wincing at the recollection*). To me it sounded like—thunder!

JIM. Well, well, well, I never even noticed.

LAURA. And everybody was seated before I came in. I had to walk in front of all those people. My seat was in the back row. I had to go clumping all the way up the aisle with everyone watching!

JIM. You shouldn't have been self-conscious.

LAURA. I know, but I was. It was always such a relief when the singing started.

JIM. Aw, yes, I've placed you now! I used to call you Blue Roses. How was it that I got started calling you that?

LAURA. I was out of school a little while with pleurosis. When I came back you asked me what was the matter. I said I had pleurosis—you thought I said Blue Roses. That's what you always called me after that!

JIM. I hope you didn't mind.

LAURA. Oh, no—I liked it. You see, I wasn't acquainted with many—people. . . .

260 JIM. As I remember you sort of stuck by yourself.

LAURA. I—I—never have had much luck at —making friends.

JIM. I don't see why you wouldn't.

LAURA. Well, I—started out badly.

JIM. You mean being—

LAURA. Yes, it sort of—stood between me—

JIM. You shouldn't have let it!

LAURA. I know, but it did, and—

270 JIM. You were shy with people!

LAURA. I tried not to be but never could—

JIM. Overcome it?

LAURA. No, I—I never could!

JIM. I guess being shy is something you have to work out of kind of gradually.

LAURA (*sorrowfully*). Yes—I guess it—

JIM. Takes time!

LAURA. Yes—

JIM. People are not so dreadful when you 280 know them. That's what you have to remember! And everybody has problems, not just you, but practically everybody has got some problems. You think of yourself as having the only problems, as being the only one who is disappointed. But just look around you and you will see lots of people as disappointed as you are. For instance, I hoped when I was going to high school that I would be further along at this time, six years later, than I am now—You 290 remember that wonderful write-up I had in *The Torch?*

LAURA. Yes! (*She rises and crosses to table.*)

JIM. It said I was bound to succeed in anything I went into! (LAURA *returns with the annual.*) Holy Jeez! *The Torch!* (*He accepts it reverently. They smile across it with mutual wonder.* LAURA *crouches beside him and they begin to turn through it.* LAURA'*s shyness is dissolving in his warmth.*)

300 LAURA. Here you are in *Pirates of Penzance!*

JIM (*wistfully*). I sang the baritone lead in that operetta.

LAURA (*rapidly*). So—*beautifully!*

JIM (*protesting*). Aw—

LAURA. Yes, yes—beautifully—beautifully!

JIM. You heard me?

LAURA. All three times!

JIM. No!

LAURA. Yes!

310 JIM. All three performances?

LAURA (*looking down*). Yes.

JIM. Why?

LAURA. I—wanted to ask you to—autograph my program.

JIM. Why didn't you ask me to?

LAURA. You were always surrounded by your own friends so much that I never had a chance to.

JIM. You should have just—

320 LAURA. Well, I—thought you might think I was—

JIM. Thought I might think you was—what?

LAURA. Oh—

JIM (*with reflective relish*). I was beleaguered by females in those days.

LAURA. You were terribly popular!

JIM. Yeah—

LAURA. You had such a—friendly way—

330 JIM. I was spoiled in high school.

LAURA. Everybody—liked you!

JIM. Including you?

LAURA. I—yes, I—I did, too—(*She gently closes the book in her lap.*)

JIM. Well, well, well!—Give me that program, Laura. (*She hands it to him. He signs it with a flourish.*) There you are—better late than never!

LAURA. Oh, I—what a—surprise!

340 JIM. My signature isn't worth very much right now. But some day—maybe—it will increase in value! Being disappointed is one thing and being discouraged is something else. I am disappointed but I am not discouraged. I'm twenty-three years old. How old are you?

LAURA. I'll be twenty-four in June.

JIM. That's not old age!

LAURA. No, but—

JIM. You finished high school?

350 LAURA (*with difficulty*). I didn't go back.

JIM. You mean you dropped out?

LAURA. I made bad grades in my final examinations. (*She rises and replaces the book and the program. Her voice strained.*) How is —Emily Meisenbach getting along?

JIM. Oh, that kraut-head!

LAURA. Why do you call her that?

JIM. That's what she was.

LAURA. You're not still—going with her?

360 JIM. I never see her.

LAURA. It said in the Personal Section that you were—engaged!

JIM. I know, but I wasn't impressed by that —propaganda!

LAURA. It wasn't—the truth?

JIM. Only in Emily's optimistic opinion!

LAURA. Oh—

(LEGEND: "WHAT HAVE YOU DONE SINCE HIGH SCHOOL?")

370 (JIM *lights a cigarette and leans indolently back on his elbows smiling at* LAURA *with a warmth and charm which lights her inwardly with altar candles. She remains by the table and turns in her hands a piece of glass to cover her tumult.*)

JIM (*after several reflective puffs on a cigarette*). What have you done since high school? (*She seems not to hear him.*) Huh? (LAURA *looks up.*) I said what have you done since high school, Laura?

380 LAURA. Nothing much.

JIM. You must have been doing something these six long years.

LAURA. Yes.

JIM. Well, then, such as what?

LAURA. I took a business course at business college—

JIM. How did that work out?

LAURA. Well, not very—well—I had to drop out, it gave me—indigestion—

390 (JIM *laughs gently.*)

JIM. What are you doing now?

LAURA. I don't do anything—much. Oh, please don't think I sit around doing nothing! My glass collection takes up a good deal of time. Glass is something you have to take good care of.

JIM. What did you say—about glass?

LAURA. Collection I said—I have one—(*She clears her throat and turns away again, acutely* 400 *shy.*)

JIM (*abruptly*). You know what I judge to be the trouble with you? Inferiority complex! Know what that is? That's what they call it when someone low-rates himself! I understand it because I had it, too. Although my case was not so aggravated as yours seems to be. I had it until I took up public speaking, developed my voice, and learned that I had an aptitude for science. Before that time I never thought of myself as being outstanding in any way whatso- 410 ever! Now I've never made a regular study of it, but I have a friend who says I can analyze people better than doctors that make a profession of it. I don't claim that to be necessarily true, but I can sure guess a person's psychology, Laura! (*Takes out his gum.*) Excuse me, Laura. I always take it out when the flavor is gone. I'll use this scrap of paper to wrap it in. I know how it is to get it stuck on a shoe. Yep—that's what I judge to be your principal trouble. A 420 lack of confidence in yourself as a person. You don't have the proper amount of faith in yourself. I'm basing that fact on a number of your remarks and also on certain observations I've made. For instance that clumping you thought was so awful in high school. You say that you even dreaded to walk into class. You see what you did? You dropped out of school, you gave up an education because of a clump, which as far as I know was practically non-existent! A 430 little physical defect is what you have. Hardly noticeable even! Magnified thousands of times by imagination! You know what my strong advice to you is? Think of yourself as *superior* in some way!

LAURA. In what way would I think?

JIM. Why, man alive, Laura! Just look about you a little. What do you see? A world full of common people! All of 'em born and all of 'em going to die! Which of them has one-tenth of 440 your good points! Or mine! Or anyone else's, as far as that goes—Gosh! Everybody excels in some one thing. Some in many! (*Unconsciously glances at himself in the mirror.*) All you've got to do is discover in *what!* Take me, for instance. (*He adjusts his tie at the mirror.*) My interest happens to lie in electro-dynamics. I'm taking a course in radio engineering at night school, Laura, on top of a fairly responsible job at the warehouse. I'm taking that course and 450 studying public speaking.

LAURA. Ohhhh.

JIM. Because I believe in the future of television! (*Turning back to her.*) I wish to be ready to go up right along with it. Therefore I'm planning to get in on the ground floor. In fact I've already made the right connections and all that remains is for the industry itself to get under way! Full steam—(*His eyes are starry.*) 460 *Knowledge*—Zzzzzp! *Money*—Zzzzzzp!—*Power!* That's the cycle democracy is built on! (*His attitude is convincingly dynamic.* LAURA *stares at him, even her shyness eclipsed in her absolute wonder. He suddenly grins.*) I guess you think I think a lot of myself!

LAURA. No—o-o-o, I—

JIM. Now how about you? Isn't there something you take more interest in than anything else?

470 LAURA. Well, I do—as I said—have my—glass collection—

(*A peal of girlish laughter from the kitchen.*)

JIM. I'm not right sure I know what you're talking about. What kind of glass is it?

LAURA. Little articles of it, they're ornaments mostly! Most of them are little animals made out of glass, the tiniest little animals in the world. Mother calls them a glass menagerie! Here's an example of one, if you'd like to see it! This one 480 is one of the oldest. It's nearly thirteen. (MUSIC: "THE GLASS MENAGERIE.") (*He stretches out his hand.*) Oh, be careful—if you breathe, it breaks!

JIM. I'd better not take it. I'm pretty clumsy with things.

LAURA. Go on, I trust you with him! (*Places it in his palm.*) There now—you're holding him gently! Hold him over the light, he loves the light! You see how the light shines through him?

490 JIM. It sure does shine!

LAURA. I shouldn't be partial, but he is my favorite one.

JIM. What kind of a thing is this one supposed to be?

LAURA. Haven't you noticed the single horn on his forehead?

JIM. A unicorn, huh?

LAURA. Mmm-hmmm!

JIM. Unicorns, aren't they extinct in the 500 modern world?

LAURA. I know!

JIM. Poor little fellow, he must feel sort of lonesome.

LAURA (*smiling*). Well, if he does he doesn't complain about it. He stays on a shelf with some horses that don't have horns and all of them seem to get along nicely together.

JIM. How do you know?

LAURA (*lightly*). I haven't heard any arguments among them! 510

JIM (*grinning*). No arguments, huh? Well, that's a pretty good sign! Where shall I set him?

LAURA. Put him on the table. They all like a change of scenery once in a while!

JIM (*stretching*). Well, well, well, well—Look how big my shadow is when I stretch!

LAURA. Oh, oh, yes—it stretches across the ceiling!

JIM (*crossing to door*). I think it's stopped 520 raining. (*Opens fire-escape door.*) Where does the music come from?

LAURA. From the Paradise Dance Hall across the alley.

JIM. How about cutting the rug a little, Miss Wingfield?

LAURA. Oh, I—

JIM. Or is your program filled up? Let me have a look at it. (*Grasps imaginary card.*) Why, every dance is taken! I'll just have to 530 scratch some out. (WALTZ MUSIC: "LA GOLONDRINA") Ahhh, a waltz! (*He executes some sweeping turns by himself then holds his arms toward* LAURA.)

LAURA (*breathlessly*). I—can't dance!

JIM. There you go, that inferiority stuff!

LAURA. I've never danced in my life!

JIM. Come on, try!

LAURA. Oh, but I'd step on you!

JIM. I'm not made out of glass. 540

LAURA. How—how—how do we start?

JIM. Just leave it to me. You hold your arms out a little.

LAURA. Like this?

JIM. A little bit higher. Right. Now don't tighten up, that's the main thing about it—relax.

LAURA (*laughing breathlessly*). It's hard not to.

JIM. Okay. 550

LAURA. I'm afraid you can't budge me.

JIM. What do you bet I can't? (*He swings her into motion.*)

LAURA. Goodness, yes, you can!

JIM. Let yourself go, now, Laura, just let yourself go.

LAURA. I'm—

JIM. Come on!

LAURA. Trying!

560 JIM. Not so stiff—Easy does it!

LAURA. I know but I'm—

JIM. Loosen th' backbone! There now, that's a lot better.

LAURA. Am I?

JIM. Lots, lots better! (*He moves her about the room in a clumsy waltz.*)

LAURA. Oh, my!

JIM. Ha-ha!

LAURA. Oh, my goodness!

570 JIM. Ha-ha-ha! (*They suddenly bump into the table.* JIM *stops.*) What did we hit on?

LAURA. Table.

JIM. Did something fall off it? I think—

LAURA. Yes.

JIM. I hope that it wasn't the little glass horse with the horn!

LAURA. Yes.

JIM. Aw, aw, aw. Is it broken?

LAURA. Now it is just like all the other

580 horses.

JIM. It's lost its—

LAURA. Horn! It doesn't matter. Maybe it's a blessing in disguise.

JIM. You'll never forgive me. I bet that that was your favorite piece of glass.

LAURA. I don't have favorites much. It's no tragedy, Freckles. Glass breaks so easily. No matter how careful you are. The traffic jars the shelves and things fall off them.

590 JIM. Still I'm awfully sorry that I was the cause.

LAURA (*smiling*). I'll just imagine he had an operation. The horn was removed to make him feel less—freakish! (*They both laugh.*) Now he will feel more at home with the other horses, the ones that don't have horns . . .

JIM. Ha-ha, that's very funny! (*Suddenly serious.*) I'm glad to see that you have a sense of humor. You know—you're—well—very dif-

600 ferent! Surprisingly different from anyone else I know! (*His voice becomes soft and hesitant with a genuine feeling.*) Do you mind me telling you that? (LAURA *is abashed beyond speech.*) I mean it in a nice way . . . (LAURA *nods shyly, looking away.*) You make me feel sort of—I don't know how to put it! I'm usually pretty good at expressing things, but—This is something that I don't know how to say! (LAURA *touches her throat and clears it—turns the broken unicorn in her hands.*) (*Even softer.*) Has anyone ever 610 told you that you were pretty? (PAUSE: MUSIC.) (LAURA *looks up slowly, with wonder, and shakes her head.*) Well, you are! In a very different way from anyone else. And all the nicer because of the difference, too. (*His voice becomes low and husky.* LAURA *turns away, nearly faint with the novelty of her emotions.*) I wish that you were my sister. I'd teach you to have some confidence in yourself. The different people are not like other people, but being different 620 is nothing to be ashamed of. Because other people are not such wonderful people. They're one hundred times one thousand. You're one times one! They walk all over the earth. You just stay here. They're common as—weeds, but—you—well, you're—*Blue Roses!*

(IMAGE ON SCREEN: BLUE ROSES.)

(MUSIC CHANGES.)

LAURA. But blue is wrong for—roses . . .

JIM. It's right for you—You're—pretty! 630

LAURA. In what respect am I pretty?

JIM. In all respects—believe me! Your eyes—your hair—are pretty! Your hands are pretty! (*He catches hold of her hand.*) You think I'm making this up because I'm invited to dinner and have to be nice. Oh, I could do that! I could put on an act for you, Laura, and say lots of things without being very sincere. But this time I am. I'm talking to you sincerely. I happened to notice you had this inferiority com- 640 plex that keeps you from feeling comfortable with people. Somebody needs to build your confidence up and make you proud instead of shy and turning away and—blushing—Somebody ought to—Ought to—*kiss* you, Laura! (*His hand slips slowly up her arm to her shoulder.*) (MUSIC SWELLS TUMULTUOUSLY.) (*He suddenly turns her about and kisses her on the lips.*) (*When he releases her* LAURA *sinks on the sofa with a bright, dazed look.*) (JIM *backs* 650 *away and fishes in his pocket for a cigarette.*) (LEGEND ON SCREEN: "SOUVENIR.") Stumble-john! (*He lights the cigarette, avoiding her look.*) (*There is a peal of girlish laughter from* AMANDA *in the kitchen.*) (LAURA *slowly raises and opens her hand. It still contains the little broken glass animal. She looks at it with a tender, bewildered expression.*) Stumble-john! I shouldn't have done that—That was way off the beam. You don't smoke, do you? (*She looks up, smiling, not hearing the question.*) (*He sits beside her a little gingerly. She looks at him speechlessly—waiting.*) (*He coughs decorously and moves a little farther aside as he considers the situation and senses her feelings, dimly, with perturbation.*) (*Gently.*) Would you—care for a—mint? (*She doesn't seem to hear him but her look grows brighter even.*) Peppermint—Life Saver? My pocket's a regular drug store—wherever I go . . . (*He pops a mint in his mouth. Then gulps and decides to make a clean breast of it. He speaks slowly and gingerly.*) Laura, you know, if I had a sister like you, I'd do the same thing as Tom. I'd bring out fellows and—introduce her to them. The right type of boys of a type to—appreciate her. Only—well—he made a mistake about me. Maybe I've got no call to be saying this. That may not have been the idea in having me over. But what if it was? There's nothing wrong about that. The only trouble is that in my case —I'm not in a situation to—do the right thing. I can't take down your number and say I'll phone. I can't call up next week and—ask for a date. I thought I had better explain the situation in case you misunderstood it and—hurt your feelings. . . . (*Pause.*)

(*Slowly, very slowly,* LAURA'S *look changes, her eyes returning slowly from his to the ornament in her palm.*)

(AMANDA *utters another gay laugh in the kitchen.*)

LAURA (*faintly*). You—won't—call again?

JIM. No, Laura, I can't. (*He rises from the sofa.*) As I was just explaining, I've—got strings on me, Laura, I've—been going steady! I go out all the time with a girl named Betty. She's a home-girl like you, and Catholic, and Irish, and in a great many ways we—get along fine. I met her last summer on a moonlight boat trip up the river to Alton, on the *Majestic*. Well—right away from the start it was—love! (LEGEND: "LOVE!") (LAURA *sways slightly forward and the arm of the sofa. He fails to notice, now enrapt in his own comfortable being.*) Being in love has made a new man of me! (*Leaning stiffly forward, clutching the arm of the sofa,* LAURA *struggles visibly with her storm. But* JIM *is oblivious, she is a long way off.*) The power of love is really pretty tremendous! Love is something that—changes the whole world, Laura! (*The storm abates a little and* LAURA *leans back. He notices her again.*) It happened that Betty's aunt took sick, she got a wire and had to go to Centralia. So Tom—when he asked me to dinner—I naturally just accepted the invitation, not knowing that you—that he—that I—(*He stops awkwardly.*) Huh—I'm a stumble-john! (*He flops back on the sofa.*) (*The holy candles in the altar of* LAURA'S *face have been snuffed out. There is a look of almost infinite desolation.*) (JIM *glances at her uneasily.*) I wish that you would—say something. (*She bites her lip which was trembling and then bravely smiles. She opens her hand again on the broken glass ornament. Then she gently takes his hand and raises it level with her own. She carefully places the unicorn in the palm of his hand, then pushes his fingers closed upon it.*) What are you—doing that for? You want me to have him?—Laura? (*She nods.*) What for?

LAURA. A—souvenir . . .

(*She rises unsteadily and crouches beside the victrola to wind it up.*)

(LEGEND ON SCREEN: "THINGS HAVE A WAY OF TURNING OUT SO BADLY!")

(OR IMAGE: "GENTLEMAN CALLER WAVING GOOD-BYE!—GAILY.")

(*At this moment* AMANDA *rushes brightly back in the front room. She bears a pitcher of fruit punch in an old-fashioned cut-glass pitcher and a plate of macaroons. The plate has a gold border and poppies painted on it.*)

AMANDA. Well, well, well! Isn't the air delightful after the shower? I've made you children a little liquid refreshment. (*Turns gaily to the gentleman caller.*) Jim, do you know that song about lemonade?
"Lemonade, lemonade
Made in the shade and stirred with a spade—
Good enough for any old maid!"

JIM (*uneasily*). Ha-ha! No—I never heard it.

AMANDA. Why, Laura! You look so serious!

JIM. We were having a serious conversation.

AMANDA. Good! Now you're better acquainted!

JIM (*uncertainly*). Ha-ha! Yes.

760 AMANDA. You modern young people are much more serious-minded than my generation. I was so gay as a girl!

JIM. You haven't changed, Mrs. Wingfield.

AMANDA. Tonight I'm rejuvenated! The gaiety of the occasion, Mr. O'Connor! (*She tosses her head with a peal of laughter. Spills lemonade.*) Oooo! I'm baptizing myself!

JIM. Here—let me—

AMANDA (*setting the pitcher down*). There 770 now. I discovered we had some maraschino cherries. I dumped them in, juice and all!

JIM. You shouldn't have gone to that trouble, Mrs. Wingfield.

AMANDA. Trouble, trouble? Why it was loads of fun! Didn't you hear me cutting up in the kitchen? I bet your ears were burning! I told Tom how outdone with him I was for keeping you to himself so long a time! He should have brought you over much, much sooner! Well, 780 now that you've found your way, I want you to be a very frequent caller! Not just occasional but all the time. Oh, we're going to have a lot of gay times together! I see them coming! Mmm, just breathe that air! So fresh, and the moon's so pretty! I'll skip back out—I know where my place is when young folks are having a—serious conversation!

JIM. Oh, don't go out, Mrs. Wingfield. The fact of the matter is I've got to be going.

790 AMANDA. Going, now? You're joking! Why, it's only the shank of the evening, Mr. O'Connor!

JIM. Well, you know how it is.

AMANDA. You mean you're a young workingman and have to keep workingmen's hours. We'll let you off early tonight. But only on the condition that next time you stay later. What's the best night for you? Isn't Saturday night the best night for you workingmen?

800 JIM. I have a couple of time-clocks to punch, Mrs. Wingfield. One at morning, another one at night!

AMANDA. My, but you *are* ambitious! You work at night, too?

JIM. No, Ma'am, not work but—Betty! (*He crosses deliberately to pick up his hat. The band at the Paradise Dance Hall goes into a tender waltz.*)

AMANDA. Betty? Betty? Who's—Betty!

(*There is an ominous cracking sound in the sky.*) 810

JIM. Oh, just a girl. The girl I go steady with! (*He smiles charmingly. The sky falls.*)

(LEGEND: "THE SKY FALLS.")

AMANDA (*a long-drawn exhalation*). Ohhhh . . . Is it a serious romance, Mr. O'Connor?

JIM. We're going to be married the second Sunday in June.

AMANDA. Ohhhh—how nice! Tom didn't mention that you were engaged to be married. 820

JIM. The cat's not out of the bag at the warehouse yet. You know how they are. They call you Romeo and stuff like that. (*He stops at the oval mirror to put on his hat. He carefully shapes the brim and the crown to give a discreetly dashing effect.*) It's been a wonderful evening, Mrs. Wingfield. I guess this is what they mean by Southern hospitality.

AMANDA. It really wasn't anything at all.

JIM. I hope it don't seem like I'm rushing 830 off. But I promised Betty I'd pick her up at the Wabash depot, an' by the time I get my jalopy down there her train'll be in. Some women are pretty upset if you keep 'em waiting.

AMANDA. Yes, I know—The tyranny of women! (*Extends her hand.*) Good-bye, Mr. O'Connor. I wish you luck—and happiness—and success! All three of them, and so does Laura!—Don't you, Laura?

LAURA. Yes! 840

JIM (*taking her hand*). Good-bye, Laura. I'm certainly going to treasure that souvenir. And don't you forget the good advice I gave you. (*Raises his voice to a cheery shout.*) So long, Shakespeare! Thanks again, ladies—Good night!

(*He grins and ducks jauntily out.*)

(*Still bravely grimacing,* AMANDA *closes the door on the gentleman caller. Then she turns back to the room with a puzzled expression. She and* 850

LAURA *don't dare to face each other.* LAURA *crouches beside the victrola to wind it.*)

AMANDA (*faintly*). Things have a way of turning out so badly. I don't believe that I would play the victrola. Well, well—well—Our gentleman caller was engaged to be married! Tom!

TOM (*from back*). Yes, Mother?

AMANDA. Come in here a minute. I want to tell you something awfully funny. 860

TOM (*enters with macaroon and a glass of the lemonade*). Has the gentleman caller gotten away already?

AMANDA. The gentleman caller has made an early departure. What a wonderful joke you played on us!

TOM. How do you mean?

AMANDA. You didn't mention that he was engaged to be married.

TOM. Jim? Engaged? 870

AMANDA. That's what he just informed us.

TOM. I'll be jiggered! I didn't know about that.

AMANDA. That seems very peculiar.

TOM. What's peculiar about it?

AMANDA. Didn't you call him your best friend down at the warehouse?

TOM. He is, but how did I know?

AMANDA. It seems extremely peculiar that you wouldn't know your best friend was going to be married! 880

TOM. The warehouse is where I work, not where I know things about people!

AMANDA. You don't know things anywhere! You live in a dream; you manufacture illusions! (*He crosses to door.*) Where are you going?

TOM. I'm going to the movies.

AMANDA. That's right, now that you've had us make such fools of ourselves. The effort, the preparations, all the expense! The new floor lamp, the rug, the clothes for Laura! All for what? To entertain some other girl's fiancé! Go to the movies, go! Don't think about us, a mother deserted, an unmarried sister who's crippled and has no job! Don't let anything interfere with your selfish pleasure! Just go, go, go —to the movies! 890

TOM. All right, I will! The more you shout about my selfishness to me the quicker I'll go, and I won't go to the movies! 900

AMANDA. Go, then! Then go to the moon—you selfish dreamer!

(TOM *smashes his glass on the floor. He plunges out on the fire-escape, slamming the door.* LAURA *screams—cut by door.*)

(*Dance-hall music up.* TOM *goes to the rail and grips it desperately, lifting his face in the chill white moonlight penetrating the narrow abyss of the alley.*)

(LEGEND ON SCREEN: "AND SO GOOD-BYE . . .") 910

(TOM'S *closing speech is timed with the interior pantomime. The interior scene is played as though viewed through soundproof glass.* AMANDA *appears to be making a comforting speech to* LAURA *who is huddled upon the sofa. Now that we cannot hear the mother's speech, her silliness is gone and she has dignity and tragic beauty.* LAURA'S *dark hair hides her face until at the end of the speech she lifts it to smile at her mother.* AMANDA'S *gestures are slow and graceful, almost dancelike, as she comforts the daughter. At the end of her speech she glances a moment at the father's picture—then withdraws through the portieres. At close of* TOM'S *speech,* LAURA *blows out the candles, ending the play.*) 920

TOM. I didn't go to the moon. I went much further—for time is the longest distance between two places—Not long after that I was fired for writing a poem on the lid of a shoe-box. I left Saint Louis. I descended the steps of this fire-escape for a last time and followed, from then on, in my father's footsteps, attempting to find in motion what was lost in space—I traveled around a great deal. The cities swept about me like dead leaves, leaves that were brightly colored but torn away from the branches. I would have stopped, but I was pursued by something. It always came upon me unawares, taking me altogether by surprise. Perhaps it was a familiar bit of music. Perhaps it was only a piece of transparent glass—Perhaps I am walking along a street at night, in some strange city, before I have found companions. I pass the lighted window of a shop where perfume is sold. The window is filled with pieces of colored glass, tiny transparent bottles in delicate colors, like bits of a shattered rainbow. Then all at 930 940 once my sister touches my shoulder. I turn around and look into her eyes . . . Oh, Laura, Laura, I tried to leave you behind me, but I am more faithful than I intended to be! I reach for a cigarette, I cross the street, I run into the movies or a bar, I buy a drink, I speak to the nearest stranger—anything that can blow your candles out! (LAURA *bends over the candles.*)—for nowadays the world is lit by lightning! Blow out your candles, Laura—and so good-bye. . . .

(*She blows the candles out.*)

THE SCENE DISSOLVES

Review Questions

1. What sort of characters are in *The Glass Menagerie?*
2. Comment on the effectiveness of Laura's glass menagerie as a symbol.
3. How does the setting contribute to the total effect of the play?
4. Why does the playwright have his characters pantomime the eating of food without the actual stage properties?
5. Describe Amanda. By what means is her character revealed?
6. In what way does Tom resemble his father?
7. What is the social background of the play? How is this made known to the audience? Cite specific evidence.
8. What is the structural arrangement of the play? Do the episodes seem appropriate for the playwright's purpose?
9. To what extent does Williams make use of music?
10. What is the tone of the play?
11. Comment on Laura as a dramatic character. What motivates her? What forces have shaped her? How does she elicit our sympathy?
12. How is the Gentleman Caller's entrance prepared for?
13. Describe the preparations for the coming of the Gentleman Caller. What sort of person is he?
14. Comment on Tom's line: "People go to the movies instead of moving."
15. Evaluate the use of Tom as the Narrator.
16. What is the range of emotions in the play?
17. How would you describe the dialogue? What recurring imagery do you find?
18. Describe the scene between Laura and the Gentleman Caller.
19. What is the effect of the ending? What will happen to Amanda and Laura?
20. What is Williams' purpose in this play?
21. What are the problems of production?
22. Who is to blame for the problems of the Wingfield family?
23. How are the various moods created?
24. The motion picture version of this play showed Laura greeting another gentleman caller. Does this seem justified?
25. Comment on the use of humor.

THE LEADER

Eugene Ionesco (1912-   )

**TRANSLATED BY
DEREK PROUSE**

Rumanian born Ionesco first attracted critical attention with his play *The Chairs* in 1952 and soon came to be recognized as one of the most important of the "absurdist" playwrights. The "theater of the absurd" projects a nihilistic philosophy in which the traditional views of man and his universe are rejected. The "anti-theater" approach of the absurdists caused them to ignore the conventions of dramatic structure and the usual processes of communication. Ionesco usually begins his plays by establishing a familiar situation into which he introduces unfamiliar elements leading to disintegration. He has been widely produced in the *avant-garde* theater. His best known works are *The Rhinoceros, The Killer, The Bald Soprano, The Lesson, Amedée* and *The New Tenant.*

Ionesco's point of view is indicated in his remarks about *The Chairs:*

> I have tried to deal with themes that obsess me; with emptiness, with frustration, with this world, at once fleeting and crushing, with despair and death. The characters I have used are not fully conscious of their spiritual rootlessness, but they feel it instinctively and emotionally.

Ionesco's approach to the theater is further evident from the following excerpt of his "Experience of the Theatre."

> So if the essence of the theatre lay in magnifying its effects, they had to be magnified still further, underlined and stressed to the maximum. To push drama out of that intermediate zone where it is neither theatre nor literature is to restore it to its own domain, to its natural frontiers. It was not for me to conceal the devices of the theatre, but rather make them still more evident, deliberately obvious, go all-out for caricature and the grotesque, way beyond the pale of witty drawing-room comedies. No drawing-room comedies, but farce, the extreme exaggeration of parody. Humor, yes, but using methods of burlesque. Comic

effects that are firm, broad and outrageous. No dramatic comedies either. But back to the unendurable. Everything raised to paroxysm, where the source of tragedy lies. A theatre of violence; violently comic, violently dramatic.

Avoid psychology or rather give it a metaphysical dimension. Drama lies in extreme exaggeration of the feelings, exaggeration that dislocates flat everyday reality. Dislocation, disarticulation of language too.

Moreover, if the actors embarrassed me by not seeming natural enough, perhaps it was because they also were, or tried to be, *too* natural; by trying to be, perhaps they will appear natural, but in a different way. They must not be afraid of not being natural.

BELOW. The announcer, played by James Horwood, from the American premiere of Ionesco's play at the 1965 Buffalo Festival of The Arts Today, staged at the State University College of Buffalo.

Sherwin Greenberg, McGranahan & Man, Inc.

RIGHT. The leader arrives.

Characters

The Announcer
The Young Lover
The Girl-Friend
The Admirer
The Girl Admirer
The Leader

THE LEADER

(Standing with his back to the public, centre-stage, and with his eyes fixed on the up-stage exit, the ANNOUNCER *waits for the arrival of the* LEADER. *To right and left, riveted to the walls, two of the* LEADER'S ADMIRERS, *a man and a girl, also wait for his arrival.)*

ANNOUNCER *(after a few tense moments in the same position).* There he is! There he is! At the end of the street! *(Shouts of 'Hurrah!' etc., are heard.)* There's the leader! He's coming, he's coming nearer! *(Cries of acclaim and applause are heard from the wings.)* It's better if he doesn't see us . . . *(The* TWO ADMIRERS *hug the wall even closer.)* Watch out! *(The* ANNOUNCER *gives vent to a brief display of enthusiasm.)* Hurrah! Hurrah! The leader! The leader! Long live the leader! *(The* TWO ADMIRERS, *with their bodies rigid and flattened against the wall, thrust their necks and heads as far forward as they can to get a glimpse of the* LEADER.) The leader! The leader! *(The* TWO ADMIRERS *in unison:)* Hurrah! Hurrah! *(Other 'Hurrahs!' mingled with 'Hurrah! Bravo!' come from the wings and gradually die down.)* Hurrah! Bravo!

(The ANNOUNCER *takes a step up-stage, stops, then up-stage, followed by the* TWO ADMIRERS, *saying as he goes: 'Ah! Too bad! He's going away! He's going away! Follow me quickly! After him!' The* ANNOUNCER *and the* TWO ADMIRERS *leave, crying: 'Leader! Leeeeader! Lee-ee-eader!' [This last 'Lee-ee-eader!' echoes in the wings like a bleating cry.])*

(Silence. The stage is empty for a few brief moments. The YOUNG LOVER *enters right, and his* GIRL-FRIEND *left; they meet centre-stage.)*

YOUNG LOVER. Forgive me, Madame, or should I say Mademoiselle?

GIRL-FRIEND. I beg your pardon, I'm afraid I don't happen to know you!

YOUNG LOVER. And I'm afraid I don't know you either!

GIRL-FRIEND. Then neither of us knows each other.

YOUNG LOVER. Exactly. We have something in common. It means that between us there is a basis of understanding on which we can build the edifice of our future.

GIRL-FRIEND. That leaves me cold, I'm afraid.

(She makes as if to go.)

YOUNG LOVER. Oh, my darling, I adore you.

GIRL-FRIEND. Darling, so do I!

(They embrace.)

YOUNG LOVER. I'm taking you with me, darling. We'll get married straightaway.

(They leave left. The stage is empty for a brief moment.)

ANNOUNCER *(enters up-stage followed by the* TWO ADMIRERS). But the leader swore that he'd be passing here.

ADMIRER. Are you absolutely sure of that?

ANNOUNCER. Yes, yes, of course.

GIRL ADMIRER. Was it really on his way?

ANNOUNCER. Yes, yes. He should have passed by here, it was marked on the Festival programme . . .

ADMIRER. Did you actually see it yourself and hear it with your own eyes and ears?

ANNOUNCER. He told someone. Someone else!

ADMIRER. But who? Who was this someone else?

GIRL ADMIRER. Was it a reliable person? A friend of yours?

ANNOUNCER. A friend of mine who I know very well. (*Suddenly in the background one hears renewed cries of 'Hurrah!' and 'Long live* 70 *the leader!'*) That's him now! There he is! Hip! Hip! Hurrah! There he is! Hide yourselves! Hide yourselves!

(*The* TWO ADMIRERS *flatten themselves as before against the wall, stretching their necks out towards the wings from where the shouts of acclamation come; the* ANNOUNCER *watches fixedly upstage his back to the public.*)

ANNOUNCER. The leader's coming. He approaches. He's bending. He's unbending. (*At* 80 *each of the* ANNOUNCER'S *words, the* ADMIRERS *give a start and stretch their necks even farther; they shudder.*) He's jumping. He's crossed the river. They're shaking his hand. He sticks out his thumb. Can you hear? They're laughing. (*The* ANNOUNCER *and the* TWO ADMIRERS *also laugh.*) Ah . . . ! they're giving him a box of tools. What's he going to do with them? Ah . . . ! he's signing autographs. The leader is stroking a hedgehog, a superb hedgehog! The 90 crowd applauds. He's dancing, with the hedgehog in his hand. He's embracing his dancer. Hurrah! Hurrah! (*Cries are heard in the wings.*) He's being photographed, with his dancer on one hand and the hedgehog on the other . . . He greets the crowd . . . He spits a tremendous distance.

GIRL ADMIRER. Is he coming past here? Is he coming in our direction?

ADMIRER. Are we really on his route?

100 ANNOUNCER (*turns his head to the* TWO ADMIRERS). Quite, and don't move, you're spoiling everything . . .

GIRL ADMIRER. But even so . . .

ANNOUNCER. Keep quiet, I tell you! Didn't I tell you he'd promised, that he had fixed his itinerary himself. . . . (*He turns back up-stage and cries.*) Hurrah! Hurrah! Long live the leader! (*Silence*) Long live, long live, the leader! (*Silence*) Long live, long live, long live the 110 lead-er! (*The* TWO ADMIRERS, *unable to contain themselves, also give a sudden cry of:*) Hurrah! Long live the leader!

ANNOUNCER (*to the* ADMIRERS). Quiet, you two! Calm down! You're spoiling everything! (*Then, once more looking up-stage, with the* ADMIRERS *silenced.*) Long live the leader! (*Wildly enthusiastic.*) Hurrah! Hurrah! He's changing his shirt. He disappears behind a red screen. He reappears! (*The applause intensifies.*) Bravo! Bravo! (*The* ADMIRERS *also long to cry* 120 *'Bravo' and applaud; they put their hands to their mouths to stop themselves.*) He's putting his tie on! He's reading his newspaper and drinking his morning coffee! He's still got his hedgehog . . . He's leaning on the edge of the parapet. The parapet breaks. He gets up . . . he gets up unaided! (*Applause, shouts of 'Hurrah!'*) Bravo! Well done! He brushes his soiled clothes.

TWO ADMIRERS (*stamping their feet*). Oh! 130 Ah! Oh! Oh! Ah! Ah!

ANNOUNCER. He's mounting the stool! He's climbing piggyback, they're offering him a thin-ended wedge, he knows it's meant as a joke, and he doesn't mind, he's laughing.

(*Applause and enormous acclaim.*)

ADMIRER (*to the* GIRL ADMIRER). You hear that? You hear? Oh! If I were king . . .

GIRL ADMIRER. Ah . . . ! the leader!

(*This is said in an exalted tone.*) 140

ANNOUNCER (*still with his back to the public*). He's mounting the stool. No. He's getting down. A little girl offers him a bouquet of flowers . . . What's he going to do? He takes the flowers . . . He embraces the little girl . . . calls her 'my child' . . .

ADMIRER. He embraces the little girl . . . calls her 'my child' . . .

GIRL ADMIRER. He embraces the little girl . . . calls her 'my child' . . . 150

ANNOUNCER. He gives her the hedgehog. The little girl's crying . . . Long live the leader! Long live the leead-er!

ADMIRER. Is he coming past here?

GIRL ADMIRER. Is he coming past here?

ANNOUNCER (*with a sudden run, dashes out up-stage*). He's going away! Hurry! Come on!

(*He disappears, followed by the* TWO ADMIRERS, *all crying 'Hurrah! Hurrah!'*)

160 (*The stage is empty for a few moments. The* TWO LOVERS *enter, entwined in an embrace; they halt centre-stage and separate; she carries a basket on her arm.*)

GIRL-FRIEND. Let's go to the market and get some eggs!

YOUNG LOVER. Oh! I love them as much as you do!

(*She takes his arm. From the right the* ANNOUNCER *arrives running, quickly regaining his* 170 *place, back to the public, followed closely by the* TWO ADMIRERS, *arriving one from the left and the other from the right; the* TWO ADMIRERS *knock into the* TWO LOVERS *who were about to leave right.*)

ADMIRER. Sorry!

YOUNG LOVER. Oh! Sorry!

GIRL ADMIRER. Sorry! Oh! Sorry!

GIRL-FRIEND. Oh! Sorry, sorry, sorry, so sorry!

ADMIRER. Sorry, sorry, sorry, oh! sorry, sorry, 180 so sorry!

YOUNG LOVER. Oh, oh, oh, oh, oh, oh! So sorry, everyone!

GIRL-FRIEND (*to her* LOVER). Come along, Adolphe! (*To the* TWO ADMIRERS:) No harm done!

(*She leaves, leading her* LOVER *by the hand.*)

ANNOUNCER (*watching up-stage*). The leader is being pressed forward, and pressed back, and now they're pressing his trousers! (*The* TWO ADMIRERS *regain their places.*) The leader is 190 smiling. Whilst they're pressing his trousers, he walks about. He tastes the flowers and the fruits growing in the stream. He's also tasting the roots of the trees. He suffers the little children to come unto him. He has confidence in everybody. He inaugurates the police force. He pays tribute to justice. He salutes the great victors and the great vanquished. Finally he recites a poem. The people are very moved.

200 TWO ADMIRERS. Bravo! Bravo! (*Then, sobbing:*) Boo! Boo! Boo!

ANNOUNCER. All the people are weeping. (*Loud cries are heard from the wings; the* ANNOUNCER *and the* ADMIRERS *also start to bellow.*) Silence! (*The* TWO ADMIRERS *fall silent; and there is silence from the wings.*) They've given the leader's trousers back. The leader puts them on. He looks happy! Hurrah! (*'Bravos', and acclaim from the wings. The* TWO ADMIRERS *also shout their acclaim, jump about, without being* 210 *able to see anything of what is presumed to be happening in the wings.*) The leader's sucking his thumb! (*To the* TWO ADMIRERS:) Back, back to your places, you two, don't move, behave yourselves and shout: 'Long live the leader!'

TWO ADMIRERS (*flattened against the wall, shouting*). Long live, long live the leader!

ANNOUNCER. Be quiet, I tell you, you'll spoil everything! Look out, the leader's coming!

ADMIRER (*in the same position*). The leader's 220 coming!

GIRL ADMIRER. The leader's coming!

ANNOUNCER. Watch out! And keep quiet! Oh! The leader's going away! Follow him! Follow me!

(*The* ANNOUNCER *goes out up-stage, running; the* TWO ADMIRERS *leave right and left, whilst in the wings the acclaim mounts, then fades. The stage is momentarily empty. The* YOUNG LOVER, *followed by his* GIRL-FRIEND, *appear left running* 230 *across the stage right.*)

YOUNG LOVER (*running*). You won't catch me! You won't catch me!

(*Goes out.*)

GIRL-FRIEND (*running*). Wait a moment! Wait a moment!

(*She goes out. The stage is empty for a moment; then once more the* TWO LOVERS *cross the stage at a run, and leave.*)

YOUNG LOVER. You won't catch me! 240

GIRL-FRIEND. Wait a moment!

(*They leave right. The stage is empty. The* ANNOUNCER *reappears up-stage, the* ADMIRER *from the right, the* GIRL ADMIRER *from the left. They meet centre.*)

ADMIRER. We missed him!

GIRL ADMIRER. Rotten luck!

ANNOUNCER. It was your fault!

ADMIRER. That's not true!

GIRL ADMIRER. No, that's not true! 250

ANNOUNCER. Are you suggesting it was mine?

ADMIRER. No, we didn't mean that!
GIRL ADMIRER. No, we didn't mean that!

(Noise of acclaim and 'Hurrahs' from the wings.)

ANNOUNCER. Hurrah!

GIRL ADMIRER. It's from over there! *(She points up-stage.)*

260 ADMIRER. Yes, it's from over there! *(He points left.)*

ANNOUNCER. Very well. Follow me! Long live the leader!

(He runs out right, followed by the TWO ADMIRERS, *also shouting.)*

TWO ADMIRERS. Long live the leader!

(They leave. The stage is empty for a moment. The YOUNG LOVER *and his* GIRL-FRIEND *appear left; the* YOUNG LOVER *exits up-stage; the* GIRL-270 FRIEND, *after saying 'I'll get you!', runs out right. The* ANNOUNCER *and the* TWO ADMIRERS *appear from up-stage. The* ANNOUNCER *says to the* ADMIRERS:) Long live the leader! *(This is repeated by the* ADMIRERS. *Then, still talking to the* ADMIRERS, *he says:)* Follow me! Follow the leader! *(He leaves up-stage, still running and shouting:)* Follow him!

(The ADMIRER *exits right, the* GIRL ADMIRER *left into the wings. During the whole of this, the ac-280 claim is heard louder or fainter according to the rhythm of the stage action; the stage is empty for a moment, then the* LOVERS *appear from right and left, crying:)*

YOUNG LOVER. I'll get you!
GIRL-FRIEND. You won't get me!

(They leave at a run, shouting:) Long live the leader! *(The* ANNOUNCER *and the* TWO ADMIRERS *emerge from up-stage, also shouting: 'Long live the leader', followed by the* TWO LOVERS. *They 290 all leave right, in single file, crying as they run: 'The leader! Long live the leader! We'll get him! It's from over here! You won't get me!') (They enter and leave, employing all the exits; finally, entering from left, from right, and from up-stage they all meet centre, whilst the acclaim and the applause from the wings becomes a fearful din. They embrace each other feverishly, crying at the tops of their voices:)* Long live the leader! Long live the leader! Long live the leader! 300

(Then, abruptly, silence falls.)

ANNOUNCER. The leader is arriving. Here's the leader. To your places! Attention!

(The ADMIRER *and the* GIRL-FRIEND *flatten themselves against the wall right; the* GIRL ADMIRER *and the* YOUNG LOVER *against the wall left; the two couples are in each other's arms, embracing.)*

ADMIRER and
GIRL-FRIEND. My dear, my darling!
GIRL ADMIRER and 310
YOUNG LOVER. My dear, my darling!

(Meanwhile the ANNOUNCER *has taken up his place, back to the audience, looking fixedly up-stage; a lull in the applause.)*

ANNOUNCER. Silence. The leader has eaten his soup. He is coming. He is nigh.

(The acclaim redoubles its intensity; the TWO ADMIRERS *and the* TWO LOVERS *shout:)*

ALL. Hurrah! Hurrah! Long live the leader!

(They throw confetti before he arrives. Then 320 the ANNOUNCER *hurls himself suddenly to one side to allow the* LEADER *to pass; the other four characters freeze with outstretched arms holding confetti; but still say:)* Hurrah! *(The* LEADER *enters from up-stage, advances down-stage to centre; to the footlights, hesitates, makes a step to left, then takes a decision and leaves with great, energetic strides by right, to the enthusiastic 'Hurrahs!' of the* ANNOUNCER *and the feeble, somewhat astonished 'Hurrahs!' of the 330 other four; these, in fact, have some reason to be surprised, as the* LEADER *is headless, though wearing a hat. This is simple to effect: the actor playing the* LEADER *needing only to wear an overcoat with the collar turned up round his forehead and topped with a hat. The-man-in-an-overcoat-with-a-hat-without-a-head is a somewhat surprising apparition and will doubtless produce a certain sensation. After the* LEADER'S *disappearance, the* GIRL ADMIRER *says:)* 340

GIRL ADMIRER. But . . . but . . . the leader hasn't got a head!

ANNOUNCER. What's he need a head for when he's got genius!

YOUNG LOVER. That's true! (*To the* GIRL-FRIEND:) What's your name?

(*The* YOUNG LOVER *to the* GIRL ADMIRER, *the* GIRL ADMIRER *to the* ANNOUNCER, *the* ANNOUNCER *to the* GIRL-FRIEND, *the* GIRL-FRIEND *to the* YOUNG LOVER:) What's yours? What's yours? What's yours? (*Then, all together, one to the other:*) What's your name? 350

CURTAIN

Review Questions

1. Describe the preparations for the Leader's coming.
2. What are the comic aspects of the play?
3. Describe the use of language citing specific evidence.
4. What is satirical about the Leader's action?
5. What is "absurd"?
6. Cite the Biblical references used by Ionesco.
7. What is the meaning of the play?
8. What is Ionesco's point of view toward life?
9. Could the idea of the play be reduced to a pantomime as Beckett's *Act Without Words, I?*
10. What are the requirements of production?
11. What is the effect of the Leader's entrance?
12. What part do the lovers play?
13. Does the play have universality?
14. Comment on the use of repetition as a comic device.
15. Read Ionesco's statements in the introductory note and relate them to *The Leader*.

ACT WITHOUT WORDS, I

MIME FOR ONE PLAYER

Samuel Beckett (1906-)

TRANSLATED FROM THE FRENCH
BY THE AUTHOR

Like George Bernard Shaw, Beckett was born in Ireland of Protestant middle-class stock. He was an exceptional student in boarding school and at Trinity College, Dublin, where he received his B.A. in 1927. The following year he took a position as a lecturer at Ecole Normale in Paris. He met James Joyce and began his career as a writer, at first with essays and poetry. After returning to Dublin, his wanderlust caught up with him until he made a permanent home in Paris in 1937. His reputation as a playwright began with his *Waiting for Godot,* which was given its *première* in Paris in 1953. It had a wide appeal and played more than four hundred performances to establish Beckett as one of the foremost playwrights in the world. His best known plays are *Endgame, Krapp's Last Tape* and *Happy Days.*

Act Without Words was first produced at the Royal Court Theater in London on April 3, 1957, as a companion piece to *Endgame.*

Ilse Buhs

Ilse Buhs

LEFT, TOP RIGHT & OUTSIDE RIGHT. Deryk Mendel in the 1962 performance at the Academy of Art in Berlin.

Ilse Buhs

INSIDE BELOW. Erwin Bredow in the 1957 Schlosspark-Theatre, Berlin, production.

Ilse Buhs

ACT WITHOUT WORDS, I

Desert. Dazzling light.

The man is flung backwards on stage from right wing. He falls, gets up immediately, dusts himself, turns aside, reflects.

Whistle from right wing.

He reflects, goes out right.

Immediately flung back on stage he falls, gets up immediately, dusts himself, turns aside, reflects.

10 Whistle from left wing.

He reflects, goes out left.

Immediately flung back on stage he falls, gets up immediately, dusts himself, turns aside, reflects.

Whistle from left wing.

He reflects, goes towards left wing, hesitates, thinks better of it, halts, turns aside, reflects.

A little tree descends from flies, lands. It has a single bough some three yards from ground and
20 at its summit a meager tuft of palms casting at its foot a circle of shadow.

He continues to reflect.

Whistle from above.

He turns, sees tree, reflects, goes to it, sits down in its shadow, looks at his hands.

A pair of tailor's scissors descends from flies, comes to rest before tree, a yard from ground.

He continues to look at his hands.

Whistle from above.

He looks up, sees scissors, takes them and starts 30
to trim his nails.

The palms close like a parasol, the shadow disappears.

He drops scissors, reflects.

A tiny carafe, to which is attached a huge label inscribed WATER, descends from flies, comes to rest some three yards from ground.

He continues to reflect.

Whistle from above.

He looks up, sees carafe, reflects, gets up, goes 40
and stands under it, tries in vain to reach it, renounces, turns aside, reflects.

A big cube descends from flies, lands.

He continues to reflect.

Whistle from above.

He turns, sees cube, looks at it, at carafe, reflects, goes to cube, takes it up, carries it over and sets it down under carafe, tests its stability, gets up on it, tries in vain to reach carafe, re-

50 nounces, gets down, carries cube back to its place, turns aside, reflects.

A second smaller cube descends from flies, lands.

He continues to reflect.

Whistle from above.

He turns, sees second cube, looks at it, at carafe, goes to second cube, takes it up, carries it over and sets it down under carafe, tests its stability, gets up on it, tries in vain to reach carafe, renounces, gets down, takes up second
60 cube to carry it back to its place, hesitates, thinks better of it, sets it down, goes to big cube, takes it up, carries it over and puts it on small one, tests their stability, gets up on them, the cubes collapse, he falls, gets up immediately, brushes himself, reflects.

He takes up small cube, puts it on big one, tests their stability, gets up on them and is about to reach carafe when it is pulled up a little way and comes to rest beyond his reach.

70 He gets down, reflects, carries cubes back to their place, one by one, turns aside, reflects.

A third still smaller cube descends from flies, lands.

He continues to reflect.

Whistle from above.

He turns, sees third cube, looks at it, reflects, turns aside, reflects.

The third cube is pulled up and disappears in flies.

80 Beside carafe a rope descends from flies, with knots to facilitate ascent.

He continues to reflect.

Whistle from above.

He turns, sees rope, reflects, goes to it, climbs up it and is about to reach carafe when rope is let out and deposits him back on ground.

He reflects, looks around for scissors, sees them, goes and picks them up, returns to rope and starts to cut it with scissors.

The rope is pulled up, lifts him off ground, 90 he hangs on, succeeds in cutting rope, falls back on ground, drops scissors, falls, gets up again immediately, brushes himself, reflects.

The rope is pulled up quickly and disappears in flies.

With length of rope in his possession he makes a lasso with which he tries to lasso carafe.

The carafe is pulled up quickly and disappears in flies.

He turns aside, reflects. 100

He goes with lasso in his hand to tree, looks at bough, turns and looks at cubes, looks again at bough, drops lasso, goes to cubes, takes up small one, carries it over and sets it down under bough, goes back for big one, takes it up and carries it over under bough, makes to put it on small one, hesitates, thinks better of it, sets it down, takes up small one and puts it on big one, tests their stability, turns aside and stoops to pick up lasso. 110

The bough folds down against trunk.

He straightens up with lasso in his hand, turns and sees what has happened.

He drops lasso, turns aside, reflects.

He carries back cubes to their place, one by one, goes back for lasso, carries it over to cubes and lays it in a neat coil on small one.

He turns aside, reflects.

Whistle from right wing.

He reflects, goes out right. 120

Immediately flung back on stage he falls, gets up immediately, brushes himself, turns aside, reflects.

Whistle from left wing.

He does not move.

He looks at his hands, looks around for scissors, sees them, goes and picks them up, starts to trim his nails, stops, reflects, runs his finger along blade of scissors, goes and lays them on small cube, turns aside, opens his collar, frees his neck and fingers it.

130

The small cube is pulled up and disappears in flies, carrying away rope and scissors.

He turns to take scissors, sees what has happened.

He turns aside, reflects.

He goes and sits down on big cube.

The big cube is pulled from under him. He falls. The big cube is pulled up and disappears in flies.

140

He remains lying on his side, his face towards auditorium, staring before him.

The carafe descends from flies and comes to rest a few feet from his body.

He does not move.

Whistle from above.

He does not move.

The carafe descends further, dangles and plays about his face.

He does not move.

150

The carafe is pulled up and disappears in flies.

The bough returns to horizontal, the palms open, the shadow returns.

Whistle from above.

He does not move.

The tree is pulled up and disappears in flies.

He looks at his hands.

CURTAIN

Review Questions

1. What is the point of the play?
2. What effect does the play have on the reader? Would it be a different effect for the spectator in the theater?
4. Describe the central pattern of action.
3. Is there any significance to the objects being raised and lowered from above?
5. What are the demands placed upon the actor by the writer?
6. Comment on the playwright's ingenuity in devising the action.
7. What is the effect of repetition?
8. Is there any comedy in the action?
9. Is there a beginning, a middle and an end?
10. Does the man learn from his experience or does he quit in frustration?
11. In the light of the objects that are used to tantalize the man, do you feel the play has any meaning about a person's objectives?
12. Is the play negative?
13. What are its dramatic values?
14. Compare it with *The Leader.*

BIBLIOGRAPHY

Anderson, Maxwell, *The Essence of Tragedy,* Washington, 1939.

Bentley, Eric, *In Search of Theater,* New York, 1953.

Bentley, Eric, *The Playwright As A Thinker,* New York, 1947.

Brockett, Oscar G., *The Theatre: An Introduction,* New York, 1964.

Brooks, Robert and R. B. Heilman, *Understanding Drama,* New York, 1945.

Brown, John Mason, *The Theatre in Revolt,* New York, 1929.

Chandler, Frank W., *Modern Continental Playwrights,* New York, 1931.

Chiari, Joseph, *The Contemporary French Theatre: The Flight from Naturalism,* New York, 1959.

Clark, Barrett H., *European Theories of Drama,* New York, 1925.

Cole, Toby (editor), *Playwrights on Playwriting,* New York, 1960.

Clurman, Harold, *Lies Like Truth,* New York, 1958.

Corrigan, Robert W. and James L. Rosenberg (editors), *The Context and Craft of Drama,* San Francisco, 1964.

Corrigan, Robert W. (editor), *Tragedy: Vision and Form,* San Francisco, 1965.

Corrigan, Robert W. (editor), *Comedy: Meaning and Form,* San Francisco, 1965.

Downer, Alan S., *Fifty Years of American Drama, 1900–1950,* Chicago, 1951.

Eastman, Max, *The Enjoyment of Laughter,* New York, 1942.

Else, Gerald F., *Aristotle's Poetics: The Argument,* Cambridge, Mass., 1957.

Enck, John J., Elizabeth T. Forter and Alvin Whitley (editors), *The Comic in Theory and Practice,* New York, 1960.

Esslin, Martin, *The Theatre of the Absurd,* New York, 1961.

Felheim, Marvin, *Comedy: Plays, Theory and Criticism,* New York, 1962.

Fergusson, Francis, *The Idea of A Theater,* New York, 1953.

Fowlie, Wallace, *Dionysus in Paris, A Guide to Contemporary French Theatre,* New York, 1960.

Freedley, George and John A. Reeves, *A History of the Theatre,* New York, 1941; revised, 1955.

Gassner, John, *Form and Idea in Modern Theatre,* New York, 1956.

GASSNER, John, *Masters of the Drama,* New York, 1954.

HARDISON, O. B., Jr., *Christian Rite and Christian Drama in the Middle Ages,* Baltimore, 1965.

HARTNOLL, Phyllis, *The Oxford Companion to the Theatre,* Oxford, 1951.

HEWITT, Barnard, *Theatre U.S.A., 1668–1957,* New York, 1959.

KITTO, H. D. F., *Form and Meaning in Drama,* London, 1956.

KRUTCH, Joseph Wood, *"Modernism" in Modern Drama,* Ithaca, 1953.

LEWIS, Allan, *The Contemporary Theatre,* New York, 1962.

LUMLEY, Frederick, *Trends in Twentieth Century Drama,* Fair Lawn, New Jersey, 1956.

MACGOWAN, Kenneth, and William MELNITZ, *The Living Stage,* New York, 1955.

MICHEL, Lawrence, and Richard B. SEWALL (editors), *Tragedy: Modern Essays in Criticism,* New York, 1963.

MULLER, Herbert, *The Spirit of Tragedy,* New York, 1956.

MYERS, Henry Alonzo, *Tragedy: A View of Life,* Ithaca, 1956.

NICOLL, Allardyce, *The Development of the Theater,* New York, revised edition, 1958.

NICOLL, Allardyce, *The Theory of Drama,* London, 1931.

OLSON, Elder, *Tragedy and the Theory of Drama,* Detroit, 1961.

PEACOCK, Ronald, *The Art of Drama,* London, 1957.

ROWE, Kenneth, *A Theater in Your Head,* New York, 1960.

SHAW, George Bernard, *Dramatic Opinions and Essays,* New York, 1907.

SIMON, John, *Acid Test,* New York, 1963.

STYAN, J. L., *The Elements of Drama,* Cambridge, 1960.

TYNAN, Kenneth, *Curtains,* New York, 1961.

WILLIAMS, Raymond, *Drama from Ibsen to Eliot,* London, 1952.

GLOSSARY

Acting area or "playing area." The part of the stage used for performance.

Alienation. A technique used by Bertolt Brecht in his "epic dramas" to negate the emotional involvement of his audience in order to make an intellectual appeal to his political views.

Antagonist. The character of force in opposition to the protagonist or hero.

Apron. The stage area in front of the main curtain.

Arena stage. An arrangement for "central staging" of plays with the acting area in the middle of the room surrounded by the audience.

Aside. A dramatic convention by which the actor speaks his private thoughts aloud, unnoticed by other actors.

Backing. Stage scenery used to mask the openings so as to prevent the audience from seeing the off-stage areas.

Blocking. The director's organization of the stage movement of his cast.

Business. The individual actions of the characters in a play, as for example, taking a drink, smoking a pipe, writing a letter.

Catharsis. The act of purging or cleansing, usually in connection with tragedy. Aristotle says that tragedy arouses fear and pity, and that these emotions are purged away and leave the audience in a state of purification. (See pp. 28, 29.)

Chorus. In Greek drama a group, varying in size from twelve to fifty, that recited lines in unison. As the first element to develop in Greek drama, it provided information and, in its most elaborate state, commentary on past actions and forebodings about future ones. With the invention of the second and third actors, the chorus became gradually less important. In later drama, the chorus was a single actor who communicated directly with the audience in giving them essential information.

Classical drama. Usually refers to the dramas of ancient Greece and Rome. See also "neoclassicism."

Climax. The strongest point of emotional tension. Most plays have a series of climaxes which cumulate in a major climax. (See p. 14.)

Comedy. Drama designed to entertain the audience, usually resulting in a happy ending.

Comedy of humours. Comedy of character based upon a dominant trait such as greed or jealousy. Popularized by the Elizabethan playwright Ben Jonson.

Comedy of manners. Social comedy that satirized characters wittily in terms of their shortcomings as measured against a specific code of conduct. For example, *The School for Scandal.*

Commedia dell'arte. Improvised Italian comedy of the sixteenth, seventeenth and eighteenth centuries put together out of stock roles in formula situations. Performed during this period by small companies of professional actors who were very popular all over Europe.

Complication. Any new force introduced into a play which affects the duration of the course of action. (See p. 13.)

Confidant. A minor character paired with a major one and who shares the latter's confidences, usually for expository purposes.

Contamination. The practice of combining plot materials from two or more plays to make a new one. Originally used to describe the practices of Plautus and Terence in reference to their borrowings from Greek comedy, the term was extended to the general practice of the Elizabethans in making new plays from old material.

Conventions. Common agreements between theater-worker and spectator concerning the manner of production, that is, certain "ground rules" that determine how the game is played; for example, the physical separation of actor and spectator.

Crisis. A time of decision; a turning point. (See p. 15.)

Cyclorama. Drapery or canvas usually hung in a half circle to mask the wings and backstage areas. Often represents the sky, or it may be a simple drape setting.

Denouement. The resolution or unravelling of a plot so that an equilibrium is usually restored. (See p. 15.)

Deus ex Machina. In the Greek theater the "God of the machine." A mechanical device used for the intervention of some outside agent to resolve the plot. As a general term, it refers to the intervention of any outside force to bring about a desired ending.

Discovery. The revelation of important information about the characters, their motivations, feelings and relationships. Discovery is often accompanied by recognition (*anagnorisis*) when a character learns the truth about himself. (See p. 12.)

Downstage. The area of the stage closest to the audience.

Drame. Any play that deals seriously with themes, characters and ideas of the present day and is of a keen and sober interest to a middle-class audience. (See p. 35.)

Exposition. Dramatic techniques for acquainting the audience with antecedent information and background material. (See p. 11.)

Expressionism. A style of drama in which an attempt is made to present "inner reality," the man beneath the skin. Often distorts the normal to present symbolic action in dreamlike sequences.

Farce. Low comedy, written for amusement, usually emphasizing physical action.

Flat. The most useful element of stage scenery, consisting of a wooden frame generally covered with muslin or canvas to represent walls.

Flies. The space above the stage out of sight of the audience—where scenery can be "flown."

Foreshadowing. Techniques for preparing the audience for the action that follows. (See p. 13.)

Forestage. In the modern theater, the area in front of the proscenium arch. In the Elizabethan theater, the forestage was a large projecting platform that was the main acting area.

Gridiron. ("grid"). The open framework above the stage from which suspended scenery is hung.

High Comedy. A general term referring to that kind of comedy which evokes "thoughtful laughter" through its concern with character, thought and dialogue.

Imagery. Communication by means of concrete and particular meanings through the use of language devices such as metaphors, similes and clusters of related words.

Irony. A discrepancy between what a character plans and anticipates, and what actually occurs.

Melodrama. Pseudo-serious drama that is played at the game level and exploits exciting action.

Motivation. A logical justification, or a showing of plausible reasons, for the behavior of the characters in a play.

Naturalism. An exaggerated form of realism which emphasizes a sordid and deterministic view of life. First appeared in France in the late nineteenth century as a response to the scientific revolution.

Neoclassicism. An attempt in the sixteenth, seventeenth and eighteenth centuries to "regularize" dramatic techniques by following scrupulously what were thought to be the practices of the ancients, e.g., adherence to the "unities," use of a chorus, preservation of "decorum" in language and action, avoiding acts of violence on stage, and use of only royal or noble characters.

Plot. The structure of the incidents; that which gives drama its form; dramatic composition. (See pp. 9 ff., 28, 45.)

Probability. An attempt by the playwright to establish credibility, or as Aristotle says, to make the action of a play seem "necessary and probable."

Properties ("props"). Includes objects used by the actors in the production of a play such as letters, weapons, food.

Proscenium arch. The architectural frame through which the spectator views the stage.

Protagonist. The chief character in a play.

Realism. Drama that attempts to establish authenticity through the use of the observed facts of daily existence.

Recognition. See "discovery."

Romanticism. In contrast with the classical drama, romantic drama adventurous, emotionally loaded characters in remote and exotic circumstances.

Reversal. An Aristotelian critical term (*peripety*) referring to a sudden change in the fortunes of the protagonist. (See p. 12.)

Skene. Originally a small hut at the back of the orchestra in the Greek theater; later became the stage-house.

"Slice of-life" play. An attempt to give the impression that the action of a play is unorganized actuality, without an apparent beginning, middle or end. Used principally in naturalistic drama.

Soliloquy. A "solo" speech of a single character.

Spectacle. The visual aspects of a produced play.

Stage left or right. Left or right side of the stage from the actor's point of view as he faces the audience.

Thought. The reasoning aspect of drama—the argument, the theme, the meaning.

Tragic flaw. An Aristotelian concept of an "error in judgment," a frailty in an otherwise good and prominent man that leads to his downfall.

Unity of action. All parts of the play are essential and organic, free from sub-plots or extraneous diversions. (See p. 17.)

Unity of place. All of the action occurs in one locale. (See p. 16.)

Unity of time. The action of a play takes place as Aristotle suggested "within the single revolution of the sun." The play covers a short span of time. (See p. 16.)

Upstage. The acting area farthest from the audience.

"Well-made play." Dramatic technique perfected by the French playwright, Scribe, in which all aspects of plot were carefully worked out in a logical cause and effect relationship.

Wings. The area offstage of the acting area.